PHILIP'S

STRE ‖‖‖‖‖‖‖‖‖‖‖ 5

C000255607

SOU...

Hampshire

First published in 1994 by

Philip's, a division of
Octopus Publishing Group Ltd
2-4 Heron Quays, London E14 4JP

Third colour edition 2006
First impression 2006
SHACA

ISBN-10   0-540-08773-4 (pocket)
ISBN-13   978-0-540-08773-0 (pocket)

© Philip's 2006

Ordnance Survey®

This product includes mapping data licensed from
Ordnance Survey® with the permission of the
Controller of Her Majesty's Stationery Office.
© Crown copyright 2006. All rights reserved.
Licence number 100011710.

Printed by Toppan, China

Contents

III	**Key to map symbols**
IV	**Key to map pages**
VI	**Route planning**
VIII	**Administrative and Postcode boundaries**
1	**Street maps** at 2⅔ inches to 1 mile
216	**Street map of Portsmouth city centre** at 5⅓ inches to 1 mile
217	**Index** of towns and villages
220	**Index** of streets, hospitals, industrial estates, railway stations, schools, shopping centres, universities and places of interest

Digital Data

The exceptionally high-quality mapping found in this atlas is available as digital data in TIFF
format, which is easily convertible to other bitmapped (raster) image formats.

The index is also available in digital form as a standard database table. It contains all the details
found in the printed index together with the National Grid reference for the map square in which
each entry is named.

For further information and to discuss your requirements, please contact Philip's on
020 7644 6932 or james.mann@philips-maps.co.uk

Motorway with junction number	
Primary route – dual/single carriageway	
A road – dual/single carriageway	
B road – dual/single carriageway	
Minor road – dual/single carriageway	
Other minor road – dual/single carriageway	
Road under construction	
Tunnel, covered road	
Rural track, private road or narrow road in urban area	
Gate or obstruction to traffic (restrictions may not apply at all times or to all vehicles)	
Path, bridleway, byway open to all traffic, road used as a public path	
Pedestrianised area	
Postcode boundaries DY7	
County and unitary authority boundaries	
Railway, tunnel, railway under construction	
Tramway, tramway under construction	
Miniature railway	
Railway station Walsall	
Private railway station	
Metro station South Shields	
Tram stop, tram stop under construction	
Bus, coach station	

◆	**Ambulance station**
◆	**Coastguard station**
◆	**Fire station**
◆	**Police station**
✚	**Accident and Emergency entrance to hospital**
H	**Hospital**
+	**Place of worship**
i	**Information Centre** (open all year)
🛒	**Shopping Centre**
P P&R	**Parking, Park and Ride**
PO	**Post Office**
Δ 🚐	**Camping site, caravan site**
▶ ✕	**Golf course, picnic site**
Prim Sch	**Important buildings, schools, colleges, universities and hospitals**
	Built up area
	Woods
River Medway	**Water name**
	River, weir, stream
	Canal, lock, tunnel
	Water
	Tidal water
Church	**Non-Roman antiquity**
ROMAN FORT	**Roman antiquity**
87	**Adjoining page indicators and overlap bands** The colour of the arrow and the band indicates the scale of the adjoining or overlapping page (see scales below)
237	

Acad	**Academy**	Inst	**Institute**	Recn Gd	**Recreation Ground**
Allot Gdns	**Allotments**	Ct	**Law Court**		
Cemy	**Cemetery**	L Ctr	**Leisure Centre**	Resr	**Reservoir**
C Ctr	**Civic Centre**	LC	**Level Crossing**	Ret Pk	**Retail Park**
CH	**Club House**	Liby	**Library**	Sch	**School**
Coll	**College**	Mkt	**Market**	Sh Ctr	**Shopping Centre**
Crem	**Crematorium**	Meml	**Memorial**	TH	**Town Hall/House**
Ent	**Enterprise**	Mon	**Monument**	Trad Est	**Trading Estate**
Ex H	**Exhibition Hall**	Mus	**Museum**	Univ	**University**
Ind Est	**Industrial Estate**	Obsy	**Observatory**	W Twr	**Water Tower**
IRB Sta	**Inshore Rescue Boat Station**	Pal	**Royal Palace**	Wks	**Works**
		PH	**Public House**	YH	**Youth Hostel**

■ The small numbers around the edges of the maps identify the 1 kilometre National Grid lines
■ The dark grey border on the inside edge of some pages indicates that the mapping does not continue onto the adjacent page

Enlarged mapping only

	Railway or bus station building
	Place of interest
	Parkland

The scale of the maps on the pages numbered in blue is 4.2 cm to 1 km • 2⅔ inches to 1 mile • 1: 23810

0 — ¼ — ½ — ¾ — 1 mile
0 — 250m — 500m — 750m — 1 kilometre

The scale of the maps on the pages numbered in red is 8.4 cm to 1 km • 5⅓ inches to 1 mile • 1: 11900

0 — 220 yards — 440 yards — 660 yards — ½ mile
0 — 125m — 250m — 375m — ½ kilometre

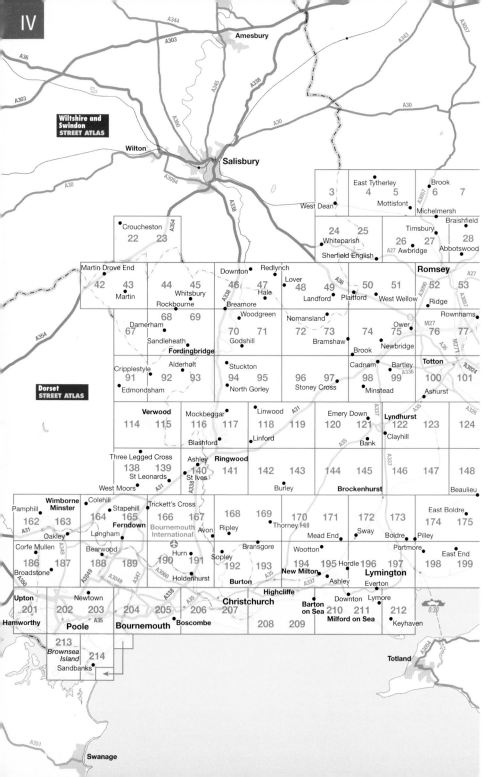

IV

A344
Amesbury
A303
A343
A3057
A36
A303
A345
A338
A30
A30
A303
A380

Wiltshire and Swindon STREET ATLAS

Wilton

A3094

Salisbury

A30
A354
A338

3 East Tytherley **4** **5** Mottisfont **6** Brook **7**
West Dean A3057 Michelmersh Braishfield

A354
22 Croucheston **23**
24 Whiteparish **25** Timsbury **26** Awbridge **27** **28** Abbotswood
Sherfield English A27

Romsey A27

Martin Drove End
42 **43** Martin **44** **45** Whitsbury **46** **47** Hale **48** Lover **49** **50** Plaitford **51** West Wellow **52** **53**
Downton Redlynch A36 Landford Ridge Rownhams
A354 Rockbourne Breamore **68** **69** Woodgreen Nomansland Ower **75** **76** M27 **77**
Damerham **67** **70** Godshill **71** **72** **73** Bramshaw **74** Brook Newbridge M271
Sandleheath **Fordingbridge** Cadnam Bartley **Totton** A336
Cripplestyle Alderholt **91** **92** **93** Stuckton **94** **95** **96** **97** Stoney Cross **98** Minstead **99** **100** **101** Ashurst
Edmondsham North Gorley A326

Dorset STREET ATLAS

A354
Linwood A37 Emery Down A337 **Lyndhurst**
Verwood Mockbeggar **114** **115** **116** **117** **118** **119** **120** **121** **122** **123** **124**
Blashford Linford A35 Bank Clayhill A337 A326
Three Legged Cross Ashley **Ringwood** A35
138 **139** **140** **141** **142** **143** **144** **145** **146** **147** **148**
St Leonards St Ives A337 Beaulieu
West Moors A31 A338 Burley **Brockenhurst**

Wimborne Colehill Trickett's Cross East Boldre
Pamphill **Minster** Stapehill **164** **165** **166** **167** **168** **169** **170** **171** **172** **173** **174** **175**
162 A31 **Ferndown** **Bournemouth** Avon Ripley Thorney Hill Sway Boldre Pilley
Oakley Longham **International** Mead End Portmore East End
Corfe Mullen Bearwood **186** **187** **188** **189** **190** Hurn **191** **192** **193** **194** **195** Hordle **196** **197** **198** **199**
Broadstone A3049 A347 A3060 Holdenhurst Sopley Bransgore Wootton **New Milton** Ashley **Lymington**
A350 A349 Burton A337 Everton
Upton Newtown A35 Highcliffe Lymore
201 **202** **203** **204** **205** **206** **207** **Christchurch** Barton Downton Lymore **212**
Hamworthy A35 **Boscombe** on Sea **210** **211** Keyhaven
Poole **Bournemouth** Boscombe **208** **209** **Milford on Sea**

213
Brownsea Island **214**
Sandbanks

Totland

A3054
0.30

A351

Swanage

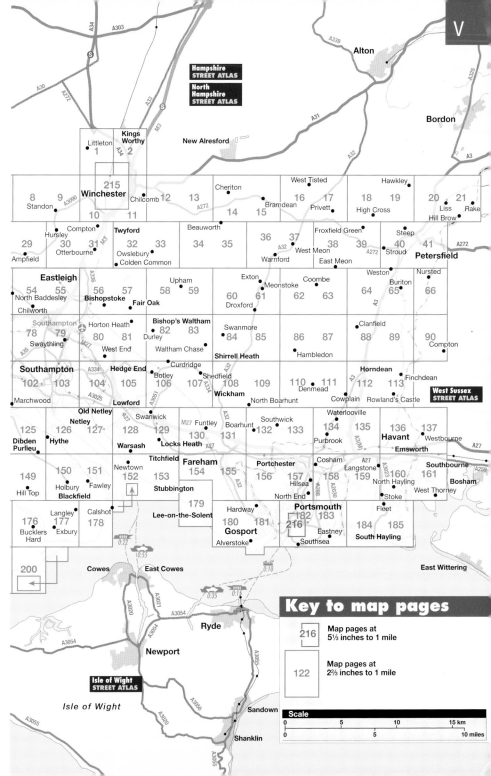

V

Alton

Bordon

New Alresford

Littleton **1**

Kings Worthy **2**

215 Winchester

Chilcomb **12** | **13**

Cheriton

West Tisted

Hawkley

8 | 9 | Winchester
Standon | | **10** | **11**

16 | **17** | **18** | **19** | **20** | **21**
Bramdean | Privett | High Cross | | Liss | Rake
14 | **15** | | | Hill Brow

29 | Hursley Compton | Twyford | Beauworth | | | Froxfield Green | Steep | **40** | **41**
Ampfield | **30** Otterbourne | **31** | **32** Owslebury | **33** Colden Common | **34** | **35** | **36** | **37** West Meon | **38** | **39** | Stroud | Petersfield
| | | | | | | | East Meon | **41**

Eastleigh | Upham | Exton | Coombe | Weston | Nursted
54 | **55** | **56** | **57** | **58** | **59** | **60** | **61** Meonstoke | **62** | **63** | **64** | **65** Buriton | **66**
North Baddesley | Bishopstoke | Fair Oak | | Droxford | | | | Weston

Chilworth

Southampton | Horton Heath | Bishop's Waltham | Swanmore | | Clanfield
78 | **79** | **80** | **81** | **82** | **83** | **84** | **85** | **86** | **87** | **88** | **89** | **90**
Swaythling | | West End Durley | Waltham Chase | | | | | | Compton
| | | | Shirrell Heath | Hambledon

Southampton | Curdridge | Horndean | Finchdean
102 | **103** | **104** | **105** | **106** Botley | **107** Shedfield | **108** | **109** | **110** Denmead | **111** | **112** | **113**
Marchwood | Lowford | Hedge End | | Wickham | | | | Cowplain Rowland's Castle | | West Sussex STREET ATLAS
| | | | North Boarhunt | | | |

Old Netley | Swanwick | Funtley | Southwick | Waterlooville
Netley | **126** | **127** | **128** | **129** | Boarhunt | **132** | **133** | **134** | **135** | **136** | **137**
125 | Hythe | | Warsash | **130** | **131** | | | Purbrook | | Havant | Westbourne
Dibden Purlieu | | | Locks Heath | | | | | | Emsworth

Titchfield | Fareham | Portchester | Cosham | Southbourne
149 | **150** | **151** | Newtown **152** | **153** | **154** | **155** | **156** | **157** | **158** | **159** | **160** | **161**
Hill Top | Holbury Fawley | | Stubbington | | | Hilsea | | Langstone | North Hayling | Bosham
Blackfield | | | | | | North End | | | West Thorney

Hardway | Portsmouth | Stoke | Fleet
176 | **177** | **178** | **179** | **180** | **181** | **182** | **183** | **184** | **185**
Bucklers Hard | Langley Exbury | Calshot | Lee-on-the-Solent | Gosport | **216** | Eastney | South Hayling
| | | | | Alverstoke | Southsea

200

Cowes | East Cowes | | East Wittering

Ryde

Newport

Isle of Wight STREET ATLAS

Isle of Wight

Sandown

Shanklin

Key to map pages

| 216 | Map pages at 5⅓ inches to 1 mile |

| 122 | Map pages at 2⅔ inches to 1 mile |

Scale

| 0 | | 5 | | 10 | | 15 km |
| 0 | | | 5 | | | 10 miles |

Route planning

Scale

0 5 10 km
0 1 2 3 4 5 6 miles

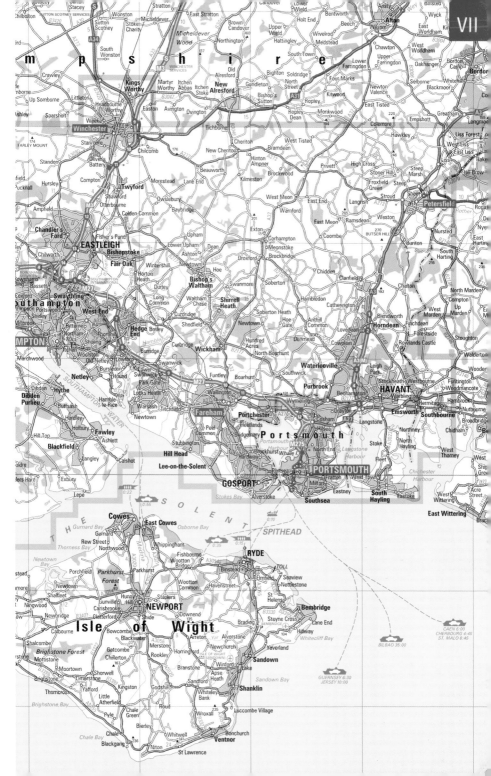

Major administrative and Postcode boundaries

Scale

0 5 10 15 Km
0 5 10 miles

County and unitary authority boundaries
District boundaries
Postcode boundaries

Surrey

West Sussex

Bracknell Forest

Wokingham

West Berkshire

Basingstoke and Deane

Hart

East Hampshire

Hampshire

Winchester

Test Valley

New Forest

City of Southampton

Eastleigh

City of Portsmouth

Fareham

Gosport

Havant

Isle of Wight

Wiltshire

Dorset

Bournemouth

Poole

Camberley · Frimley · GU16 · Farnborough
GU15 · GU14 · GU11 · GU12 · Aldershot
GU46 · GU17 · GU51 · Odiham · Fleet · GU9 · Farnham
RG40 · Yateley · GU27 · Hook · GU52 · GU10 · Bentley
RG7 · Tadley · RG27 · Chineham · GU35 · Bordon · Liphook · GU27
Mortimer · RG26 · Bramley · RG24 · Basingstoke · GU34 · Grayshott · Haslemere
RG19 · Kingsclere · RG23 · RG21 · Alton · GU31 · GU33 · Liss
RG14 · RG20 · Oakley · RG22 · Medstead · East Tisted · Petersfield
Newbury · Burghclere · North · RG25 · Ellisfield · West Meon · GU32 · PO18
RG17 · St Mary Bourne · Whitchurch · Waltham · SO24 · Meonstoke · Horndean · PO8 · PO9 · Havant · PO10 · Thorney Island
Vernham Dean · RG28 · New · Alresford · PO7 · PO10 · PO11 · Hayling Island
SN8 · Tangley · Micheldever · Abbas · Itchen · SO21 · SO23 · Bishop's · Wickham · PO17 · PO16 · PO13 · Portsmouth · PO5
SP11 · Andover · South · SO22 · Twyford · Waltham · SO32 · PO14 · PO4
SP10 · Wherwell · Wonston · SO53 · West End · SO31 · PO15 · PO12
Thruxton · Over · SO20 · SO50 · SO30 · Netley · SO19 · Fareham · PO2 · PO3
SP9 · SP4 · Wallow · Broughton · SO51 · Romsey · SO18 · Eastleigh · SO45 · Fawley
West Dean · Mottisfont · SO52 · SO16 · SO17 · Hythe · SO42
SP5 · West Wellow · SO40 · Southampton · SO14 · Beaulieu
SP6 · Cadnam · SO43 · Totton · SO41 · Lymington
Wick · Lyndhurst · Brockenhurst · Sway · Barton on Sea
Martin · Fordingbridge · Burley · BH25 · BH23 · BH6 · BH5
Croucheston · SP6 · Ibsley · BH24 · Ringwood · Ferndown · BH7 · BH1 · BH2 · BH4
BH3 · BH22 · Burley · BH23 · Christchurch · Bournemouth · BH8 · BH9
Verwood · BH21 · Wimborne Minster · BH10 · BH3 · BH11 · BH12 · BH14 · BH7
BH18 · BH21 · BH17 · BH15 · BH12 · Poole · BH13 · BH3
BH16 · BH15 · Poole · BH14

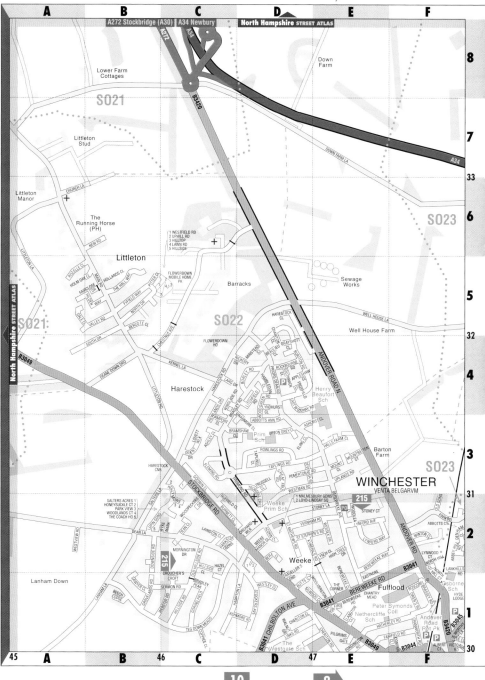

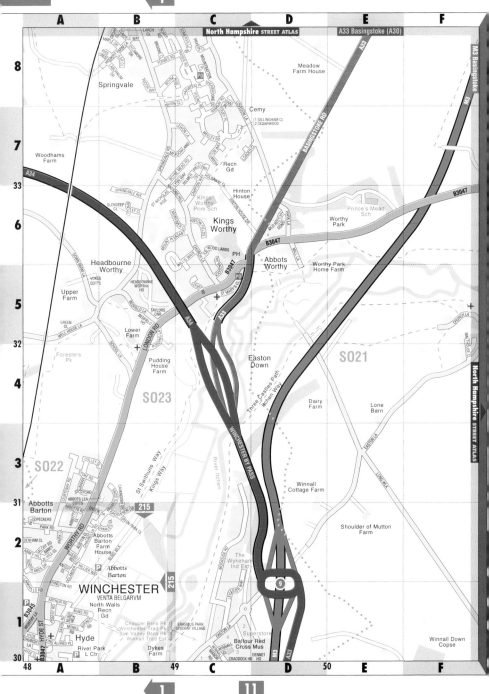

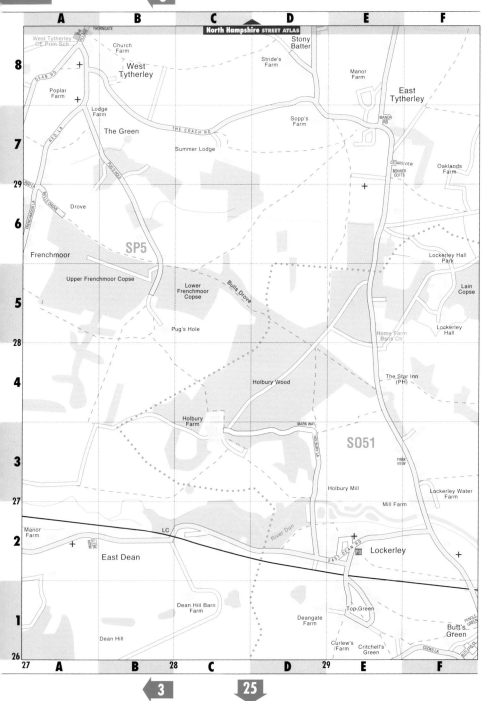

West Tytherley
CE Prim Sch

THORNGATE

Church
Farm

West
Tytherley

Stride's
Farm

Stony
Batter

Manor
Farm

East
Tytherley

+

+

DEAN RD

Poplar
Farm

Lodge
Farm

Sopp's
Farm

MANOR
RD

RED LA

The Green

THE COACH RD

Summer Lodge

CEDARS VIEW
BONNER
COTTS

Oaklands
Farm

RED LA

29

+

POST LA DVE

FRENCHMOOR LA

BULLS DROVE

Drove

6

Lockerley Hall
Park

Frenchmoor

SP5

Upper Frenchmoor Copse

Lower
Frenchmoor
Copse

Bulls Drove

Lain
Copse

5

Pug's Hole

Home Farm
Bsns Ctr

Lockerley
Hall

28

4

Holbury Wood

The Star Inn
(PH)

Holbury
Farm

MARK WAY

SO51

HOLBURY LA

3

PARK
VIEW

27

Holbury Mill

Lockerley Water
Farm

Mill Farm

Manor
Farm

+

LC

MILL GLEBE

River Dun

EAST DEAN RD

+

PO

Lockerley

+

2

East Dean

Dean Hill Barn
Farm

Deangate
Farm

Top Green

PENDLE
GREEN

Butt's
Green

1

Dean Hill

Curlew's
Farm

Critchell's
Green

COOKS LA

BUTTS LA

26

Redhills
Copse

SP5

Little Bentley
Farm

Hackpits
Copse

Deborah
Copse

Pittleworth
Manor

Pittleworth
Farm

Great Bentley
Farm

Holm Moor
Copse

SO20

Bentley
Firs

Blackpits Wood

The
Bungalow

Lain Copse

Great
Copse

Clapgate
Copse

Snook's
Copse

Spearywell Wood

SO51

Newlyns
Farm

BACK LA

Blackmoor Firs

Culver
Leaze

Bushy
Copse

Woodland
Walk

Cadbury
Farm

Spearywell

OAKLEY LA

Dummer
Copse

Test Way
Monarch's Way

Mottisfont Abbey

Gardens

Priory

OAKLEY RD

BENGER'S LA

Abbey
Farm

KEEPERS LA

Mottisfont

Glebe
Farm

HATT LA

Drove Copse

Hatt Farm
Hatt Hill

Monarch's Way

CHURCH LA

River Test

River Dun

Lockerley
CE Prim Sch

LOCKERLEY RD

The
School
Farm

Dunbridge

LC

B3084

LC

River Dun

Dunbridge

RUSSELL DR 1
MILL RISE 2

PH

LOCKERLEY RD

DUNBRIDGE LA

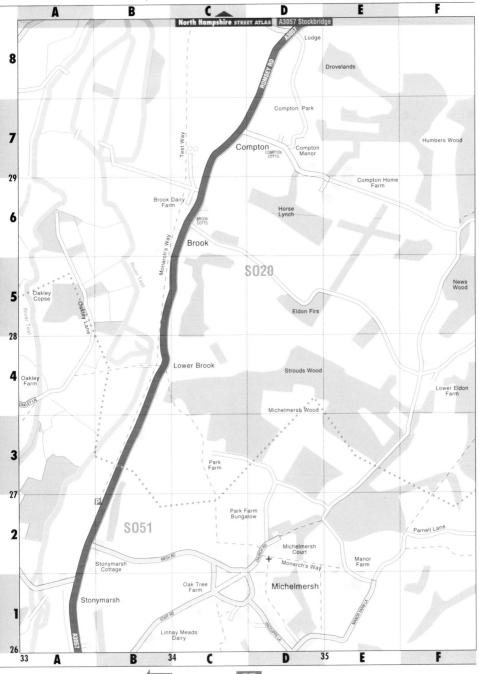

A B C D E F

8

7

29

6

5

28

4

3

27

2

1

26

ROMSEY RD

A3057

Lodge

Drovelands

Compton Park

Humbers Wood

Compton

Compton Manor

COMPTON COTTS

Test Way

Compton Home Farm

Brook Dairy Farm

Horse Lynch

BROOK COTTS

Monarch's Way

Brook

SO20

News Wood

River Test

Oakley Copse

Oakley Lane

Eldon Firs

River Test

Lower Brook

Strouds Wood

Oakley Farm

Lower Eldon Farm

OAKLEY LA

Michelmersh Wood

Park Farm

P

SO51

Park Farm Bungalow

Parnell Lane

MESH RD

CHURCH RD

Michelmersh Court

Monarch's Way

Manor Farm

Stonymarsh Cottage

Oak Tree Farm

Michelmersh

Stonymarsh

MANOR FARM LA

A3057

STAFF RD

INCLOSED LA

Linhay Meads Dairy

33 A B 34 C D 35 E F

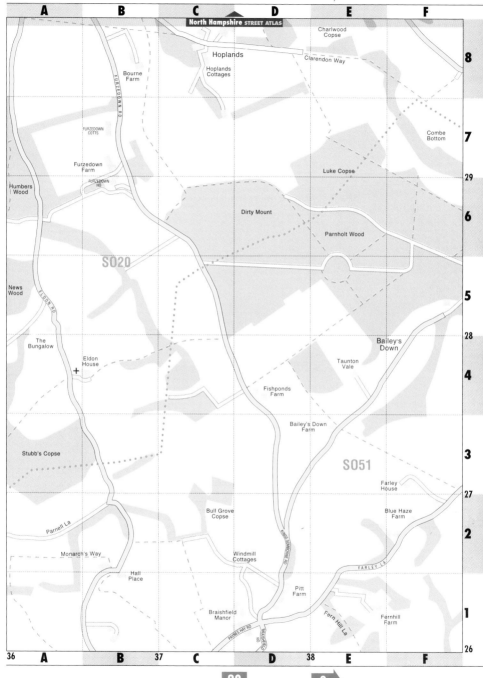

A B C D E F

8

8

7

29

6

5

28

4

3

27

2

1

26

36 A B 37 C D 38 E F

28

8

Charlwood Copse

Hoplands

Clarendon Way

Hoplands Cottages

Combe Bottom

Bourne Farm

FURZEDOWN RD

FURZEDOWN COTTS

Furzedown Farm

FURZEDOWN HO

Humbers Wood

Luke Copse

Dirty Mount

SO20

Parnholt Wood

News Wood

ELDON RD

The Bungalow

Bailey's Down

Eldon House

Taunton Vale

Fishponds Farm

Bailey's Down Farm

Stubb's Copse

SO51

Farley House

Bull Grove Copse

Blue Haze Farm

KINGS SOMBORNE RD

Parnell La

Monarch's Way

Windmill Cottages

FARLEY LA

Hall Place

Pitt Farm

Fernhill Farm

Braishfield Manor

Fern Hill La

PAINS HAY RD

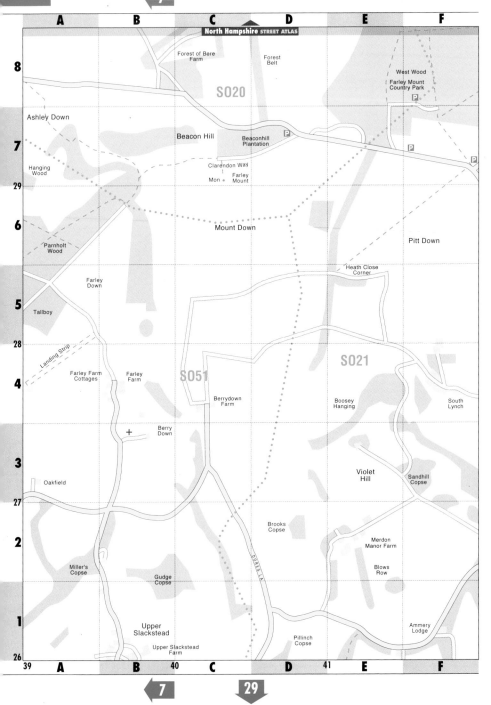

North Hampshire STREET ATLAS

8

SO20

West Wood

Forest of Bere Farm

Forest Belt

Farley Mount Country Park

Ashley Down

7

Beacon Hill

Beaconhill Plantation

Hanging Wood

29

Clarendon Way

Mon · Farley Mount

6

Mount Down

Pitt Down

Parnholt Wood

Heath Close Corner

Farley Down

5

Tallboy

28

Landing Strip

SO021

4

Farley Farm Cottages

Farley Farm

SO51

Berrydown Farm

Boosey Hanging

South Lynch

Berry Down

3

Violet Hill

Sandhill Copse

Oakfield

27

Brooks Copse

2

Merdon Manor Farm

Miller's Copse

Gudge Copse

Blows Row

DORES LA

1

Upper Slackstead

Ammery Lodge

26

Upper Slackstead Farm

Pillinch Copse

39   A   B   40   C   D   41   E   F

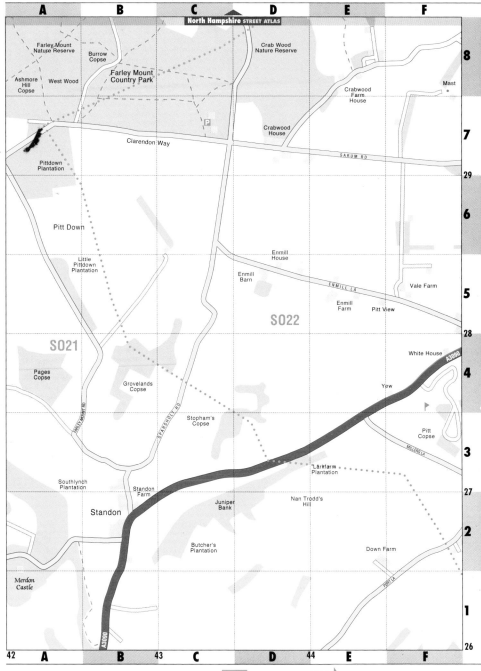

Farley Mount
Nature Reserve

Burrow
Copse

Crab Wood
Nature Reserve

Ashmore
Hill
Copse

West Wood

Farley Mount
Country Park

Crabwood
Farm
House

Mast

Crabwood
House

Clarendon Way

SARUM RD

Pittdown
Plantation

Pitt Down

Little
Pittdown
Plantation

Enmill
House

Enmill
Barn

ENMILL LA

Vale Farm

Enmill
Farm

Pitt View

SO22

SO21

Pages
Copse

Grovelands
Copse

White House

A3090

Yew

Stopham's
Copse

Pitt
Copse

MILLERS LA

Larkfarm
Plantation

Southlynch
Plantation

Standon
Farm

Juniper
Bank

Nan Trodd's
Hill

Standon

Butcher's
Plantation

Down Farm

Merdon
Castle

PORT LA

FARLEY MOUNT RD

SPARSHOLT RD

A3090

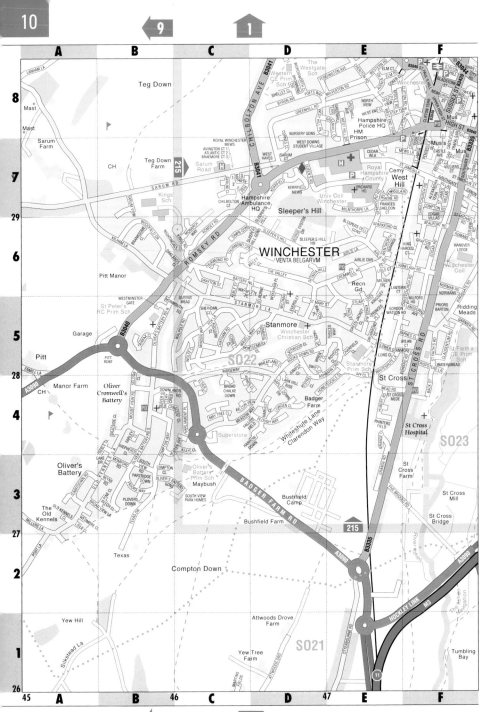

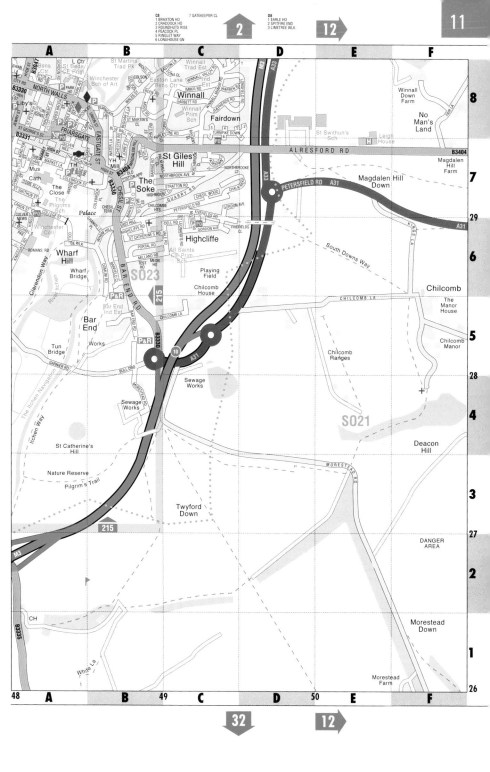

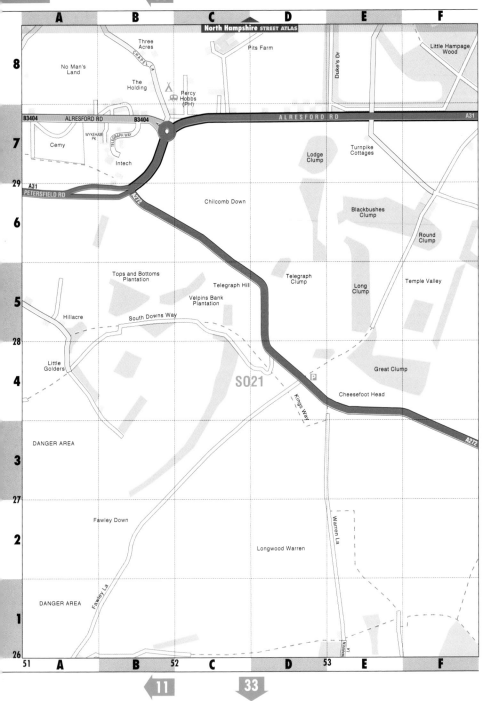

North Hampshire STREET ATLAS

A **B** **C** **D** **E** **F**

8

Three Acres

Little Hampage Wood

Pits Farm

No Man's Land

The Holding

Percy Hobbs (PH)

Duke's Dr

B3404 ALRESFORD RD B3404 ALRESFORD RD A31

7

Cemy

WYKEHAM PK

TELEGRAPH WAY

Intech

Lodge Clump

Turnpike Cottages

29 A31
PETERSFIELD RD

A272

Chilcomb Down

Blackbushes Clump

6

Round Clump

Tops and Bottoms Plantation

Telegraph Hill

Telegraph Clump

Long Clump

Temple Valley

5

Velpins Bank Plantation

Hillacre

South Downs Way

SO21

Great Clump

28

Little Golders

Cheesefoot Head

4

Kings Way

P

A272

DANGER AREA

27

Fawley Down

Warren La

2

Longwood Warren

DANGER AREA

Fawley La

1

Warren La

26
51 **A** 52 **B** **C** 52 **D** 53 **E** **F**

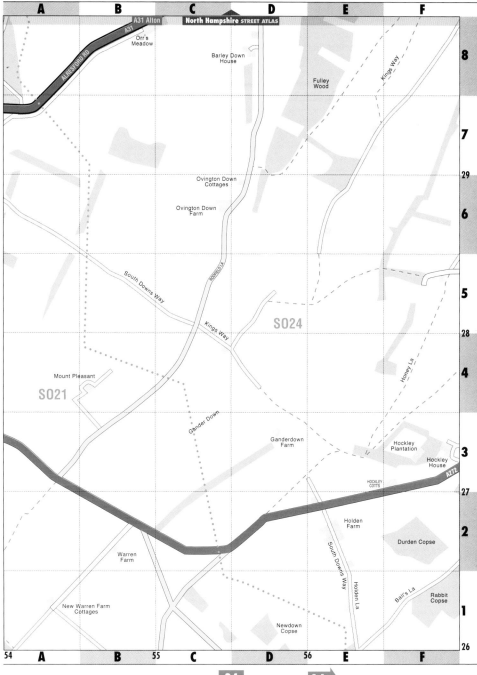

North Hampshire STREET ATLAS

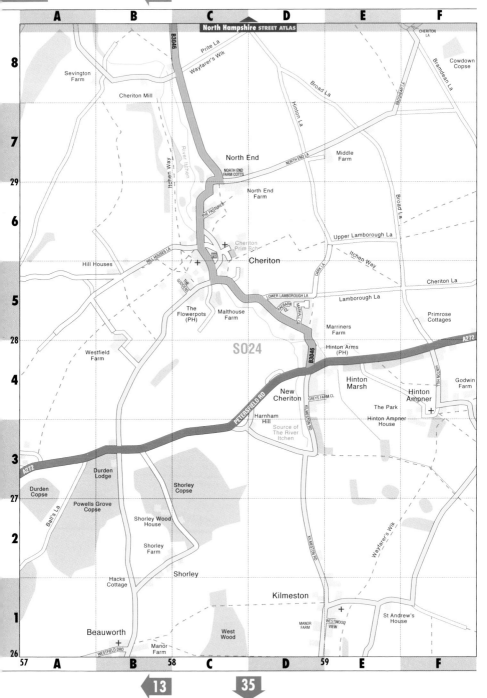

North Hampshire STREET ATLAS

A **B** **C** **D** **E** **F**

8

Sevington Farm

Cheriton Mill

Prite La

Wayfarer's Wik

B3046

Broad La

Cowdown Copse

CHERITON LA

BRAMDEAN LA

7

River Itchen

Itchen Way

North End

NORTH END LA

Middle Farm

Hinton La

29

NORTH END FARM COTTS

North End Farm

Broad La

6

THE PASTURES

Cheriton Prim Sch

Upper Lamborough La

Itchen Way

Hill Houses

HILL HOUSES LA

THE GODOLNS

Cheriton

DUCK LA

Cheriton La

5

The Flowerpots (PH)

Malthouse Farm

LOWER LAMBOROUGH LA

Lamborough La

Primrose Cottages

A272

28

Westfield Farm

MARSHAL CL

SALEARN CL

S024

Marriners Farm

B3046

Hinton Arms (PH)

HINTON HILL

Godwin Farm

4

PETERSFIELD RD

New Cheriton

Harnham Hill

GREYS FARM CL

Hinton Marsh

Hinton Ampner

The Park

Hinton Ampner House

3

A272

Durden Lodge

Source of The River Itchen

KILMESTON RD

KILMESTON RD

Wayfarer's Wik

27

Durden Copse

Ball's La

Powells Grove Copse

Shorley Copse

2

Shorley Wood House

Shorley Farm

Shorley

1

Hacks Cottage

Kilmeston

MANOR FARM

WESTWOOD VIEW

St Andrew's House

26

Beauworth

WESTFIELD DRO

Manor Farm

West Wood

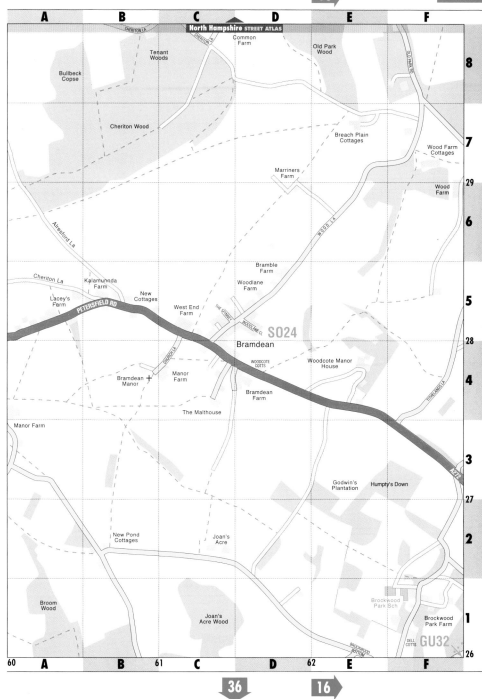

North Hampshire STREET ATLAS

A   **B**   **C**   **D**   **E**   **F**

CHERITON LA

CHERITON

Common Farm

Old Park Wood

OLD PARK RD

8

Bullbeck Copse

Tenant Woods

Cheriton Wood

Breach Plain Cottages

Wood Farm Cottages

7

Marriners Farm

Wood Farm

29

Alresford La

WOOD LA

6

Cheriton La

Kalamunnda Farm

Lacey's Farm

New Cottages

Bramble Farm

Woodlane Farm

West End Farm

THE SPINNEY

WOODLANE CL

SO24

5

PETERSFIELD RD

Bramdean

28

CHURCH LA

Manor Farm

WOODCOTE COTTS

Woodcote Manor House

THE HANGERS LA

4

Bramdean Manor

Bramdean Farm

The Malthouse

Manor Farm

Godwin's Plantation

Humpty's Down

A272

3

27

New Pond Cottages

Joan's Acre

2

Broom Wood

Joan's Acre Wood

Brockwood Park Sch

Brockwood Park Farm

1

BROCKWOOD BOTTOM

DELL COTTS

GU32

26

60   **A**   **B**   61   **C**   **D**   62   **E**   **F**

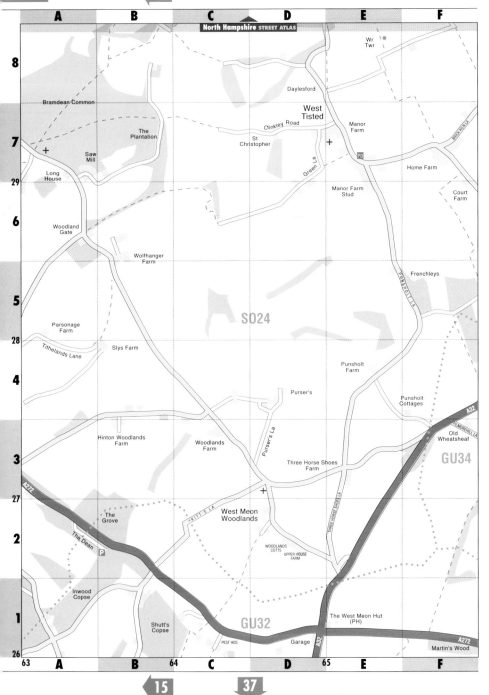

North Hampshire STREET ATLAS

Wr Twr

Daylesford

West Tisted

Clinkley Road

Bramdean Common

The Plantation

St Christopher

Manor Farm

Green La

Home Farm

Saw Mill

Long House

Manor Farm Stud

Court Farm

Woodland Gate

Wolfhanger Farm

BRICK KILN LA

PUNSHOLT LA

Frenchleys

SO24

Parsonage Farm

Tithelands Lane

Slys Farm

Punsholt Farm

Purser's

Punsholt Cottages

A32

ILMOREHILL LA

Old Wheatsheaf

Hinton Woodlands Farm

Woodlands Farm

Purser's La

Three Horse Shoes Farm

GU34

A272

The Grove

The Dean

West Meon Woodlands

KITT S LA

THREE HORSE SHOES LA

Inwood Copse

Shutt's Copse

WOODLANDS COTTS
UPPER HOUSE FARM

The West Meon Hut (PH)

GU32

PEST HOS

Garage

A32

A272

Martin's Wood

29 28 26 27 63 64 65

8 7 6 5 4 3 2 1

A B C D E F

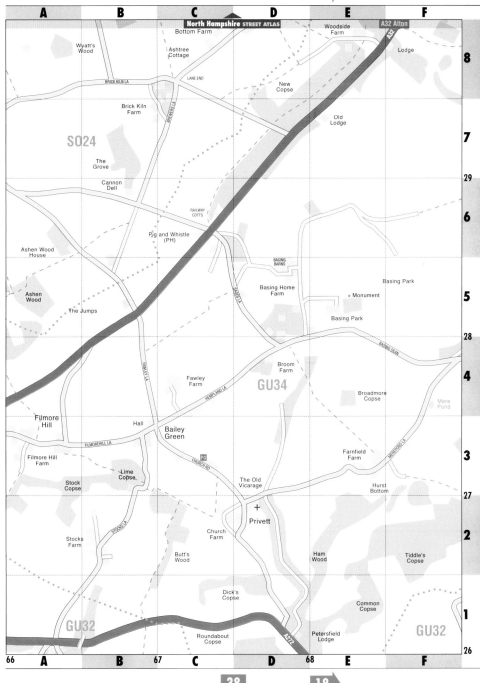

| A | B | C | D | E | F |

8

Wyatt's Wood

Bottom Farm

Ashtree Cottage

Woodside Farm

A32 Alton

Lodge

BRICK KILN LA

LANE END

New Copse

Brick Kiln Farm

SO24

7

BREWERS LA

Old Lodge

The Grove

29

Cannon Dell

RAILWAY COTTS

6

Pig and Whistle (PH)

Ashen Wood House

BASING BARNS

Basing Barns

Basing Park

5

Ashen Wood

Basing Home Farm

Monument

The Jumps

Basing Park

28

FARLEY LA

Fawley Farm

HEMPLAND LA

Broom Farm

GU34

Broadmore Copse

Mere Pond

4

Filmore Hill

Hall

BASING DEAN

MEREPOND LA

Bailey Green

FILMOREHILL LA

CHURCH RD

PO

Farnfield Farm

3

Filmore Hill Farm

Lime Copse

Stock Copse

The Old Vicarage

Hurst Bottom

27

STOCKS LA

Stocks Farm

Butt's Wood

Church Farm

✝
Privett

Ham Wood

Tiddle's Copse

2

Dick's Copse

Common Copse

1

GU32

Roundabout Copse

A272

Petersfield Lodge

GU32

26

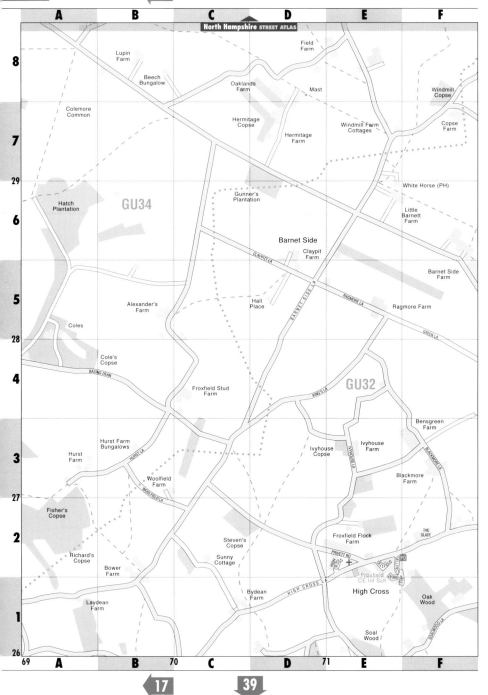

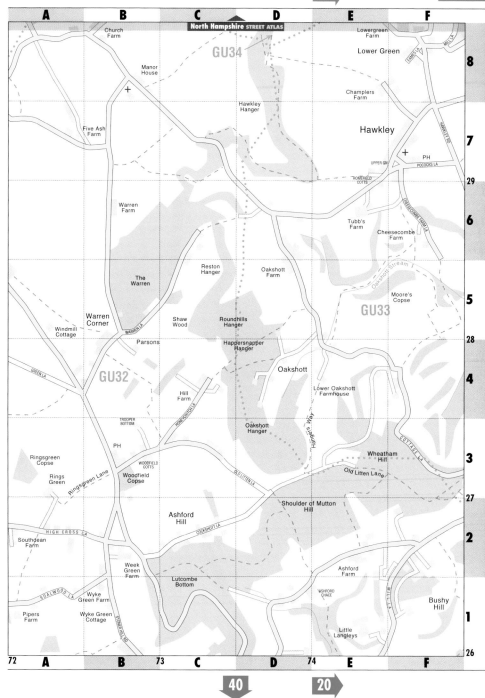

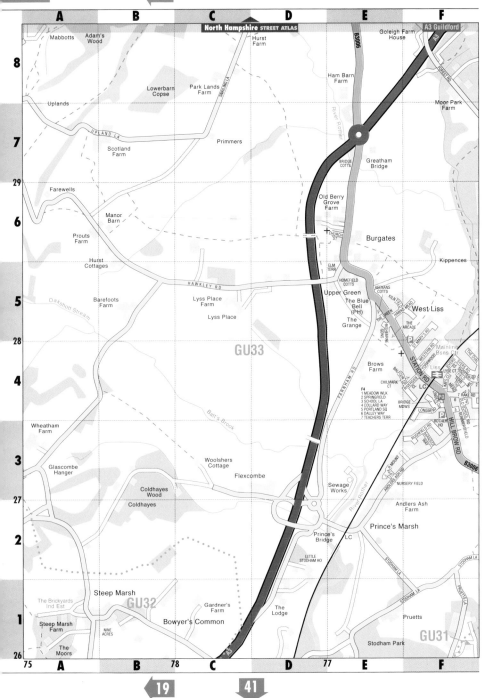

A **B** **C** **D** **E** **F**

North Hampshire STREET ATLAS

8

Mabbotts
Adam's Wood
Hurst Farm
Goleigh Farm House
A3 Guildford

B3006

FOREST RD

GU32

7

Lowerbarn Copse
Park Lands Farm
Ham Barn Farm
Moor Park Farm

SNAILING LA

Uplands
UPLAND LA
Scotland Farm
Primmers

River Rother

29

Farewells

BRIDGE COTTS
Greatham Bridge

6

Manor Barn
Prouts Farm
Hurst Cottages
Old Berry Grove Farm
CHURCH ST
Burgates
Kippences

ELM TERR

HAWKLEY RD

HOMEFIELD COTTS

Oakshott Stream

Barefoots Farm
Lyss Place Farm
Upper Green

KEENANS COTTS
KILN LA
HAWKS MEAD

West Liss

THE GREEN

THE ARCADE

5

Lyss Place
The Blue Bell (PH)
The Grange

ST MARY'S RD

WESTON RD

28

GU33

FARNHAM RD

Brows Farm
Liss
Mainline Busn Ctr
LC

BAILS CLOSE

STATION RD

THE GORE

RAKE RD

4

CHILMARK CT
F4
1 MEADOW WLK
2 SPRINGFIELD
3 SCHOOL LA
4 COLLARD WAY
5 PORTLAND SQ
6 DALLEY WAY
7 TEACHERS TERR

BRIDGE MDWS
LONGMEAD
ROTHER RD

Batt's Brook

SUMMERSFIELD
HILL BROW RD

3

Wheatham Farm
Glascombe Hanger
Woolshers Cottage
Flexcombe

Sewage Works

River Rother

FISHFIELD RD
ANDLERS ASH RD
NURSERY FIELD

B3006

27

Coldhayes Wood
Coldhayes

Andlers Ash Farm
Prince's Marsh

STODHAM LA

STODHAM LA

2

Prince's Bridge
LC

LITTLE STODHAM HO

1

The Brickyards Ind Est
Steep Marsh
GU32
Gardner's Farm
The Lodge
Pruetts

GU31

Steep Marsh Farm
NINE ACRES
Bowyer's Common
Stodham Park

26

The Moors

A3

75 **A** **B** 78 **C** **D** 77 **E** **F**

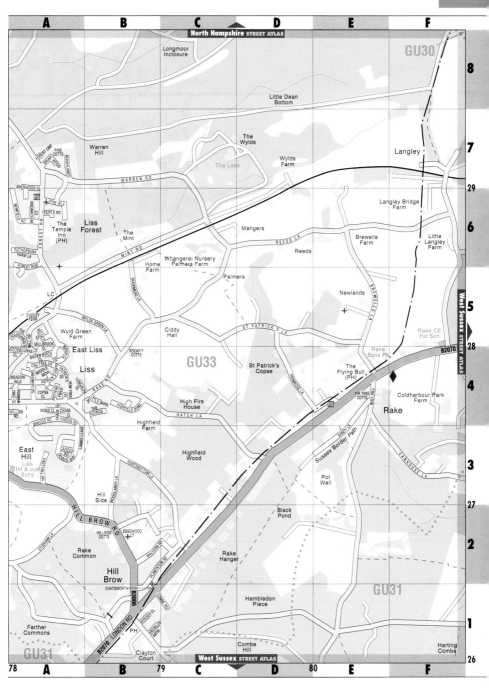

GU30

Longmoor
Inclosure

Little Dean
Bottom

8

Langley

7

The
Wylds

Warren
Hill

The Lake

Wylds
Farm

WARREN RD

29

FOREST DRR
PINE COTTS
BRIM WOOD
BERRY WOOD

SHERWOOD CL
PO
PINE WLK

NEWFIELD RD
BEECHWOOD CL
TEMPLE RD

Langley Bridge
Farm

6

Liss
Forest

The
Temple
Inn
(PH)

The
Mint

Mangers

REEDS LA

Brewells
Farm

Little
Langley
Farm

FOREST RD
ROTHERBANK
FARM LA
MINT RD

Home
Farm

Whangerei Nursery
Palmers Farm

Reeds

West Sussex STREET ATLAS

FOREST RISE

Palmers

Newlands

BREWELLS LA

5

LC

DUDLEY
TERR

St PATRICK's LA

28

Wyld Green
Farm

WYLDE GREEN LA

Ciddy
Hall

Rake CE
Fst Sch

Rake
Bsns Pk

B2070

WOODBOURNE
CL
SILVER BIRCH
MILLBROOK

East Liss

RAMMELL MW

ROCKPIT
COTTS

GU33

St Patrick's
Copse

The
Flying Bull
(PH)

4

OAK TREE DR
MIDDLE

Liss

GREENFIELDS

PRIDES LA

FIR TREE
COTTS

Coldharbour Park
Farm

MEADOW
WLK
COPSE
CL
LIME TREE WLK
RAKE RD

LITTLE BARN

HIGHFIELD GRO

High Firs
House

HATCH LA

SANDY LA

THE HILL

Rake

WILLOW
RD
MOSS CL
THE CHASE
CL
VINSON RD
THE
RIDINGS

Highfield
Farm

INWOOD RD

LAMBS LEASE

Highfield
Wood

Sussex Border Path

3

CARPENTER
RD

WITHY LEA

East
Hill
Liss
Inf & Jun
Schs

WICKHAM LA

Hill
Side

HUNTSBOTTOM LA

Pot
Well

CARHOUSE LA

27

TENNIS WAY

STODHAM LA

HILL BROW RD

HILLSIDE
COTTS
EDGEWOOD
CT

MALDEN WAY

Black
Pond

2

Rake
Common

Hill
Brow

CHATSWORTH

Rake
Hanger

Hambledon
Piece

GU31

B3006

PLANTATION RD

COMBE RD

Farther
Commons

LONDON RD

PH

BORDER CL
KNOWLE
GROW

Combe
Hill

Harting
Combe

1

GU31

B2070

Clayton
Court

West Sussex STREET ATLAS

26

78   **A**   **B**   79   **C**   **D**   80   **E**   **F**

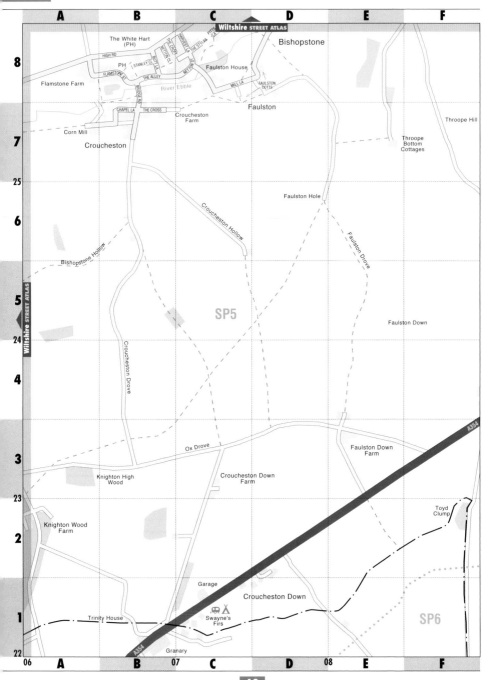

Bishopstone

The White Hart
(PH)

HIGH RD

PH

FLAMSTONE ST

THE ALLEY

STANLEY CL

THE CORT

NETTON CL

BRIDGE RD

MARKET LA

PITTS LA

THE STYLES

NETTON LA

FAULSTON CL

Faulston House

MILL LA

FAULSTON
COTTS

Flamstone Farm

River Ebble

Faulston

CHAPEL LA

THE CROSS

Croucheston
Farm

Corn Mill

Croucheston

Throope Hill

Throope
Bottom
Cottages

Faulston Hole

Croucheston Hollow

Bishopstone Hollow

SP5

Faulston Drove

Faulston Down

Croucheston Drove

Ox Drove

Faulston Down
Farm

A354

Knighton High
Wood

Croucheston Down
Farm

Toyd
Clump

Knighton Wood
Farm

Garage

Croucheston Down

SP6

Trinity House

Swayne's
Firs

A354

Granary

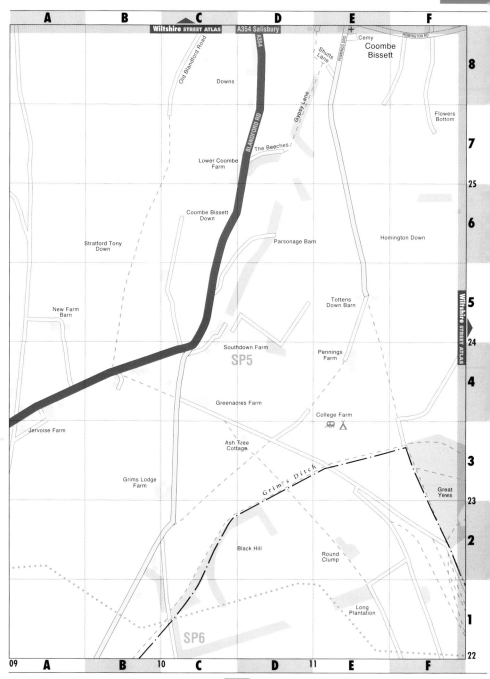

A354 Salisbury

A354

Old Blandford Road

Downs

BLANDFORD RD

Gypsy Lane

Shutts Lane

PENNINGS DRO

Cemy

Coombe Bissett

HOMINGTON RD

8

Flowers Bottom

The Beeches

7

Lower Coombe Farm

25

Coombe Bissett Down

Parsonage Barn

Homington Down

6

Stratford Tony Down

New Farm Barn

Tottens Down Barn

5

24

Southdown Farm

SP5

Pennings Farm

4

Greenacres Farm

College Farm

Jervoise Farm

Ash Tree Cottage

Grims Lodge Farm

Grim's Ditch

Great Yews

3

23

Black Hill

Round Clump

2

Long Plantation

1

SP6

22

09 A B 10 C D 11 E F

44

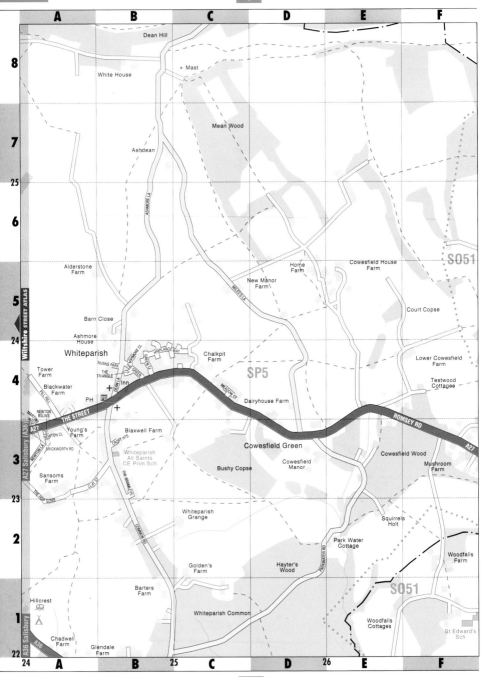

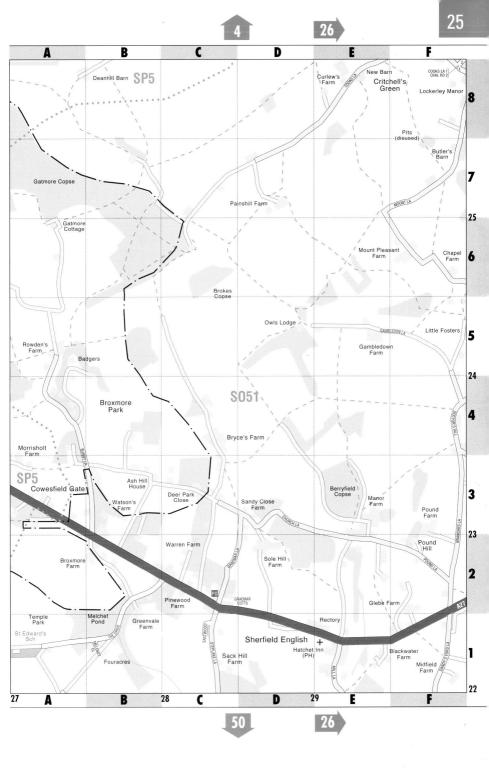

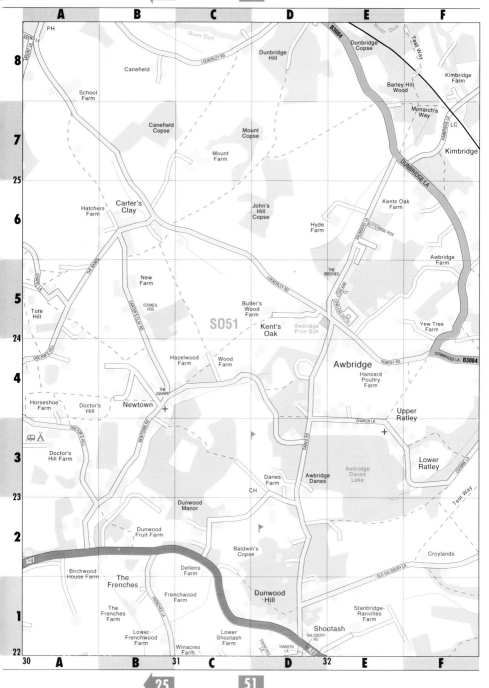

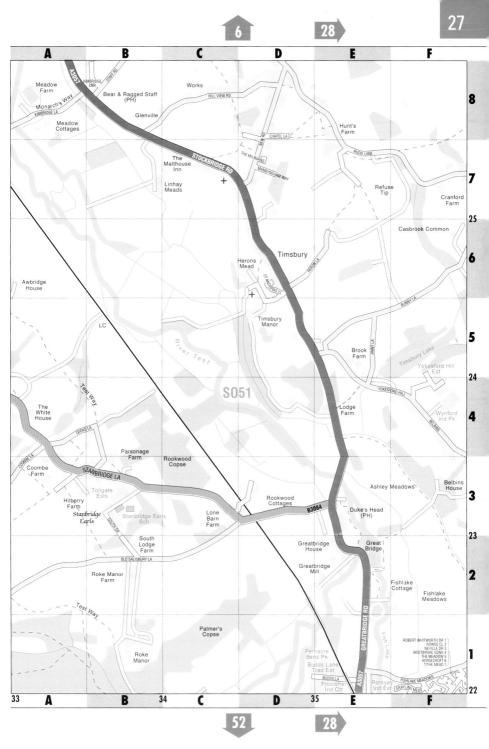

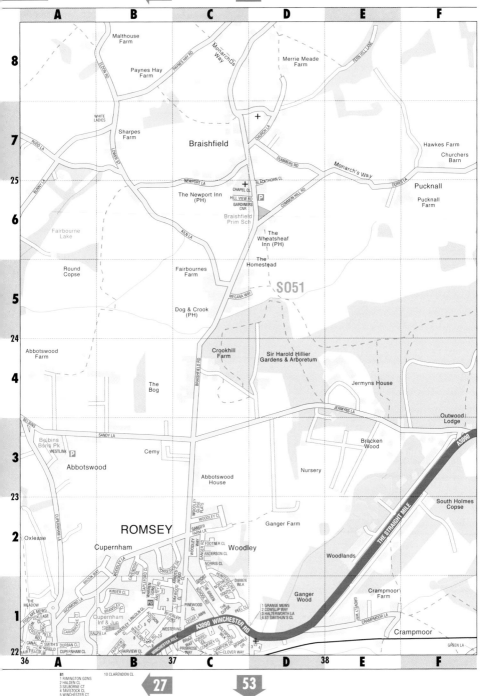

8

7

25

6

5

24

4

23

3

2

1

22

A   **B**   **C**   **D**   **E**   **F**

Malthouse
Farm

Paynes Hay
Farm

WHITE
LADIES

Sharpes
Farm

Braishfield

Merrie Meade
Farm

TEAN HILL LANE

Hawkes Farm

Churchers
Barn

NEWPORT LA

BLACKTHORN CL

DUMMERS RD

Monarch's Way

DORIE LA

Pucknall

The Newport Inn
(PH)

CHAPEL CL
HILL VIEW RD
GARDINERS
CNR

Braishfield
Prim Sch

COMMON HILL RD

Pucknall
Farm

Fairbourne
Lake

KILN LA

The
Wheatsheaf
Inn (PH)

The
Homestead

Round
Copse

Fairbournes
Farm

S051

MEGANA WAY

Dog & Crook
(PH)

Abbotswood
Farm

Crookhill
Farm

Sir Harold Hillier
Gardens & Arboretum

Jermyns House

The
Bog

BRAISHFIELD RD

Outwood
Lodge

JERMYNS LA

A3090

BELBINS

SANDY LA

Belbins
Barns Pk
WESTLINK

Cemy

Bracken
Wood

Abbotswood

CUPERNHAM LA

Abbotswood
House

Nursery

South Holmes
Copse

WOODLEY
CLOSE
FLATS

WOODLEY CL

THE STRAIGHT MILE

Oxlease

ROMSEY

Cupernham

WOODLEA LA

CAVENDISH

GANGER
FARM LA

Woodley

WOODLEY

FOOTNER CL

ANDERSON CL

NORRIS CL

Ganger Farm

Woodlands

Crampmoor
Farm

Ganger
Wood

THE MEADOW

TRELOYHAN

MOXLEASE

BIGAMOUND LA

WOODLEA LA

KINVER CL

STAFFERTON

WARREN
GDNS

BRAMLEY
CL

PINEWOOD CL

HUNTER

NORTHUMBERLAND

THE GREEN

DIBBEN
WLK

COPSE

PEEL CL

1 GRANGE MEWS
2 COWSLIP WAY
3 HALTERWORTH LA
4 ST SWITHUN'S CL

WINCHESTER HILL

A3090 WINCHESTER RD

Crampmoor

GREEN LA

THE
MEADOW

CANAL

SMITH'S
FIELD

DURBAN CL

CUPERNHAM CL

Cupernham
Inf & Jun
Sch

WAVERLEY

LINCOLN CL

FAIRVIEW

FAIRVIEW CL

WESTERING

BRIAR
WAY
PRIMROSE
WAY

COMFREY CL
LOVAGE CL

CAMPION DR

CLOVER WAY

BRAMBLE
DR

36   **A**   **B**   37   **C**   **D**   38   **E**   **F**

B1
1 RIMINGTON GDNS
2 HALDEN CL
3 SELBORNE CT
4 TAVISTOCK CL
5 WINCHESTER CT
6 SUTHERLAND CL
7 HOGARTH CL
8 WOODLANDS GDNS
9 SAVERNAKE CL

10 CLARENDON CL

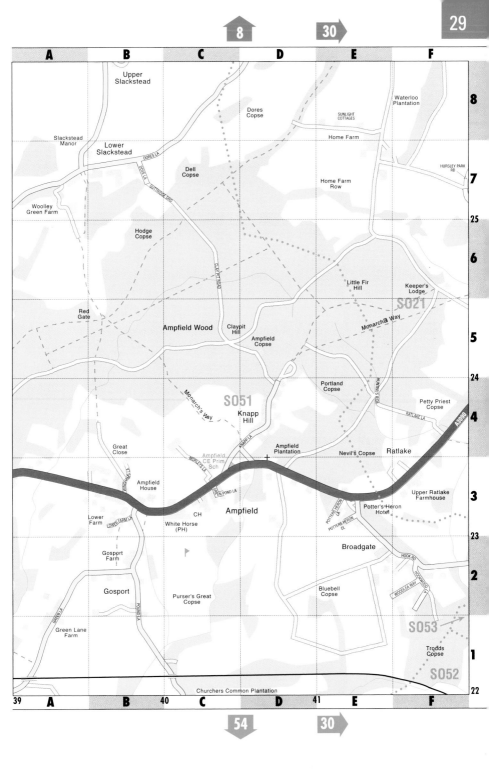

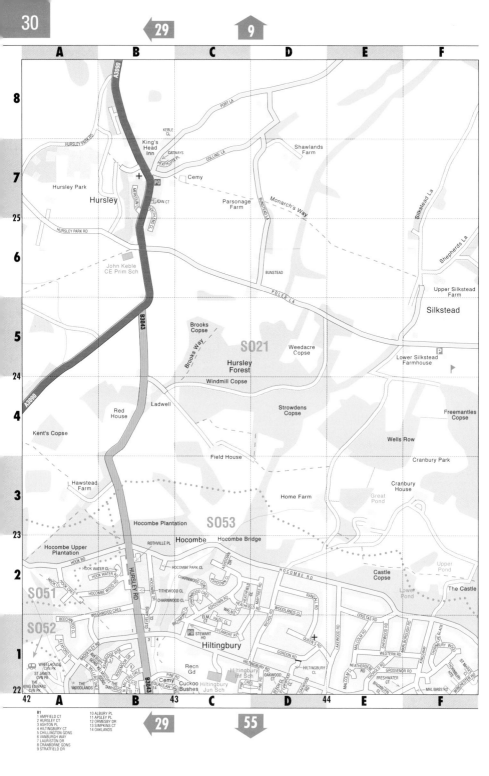

B1
1 AMPFIELD CT
2 HURSLEY CT
3 ASHTON PL
4 HILTINGBURY CT
5 CHILLINGTON GDNS
6 VANBURGH WAY
7 LAURISTON DR
8 CRANBORNE GDNS
9 STRATFIELD DR
10 ALBURY PL
11 APSLEY PL
12 ORMESBY DR
13 SIMPKINS CT
14 OAKLANDS

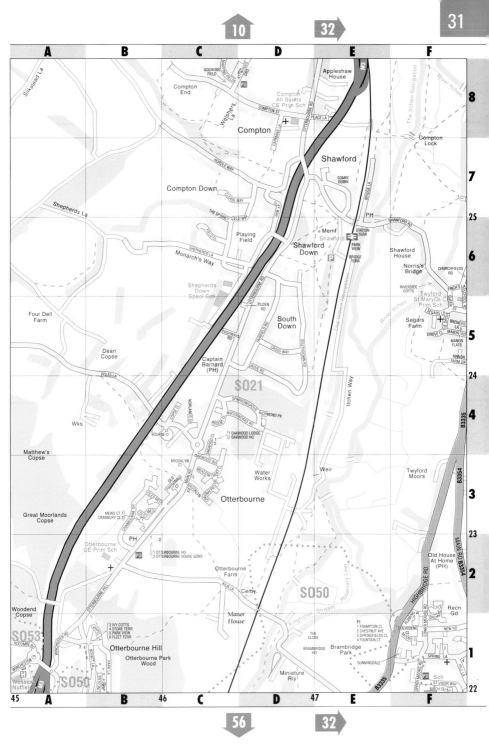

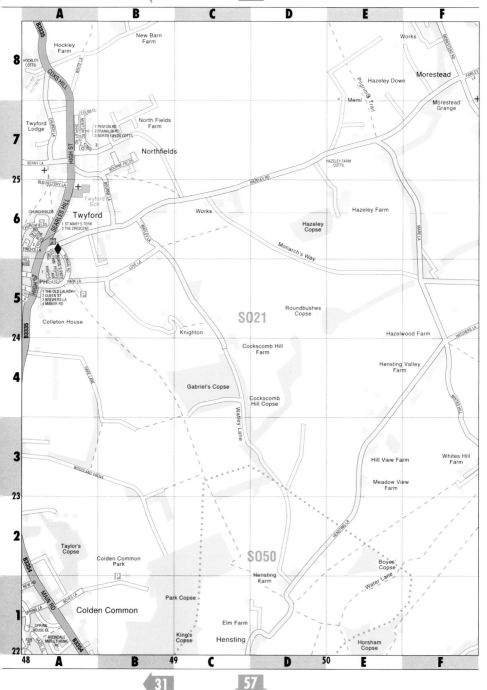

8

Hockley Farm
HOCKLEY COTTS
B3335
River Itchen
COXS HILL
New Barn Farm

Works

Morestead

MORESTEAD RD

Hazeley Down

Pilgrims' Trail

Meml

Morestead Grange

FAWLEY LA

7

Twyford Lodge
North Fields Farm

1 PENTON RD
2 FRANKLIN RD
3 NORTH FIELDS COTTS

CHURCH LA
COLES CL
NEWTON RD
SHIP LA
CUBBS

HIGH ST

Northfields

25

BERRY LA

BOURNE FIELDS

OLD RECTORY LA

Twyford Sch

HAZELEY RD

HAZELEY FARM COTTS

6

CHURCHFIELDS

Twyford

SEARLES HILL

1 ST MARY'S TERR
2 THE CRESCENT

Works

Hazeley Copse

Hazeley Farm

CHURCHFIELDS RD
PO
FINCH'S LA
HILL RISE
PH
HIGH ST
WATLEY LA
LOVE LA

NURSE'S
DOLPHIN HILL

Monarch's Way

MARE LA

5

1 THE OLD LAUNDRY
2 QUEEN ST
3 BREWERS LA
4 MANOR RD

PARK LA

Roundbushes Copse

24

B3335

Colleton House

Knighton

SO21

Cockscomb Hill Farm

Hazelwood Farm

HATCHERS LA

4

HAZEL LANE

Gabriel's Copse

Cockscomb Hill Copse

Watley Lane

Hensting Valley Farm

WHITEHILL

3

WOODLAND DRIVE

Hill View Farm

Whites Hill Farm

23

Meadow View Farm

2

Taylor's Copse

Colden Common Park

SO50

Boyes' Copse

B3354

NEW RD

MAIN RD

BOYES LA

Hensting Farm

Water Lane

HENSTING LA

1

SPRING LA

Colden Common

Park Copse

Elm Farm

22

ASH LA

SPRING HOUSE CL

HOLLY LA

AVONDALE MOBILE HOME

B3354

King's Copse

Hensting

Horsham Copse

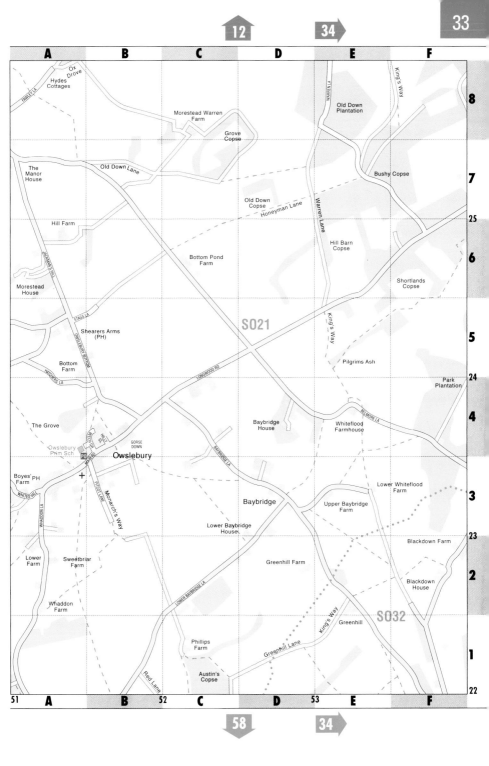

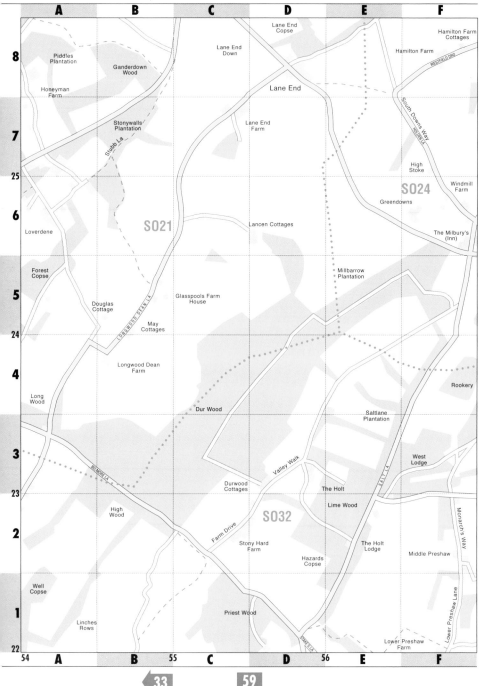

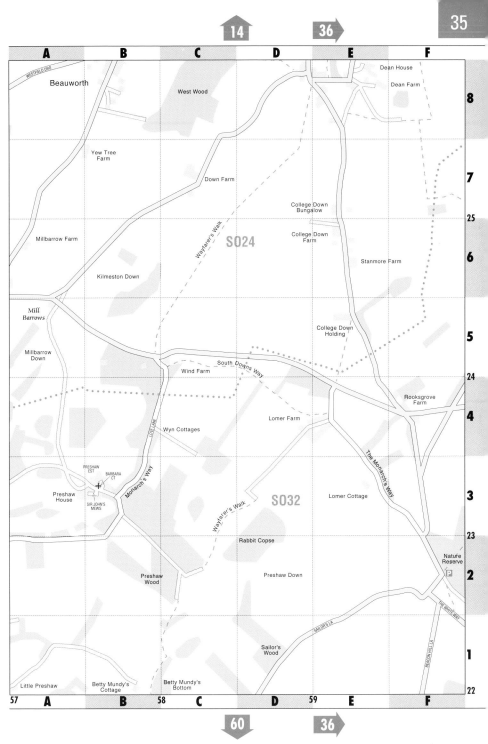

A   B   C   D   E   F

8

Beauworth

West Wood

Dean House

Dean Farm

Yew Tree
Farm

7

Down Farm

25

Millbarrow Farm

College Down
Bungalow

SO24

College Down
Farm

6

Kilmeston Down

Stanmore Farm

Mill
Barrows

5

Millbarrow
Down

College Down
Holding

Wind Farm

South Downs Way

24

Wayfarer's Walk

Rooksgrove
Farm

Wyn Cottages

Lomer Farm

4

PRESHAW
EST

BARBARA
CT

Preshaw
House

SIR JOHN'S
MEWS

Monarch's Way

LOVE LANE

Wayfarer's Walk

SO32

Lomer Cottage

The Monarch's Way

3

23

Rabbit Copse

Nature
Reserve

Preshaw
Wood

Preshaw Down

2

THE WHITE WAY

Sailor's
Wood

SAILOR'S LA.

BEACON HILL LA.

1

Little Preshaw

Betty Mundy's
Cottage

Betty Mundy's
Bottom

22

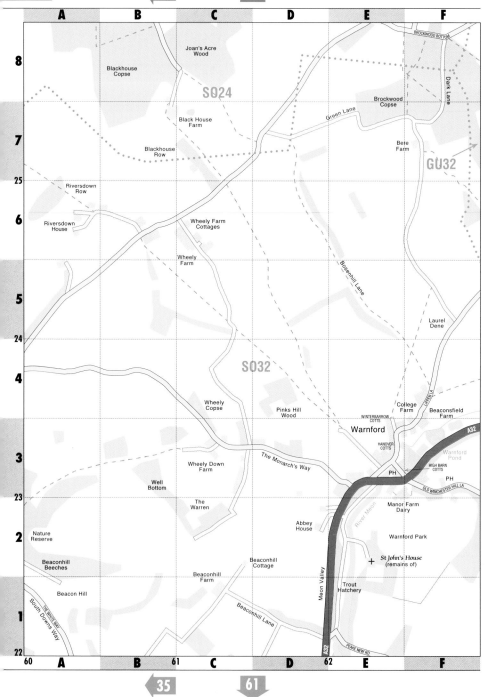

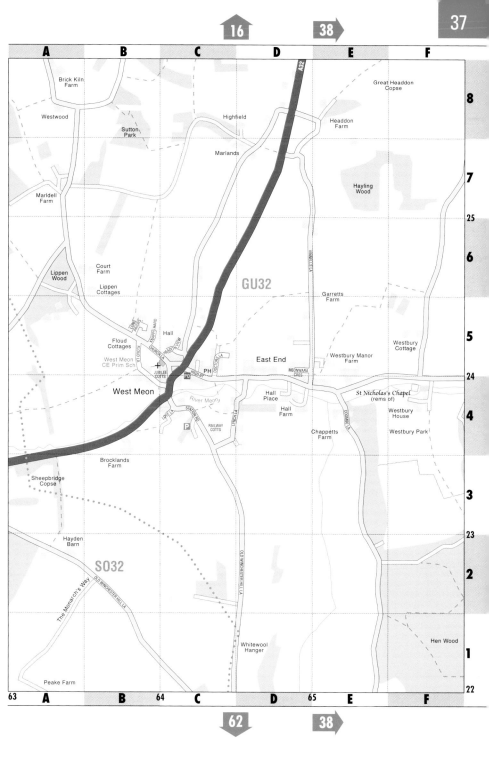

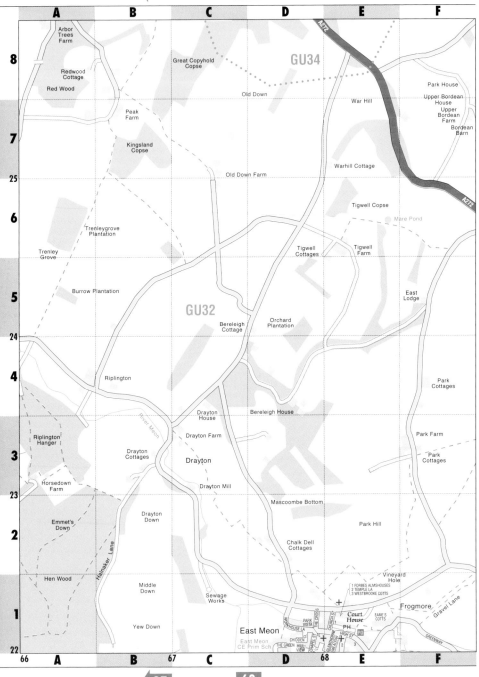

A   B   C   D   E   F

8

Arbor Trees Farm

Redwood Cottage

Red Wood

Great Copyhold Copse

Old Down

GU34

War Hill

Park House

Upper Bordean House

Upper Bordean Farm

Bordean Barn

7

Peak Farm

Kingsland Copse

25

Old Down Farm

Warhill Cottage

6

Trenleygrove Plantation

Trenley Grove

Tigwell Copse

Mare Pond

Tigwell Cottages

Tigwell Farm

5

Burrow Plantation

GU32

Bereleigh Cottage

Orchard Plantation

East Lodge

24

4

Riplington

Drayton House

Bereleigh House

Park Cottages

River Meon

Drayton Farm

Park Farm

3

Riplington Hanger

Drayton Cottages

Drayton

Park Cottages

23

Horsedown Farm

Drayton Mill

Mascoombe Bottom

2

Emmet's Down

Drayton Down

Park Hill

Hen Wood

Chalk Dell Cottages

Vineyard Hole

Frogmore

1

Halnaker Lane

Middle Down

Sewage Works

1 FORBES ALMSHOUSES
2 TEMPLE LA
3 WESTBROOKE COTTS

PARK VISTA

EAME'S COTTS

Court House

PH

Gravel Lane

GREENWAY

Yew Down

East Meon

East Meon CE Prim Sch

THE GREEN

CHIDDEN HILL VIEW

22

66   A   B   67   C   D   68   E   F

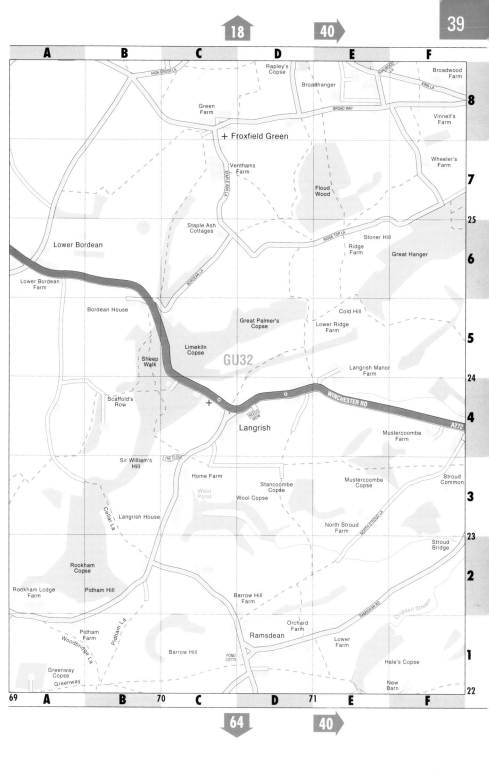

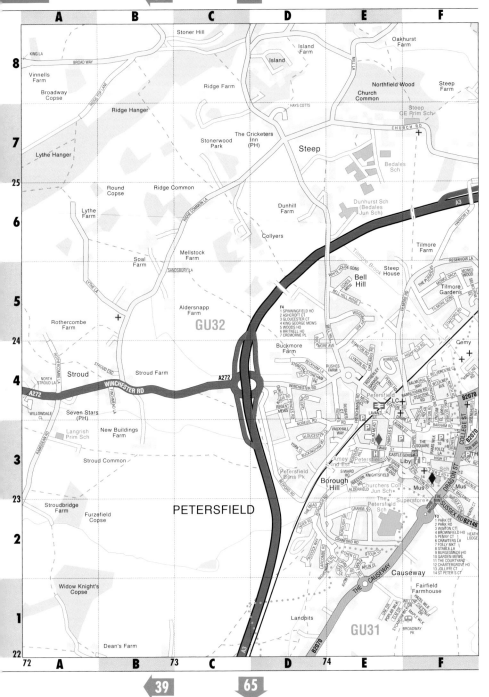

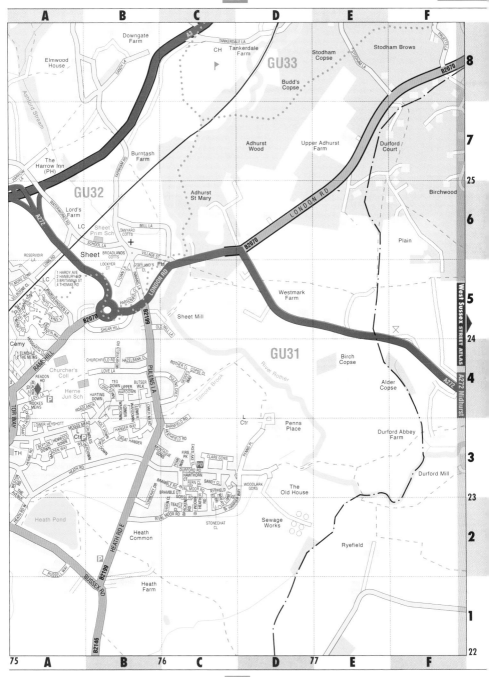

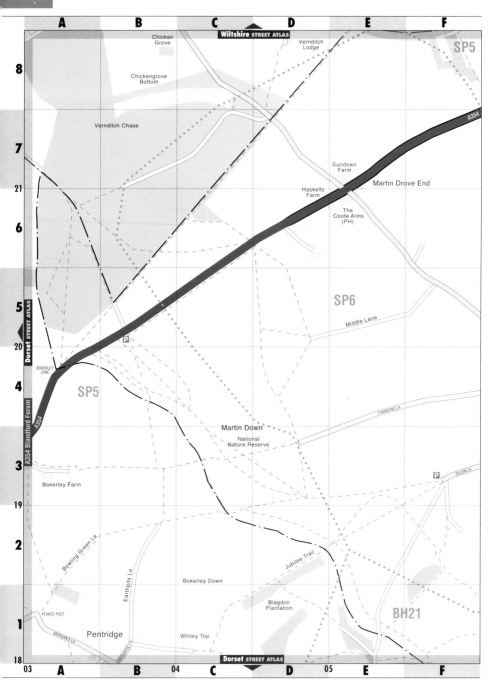

SP5

8

Chicken
Grove

Chickengrove
Bottom

Verndltch
Lodge

Verndltch Chase

A354

7

21

Sundown
Farm

Martin Drove End

Haskells
Farm

The
Coote Arms
(PH)

6

SP6

5

Middle Lane

20

BOKERLEY
JUNC

P

SP5

4

SP5

TOWNSEND LA

A354 Blandford Forum

A354

3

P

SILLEN LA

Bokerley Farm

Martin Down

National
Nature Reserve

19

2

Bowling Green La

Earthpits La

Jubilee Trail

BH21

Bokerley Down

1

PEAKED POST

Blagdon
Plantation

Pentridge

MORGAN'S LA

EARTHPITS LA

Whitey Top

18

03

04

05

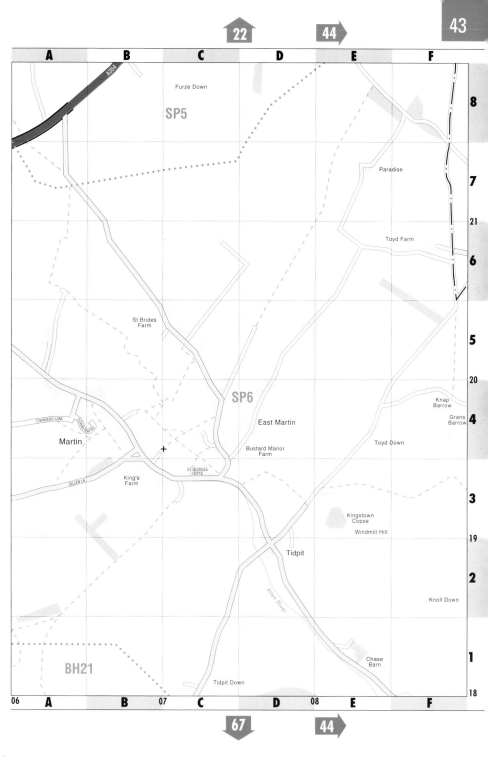

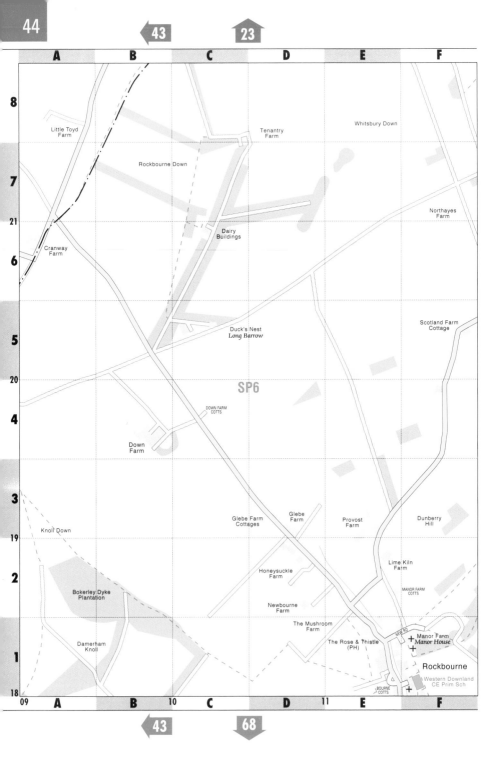

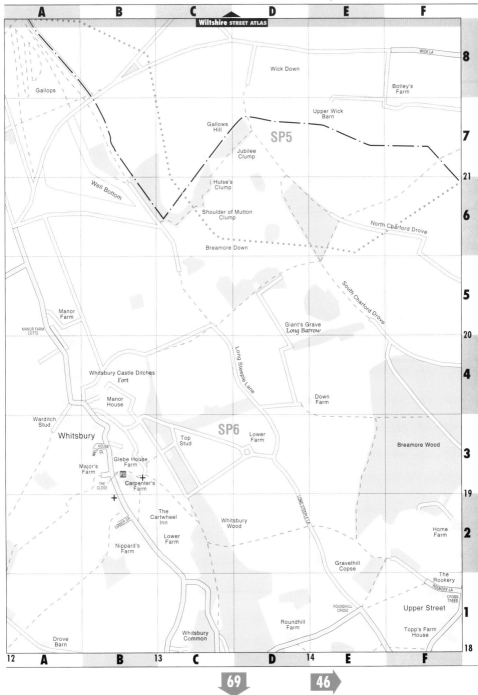

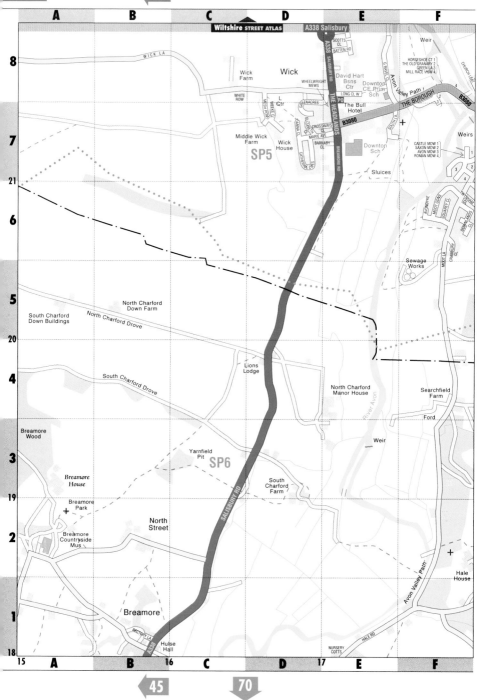

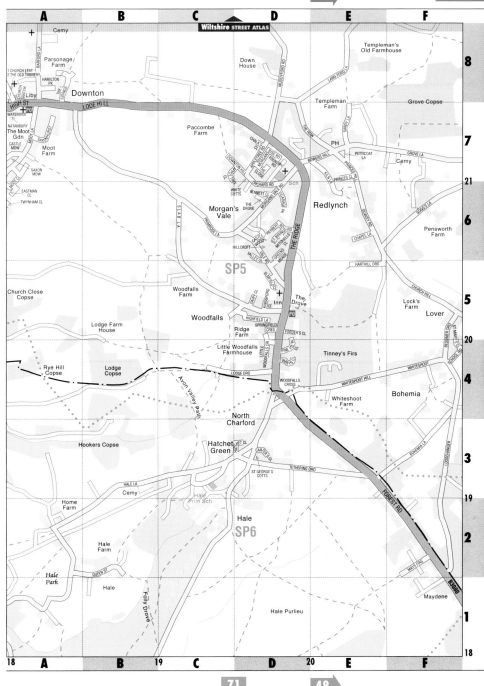

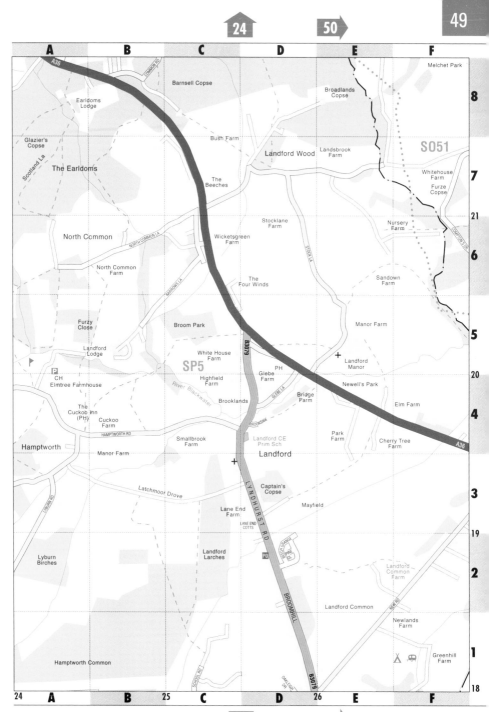

A   B   C   D   E   F

A36

Melchet Park

Barnsell Copse

Earldoms
Lodge

Broadlands
Copse

8

Glazier's
Copse

Bush Farm

Landford Wood

Landsbrook
Farm

SO51

Whitehouse
Farm

Furze
Copse

Scotland La

The Earldoms

The
Beeches

7

Stocklane
Farm

Nursery
Farm

21

North Common

NORTH COMMON LA

Wicketsgreen
Farm

STOCK LA

6

North Common
Farm

The
Four Winds

Sandown
Farm

Furzy
Close

Broom Park

Manor Farm

5

Landford
Lodge

White House
Farm

SP5

PH

Landford
Manor

B3079

Highfield
Farm

Glebe
Farm

GLEBE LA

20

CH
Elmtree Farmhouse

River Blackwater

Brooklands

Bridge
Farm

Newell's Park

Elm Farm

The
Cuckoo Inn
(PH)

Cuckoo
Farm

HAMPTWORTH RD

Smallbrook
Farm

BROOKSIDE

Landford CE
Prim Sch

Park
Farm

Cherry Tree
Farm

A36

4

Hamptworth

Manor Farm

Landford

Captain's
Copse

LYNDHURST RD

LYBURN RD

Latchmoor Drove

Lane End
Farm

Mayfield

3

Lane End
Farm

LANE END
COTTS

19

Lyburn
Birches

Landford
Larches

PO

Landford
Common
Farm

2

BROOMHILL

Landford Common

NEW RD

Newlands
Farm

SCHOOL RD

Greenhill
Farm

1

Hamptworth Common

OAK LEIGH

B3079

18

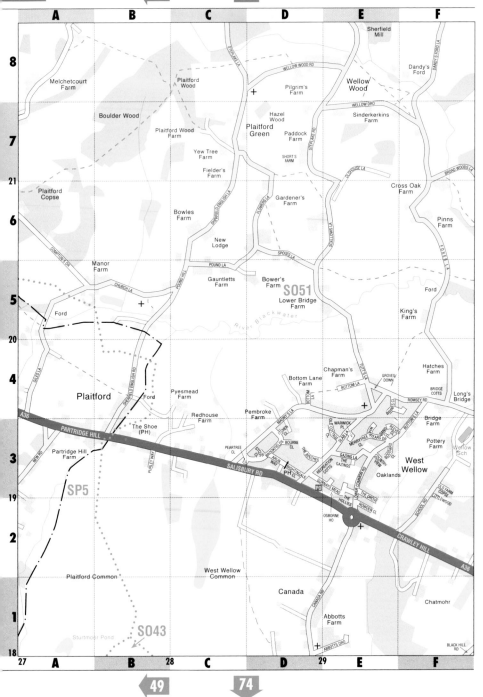

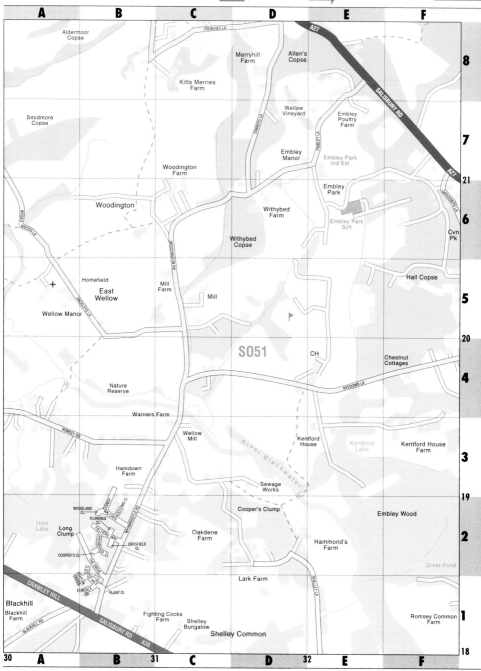

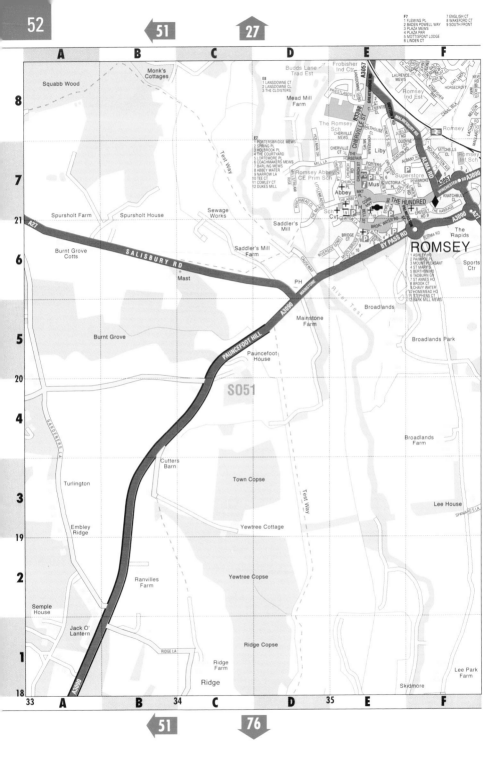

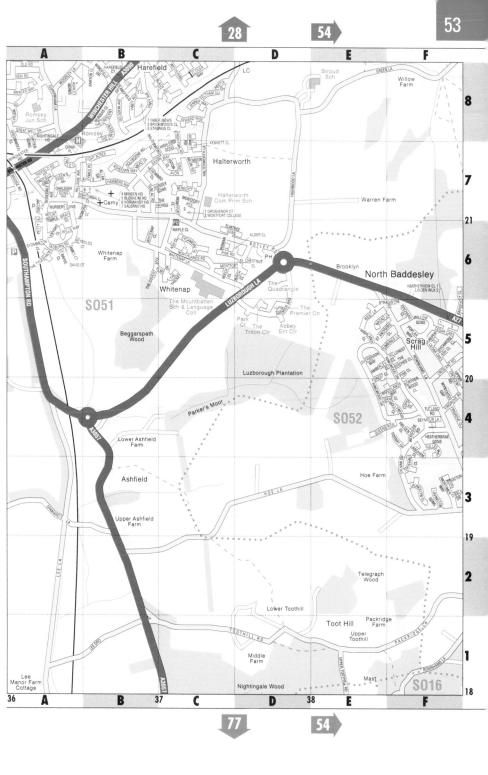

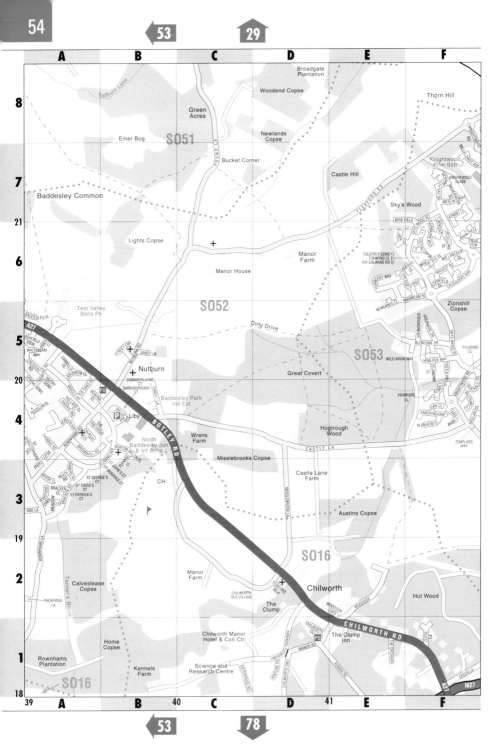

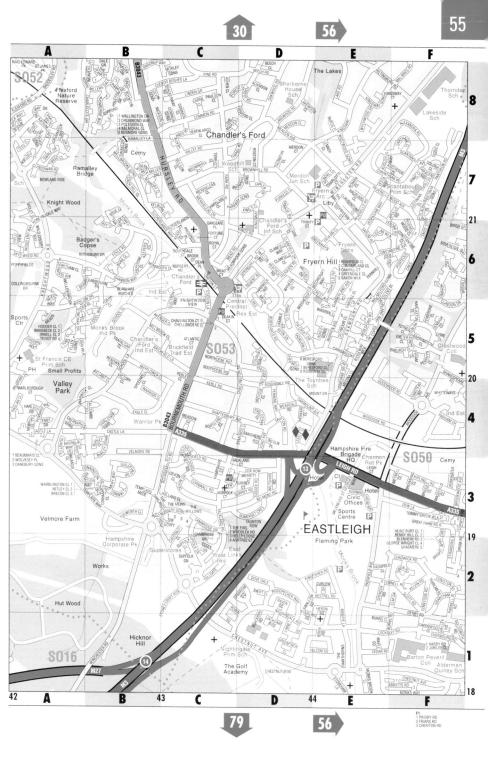

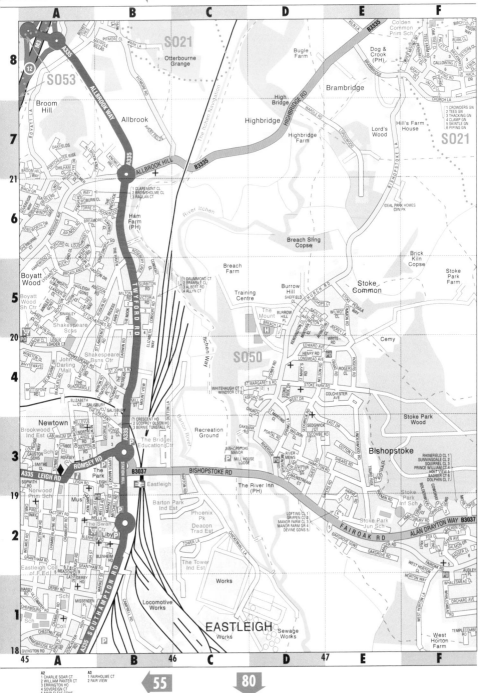

A2
1 CHARLIE SOAR CT
2 WILLIAM PANTER CT
3 ERRINGTON HO
4 SOVEREIGN CT
5 MAPLELEAF GDNS
6 THE PASTURES
7 THE CROFT
8 THE SPINNEY
9 GRANTHAM CT

A3
1 FAIRHOLME CT
2 FAIR VIEW

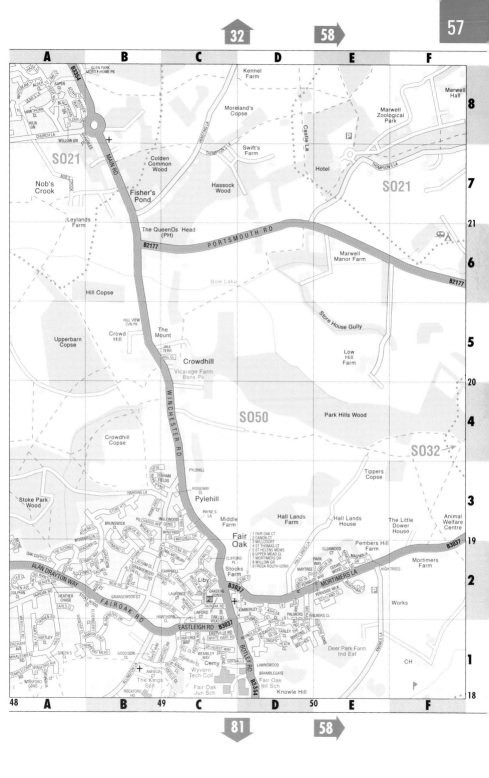

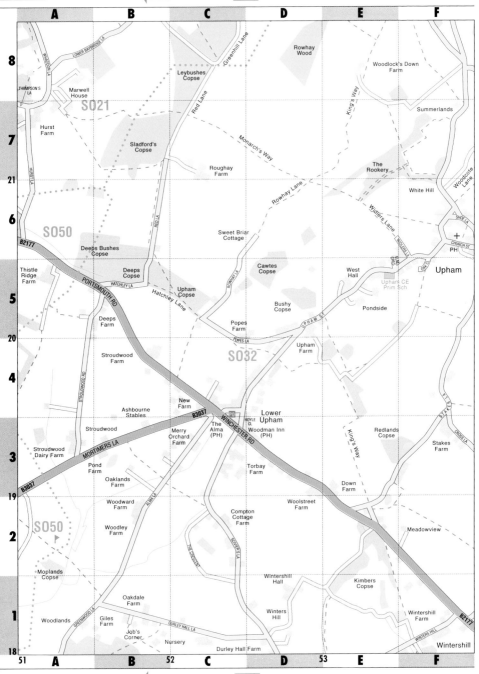

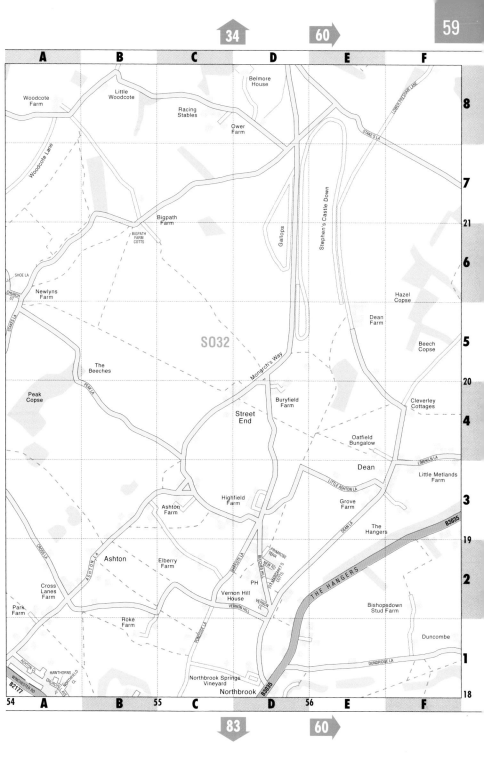

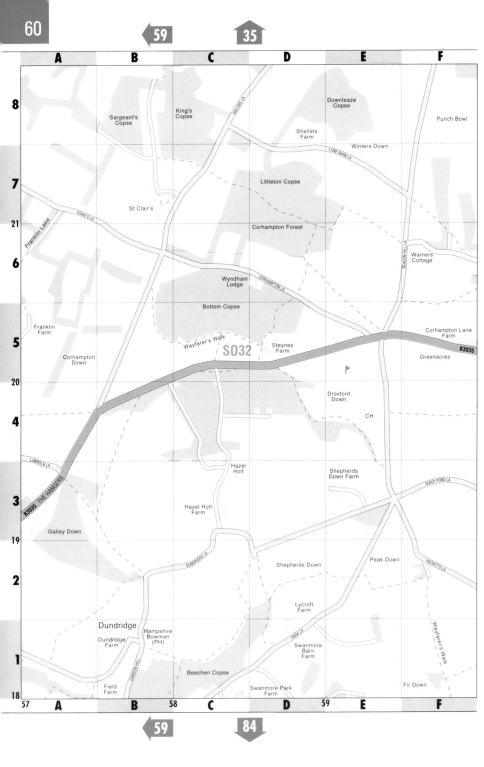

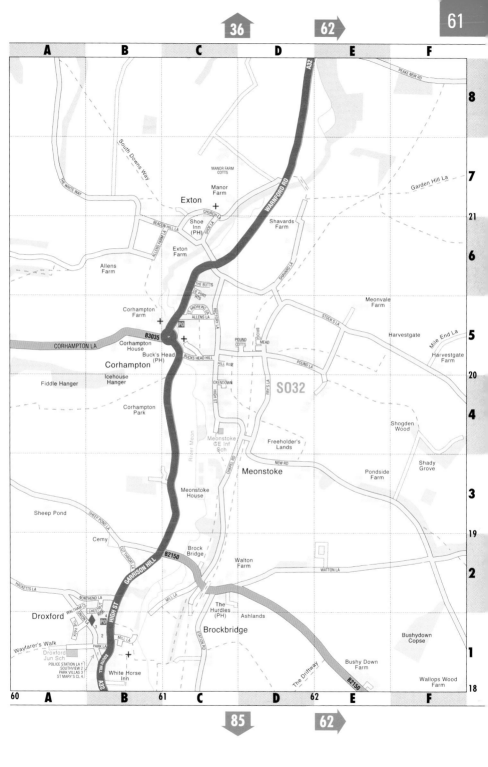

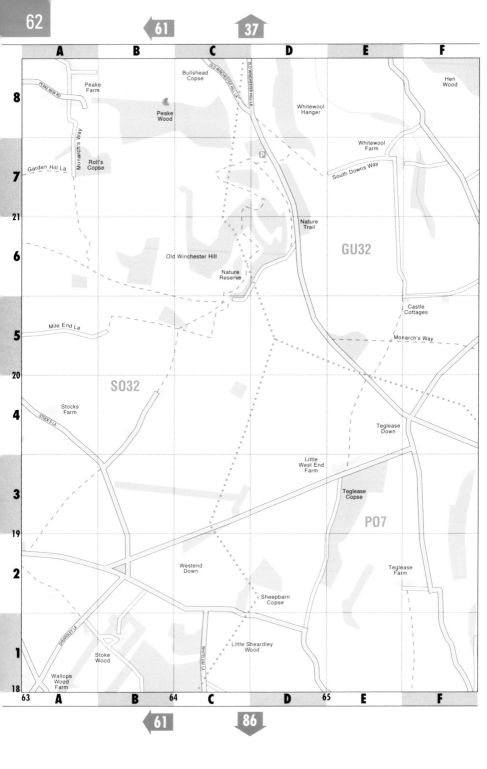

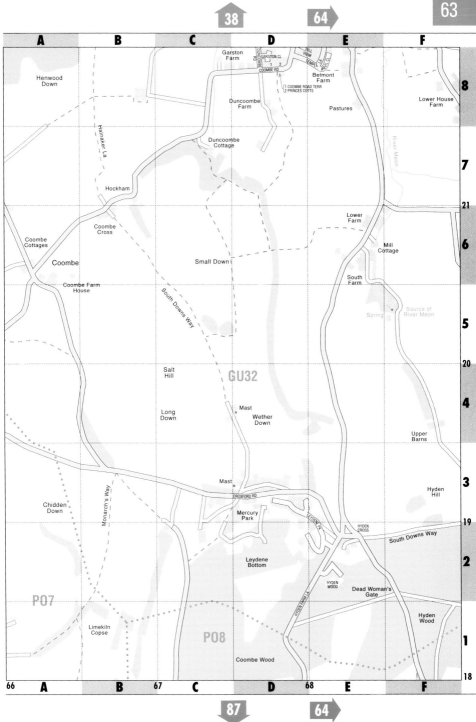

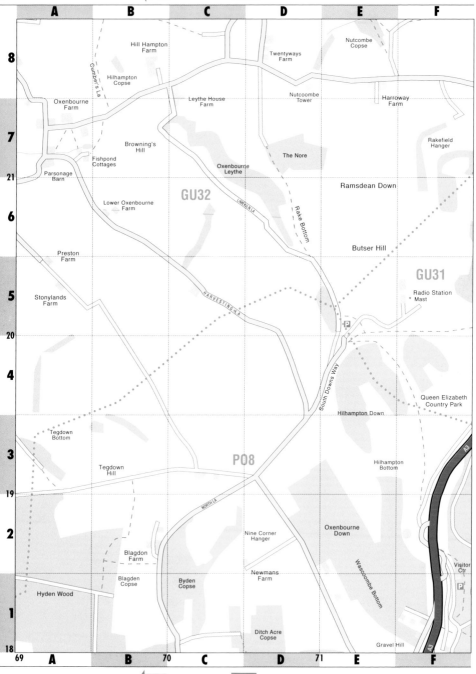

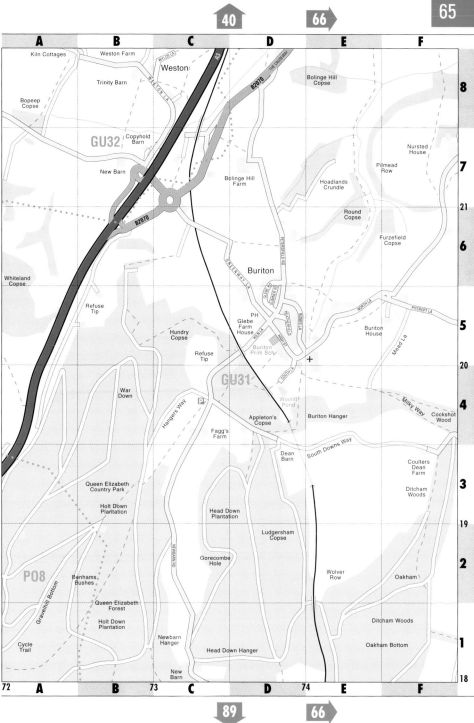

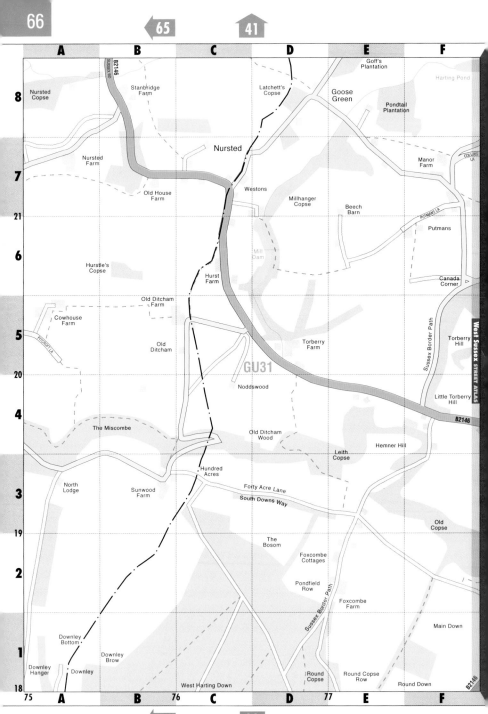

A **B** **C** **D** **E** **F**

Goff's
Plantation

Harting Pond

8

Nursted
Copse

Stanbridge
Farm

Latchett's
Copse

Goose
Green

Pondtail
Plantation

B2146
SUSSEX RD

7

Nursted
Farm

Nursted

Westons

Manor
Farm

COLINS LA

Old House
Farm

Millhanger
Copse

Beech
Barn

PUTMANS LA

21

Putmans

6

Hurstle's
Copse

Hurst
Farm

Mill
Dam

Canada
Corner

Old Ditcham
Farm

5

Cowhouse
Farm

PITCROFT LA

Old
Ditcham

Torberry
Farm

Sussex Border Path

Torberry
Hill

West Sussex STREET ATLAS

GU31

20

Noddswood

Little Torberry
Hill

4

The Miscombe

Old Ditcham
Wood

Hemner Hill

B2146

Hundred
Acres

Leith
Copse

3

North
Lodge

Sunwood
Farm

Forty Acre Lane

South Downs Way

19

The
Bosom

Old
Copse

Foxcombe
Cottages

2

Pondfield
Row

Sussex Border Path

Foxcombe
Farm

Main Down

1

Downley
Bottom

Downley
Brow

Round
Copse

Round Copse
Row

Round Down

B2146

18

Downley
Hanger

Downley

West Harting Down

A **B** 76 **C** **D** 77 **E** **F**

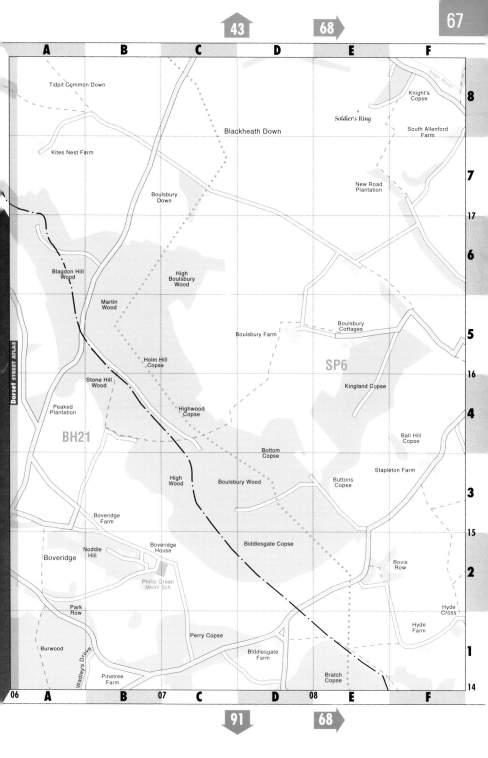

A   **B**   **C**   **D**   **E**   **F**

Tidpit Common Down

Allen River

Knight's Copse

8

Blackheath Down

Soldier's Ring

South Allenford Farm

Kites Nest Farm

7

New Road Plantation

Boulsbury Down

17

6

Blagdon Hill Wood

High Boulsbury Wood

Martin Wood

Boulsbury Cottages

Boulsbury Farm

5

SP6

Holm Hill Copse

16

Stone Hill Wood

Kingland Copse

Peaked Plantation

Highwood Copse

4

BH21

Bottom Copse

Ball Hill Copse

Stapleton Farm

High Wood

Boulsbury Wood

Buttons Copse

3

Boveridge Farm

Biddlesgate Copse

15

Noddle Hill

Boveridge House

Boveridge

Bovis Row

2

Philip Green Meml Sch

Hyde Cross

Park Row

Hyde Farm

Burwood

Perry Copse

Biddlesgate Farm

1

Wadleys Drove

Bratch Copse

Pinetree Farm

14

06   **A**   **B**   07   **C**   **D**   08   **E**   **F**

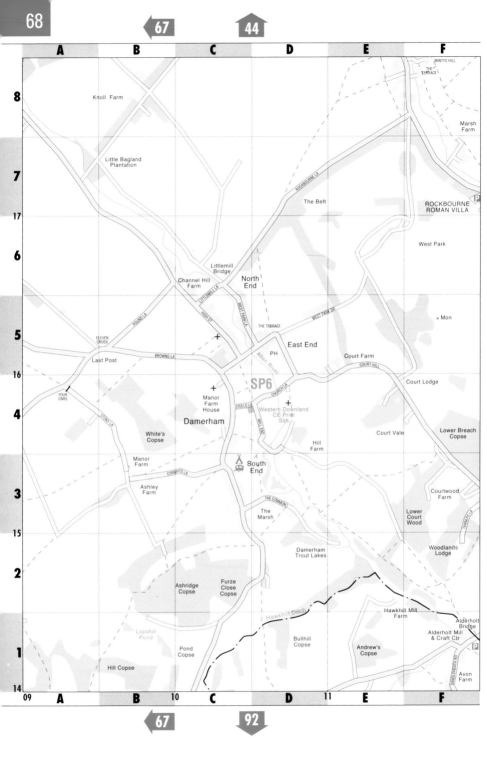

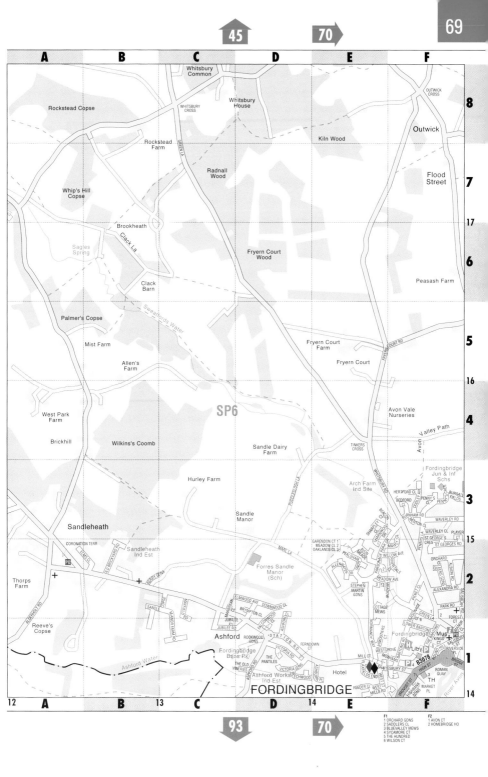

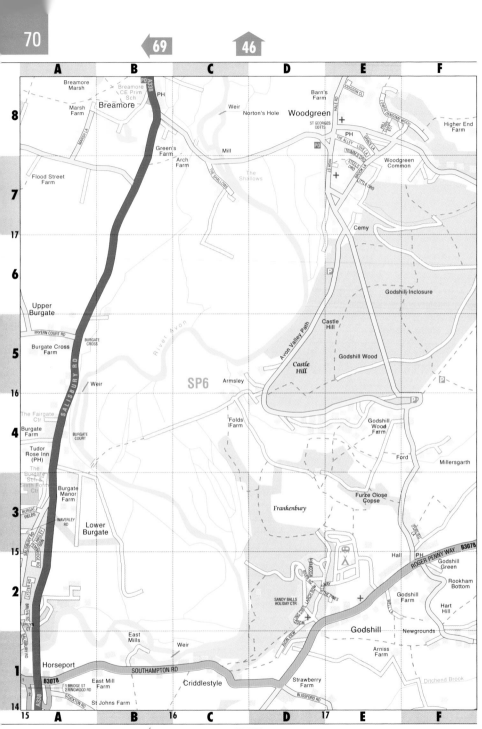

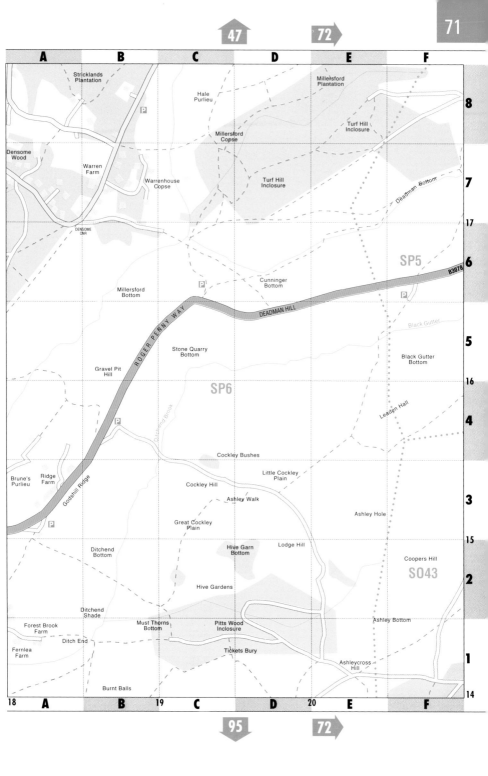

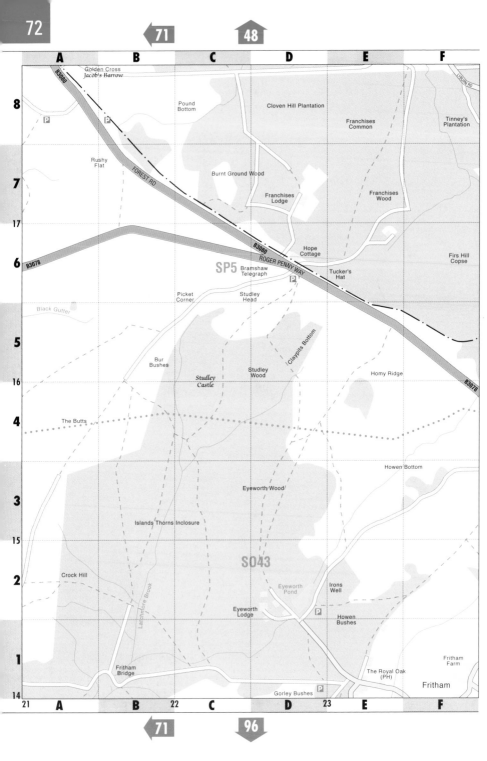

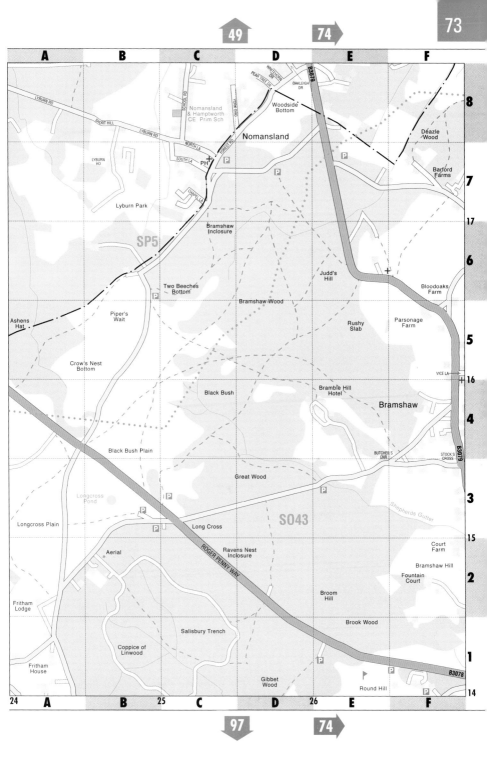

73
50

| A | B | C | D | E | F |

SP5

8

Rockingham Arms (PH)

Black Hill

P

PLANTATION RD

CANADA RD

KINGSTON PK

P

Canada Common

+

Pitts Farm

SO51

Swallow Fields

BLACK HILL RD

7

Wicksmoor Farmhouse

Penn Common

Cooper's Lane

17

Hungerford Farm

6

Furzley

Furzley Farm

FOREST LA

Penn Farm

Half Moon Common

SO43

5

Mark's Farm

Furzley Common

Penn Copse

Duck Hill

16

Stagbury Hill

Porters Farm

4

Crock Hill

STOCK'S CROSS

Blenmans Farm

Newbridge

FURZLEY RD

NEWBRIDGE RD

3

B3079

STABLE COTTS

Warrens House

Cadnam Common

Cadnam River

15

Warren's Park

Storm's Farm

2

PO

Brook Hill

Warren's Farm

SO40

Cadnam Green

Withers Farm

BROOK LANE

NEW AGE LA

SILVER LA

1

ROGER PENNY WAY

CH

Brook

The Bell Inn Hotel

Manor Farm

Springer's Farm

Dairyhouse Farm

Manor Farm

M27

OLD LYNDHURST RD

A31

B3078

14

B3079

WITTENSFORD LA

| 27 | A | B | 28 | C | D | 29 | E | F |

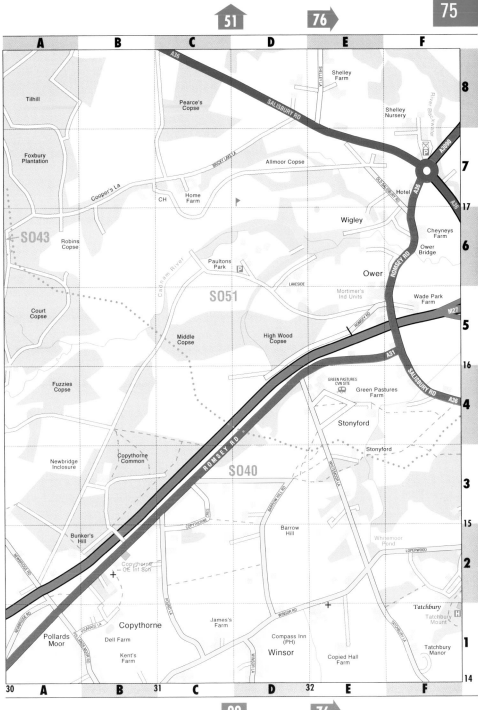

51
76
76

75
52

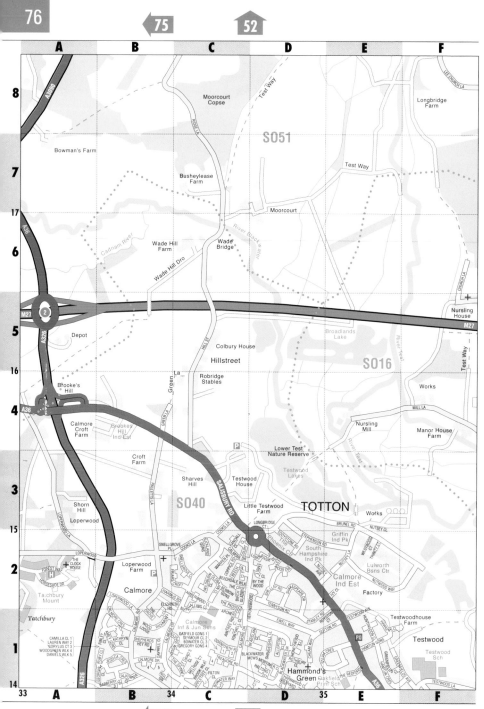

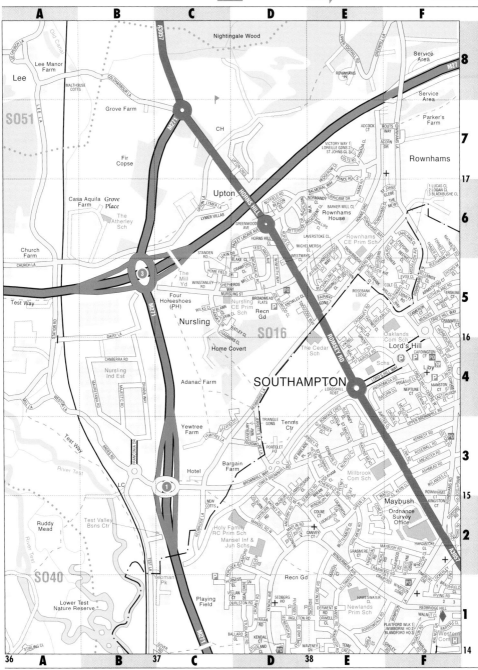

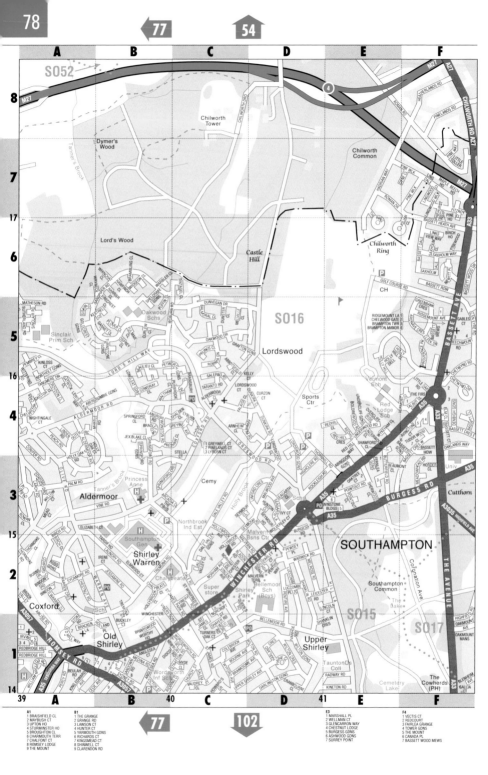

S052

Chilworth Tower

Dymer's Wood

Chilworth Common

Tanner's Brook

Lord's Wood

Castle Hill

Chilworth Ring

Chilworth Common

GOLF COURSE RD CH

SO16

Oakwood Schs

Lordswood

Sinclair Prim Sch

RIDGEMOUNT LA
CHELWOOD GATE
BRAMPTON TWR
BRAMPTON MANOR

Red Lodge Sch

Sports Ctr

Shawford

Bassett
MDW

Univ

1 GREYWELL CT
2 PINELANDS CT
3 LYBORN CT

Cemy

Cutthorn

BURGESS RD

A35

A3035 HIGHFIELD AVE

Princess Anne

Aldermoor

Northbrook Ind Est

POWINSTONE BLDGS

A35

Beaumont

Oaklands Way

Bassett

Elizabeth Ct

Southampton Gen

Shirley Warren

Chalybeate

Malvern Bsns Ctr

SOUTHAMPTON

Super store

Shirley Park

Bellemoor Sch (Boys)

Southampton Common

Colrington Ave

SO15

The Dale

THE AVENUE

Coxford

Old Shirley

Upper Shirley

SO17

SO15

ROMSEY RD

REDBRIDGE HILL
REDBRIDGE HILL

WINCHESTER RD

A3057

Taunton Ds Coll

RADWAY RD

KINETON RD

Cemetery Lake

The Cowherds (PH)

A1
1 BRAISHFIELD CL
2 MAYBUSH CT
3 UPTON HO
4 STURMINSTER HO
5 BROUGHTON CL
6 CHARMOUTH TERR
7 CHALFONT CT
8 ROMSEY LODGE
9 THE MOUNT

B1
1 THE GRANGE
2 GRANGE RD
3 LAWSON CT
4 HUNTER CT
5 YARMOUTH GDNS
6 RICHARDS CT
7 KINGSMEAD CT
8 SHINWELL CT
9 CLARENDON RD

E3
1 MARSHALL PL
2 WELLMAN CT
3 GLENCARRON WAY
4 CHESTNUT LODGE
5 BURGESS GDNS
6 ASHWOOD GDNS
7 SURREY POINT

F4
1 VECTIS CT
2 REDCOURT
3 FAIRLEA GRANGE
4 TOWER GDNS
5 THE MOUNT
6 CANADA PL
7 BASSETT WOOD MEWS

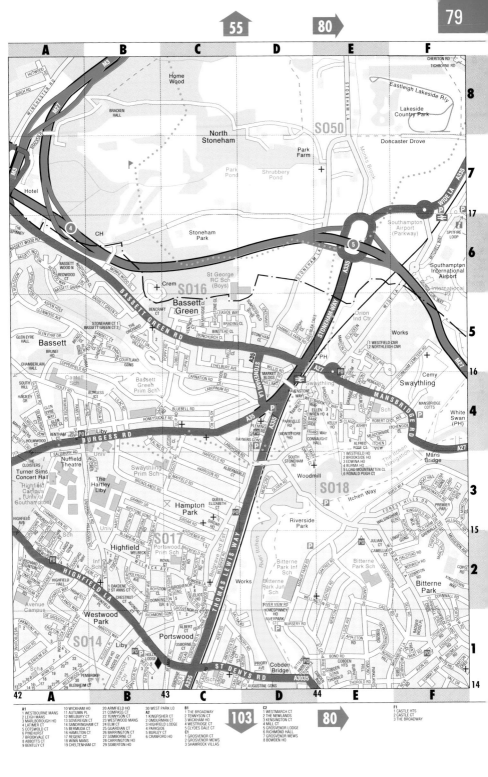

A1
1 WESTBOURNE MANS
2 LEIGH MANS
3 MARLBOROUGH HO
4 LATIMER CT
5 COTSWOLD CT
6 PINEHURST
7 BROOKVALE CT
8 ABBOTTS CT
9 BENTLEY CT

10 WICKHAM HO
11 AUTUMN PL
12 MELBURY CT
13 SOVEREIGN CT
14 SANDRINGHAM CT
15 BERMUDA CT
16 HAMILTON CT
17 REGENT CT
18 WINN MANS
19 CHELTENHAM CT

20 ARMFIELD HO
21 COMPASS CT
22 TENNYSON CT
23 WESTWOOD MANS
24 ELM CT
25 GUARDIAN CT
26 BARRINGTON CT
27 SOMBORNE CT
28 CARRINGTON HO
29 SOBERTON HO

30 WEST PARK LO
A2
1 KINGFISHER CT
2 OMDURMAN CT
3 HIGHFIELD LODGE
4 PARKSIDE
5 BURLEY CT
6 CRANFORD HO

B1
1 THE BROADWAY
2 TENNYSON CT
3 WICKHAM HO
4 WESTRIDGE CT
5 GROSVENOR LODGE
6 RICHMOND HALL
7 GROSVENOR MEWS
8 BOWDEN HO

C1
1 GROSVENOR CT
2 GROSVENOR MEWS
3 SHAMROCK VILLAS

C2
1 WESTMARCH CT
2 THE NEWLANDS
3 KENSINGTON CT
4 MILL CT
5 GROSVENOR LODGE
6 RICHMOND HALL
7 GROSVENOR MEWS
8 BOWDEN HO

F1
1 CASTLE HTS
2 CASTLE CT
3 THE BROADWAY

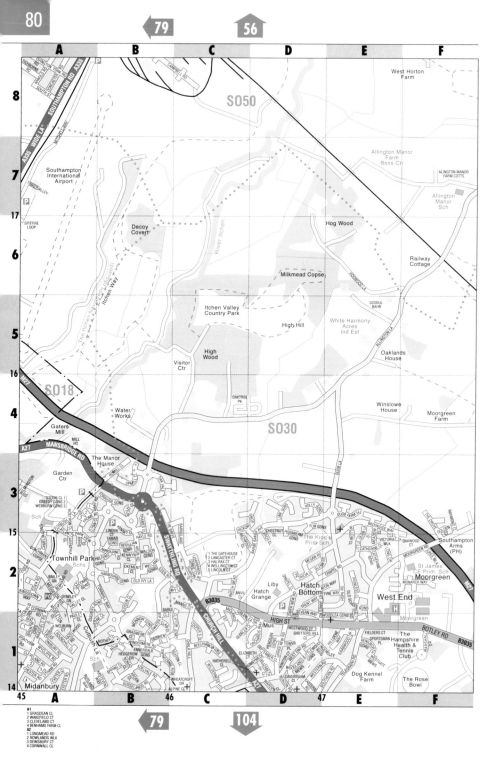

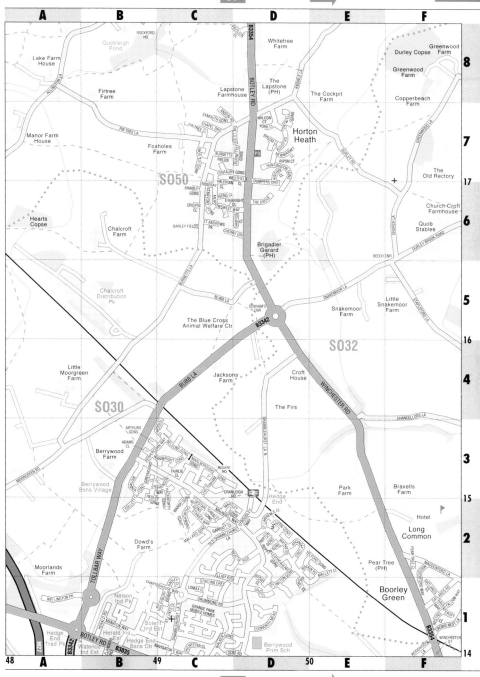

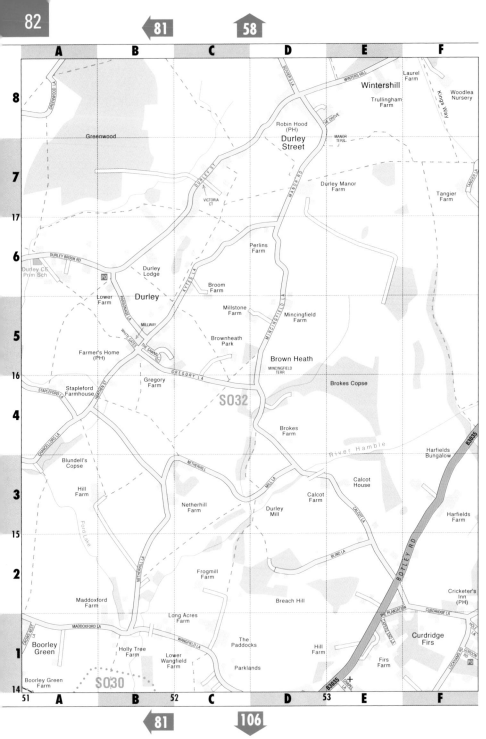

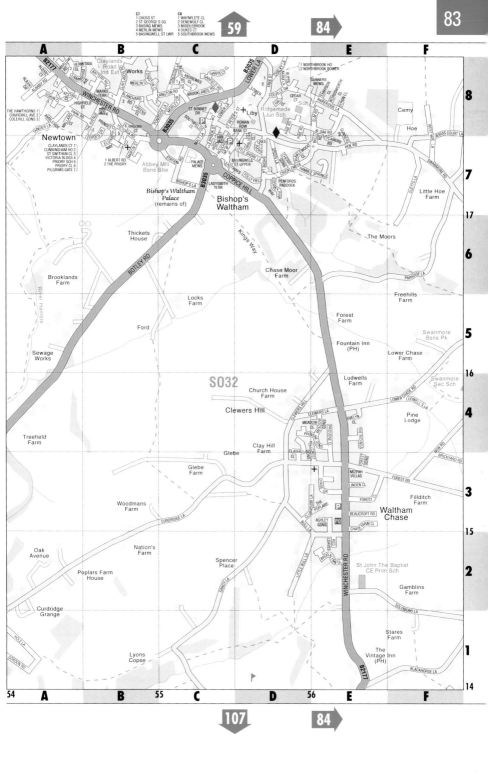

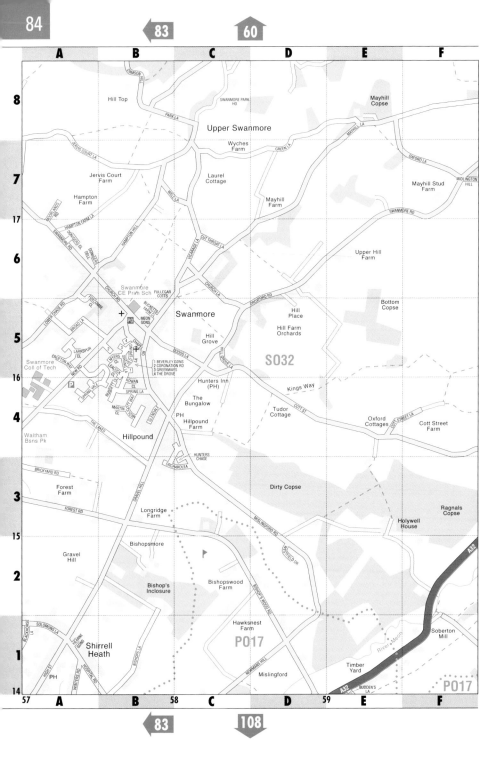

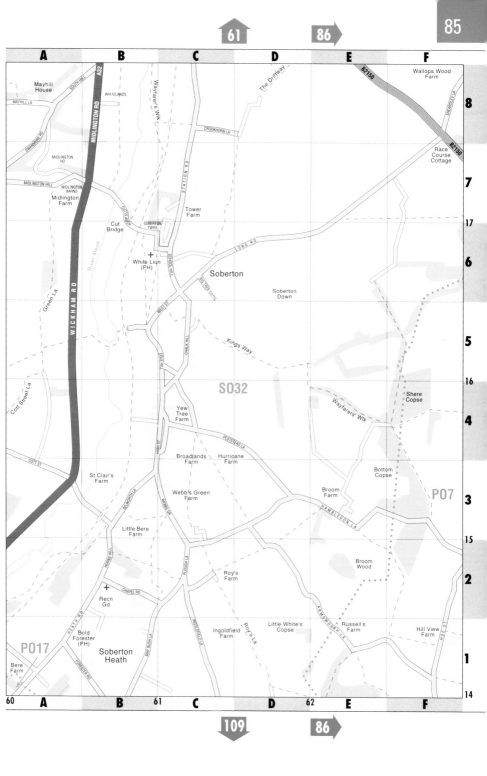

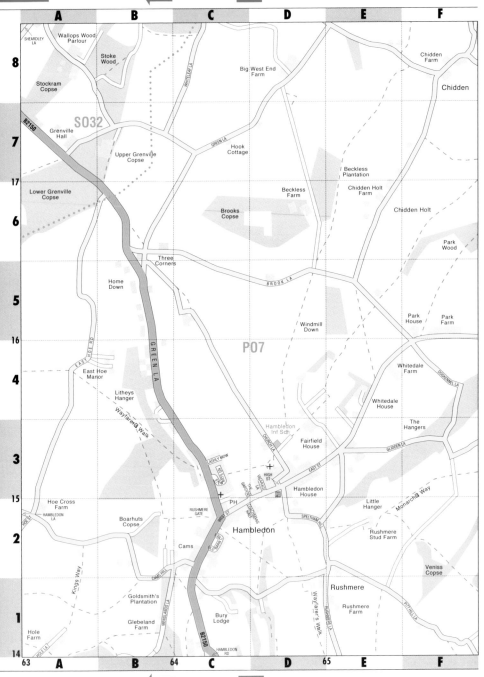

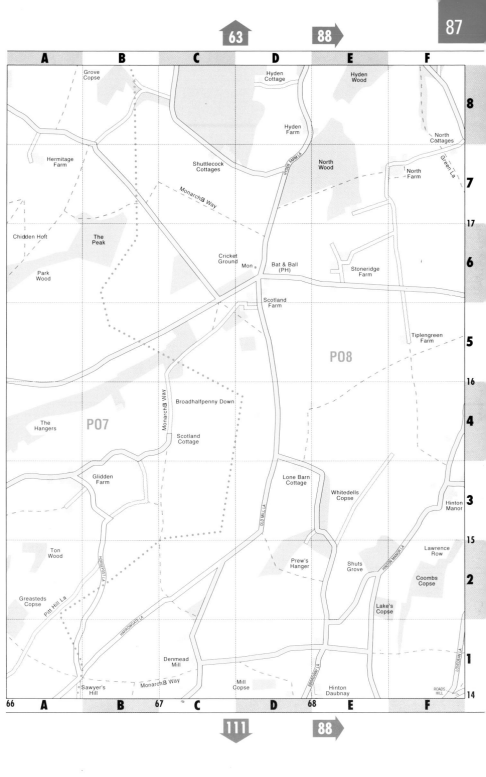

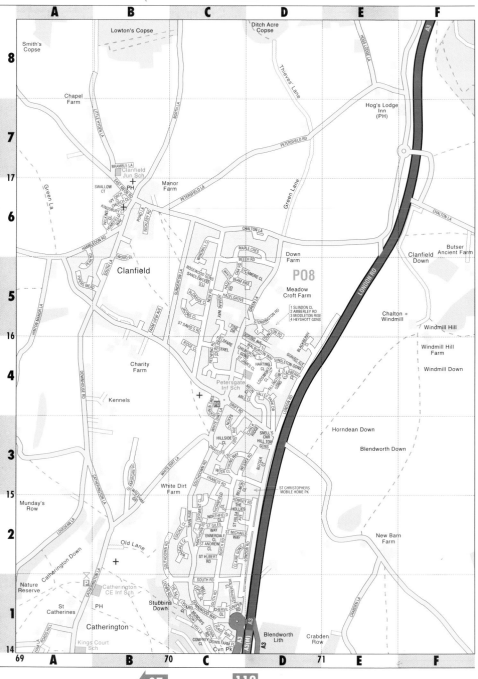

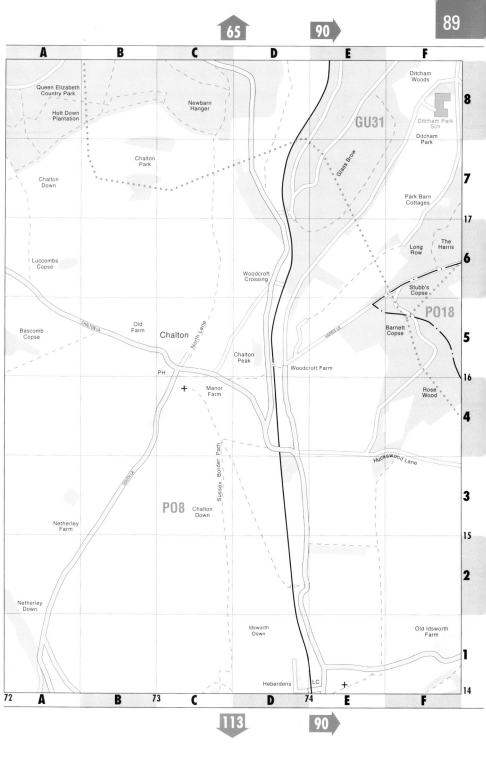

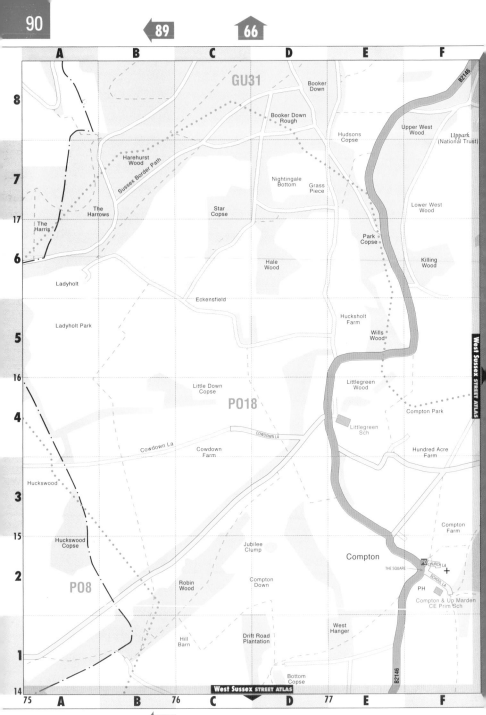

A   B   C   D   E   F

8

GU31

Booker
Down

Booker Down
Rough

Upper West
Wood

Uppark
(National Trust)

Hudsons
Copse

Harehurst
Wood

7

Sussex Border Path

Nightingale
Bottom

Grass
Piece

Lower West
Wood

17

The
Harrows

Star
Copse

Park
Copse

The
Harris

6

Ladyholt

Hale
Wood

Killing
Wood

Eckensfield

Ladyholt Park

Hucksholt
Farm

5

Wills
Wood

16

Little Down
Copse

Littlegreen
Wood

PO18

Compton Park

4

Cowdown La

COWDOWN LA

Littlegreen
Sch

Huckswood

Cowdown
Farm

Hundred Acre
Farm

3

Huckswood
Copse

15

Jubilee
Clump

Compton
Farm

2

PO8

Robin
Wood

Compton
Down

Compton

THE SQUARE

PO
CHURCH LA

SCHOOL LA

PH

Compton & Up Marden
CE Prim Sch

Hill
Barn

Drift Road
Plantation

West
Hanger

1

Bottom
Copse

14

75   A   B   76   C   D   77   E   F

B2146

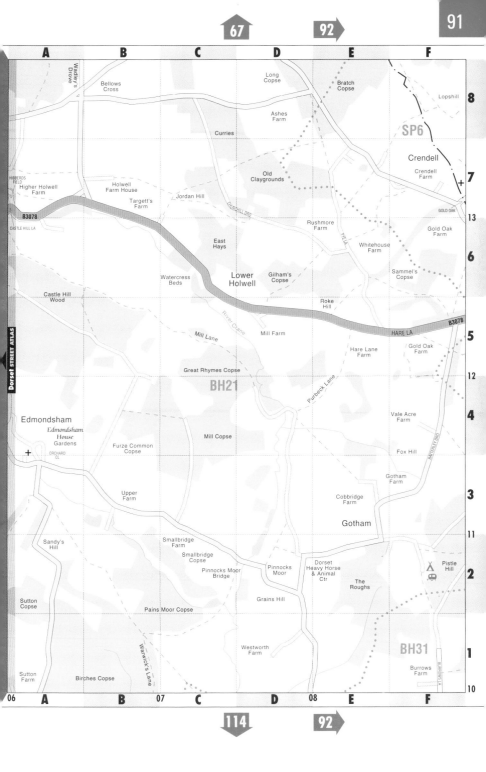

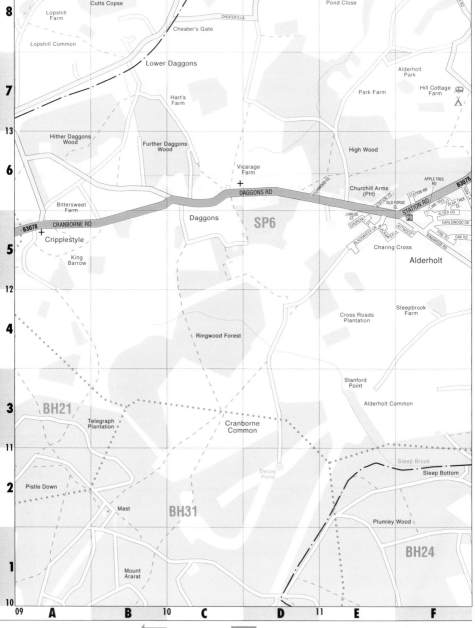

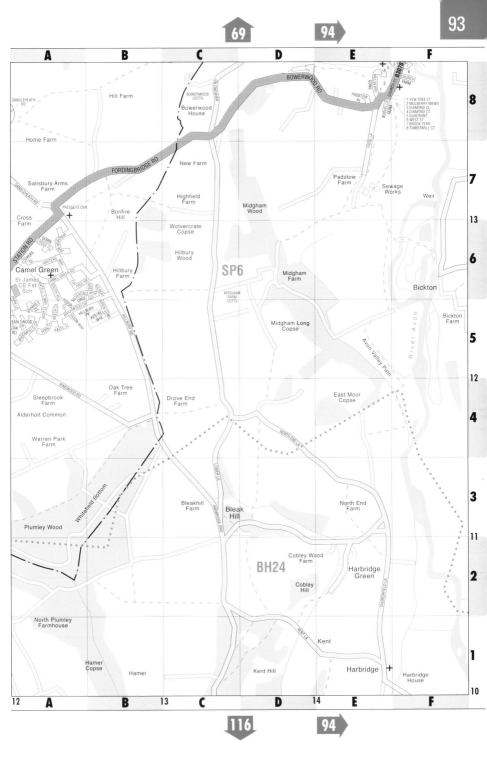

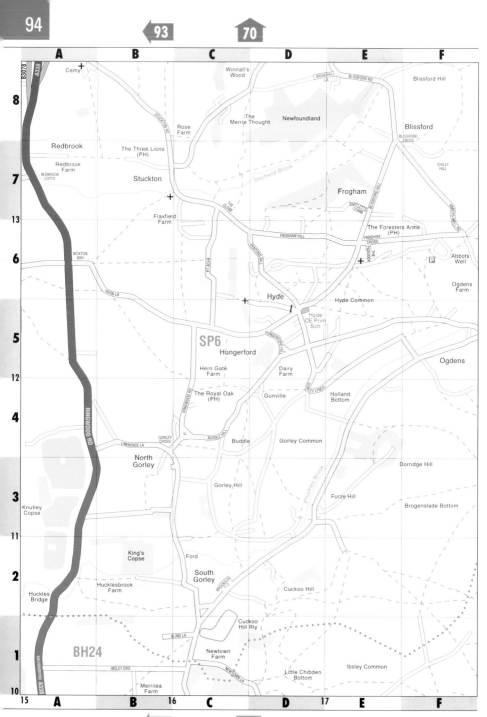

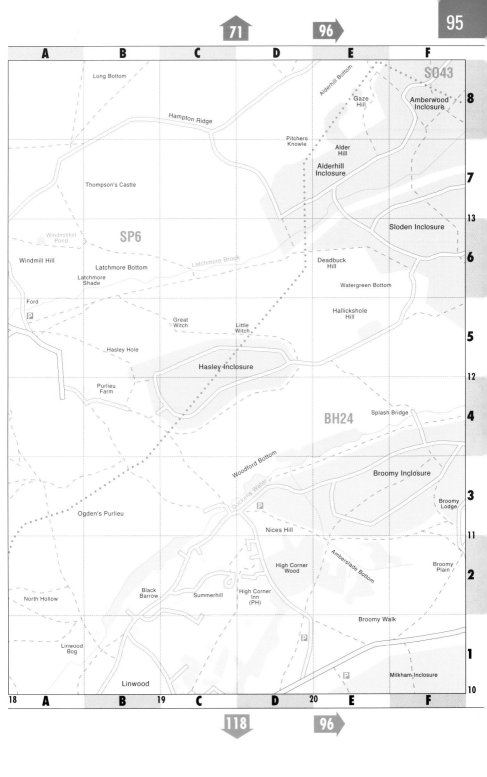

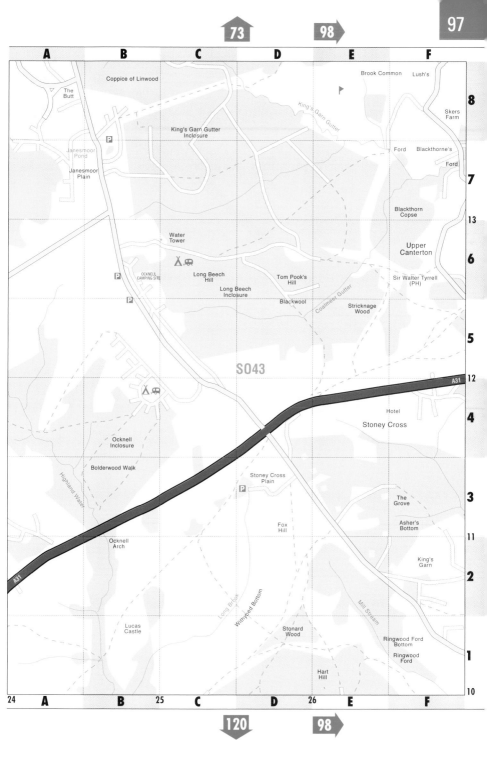

A   B   C   D   E   F

The Butt

Coppice of Linwood

Brook Common   Lush's

8

Skers Farm

King's Garn Gutter

King's Garn Gutter Inclosure

Janesmoor Pond

Ford   Blackthorne's

Ford

7

Janesmoor Plain

Blackthorn Copse

13

Water Tower

Upper Canterton

6

Long Beech Hill

OCKNELL CAMPING SITE

Long Beech Inclosure

Tom Pook's Hill

Sir Walter Tyrrell (PH)

Blackwool

Stricknage Wood

Coalmeer Gutter

5

SO43

12

A31

Hotel

Stoney Cross

4

Ocknell Inclosure

Bolderwood Walk

Stoney Cross Plain

The Grove

Asher's Bottom

3

Highland Water

Fox Hill

11

Ocknell Arch

King's Garn

2

Mill Stream

Long Brook

Withybed Bottom

Lucas Castle

Stonard Wood

Ringwood Ford Bottom

Ringwood Ford

1

Hart Hill

10

24   A   B   25   C   D   26   E   F

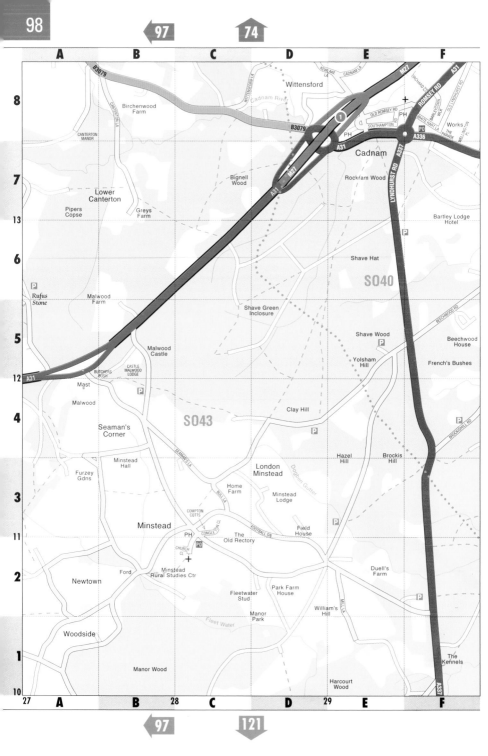

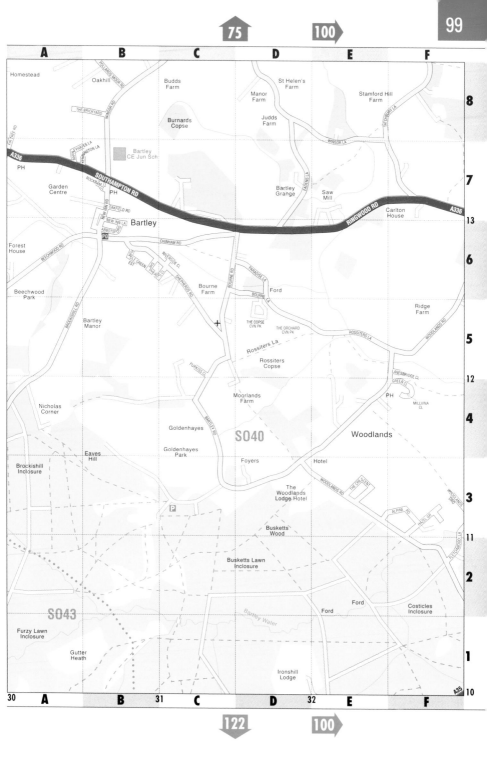

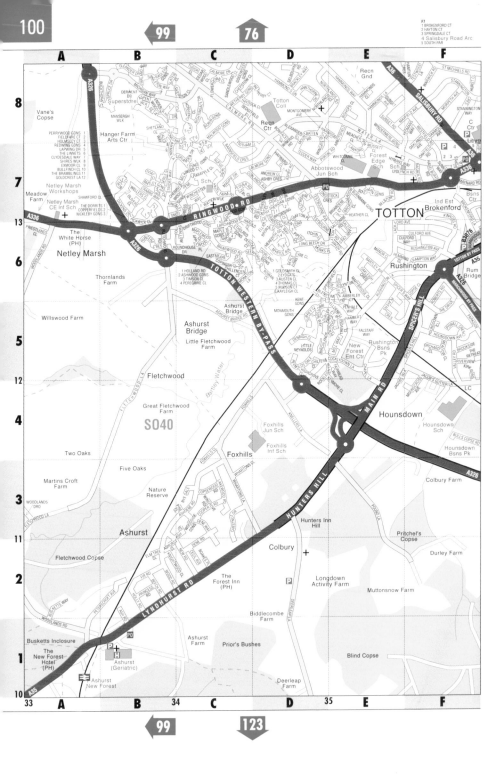

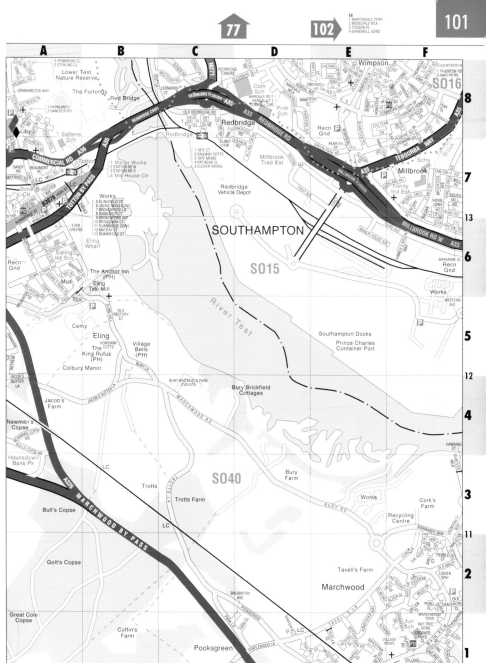

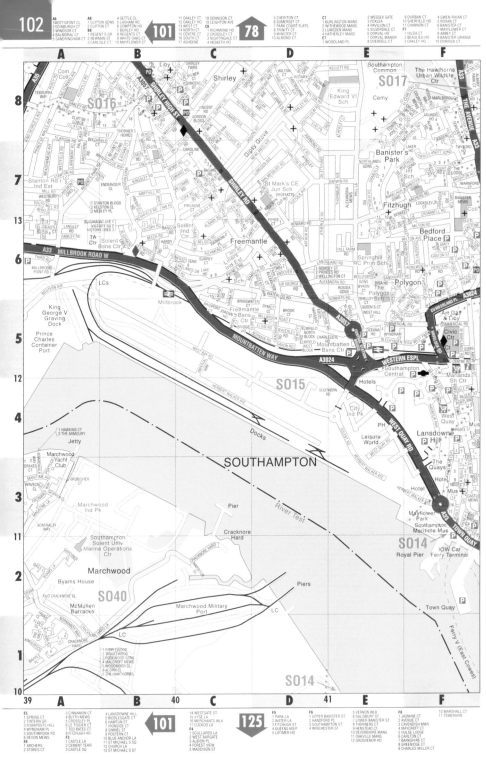

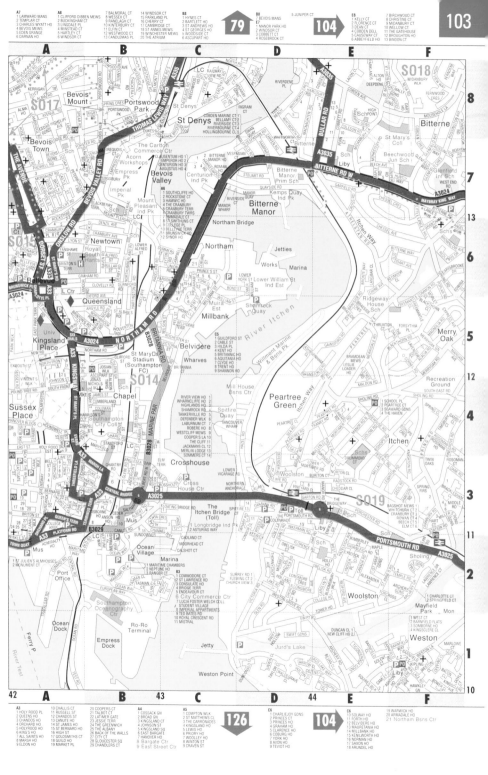

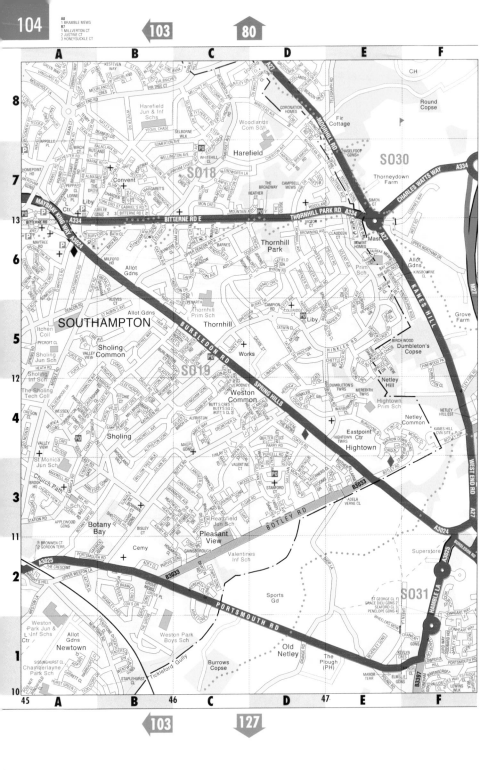

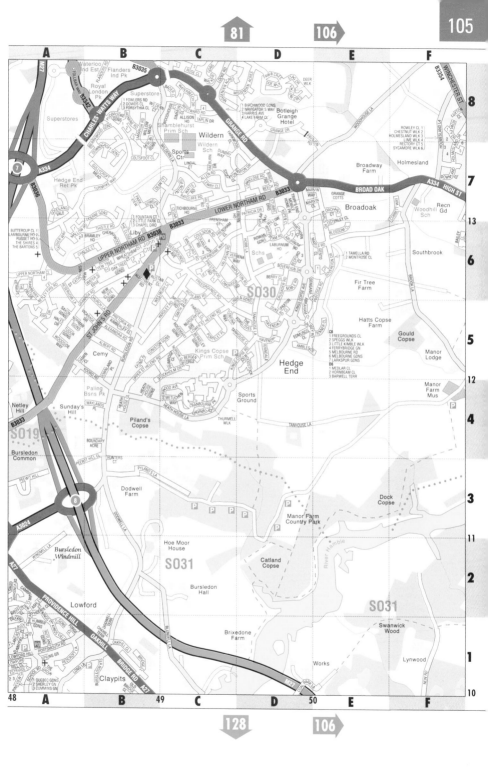

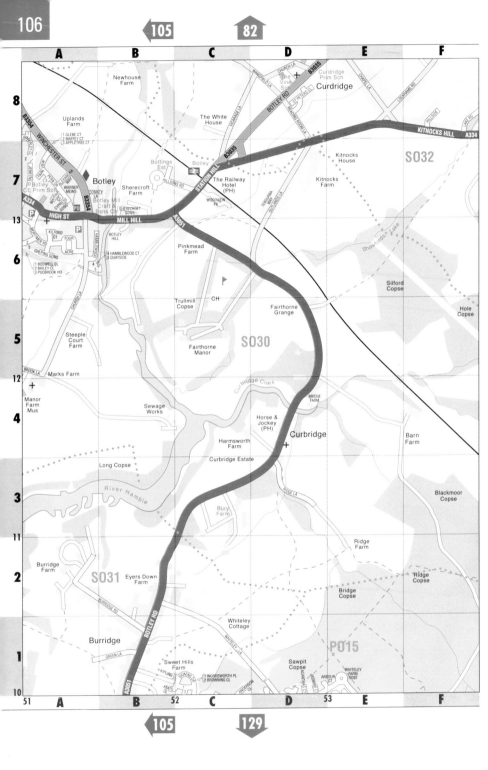

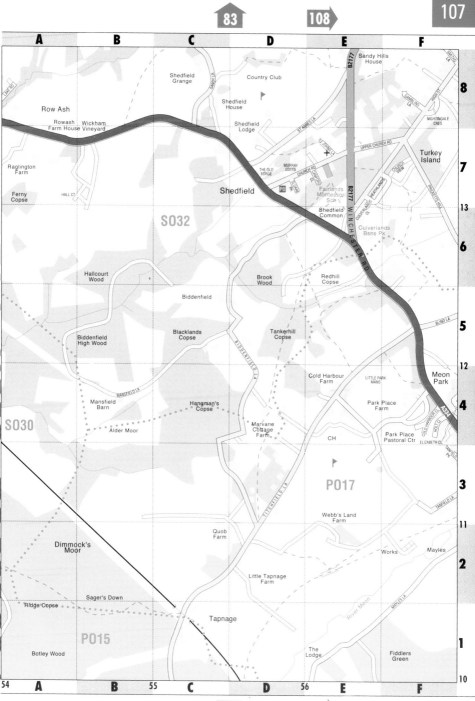

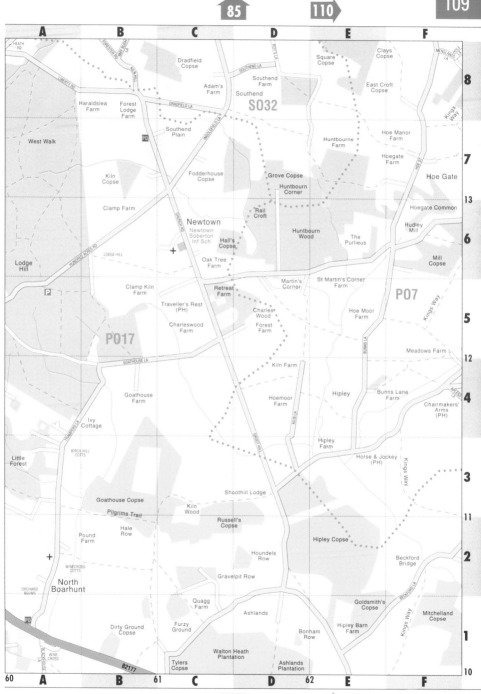

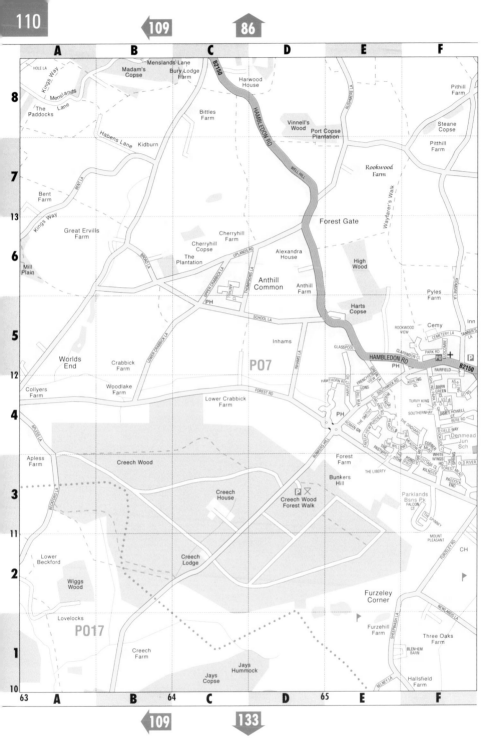

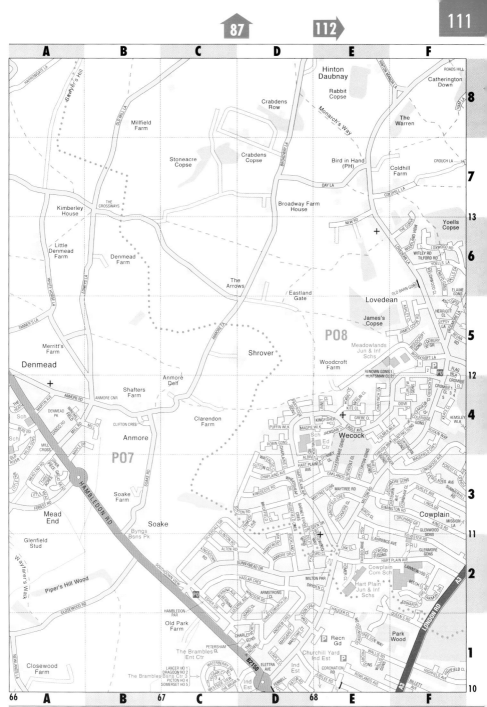

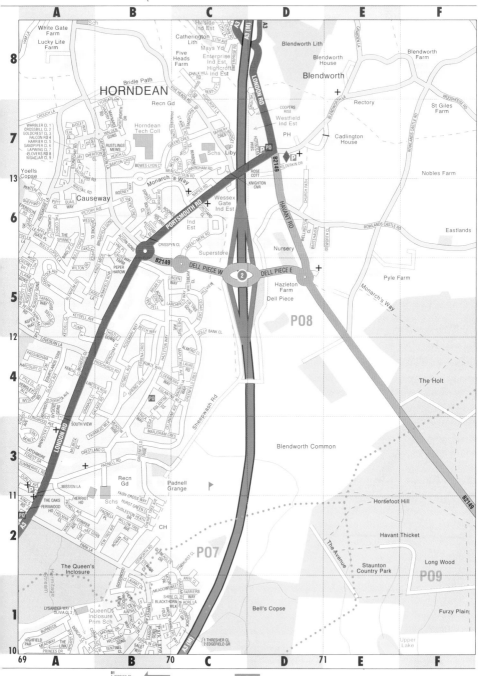

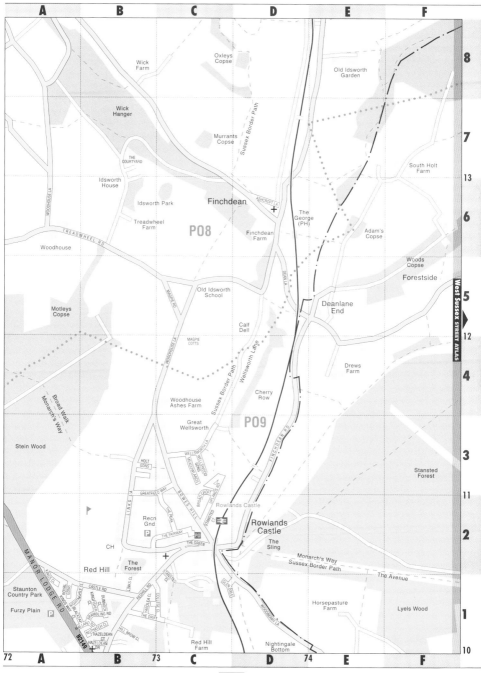

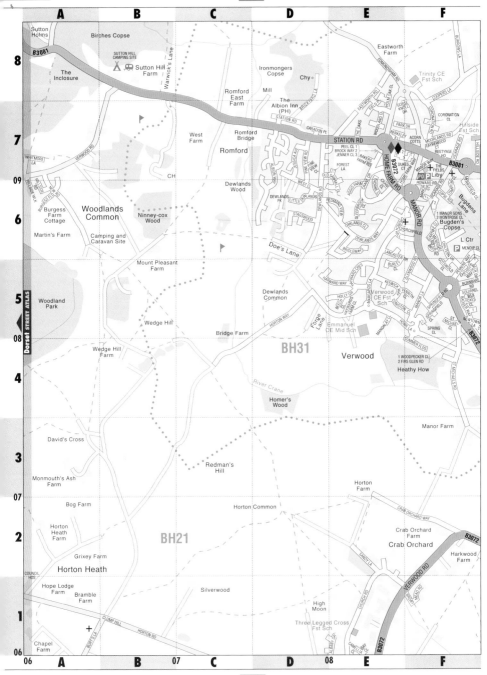

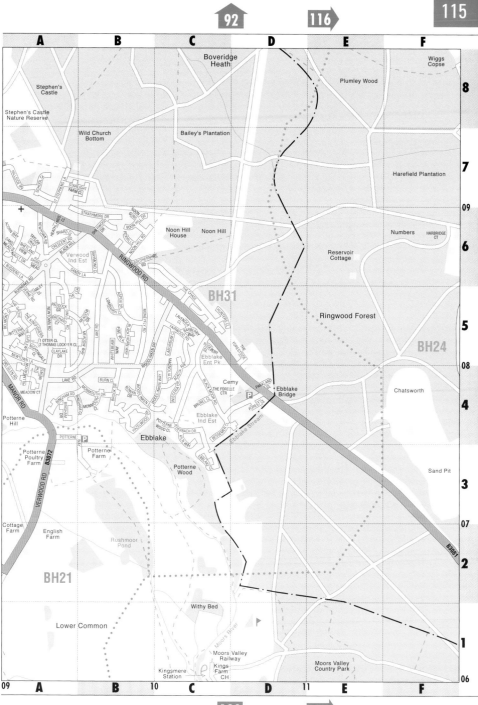

92
116

Boveridge
Heath

Plumley Wood

Wiggs
Copse

Stephen's
Castle

8

Stephen's Castle
Nature Reserve

Bailey's Plantation

Wild Church
Bottom

Harefield Plantation

7

09

SCHOOL LA
HILL SIDE RD
ST STEPHEN'S LA
STARLIGHT
FARM CL

STRATHMORE DR

Noon Hill
House

Noon Hill

Numbers

HARBRIDGE
CT

6

NEWTOWN RD
SHARD CL
CRESENT RD
BLACK HILL
DIAMOND CL
NOON HILL DR
NOON HILL RD
POODLE LA
SOUTHERNHAY RD

Verwood
Ind Est

RINGWOOD RD

BH31

Reservoir
Cottage

ACORN WAY
OAKS
MILFORD WAY
SKET LAND
VIEW CL
TAKE CROFT
PEDDLERS WAY

SANDY LA

THE CHASE

HUNTER CL

09

ACHURN RISE
BUGDENS LA
STALEY
THE NOOK
ASPEN CL

Ringwood Forest

5

BITTERNE
LAWNS DR
OLD RECTORY
PADDOCK GR
ORCHARD CT
THE HOLT
LONGSPEY CL
MINE FLY RD
BLACK THORN WAY
LAVENDER CL
FAIRWOOD WAY
LABURNUM CL
FERN CL
THE FOREST SIDE

BH24

BELMOUR
WAY
GRETE
LINE CRESS
CORE CL
EDE CROFT ME...
SHELLEY CL
OTTER CL
2 THOMAS LOCKYER CL
CLAYLAKE
DR
PINE VIEW CL
BARBERRY WAY
AGATE LA
ROSEBERY
AVE

08

NEWTOWN LA
THE MEARS
EDE GLEN RD
LAKE RD
BURN CL
MEADOW WAY
KILN WAY
WOOD LARKS CL
ROMAN WAY
WISTERIA CL
LADYLAVEN WAY
Ebblake
Ent Pk

Chatsworth

MANOR RD

MEADOW CT

BINGHAM RD
MONMOUTH DR
MONKEY CT
HAZELWOOD
Cemy
THE FORELLE
CTR

Ebblake
Bridge

4

Potterne
Hill

LAKE RD
BURN CL
BINGHAM RD
MONMOUTH DR
BRUNEL CL RD
CORBACH DR
BLACK BARROW DR
BESSEMER
PARKLAND
FOREST CL
Ebblake Stream

P

Ebblake
Ind Est

POTTERNE
WAY
B3072

P

Potterne
Farm

Ebblake

POTTERNE
WOOD CL
THE GLEN

Ebblake
Stream

Sand Pit

Potterne
Poultry
Farm

Potterne
Wood

3

07

Cottage
Farm

English
Farm

Rushmoor
Pond

B3081

2

BH21

Lower Common

Withy Bed

Moors River

1

Moors Valley
Railway

Kings
Farm
CH

Moors Valley
Country Park

Kingsmere
Station

06

	A	B	C	D	E	F

8

Gravel Pit

Turmer Hill

Harbridge Farm

Avon Valley Path

Ibsley Bridge

Hamer Brook

Turmer

Weir

Harbridge Lodge

Plumley Farm

7

Lower Turmer

Mill Stream

PH

09

Turmer Brook

SHEPHERDS LA.

6

Shepherds Cottage

Shepherds Hill

Home Wood

Dog Kennel Wood

Gravel Pit

Ibsley Water

Riverbank Covert

CHESTNUT AVE.

Whitehoe Cottages

5

New Barn Cottages

Old Somerley

ELLINGHAM DR.

New Bridge

Ellingham Farm

Ellingham

ELLINGHAM CROSS

ELLINGHAM DRO.

SALISBURY RD

The Bothy

BH24

Nursery Cottages

Somerley Park

NEA DR.

08

Broad Close Covert

Old Laundry Cottage

Somerley

Gravel Works

4

Park Cottage

The Belt

Ringwood Forest

3

River Avon

Meadow Lake

Blashford Farm

DUNCOMBE DR.

A338

07

Sand Pit

ASHLEY DR.

Dockens Water

SALISBURY RD

B3081

2

Sunderton Wood

Weir

Lifeland Copse

Upper Hurst Farm

A338

VERWOOD RD.

Duncombe Lodge

Ashley Farm

King Stream

Gouldings Farm

B3081

1

Baker's Hanging

Up Mead

Hurst Old Farm

Lin Brook

06

| 12 | A | B | 13 | C | D | 14 | E | F |

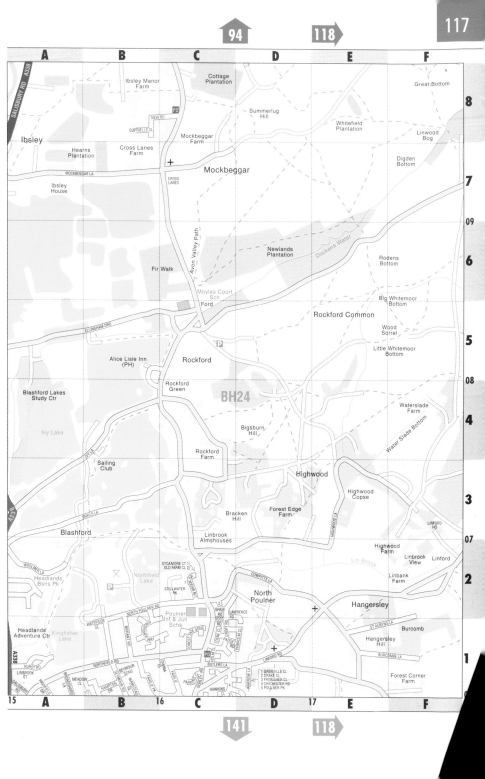

117
95

	A	B	C	D	E	F

8

Linwood

Amie's Wood

Milkham Inclosure

Toms Farm

Webb's Copse

7

Appleslade Farm

The Red Shoot Inn (PH)

Linwood Farm

Amie's Corner

King's Garden

Appleslade Bottom

TOMS LA

09

Mount Hill

Lin Wood

Castle Piece

Roe Inclosure

6

Appleslade Inclosure

Linford Brook

5

Red Shoot Plain

Red Shoot Wood

Green Ford

Buckherd Bottom

08

Great Linford Inclosure

White Hill

Greenford Bottom

BH24

Collier's Thorns

4

Pinnick Wood

Akercombe Bottom

Handy Cross

A31

3

Linford Bottom

Little Linford Inclosure

Handy Cross Plain

07

Marrowbones Hill

2

Linford

Picket Bottom

Ridley Plain

Brook Farm

Picket Hill

Old Gate

Little Wood

Harvest Slade

1

Shobley

Ridley Bottom

Ridley Wood

Shobley Bottom

A31

Picket Post

A	B	19	C	D	20	E	F

117
142

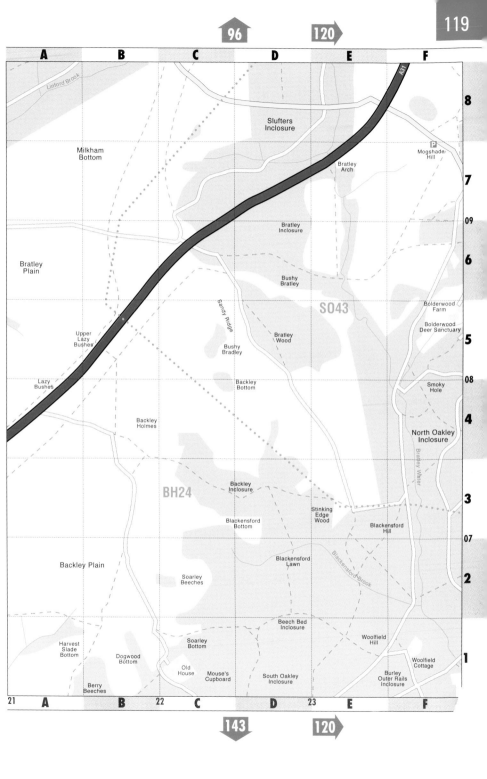

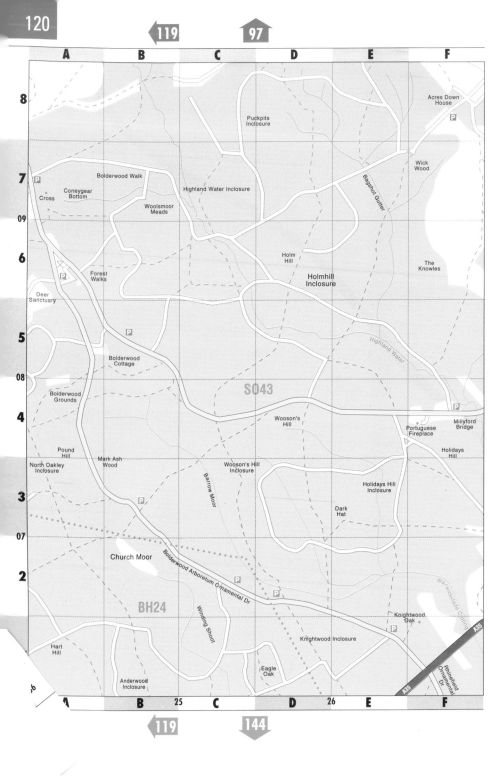

A B C D E F

8

Acres Down
House

P

7

Bolderwood Walk

Highland Water Inclosure

Wick
Wood

Coneygear
Bottom

P

Cross

Woolsmoor
Meads

Bagshot Gutter

09

Holm
Hill

6

P

Forest
Walks

Holmhill
Inclosure

The
Knowles

Deer
Sanctuary

Highland Water

5

Bolderwood
Cottage

08

SO43

Bolderwood
Grounds

P

4

Wooson's
Hill

Millyford
Bridge

Portuguese
Fireplace

Pound
Hill

Mark Ash
Wood

Wooson's Hill
Inclosure

Holidays
Hill

North Oakley
Inclosure

Holidays Hill
Inclosure

3

Barrow Moor

P

Dark
Hat

07

Church Moor

Bolderwood Arboretum Ornamental Dr

Warwickslade Cutting

2

BH24

P

P

Winding Shoot

Knightwood
Oak

A35

P

Knightwood Inclosure

Hart
Hill

A35

Rhinefield
Ornamental

Eagle
Oak

Anderwood
Inclosure

.6

A B 25 C D 26 E F

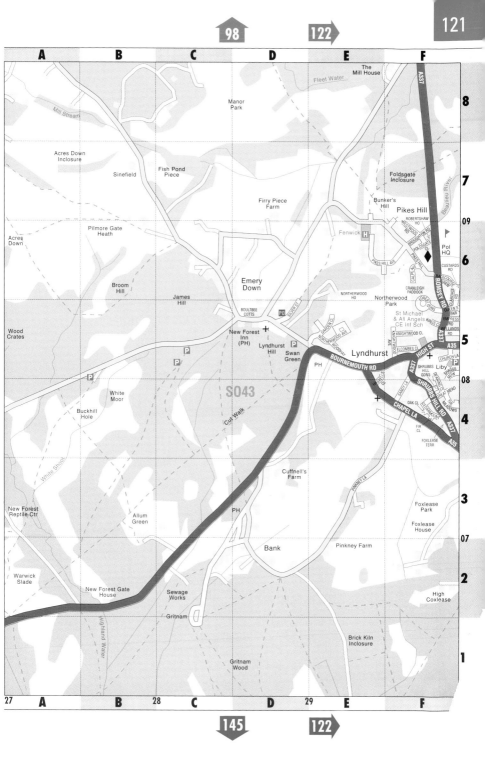

121
99

A
B
C
D
E
F
8
7
09
6
5
08
4
3
07
2
06
31
32
Fox Hill
Rushpole Wood
Redbridge Hill
Ironshill Inclosure
Lodgehill Inclosure
A35
Whitebridge Hill
Fair Cross
Lodgehill Cottage
Beaulieu River
Mallard Wood
Dunces Arch Inclosure
SO40
Beaulieu River
CH
Dunces Arch
THE CUSTARDS
PEMBERTON RD
Custards
THATCHED COTTAGE CVN PK
SOUTHAMPTON RD
QUEENS RD
PRINCES CRES
1 QUEEN'S PAR
2 EMPRESS RD
WELLANDS RD
Longwater Lawn
Fox Hill
Row Hill
PRINCES CT
PO
HIGH ST
A35
Meml
Cemy
RUFUS CT
Hotel
New Forest Mus
B3056
Bolton's Bench
White Moor
SO43
SHAGGS MDW
THE MEADOWS
GOSPORT LA
The Ridge
The Bench
Goose Green
A35
BEAULIEU RD
BROOKLANDS
A337
Irons Hill Walk
B3056
Clayhill
Matley Ridge
BEECHEN LA
PARK CL
HILLARY CL
Pondhead Inclosure
The Crown & Stirrup (PH)
CLAY HILL
Parkhill (Hotel)
Pondhead
Beechen La
Parkhill Lawn
Holmhill Passage
Little Holmhill Inclosure
Park Ground Inclosure
Park Hill
Denny Inclosure
Little Holmhill

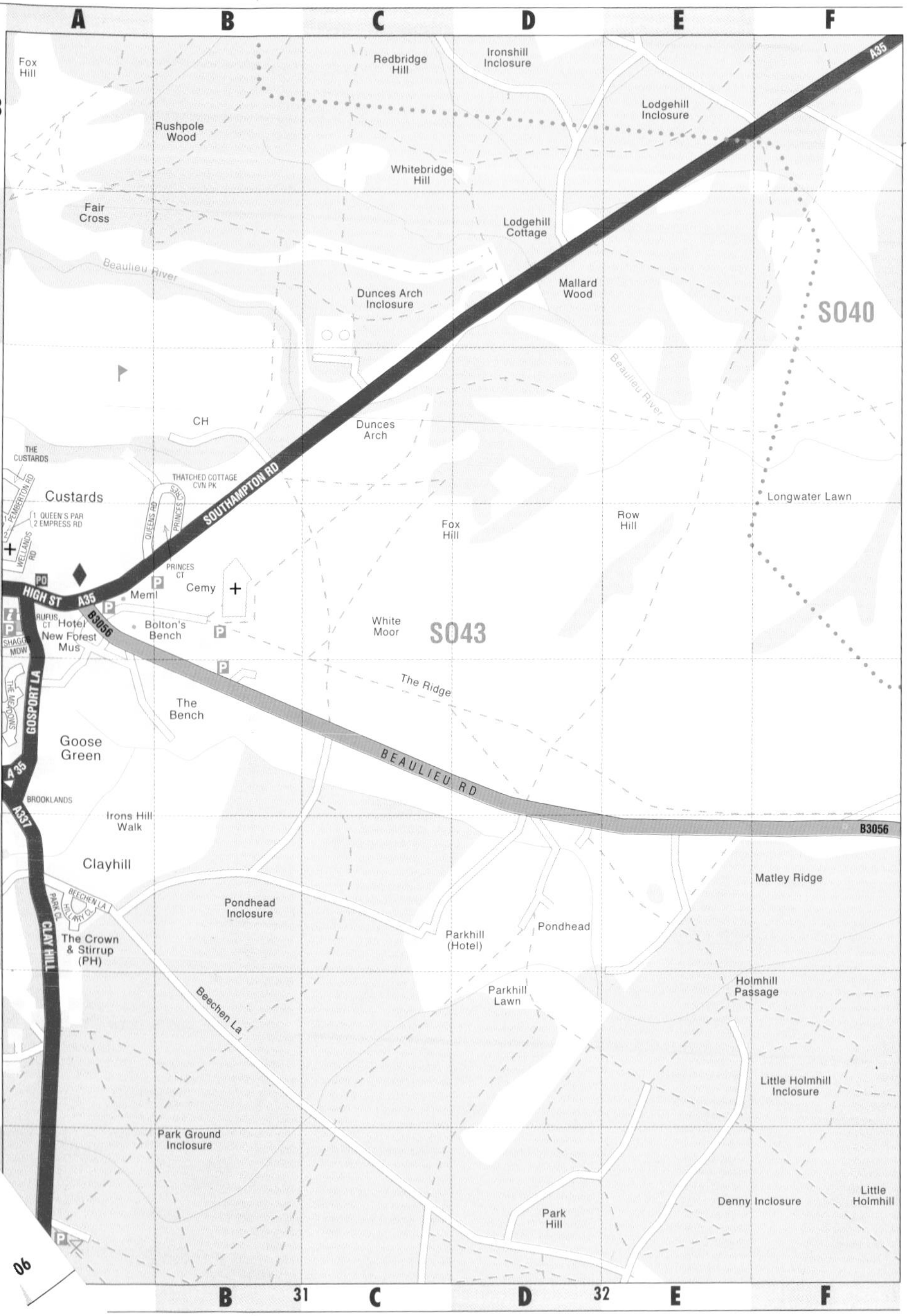

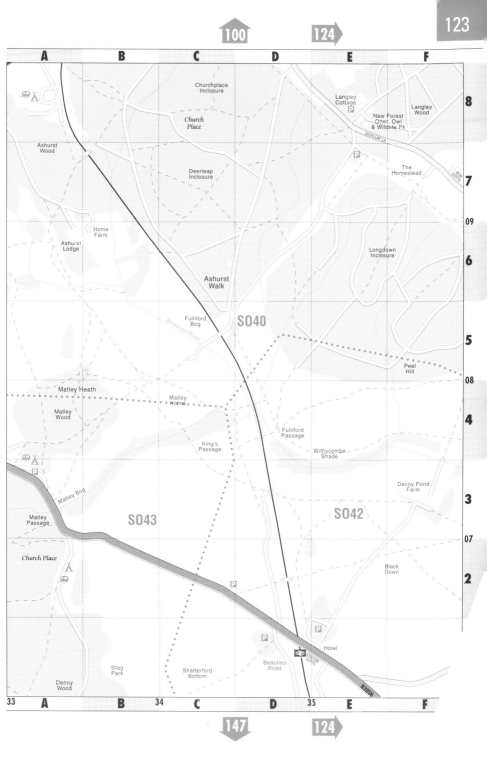

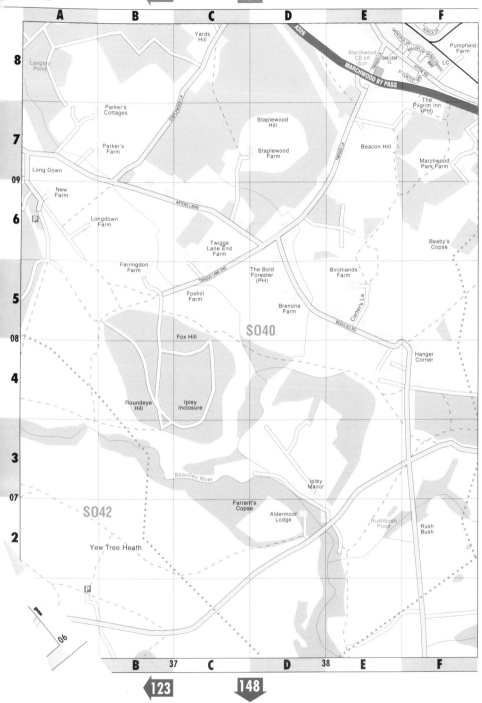

A B C D E F

8

Yards
Hill

A326

Pumpfield
Farm

Langley
Pond

Marchwood
CE Inf
Sch

LARROF DR

WILLOW PL

SPINDLEWOOD

TYTHE RD

OAK LEAF
CL

ST CONTEST WY

LC

MARCHWOOD BY PASS

The
Pilgrim Inn
(PH)

7

Parker's
Cottages

Staplewood
Hill

STAPLEWOOD LA

Beacon Hill

Marchwood
Park Farm

Parker's
Farm

Staplewood
Farm

TWIGGS LA

09

Long Down

New
Farm

ARTERS LAWN

6

P

Longdown
Farm

Twiggs
Lane End
Farm

Beaby's
Copse

Farringdon
Farm

The Bold
Forester
(PH)

Birchlands
Farm

Carter's La

5

Foxhill
Farm

TWIGGS LANE END

Brenona
Farm

BEAULIEU RD

08

Fox Hill

SO40

Hanger
Corner

4

Roundeye
Hill

Ipley
Inclosure

3

Beaulieu River

Ipley
Manor

07

SO42

Farrant's
Copse

Aldermoor
Lodge

Rushbush
Pond

Rush
Bush

2

Yew Tree Heath

P

06

B 37 C D 38 E F

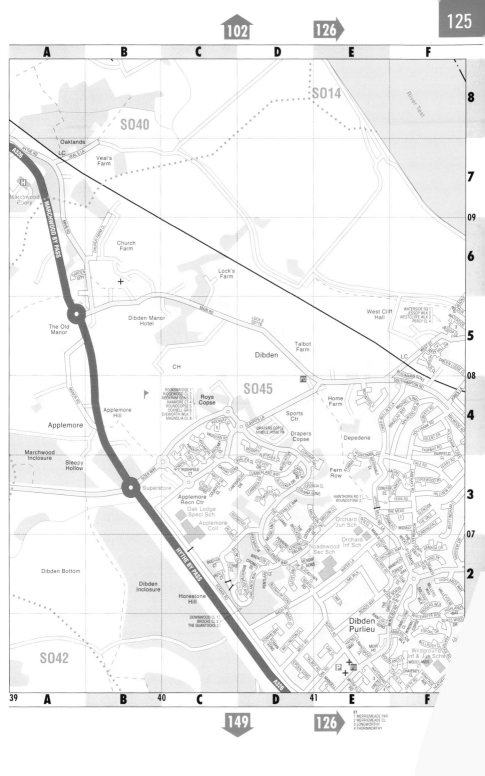

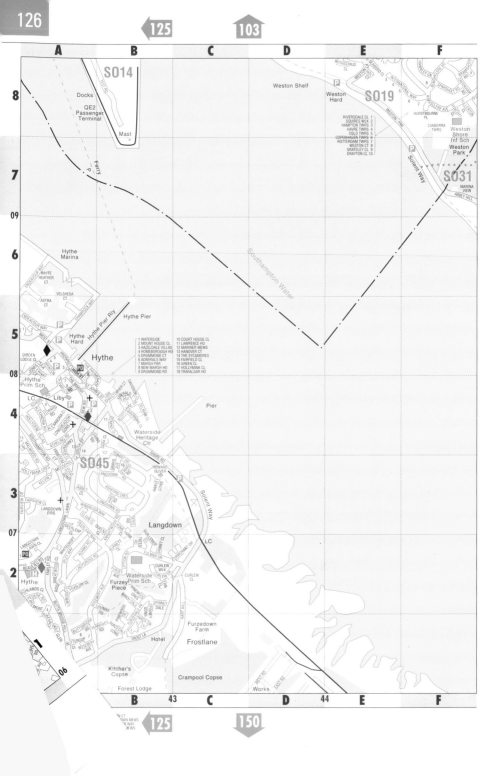

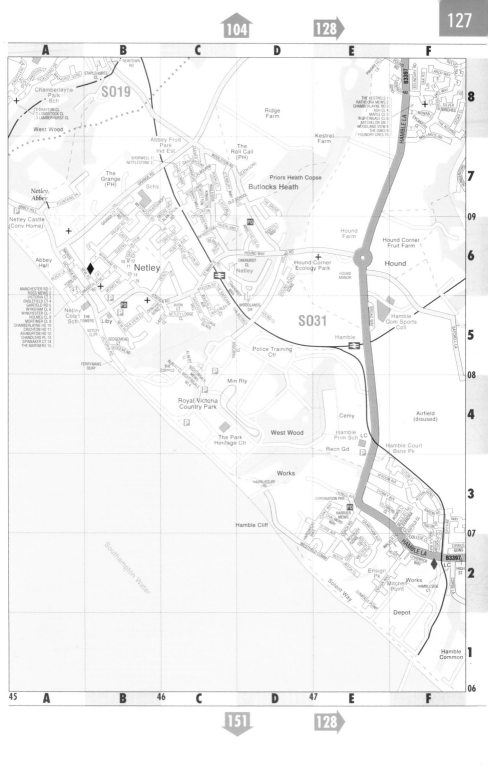

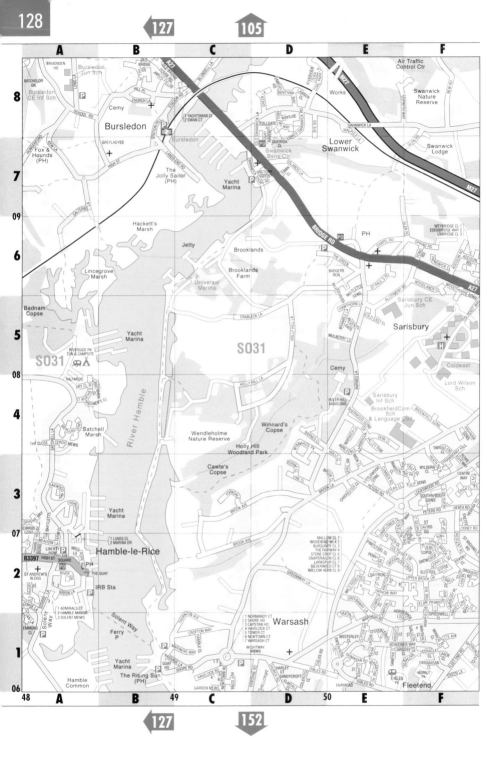

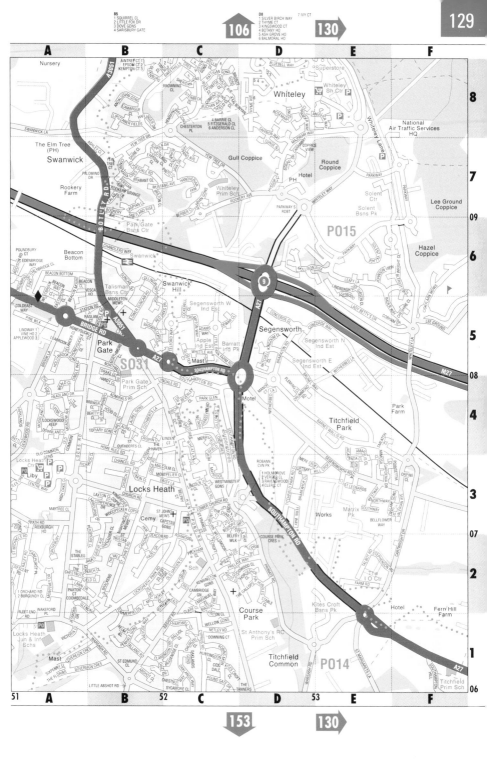

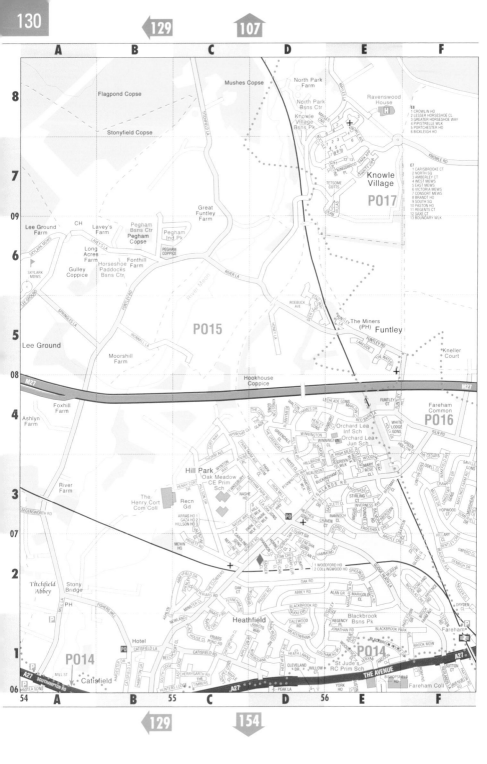

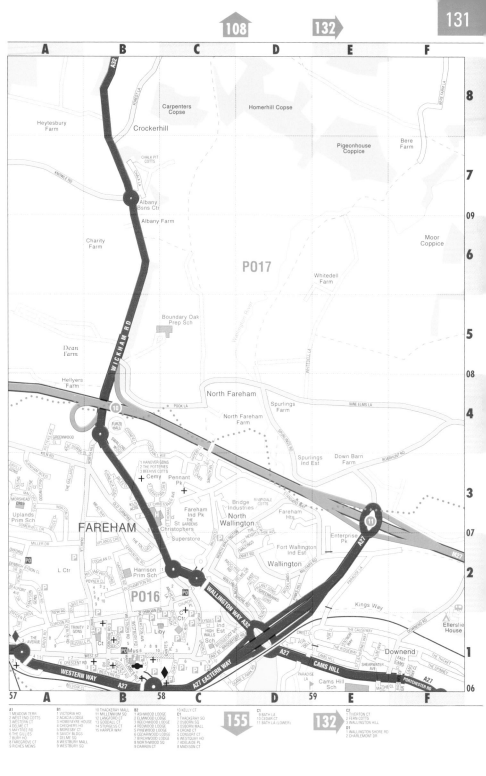

A B C D E F

8

Heytesbury
Farm

Carpenters
Copse

Homerhill Copse

Crockerhill

CHALK PIT
COTTS

Pigeonhouse
Coppice

Bere
Farm

7

KNOWLE RD

FORREST LA

Albany
Bsns Ctr

Albany Farm

BERE FARM LA

A27

09

Charity
Farm

PO17

Moor
Coppice

6

Whitedell
Farm

WICKHAM RD

Boundary Oak
Prep Sch

5

Dean
Farm

WHITEDELL LA

Wallington River

Hellyers
Farm

North Fareham

Spurlings
Farm

NINE ELMS LA

08

4

10

FURZE
HALL

POOK LA

North Fareham
Farm

Spurlings
Ind Est

Down Barn
Farm

BOARHUNT RD

SPURLINGS RD

GREENWOOD
CL

KILN RD

1 HANOVER GDNS
2 THE POTTERIES
3 BEEHIVE COTTS

Cemy

Pennant
Pk

RIVERDALE
COTTS

STUBBINGTON LA

Bridge
Industries

Fareham
Ind Pk

North
Wallington

Fareham
Hts

Enterprise
Pk

11

A27

M27

07

3

Uplands
Prim Sch

MORSHEAD

FAREHAM

ST CHRISTOPHERS

THE
ST GARDENS
Christophers

Superstore

Fort Wallington
Ind Est

Wallington

2

Harrison
Prim Sch

PO16

PO

Liby

CHURCH
PL

Ind
High St
Sch

WALLINGTON WAY A32

Kings Way

Ellerslie
House

THE CAUSEWAY

1

L Ctr

WESTERN WAY

A27

Mus

A27 EASTERN WAY

A27

CAMS HILL

Cams Hill
Sch

Downend

PORTCHESTER RD

THE SPINNEY

A27

06

57 A 58 B C D 59 E F

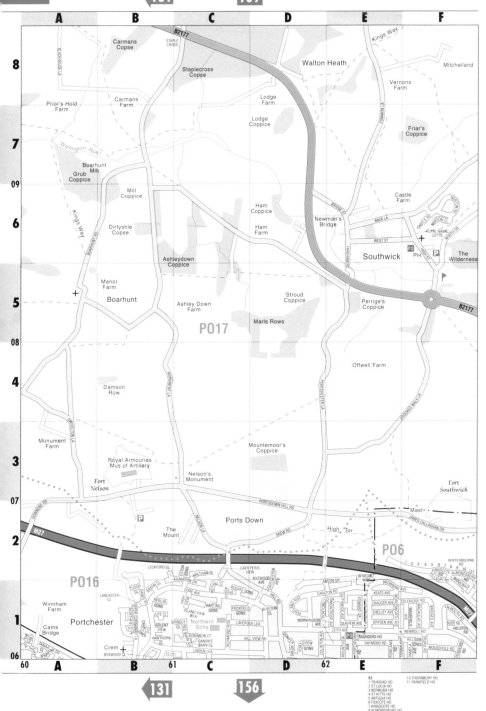

F2
1 TRINIDAD HO
2 ST LUCIA HO
3 BERMUDA HO
4 ST KITTS HO
5 ANTIGUA HO
6 FOXCOTE HO
7 KINGSCOTE HO
8 ALMONDSBURY HO
9 OAKLANDS HO
10 THORNBURY HO
11 PARKFIELD HO

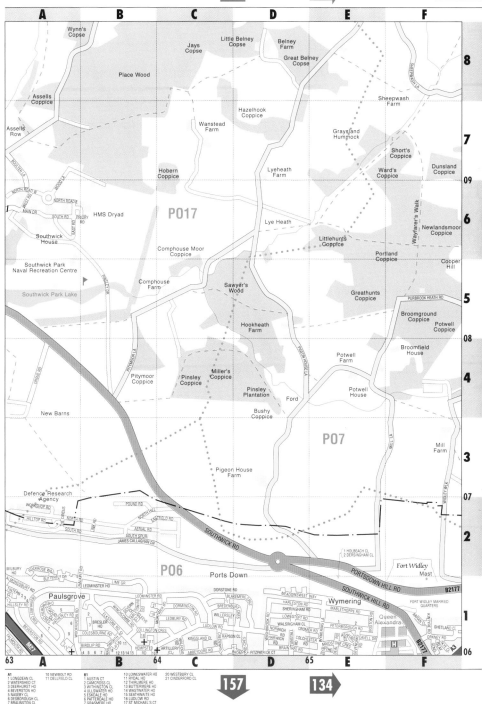

A   B   C   D   E   F

8

Wynn's
Copse

Place Wood

Little Belney
Copse

Jays
Copse

Belney
Farm

Great Belney
Copse

Sheepwash
Farm

Assells
Coppice

Hazelhook
Coppice

7

Assells
Row

Wanstead
Farm

Grays and
Hummock

Short's
Coppice

Dunsland
Coppice

Ward's
Coppice

09

Hobern
Coppice

Lyeheath
Farm

NORTH ROAD W
POOL LA
ROUTLER LA
NORTH RD W
WEST RD
MAIN DR
SOUTH RD
EAST RD
PRIORY RD
NORTH ROAD E

HMS Dryad

PO17

Lye Heath

Littlehunts
Coppice

Wayfarer's Walk

Newlandsmoor
Coppice

6

Southwick
House

Comphouse Moor
Coppice

Portland
Coppice

Cooper
Hill

Southwick Park
Naval Recreation Centre

Comphouse
Farm

Sawyer's
Wood

Greathunts
Coppice

PURBROOK HEATH RD

5

Southwick Park Lake

Hookheath
Farm

Broomground
Coppice

Potwell
Coppice

08

PITYMOOR LA
PINSLEY DR

Pitymoor
Coppice

Pinsley
Coppice

Miller's
Coppice

Potwell
Farm

Broomfield
House

4

PIGEON HOUSE LA

New Barns

Pinsley
Plantation

Ford

Potwell
House

Bushy
Coppice

PO7

MILL LA

Mill
Farm

3

DROVE RD

Pigeon House
Farm

WIDLEY WLK

07

Defence Research
Agency

WORKSHOP RD
NORTH HILL
EASTFIELD RD
POUND RD

HILLTOP RD
SOUTH RD
LINK RD
AERIAL RD
SOUTH SPUR
JAMES CALLAGHAN DR

SOUTHWICK RD

1 HOLBEACH CL
2 DERSINGHAM CL

2

MILBURY HO
ROCKROSE WAY
BUTTERFLY DR
CHALKPIT HO
LEOMINSTER HO
LIME GR

PO6

Ports Down

PORTSDOWN HILL RD

SOUTHWICK HILL RD

Fort Widley
Mast

B2177

Paulsgrove

Wymering

Queen
Alexandra

FORT WIDLEY MARRIED
QUARTERS

SHETLAND CL
ORKNEY CL
A3

1

M27

Dorstone Rd
Blakemere Dr
Bredenbury
Willersley
Ludlow Rd

Meadowsweet Way
Harleston Rd
Sheringham Rd
Lowestoft Rd
Walsingham Cl
Norwich
Harwich
Colchester
Braintree Rd

Mablethorpe Rd
Peterborough Rd
Cromer Rd
Zavell Dr
Maidstone Cres
Hythe

H
B2177

06

63   A   B   64   C   D   65   E   F

A1
1 LONGDEAN CL
2 WATERSHED CT
3 DEERHURST HO
4 BEVERSTON HO
5 NASEBY CL
6 DESBOROUGH CL
7 BRAUNSTON CL
8 BRIXWORTH CL
9 ROTHWELL CL

10 NEWBOLT RD
11 DELLFIELD CL

B1
1 AUSTIN CT
2 CAMCROSS CL
3 WITHINGTON CL
4 ULLSWATER HO
5 ESKDALE HO
6 PATTERDALE HO
7 GRASMERE HO
8 CONISTON HO
9 RYDAL CL

10 LOWESWATER HO
11 RYDAL HO
12 THIRLMERE HO
13 BUTTERMERE HO
14 WASTWATER HO
15 SEATHWAITE HO
16 LUDLOW RD
17 ST MICHAEL'S CT
18 EDWARD'S CL
19 HUNTLEY CL

20 WESTBURY CL
21 CINDERFORD CL

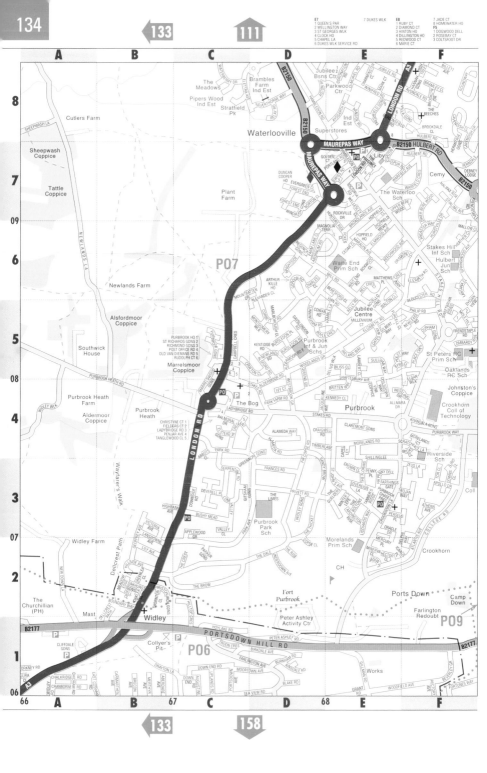

112
136

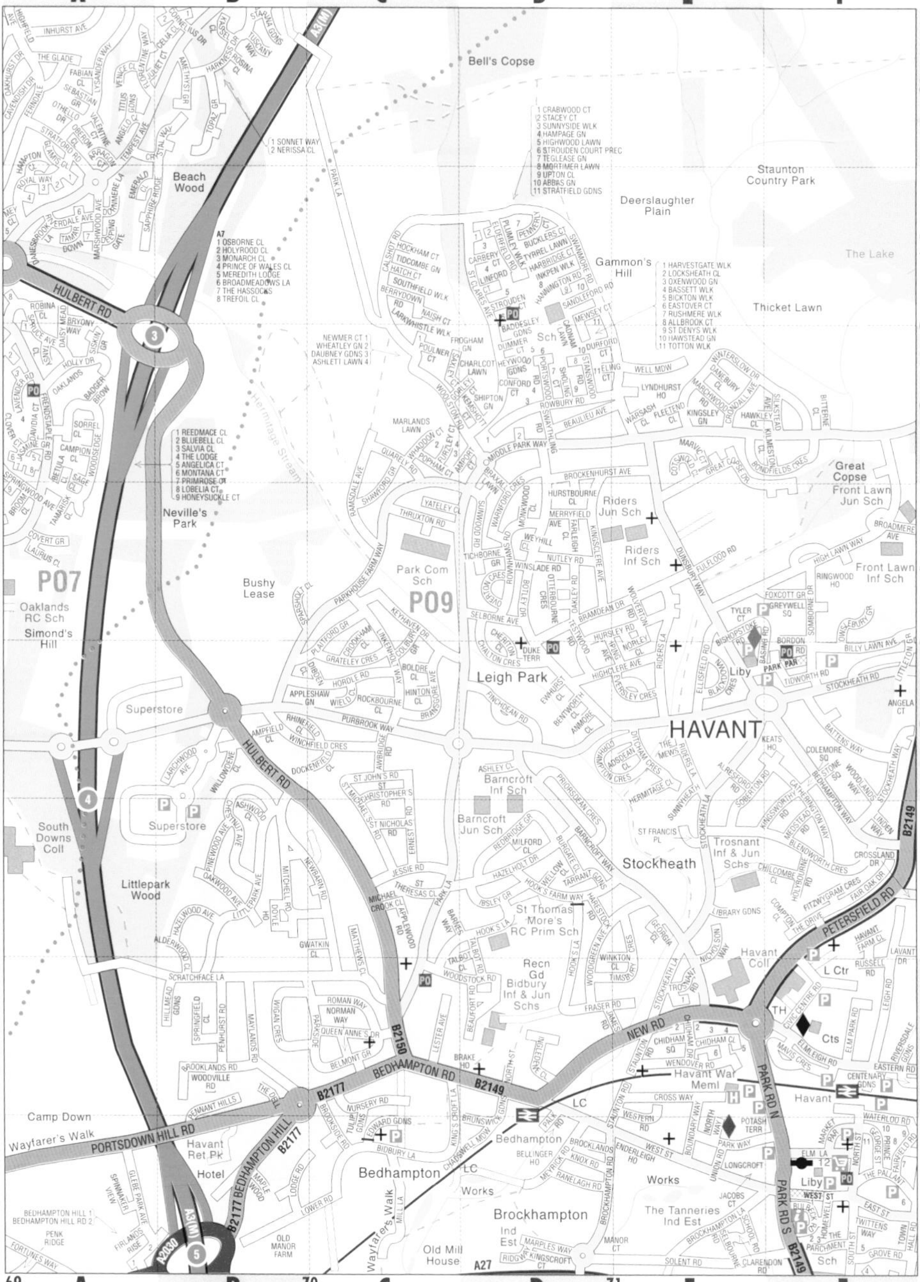
A B C D E F
8
7
09
6
5
08
4
3
07
2
1
06
69 70 71
Bell's Copse
1 CRABWOOD CT
2 STACEY CT
3 SUNNYSIDE WLK
4 HAMPAGE GN
5 HIGHWOOD LAWN
6 STROUDEN COURT PREC
7 TEGLEASE GN
8 MORTIMER LAWN
9 UPTON CL
10 ABBAS GN
11 STRATFIELD GDNS
Staunton Country Park
Deerslaughter Plain
Beach Wood
1 SONNET WAY
2 NERISSA CL
A7
1 OSBORNE CL
2 HOLYROOD CL
3 MONARCH CL
4 PRINCE OF WALES CL
5 MEREDITH LODGE
6 BROADMEADOWS LA
7 THE HASSOCKS
8 TREFOIL CL
Gammon's Hill
1 HARVESTGATE WLK
2 LOCKSHEATH CL
3 OXENWOOD GN
4 BASSETT WLK
5 BICKTON WLK
6 EASTOVER CT
7 RUSHMERE WLK
8 ALLBROOK CT
9 ST DENYS WLK
10 HAWSTEAD GN
11 TOTTON WLK
The Lake
Thicket Lawn
HULBERT RD
NEWMER CT 1
WHEATLEY GN 2
DAUBNEY GDNS 3
ASHLETT LAWN 4
1 REEDMACE CL
2 BLUEBELL CL
3 SALVIA CL
4 THE LODGE
5 ANGELICA CT
6 MONTANA CT
7 PRIMROSE CT
8 LOBELIA CT
9 HONEYSUCKLE CT
Neville's Park
Hermitage Stream
Great Copse
Front Lawn Jun Sch
Riders Jun Sch
Riders Inf Sch
Front Lawn Inf Sch
Park Com Sch
PO7
PO9
Bushy Lease
Oaklands RC Sch
Simond's Hill
Leigh Park
Superstore
HAVANT
Barncroft Inf Sch
Barncroft Jun Sch
South Downs Coll
Littlepark Wood
Stockheath
Trosnant Inf & Jun Schs
St Thomas More's RC Prim Sch
Recn Gd
Bidbury Inf & Jun Schs
Havant Coll
L Ctr
Cts
Havant War Meml
Havant
Camp Down
Wayfarer's Walk
PORTSDOWN HILL RD
Havant Ret Pk
Hotel
B2177 BEDHAMPTON HILL
BEDHAMPTON RD
B2149
B2150
NEW RD
PARK RD N
PARK RD S
PETERSFIELD RD
Bedhampton
Brockhampton
Brockhampton Ind Est
Works
The Tanneries Ind Est
Old Mill House
OLD MANOR FARM
BEDHAMPTON HILL 1
BEDHAMPTON HILL RD 2
A27
A3(M)
A2030
Liby
Sch

E2
1 BROOKFIELD CL
2 CHIDHAM WLK
3 WHYKE CT
4 COMPTON CT
5 WESTBOURNE CT
6 THE FORUM

F1
1 MILESTONE POINT
2 WATERMILL CT
3 SPRINGWELL
4 SLINDON GDNS
5 GROVE CT
6 EMPIRE CT
7 FAIRFIELD TERR
8 MANOR CL
9 EAST VIEW TERR
10 WELLINGTON CT
11 NORTH STREET ARC
12 Meridian Ctr

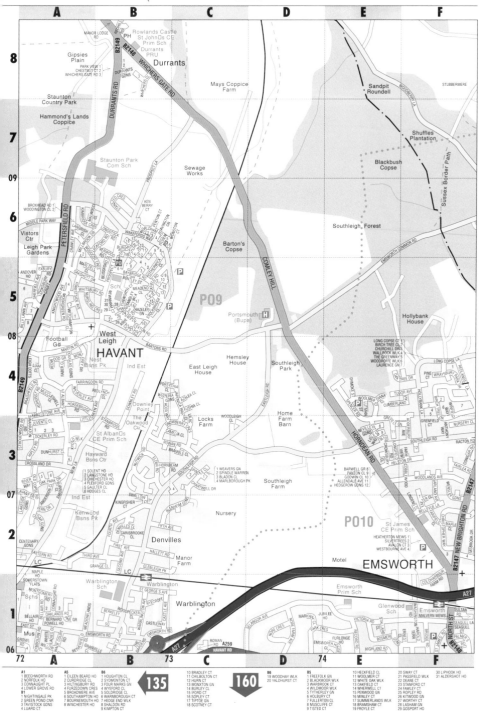

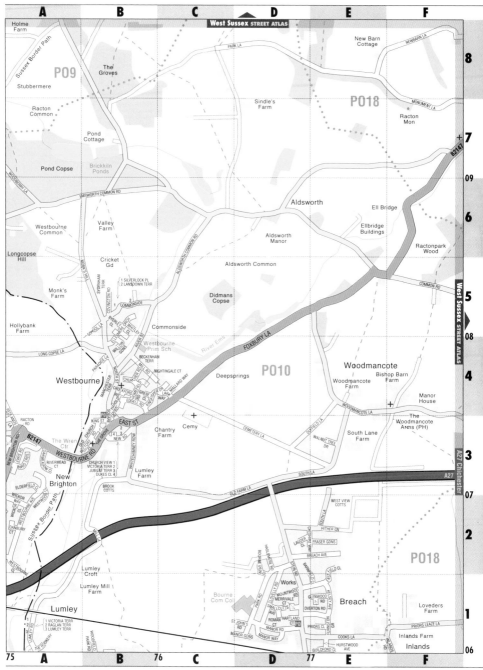

PO9

PO18

PO10

PO18

West Sussex STREET ATLAS

A27 Chichester

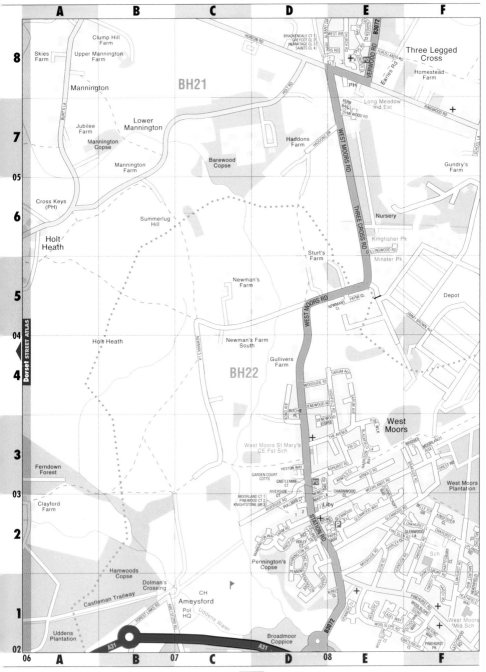

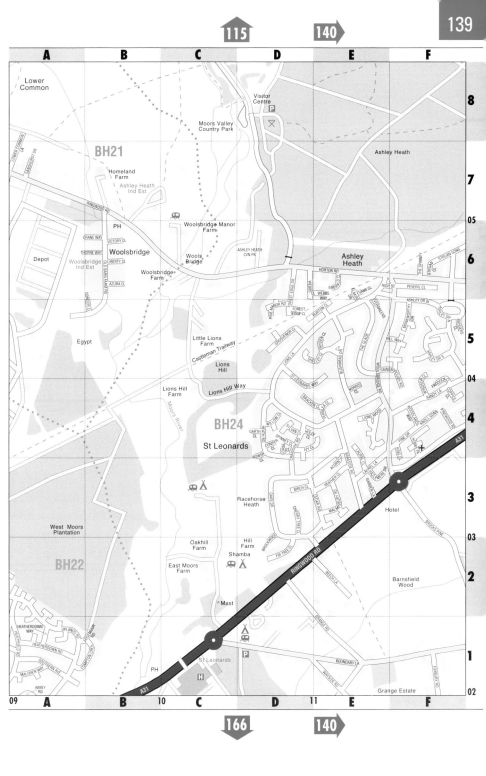

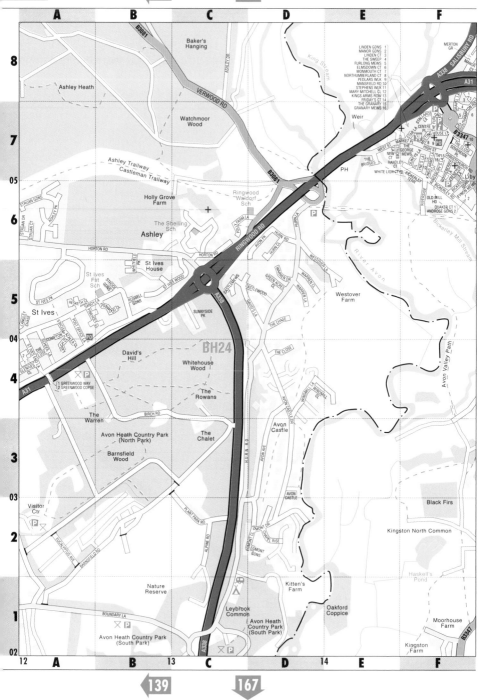

139
116

1 LINDEN GDNS
2 MANOR GDNS
3 LINDEN CT
4 THE SWEEP
5 FURLONG MEWS
6 ELMSDOWN CT
7 MONMOUTH CT
8 NORTHUMBERLAND CT
9 PEDLARS WLK
10 MANSFIELD RD
11 STEPHENS WLK
12 MARY MITCHELL CL
13 KINGS ARMS ROW
14 FRIDAY'S CT
15 THE GRANARY
16 GRANARY MEWS

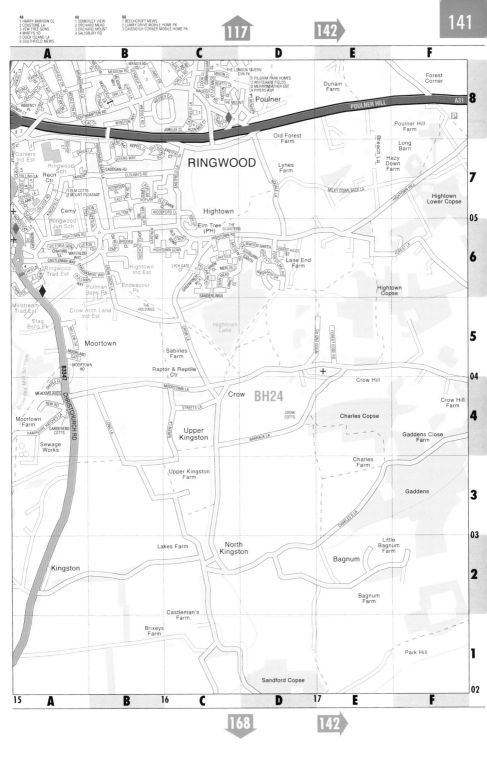

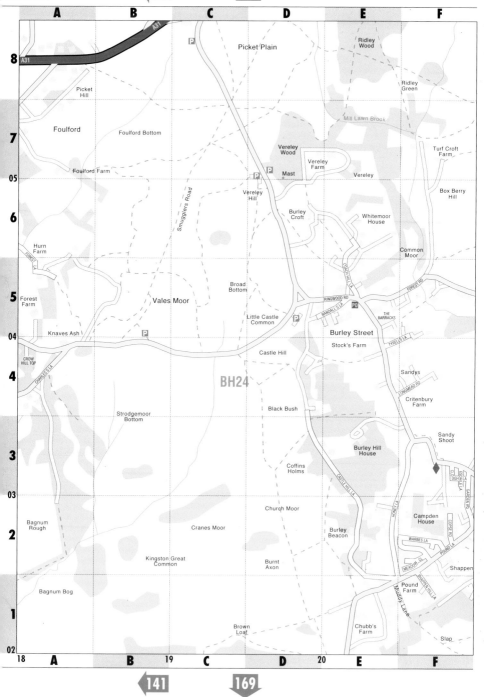

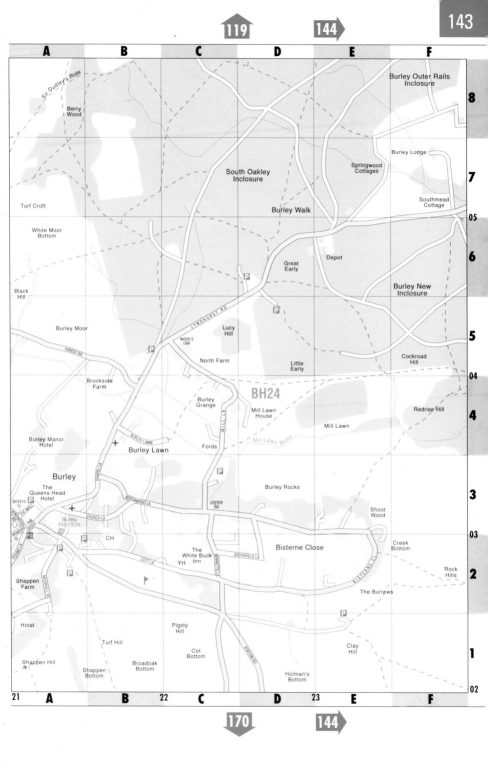

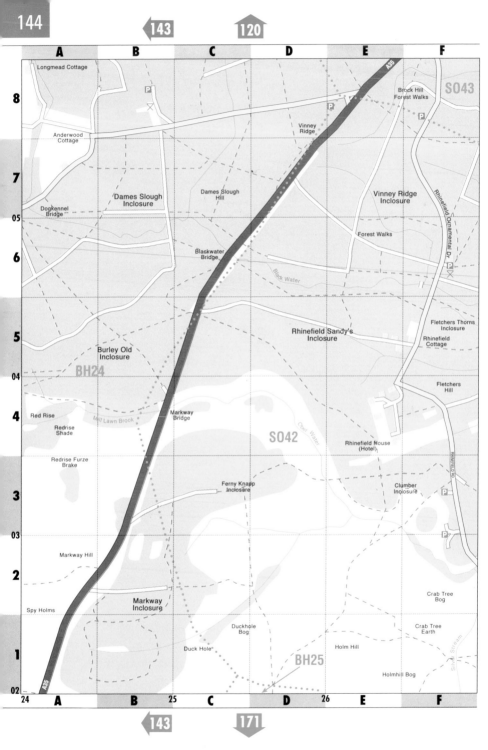

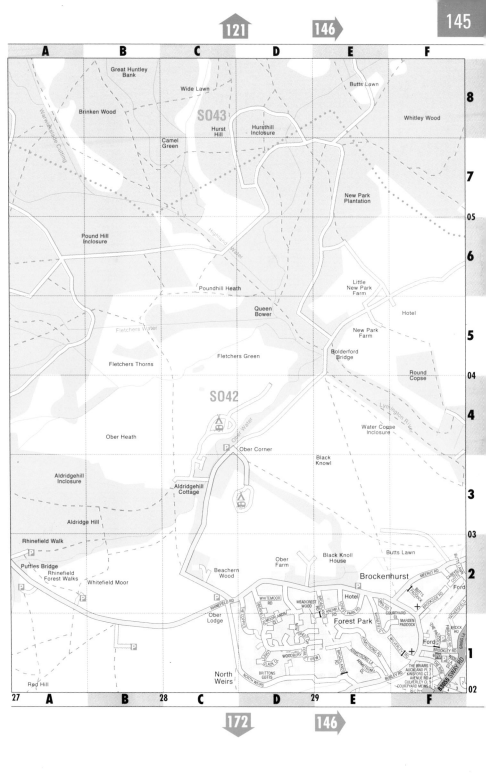

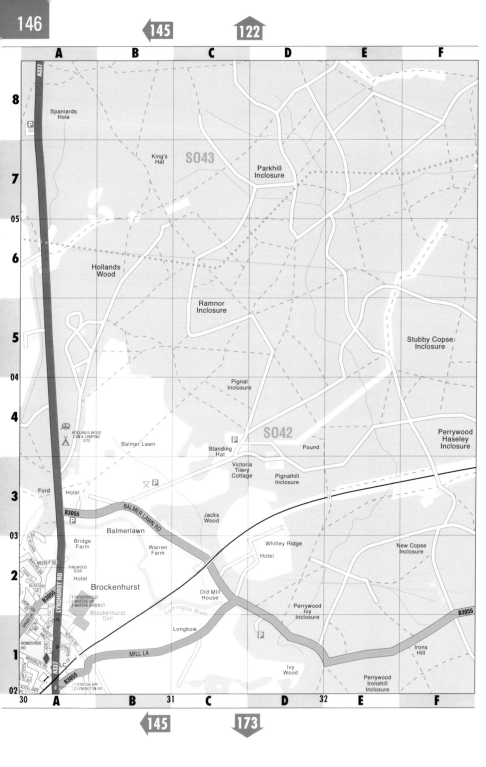

A B C D E F

8

S043

Denny
Wood

Denny
Lodge

Stephill
Bottom

7

Woodfidley
Passage

05

Furzy
Brow

Bishop of
Winchester's
Purlieu

6

Denny Lodge
Inclosure

Penny
Moor

Woodfidley

5

S042

Rowbarrow

04

LC

4

Frame Heath
Inclosure

Frame
Wood

3

03

Ladycross
Inclosure

Moon
Hill

2

Ladycross
Lodge

Worts Gutter

Hawkhill
Inclosure

1

Lodge
Heath

Stockley
Inclosure

Little
Wood

02

33 A B 34 C D 35 E F

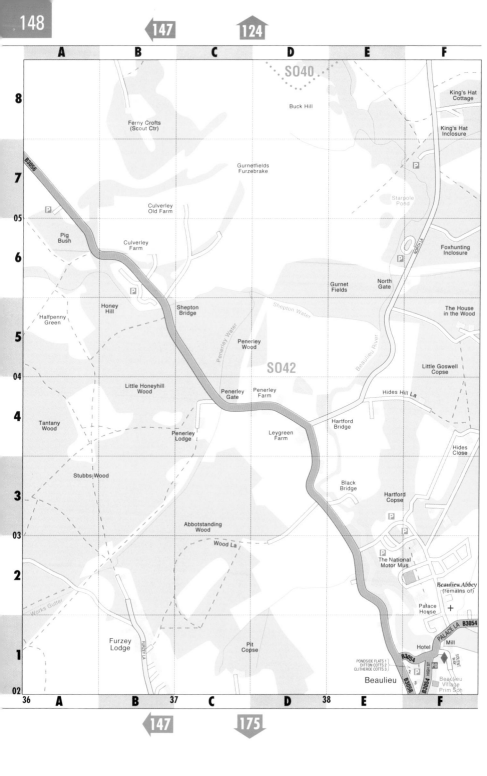

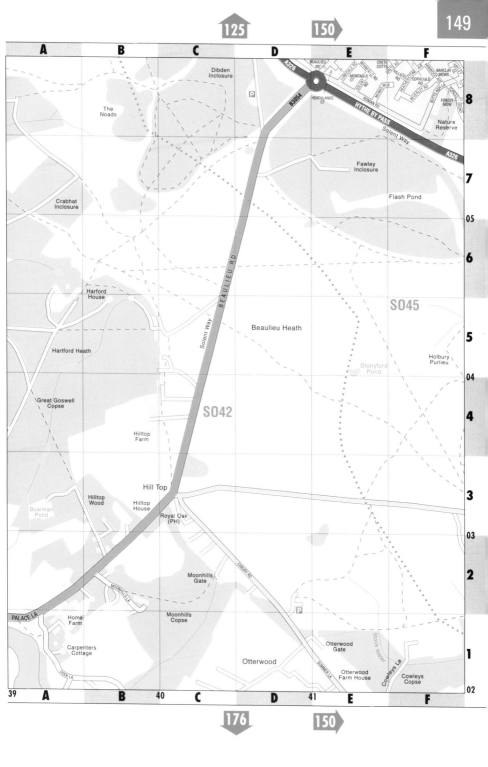

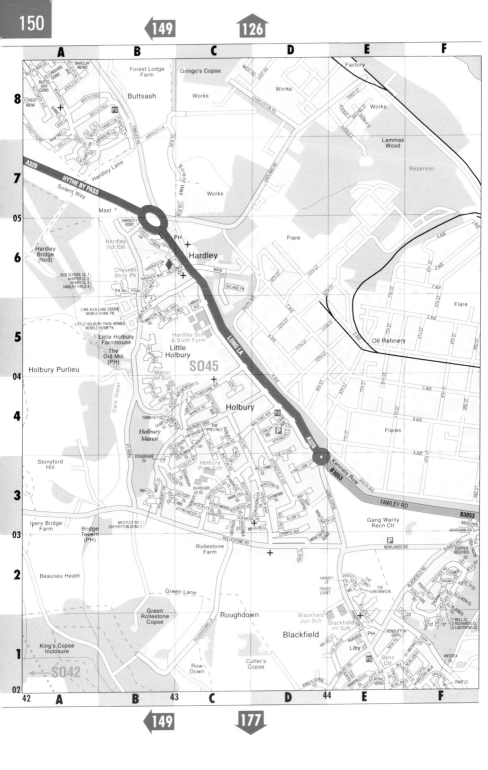

127
152
178
152

A   B   C   D   E   F

8
05
7
6
05
5
04
4
3
03
2
03
1
02

Jetty

Southampton Water

Cadland Creek

Pier

Marine Terminal

FORESHORE LA
FORESHORE S
NORTH TRESTLE RD
PI.FH. RD
BURMAH RD
BURMAH ROAD S
JETTY RD
SOUTH TRESTLE RD
Pier

CADLAND RD
OLD AGWI RD
AGITATOR RD
SEPS 4 RD
FLUME RD
ROTARNEX RD

Pier

E. AVE
2 AVE
E. AVE
D.AVE
C.AVE
B.AVE
A.AVE

S045

Ashlett Creek

RYE PADDOCK LA
MANORDA LA
CHURCH RD
CHURCHELL LA
COPTHORNE COTTS
COPTHORNE LA

Fawley

ASHLETT CL
ASHLETT RD
STONEHILLS

The Jolly Sailor (PH)

Fawley Inf Sch
Fawley Bsns Ctr
SOUTH AVE
BLACKFELD
CHURCH LA
SCHOOL RD
SCHOOL RD
ARCANGELS
NEWPOOLS RD
LITTLE
AGINCOURTS
FORD
THE
DENNY
ADMIRALS CL
Liby

Ashlett

FAWLEY RD
FAWLEY BY PASS

THE PENTAGON
HAMLET CT   1
MEADOW WAY   2
THE PADDOCKS   3
CHARLES LEY CT   4
WHITES LA   5
FORGE LA   6
ASHLETT MEWS   7
RHYME HALL MEWS 8
THE LANE   9
MERLIN COTTS   10

Stone Hill Farm

Stonehills

NORTHERN ACCESS RD

NORTHERN RD
SWITCH HOUSE RD
EASTERN RD
CENTRAL WEST W
CALDRON RD
CENTRAL RD
WESTERN RD
BOILER
PRIORY WAY
CHANNEL MOUTH RD
SOUTHERN RD
QUAYSIDE RD

Fawley Power Station

Fields Farm

Fields Heath

BADMINSTON LA

Badminston Farm

Chy

Swing Bridge

Tom's Down

Badminston Common

BADMINSTON DRO

B3053

45   46   47
A   B   C   D   E   F

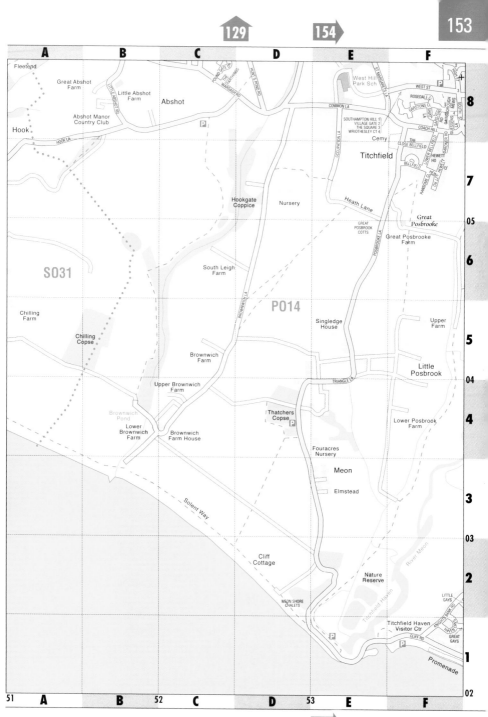

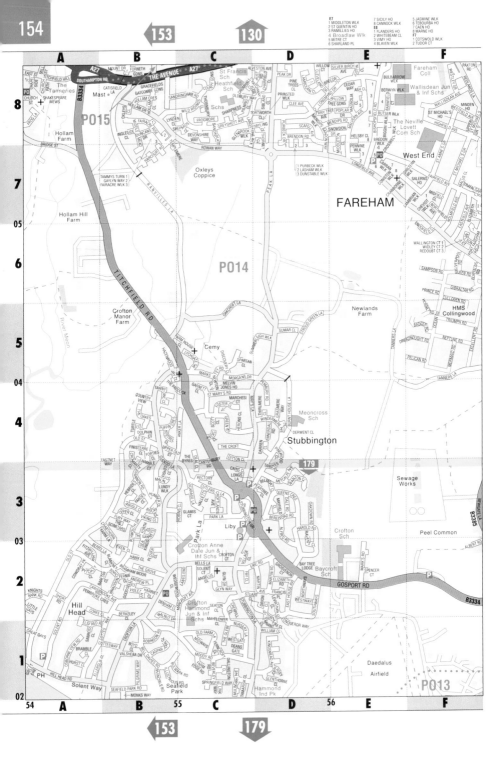

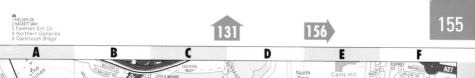

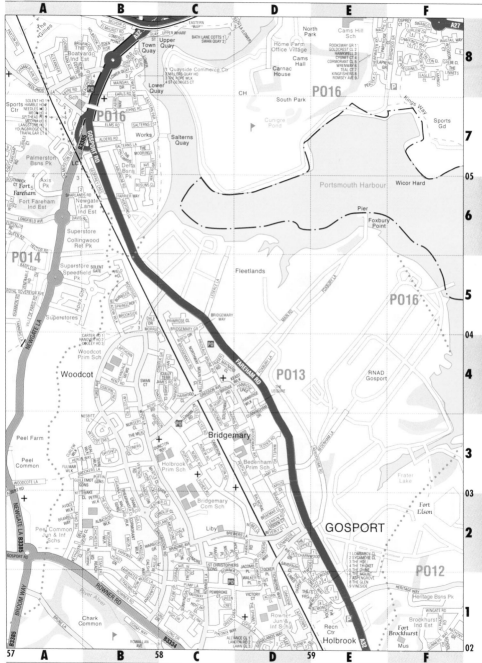

A6
1 FIELDER DR
2 HACKETT WAY
3 Fareham Ent Ctr
4 Northern Galleries
5 Dartmouth Bldgs

A   B   C   D   E   F

The Gilles

North Park

Cams Hill Sch

A27

ROOKSWAY GR 1
GOLDCREST CL 2
HAWKWELL 3
CYGNET CL 4
CORMORANT CL 5
WRENWAY 6
TEAL CT 7
KINGFISHERS 8
ROMSEY AVE 9

Home Farm
Office Village

Cams
Hall

Carnac
House

PO16

8

South Park

Boatyard
Ind Est

Upper
Town Quay

Upper
Quay

Quayside Commerce Ctr
1 MILLERS QUAY HO
3 THE POPE WLK
4 ST GEORGES CT

Lower
Quay

BATH LANE COTTS 1
SWAN QUAY 2

CH

Kings Way

Sports
Gd

Sports
Ctr

Solent HO 1
HAMBLE HO 2
NEEDLES 3
MEON 4
SPITHEAD 5
MEDINA 6
LANGSTONE 7
YOUNGBRIDGE CT 8
TRAFALGAR CT 9

PO16

Salterns Est

Salterns
Quay

Cunigre
Pond

05

Portsmouth Harbour

Wicor Hard

7

Works

The
Moorings

Palmerston
Bsns Pk

Delta
Bsns
Pk

Pier

Foxbury
Point

6

Southwick
CT
Fort
Fareham

Axis
Pk

Fort Fareham
Ind Est

Sharlands Rd
Newgate
Lane Ind Est

BOSUNS CL

FARRIER WAY

PO14

Superstore

Collingwood
Ret Pk

Superstore
Speedfield
Pk

Solent
Speedfield
Gate

Portsmouth Harbour

Fleetlands

PO16

5

Superstores

Royal Sovereign Ave

Woodcot
Prim Sch

Primrose Cl

Bridgemary
Way

04

Bridgemary Gr

Woodcot

Dale
Dr

Carter Ho 1
Hanover Ho 2
Cooley Ho 3

Main Rd

RNAD
Gosport

4

SWAN
CT

Bridgemary

PO13

THE
LEISURE

Peel Farm

Peel
Common

Nesbitt
Cl

Nursery Cl

The Meads

Holbrook
Prim Sch

Bedenham
Prim Sch

Frater
Lake

3

Fort
Elson

WOODCOTE LA

Bridgemary
Com Sch

03

Peel Common
Jun & Inf
Schs

Liby

Brewers La

GOSPORT

LOMBARD CL 1
SYCAMORE CL 2
THE HOE 3
THE THICKET 4
THE DRIVE 5
THE MOUNT 6
ASPENGROVE 7
THE GLEN 8
VINESIDE 9

PO12

2

BROOM WAY   B3385

ROWNER RD

River Alver

Chark
Common

St Christophers
Gdns

PO

Pembroke
Ct

Victory
Ct

Rowner
Jun & Inf Sch

The
Firs

ALMONDSIDE

Heritage Bsns Pk

Fort
Brockhurst
Ind Est

WINGATE RD

1

BROOM WAY   B3385

GOSPORT RD

B3334

ALLIANCE CL 1
LANDON RD 2
LAWN CL 3

GOSDENSWAY

Recn
Ctr
Holbrook

A32

Fort
Brockhurst
Mus

02

57   A   58   B   C   58   D   59   E   F

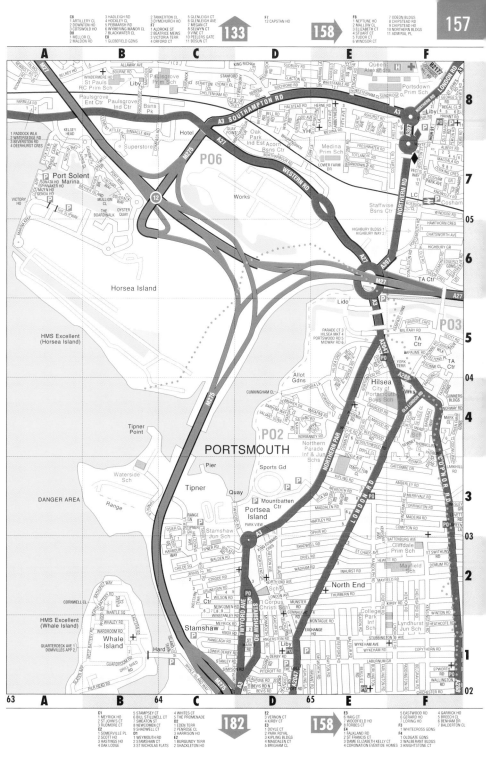

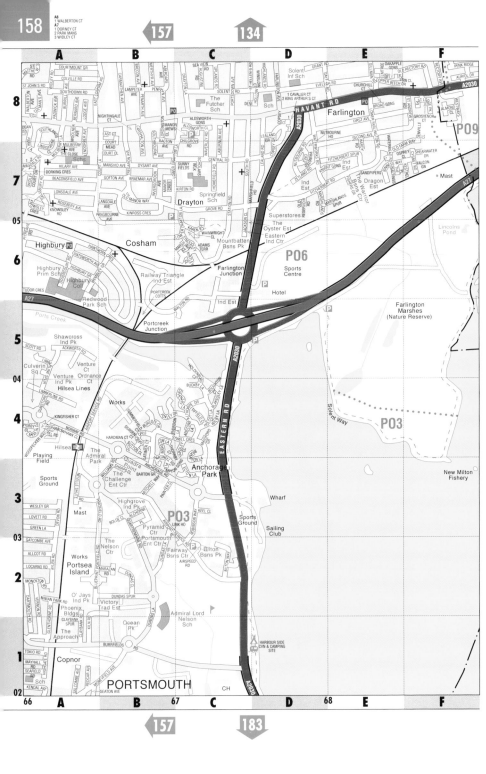

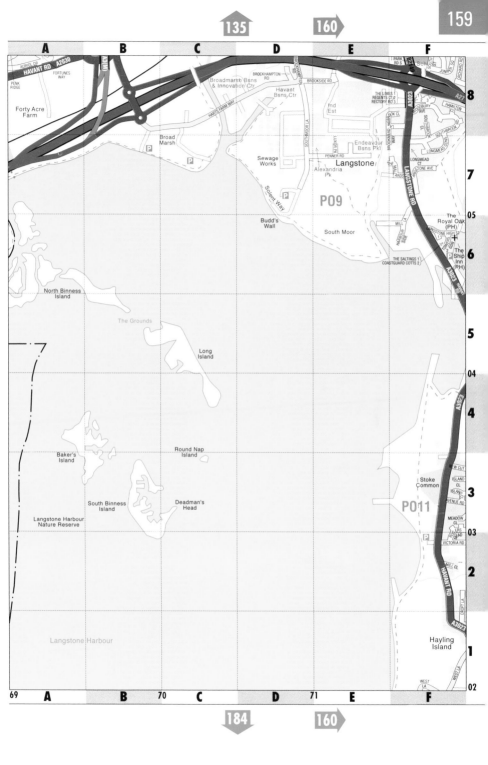

159
136

F8
1 CHURCH PATH
2 MEADOW CT
3 WARWICK CT
4 KING'S TERR
5 OYSTER MEWS
6 FROBISHER GDNS

7 ST PETER'S SQ
8 HARBOUR CT

HAVANT RD
PARK CRES
EMSWORTH HOUSE
CONVENT CT
HIGHLAND CL
NORE FARM AVE
NORE FARM CL
BARN CL
BROOK GDNS
WEST RD

EMSWORTH

PO10

A27
HAVANT-BY-PASS
HAVANT RD

Victoria Cott
A259
B2148

Wade
Court

ORCHARD
RD

PUCK LA

PO9

Cemy

Solent Way

Church Path

Wayfarer's Walk

WESTERN
PAR

Swimming
Pool

Conigar Point

8

7

05

6

Fowley
Island

Nore Rithe

Fowley Rithe

Langstone
Bridge

A3023
HAVANT RD

New Cut

Duckard Point

Marina

Hotel

North
Common

Boating
Lake

Sweare Deep

Wickor
Point

5

04

4

NORTHNEY RD

SPINNAKER GRANGE

Northney

NORTHNEY LA

CLOVELLY RD

PO10

Sussex Border Path

North Hayling

PYCROFT CL

CHURCH LA

Church Farm

Thorney
Island

3

03

PO11

NEW CUT

KINGSWAY

QUEENSWAY

AVENUE RD

VICTORIA RD

ST PETER'S AVE

THORNEY
VIEW

ELM GROVE

Emsworth Channel

2

Northwood
Farm

NORTHWOOD LA

WEST LA

Stoke

Upper Tye
Farm

Tye

CHICHESTER RD

GUTNER LA

Gutner
Farm

Marker Point

1

02

A3023
HAVANT RD

CASTLEMANS LA

Finchwood Farm
Ind Units

GEORGE LA

LOWER TYE
CVN &
CAMPING CTR

WOODGASTON LA

72

A

73

B

C

74

D

E

F

159
185

A8
1 ST PETERS CT
2 SPRING GDNS
3 PELHAM TERR
4 FRANKLAND TERR
5 RIVERSIDE TERR
6 SPINNAKER PL
7 LUMLEY PATH
8 CHEQUERS QUAY
9 SADLERS WLK
10 JOHN KING SHIPYARD

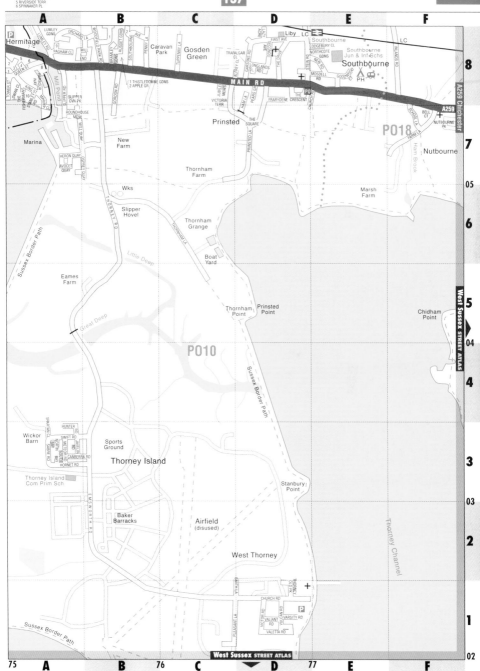

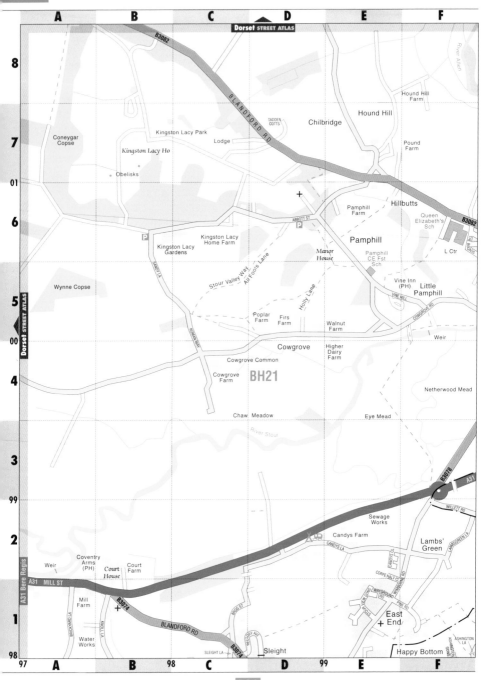

A B C D E F

8

7

01

6

5

00

4

3

99

2

1

98

97 A B 98 C D 99 E F

B3082

BLANDFORD RD

TADDEN COTTS

Chilbridge

Hound Hill

Hound Hill Farm

Coneygar Copse

Kingston Lacy Park

Lodge

Pound Farm

Kingston Lacy Ho

Obelisks

Hillbutts

Pamphill Farm

B3082

Queen Elizabeth's Sch

ABBOTT ST

L Ctr

P

Kingston Lacy Gardens

Kingston Lacy Home Farm

Manor House

Pamphill

Pamphill CE Fst Sch

P

Stour Valley Way

Aul Fools Lane

Holly Lane

Vine Inn (PH)

Little Pamphill

Wynne Copse

ROMAN WAY

VINE HILL

LONGROVE RD

Poplar Farm

Firs Farm

Walnut Farm

Weir

Dorset STREET ATLAS

Cowgrove

Higher Dairy Farm

Cowgrove Common

BH21

Netherwood Mead

Cowgrove Farm

Chaw Meadow

Eye Mead

River Stour

B3078

A31

Sewage Works

WILLETT RD

Candys Farm

CANDYS LA

Lambs' Green

LAMBSGREEN LA

LB

Coventry Arms (PH)

Court House

Court Farm

CANDYS CL

CORFE HALT CL

PINE RD

WAYGROUND RD

A31 Bere Regis

A31 MILL ST

Weir

Mill Farm

BIRCHYARD LA

KNOLL LA

B3074

BLANDFORD RD

BOG ST

ABBOTT RD

ASHINGTON LA

East End

Water Works

B3074

SLEIGHT LA

Sleight

Happy Bottom

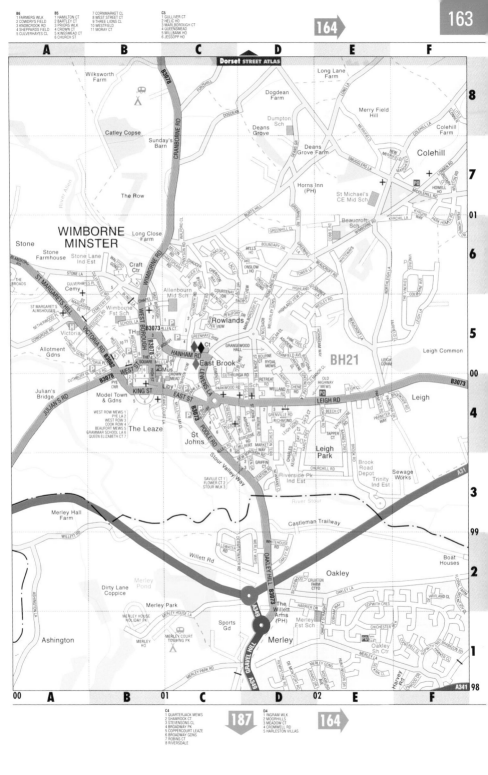

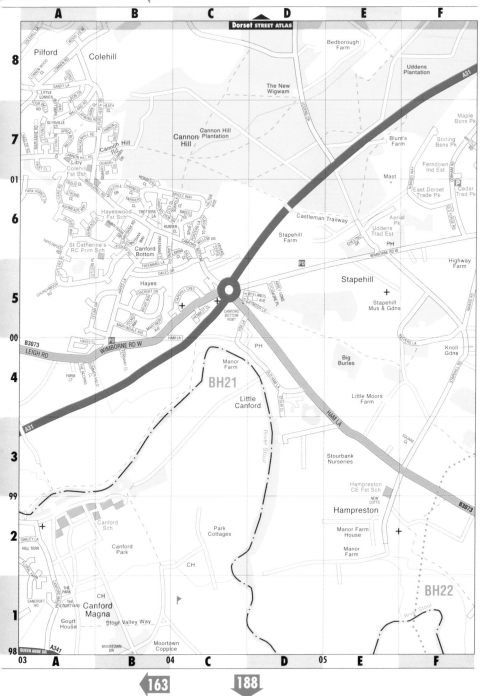

Dorset STREET ATLAS

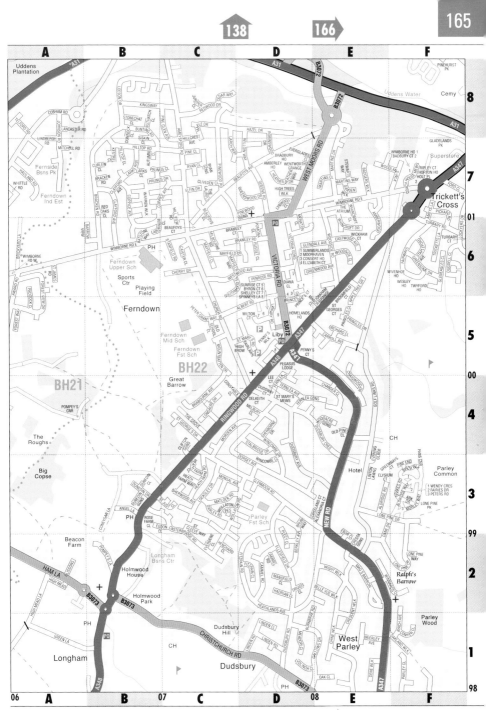

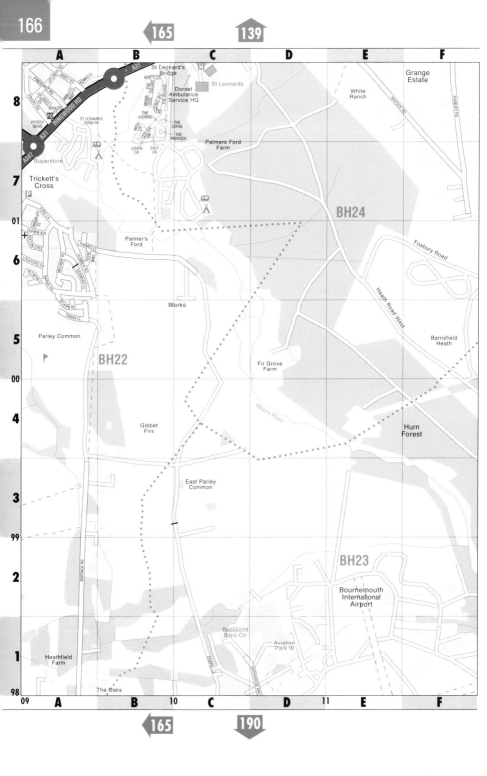

167
141

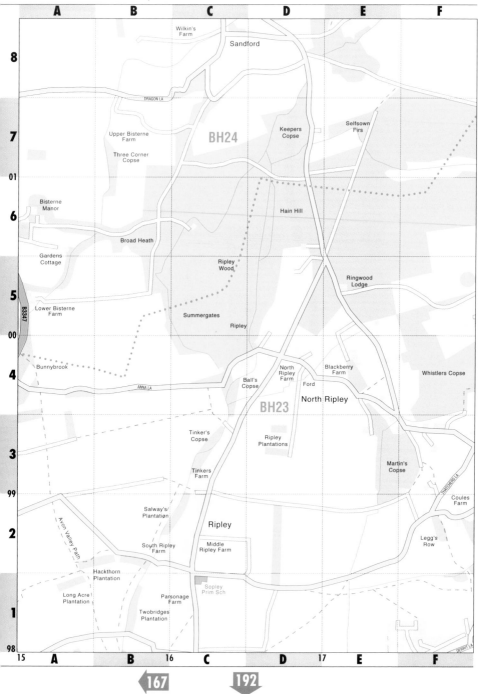

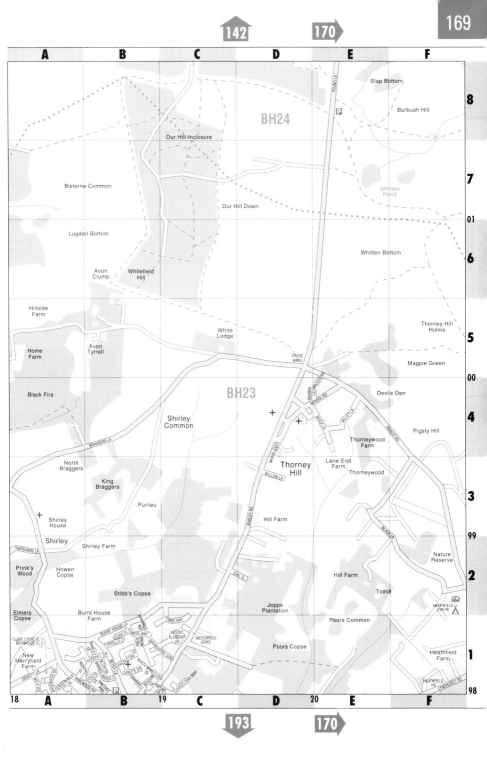

169
143

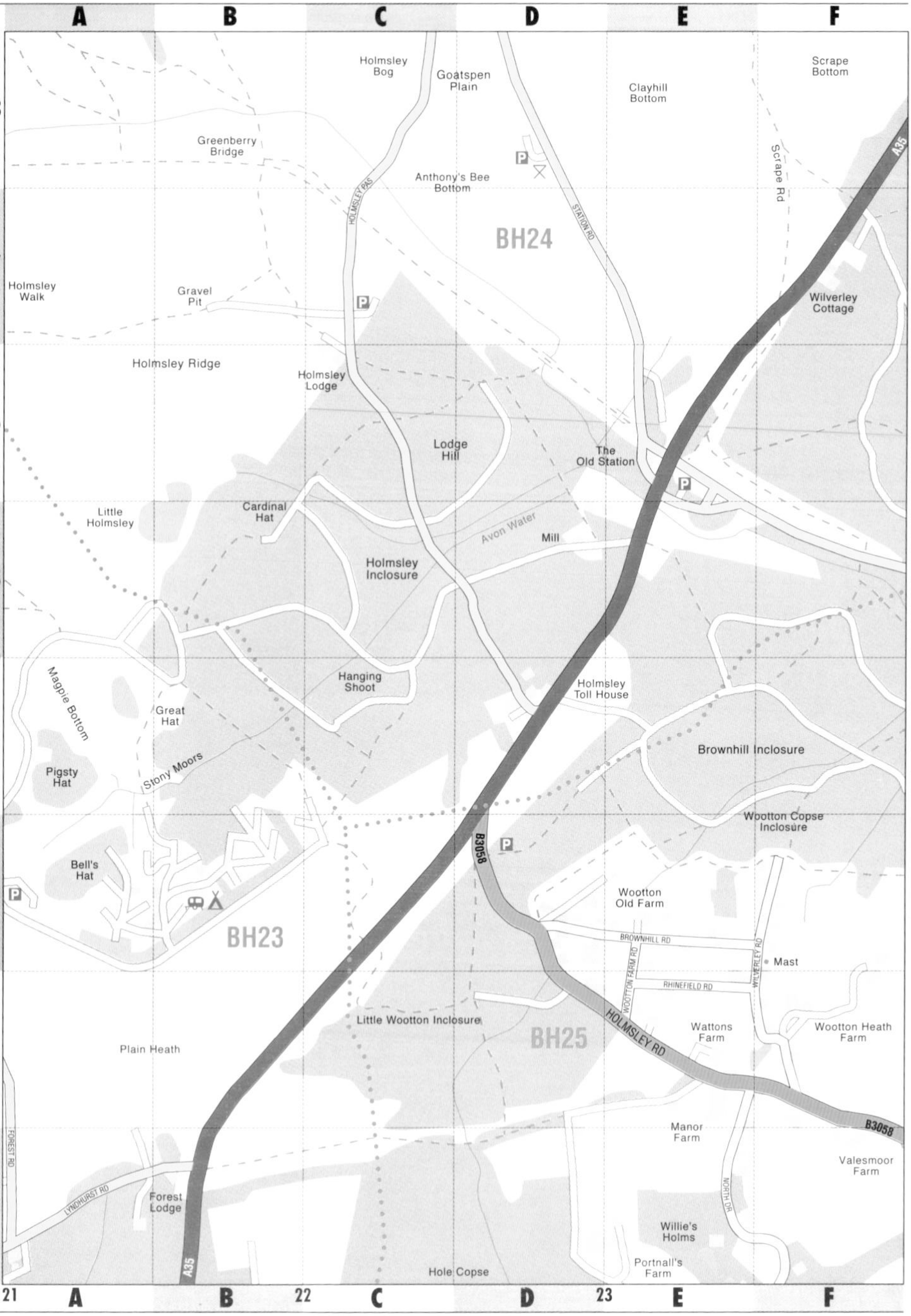

A **B** **C** **D** **E** **F**

8

Holmsley
Bog

Goatspen
Plain

Clayhill
Bottom

Scrape
Bottom

Greenberry
Bridge

Anthony's Bee
Bottom

BH24

Scrape Rd

A35

7

Holmsley
Walk

Gravel
Pit

Wilverley
Cottage

01

Holmsley Ridge

Holmsley
Lodge

6

Lodge
Hill

The
Old Station

Little
Holmsley

Cardinal
Hat

Avon Water

Mill

5

Holmsley
Inclosure

00

Magpie Bottom

Hanging
Shoot

Holmsley
Toll House

4

Great
Hat

Stony Moors

Brownhill Inclosure

Pigsty
Hat

Wootton Copse
Inclosure

3

Bell's
Hat

BH23

Wootton
Old Farm

Mast

BROWNHILL RD

WOOTTON FARM RD

RHINEFIELD RD

WILVERLEY RD

Wootton Heath
Farm

99

Little Wootton Inclosure

BH25

HOLMSLEY RD

Wattons
Farm

2

Plain Heath

B3058

Manor
Farm

Valesmoor
Farm

1

FOREST RD

LYNDHURST RD

Forest
Lodge

A35

Willie's
Holms

RD HUICH

Portnall's
Farm

98

Hole Copse

A **B** **C** **D** **E** **F**

21   22   23

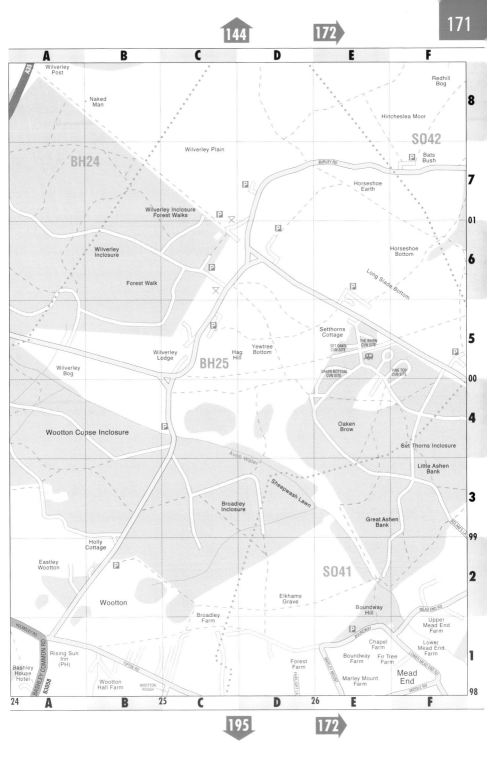

171
145

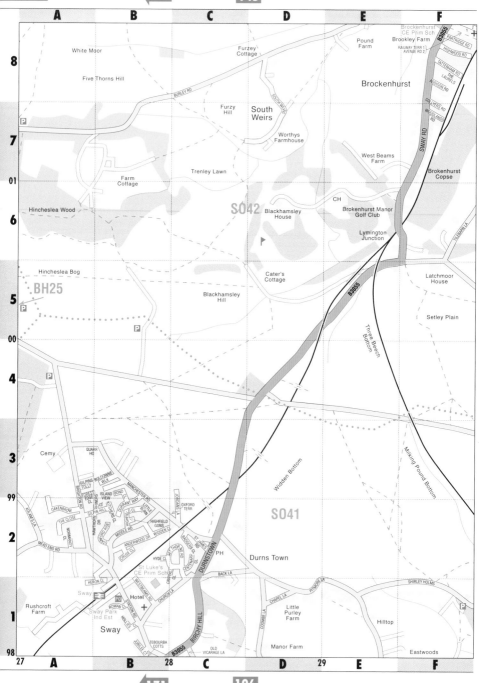

171
196

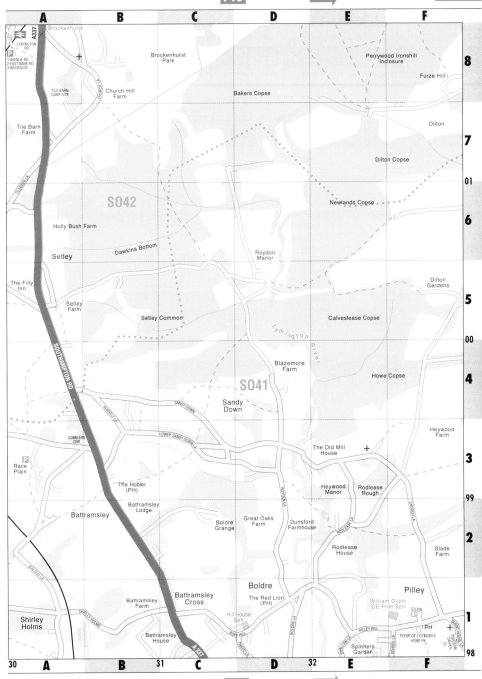

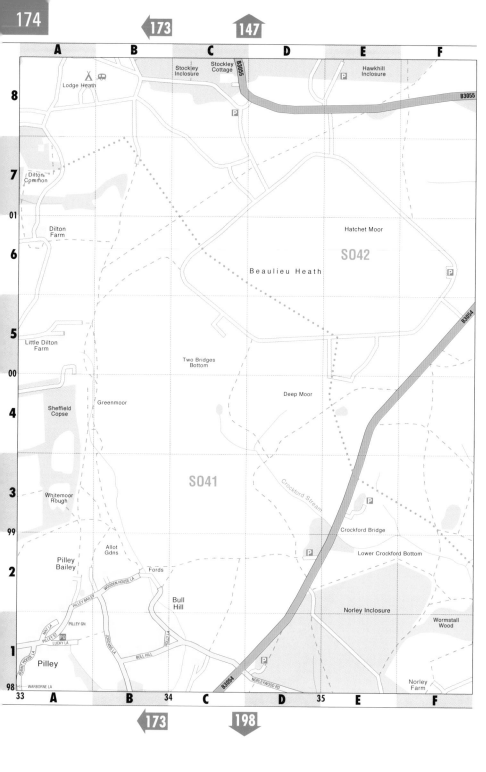

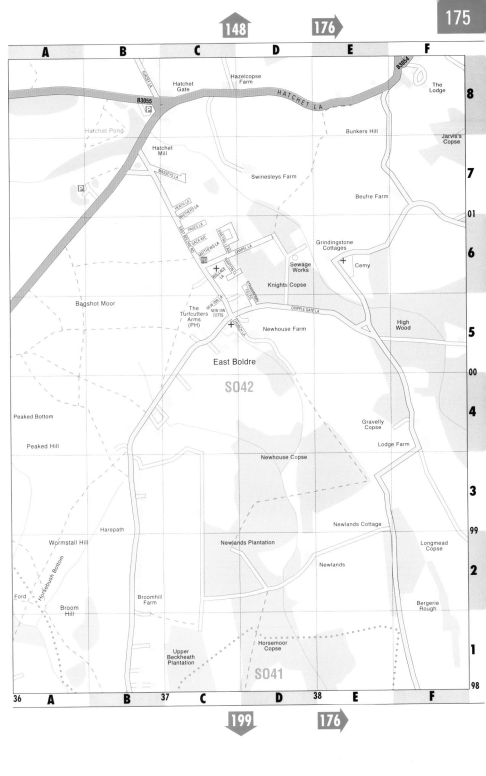

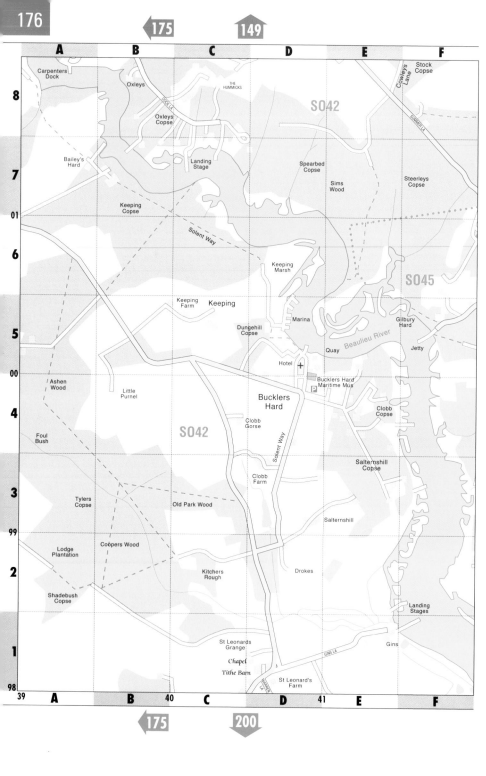

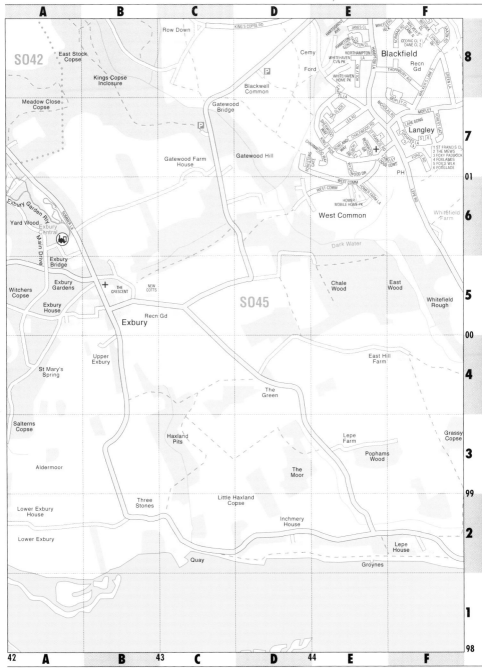

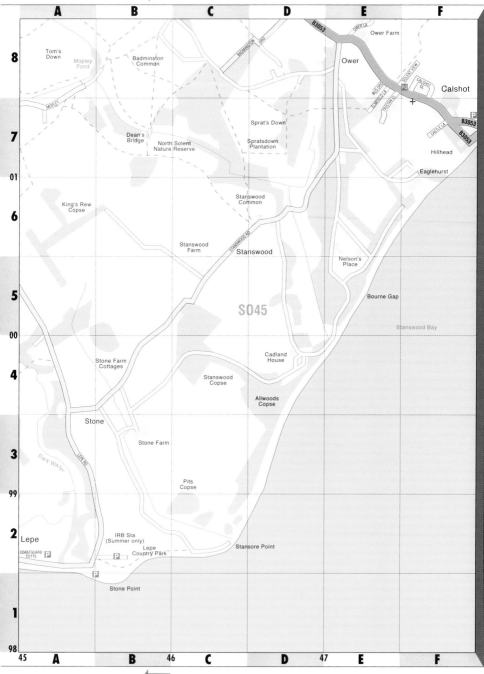

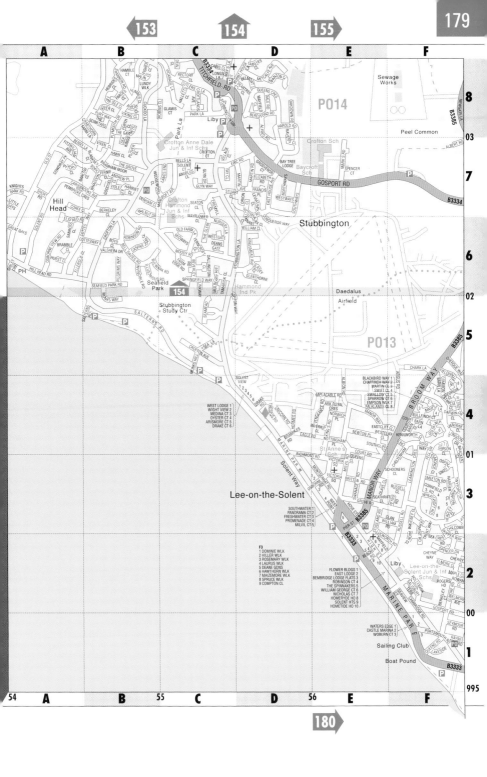

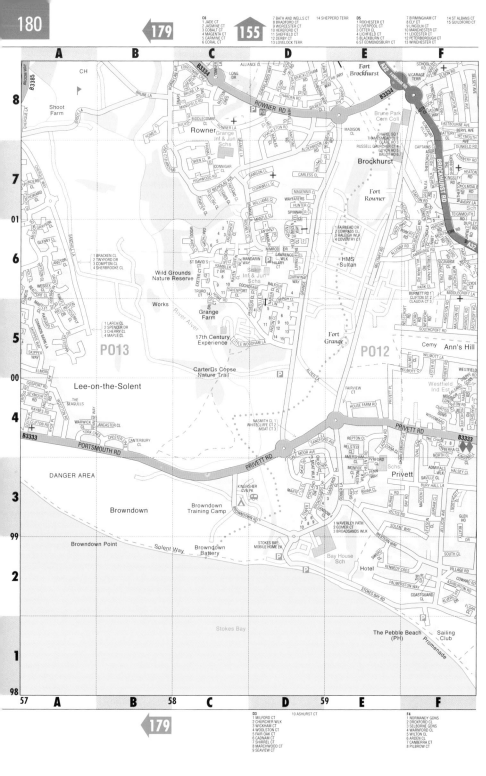

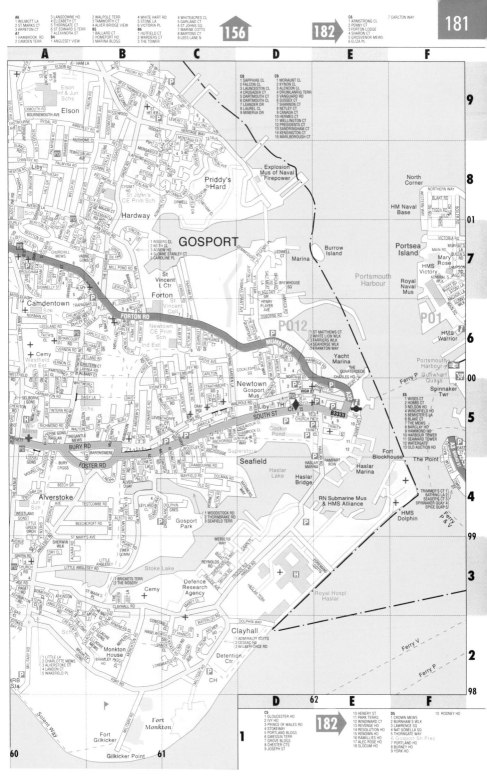

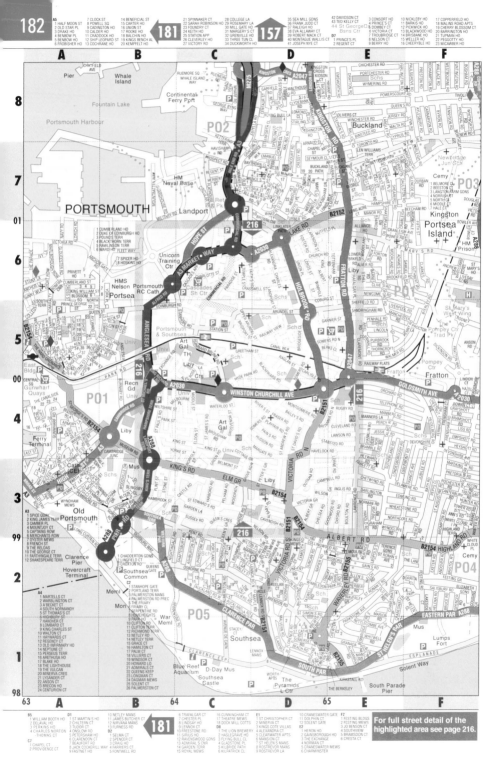

A5
1 ANSON RD
2 VERNON MEWS
3 MILTON CT
4 WASHINGTON CT

A8
1 SIDMOUTH AVE
2 MONEYFIELD AVE
3 MONEYFIELD LA
4 CONISTON AVE
5 MANOR PARK AVE
6 STAPLETON RD

B5
1 BLENDWORTH RD
2 AVOCET HO
3 CURLEW PATH
4 CHEVENING CT
5 OXTED CT
6 TERN WLK

158

184

8

Langstone Harbour

Great Salterns Quay

Great Salterns Lake

Portsea Island

Westover Prim Sch

Baffins

P03

Liby

Baffins Pond

Portsmouth Coll

Eastern Rd

Solent Way

7

Hayling Ave

Jenkins Gr

Cedar Gr

01

PORTSMOUTH

Central Point

East Shore Sch

1 SCHOONER WAY
2 SOVEREIGN CL
3 ATALANTA CL
4 WAYFARER CL
5 MAYFLOWER DR
6 LONGFIELD CL

6

St Mary's East Wing

Langstone Rd

Moorings Way Inf Sch

Moorings Way

Miltoncross Sch

Cemy

St Georges

A2030 VELDER AVE

Univ of Portsmouth (Langstone Campus)

5

Cluster Ind Est

St James

Waterside Sch (Unit)

Landing Stage

Landing Stage

Ferry (F)

Frattoft Ind Est

MILTON LA Football Gd

P04

Milton

IRB Sta

The Ferry Boat Inn (PH)

CH

P011

00

Liby
1 RHYS CT
2 ANVIL CT

4

Goldsmith Ave A2030

A288

Dickens Ho

1 COACH-HOUSE MEWS
2 TOWPATH MEAD
3 MAURICE RD
4 FAIR OAK RD
5 OAKDEAN RD
6 CHERITON RD

Allot Gdns

1 EASTLAKE HTS 1
HORSE SANDS CL 2
LANGSTONE MARINA HTS 3
SPITHEAD HTS 4
SOLENT HTS 5
VANGUARD CT 6

Marina

Bransbury Park

Friendly Societies Homes

Bransbury Rd

Sea Breeze Gdns

Henderson Pk

Gibraltar

Fort Cumberland

3

Highland Rd B2154

High Ct

Eastney

Royal Marines Mus

Southsea Cvn Pk

99

Solent Way

Eastern Par

Esplanade

2

1

98

66 A   B   67 C   D   68 E   F

184

A2
1 NETTLESTONE RD
2 CULVER RD
3 EASTERN TERR
4 HIGHLAND ST
5 PRIORY RD
6 EASTNEY ST

A3
1 HATFIELD RD
2 COVINDALE HO
3 WYN SUTCLIFFE CT
4 CARPENTER CL

B2
1 CLOCKTOWER DR
2 TEAPOT ROW
3 CHURCHILL SQ
4 FLINDERS CT
5 SAUNDERS MEWS
6 MOUNTBATTEN SQ
7 DRYSDALE MEWS
8 PITCAIRN MEWS
9 BAMFORD HO

10 DOWELL HO
11 FINCH HO
12 HALLIDAY HO
13 HARVEY HO
14 PRETTYJOHN HO
15 WILKINSON HO

B3
1 GRAND DIVISION ROW

B4
1 MILTON PARK AVE
2 ARTILLERY TERR
3 OLD CANAL
4 MILFORD CT
5 WILLIAM CT

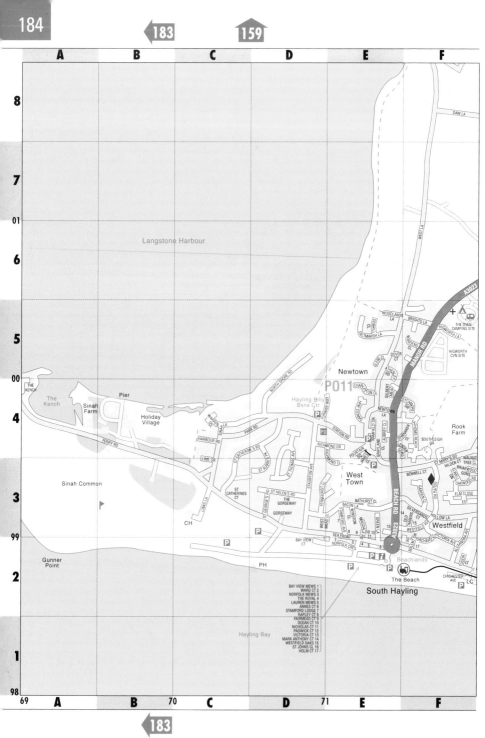

Langstone Harbour

THE KENCH
The Kench
Sinah Farm
Pier
Holiday Village
FERRY RD
HARBOUR RD
Sinah Common
Gunner Point
CH
LIME GR
ST CATHERINES CT
WALHON LA
PARK RD
ST CATHERINE'S RD
ST ANDREWS
ST GEORGE'S RD
ST THOMAS AVE
STAUNTON AVE
Hayling Billy Bsns Ctr
NORTH SHORE RD
STATION RD
RICHMOND DR
RICHMOND CL
Newtown
PO11
West Town
FOUNTAIN
BACON LA
BATHURST CL
WEST MEAD
SEA FRONT
NORFOLK CRES
BAY VIEW CT
PH
WINSTON
ST HELEN'S RD
THE GORSEWAY
GORSEWAY
Hayling Bay
WOODLANDS LA
BRIGHTS LA
SALTMARSH LA
DOVER CT
CHAPELTON CL
MANOR RD
HIGWORTH LA
THE OVEN CAMPING SITE
HIGWORTH CVN SITE
Rook Farm
A3023
WEST LA
DAW LA
GILBERT
SOUTHLEIGH GR
MARY'S RD
HILDEN CT
WALNUT TREE CL
BRIARWOOD GDNS
OAKWO RD
ELM CLOSE EST
BENWELL CT
SILVERSANDS
HOLLOW LA
Westfield
WESTFIELD
VICTORIA AVE
ORCHARD
CHICHESTER AVE
LC
The Beach
Beachlands
South Hayling

BAY VIEW MEWS 1
WARD CT 2
NORFOLK MEWS 3
THE ROYAL 4
LAUREN MEWS 5
ANNES CT 6
STAMFORD LODGE 7
RAPLEY CT 8
FAIRMEAD CT 9
OCEAN CT 10
NICHOLAS CT 11
PADWICK CT 12
VICTORIA CT 13
MARK ANTHONY CT 14
WESTFIELD OAKS 15
ST JOHNS CL 16
HOLM CT 17

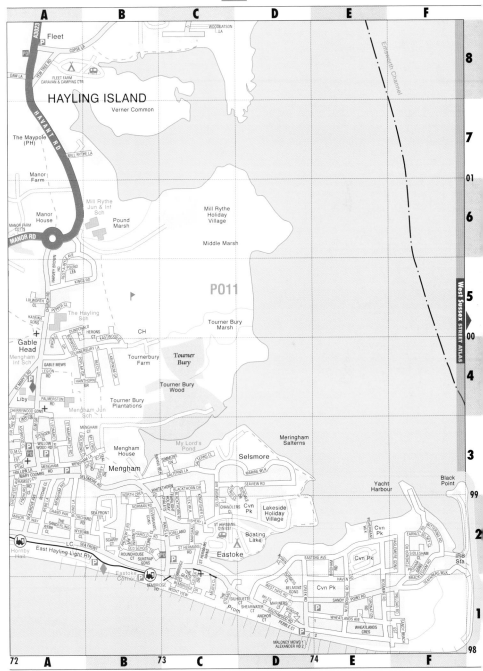

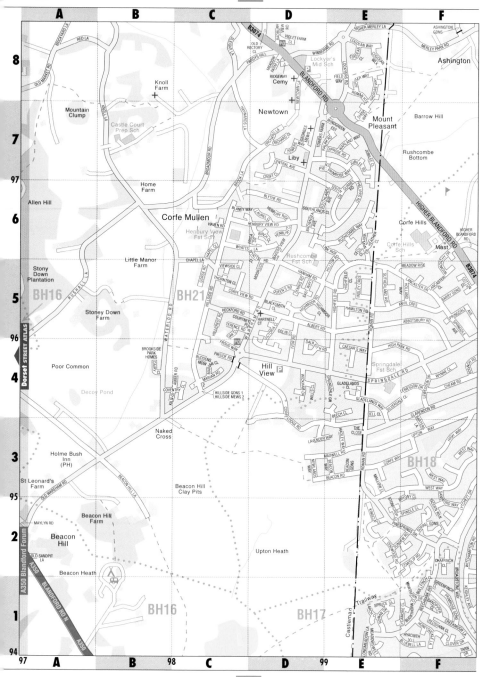

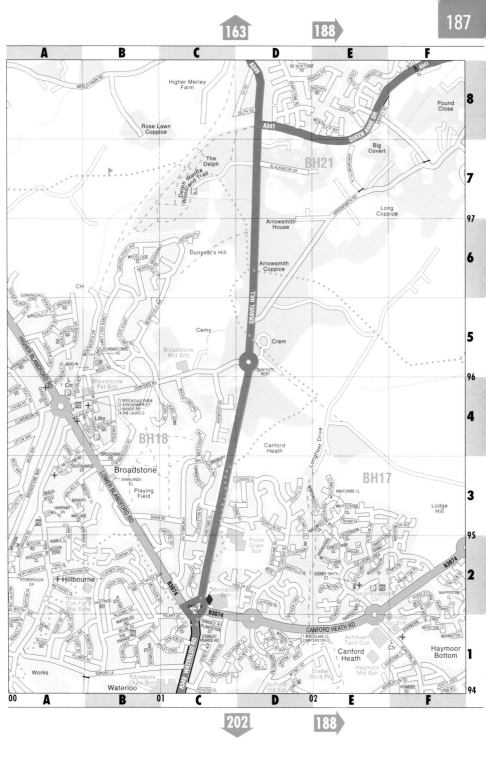

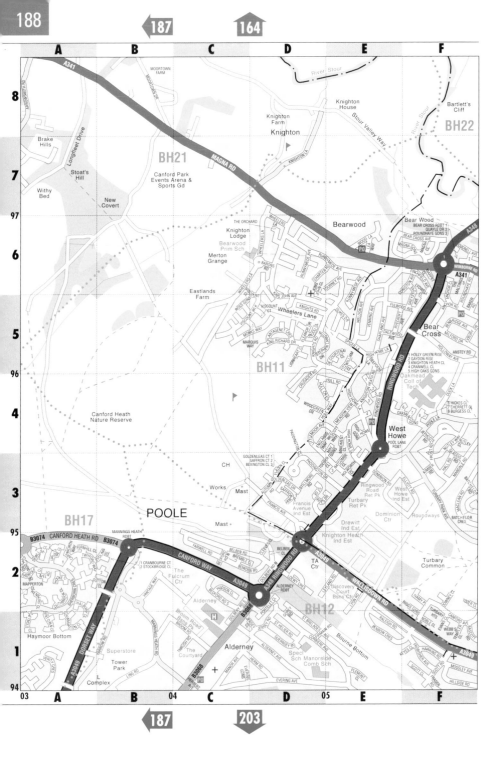

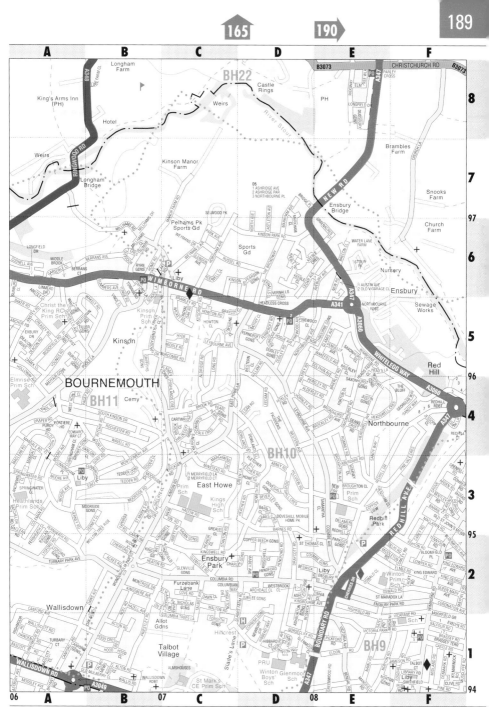

A B C D E F

8

BH22

B3073 CHRISTCHURCH RD

BARRACK RD

Portfield Sch

East Parley

CHAPEL LA

Aviation Park Way

ENTERPRISE WAY

CHAPEL GATE

Bournemouth International Airport

College of Air Traffic Control

PARLEY LA

New Cottages

BH23

Alice in Wonderland Family Fun Park

Merritown

B3073

7

Parley Court

PARLEY GREEN LA

Parley Green

River Stour

Stour Valley Way

DALES LA

MERRITOWN LA

West Hurn

97

HURN COURT LA

West Lodge

6

BH10

Works

Mucclesshell Farm

Hurn Court Farm

Leaden Stour

5

Berry Hill

THE FRANK WAREHAM COTTAGE HOMES

BH9

MUSCLIFF LA

Hicks Farm

WOOD ROW

Weir

Throop Mill

West Lodge

96

BOURNEMOUTH

Muscliff

Nursery

Muscliff Prim Sch

Cemy

River Farm Throop

1 DOWNTON CL
2 CALMORE CL
3 FRITHAM GDNS
4 BRAMSHAW GDNS

Westover Retail Pk

THE GROVE

A3060

BH8

4

VICARAGE COTTS

Blue Roof Farm

3

Nurseries

MOUNTBATTEN GDNS 1
IBBERTSON CL 2
BOURNEMOUTH MEMORIAL HOMES 3

95

CHARMINSTER RD

ASHSTEAD GDNS

LUCKHAM GDNS

SHAWFORD GDNS 1
MICHELMERSH GN 2
SHERFIELD CL 3
WHITSBURY CL 4

CASTLE LA W

Castlepoint

Liby

Yeomans Ind Pk

EVENLODE HOMES

2

Moordown

CHARMINSTER CL

Charminster

Bournemouth Sch for Girls

Strouden

Liby

A3060

Bournemouth Sch

Sports Ctr

EAST WAY

Queen's Park Jun & Inf Schs

The Bishop of Winchester Comp Sch

Haddon Hill

1

B3063

MORTIMER RD

SUTTON RD

CHIGWELL RD

Cemy

MALLARD RD

PARKWAY DR

94

09 A B 10 C D 11 E F

A2
1 ROSEBUD AVE
2 McWILLIAM RD
3 MINTERNE RD
4 MALVERN CT
A3
1 COMBER RD
2 MEADOW CT
3 PRIORY VIEW PL

A4
1 REDHILL CT
2 PORTSWOOD DR
3 THE CIRCLE
B4
1 STURMINSTER RD
2 SIDNEY GDNS

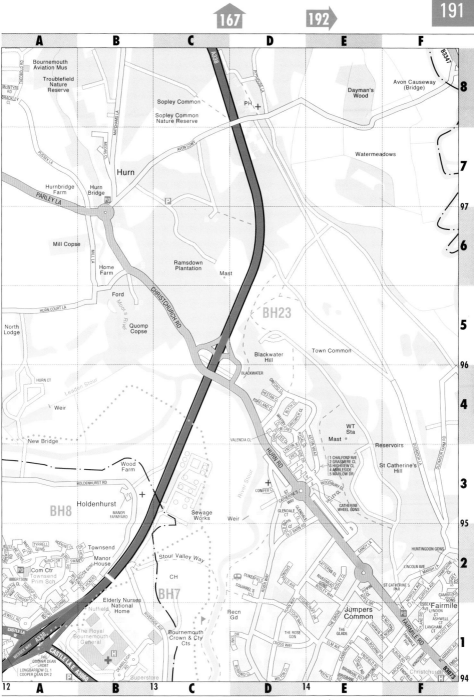

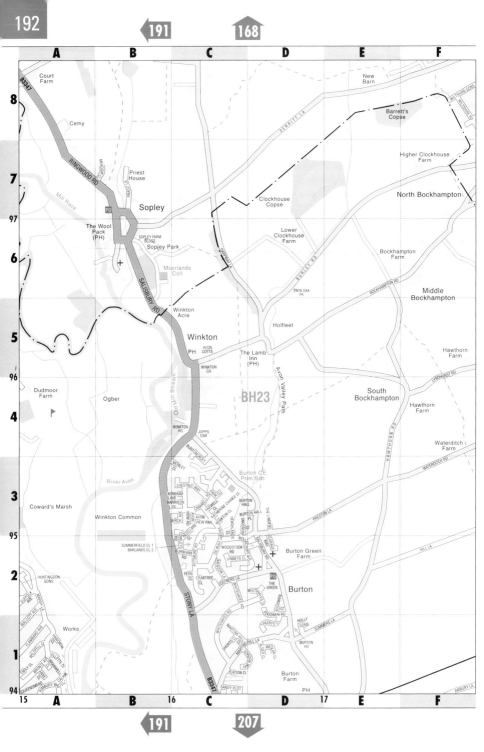

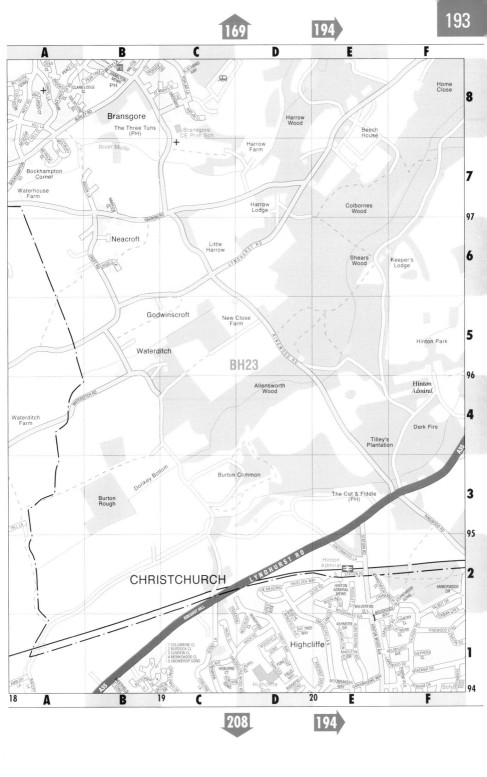

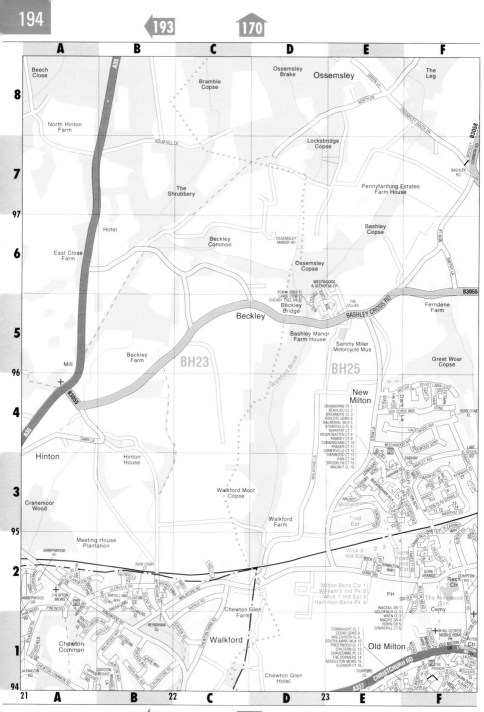

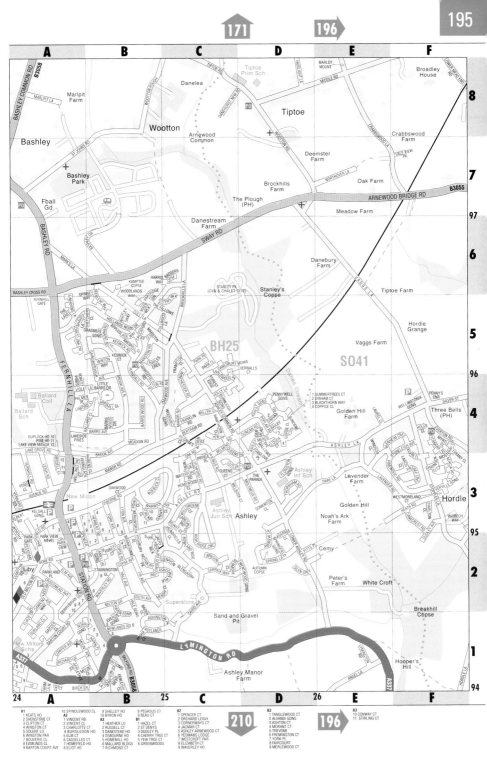

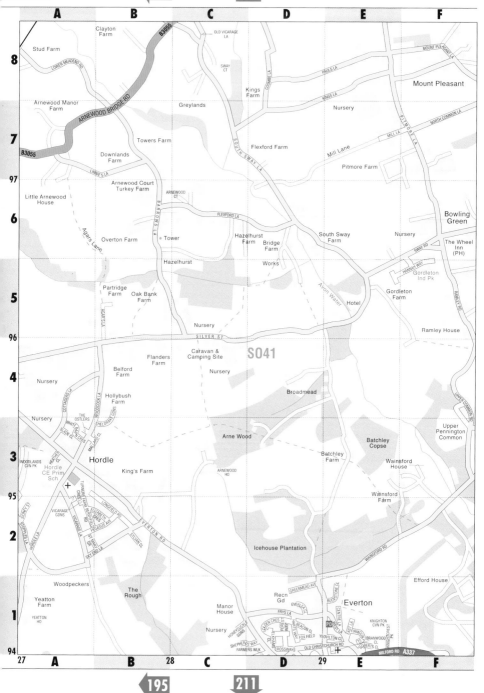

195
172

A **B** **C** **D** **E** **F**

8

Stud Farm

Clayton Farm

OLD VICARAGE LA

LOWER MEADEND RD

B3055

SWAY CT

Kings Farm

COOMBE LA

PAULS LA

KINGS LA

MOUNT PLEASANT LA

Mount Pleasant

Arnewood Manor Farm

Greylands

Nursery

NORTH COMMON LA

7

ARNEWOOD BRIDGE RD

B3055

Towers Farm

Downlands Farm

LINNIES LA

SOUTH SWAY LA

Flexford Farm

Mill Lane

Pitmore Farm

ROPEHILL

MILL LA

97

Arnewood Court Turkey Farm

ARNEWOOD CT

Bowling Green

Little Arnewood House

BARROWS LA

FLEXFORD LA

South Sway Farm

Nursery

The Wheel Inn (PH)

6

Agars Lane

Overton Farm

Tower

Hazelhurst Farm

Bridge Farm

SWAY RD

Hazelhurst

Works

HANNAH WAY

Gordleton Ind Pk

Avon Water

Gordleton Farm

RAMLEY RD

5

AGARS LA

Partridge Farm

Oak Bank Farm

Nursery

Hotel

Ramley House

96

SILVER ST

Caravan & Camping Site

SO41

Flanders Farm

Belford Farm

4

Nursery

Nursery

Broadmead

LOWER COMMON RD

Hollybush Farm

COTTAGERS LA

PT WOODDOORS

SHELDRAKE GDNS

Upper Pennington Common

Nursery

THE OSTLERS

WHIT...

SLOE CL

MALLARD CL

Arne Wood

Batchley Copse

3

WOODLANDS CVN PK

HEATHER CL

Hordle

Hordle CE Prim Sch

King's Farm

ARNEWOOD HO

Batchley Farm

Wainsford House

95

TURNER FARM RD

CREST

LONGFIELD RD

ELIZABETH RD

PEGASUS AVE

VICARAGE GDNS

VICARAGE LA

ST MARY CL

EVERTON RD

Wainsford Farm

2

STOPPLES LA

STOPPLES LA

DIBBLES LA

SKY END LA

SYLVAN CL

Icehouse Plantation

WAINSFORD RD

Efford House

1

Woodpeckers

Yeatton Farm

YEATTON HO

The Rough

Manor House

Nursery

Recn Gd

GREENMEAD AVE

EVERLEA

Everton

BUCKLAND

CENTRAL

KNIGHTON CVN PK

PO

HONEYSUCKLE GDNS

MAIDEN CRES

FRYS LA

BEACON CL

FOX FIELD

YEOVILTON CL

FIRMST

BRANWOOD

ROBERTS CL

Efford House

SHEPHERDS WAY

FARMERS WLK

CROSSWAYS

OLD CHRISTCHURCH RD

MILFORD RD A337

94

27 **A** **B** 28 **C** **D** 29 **E** **F**

195
211

A B C D E F

8 7 97 6 5 96 4 3 95 2 1 94

LYMINGTON

S041

Passford House Hotel
Mount Pleasant
Springhill
St Austins
Starve Croft Bottom
Tuckermill Copse
Galley Hill
Passford Hill
Passford Water
Great Fry's Hill Copse
Nursery
Vicars Hill Farm
Warborne
Southlands Sch & The Wing Ctr
Vicars Hill
St Rose
Wr Twr
Buckland Rings
Ampress Pk
Buckland Manor Farm
Nursery
Buckland
Lower Buckland
Lymington River
St Cyres Memorial Cotts
Cowley Farm
Yaldhurst Copse
Yaldhurst
Our Lady & St Joseph RC Prim Sch
Lymington Town
Island Point
Superstore
Pennington CE Jun Sch
Priestlands Sch
Recn Ctr
Upper Pennington
War Meml
The Square
Pennington Cross
Upper Rough
Newlease Copse
Vineyard
Pennington
Efford Farm Cotts
Efford Farm House
Works
Efford Bridge
Woodside Gdns
Woodside
De La Warr House
Nursery
Nursery

E2
1 BELMORE HO
2 SALTERNE HO
3 PYRFORD GDNS
4 VICTORIA PL
5 GOLD MEAD CL
6 PEARMAIN DR
7 PEARTREE CT
8 PIPPIN CL
9 CHURCH MEAD
10 WOODSIDE CL

E4
1 LIME TREE HO
2 BARFIELDS CT
3 COURTLANDS
4 CARLTON HO

F2
1 WORCESTER PL
2 BROADMEAD CL
3 RUSSET CL
4 MONKS CT
5 CONFERENCE PL

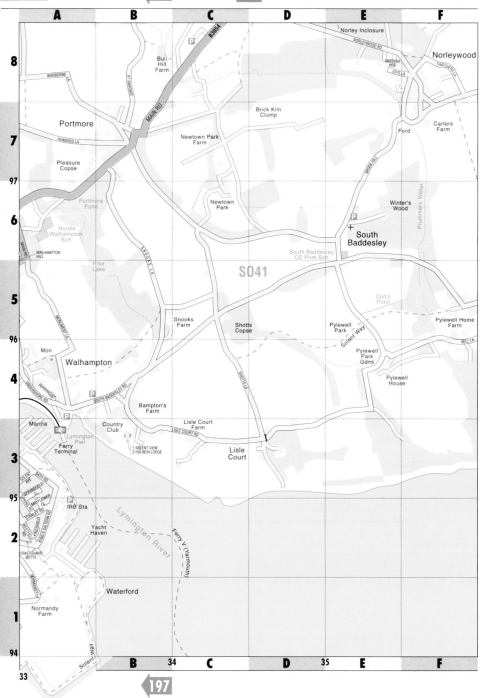

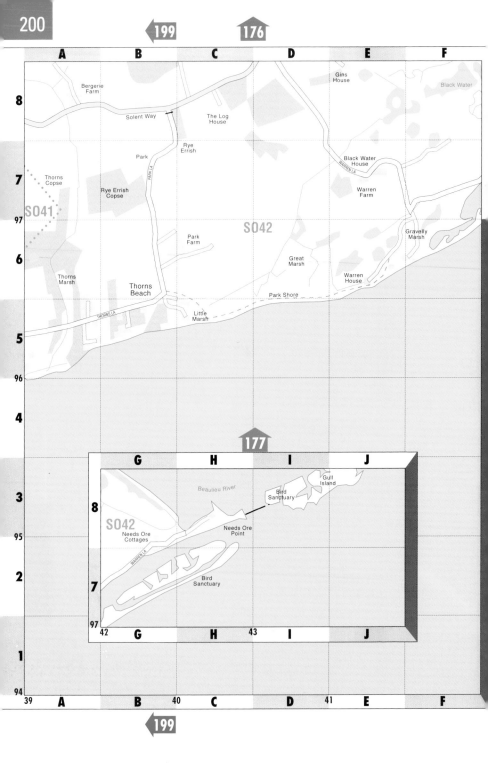

A   B   C   D   E   F

8

Bergerie
Farm

Solent Way

The Log
House

Gins
House

Black Water

Rye
Errish

Park

PARK LA

7

Thorns
Copse

Rye Errish
Copse

Black Water
House

WARREN LA

Warren
Farm

SO41

97

SO42

Gravelly
Marsh

6

Thorns
Marsh

Park
Farm

Great
Marsh

Warren
House

Thorns
Beach

Park Shore

THORNS LA

Little
Marsh

5

96

4

G   H   I   J

Beaulieu River

Gull
Island

Bird
Sanctuary

3

8

SO42

Needs Ore
Cottages

Needs Ore
Point

95

WARREN LA

2

Bird
Sanctuary

7

97

42   G   43   I   J
      H

1

94

39   A   B   40   C   D   41   E   F

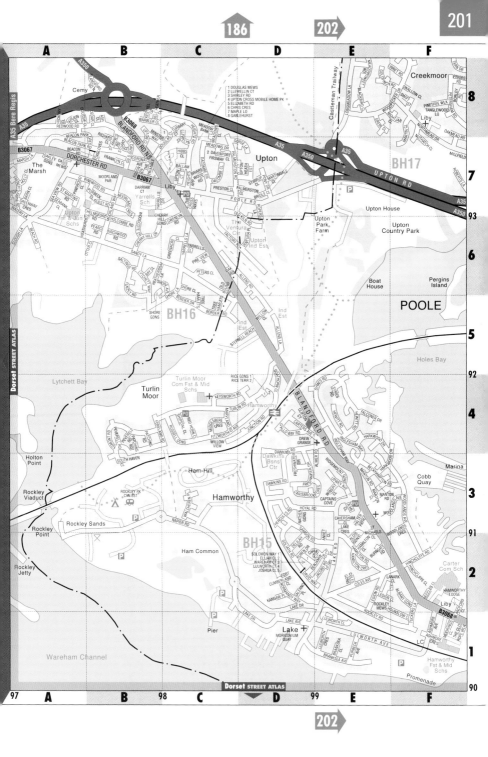

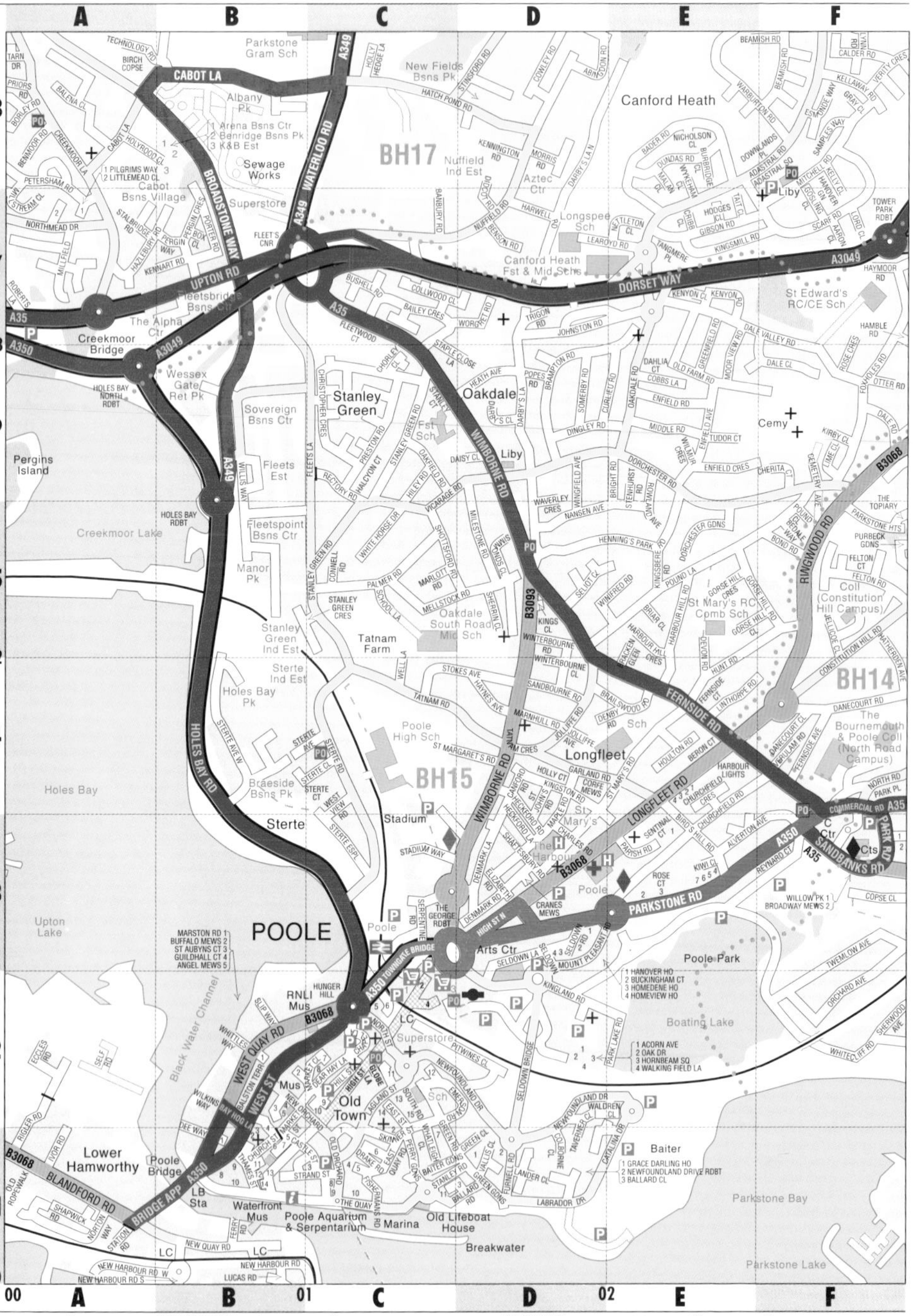

A B C D E F

8 7 93 6 5 92 4 3 91 2 1 90

BH17

Canford Heath

Canford Heath Fst & Mid Sch

DORSET WAY

A3049

St Edward's RC/CE Sch

TOWER PARK RDBT

Oakdale

Liby

Cemy

BH14

The Bournemouth & Poole Coll (North Road Campus)

Coll (Constitution Hill Campus)

Creekmoor Bridge

Pergins Island

Creekmoor Lake

Holes Bay RDBT

Stanley Green

Stanley Green Ind Est

Sterte Ind Est

Poole High Sch

Tatnam Farm

BH15

Longfleet

Holes Bay

Upton Lake

POOLE

Poole Park

THE GEORGE RDBT

Arts Ctr.

PARKSTONE RD

Old Town

Lower Hamworthy

Poole Bridge

RNLI Mus

HUNGER HILL

Waterfront Mus

Poole Aquarium & Serpentarium

Marina

Old Lifeboat House

Breakwater

Baiter

Boating Lake

Parkstone Bay

Parkstone Lake

00 A 01 C 02 E F

← 201 213 187

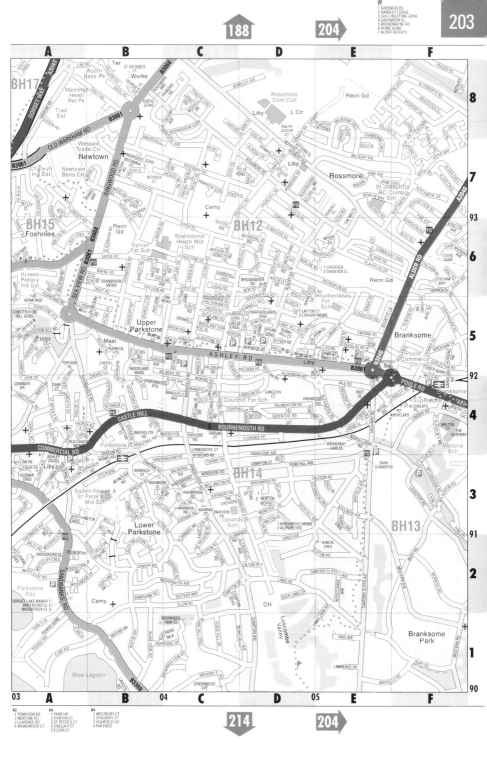

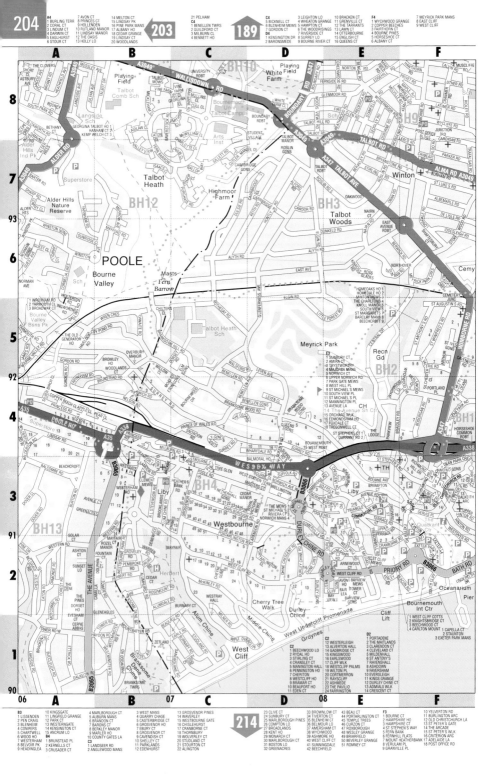

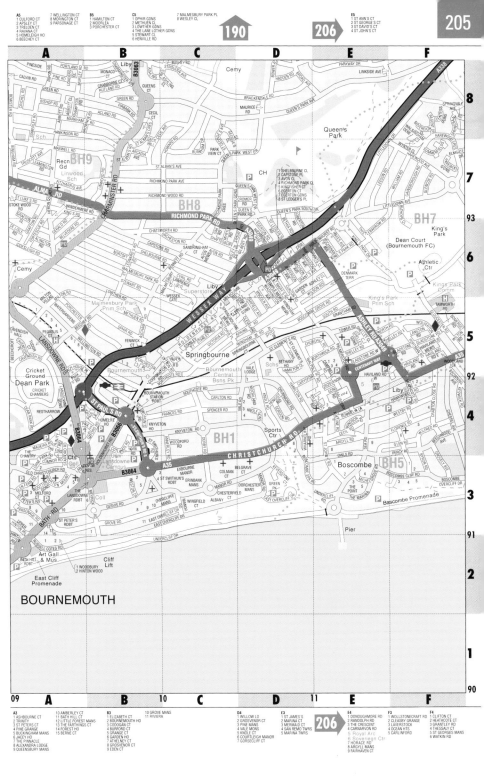

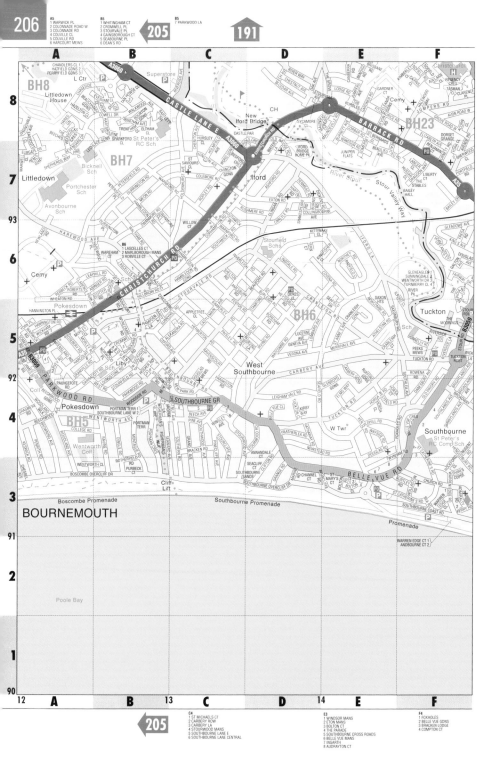

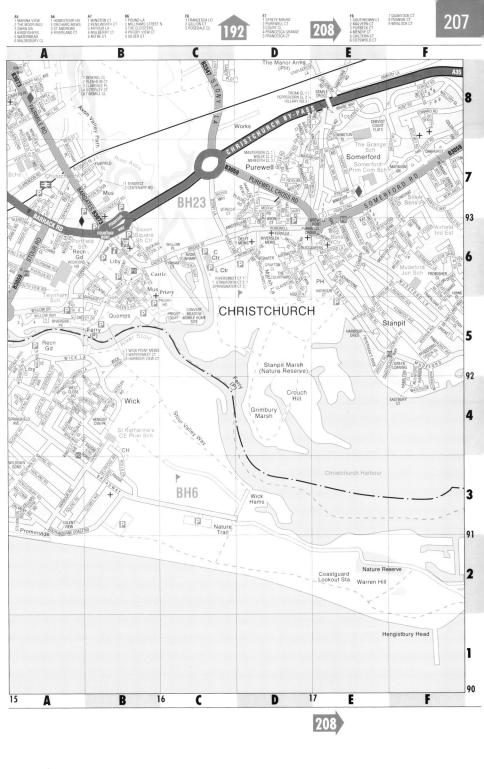

207
193

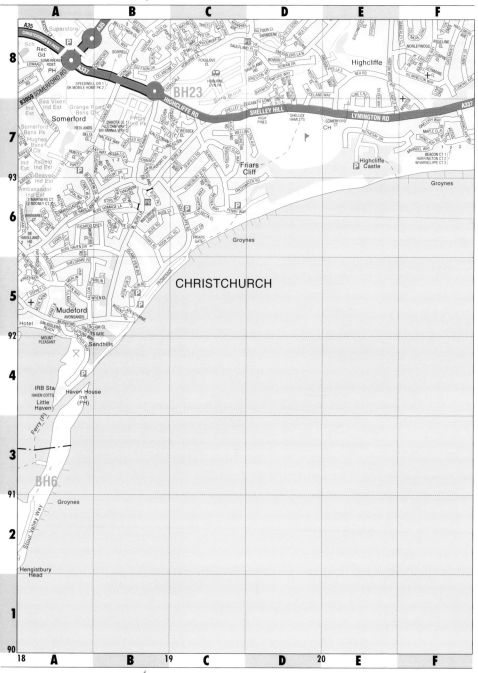

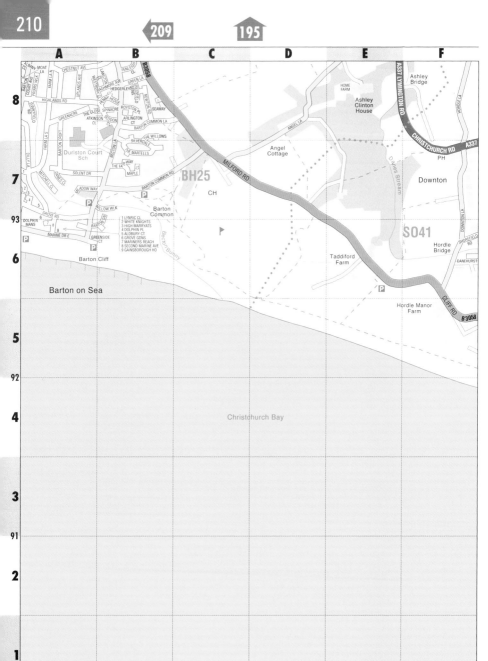

Barton on Sea

Christchurch Bay

BH25

S041

Downton

Ashley Clinton House

Angel Cottage

Taddiford Farm

Hordle Bridge

Hordle Manor Farm

Barton Common

Barton Cliff

Duriston Court Sch

1 LYNRIC CL
2 WHITE KNIGHTS
3 HIGH MARRYATS
4 DOLPHIN PL
5 ALDBURY CT
6 GROVE GDNS
7 MARINERS REACH
8 SECOND MARINE AVE
9 GAINSBOROUGH HO

196
212

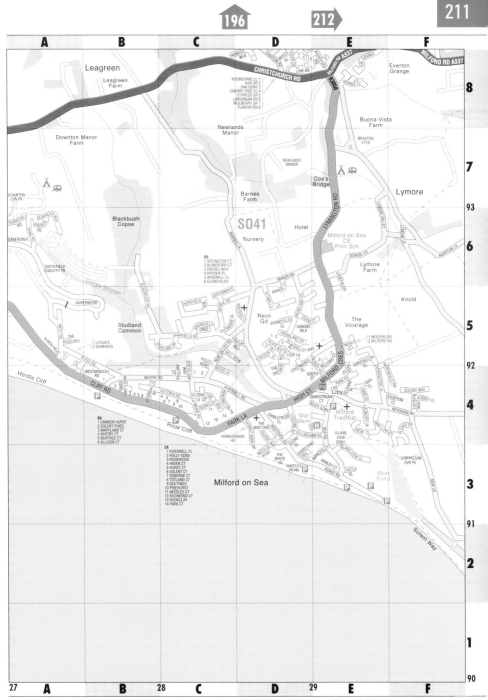

212

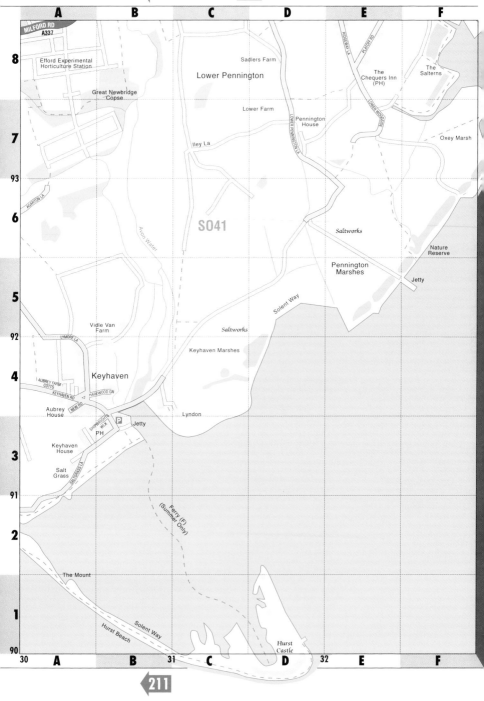

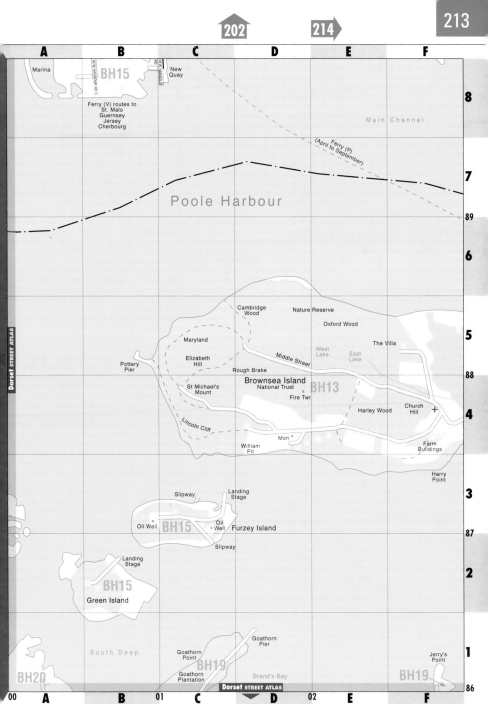

Marina

New Quay

Ferry (V) routes to
St. Malo
Guernsey
Jersey
Cherbourg

8

Main Channel

Ferry (P)
(April to September)

7

Poole Harbour

89

6

Cambridge Wood

Nature Reserve

Oxford Wood

5

Maryland

West Lake

The Villa

East Lake

Pottery Pier

Elizabeth Hill

Middle Street

Rough Brake

88

St Michael's Mount

Brownsea Island
National Trust

BH13

Fire Twr

Lincoln Cliff

Harley Wood

Church Hill

4

Mon

Farm Buildings

William Pit

Harry Point

Slipway

Landing Stage

3

Oil Well

BH15

Oil Well

Furzey Island

87

Slipway

Landing Stage

2

BH15

Green Island

South Deep

Goathorn Pier

1

Goathorn Point

Jerry's Point

BH19

BH20

Goathorn Plantation

Brand's Bay

BH19

86

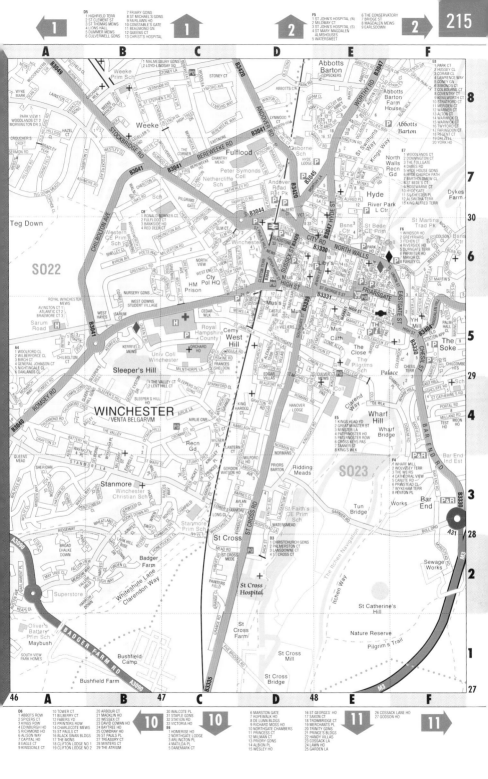

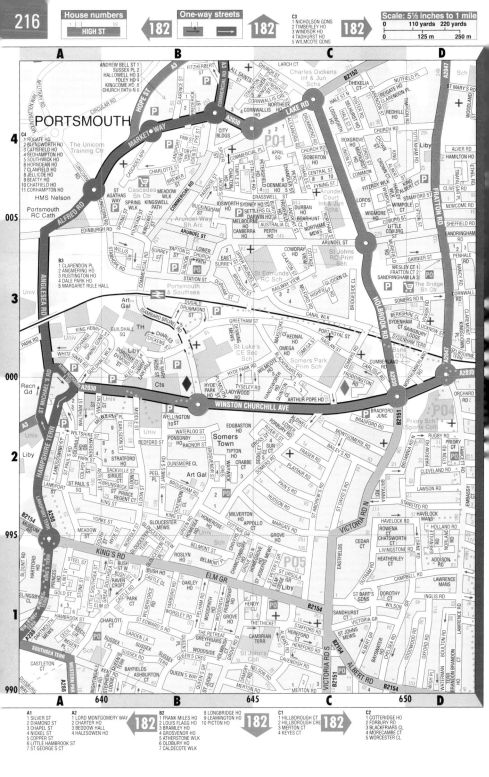

Index

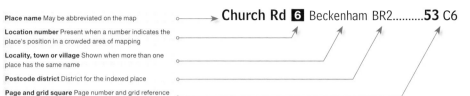

Place name May be abbreviated on the map

Location number Present when a number indicates the place's position in a crowded area of mapping

Locality, town or village Shown when more than one place has the same name

Postcode district District for the indexed place

Page and grid square Page number and grid reference for the standard mapping

Church Rd 6 Beckenham BR2.........53 C6

Public and commercial buildings are highlighted in magenta. Places of interest are highlighted in blue with a star*

Abbreviations used in the index

Acad	Academy	Comm	Common	Gd	Ground	L	Leisure	Prom	Promenade
App	Approach	Cott	Cottage	Gdn	Garden	La	Lane	Rd	Road
Arc	Arcade	Cres	Crescent	Gn	Green	Lby	Library	Recn	Recreation
Ave	Avenue	Cswy	Causeway	Gr	Grove	Mdw	Meadow	Ret	Retail
Bglw	Bungalow	Ct	Court	H	Hall	Meml	Memorial	Sh	Shopping
Bldg	Building	Ctr	Centre	Ho	House	Mkt	Market	Sq	Square
Bsns, Bus	Business	Ctry	Country	Hospl	Hospital	Mus	Museum	St	Street
Bvd	Boulevard	Cty	County	HQ	Headquarters	Orch	Orchard	Sta	Station
Cath	Cathedral	Dr	Drive	Hts	Heights	Pal	Palace	Terr	Terrace
Cir	Circus	Dro	Drove	Ind	Industrial	Par	Parade	TH	Town Hall
Cl	Close	Ed	Education	Inst	Institute	Pas	Passage	Univ	University
Cnr	Corner	Emb	Embankment	Int	International	Pk	Park	Wk, Wlk	Walk
Coll	College	Est	Estate	Intc	Interchange	Pl	Place	Wr	Water
Com	Community	Ex	Exhibition	Junc	Junction	Prec	Precinct	Yd	Yard

Index of localities, towns and villages

A

Abbotswood 28 A3
Abbotts Barton . . . 215 E8
Abshot 153 C8
Alderholt 92 F5
Aldermoor 78 A3
Alderney 188 C1
Aldsworth 137 D6
Allbrook 56 B7
Alverstoke 181 A4
Ameysford 138 C1
Ampfield 29 C3
Anchorage Park . . . 158 C3
Anmore 111 B4
Ann's Hill 180 F5
Anthill Common . . . 110 D6
Applemore 125 A4
Appleslade Bottom . . 118 A7
Ashfield 53 B3
Ashford 69 C1
Ashington 163 A1
Ashlett 151 D3
Ashley
New Milton 195 D3
St Leonards 140 B6
Ashley Heath 139 E6
Ashton 59 B2
Ashurst 100 B3
Ashurst Bridge 100 C5
Avon 167 F2
Avon Castle 140 D3
Awbridge 26 E4

B

Baffins 183 B7
Bagnum 141 E2
Balmerlawn 146 B3
Banister's Park 102 F7
Bank 121 D2
Bar End 215 F3
Bartley 99 B6
Barton on Sea 209 F6
Bashley 195 A7
Bassett 79 A5
Battramsley 173 B2
Battramsley Cross . . 173 C1
Baybridge 33 D3
Beacon Hill 186 A2

Bear Cross 188 F5
Bearwood 188 E6
Beaulieu 148 E1
Beauworth 34 A8
Beckley 194 C5
Bedford Place 102 F6
Bedhampton 135 C1
Bellevue 103 A6
Bell Hill 40 C5
Belvidere 103 C5
Bevois Mount 103 A8
Bevois Town 103 A7
Bevois Valley 103 B7
Bickton 93 F6
Bishopstoke 56 E3
Bishopstone 22 D8
Bishop's Waltham . . . 83 C7
Bisterne 167 F6
Bisterne Close 143 D2
Bitterne 103 F8
Bitterne Manor . . . 103 D7
Bitterne Pk 79 F2
Blackfield 150 D1
Blackwater 191 D4
Blashford 117 A3
Bleak Hill 93 C3
Blendworth 112 D8
Blissford 94 F8
Boarhunt 132 B5
Bohemia 47 F4
Boldre 173 D1
Boorley Green 81 F2
Borough Hill 40 E3
Boscombe 205 E3
Botany Bay 104 A3
Botley 106 D7
Bournemouth 205 A2
Bourne Valley 204 B6
Boveridge 67 A2
Bowling Green 196 F6
Boyatt Wood 56 A5
Braishfield 28 C7
Brambridge 56 E8
Bramdean 15 D4
Bramshaw 73 F4
Branksome 203 F5
Branksome Park . . . 203 F1
Bransgore 193 B8
Breach 137 E1
Breamore 70 B8
Bridgemary 155 C3
Broadgate 29 E2

Broadoak 105 E7
Broadstone 187 B3
Brockbridge 61 C1
Brockenhurst 145 E2
Brockhampton 135 D1
Brockhurst 180 E7
Brokenford 100 F7
Brook 74 A1
Brook Hill 74 A7
Broom Hill 56 A7
Brown Heath 82 D5
Buckland
Lymington 197 D5
Portsmouth 182 E8
Bucklers Hard 200 D4
Bunstead 30 D6
Buriton 65 D6
Burley 143 A3
Burley Lawn 143 B4
Burley Street 142 E5
Burridge 106 B1
Bursledon 128 B8
Burton 192 D2
Butlocks Heath 127 D7
Buttsash 150 B8

C

Cadnam 98 E7
Calmore 76 B2
Calshot 178 F8
Camdentown 181 A6
Camel Green 93 A6
Canada 50 D1
Canford Cliffs 214 E8
Canford Heath 187 E1
Canford Magna . . . 164 A1
Carter's Clay 26 B6
Catherington 88 B1
Catisfield 130 A1
Causeway
Horndean 112 A3
Petersfield 40 F2
Chalton 89 C5
Chandler's Ford . . . 55 C8
Chapel 103 B4
Charminster 190 C2
Cheriton 14 D6
Chidden 86 F8
Chilbridge 162 E7
Chilcomb 11 F6

Chilworth 54 D2
Christchurch 207 D5
Clanfield 88 B5
Clayhall 181 D2
Clayhill 122 A3
Claypits 105 B1
Clewers Hill 83 D4
Colbury 100 D2
Colden Common . . . 32 A1
Colehill 164 B8
Compton
Brook 6 D7
Horndean 90 E1
Shawford 31 D8
Compton Down . . . 31 C7
Coombe Bissett . . . 23 E8
Copnor 158 A1
Copythorne 75 B1
Corfe Mullen 186 C6
Corhampton 61 B5
Cosham 158 B6
Course Park 129 D2
Cowesfield Gate . . . 25 D1
Cowgrove 162 D4
Cowplain 111 F3
Coxford 78 A2
Crab Orchard 114 F2
Crampmoor 28 F1
Creekmoor 201 F8
Crendell 91 F7
Criddlestyle 70 C1
Cripplestyle 92 A5
Critchell's Green . . . 25 F8
Crockerhill 131 B8
Crosshouse 103 C3
Croucheston 22 B7
Crow 141 C4
Crowdhill 57 C5
Crowesfield Green . . 24 D3
Cupernham 28 B2
Curbridge 106 D4
Curdridge 106 D8
Curdridge Firs 82 F1
Custards 122 A6

D

Daggons 92 C5
Damerham 68 C4
Dean 59 E3
Deanlane End 113 E5

Dean Park 205 A4
Denmead 111 A5
Denvilles 136 B2
Dibden 125 D5
Dibden Purlieu 125 E1
Downend 131 F1
Downton
Milford on Sea . . . 210 F7
Redlynch 47 A8
Drayton
Cosham 158 C2
East Meon 38 C3
Droxford 61 C1
Dudsbury 165 C1
Dunbridge 5 D1
Dundridge 60 B1
Dunwood Hill 26 C1
Durley 82 B5
Durley Street 82 D7
Durns Town 172 D2
Durrants 136 B8

E

East Boldre 175 C5
East Brook 163 C5
East Dean 4 B2
East End
Corfe Mullen . . . 162 E1
Damerham 68 D5
East Boldre 199 B7
East Howe 189 C3
Eastleigh 56 C1
East Meon 38 C1
Eastney 183 C3
Eastoke 185 C2
Easton Down 2 D4
East Parley 190 B8
East Tytherley 4 B2
Ebblake 115 C3
Edmondsham 91 A4
Eling 101 B5
Ellingham 116 E5
Elson 181 A9
Emery Down 121 D6
Emsworth 136 E2
Ensbury 189 F6
Ensbury Park 189 C2
Everton 196 E1
Exbury 177 B5
Exton 61 C7

F

Fairmile ... 191 F1
Fair Oak ... 57 D2
Fareham ... 131 B3
Farlington ... 158 E8
Faulston ... 22 D7
Fawley ... 151 A3
Ferndown ... 165 B5
Finchdean ... 113 D6
Fisher's Pond ... 57 B7
Fitzhugh ... 102 E7
Fleet ... 185 A8
Fleetend ... 128 F1
Fletchwood ... 100 B5
Flood Street ... 69 F7
Fordingbridge ... 69 D1
Forest Gate ... 110 E6
Forest Park ... 145 E1
Forestside ... 113 F5
Forton ... 181 C7
Foulford ... 142 A7
Foxhills ... 100 C4
Foxholes ... 203 A6
Fratton ... 182 F5
Freemantle ... 102 C6
Friars Cliff ... 208 D7
Fritham ... 72 F1
Frogham ... 94 E7
Frostlane ... 126 C1
Froxfield Green ... 39 D8
Fryern Hill ... 55 E6
Fulflood ... 215 D7
Funtley ... 130 E5
Furzeley Corner ... 110 E2
Furzey Lodge ... 148 B1
Furzley ... 74 C6

G

Gable Head ... 185 A4
Godshill ... 70 E2
Godwinscroft ... 193 C5
Goose Green ... 122 A4
Gosden Green ... 161 C8
Gosport
  Ampfield ... 29 B2
  Portsmouth ... 181 C7
Gotham ... 91 E3
Grange Estate ... 166 F8

H

Haddon Hill ... 190 E1
Hale ... 47 D2
Halterworth ... 53 C7
Hambledon ... 86 C2
Hamble-le-Rice ... 128 B2
Hammond's Green ... 76 D1
Hampreston ... 164 E2
Hamptworth ... 49 A4
Hamworthy ... 201 C4
Hangersley ... 117 E2
Happy Bottom ... 162 F1
Harbridge ... 93 E1
Harbridge Green ... 93 E2
Hardley ... 150 C6
Hardway ... 181 B8
Harefield
  Romsey ... 53 B8
  Southampton ... 104 C7
Hatch Bottom ... 80 D2
Hatchet Green ... 47 C3
Havant ... 135 E4
Hawkley ... 19 E7
Hayling Island ... 183 A8
Haymoor Bottom ... 187 F1
Heathfield ... 130 C1
Hedge End ... 105 D5
Hensting ... 32 C1
Hermitage ... 161 A8
Highbridge ... 56 D7
Highbury ... 158 A6
Highcliffe ... 208 E8
High Cross ... 18 C1
Highfield ... 79 B2
Highrown ... 141 E4
Hightown ... 104 E4
High Wood ... 117 D3
Hillbourne ... 187 A2
Hill Brow ... 21 B2
Hillbutts ... 162 F6
Hill Head ... 179 A7
Hill Park ... 130 C3
Hillpound ... 84 B4
Hillstreet ... 76 C5
Hill Top ... 149 B3
Hill View ... 186 D4
Hilsea ... 157 E4
Hiltingbury ... 30 C1
Hinton ... 194 A3
Hinton Daubnay ... 111 E8
Hocombe ... 30 C2
Hoe Gate ... 109 F7
Holbrook ... 155 C1
Holbury ... 150 C4
Holdenhurst ... 191 B3
Holt Heath ... 138 A6
Hook ... 153 A8
Hordle ... 195 F3
Horndean ... 112 B8
Horsea Island ... 157 B6

Horseport ... 70 A1
Horton Heath
  Fair Oak ... 81 D7
  Three Legged Cross ... 114 A2
Hound ... 127 F6
Hound Hill ... 162 E7
Houndsdown ... 100 E4
Hungerford ... 94 C5
Hurn ... 191 B7
Hursley ... 30 B7
Hyde
  Frogham ... 94 D6
  Winchester ... 215 E7
Hythe ... 126 B5

I

Ibsley ... 117 A8
Iford ... 206 D7
Inlands ... 137 F1
Itchen ... 103 F4

J

Jumpers Common ... 191 E1

K

Keeping ... 176 C5
Kent's Oak ... 26 D5
Keyhaven ... 212 B4
Kilmeston ... 14 D1
Kimbridge ... 26 F7
Kingsland Place ... 103 A5
Kingsmead ... 108 C7
Kingston
  Portsmouth ... 182 F7
  Ringwood ... 141 A2
Kings Worthy ... 2 C6
Kinson ... 189 B5
Knapp Hill ... 29 D4
Knighton ... 188 D8
Knowle Village ... 130 E7

L

Lake ... 201 D1
Lambs' Green ... 162 F2
Landford ... 49 D3
Landford Wood ... 49 D7
Landport ... 182 C7
Lane End ... 34 D8
Langdown ... 126 C2
Langley ... 177 F7
Langrish ... 39 D4
Langstone ... 159 E7
Lansdowne Hill ... 102 F4
Leagreen ... 211 B8
Lee ... 77 A8
Lee-on-the-Solent ... 179 D3
Leigh ... 163 F4
Leigh Park
  Havant ... 135 D4
  Wimborne Minster ... 163 E4
Lepe ... 178 A2
Lilliput ... 214 C8
Linford ... 118 A2
Linwood ... 118 B8
Lisle Court ... 198 C3
Liss ... 21 A4
Little Canford ... 164 D4
Littledown ... 206 A7
Little Holbury ... 150 C5
Little Pamphill ... 162 F5
Little Posbrook ... 153 F5
Littleton ... 1 B5
Lockerley ... 4 E2
Locks Heath ... 129 B3
London Minstead ... 98 D3
Long Common ... 81 F2
Longfleet ... 202 D4
Longham ... 165 A1
Lord's Hill ... 77 F4
Lordswood ... 78 D5
Lovedean ... 111 E5
Lover ... 48 A5
Lower Bordean ... 39 A6
Lower Buckland ... 197 C5
Lower Burgate ... 70 A3
Lower Canterton ... 98 A7
Lower Daggons ... 92 B7
Lower Hamworthy ... 202 A1
Lower Holwell ... 91 D6
Lower Mannington ... 138 B7
Lower Parkstone ... 203 B3
Lower Pennington ... 212 D8
Lower Ratley ... 26 F3
Lower Slackstead ... 29 A7
Lower Swanwick ... 128 E2
Lower Upham ... 58 D3
Lowford ... 105 A2
Lumley ... 137 A1
Lymington ... 197 C5
Lymore ... 211 F2
Lyndhurst ... 121 E5

M

Mannington ... 138 A8
Marchwood ... 101 E2

Martin ... 43 A4
Maybush ... 77 F2
Mead End
  Horndean ... 111 A3
  Sway ... 171 F1
Mengham ... 185 B3
Meon ... 153 E3
Meon Park ... 108 A4
Moonstoke ... 61 D3
Merley ... 163 D1
Merritown ... 190 E7
Merry Oak ... 103 F5
Michelmersh ... 6 D1
Midanbury ... 80 A1
Middle
  Bockhampton ... 192 F6
Milford on Sea ... 211 D3
Millbank ... 103 C5
Millbrook ... 101 F7
Milton ... 183 C4
Minstead ... 98 B3
Mockbeggar ... 117 C2
Moordown ... 101 D8
Moorgreen ... 80 F2
Moortown ... 141 B5
Morestead ... 32 F8
Morgan's Vale ... 47 C5
Mottisfont ... 5 E2
Mount Pleasant
  Corfe Mullen ... 186 E7
  Lymington ... 196 F8
Mudeford ... 208 C4
Muscliffe ... 190 C4

N

Neacroft ... 193 B6
Netley ... 127 B6
Netley Marsh ... 100 A5
Newbridge ... 74 F3
New Brighton ... 137 A3
New Milton ... 194 E5
Newtown
  Awbridge ... 26 B4
  Bishop's Waltham ... 83 A7
  Corfe Mullen ... 186 D7
  Eastleigh ... 56 A3
  Gosport ... 181 D5
  Minstead ... 98 A2
Nob's Crook ... 57 A7
Nomansland ... 73 D8
Norleywood ... 198 F8
Northam ... 103 C6
North Baddesley ... 53 F6
North Boarhunt ... 109 A2
North
  Bockhampton ... 192 F7
Northbourne ... 189 E4
Northbrook ... 59 D1
North Charford ... 47 D3
North Common ... 49 B6
North End
  Damerham ... 68 C6
  Portsmouth ... 157 E2
North Fareham ... 131 C4
Northfields ... 32 B7
North Gorley ... 94 B3
North Hayling ... 160 C3
North Kingston ... 141 C2
Northney ... 160 C4
North Poulner ... 117 D2
North Ripley ... 168 D4
North Street ... 46 B2
North Wallington ... 131 C3
North Weirs ... 145 C1
Nursling ... 77 C5
Nursted ... 66 C7
Nutbourne ... 161 F7
Nutburn ... 54 B5

O

Oakdale ... 202 D6
Oakley ... 163 E2
Ogdens ... 94 F5
Old Milton ... 194 E1
Old Netley ... 104 D1
Old Portsmouth ... 182 A3
Old Shirley ... 78 B1
Old Town ... 202 C2
Ossemsley ... 194 E8
Otterbourne ... 31 C3
Otterbourne Hill ... 31 A2
Otterwood ... 149 D1
Outwick ... 69 F8
Ower
  Calshot ... 178 E8
  Romsey ... 75 E6
Owslebury ... 33 B3

P

Pamphill ... 162 E6
Park Gate ... 129 B5
Parley Green ... 190 C7
Paulsgrove ... 133 A1

Peartree Green ... 103 D4
Pennington ... 197 B1
Pentridge ... 42 B1
Petersfield ... 40 C2
Pikes Hill ... 121 F7
Pilford ... 164 A8
Pilley ... 174 A1
Pilley Bailey ... 174 A2
Plaitford ... 50 B4
Plaitford Green ... 50 D7
Pleasant View ... 104 C3
Pokesdown ... 206 A4
Pollards Moor ... 75 A1
Polygon ... 102 E6
Pooksgreen ... 101 C1
Poole ... 202 B3
Portchester ... 156 C7
Portmore ... 198 A7
Ports Down ... 134 F2
Portsea ... 182 B6
Portsea Island ... 182 F6
Portsmouth ... 216 A4
Port Solent ... 157 A7
Portswood ... 79 C1
Portswood Park ... 103 B8
Poulner ... 141 D8
Priddy's Hard ... 181 C8
Prinsted ... 161 C7
Privett
  Gosport ... 180 F3
  West Meon ... 17 D2
Puckenall ... 28 F6
Purbrook ... 134 E4
Purewell ... 207 D7
Pylehill ... 57 C3

Q

Queensland ... 103 B5

R

Rake ... 21 F4
Ramsdean ... 39 D1
Ratlake ... 29 F4
Redbridge ... 101 C8
Redbrook ... 94 A7
Red Hill
  Bournemouth ... 189 F5
  Rowlands Castle ... 113 B2
Redlynch ... 47 E6
Ridge ... 52 C1
Ringwood ... 141 C7
Ripley ... 168 C2
Rockbourne ... 44 F1
Rockford ... 117 C5
Romford ... 114 C7
Romsey ... 52 F6
Rossmore ... 203 E2
Roughdown ... 150 C1
Row Ash ... 107 A8
Rowlands ... 163 C5
Rowlands Castle ... 113 D2
Rowner ... 180 C8
Rownhams ... 77 F7
Rushington ... 100 F6
Rushmere ... 86 E1

S

St Cross ... 215 C8
St Denys ... 103 C8
St Ives ... 140 A5
St Johns ... 163 C4
St Leonards ... 139 C4
Sandbanks ... 214 C3
Sandford ... 168 C8
Sandleheath ... 69 A3
Sandy Down ... 173 C4
Sarisbury ... 128 F5
Scrag Hill ... 53 F5
Seafield ... 181 D4
Seaman's Corner ... 98 B4
Segensworth ... 129 D5
Selsmore ... 185 D3
Setley ... 173 A6
Shawford ... 31 E7
Shawford Down ... 31 D6
Sheffield ... 107 D7
Sherfield English ... 25 D1
Shirley
  Bransgore ... 169 A2
  Southampton ... 102 C8
Shirley Holms ... 173 A1
Shirley Warren ... 78 B2
Shirrell Heath ... 84 A1
Shobley ... 118 A1
Sholing ... 104 B4
Sholing Common ... 104 B5
Shootash ... 26 D1
Shrover ... 111 D5
Silkstead ... 30 F5
Sleeper's Hill ... 215 B5
Sleight ... 162 D1
Soake ... 111 B3
Soberton ... 85 C6
Soberton Heath ... 85 B1
Somerford ... 207 E2
Sopley ... 192 B7
Southampton ... 102 D3
South Baddesley ... 198 E6
South Bockhampton ... 192 E4

Southbourne
  Bournemouth ... 206 F4
  Havant ... 161 E8
South Down ... 31 D5
South End ... 68 D3
South Gorley ... 94 C2
South Hayling ... 184 E2
Southsea ... 182 C1
South Weirs ... 172 D7
Southwick ... 132 E6
Springbourne ... 205 C5
Stamshaw ... 157 C1
Stanley Green ... 202 C6
Stanmore ... 215 B3
Stanpit ... 207 F5
Stanswood ... 178 D6
Stapehill ... 164 E5
Steep ... 40 D7
Steep Marsh ... 20 B1
Sterte ... 202 B3
Stockheath ... 135 E3
Stoke ... 160 A1
Stoke Common ... 56 E5
Stone
  Langley ... 178 A3
  Wimborne Minster ... 163 A6
Stoney Cross ... 97 E4
Stonyford ... 75 E4
Street End ... 59 D4
Stroud ... 40 A4
Strouden ... 190 E1
Stubbington ... 179 D4
Stuckton ... 94 B7
Sussex Place ... 103 A4
Swanmore ... 84 C5
Swanwick ... 129 A7
Sway ... 172 B1
Swaythling ... 79 F4

T

Talbot Heath ... 204 B7
Talbot Village ... 189 C1
Talbot Woods ... 204 C7
Tapnage ... 107 C1
Teg Down ... 215 A6
Testwood ... 76 F1
The Earldoms ... 49 A7
The Frenches ... 26 B1
The Marsh ... 201 A7
The Soke ... 215 C7
Thorney Hill ... 169 D3
Thorney Island ... 161 B3
Thornhill ... 104 C5
Thornhill Park ... 104 B6
Thorns Beach ... 200 B6
Three Legged Cross ... 138 F8
Throop ... 190 E4
Timsbury ... 27 D6
Tipner ... 157 C3
Tiptoe ... 195 D8
Titchfield ... 153 E2
Titchfield Common ... 129 D1
Titchfield Park ... 129 E4
Toot Hill ... 53 E1
Totton ... 100 E7
Townhill Park ... 80 A2
Trickett's Cross ... 165 F7
Tuckton ... 206 F5
Turkey Island ... 107 F7
Turlin Moor ... 201 B4
Turmer ... 116 B8
Twyford ... 32 A6
Tye ... 161 C1

U

Upham ... 58 F5
Upper Burgate ... 70 A2
Upper Canterton ... 97 F6
Upper Kingston ... 141 C4
Upper Parkstone ... 203 B5
Upper Pennington ... 197 A3
Upper Ratley ... 26 E4
Upper Shirley ... 78 D1
Upper Slackstead ... 29 B8
Upper Street ... 45 F1
Upper Swanmore ... 84 C8
Upton
  Poole ... 201 D7
  Southampton ... 77 C6

V

Valley Park ... 55 A4
Verwood ... 114 E4

W

Walhampton ... 198 A4
Walkford ... 194 C1
Wallington ... 131 D2
Wallisdown ... 189 A2
Waltham Chase ... 83 F3
Warblington ... 136 C1
Warborne ... 197 F4
Warnford ... 36 E3
Warren Corner ... 19 B5
Warsash ... 128 C1
Waterditch ... 193 B5
Waterford ... 198 B1

1

1st St SO45 .... 151 A4

2

2nd St SO45 .... 151 A4

3

3rd St SO45 .... 150 F4

4

4th St SO45 .... 150 F4

5

5th St Blackfield SO45 .... 150 E4
Fawley SO45 .... 150 F5

6

6th St Fawley SO45 .... 150 E4
Fawley SO45 .... 150 F6

7

7th St Fawley SO45 .... 150 E4
Fawley SO45 .... 150 E5

8

8th St SO45 .... 150 E4

9

9th St SO45 .... 150 D4

1

10th St SO45 .... 150 D5
11th St SO45 .... 150 D5
12th St SO45 .... 150 D5
13th St SO45 .... 150 D6
14th St SO45 .... 150 D6
17th Century Experience*
POI3 .... 180 C5

A

A Ave SO45 .... 150 D4
A'Becket Ct **3** PO1 .... 182 A4
Aaron Cl BH17 .... 202 F7
Aaron Ct SO40 .... 101 F2
Abbas Gn PO4 .... 135 D7
Abbey Cl SO45 .... 126 A3
Abbey Ct **8** SO15 ..... 102 F7
Abbey Ent Ctr SO51 ...... 53 D5
Abbey Fruit Park Ind Est
SO31 .... 127 C7
Abbey Gdns BH21 .... 164 D5
Abbey Hill SO31 .... 127 A7
Abbey Hill Cl SO23 ...... 215 E8
Abbey Hill Rd SO23 ...... 215 E8
Abbey Mill Bsns Site
SO32 .... 83 C7
Abbey Pas SO23 .... 215 E5
Abbey Rd Fareham PO15 ... 130 D2
West Moors BH22 .... 166 A8
Abbey The SO51 .... 52 E7
Abbey Water **6** SO45 .. 133 C1
Abbeydore Rd PO6 .... 133 C1
Abbeyfield Dr PO11 ...... 130 C2
Abbeyfield Ho **6** SO18 . 103 C8
Abbeyfields Cl SO31 ..... 127 D6
Abbeymede PO6 .... 157 E8
Abbots Cl
Christchurch BH23 ...... 208 F7
Waterlooville PO7 ...... 134 C4
Abbots Lea Cotts SO23 ... 2 B3
Abbots Row **1** SO22 ... 215 D6
Abbots Way
Fareham PO15 .... 130 D1
Netley SO31 .... 127 D6
Abbots Well Rd SP6 ...... 94 F7
Abbotsbury Rd
Bishopstoke SO50 .... 56 F2
Corfe Mullen BH18 ...... 186 F5
Abbotsfield SO40 .... 100 E8
Abbotsfield Cl SO16 ..... 78 C5
Abbotsford SO40 .... 99 B6
Abbotstone Ave PO9 ...... 136 A4
Abbotswood Cl SO51 ...... 28 E5
Abbotswood Jun Sch
SO51 .... 28 E5
Abbott Cl BH9 .... 205 A8
Abbott Rd BH9 .... 205 A8
Abbott St BH21 .... 162 D6
Abbotts Ann Rd SO22 ..... 1 D3
Abbotts Cl SO23 .... 215 E8
Abbotts Ct
8 Southampton SO17 ... 79 A1

Abbotts Ct continued
Winchester SO22 .... 215 D8
Abbotts Dro SO51 .... 50 E1
Abbotts Rd Eastleigh SO50 . 55 F1
Winchester SO23 .... 215 E8
Abbotts Way
Southampton SO17 .... 79 B1
West Moors BH22 .... 166 A8
Abercrombie Sch SO16 .... 78 A4
Aberdare Ave PO6 .... 158 B8
Aberdare Rd BH10 .... 189 E3
Aberdeen Cl PO15 .... 130 E3
Aberdeen Rd SO17 .... 79 C1
Aberdour Cl SO18 .... 104 B8
Abingdon Cl PO12 .... 181 B5
Abingdon Dr BH23 .... 209 C8
Abingdon Gdns SO16 ..... 78 E3
Abingdon Rd BH17 .... 202 D8
Abinger Rd BH7 .... 206 B6
Abney Rd BH10 .... 189 D3
Above Bar St SO14 ...... 102 F5
Abraham Cl SO30 .... 105 D5
Abshot Cl PO14 .... 129 C1
Abshot Rd PO14 .... 129 C1
Acacia Ave BH31 .... 115 C4
Acacia Gdns PO8 .... 112 B5
Acacia Lodge **2** PO16 .. 131 B1
Acacia Rd Hordle SO41 ... 195 F3
Southampton SO19 .... 103 F5
Acanthas Ct PO15 .... 106 D1
Acer Way PO9 .... 136 B8
Ackworth Rd PO3 .... 158 A5
Acland Rd BH9 .... 205 B8
Acorn Ave BH15 .... 202 D2
Acorn Bsns Ctr PO6 ..... 157 D7
Acorn Bsns Pk BH12 ..... 203 B8
Acorn Cl
Christchurch BH23 ...... 206 F8
Farlington PO6 .... 158 E8
Gosport PO13 .... 155 D1
Marchwood SO40 .... 102 A1
New Milton BH25 .... 195 C4
St Leonards BH24 .... 139 E3
Winchester SO22 .... 215 B8
Acorn Cotts BH31 .... 114 F7
Acorn Ct SO31 .... 127 F3
Acorn Dr SO16 .... 77 F7
Acorn Gdns PO8 .... 112 B6
Acorn Gr SO53 .... 54 F4
Acorn Way BH31 .... 115 A6
Acorn Workshops SO14 ... 103 B7
Acorns The
Burslledon SO31 .... 127 F8
West Moors BH22 .... 166 B8
Wimborne Minst BH21 .... 164 A4
Acre La PO7 .... 112 C1
Acres Rd BH11 .... 189 B2
Acton Rd BH10 .... 189 B1
Ad Astro Fst Sch BH17 ... 187 F1
Adair Rd PO4 .... 183 A2
Adames Rd PO1 .... 182 E6
Adams Cl SO30 .... 81 B3
Adastral Rd BH17 .... 202 F8
Adastral Sq BH17 .... 202 F8
Adcock Ct SO16 .... 126 A2
Adderbury Ave PO10 ..... 136 F3
Addington Ct **1** SO41 . 211 D5
Addington Pl BH23 ...... 207 D6
Addis Ho SO17 .... 79 B1
Addis Sq SO17 .... 79 B1
Addiscombe Rd BH23 ..... 207 A7
Addison Cl Romsey SO51 .. 28 B1
Winchester SO22 .... 215 A3
Addison Rd
Brockenhurst SO42 ...... 172 F8
Eastleigh SO50 .... 56 B5
Locks Heath SO31 ...... 129 A6
Portsmouth PO4 .... 216 D1
Sarisbury SO31 .... 128 F6
Addison Sq PO14 .... 141 B7
Adela Verne Cl SO19 .... 104 E3
Adelaide Cl BH23 .... 206 F8
Adelaide Ct SO41 .... 197 F4
Adelaide La **17** BH1 ... 204 F3
Adelaide Pl **7** PO1 ... 131 C1
Adelaide Rd SO17 .... 103 C8
Adeline Rd BH1,BH5 ..... 205 E4
Adey Cl SO19 .... 104 B2
Admiral Lord Nelson Sch
PO3 .... 158 B1
Admiral Park The PO3 ... 158 A4
Admiral Pl **11** PO6 ... 157 F8
Admiral's Cnr **13** PO5 . 182 D2
Admiral's Wlk PO1 ...... 181 F7
Admirals Cl SO45 .... 151 B3
Admirals Ct
Hamble-le-R SO31 .... 128 A2
Lymington SO41 .... 197 F4
21 Portsmouth PO5 ... 182 C2
Admirals Ho SO31 .... 152 C10
Admirals Rd SO31 .... 129 B4
Admirals Way SO45 ..... 126 A5
Admirals Wlk
18 Bournemouth BH2 .. 204 D2
Gosport PO12 .... 180 F3
Admiralty Cl PO12 ...... 181 C8
Admiralty Cotts PO12 ... 181 C2
Admiralty Way SO14 ..... 103 A2
Admiralty Rd
Bournemouth BH6 .... 206 F3

Admiralty Rd continued
Portsmouth PO1 .... 182 A5
Admiralty Way SO40 ..... 101 F3
Adsdean Cl PO9 .... 135 E4
Adstone La PO3 .... 158 C4
Adur Cl Gosport PO12 ... 180 F7
West End SO18 .... 80 B1
Aerial Pk BH21 .... 164 E6
Aerial Rd PO4 .... 133 B2
Aerodrome Rd PO13 ..... 155 E3
Africa Dr SO40 .... 124 F8
Agar's La SO41 .... 196 B5
Agarton La SO41 .... 211 F6
Aggis Farm BH31 .... 114 E6
Agincourt Rd PO2 ...... 182 D7
Agitator Rd SO41 ...... 151 C4
Agnew Rd PO12 .... 181 B7
Agnew Rd PO13 .... 155 C3
Aikman La SO40 .... 100 B7
Ailsa La SO19 .... 103 D4
Ainsdale Rd PO6 .... 134 D1
Ainsley Gdns SO50 ..... 56 A5
Aintree Cl SO50 .... 81 D7
Aintree Ct SO31 .... 129 B8
Aintree Dr PO7 .... 112 B1
Aintree Rd SO40 .... 76 C1
Airetons Cl BH18 ...... 187 C3
Airfield Ind Est
Christchurch BH23 ..... 207 F6
Christchurch BH23 ..... 208 A7
Airfield Rd BH23 ...... 207 F7
Airfield Way BH23 ..... 207 F7
Airlie Cnr SO22 .... 215 C4
Airlie La SO22 .... 215 C4
Airlie Rd SO22 .... 215 C4
Airport Service Rd
Portsmouth PO3 .... 158 A4
Portsmouth PO3 .... 158 B3
Airspeed Rd
Christchurch BH23 ..... 208 B7
Portsmouth PO3 .... 158 C2
Ajax Cl PO14 .... 179 D6
Akeshill Cl BH25 ...... 195 B5
Alameda Rd PO7 .... 134 D4
Alameda Way PO7 .... 134 D4
Alan Chun Ho SO31 ..... 127 C7
Alan Cl **16** BH23 .... 209 B7
Alan Drayton Way SO50 .. 56 F2
Alan Gr SO53 .... 130 E2
Alandale Rd SO19 ...... 104 D4
Albacore Ave PO6 ...... 128 F1
Albany BH1 .... 205 C3
Albany Bsns Ctr PO17 ... 131 B7
Albany Cl BH25 .... 194 F1
Albany Ct
Bishop's Waltham SO32 .. 83 A8
3 Bournemouth BH2 .. 204 F4
Gosport PO12 .... 181 B6
Albany Dr
Bishop's Waltham SO32 .. 83 A8
Three Legged Cross BH21 . 114 E1
Albany Gdns BH15 ...... 202 F7
Albany Ho **1** BH3 .... 204 A4
Albany Park Ct SO17 ... 102 F8
Albany Pk BH17 .... 202 B8
Albany Rd
Bishop's Waltham SO32 .. 83 A8
Holbury SO45 .... 150 C4
Portsmouth PO5 .... 216 C1
Romsey SO51 .... 52 F7
Southampton SO15 ...... 102 C6
Albany The **25** SO14 . 103 A3
Albatross Wlk PO13 .... 155 B2
Albemarle Ave PO12 .... 181 B9
Albemarle Rd BH3 ...... 204 F7
Albemarle St SO17 ..... 79 C3
Albert Cl SO31 .... 127 C5
Albert Ct
Southampton SO17 ...... 79 C1
Winchester SO23 .... 215 D7
Albert Gr PO5 .... 216 C1
Albert Rd
Bishop's Waltham SO32 .. 83 B7
Bournemouth BH1 .... 204 F3
Corfe Mullen BH21 ..... 186 D5
Cosham PO6 .... 157 F7
Eastleigh SO50 .... 56 B5
Ferndown BH22 .... 165 D5
Hedge End SO30 .... 105 B5
New Milton BH25 .... 194 F2
Poole BH12 .... 203 D6
Portsmouth PO4,PO5 .... 182 E2
Stubbington PO14 ...... 179 D8
Albert Rd N SO14 ...... 103 B3
Albert Rd S SO14 ...... 103 B3
Albert St PO12 .... 181 C6
Albion Cl Poole BH12 ... 203 B7
Portchester PO16 ...... 156 B6
Albion Pl
3 Southampton SO14 . 102 F7
14 Winchester SO23 .. 215 E6
Albion Rd
Christchurch BH23 ..... 191 F1
Fordingbridge SP6 ..... 69 F2
Lee-on-t-S PO13 .... 179 E4
Albion Twrs SO31 ...... 103 B4
Albion Way BH31 .... 114 D7
Albretia Ave PO8 ...... 111 E3
Albury PO10 .... 30 B1
Alby Rd PO12 .... 203 F5
Alcantara Cres SO14 ... 103 B2
Alcester Rd BH12 ...... 203 D3
Alchorne Pl PO3 .... 158 B3
Aldbury Ct BH25 .... 210 A2
Alder Cl Burton BH23 ... 192 D1
Colden Common SO21 .... 57 A8
Hythe SO45 .... 125 D4
Marchwood SO40 .... 101 F2

Alder Cl continued
Romsey SO51 .... 53 D6
Alder Cres BH12 .... 203 F7
Alder Dr SP6 .... 92 F5
Alder Hill Dr SO40 .... 100 B8
Alder Hills BH12 ...... 204 A7
Alder Hills Ind Pk BH12 . 204 A7
Alder Hills Nature Reserve*
BH12 .... 204 A7
Alder Hts BH12 .... 204 A7
Alder La PO12,PO13 .... 180 D5
Alder Rd Poole BH12 ... 203 F6
Southampton SO16 ...... 78 A3
Alderfield GU32 .... 40 E3
Alderholt Mill & Craft Ctr*
SP6 .... 68 F1
Alderholt Rd SP6 ...... 69 C2
Alderley Rd BH10 ...... 189 D4
Alderman Quilley Sch
SO50 .... 55 F1
Alderman Quilley Sch The
SO50 .... 56 A1
Aldermoor Ave SO16 .... 78 A4
Aldermoor Cl SO16 ..... 78 C4
Aldermoor Rd
Gosport PO13 .... 180 D7
Southampton SO16 ...... 78 B4
Waterlooville PO7 ..... 134 D4
Aldermoor Rd E PO7 .... 134 D5
Alderney Ave PO7 ...... 134 D4
Alderney Cl SO16 ...... 77 E4
Alderney Hospl BH12 ... 188 D2
Alderney Rdbt BH12 .... 188 D2
Alders Rd PO16 .... 155 B7
Aldershot Ho **51** PO9 . 136 B5
Alderwood Ave SO53 .... 55 A6
Alderwood Cl PO9 ...... 135 B3
Aldis Gdns BH15 .... 201 E2
Aldrich Rd PO1 .... 182 A6
Aldridge Cl PO8 .... 88 C5
Aldridge Rd
Bournemouth BH10 ...... 189 C5
Ferndown BH22 .... 165 E3
Aldridge Way BH22 ..... 165 F3
Aldroke St **1** PO6 ... 158 C8
Aldsworth Cl PO6 ...... 158 C8
Aldsworth Common Rd
PO10 .... 137 C6
Aldsworth Gdns PO6 .... 158 C8
Aldwell St PO5 .... 216 C2
Alec Rose Ho **17** PO12 . 181 C5
Alec Rose La PO1 ...... 216 B3
Alec Wintle Ho PO7 .... 182 D8
Alecto Rd PO12 .... 181 B4
Alencon Cl **3** PO12 .. 181 C9
Alexander Cl
Christchurch BH23 ..... 207 E6
Totton SO40 .... 100 D8
Waterlooville PO7 ..... 134 A4
Alexander Ct
Southampton SO15 ...... 102 D6
Southampton,Woolston
SO19 .... 103 E2
Alexander Gr PO16 ..... 155 A8
Alexander Ho PO11 ..... 185 E1
Alexandra Ave PO11 .... 184 F2
Alexandra Cl SO45 ..... 126 A4
Alexandra Ct
Hamble-le-R SO31 ...... 127 F3
4 Portsmouth PO1 ... 182 E6
Alexandra Lodge **8**
BH1 .... 205 A3
Alexandra Mews SO15 ... 102 E7
Alexandra Rd
Bournemouth BH6 .... 206 C5
Chandler's Ford SO53 .. 55 F5
Fordingbridge SP6 ..... 69 F2
Hedge End SO30 .... 105 B5
Lymington SO41 .... 197 C5
Poole BH14 .... 203 D5
Portsmouth PO1 .... 216 C4
Southampton SO15 ...... 102 E6
Alexandra St **7** PO12 . 181 A7
Alexandra Terr SO23 ... 215 D5
Alexandra Way SO30 .... 106 A7
Alexandra Cl BH22 ..... 165 E3
Alexandra Pk PO9 ...... 159 F7
Alford Rd BH1 .... 204 F3
Alfred Cl SO40 .... 100 C7
Alfred Rd
Portsmouth PO1 .... 216 A4
Stubbington PO14 ...... 179 D8
Alfred Rose Ct SO18 ... 79 E4
Alfred St SO14 .... 103 B6
Alfrey Cl PO10 .... 161 D8
Alfriston Ct SO19 ..... 104 C4
Alfriston Gdns SO19 ... 104 B4
Algiers Rd PO3 .... 183 B8
Alhambra Rd PO4 ...... 182 E1
Alice in Wonderland Family
Fun Pk* BH23 .... 190 E7
Alington Cl BH4 .... 204 C3
Alington Ct BH14 ...... 214 C7
Alington Ho BH14 ...... 214 C7
Alington Manor Farm Cotts
SO50 .... 80 F7
Alington Rd
Bournemouth BH3 .... 205 B6
Poole BH14 .... 214 C7
Alipore Cl BH14 .... 203 D3
Alipore Mts BH14 ...... 203 D3
Alison Way **6** SO22 .. 215 B6
All Saint's Rd PO1 .... 182 D7
All Saints CE Prim Sch
SO50 .... 55 F1
All Saints Ho **7** SO14 . 103 A3
All Saints Rd SO41 .... 197 F2

All Saints' St PO1 .... 216 B4
Allan Gr SO51 .... 53 B7
Allaway Ave PO6 .... 157 B8
Allbrook Ct PO7 .... 135 D6
Allbrook Hill SO50 .... 56 B7
Allbrook Knoll SO50 ... 56 A7
Allbrook Way SO50 ..... 56 B7
Allcot Rd PO3 .... 158 A2
Allen Ct BH21 .... 163 C5
Allen Rd Hedge End SO30 . 105 C7
Wimborne Minst BH21 ... 163 C4
Allen's Rd PO4 .... 182 E2
Allenbourn Mid Sch
BH21 .... 163 C5
Allenby Cl BH17 .... 187 B2
Allenby Gr PO16 .... 156 C7
Allenby Rd Gosport PO12 . 180 E6
Poole BH17 .... 187 B2
Allendale Ave PO10 .... 136 C3
Allens Farm La SO32 ... 61 B6
Allens La Meonstoke SO32 . 61 C5
Upton BH16 .... 201 D5
Allen's Rd BH16 .... 201 D6
Allenview Rd BH21 ..... 163 C5
Allenwater Dr SP6 ..... 69 E2
Allerton Cl SO40 ...... 76 D1
Alley The Bishopstone SP5 . 22 B8
Woodgreen SP6 .... 70 E8
Alliance Cl PO13 ...... 180 D8
Alliance Ho PO1 .... 182 E6
Allington La SO30 ..... 80 E5
Allington Manor Farm Bsns
Ctr SO50 .... 80 E7
Allington Manor Sch
SO50 .... 80 F7
Allington Rd SO15 ..... 101 D7
Allison Ct **6** SO41 .. 211 B4
Allison Ho SO30 .... 105 C8
Allmara Dr PO7 .... 134 F4
Allotment Rd
Hedge End SO30 .... 105 B6
Sarisbury SO31 .... 128 E3
Allyn Ct SO50 .... 56 B5
Alma Ho SO14 .... 103 A8
Alma La SO32 .... 58 B2
Alma Rd
Bournemouth BH9 ...... 205 A7
Romsey SO51 .... 52 F7
Southampton SO14 ..... 103 A8
Alma St SO12 .... 181 B7
Alma Terr PO4 .... 183 A3
Almatade Rd BH15 ..... 201 E8
Almer Rd BH15 .... 201 E8
Almond Cl Havant PO9 .. 158 F8
Waterlooville PO8 ..... 102 C6
Almond Gr BH12 .... 203 D7
Almond Gr SO15 .... 102 C6
Almondsbury Ho **8**
PO6 .... 132 F2
Almondsbury Rd PO6 .... 132 F2
Almondside PO13 ...... 155 A1
Almshouses PO1 .... 182 E6
Alpha Ctr The BH17 .... 202 B7
Alphage Rd PO12 ...... 155 F1
Alpine Cl SO18 .... 104 B8
Alpine Rd
St Leonards BH24 ..... 140 C2
Woodlands SO40 .... 99 F3
Alresford Rd
Chilcomb SO21 .... 12 D7
Havant PO9 .... 135 E4
Winchester SO23 ...... 11 D7
Alsford Rd PO7 .... 134 D5
Alswitha Terr **12** SO23 . 215 E7
Alten Rd PO7 .... 111 C2
Althorpe Dr PO3 ...... 158 C4
Alton Cl SO30 .... 57 B2
Alton Ct **8** SO23 ... 215 E8
Alton Gr PO16 .... 156 C6
Alton Ho SO18 .... 103 E8
Alton Rd
Bournemouth BH10 ..... 189 C1
Poole BH14 .... 203 C3
Alton Rd E BH14 ...... 203 D2
Alum Chine Rd BH4 .... 204 B3
Alum Ct SO45 .... 150 D3
Alum Way
Portchester PO16 ..... 131 E1
Southampton SO18 ..... 104 B7
Alumdale Rd BH4 ...... 204 B2
Alumhurst Rd BH4 ..... 204 B2
Alvandi Gdns **2** BH25 . 195 B3
Alvara Rd PO12 .... 181 A3
Alver Bridge View **4**
PO12 .... 181 B4
Alver Rd Gosport PO12 .. 181 B4
Portsmouth PO2 .... 182 E6
Alvercliffe Dr PO12 ... 180 F2
Alverstoke CE Jun Sch
PO12 .... 181 A4
Alverstoke Com Inf Sch
PO12 .... 181 A3
Alverstoke Ct PO12 ... 181 A3
Alverstone Rd PO4 .... 183 A5
Alverton Ave BH15 .... 202 F3
Alverton Ho PO14 ..... 154 D8
Alveston Ave PO14 .... 154 D8
Alyne Ho SO15 .... 102 F8
Alyth Rd BH3 .... 204 D6
Amaryllis Cl PO15 .... 129 E4
Ambassador Cl BH23 ... 208 A6
Ambassador Ind Est
BH23 .... 208 A6
Amber Rd BH21 .... 186 C4
Amberley Cl Botley SO30 . 106 A8
Christchurch BH23 .... 208 F8

Amberley Cl continued
North Baddesley SO52 .....53 E5
Amberley Ct
6 Bournemouth BH1 .....205 A3
3 Knowle Village PO17 ...130 E7
Totton SO40 ....100 E6
Amberley Ho BH22 ......165 D7
Amberley Rd
Clanfield PO8 ....88 D5
Gosport PO12 ....181 A9
Portsmouth PO2 ....157 F3
Amberslade Wlk SO45 ..125 F1
Amberwood
Ferndown BH22 ....165 E7
Milford on S SO41 ....211 B5
Amberwood Cl SO40 .....76 C2
Amberwood Dr BH23 ....193 F2
Amberwood Gdns BH23 .194 A2
Amberwood Ho PO7 .....194 A3
Ambledale SO31 ....128 E4
Ambleside
Bishop's Waltham SO32 ..83 A8
Christchurch BH23 ....191 C3
Hedge End SO30 ....105 D5
Ambleside Gdns SO19 ...104 A3
Ambleside Rd SO41 .....197 F3
Ambury La BH23 ....207 F8
Amersham Cl PO12 ......180 E4
Amersham Ct PO9 ......135 C3
Amesbury Rd BH6 ......206 C6
Amethyst Gr PO7 ....135 B8
Amethyst Rd BH23 ......207 F7
Amey Gdns SO40 ....76 B1
Amey Ind Est GU32 ......40 E3
Ameys La BH22 ....165 E7
Ameysford Rd
Ameysford BH22 ....138 B1
Ferndown BH22 ....165 C7
Amira Ct 3 BH2 ....204 E3
Amoy St SO15 ....102 F6
Ampfield CE Prim Sch
SO51 ....29 C3
Ampfield Cl PO9 ....135 B4
Ampfield Ct 1 SO53 ......30 E1
Ampfield Rd BH8 ....190 D3
Amport Cl SO22 ....1 C3
Amport Ct PO9 ....135 C6
Ampress La SO41 ....197 D6
Ampress Pk SO41 ....197 D6
Ampthill Rd SO15 ....102 B7
Amsterdam Sq BH23 ....207 D6
Amyas Ct PO4 ....183 C4
Ancasta Rd SO14 ....103 B7
Anchor Cl
Bournemouth BH11 ......188 F6
Christchurch BH23 ....208 A5
Anchor Ct PO11 ....185 D1
Anchor Gate Rd PO1 ...182 A6
Anchor La PO1 ....182 A6
Anchor Mews SO41 .....197 E4
Anchor Rd BH11 ....188 F5
Anchorage Rd PO3 .....158 B3
Anchorage The PO12 ...181 C5
Anchorage Way SO41 ..197 D3
Ancrum Lo 15 BH4 ......204 B3
Anderson Cl Havant PO9 .136 A3
Romsey SO51 ....28 C2
Swanwick PO15 ....129 C8
Anderson's Rd SO14 ....103 B3
Anderwood Dr SO41 ....172 B2
Andes Cl SO14 ....103 C3
Andes Rd SO16 ....77 B3
Andlers Ash Rd GU33 ....20 E3
Andover Cl BH23 ....208 B7
Andover Ho PO9 ....136 A5
Andover Rd
Portsmouth PO4 ....182 F2
Southampton SO15 ......102 D6
Winchester SO23 ....215 D8
Andover Road N SO22 ....1 E4
Andover Road Ret Pk
SO23 ....215 D7
Andre Ct BH23 ....209 B8
Andrew Bell St PO1 .....216 B4
Andrew Cl
3 Hythe SO45 ....126 A1
Portsmouth PO1 ....182 F6
Totton SO40 ....100 D7
Andrew Cres PO7 ....111 D1
Andrew La BH25 ....195 D2
Andrew Pl PO14 ....179 B7
Andrew's Lodge SO41 ..197 D5
Andrewes Cl SO32 ....83 C8
Andrews Cl BH11 ....189 A3
Andromeda Rd SO16 .....77 F4
Androse Gdns BH24 ....140 F6
Anfield Cl SO50 ....57 C1
Anfield Ct SO50 ....57 B1
Angel Cres SO18 ....104 A6
Angel Ct SO41 ....197 E4
Angel La
Barton on S BH25 ....210 D8
Ferndown BH22 ....165 B3
Angel Mews BH15 ......202 B2
Angela Ct PO9 ....135 F4
Angelica Ct PO7 ....135 A6
Angelica Gdns SO50 .....81 C7
Angelica Way PO15 ....129 E8
Angeline Cl BH23 ......208 F8
Angelo Cl PO7 ....135 A8
Angelus Ct PO14 ....179 C7
Angerstein Rd PO2 .....157 D1
Anglers Way SO31 .....128 D8
Anglesea Ct PO1 ....182 B5
Anglesea SO15 ....78 B1

Anglesea Rd
Lee-on-t-S PO13 ....180 A4
Portsmouth PO1 ....216 A3
Southampton SO15 ....78 B1
Anglesea Terr SO14 ....103 B3
Anglesey Arms Rd
PO12 ....181 A3
Anglesey Rd PO12 .....181 A3
Anglesey View 1 PO12 .181 B4
Anglewood Mans 2
BH4 ....204 C3
Anglo-European Coll of
Chiropractic BH5 ....206 A4
Angmering Ho 2 PO1 ..216 B3
Angus Cl PO15 ....130 E3
Anjou Cl BH11 ....188 D5
Anjou Cres PO15 ....130 D2
Anker La PO14 ....154 C4
Ankerwyke PO13 ....155 B1
Anmore Cl PO9 ....135 D4
Anmore Dr PO7 ....111 B4
Anmore Dr PO7 ....111 C2
Anmore La PO7,PO8 ....111 C5
Anmore Rd PO7 ....111 A4
Ann's Hill Rd PO12 .....181 A6
Anna La BH23 ....168 B4
Annandale Ct BH6 ......206 D4
Anne Cl BH23 ....192 A1
Anne Cres PO7 ....134 E6
Annerley Rd BH1 ....205 C4
Annes Ct PO11 ....184 E2
Annet Cl BH15 ....201 E2
Argyle Rd
Christchurch BH23 ....207 E5
Southampton SO14 ......103 B5
Argyll Mans 8 BH5 .....205 E4
Argyll Rd
Bournemouth BH5 ....205 E4
Poole BH12 ....203 D6
Ariel Cl BH6 ....207 B4
Ariel Dr BH6 ....207 B4
Ariel Rd PO1 ....182 E5
Arismore Ct PO13 ......179 D4
Ark Dr BH22 ....165 A3
Ark Royal Cres PO13 ...179 E4
Ark Cl PO8 ....88 C4
Arley Rd BH14 ....203 A2
Arlington Ct BH25 .....210 B8
Arlington Pl 3 SO23 ...215 E6
Arliss Rd SO16 ....78 A1
Arlott Ct SO15 ....102 E7
Armada Cl SO16 ....77 E7
Armada Dr SO45 ....125 F2
Armadale Ho 20 SO14 ..103 C4
Armfield Rd 20 SO17 ....79 A1
Arminers Cl PO12 .....181 B2
Armitage Ave SO45 ....125 F1
Armory La PO1 ....182 A4
Armoury The SO40 ....102 A3
Armstrong Cl
Brockenhurst SO42 ......145 E1
1 Gosport PO12 ....181 C6
Waterlooville PO7 ....111 D1
Armstrong Ct SO16 ......77 F5
Armstrong La SO42 ....145 E1
Armstrong Rd SO42 ....145 E1
Armsworth La PO7,SO32 .85 E1
Arnaud Cl PO2 ....182 D7
Arne Ave BH12 ....203 E7
Arne Cres BH12 ....203 F7
Arnewood Bridge Rd
SO41 ....196 B7
Arnewood Ct
Bournemouth BH2 ....204 E2
Sway SO41 ....196 C6
Arnewood Ho SO41 ....196 C6
Arnewood Rd BH6 ......206 D5
Arnewood Sch The
BH25 ....194 F2
Arnheim Cl SO16 ....78 C4
Arnheim Rd SO16 ....78 D4
Arnold Cl BH22 ....138 E3
Arnold Rd Eastleigh SO50 ..80 A8
Southampton SO17 ....79 C2
West Moors BH22 ....138 E3
Arnolds Cl BH25 ....209 F8
Arnside Rd PO7 ....134 E8
Arnwood Ave SO45 ....149 F8
Arragon Ct PO7 ....135 A8
Arran Cl PO6 ....133 F1
Arran Way BH23 ....194 B1
Arras Ho PO15 ....130 C3
Arreton SO31 ....127 C6
Arreton Ct 3 PO12 .....181 A6
Arrow Cl Eastleigh SO50 ..56 A4
Southampton SO19 ......103 D1
Arrowsmith Ct BH18 ...187 A2
Arrowsmith La BH21 ...187 E7
Arrowsmith Rd BH21 ...187 E7
Arters Lawn SO40 .....124 C6
Arthur Cl BH2 ....204 F5
Arthur Kille Ho PO7 ....134 D6
Arthur La 3 BH23 .....207 A7
Arthur Pope Ho PO5 ...216 B1
Arthur Rd
Christchurch BH23 ....207 A7
Eastleigh SO50 ....56 A4
Southampton SO15 ......102 D6
Winchester SO23 ....215 D7
Arthur St PO2 ....182 E7
Arthurs Gdns SO30 .....81 B3
Artillery Cl 1 PO6 ......157 C8
Artillery Terr 2 PO4 ...183 B4
Arts Inst of Bournemouth The
BH12 ....203 F8
Arun Cl GU31 ....40 E2
Arun Rd SO18 ....80 B2
Arun Way SO51 ....196 C5
Arundel Cl BH25 ....194 E3

Arcadia Cl SO16 ....78 B3
Arcadia Rd BH23 ....191 E1
Arch Farm Ind Site SP6 ..69 E3
Archdale Cl BH12 ......189 D2
Archer Ho PO12 ....181 C2
Archers 1 SO15 ....102 E6
Archers Cl SO40 ....76 C1
Archers Rd Eastleigh SO50 ..56 A3
Southampton SO15 ......102 F7
Archery Gdns SO19 ....103 F2
Archery Gr SO19 ......103 F2
Archery La
Fareham PO16 ....131 C2
Winchester SO23 ....215 D5
Archery Rd SO19 ......103 E1
Archgate SO41 ....197 E4
Archway Rd BH14 .....203 E4
Arden Cl
6 Gosport PO12 ....180 F4
Southampton SO18 ....80 B1
Arden Rd BH9 ....189 F3
Arden Wlk BH25 ....195 B2
Ardingly Cres SO30 .....81 D2
Ardington Rise PO7 ....134 E3
Ardington Terr BH14 ...203 B4
Ardnave Cres SO16 ....77 F5
Arena Bsns Ctr BH17 ...202 B8
Arethusa Ho 18 PO1 ...182 A4
Argosy Cl SO31 ....128 F1
Argus Rd PO13 ....179 F4
Argyle Cres PO15 ......130 F2

Arundel Ct Inf Sch PO1 .216 C4
Arundel Ct Jun Sch
PO1 ....216 B3
Arundel Dr PO16 ....131 A2
Arundel Ho
Southampton,Banister's Pk
SO15 ....102 F8
18 Southampton,Northam
SO14 ....103 C6
Arundel Rd Eastleigh SO50 ..56 A6
Fordingbridge SP6 ....69 C1
Totton SO40 ....101 A8
Arundel St PO1 ....216 C3
Arundel Way BH23 ....208 F7
Arundel Way Sh Arc
PO1 ....216 B3
Ascham Rd BH8 ....205 B5
Ascot Cl PO14 ....129 C2
Ascot Rd
Broadstone BH18 ....187 A4
Horton Heath SO50 ......81 D7
Portsmouth PO3 ....183 A7
Ascupart Ho 6 SO17 ...103 B8
Ascupart St SO14 ......103 B4
Asford Gr SO50 ....56 C4
Ash Cl Alderholt SP6 ....93 A5
Bursledon SO31 ....127 F8
Colden Common SO21 ....32 A1
Fareham PO14 ....154 E8
Gosport PO12 ....181 B5
Hythe SO45 ....150 A8
North Baddesley SO52 ....53 F5
Romsey SO51 ....53 C6
Southampton SO19 ......104 C6
Upton BH16 ....201 B8
Waterlooville PO8 ....111 E2
Ash Copse PO8 ....111 F5
Ash Gr Ashurst SO40 ...100 C3
Hordle SO41 ....211 D8
Ringwood BH24 ....141 C6
Ash Grove Ho 5 PO15 ..129 D8
Ash Rd SO40 ....100 B2
Ashburn Cres SO22 ....215 C3
Ashbourne Cl 1 BH1 ...205 A3
Ashbourne Rd BH5 ....206 B5
Ashbridge Rise SO53 ....30 B1
Ashburn Garth BH24 ...141 D6
Ashburn Pl SP6 ....69 E1
Ashburnham Cl SO19 ..103 D5
Ashburton Cl SO45 ....125 D3
Ashburton Ct PO5 .....216 B1
Ashburton Gdns BH10 .189 D1
Ashburton Ho SO31 ...127 B6
Ashburton Rd
Gosport PO12 ....180 F2
Portsmouth PO5 ....182 C2
Ashby Cres SO40 ......100 D7
Ashby Pl PO5 ....182 C2
Ashby Rd
Southampton SO19 ......104 B3
Totton SO40 ....100 D7
Ashcroft Ct 2 GU32 .....40 F4
Ashcroft La PO8 ....113 D6
Ashdene 17 SO15 .....102 B8
Ashdene Cl BH21 ......163 D5
Ashdene Rd SO40 .....100 C3
Ashdown
8 Bournemouth BH2 ...204 D2
Fawley SO45 ....150 F3
Gosport PO13 ....155 D1
Ashdown Cl
Chandler's Ford SO53 ....30 C2
Poole BH17 ....187 F1
Ashdown Dr SO53 ......30 C2
Ashdown Rd
Blackfield SO45 ....150 F2
Chandler's Ford SO53 ....30 C2
Ashdown Tech Coll
BH17 ....187 E1
Ashdown Way SO51 ....53 B7
Ashdown Wlk BH25 ...195 C2
Ashe Rd PO9 ....136 B5
Ashen Cl SO53 ....55 C8
Ashfield View SO52 .....54 A5
Ashford Chace GU32 ...19 E1
Ashford Cl
Fordingbridge SP6 ....69 C1
Portsmouth PO6 ....133 C1
Ashford Cres SO45 ....126 B3
Ashford Rd
Bournemouth BH6 ....206 D7
Fordingbridge SP6 ....93 C8
Ashford Works Ind Est
SP6 ....69 C1
Ashington Cl PO8 .....112 A3
Ashington Gdns BH21 ..186 F8
Ashington La BH21 ....163 A1
Ashington Pk BH25 ....195 B1
Ashlea Cl SO50 ....57 D2
Ashleigh Cl SO45 ......150 A8
Ashleigh Rise BH10 ....189 D2
Ashlet Gdns BH25 ....195 D4
Ashlett Cl SO45 ....151 C3
Ashlett Lawn PO9 ....135 C6
Ashlett Mews SO45 ...151 C3
Ashlett Rd SO45 ......151 C3
Ashley Arnewood Ct 5
BH25 ....195 B2
Ashley Common Rd
BH25 ....195 C4
Ashley Cres SO19 .....104 C1

Ashley Cross BH14 ....203 A4
Ashley Ct
Bursledon SO31 ....105 A2
Gosport PO12 ....181 A6
West Moors BH22 ......166 A8
Ashley Dr BH24 ....116 C3
Ashley Drive N BH25 ..139 F5
Ashley Drive S BH25 ..139 F5
Ashley Drive W BH24 ..139 F5
Ashley Gdns
Chandler's Ford SO53 ....55 E5
Waltham Chase SO32 ....83 E3
Ashley Heath Cvn Pk
BH24 ....139 D6
Ashley Heath Ind Est
BH21 ....139 B7
Ashley Ho SO51 ....52 E6
Ashley Inf Sch BH25 ..195 D3
Ashley Jun Sch BH25 ..195 C3
Ashley La
Hordle BH25,SO41 ......195 E4
Lymington SO41 ....197 E3
Ashley Mdws SO51 .....53 A8
Ashley Meads BH25 ...195 D4
Ashley Pk BH24 ....140 A6
Ashley Rd
Bournemouth BH1 ......205 E5
New Milton BH25 ......195 C3
Poole BH14 ....203 C5
Ashleycross Cl SO45 ...150 D3
Ashling Cl
Bournemouth BH8 ......205 C8
Denmead PO7 ....111 E5
Ashling Cres BH8 ......205 B8
Ashling La PO2 ....157 D1
Ashling Park Rd PO7 ..110 F4
Ashlyn Ct PO15 ....130 C2
Ashmead Rd 4 SO16 ....77 F3
Ashmeads Cl BH21 ....164 A6
Ashmeads Cl BH21 ....164 A6
Ashmeads Way BH21 ..164 A6
Ashmore BH21 ....163 D4
Ashmore Ave
Barton on S BH25 ....210 B8
Hamworthy BH15 ......201 F1
Ashmore Cl SP5 ....24 B4
Ashmore Cres BH15 ...201 F1
Ashmore Gr BH23 .....193 C1
Ashmore Ho 10 BH4 ...204 C3
Ashmore La SP5 ....24 B6
Ashmore Rd SO22 .....215 B7
Ashridge Ave 1 BH10 ..189 D5
Ashridge Cl SO15 .....102 F8
Ashridge Gdns BH10 ..189 D5
Ashridge Par 2 BH10 ..189 D5
Ashstead Gdns BH8 ....190 C3
Ashtead Cl PO16 ......156 A8
Ashton Cl SO32 ....59 A1
Ashton Cross SO51 .....51 B1
Ashton Ct
3 New Milton BH25 ...195 B3
Poole BH13 ....204 A2
Ashton Ho SO19 ....103 F1
Ashton La SO32 ....59 B2
Ashton Pl 3 SO53 ......30 B1
Ashton Rd BH9 ....189 F2
Ashton Way PO14 .....179 C5
Ashtree Cl BH25 ....195 D2
Ashtree Ct SO53 ....55 C3
Ashtree Rd SO18 ....79 E2
Ashurst Bridge Rd
SO40 ....100 C5
Ashurst Cl Ashurst SO40 ..100 B2
Southampton SO19 ......104 A1
Winchester SO22 ....1 D3
Ashurst Ct 10 PO12 ...180 D3
Ashurst New Forest Sta
SO40 ....100 A1
Ashurst Rd
Bournemouth BH8 ......190 D3
Cosham PO6 ....157 E8
West Moors BH22 ......138 E3
Ashwell Ct BH23 ......191 F1
Ashwood Titchfield SO31 .129 C2
Whiteley PO15 ....129 E5
Ashwood Cl Havant PO9 .135 B3
South Hayling PO11 ....185 A3
Ashwood Dr BH18 .....187 C4
Ashwood Gdns
6 Southampton SO16 ...78 E3
Totton SO40 ....100 C7
Ashwood Lodge 1
PO16 ....131 A2
Aspen Ave SO31 ......152 D10
Aspen Cl
Colden Common SO21 ....57 A8
Hedge End SO30 ....105 D7
Aspen Dr BH31 ....115 B5
Aspen Gdns BH12 .....203 F7
Aspen Holt SO16 ....79 A5
Aspen Pl BH25 ....195 B1
Aspen Rd BH12 ....203 F7
Aspen Way Poole BH12 .203 F7
Waterlooville PO8 ....112 A5
Aspen Wlk SO40 ......100 B8
Aspengrove PO13 .....155 E1
Asquith Cl BH23 ....207 D6
Assheton Cl PO16 .....156 C6
Astbury Ave BH12 ....204 A8
Aster Rd SO16 ....79 C4
Astley St PO5 ....216 A2
Aston Mead BH23 .....191 E4

Aston Rd Portsmouth PO4 .182 F3
Waterlooville PO7 ....111 D1
Astra Ct SO45 ....126 A5
Astra Wlk PO12 ....181 D5
Astral Gdns SO31 ....127 F3
Astrid Cl PO11 ....185 C3
Asturias Way SO14 ....103 C3
Asylum Rd SO15 ....103 A6
Atalanta Cl PO4 ....183 C5
Atheling Rd SO45 ....126 A4
Athelney Ct **7** BH1 ....205 B3
Athelstan Rd
  Bournemouth BH6 ....206 E5
  Southampton SO19 ......103 E6
Athelston Ct SO41 ....197 D3
Athena Ave PO7 ....134 F3
Athena Cl SO50 ....57 B3
Atherfield Rd SO16 ....77 E3
Atherley Ct SO15 ....102 E8
Atherley Rd
  South Hayling PO11 .....184 E5
  Southampton SO15 ......102 D6
Atherley Sch The **5** PO5 .77 B6
Atherstone Wlk **5** PO5 .216 B2
Atkins Pl PO15 ....130 C3
Atkinson Cl
  Barton on S BH25 ....210 B8
  Gosport PO12 ....181 A3
Atlantic Cl SO14 ....103 B2
Atlantic Ct
  Chandler's Ford SO53 ....55 C5
  Winchester SO22 ....215 A5
Atlantic Park View SO18 .80 A2
Atlantis Ave PO7 ....134 F2
Atrium The
  Ferndown BH22 ....165 E7
  20 Southampton SO17 .103 A8
  29 Winchester SO23 ....215 D6
Attwood Cl SP6 ....92 F5
Attwoods Dro SO21 ......10 D1
Aubrey Cl
  Milford on S SO41 ......211 F4
  South Hayling PO11 .....184 E4
Aubrey Farm Cotts
  SO41 ....212 A4
Auburn Mans **5** BH1 ...204 B4
Auckland Ave SO42 ......146 A1
Auckland Pl SO42 ....146 A1
Auckland Rd
  Christchurch BH23 ......208 C7
  Southampton SO15 ......101 F7
Auckland Rd E PO5 ......182 C2
Auckland Rd W PO5 .....182 C2
Audemer Ct BH24 ....141 C8
Audley Pl SO50 ....56 F1
Audratyon Ct **8** BH6 ..206 E3
Audret Cl PO16 ....156 B6
Augustine Rd
  Cosham PO6 ....158 C8
  Southampton SO14 ......103 B6
Augustus Cl SO33 ....55 E7
Augustus Ho SO18 ....103 C7
Augustus Way SO53 ......55 E7
Auriol Dr PO9 ....159 A8
Aust Rd PO14 ....154 D8
Austen Ave
  Bournemouth BH10 .....189 E6
  Winchester SO22 ......215 A2
Austen Cl Totton SO40 ...100 D6
  Winchester SO23 ....215 E8
Austen Gdns PO15 ......129 C8
Austerberry Way PO13 ..180 E8
Austin Ave BH14 ....203 B1
Austin Cl BH1 ....205 D5
Austin Ct **1** PO6 ......133 B1
Australia Cl PO1 ....216 C3
Autumn Cl BH22 ....165 B7
Autumn Copse BH25 .....195 D2
Autumn Pl **11** SO17 ...79 A1
Autumn Rd
  Bournemouth BH11 ......188 D3
  Marchwood SO40 ....102 A1
Avalon BH14 ....214 C8
Avalon Ct PO10 ....136 F2
Avebury Ave BH10 ......189 E6
Avebury Gdns SO53 ......30 A1
Avenger Cl SO53 ....55 B5
Avenue C SO45 ....81 C6
Avenue C SO45 ....152 E2
Avenue Campus (Univ of
  Southampton) SO17 ......79 A2
Avenue Ct Gosport PO12 .181 A3
  Poole BH13 ....204 B3
  2 Southampton SO17 .102 F8
Avenue D SO45 ....150 E8
Avenue De Caen PO5 ....182 C1
Avenue E SO45 ....150 E8
Avenue La **18** BH2 ....204 E3
Avenue Rd
  Bournemouth BH2 ......204 E3
  Brockenhurst SO42 .....172 F8
  Christchurch BH23 ......206 F7
  Gosport PO12 ....181 C4
  Lymington SO41 ....197 E4
  New Milton BH25 ....195 A3
  North Hayling PO11 .....160 A3
  Southampton SO14 ......103 A8
  Walkford BH23 ....194 C2
  Wimborne Minst BH21 ...163 D4
  Winchester SO22 ......215 A2
Avenue Sh Ctr The **14**
  BH2 ....204 E3
Avenue The
  Bishop's Waltham SO32 ...83 B8

Avenue The continued
  Bournemouth BH9 ....189 F3
  Fareham PO14 ....130 E1
  Gosport PO12 ....181 A4
  Petersfield GU31 ....40 F3
  Poole BH13 ....204 A2
  Southampton SO17 ......78 F2
  Twyford SO21 ....32 A6
  West Moors BH22 ......138 E3
  West Moors BH24 ......166 B8
Avery Fields SO50 ....56 B7
Avery La PO12 ....181 A8
Aviation Park W
  East Parley BH23 ......190 C8
  Hurn BH23 ....166 D1
Avington Cl SO50 ....56 D5
Avington Ct
  Southampton SO16 ......78 F4
  Winchester SO22 ......215 A5
Avington Gn PO9 ....136 B6
Avlan Ct SO23 ....215 D3
Avocet Cl PO4 ....183 B5
Avocet Ho **2** PO4 .....183 B5
Avocet Quay PO10 ......161 A7
Avocet Way PO8 ....112 A7
Avocet Wlk PO13 ....155 A2
Avon Ave BH24 ....140 D4
Avon Bldgs BH23 ....207 B7
Avon Castle BH24 ....140 D3
Avon Castle Dr BH24 ....140 D3
Avon Cl
  Bournemouth BH8 ......205 D6
  Lee-on-t-S PO13 ....179 F2
  Lymington SO41 ....197 C3
  Petersfield GU31 ....40 E2
Avon Cotts BH23 ....192 C5
Avon Cres SO51 ....53 C7
Avon Cswy BH23 ....191 C5
Avon Ct
  Christchurch BH23 ......207 C6
  1 Fordingbridge SP6 ..69 F2
  Netley SO31 ....127 C5
  2 Waterlooville PO8 ..111 F4
  7 Poole BH13 ....204 A4
Avon Farm Cotts BH23 ..167 E3
Avon Gdns BH23 ....169 B1
Avon Gn SO53 ....55 D5
Avon Heath Ctry Park Visitor
  Ctr* BH24 ....140 A2
Avon Heath Ctry Pk (North
  Pk)* BH24 ....140 B3
Avon Heath Ctry Pk (South
  Pk)* BH24 ....167 B8
Avon Ho
  Bournemouth BH2 ......204 E2
  8 Southampton SO14 .103 C6
Avon Mdw SP5 ....46 F7
Avon Meade SP6 ....69 E2
Avon Mews BH4 ....205 C6
Avon Pk BH24 ....140 D6
Avon Rd
  Bournemouth BH8 ......205 C6
  Southampton SO19 ......79 F1
  West Moors BH22 ......138 E2
Avon Road E BH23 ......207 A8
Avon Road W BH23 .....206 F8
Avon Run Cl BH23 ......208 B5
Avon Run Rd BH23 .....208 B5
Avon View SO41 ....70 D1
Avon View Par BH23 ....192 C3
Avon View Rd BH23 ....192 C3
Avon Way SO30 ....80 E2
Avon Wharf BH23 ....207 C5
Avon Wlk PO16 ....156 A8
Avonborne Way SO53 ....55 B8
Avoncliffe Sch BH7 .....206 A7
Avoncliffe Rd BH6 ......206 E3
Avondale Ct SO17 ....79 B2
Avondale Mobile Home Pk
  SO21 ....32 A1
Avondale Rd
  Portsmouth PO1 ....182 F7
  Waterlooville PO7 ......134 F8
Avondyke SP5 ....46 F6
Avonsands BH23 ....208 A5
Avro Cl SO15 ....102 A7
Avro Ct SO31 ....127 F2
Award Rd
  Ferndown BH21 ....164 F5
  Wimborne Minst BH21 ..165 A6
Awbridge Prim Sch
  SO51 ....26 D5
Awbridge Rd PO9 ....135 C4
Axford Cl BH8 ....190 D3
Axis Pk PO14 ....155 A6
Aylen Rd PO3 ....158 A2
Aylesbury Rd
  Bournemouth BH1 ......205 E4
  Portsmouth PO2 ....182 F8
Ayling Cl PO13 ....180 C7
Aylward St PO1 ....182 A5
Aynsley Ct SO15 ....102 D7
Aysgarth Rd PO7 ....134 E8
Aysha Cl BH25 ....195 B1
Azalea Cl Havant PO9 ...136 C4
  St Leonards BH24 ......140 A5
Aztec Ctr BH17 ....202 D8
Azura Cl BH21 ....139 B6

B Ave Fawley SO45 ......150 F4
  Holbury SO45 ....150 D5
Back La Mottisfont SO51 ..5 E5
  Southwick PO17 ....132 E6
  Sway SO41 ....172 C2

Back of the Walls **26**
  SO14 ....103 A3
Back St SO23 ....215 D2
Bacon Cl SO19 ....103 F1
Bacon La PO11 ....184 E3
Badbury Cl BH18 ....187 C3
Badbury Ct BH22 ....165 F7
Badbury View BH21 .....163 D5
Badbury Rd BH21 ....186 D8
Baddesley Cl SO52 ......53 F6
Baddesley Gdns PO9 ....135 D6
Baddesley Park Ind Est
  SO52 ....54 B4
Baddesley Rd SO53 ......30 A1
Baden Cl BH25 ....195 B1
Baden Powell Way **2**
  SO51 ....52 F7
Baden-Powell & St Peter's
  CE Mid Sch BH14 ......203 B3
Bader Cl SO30 ....105 C8
Bader Rd BH17 ....202 E8
Bader Way PO15 ....129 F5
Badger Brow PO7 ....135 A6
Badger Cl
  Bishopstoke SO50 ......56 F2
  Fareham PO15 ....130 D2
Badger Ct SO50 ....56 F2
Badger Rd PO14 ....154 F5
Badger Way BH31 ....114 F5
Badger Wood Pl SO18 ....79 F1
Badgers Cl
  St Leonards BH24 ......139 F5
  Sway SO41 ....172 C2
Badgers Copse
  Locks Heath SO31 ......129 B5
  New Milton BH25 ....195 C6
Badgers Run SO31 ......128 E6
Badgers The SO31 ......127 C6
Badgers Wlk
  Ferndown BH22 ....165 E7
  Hythe SO45 ....125 F2
Badminton Dro SO45 ....178 C8
Badminston La SO45 ....151 C1
Badshear La SO24 ......14 F8
Baffins Rd PO3 ....183 A6
Bagber Rd SO40 ....100 F7
Bagot Ho PO12 ....180 F6
Bagshot Mews SO19 ....103 F3
Baigent Cl SO23 ....11 C8
Bailey Cl Botley SO30 ...106 A6
  New Milton BH25 ....195 A4
  Winchester SO22 ......215 B4
Bailey Cres BH15 ....202 C7
Bailey Dr BH23 ....206 F7
Bailey Gn SO18 ....80 A2
Bailey Hall BH23 ....206 A5
Bailey's Rd PO5 ....216 C2
Baiter Gdns BH15 ......202 C1
Baker Rd BH11 ....189 A5
Baker St PO1 ....182 D7
Bakers Dro SO19 ....77 E5
Bakers Farm Rd BH31 ..114 E7
Bakers View BH21 ......166 C6
Balaclava Rd SO18 .....104 B7
Balchin Ho **18** PO1 ...182 A5
Balcombe Rd BH13 .....204 A3
Balderton Ct **7** PO2 ..157 F4
Baldwin Cl BH23 ....207 D6
Balena Cl SO17 ....102 A6
Balfour Cl
  Christchurch BH23 ......208 D8
  Gosport PO13 ....180 D6
Balfour Dr GU33 ....20 F4
Balfour Rd
  Bournemouth BH9 ......189 F1
  Portsmouth PO2 ....157 E1
  Southampton SO19 ......104 C5
Balfour Red Cross Mus*
  SO23 ....2 C1
Ballam Cl BH16 ....201 C7
Ballard Cl
  New Milton BH25 ....195 B4
  Poole BH15 ....202 D1
  Southampton SO16 ......77 D1
Ballard Coll BH25 ......195 A4
Ballard Ct **1** PO12 ...181 B5
Ballard Rd BH15 ....202 D1
Ballard Sch BH25 ......195 A4
Balliol Cl PO14 ....129 C1
Balliol Rd PO2 ....182 E8
Balmer Lawn Rd SO42 ..146 B3
Balmoral Ave BH6 ......206 E6
Balmoral Cl
  Chandler's Ford SO53 ...55 B8
  Gosport PO13 ....155 D2
  Southampton SO16 ......78 C5
Balmoral Ct
  3 Christchurch BH23 .209 B7
  7 Southampton SO17 .103 A8
  4 Southampton,Millbrook
  SO15 ....102 A6
Balmoral Dr PO7 ....134 C4
Balmoral Ho
  Bournemouth BH2 ......204 C1
  6 Whiteley PO15 ......129 D8
Balmoral Rd
  Fareham PO15 ....130 E3
  Poole BH14 ....203 C3
Balmoral Way
  Petersfield GU32 ....40 F4
  Rownhams SO16 ....77 E6
Balmoral Wlk BH25 .....194 F3
Balston Rd BH14 ....203 A6
Balston Terr BH15 .....202 B2
Balston Terr BH15 ......80 E1
Bambridge Pk Gdn Ctr
  Miniature Rly* SO50 .....31 D1

Bamford Ho **9** PO4 ...183 B2
Bampton Cl SO16 ....101 E8
Bampton Ct SO53 ....55 C6
Banbury Ave SO19 ......104 C4
Banbury Rd BH17 ....202 C2
Bancroft Ct **1** BH15 ..202 E4
Bangor Rd SO15 ....102 B6
Banister Ct **6** SO15 ..102 F7
Banister Gdns SO15 ....102 F7
Banister Grange **9**
  SO15 ....102 F7
Banister Inf Sch SO15 ..102 F7
Banister Mews SO15 ....102 F7
Banister Rd SO15 ......102 F7
Bank Chambers BH14 ...203 E3
Bank Cl BH23 ....207 B6
Bank Side SO18 ....79 D4
Bank St SO32 ....83 D8
Bankhill Dr SO41 ....197 D5
Banks Rd BH13 ....214 C4
Banks The SO51 ....26 A5
Bankside SO41 ....197 D6
Bankside Ho **3** SO22 .215 C6
Bankside Rd BH9 ....190 A3
Bankview SO41 ....197 D6
Bannerman Rd GU32 ....40 F4
Banning St SO51 ....52 E6
Bannister Cl SO40 .....101 A7
Banstead Rd BH18 ....187 A5
Bapaume Rd PO3 ......157 F5
Bar End Ind Est SO23 ..215 F3
Bar End Rd SO23 ......215 F3
Bar Gate Mus* SO14 ...102 F4
Barbara Ct SO32 ....35 B3
Barbe Baker Ave SO30 ..80 D2
Barberry Dr SO40 ....76 B1
Barberry Way BH31 ....115 C5
Barbers Gate **8** BH15 .202 B1
Barbers Piles **1** BH15 .202 B1
Barbers Wharf **8** BH15 .202 B1
Barbican Mews PO16 ...156 E7
Barclay Ho **8** PO12 ..181 E5
Barclay Mans BH2 ......204 F5
Barclay Mews
  Hythe SO45 ....149 F8
  Hythe SO45 ....150 A8
Bardon Way PO14 ......154 D8
Barentin Way GU31 .....41 A4
Barfield Cl SO23 ....215 F4
Barfields SO41 ....197 E4
Barfields Ct **2** SO41 ..197 E4
Barfleur Cl PO15 ....130 D2
Barfleur Rd PO14 ......155 A5
Barford Cl SO53 ....55 B8
Barford La SP5 ....47 A8
Bargate Ctr **12** SO14 .103 A4
Bargate St SO14 ....102 F4
Bargates BH23 ....207 B7
Barham Cl PO12 ....181 B7
Barham Rd GU32 ....40 F3
Barham Way PO2 ......157 D4
Baring Rd
  Bournemouth BH6 ......207 A3
  Winchester SO23 ......215 C7
Bark Mill Mews SO51 ...52 E6
Barker Mill Cl SO16 .....77 E6
Barkis Ho **11** PO1 ....182 D7
Barkisfare Cl **7** SO15 .102 F8
Barlands Cl BH23 ......192 C2
Barle Cl SO18 ....80 B1
Barley Down Dr SO22 ..215 B2
Barley Fields SO50 ......81 C6
Barleycorn Wlk SO40 ...98 F8
Barling Mews **7** SO51 .52 E7
Barlow Cl PO14 ....154 C8
Barn Cl Emsworth PO10 .160 D8
  Upton BH16 ....201 A7
Barn End PO7 ....112 B1
Barn Green Cl PO7 .....110 F4
Barn Piece SO53 ....54 F6
Barn Rd BH18 ....187 B3
Barn Wood Rd PO15 ...130 D1
Barnaby Cl SP5 ....46 D7
Barnbrook Rd SO31 ...128 E4
Barncroft Inf Sch PO9 .135 D3
Barncroft Jun Sch PO9 .135 D3
Barncroft Way PO9 ....135 D3
Barnes Cl
  Bournemouth BH10 .....189 D3
  Sarisbury SO31 ....128 D4
  Southampton SO18 .....104 C6
  West Wellow SO51 ......50 E4
  Winchester SO23 ......215 D3
Barnes Cres
  Bournemouth BH10 .....189 D3
  Wimborne Minst BH21 ..163 A4
Barnes La
  Milford on S SO41 ......211 C6
  Sarisbury SO31 ....128 C4
Barnes Rd
  Bournemouth BH10 .....189 D3
  Portsmouth PO1 ....182 E6
  Southampton SO19 .....104 C6
Barnes Wallis Rd PO15 .129 E4
Barnes Way PO9 ....135 E4
Barnet Side La GU32,
  GU34 ....18 D5
Barney Evans Cres PO8 .111 D3
Barneyhayes La SO40 ...99 A7
Barnfield BH23 ....208 D8
Barnfield Cl
  Breach PO10 ....137 E1
  Southampton SO19 .....103 E1
Barnfield Ct
  Fareham PO14 ....154 E8
  Southampton SO19 .....103 E1
Barnfield Flats SO19 ...103 F1

Barnfield Rd
  Petersfield GU31 ....41 C3
  Southampton SO19 .....103 F1
Barney Way SO19 ......103 F1
Barns Rd BH22 ....166 A6
Barnsfield Cres SO40 ...100 C7
Barnsfield Rd BH24 ....140 B2
Barnside Way GU33 .....20 F3
Barnsland SO30 ....80 C2
Baron Rd SO31 ....127 F3
Barons Ct **7** BH12 ...204 B4
Barons Mead SO16 ......77 E3
Barons Rd BH11 ....188 D6
Baronsmede **2** BH2 ..204 D4
Baronsmere PO12 ......181 A5
Barrack La BH24 ....141 D4
Barrack Rd
  Christchurch BH23 .....206 E8
  Ferndown BH22 ....166 A2
Barracks The BH24 .....142 E5
Barratt Ind Pk PO15 ...129 C5
Barrie Cl PO15 ....129 C8
Barrie Rd BH9 ....189 F3
Barrington Cl SO50 ......55 F5
Barrington Ct **20** SO17 .79 A1
Barrington Ho **20** PO1 .182 D7
Barrow Down Gdns
  SO19 ....104 E4
Barrow Dr BH8 ....190 F2
Barrow Hill Rd SO40 ....75 D3
Barrow Rd BH8 ....190 F2
Barrow View BH22 .....165 B6
Barrow Way BH8 ....190 F2
Barrowgate Rd BH8 ....190 D3
Barrowgate Way BH8 ..190 D3
Barrows La Lanford SP5 ..49 C6
  Sway SO41 ....196 B6
Barrs Ave BH25 ....195 B4
Barrs Wood Dr BH25 ..195 B4
Barrs Wood Rd BH25 ..195 B4
Barry Gdns BH18 ......186 F5
Barry Rd SO19 ....104 B5
Barter Rd BH12 ....204 A7
Barters Cl SO16 ....77 F1
Bartless La BH18 ....186 F3
Bartholomew Cl **7**
  SO23 ....215 E7
Bartlett Cl PO15 ....130 E3
Bartlett Dr BH7 ....206 B8
Bartlett Ho **12** SO17 .103 B8
Bartletts Comm SO51 ...94 E7
Bartletts Rd The SO31 ..128 A2
Bartley Ave SO40 .....100 E6
Bartley CE Jun Sch SO40 .98 F2
Bartley Ct **2** BH21 ...163 B5
Bartley Rd SO40 ....99 C4
Barton Chase BH25 ....209 F7
Barton Cl SO51 ....53 B8
Barton Common La
  BH25 ....210 B8
Barton Common Rd
  BH25 ....210 B8
Barton Court Ave BH25 .210 A8
Barton Court Rd BH25 .195 A1
Barton Cres SO18 ....79 F1
Barton Croft BH25 .....210 A7
Barton Cross PO8 ......112 B7
Barton Dr
  Barton on S BH25 .....209 F8
  Hamble-le-R SO31 .....127 F3
  Hedge End SO30 ....105 D7
Barton Gn BH25 ....210 B6
Barton Gr PO3 ....158 B3
Barton Ho BH25 ....195 A1
Barton La Barton on S BH25 .210 A8
  Barton Park Ind Est SO50 .56 B2
  Barton Peverill Coll SO50 .55 F1
Barton Rd SO50 ....56 C3
Barton Way BH25 ......209 F8
Barton Wood Rd BH25 .209 F7
Barton Ct **6** PO12 ...181 B6
Bartons Rd
  Fordingbridge SP6 ......69 F1
  Havant PO9 ....136 B4
Bartons The
  Fordingbridge SP6 ......69 F1
  Hedge End SO30 ......105 A6
Bartonside Rd BH25 ...209 C7
Bartram Rd SO40 .....101 A6
Barwell Gr PO10 ....136 E3
Barwell Terr **8** SO30 .105 D6
Bascott Cl BH11 ....189 A1
Bascott Rd BH11 ....189 A1
Basepoint Bsns Ctr
  BH23 ....166 C1
Basepoint Ent Ctr SO14 .103 B3
Bashley Common Rd
  BH25 ....193 A8
Bashley Cross Rd BH25 .194 E5
Bashley Dr BH25 ....195 B6
Bashley Rd BH25 ......195 A6
Basin St PO2 ....182 D8
Basing Barns GU34 .....17 D5
Basing Dean GU34 .....17 E4
Basing Ho SO31 ....102 C7
Basing Mews **3** SO32 ..83 C7
Basing Rd PO9 ....135 E4
Basing Way SO53 ....55 C6
Basingstoke Rd SO21,SO23 ..2 D7
Basingwell St Lwr **5**
  SO32 ....83 C7
Basingwell St Upper
  SO32 ....83 D7
Bassett Ave SO16 ....78 F5
Bassett Cl SO16 ....78 F4
Bassett Cres E SO16 ....78 F4
Bassett Cres W SO16 ...78 F5

Bassett Ct SO16 . . . . .78 F4
Bassett Dale SO16 . . . . .78 F6
Bassett Gdns SO16 . . . . .78 F6
Bassett Gn Village SO16 . . .79 B5
Bassett Green Cl SO16 . . .79 B5
Bassett Green Dr SO16 . . .79 A6
Bassett Green Prim Sch
SO16 . . . . .79 B4
Bassett Green Rd SO16 . . .79 B5
Bassett Heath Ave SO16 . .78 F6
Bassett Mdw SO16 . . . . . .78 F4
Bassett Mews SO16 . . . . . .78 F5
Bassett Rd BH12 . . . . . . .203 B6
Bassett Row SO16 . . . . . . .78 F6
Bassett Wlk PO9 . . . . . . .135 D6
Bassett Wood Dr SO16 . . . .79 A6
Bassett Wood Mews 🔳
SO16 . . . . .79 A6
Bassett Wood N SO16 . . . .79 A6
Bassett Wood Rd SO16 . . .79 A6
Batchelor Cres BH11 . . . .188 F3
Batchelor Gn SO31 . . . . . .127 F8
Batchelor Rd BH11 . . . . . .189 A3
Batcombe Cl BH11 . . . . . .188 E3
Bath & Wells Ct 🔳
PO13 . . . . .180 C6
Bath Cl SO19 . . . . .104 B6
Bath Hill Ct 🔳 BH1 . . . . .205 A3
Bath Hill Rdbt BH1 . . . . . .205 A2
Bath La 🔳 PO16 . . . . . . .131 C1
Bath La (lower) 🔳
PO16 . . . . .131 C1
Bath Lane Cotts PO16 . . .155 C8
Bath Rd
Bournemouth BH1 . . . . . . .205 A3
Emsworth PO10 . . . . .160 F8
Lymington SO41 . . . . .198 A3
Portsmouth PO4 . . . . .182 F3
Southampton SO19 . . . . . .104 B6
Bath Sq PO1 . . . . .181 F5
Bath St SO14 . . . . .103 A7
Bathing La PO1 . . . . .181 F5
Bathurst Cl PO11 . . . . . . .184 E3
Bathurst Way PO2 . . . . . .157 B2
Batstone Way BH22 . . . . .165 B6
Batten Cl BH23 . . . . .207 D7
Batten Rd SP5 . . . . .46 E8
Battenburg Ave PO2 . . . . .157 F2
Battenburg Rd PO12 . . . .181 C6
Battens Way PO9 . . . . . . .135 F4
Batterley Dro BH21 . . . . . .91 F4
Battery Cl PO12 . . . . .180 E8
Battery Hill
Bishop's Waltham SO22 . . . .83 B8
Winchester SO22 . . . . . . .215 A4
Battery Row PO1 . . . . . . .182 A3
Battle Cl SO31 . . . . .129 A4
Battramsley Cross
SO41 . . . . .173 C1
Baverstock Rd BH12 . . . .204 B8
Baxter Rd SO19 . . . . .104 E5
Bay Cl Southampton SO19 .104 A3
Three Legged Cross BH21 .138 E8
Upton BH16 . . . . .201 B6
Bay Hog La BH15 . . . . . . .202 B2
Bay House Sch PO12 . . . .180 E2
Bay Rd Gosport PO12 . . . .180 F3
Southampton SO19 . . . . . .104 A3
Bay Tree Gdns SO40 . . . .101 F1
Bay Tree Lodge PO14 . . . .179 D7
Bay Tree Way BH23 . . . . .193 D1
Bay Trees SO19 . . . . .104 E6
Bay View BH2 . . . . .204 E2
Baybridge La SO21 . . . . . . .33 C4
Baybridge Rd PO9 . . . . . .136 B5
Bayfields PO5 . . . . .216 B1
Bayly Ave PO16 . . . . .156 D6
Baynton Ho SO41 . . . . . . .197 D4
Bays Ct SO41 . . . . .197 C4
Bays Rd SO41 . . . . .197 C3
Bayswater Ho PO5 . . . . . .216 C1
Baythorn Cl PO2 . . . . .182 D7
Baytree Ho 🔳 SO23 . . . . .215 B6
Bayview Gdns BH2 . . . . . .204 E2
Bayview Mews BH2 . . . . .204 E2
Beach Ave BH25 . . . . .209 F7
Beach Cl BH13 . . . . .214 G8
Beach Dr PO6 . . . . .156 F8
Beach La SO31 . . . . .127 A6
Beach Rd
Emsworth PO10 . . . . .160 E8
Lee-on-t-S PO13 . . . . .179 E2
Poole BH13 . . . . .214 G8
Portsmouth PO5 . . . . .182 D1
Waterlooville PO11 . . . . . .184 E3
Upton BH16 . . . . .201 A6
Beach View BH13 . . . . . . .214 C4
Beachcroft BH13 . . . . . . .204 A3
Beachlands Sta* PO11 . . .184 F2
Beachway PO16 . . . . .156 D6
Beacon Bottom SO31 . . . .129 A6
Beacon Cl Everton SO41 . .196 C2
Locks Heath SO31 . . . . . . .129 A6
Rownhams SO16 . . . . .77 D6
Beacon Ct
Christchurch BH23 . . . . . .208 F7
Fordingbridge SP6 . . . . .69 E3
Beacon Dr BH23 . . . . .208 F7
Beacon Gdns BH18 . . . . . .186 E3
Beacon Hill La
Corfe Mullen BH21 . . . . . . .186 B3
Droxford SO32 . . . . .60 F6
Meonstoke SO32 . . . . .61 C6
Beacon Mews SO30 . . . . .104 D8

Beacon Mount SO31 . . . . .129 A6
Beacon Park Cres BH16 . .201 A8
Beacon Park Rd BH16 . . .201 B7
Beacon Rd
Bournemouth BH2 . . . . . . .204 F2
Broadstone BH18 . . . . .186 E3
Upton BH16 . . . . .201 B7
West End SO30 . . . . .104 D8
Beacon Sq PO10 . . . . .160 F7
Beacon Way
Broadstone BH18 . . . . .186 E3
Locks Heath SO31 . . . . . . .129 A6
Beaconsfield Ave PO6 . . .158 A7
Beaconsfield Rd
Christchurch BH23 . . . . . .207 B7
Fareham PO16 . . . . .155 B8
Poole BH12 . . . . .203 D6
Waterlooville PO7 . . . . . . .134 E8
Bealing Cl SO16 . . . . .79 B4
Beamish Rd BH17 . . . . . . .202 F8
Bear Cross Ave BH11 . . . .188 F6
Bear Cross Rdbt BH11 . . .188 F6
Bear Mus The* GU31 . . . . .40 F3
Bearslane Cl SO40 . . . . . . .76 D1
Bearwood Prim Sch
BH11 . . . . .188 C6
Beasant Cl PO3 . . . . .183 B6
Beatrice Ct 🔳 SO41 . . . . .211 B4
Beatrice Mews 🔳 PO6 . . .157 F7
Beatrice Rd
Portsmouth PO4 . . . . .182 E2
Southampton SO15 . . . . . .102 C7
Beattie Rise SO30 . . . . .81 D2
Beatty Cl
Locks Heath SO31 . . . . . . .129 B4
Ringwood BH24 . . . . .141 C8
Beatty Ho 🔳 PO1 . . . . . . .216 C4
Beatty Rd BH9 . . . . .190 B1
Beaty Ct SO19 . . . . .104 C5
Beatty Sq PO1 . . . .
🔳 Bournemouth BH4 . . . .204 C3
🔳 New Milton BH25 . . . . .195 A3
Beauchamp Ave PO13 . . .155 D1
Beauchamp Pl BH23 . . . . .207 A7
Beauchamps Gdns BH7 . .206 A8
Beaucroft La BH21 . . . . . .163 E5
Beaucroft Rd
Waltham Chase SO32 . . . . .83 E3
Wimborne Minst BH21 . . . .163 E6
Beaucroft Sch BH21 . . . .163 E6
Beaufort Ave PO16 . . . . . .130 F2
Beaufort Cl
Christchurch BH23 . . . . . .208 B7
Lee-on-t-S PO13 . . . . .180 A6
Beaufort Dr
Bishop's Waltham SO22 . . . .83 C8
Waltham Minst BH21 . . . . .163 C5
Beaufort Ho 🔳 BH4 . . . . .204 C2
Beaufort Mews BH21 . . . .163 B4
Beaufort Rd
Bournemouth BH6 . . . . . . .206 D6
Havant PO9 . . . . .135 D2
🔳 Portsmouth PO5 . . . . . .182 D1
Winchester SO23 . . . . . . .215 D4
Beaufoys Ave BH22 . . . . .165 D7
Beaufoys Cl BH22 . . . . . . .165 C7
Beaufoys Ct BH22 . . . . . . .165 C6
Beaulieu Abbey* SO42 . . .148 F2
Beaulieu Ave
Christchurch BH23 . . . . . .206 E7
Havant PO9 . . . . .135 D6
Portchester PO16 . . . . . . .156 A8
Beaulieu Cl
New Milton BH25 . . . . . . .194 E3
Southampton SO16 . . . . . . .78 B5
Winchester SO22 . . . . .1 D1
Beaulieu Ct 🔳 PO8 . . . . .111 F4
Beaulieu Ho 🔳 SO15 . . . .102 F7
Beaulieu Rd BH21 . . . . . . .155 B2
Beaulieu Rd
Beaulieu SO42,SO45 . . . . .149 C6
Bournemouth BH4 . . . . . . .204 B1
Christchurch BH23 . . . . . .206 E7
Dibden Purlieu SO45 . . . . .125 F1
Eastleigh SO50 . . . . .56 A4
Hamble-le-R SO31 . . . . . . .127 F3
Hythe SO45 . . . . .125 F1
Marchwood SO40 . . . . . . .124 C4
Portsmouth PO2 . . . . .157 E1
Beaulieu Road Sta
SO42 . . . . .123 D1
Beaulieu Village Prim Sch
SO42 . . . . .148 F1
Beaumaris Cl SO53 . . . . . .55 A4
Beaumaris Gdns SO45 . . .125 F5
Beaumond Gn 🔳 SO23 . .215 D5
Beaumont Cl
Fareham PO15 . . . . .130 D3
Southampton SO16 . . . . . . .78 E3
🔳 Beaumont Ct PO12 . . . .181 A9
Beaumont Pl SO40 . . . . . .101 A7
Beaumont Rd
Poole BH13 . . . . .214 F7
Totton SO40 . . . . .101 A7
Beaumont Rise PO15 . . . .130 D4
Beauworth Ave SO18 . . . .104 C8
Beaver Dr SO50 . . . . .57 A2
Beaver Ind Est BH23 . . . .208 A7
Beccles Cl BH15 . . . . .201 F2
Becher Rd BH14 . . . . .203 E4
Beck Cl SO31 . . . . .128 E3
Beck St PO1 . . . . .182 B5
Beckenham Terr PO10 . . .137 B4
Beckford La PO17 . . . . . . .109 F2
Beckham La GU32 . . . . . . .40 D4
Beckhampton Rd BH15 . .201 E3

Beckley Copse BH23 . . . .194 A2
Becton La BH25 . . . . .210 B7
Becton Mead BH25 . . . . . .195 B1
Bedale Way BH15 . . . . . . .202 F5
Bedales Sch GU32 . . . . . . .40 E7
Beddow Hall 🔳 PO5 . . . . .216 A2
Bedenham La PO13 . . . . .155 E3
Bedenham Prim Sch
PO13 . . . . .155 D3
Bedfield Ho SO23 . . . . .2 B5
Bedfield La SO23 . . . . .2 B5
Bedford Ave SO19 . . . . . .103 E2
Bedford Cl
Fordingbridge SP6 . . . . .69 F3
Havant PO9 . . . . .160 B8
Hedge End SO30 . . . . .105 D6
Bedford Cres BH7 . . . . . . .206 C7
Bedford Pl SO15 . . . . .102 F6
Bedford Rd GU32 . . . . .40 D3
Bedford Rd N BH12 . . . . .188 C2
Bedford Rd S BH12 . . . . .188 C2
Bedford St Gosport PO12 .181 A7
Portsmouth PO5 . . . . .216 B2
Bedhampton Hill PO9 . . . .135 B1
Bedhampton Hill Rd
PO9 . . . . .135 A1
Bedhampton Ho 🔳 PO1 .216 C4
Bedhampton Rd
Havant PO9 . . . . .135 C2
Portsmouth PO2 . . . . .182 F8
Bedhampton Sta PO9 . . . .135 D1
Bedhampton Way PO9 . . .135 F4
Bedwell Cl SO16 . . . . .77 F6
Beech Ave
Bournemouth BH6 . . . . . . .206 C4
Christchurch BH23 . . . . . .206 D8
Southampton SO18 . . . . . .103 E7
Broadstone BH18 . . . . .186 E4
Chandler's Ford SO53 . . . . .55 D8
Hamble-le-R SO31 . . . . . . .127 E2
Hordle SO41 . . . . .211 D8
Romsey SO51 . . . . .53 C6
Verwood BH31 . . . . .114 C5
Waterlooville PO8 . . . . . . .111 F2
Winchester SO22 . . . . .10 B3
Beech Cnr SO32 . . . . .81 F6
Beech Copse SO22 . . . . . . .1 B1
Beech Cres SO45 . . . . . . .150 A8
Beech Ct
Southampton SO19 . . . . . .103 F3
Wimborne Minst BH21 . . . .163 E4
Beech Gdns SO31 . . . . . . .127 E2
Beech Gr Gosport PO12 . .181 A4
Owslebury SO21 . . . . .33 B4
South Hayling PO11 . . . . . .185 B4
Beech Grange SP5 . . . . .0 F2
Beech Ho SO16 . . . . .78 F1
Beech La BH24 . . . . .139 E2
Beech Rd Ashurst SO40 . .100 B2
Chandler's Ford SO53 . . . . .55 D8
Clanfield PO8 . . . . .88 D5
Fareham PO15 . . . . .130 C6
Hedge End SO30 . . . . .105 D7
Southampton SO15 . . . . . .102 B2
Beech Way PO8 . . . . .112 B5
Beech Wood Cl BH18 . . . .187 A3
Beecham Rd PO1 . . . . . . .182 F7
Beechbank Ave BH17 . . . .186 F1
Beechcroft BH1 . . . . .205 A5
Beechcroft Cl
Chandler's Ford SO53 . . . . .55 D6
Southampton SO15 . . . . . .130 C1
Beechcroft Mews 🔳
BH24 . . . . .141 B8
Beechcroft Rd PO12 . . . . .181 B4
Beechcroft Way SO53 . . . .55 E6
Beechdale Cl SO40 . . . . . .76 D2
Beechdale Wlk SO40 . . . . .76 C2
Beeches La SO43 . . . . . . .122 A3
Beeches Hill SO32 . . . . . . .59 D2
Beeches The
Awbridge SO51 . . . . .26 E5
Bournemouth BH7 . . . . . . .206 A8
Fair Oak SO50 . . . . .57 D1
Waterlooville PO7 . . . . . . .134 F8
West Wellow SO51 . . . . . . .50 D3
Beechwood Ave
Bournemouth BH5 . . . . . . .206 A4
New Milton BH25 . . . . . . .194 F4
Waterlooville PO7 . . . . . . .134 E6
Beechwood Cl
Chandler's Ford SO53 . . . . .30 A1
Warsash SO31 . . . . .152 D10
Beechwood Cres SO53 . . .30 B2
Beechwood Ct
Bournemouth BH4 . . . . . . .204 C2
Liss GU33 . . . . .21 A6
Beechwood Gdns
Bournemouth BH5 . . . . . . .206 A4
Southampton SO18 . . . . . .103 F8
Beechwood Jun Sch
SO18 . . . . .103 F7
Beechwood La 🔳 BH24 . .204 C2
Beechwood Lo 🔳 BH4 . . .204 C2
Beechwood Lodge 🔳
PO16 . . . . .131 B2
Beechwood Rd
Bartley SO40 . . . . .99 A6
Holbury SO45 . . . . .150 C3

Beechwood PO02 continued
Portsmouth PO2 . . . . .157 E4
West Moors BH21 . . . . . . .138 F1
Beechwood Rise SO18 . . . .80 C1
Beechwood Way SO45 . . .125 C2
Beechworth Rd 🔳 PO9 . .136 A1
Beehive Cotts SO16 . . . . .181 B3
Beehive Wlk PO1 . . . . . . .182 A4
Beeston Cl PO1 . . . . .182 E7
Beggar's La SO23 . . . . . . .215 F6
Begonia Rd SO16 . . . . .79 B4
Behrendt Cl PO12 . . . . . . .181 A7
Belben Cl BH12 . . . . .188 D3
Belben Rd BH12 . . . . .188 C2
Belbins SO51 . . . . .27 F4
Belbins Bsns Pk SO51 . . . .28 A3
Belfield Rd BH6 . . . . .206 D4
Belfry Ct SO31 . . . . .129 C3
Belfry Wlk PO14 . . . . .129 C2
Belgrave Cl BH1 . . . . .205 D3
Belgrave Ind Est SO17 . . .79 C2
Belgrave Rd Poole BH15 . .204 A2
Southampton SO17 . . . . . . .79 C2
Belgravia Rd PO2 . . . . . . .157 F1
Bell Cl SO45 . . . . .150 F2
Bell Cres PO7 . . . . .134 E6
Bell Ct PO18 . . . . .161 F7
Bell Davies Rd PO14 . . . .179 B6
Bell Heather Cl BH16 . . . .201 B8
Bell Hill GU32 . . . . .40 E5
Bell Hill Ridge GU32 . . . . .40 E5
Bell Rd PO6 . . . . .157 D8
Bell St Romsey SO51 . . . . .52 E7
Southampton SO14 . . . . . .103 A3
Bellair Ho PO7 . . . . .134 B1
Bellair Rd PO9 . . . . .136 A1
Bellamy Ct SO17 . . . . .79 C2
Belle Vue Cres BH6 . . . . .206 D4
Belle Vue Cres BH6 . . . . .206 D4
Belle Vue Gr 🔳 BH6 . . . .206 F4
Belle Vue La BH24 . . . . . .138 F2
Belle Vue Mans 🔳 BH6 . .206 E3
Belle Vue Rd
Bournemouth BH6 . . . . . . .206 E3
Poole BH14 . . . . .203 C3
Belle Vue Wlk BH22 . . . . .165 E7
Bellemoor Rd SO15 . . . . . .78 D1
Bellemoor Sch (Boys)
SO15 . . . . .78 D2
Bellevue La 🔳 PO10 . . . .137 A6
Bellevue Rd
Eastleigh SO50 . . . . .56 A3
Southampton SO15 . . . . . .103 A3
Bellevue Terr
🔳 Portsmouth PO5 . . . . .216 A1
🔳 Southampton SO14 . . . .103 A6
Bellflower Cl PO14 . . . . . .153 F7
Bellflower Ct 🔳 BH23 . . .208 B8
Bellflower Way
Chandler's Ford SO53 . . . . .54 F7
Titchfield PO15 . . . . .129 F3
Bellinger Ho PO9 . . . . . . .135 C2
Bells Ho PO1 . . . . .163 D6
Bells La PO14 . . . . .129 C7
Belmont Ave BH8 . . . . . . .190 C2
Belmont Cl Horndean PO8 .88 C3
Hythe SO45 . . . . .126 A2
Stubbington PO14 . . . . . . .179 D8
Verwood BH31 . . . . .115 A5
Belmont Gdns PO11 . . . . .185 D1
Belmont Gr PO9 . . . . .135 C2
Belmont Pl PO5 . . . . .216 B1
Belmont Rd
Chandler's Ford SO53 . . . . .55 D6
New Milton BH25 . . . . . . .195 C4
Poole BH14 . . . . .203 A3
Southampton SO17 . . . . . . .79 C1
Belmont St SO15 . . . . . . .102 F6
Belmore Cl PO1 . . . . .182 E7
Belmore Ct SO41 . . . . . . .197 E2
Belmore La
Lymington SO41 . . . . .197 E2
Owslebury SO21 . . . . .33 E4
Upham SO21,SO32 . . . . . . .34 B3
Belmore Rd SO41 . . . . . . .197 D3
Belmour Lo 🔳 BH4 . . . . .204 C2
Belney Ho PO9 . . . . .157 A8
Belney La PO7 . . . . .110 E1
Belstone Rd SO40 . . . . . . .100 E7
Belton Rd SO19 . . . . .104 B5
Belvedere Rd
Bournemouth BH3 . . . . . . .205 A6
Christchurch BH23 . . . . . .207 D6
Hythe SO45 . . . . .126 A2
Belverderre Cl GU32 . . . . .40 F4
Belvidere Ho 🔳 SO14 . . .103 C5
Belvidere Rd SO14 . . . . . .103 C5
Belvidere Terr SO14 . . . . .103 C5
Belvoir Cl PO16 . . . . .155 D8
Belvoir Pk 🔳 BH31 . . . . .204 C2
Bembridge 🔳 SO31 . . . . .127 C6
Bembridge Cl SO16 . . . . . .78 F3
Bembridge Cres PO4 . . . .182 E1
Bembridge Ct PO11 . . . . .185 D1
Bembridge Ho 🔳 PO11 . .185 D1
Bembridge Lodge Flats
PO13 . . . . .179 E2
Bemister Rd BH9 . . . . . . .205 A8
Bemister's La 🔳 SO23 . . .215 E5
Benbow Cl PO8 . . . . .112 C7
Benbow Cres PO13 . . . . . .155 C6
Benbow Gdns SO40 . . . . . .76 C2
Benbow Ho 🔳 PO1 . . . . .182 A5
Benbow Pl 🔳 PO1 . . . . . .182 A5
Bengal Rd BH9 . . . .
Bembridge Ave BH11 . . . .188 F5
Bencraft Cl SO16 . . . . .79 B5

Bendigo Rd BH23 . . . . . . .206 E8
Benedict Cl SO31 . . . . .53 C7
Benedict Way PO16 . . . . .132 E1
Beneficial St 🔳 PO1 . . . .182 A5
Benellen Ave SO16 . . . . . .204 C4
Benellen Gdns BH4 . . . . .204 D4
Benellen Rd BH4 . . . . . . .204 C4
Benellen Twrs 🔳 BH4 . . .204 C4
Benga! Rd BH9 . . . . .204 E8
Benger's La SO51 . . . . .5 E2
Benham Dr 🔳 PO3 . . . . . .157 F4
Benham Gr PO16 . . . . . . .156 D6
Benhams Farm Cl 🔳
SO18 . . . . .80 A1
Benhams Rd SO18 . . . . . . .80 A2
Benjamin Ct BH23 . . . . . .206 F7
Benjamin Rd BH15 . . . . . .201 D2
Benmoor Rd PO17 . . . . . .202 A8
Benmore Cl BH25 . . . . . . .195 C2
Benmore Gdns SO18 . . . . .55 B8
Benmore Rd BH9 . . . . . . .190 A1
Bennett Cl SO45 . . . . .47 D6
Bennett Ho 🔳 BH4 . . . . .204 C4
Bennett Rd BH8 . . . . .205 C6
Bennetts La BH24 . . . . . . .143 C2
Bennion Rd BH10 . . . . . . .189 C3
Benny Hill Cl SO40 . . . . . . .55 F3
Benridge Cl BH18 . . . . . . .187 A3
Benson Cl PO23 . . . . .169 B1
Benson Rd Poole BH17 . . .202 D7
Southampton SO15 . . . . . .102 B8
Bent La PO7 . . . . .110 A7
Bentham Ct SO16 . . . . . . .79 A4
Bentham Rd PO12 . . . . . .181 B4
Bentham Way SO31 . . . . .128 D8
Bentley Cl BH31 . . . . .114 C5
Bentley Ct Horndean PO8 .112 C8
Knights Worthy SO23 . . . . . .2 B6
Bentley Cres PO16 . . . . . .130 F2
Bentley Ct Havant PO9 . . .136 B5
🔳 Southampton SO17 . . . .79 A1
Bentley Gn SO18 . . . . . . .104 C8
Bentley Rd BH9 . . . . .189 F3
Bentley Way SO41 . . . . . .197 B6
Bentworth Cl PO9 . . . . . . .135 D4
Benvenue Cl BH14 . . . . . .203 D4
Bepton Down GU31 . . . . . .41 A3
Berber Cl PO15 . . . . .129 C7
Bercote Cl SO22 . . . . .1 B5
Bere Cl
Chandler's Ford SO53 . . . . .55 A8
Poole BH17 . . . . .187 D2
Winchester SO22 . . . . . . .215 B8
Bere Farm La PO17 . . . . .131 F8
Bere Rd PO7 . . . . .110 F4
Beresford Cl
Chandler's Ford SO53 . . . . .55 D5
Waterlooville PO7 . . . . . . .134 E6
Beresford Gdns
Chandler's Ford SO53 . . . . .55 D5
Christchurch BH23 . . . . . .207 E6
Beresford Rd
Bournemouth BH6 . . . . . . .206 B4
Chandler's Ford SO53 . . . . .55 D5
Lymington SO41 . . . . .197 C4
Poole BH12 . . . . .203 D6
Portsmouth PO2 . . . . .157 E1
Stubbington PO14 . . . . . . .179 D8
Bereweeke Ave SO22 . . . .215 C8
Bereweeke Cl SO22 . . . . .215 C7
Bereweeke Ho SO22 . . . . .215 C7
Bereweeke Way SO22 . . .215 C8
Bergen Cres SO30 . . . . . .105 C5
Berkeley Cl
Southampton SO15 . . . . . .102 E7
Verwood BH31 . . . . .179 B7
Berkeley Ct PO13 . . . . . . .179 E2
Berkeley Gdns SO30 . . . . .105 C5
Berkeley Rd
Bournemouth BH3 . . . . . . .204 E7
Southampton SO15 . . . . . .102 F6
Berkeley Sq PO9 . . . . . . .136 B1
Berkeley The PO5 . . . . . . .182 E1
Berkley Ave BH22 . . . . . . .165 D2
Berkley Manor 🔳 PO1 . . .216 D3
Berkshire Cl PO1 . . . . . . .216 D3
Bermuda Ct
🔳 Christchurch BH23 . . . .209 A7
🔳 Southampton SO17 . . . .79 A1
Bermuda Ho 🔳 PO4 . . . .132 F2
Bernard Ave PO6 . . . . . . .158 A8
Bernard Powell Ho PO9 . .136 A1
Bernard St SO14 . . . . . . .103 A3
Bernards Cl BH23 . . . . . . .206 E7
Berne Ct 🔳 BH1 . . . . . . .205 A3
Berney Rd PO4 . . . . .183 C4
Bernie Tunstall Pl SO50 . .56 B3
Bernina Ave PO7 . . . . . . .111 C2
Bernina Cl PO7 . . . . .111 C2
Bernwood Gr SO45 . . . . . .177 F7
Berrans Ave BH11 . . . . . .189 B6
Berry Cl SO30 . . . . .105 C8
Berry Ho 🔳 PO1 . . . . . . .182 A4
Berrydown Rd PO9 . . . . . .135 C2
Berryfield Rd SO41 . . . . . .196 A2
Berrylands GU33 . . . . .21 A7

Berrywood Bsns Village
SO30 ....81 B3
Berrywood Gdns SO30 ...105 B8
Berrywood Prim Sch
SO30 ....81 D1
Berthon Ho SO51 ....52 E6
Bertie Rd PO4 ....183 B4
Bertram Rd BH25 ....195 C4
Berwick Rd BH3 ....204 E6
Berwyn Wlk PO14 ....154 E8
Beryl Ave PO12 ....180 F8
Beryton Cl PO12 ....181 A7
Beryton Rd PO12 ....181 A7
Besomer Dro SP5 ....47 F5
Bessborough Rd BH13 ...214 E7
Bessemer Cl BH31 ....115 C4
Beswick Ave BH10 ....189 D2
Bethany Ct BH12 ....204 A7
Bethany Ho BH1 ....205 D5
Bethany Jun CE Sch
BH1 ....205 D5
Bethia Cl BH8 ....205 D6
Bethia Rd BH8 ....205 D6
Betsy Cl BH23 ....169 B1
Betsy La BH23 ....169 B1
Betteridge Dr SO16 ....77 D6
Bettesworth Rd PO1 ....182 C7
Bettiscombe Cl BH17 ....187 E2
Betula Cl PO7 ....135 A6
Beulah Rd SO16 ....78 A1
Bevan Cl SO19 ....103 E1
Bevan Rd PO8 ....111 F5
Beverley Cl SO31 ....129 C4
Beverley Gdns
Bournemouth BH10 ....189 D3
Bursledon SO31 ....104 E1
Romsey SO51 ....28 B1
Swanmore SO32 ....84 B5
Beverley Gr PO6 ....134 F1
Beverley Grange 50
BH4 ....204 C3
Beverley Hts SO18 ....79 F3
Beverley Rd Hythe SO45 ..149 F8
Stubbington PO14 ....179 C6
Beverly Cl PO13 ....155 D2
Beverston Ho 4 PO6 ....133 A1
Beverston Rd PO6 ....133 A1
Bevis Cl Blackfield SO45 ...150 F2
Warsash SO31 ....152 D10
Bevis Rd Gosport PO12 .....181 B6
Portsmouth PO2 ....183 C7
Bevis Rd N PO2 ....157 D1
Bevis Rd PO2 ....157 D1
Bevois Gdns SO14 ....103 A7
Bevois Hill SO14 ....103 B8
Bevois Mans 7 SO14 ....103 B8
Bevois Mews 4 SO14 ......103 A7
Bevois Town Prim Sch
SO14 ....103 A7
Bevois Valley Rd SO14 .....103 A7
Bexington Cl BH11 ....188 E3
Beyne Rd SO22 ....10 B3
Bickerley Gdns BH24 ....140 F6
Bickerley Rd BH24 ....140 F6
Bickerley Terr BH24 ....140 F7
Bickleigh Ho 6 BH17 ....204 B4
Bicknell Cl 3 BH4 ....204 C4
Bicknell Sch BH7 ....206 A7
Bickton Ash SP6 ....94 A6
Bickton Wlk PO9 ....135 D6
Bicton Rd BH11 ....189 D3
Bidbury Inf Sch PO9 ....135 C3
Bidbury Jun Sch PO9 ....135 D2
Bidbury La PO9 ....135 C1
Biddenfield La SO32,
PO17 ....107 D5
Biddlecombe Cl PO13 ......180 C8
Biddlesgate Ct 5 SO14 ...102 F3
Bideford Cl SO16 ....77 E1
Big Tree Cotts SO32 ....85 C6
Biggin Wlk PO14 ....154 E8
Bigpath Farm Cotts SO32 .59 B6
Bilberry Cl SO31 ....128 F2
Bilberry Cl 11 SO22 ....215 D6
Bilberry Dr SO40 ....101 E2
Bill Stillwell Ct 2 PO7 ......157 C2
Billett Ave PO7 ....111 F1
Billing Cl PO4 ....183 B3
Billington Gdns SO30 ....81 D1
Billington PI SO41 ....197 D2
Billy Lawn Ave PO9 ....135 F4
Bilton Bsns Pk PO3 ....158 C2
Bilton Way PO3 ....158 C2
Bindon Cl Poole BH12 ......203 E7
Southampton SO16 ....78 A2
Bindon Ct 13 SO18 ....203 E8
Bindon Rd SO16 ....78 A2
Bingham Ave BH14 ....214 D8
Bingham Cl
Christchurch BH23 ....207 E7
Verwood BH31 ....115 B4
Bingham Dr
Lymington SO41 ....197 E3
Verwood BH31 ....115 A4
Bingham Rd
Bournemouth BH9 ....205 A7
Christchurch BH23 ....207 E7
Verwood BH31 ....115 A4
Binnacle Way PO6 ....157 B8
Binness Way PO6 ....158 E2
Binnie Rd BH12 ....203 E6
Binsey Cl SO16 ....101 E8
Binstead Cl SO16 ....79 C5
Birch Ave Beckley BH25 ...194 D5
Burton BH23 ....192 C3

Birch Ave continued
Ferndown BH22 ....165 F1
Birch Cl
Colden Common SO21 ....56 F8
Corfe Mullen BH21 ....186 D6
Liss GU33 ....21 A4
Poole BH14 ....203 E3
Romsey SO51 ....53 D6
Southampton SO16 ....78 A2
St Leonards BH24 ....139 D3
Waterlooville PO8 ....111 E3
Birch Copse BH17 ....202 A8
Birch Cl Lymington SO41 ..197 B2
3 Winchester SO22 ....215 A4
Birch Dale SO45 ....128 B2
Birch Dr
Bournemouth BH8 ....191 A2
Gosport PO13 ....155 C4
Birch Gr Eastleigh SO50 ....56 A6
Old Milton BH25 ....195 A1
West Moors BH22 ....138 D2
Birch Hill Cotts PO17 ....109 A3
Birch Ho SO16 ....78 F7
Birch Rd Chilworth SO16 ....79 A8
Hedge End SO30 ....105 D7
Southampton SO16 ....78 A3
St Leonards BH24 ....140 B4
Birch Tree Cl PO10 ....136 F4
Birch Tree Dr PO10 ....136 F4
Birch Wlk BH22 ....165 F3
Birch Way SO19 ....104 E5
Birchdale Cl SO31 ....152 D10
Birchdale Rd BH21 ....163 D5
Birchen Cl SO31 ....129 C4
Birchen Rd SO31 ....129 C4
Birches Cl The SO52 ....54 F3
Birches The SO18 ....104 B8
Birchglade SO40 ....76 C2
Birchlands SO40 ....100 D5
Birchmore Cl PO13 ....155 C2
Birchwood Cl BH23 ....208 E8
Birchwood Ct 7 SO18 ......103 E8
Birchwood Dr SP6 ....93 A5
Birchwood Gdns SO30 .....105 C8
Birchwood Lodge 7
PO16 ....131 B2
Birchwood Mews BH14 ....203 D3
Birchwood Rd
Poole BH14 ....203 D3
Upton BH16 ....201 B6
Birchy Hill SO41 ....172 C1
Bird Field SO53 ....54 F7
Bird's Hill Rd BH15 ....202 E3
Birdham Rd PO11 ....185 E2
Birdip Cl PO8 ....112 A6
Birdlip Rd PO8 ....112 A6
Birds Hill Gdns 1 BH15 ...202 E3
Birdwood Gr PO16 ....155 F8
Birinus Rd SO23 ....215 E7
Birkdale Ave BH14 ....203 A7
Birkdale Cl BH18 ....187 A5
Birkdale Rd BH18 ....187 A5
Birmingham Ct 7 PO13 ...180 D5
Biscay Cl PO14 ....179 B8
Bishearne Gdns GU33 ......20 E5
Bishop Cl BH12 ....204 C7
Bishop of Winchester Comp
Sch The BH8 ....190 D1
Bishop Rd BH9 ....205 A8
Bishop St PO1 ....182 A5
Bishop's La SO32 ....83 C7
Bishop's Waltham Inf Sch
SO32 ....83 D8
Bishop's Waltham Pal*
SO32 ....84 D2
Bishops Cl
Bournemouth BH7 ....205 F4
Totton SO40 ....100 E8
Bishops Cres SO19 ....103 F4
Bishops Ct
Bishopstoke SO50 ....56 D5
Broadstone BH18 ....187 A3
Bishops Gate PO14 ....129 D3
Bishops La SO32 ....84 B1
Bishops Rd SO19 ....103 E4
Bishopsfield Rd PO14 ....154 E8
Bishopstoke La SO50 ....56 C3
Bishopstoke Manor SO50 ..56 C3
Bishopstoke Rd
Eastleigh SO50 ....56 C3
Havant PO9 ....135 E5
Bisley Ct SO19 ....104 B3
Bisterne Cl BH24 ....143 E2
Bittern Cl PO12 ....181 B8
Bitterne CE Inf Sch
SO19 ....103 F6
Bitterne Cl PO9 ....135 F6
Bitterne Cres SO19 ....104 A6
Bitterne Manor Ho
SO18 ....103 C7
Bitterne Manor Prim Sch
SO18 ....103 D7
Bitterne Park Inf Sch
SO17 ....79 D2
Bitterne Park Jun Sch
SO17 ....79 D2
Bitterne Park Sch SO18 ...79 E2
Bitterne Park Triangle
SO18 ....79 D1
Bitterne Rd SO18 ....104 A6
Bitterne Rd E SO18 ....104 C7
Bitterne Rd W SO18 ....103 E7

Bitterne Sta SO18 ....103 D7
Bitterne Way
Lymington SO41 ....197 D2
Southampton SO19 ....103 F6
Verwood BH31 ....115 A5
Bitumen Rd SO45 ....151 B4
Black Hill BH31 ....115 A6
Black Hill Rd SO43,SO51 ...74 E7
Black La Bransgore BH23 ..169 E3
Redlynch SP5 ....48 B4
Black Moor Rd BH31 ....115 C4
Black Swan Bldgs 16
SO22 ....215 D6
Blackberry Cl PO8 ....88 D4
Blackberry Dr SO50 ....57 B1
Blackberry La PO13 ....207 F6
Blackberry Terr SO14 ....103 B7
Blackbird Cl
Broadstone BH17 ....201 E8
Waterlooville PO8 ....111 F4
Blackbird Rd SO50 ....55 D2
Blackbird Way
Bransgore BH23 ....193 C8
Lee-on-t-S PO13 ....179 F4
Blackbrook Bsns Pk
PO15 ....130 E1
Blackbrook House Dr
PO14 ....130 E1
Blackbrook Park Ave
PO15 ....130 E1
Blackbrook Rd PO15 ....130 D2
Blackburn Ct 5 PO13 ......180 D5
Blackburn Rd BH12 ....203 B6
Blackbush Rd SO41 ....211 B5
Blackbushe Cl SO16 ....77 F5
Blackcap PO14 ....125 D2
Blackdown Cres PO9 ....135 F3
Blackfield Inf Sch SO45 ...150 E1
Blackfield Jun Sch
SO45 ....150 E1
Blackfield La BH22 ....138 E3
Blackfield Rd
Blackfield SO45 ....150 F2
Bournemouth BH8 ....190 D3
Blackfriars Cl 3 PO5 ....216 C2
Blackfriars Rd PO5 ....216 C3
Blackhorse La SO32 ....83 F1
Blackhouse La
North Boarhunt PO17 ....132 A8
Soberton PO17 ....109 A1
Blackmoor Wlk 2 PO9 ......136 B5
Blackmore La GU32 ....18 F3
Blacksmith Cl BH23 ....186 D5
Blackthorn Cl
Braishfield SO51 ....28 D6
Lymington SO41 ....197 B2
Southampton SO19 ....103 F5
Blackthorn Dr
Gosport PO12 ....156 A1
South Hayling PO11 ....185 C3
Blackthorn Rd
South Hayling PO11 ....185 C2
Southampton SO19 ....103 F5
Blackthorn Terr PO1 ....182 A6
Blackthorn Way
New Milton BH25 ....195 D4
Waterlooville PO8 ....111 B5
Blackthorn Wlk PO7 ....112 C1
Blackwater BH21 ....191 D4
Blackwater Cl
Alderholt SP6 ....92 E5
7 Cosham PO6 ....157 D8
Blackwater Dr
Oakley BH21 ....187 D7
Totton SO40 ....76 D1
Blackwater Gr SP6 ....92 E5
Blackwood La BH24 ....76 B1
Blackwood Ho 15 PO1 .....182 D7
Bladon Cl PO9 ....136 C3
Bladon Rd SO16 ....78 C2
Blair Ave BH14 ....203 C4
Blake Ave PO11 ....194 E3
Blake Cl SO16 ....77 D5
Blake Ct 6 PO12 ....181 B5
Blake Dene Rd BH14 ....203 B1
Blake Hill Ave BH14 ....203 C1
Blake Hill Cres BH14 ....203 C1
Blake Ho 17 PO1 ....182 A4
Blake Rd Cosham PO6 ......134 C1
Gosport PO12 ....181 C6
Portsmouth PO1 ....181 F8
Blakemere Cres PO6 ....133 D1
Blakeney Rd SO16 ....77 D2
Blakesley La PO13 ....158 C4
Blanchard Rd SO32 ....83 B8
Blandford Cl BH15 ....201 F2
Blandford Ct 2 SO41 ....211 D5
Blandford Ho SO16 ....77 F1
Blandford Rd
Coombe Bissett SP5 ....23 D7
Corfe Mullen BH21 ....186 D8
Hamworthy BH16 ....201 D4
Pamphill BH21 ....162 D7
Blandford Rd N
Upton BH16 ....201 B7
Upton BH16 ....201 B8
Blaney Way PO12 ....186 C6
Blankney Cl PO14 ....179 B7
Blann Cl SO16 ....77 C5
Blashford Lakes Study Ctr
BH24 ....124 A4
Blaven Wlk 4 PO14 ....154 E8
Bleaklow Cl SO16 ....101 F8
Blechynden Terr SO15 .....102 E5
Blencowe Dr PO9 ....54 F5
Blendworth Cres PO9 ....135 F3

Blendworth Ho 2 PO1 .....216 C4
Blendworth La
Blendworth PO8 ....112 E7
Southampton SO18 ....104 C7
Blendworth Rd 11 PO4 .....183 B5
Blenheim 3 BH13 ....204 B3
Blenheim Ave SO17 ....79 A1
Blenheim Cl
Chandler's Ford SO53 ....54 F4
Totton SO40 ....100 E6
Blenheim Cres SO41 ....195 F4
Blenheim Ct
58 Bournemouth BH4 ....204 C3
Christchurch BH23 ....207 A8
Portsmouth PO4 ....183 A3
Southampton SO17 ....79 B2
Blenheim Dr BH23 ....208 B6
Blenheim Gdns
Gosport PO12 ....181 B9
Havant PO9 ....136 C2
Hythe SO45 ....125 D2
Southampton SO17 ....79 B2
Blenheim Ho
Eastleigh SO50 ....56 B2
Romsey SO51 ....53 B7
Blenheim Mews 8 BH4 ....204 C4
Blenheim Rd
Eastleigh SO50 ....56 A2
Waterlooville PO8 ....112 A5
Blenheim Barn PO17 ....183 B6
Bleriot Cres PO15 ....129 F6
Blighmont Ave SO15 ....102 B6
Blighmont Cres SO15 ....102 B6
Blind La Curdridge SO32 ...82 E2
Horton Heath SO30 ....81 C5
Ibsley SP6 ....94 C1
Wickham PO17 ....107 F5
Wimborne Minst BH21 ......163 B5
Bliss Cl PO7 ....134 A6
Blissford Cl PO9 ....136 B5
Blissford Cross SP6 ....94 E8
Blissford Hill SP6 ....94 E7
Blissford Rd SP6 ....94 E8
Bloomfield Ave BH9 ....189 F2
Bloomfield PI BH9 ....189 F2
Bloomsbury Wlk SO41 .....103 E2
Blossom Cl SO19 ....105 E6
Blossom Sq PO1 ....182 A6
Blount Rd PO1 ....182 B3
Bloxworth Rd PO12 ....181 A6
Blue Anchor La 10 SO14 ..102 F3
Blue Cedars La GU32 ....18 F3
Bluebell Cl
Christchurch BH23 ....208 B8
Waterlooville PO7 ....135 A6
Bluebell Copse SO31 ....128 F2
Bluebell La BH17 ....186 F1
Bluebell Rd SO16 ....79 C4
Bluebell Way PO15 ....129 D8
Blueprint Portfield Rd
PO3 ....158 A2
Bluestar Gdns SO30 ....81 C2
Bluevalley Mews 3 SP6 ....69 F1
Bluff The BH10 ....189 F4
Blundell La SO31 ....105 C1
Blyth Cl
Christchurch BH23 ....191 D4
Southampton SO16 ....77 D2
Blyth Mews 4 SO15 ....102 E6
Blythe Rd BH21 ....186 D6
Blythswood Ct BH25 ....209 F7
Boakes PI SO40 ....100 C2
Boardwalk The PO1 ....157 B7
Boardwalk Way SO40 ......102 A3
Boarhunt Cl PO1 ....216 C3
Boarhunt Rd
Boarhunt PO17 ....132 A6
Fareham PO17 ....131 E3
Boatyard Ind Est The
PO16 ....155 A8
Bob Hann Cl BH12 ....203 D5
Bockhampton Rd BH23 ...192 E6
Bodley Rd BH23 ....214 F7
Bodmin Rd
Bishopstoke SO50 ....56 E2
Portchester PO6 ....157 A8
Bodorgan Rd PO2 ....157 A8
Bodowen Cl BH23 ....192 D3
Bodowen Rd BH23 ....192 D3
Bodycoats Rd SO53 ....55 D5
Bognor Rd BH18 ....186 F4
Bohemia La SP5,SP6 ....47 F3
Boiler Rd Fawley SO45 .....151 E1
Bokerley Junc SP5 ....42 A4
Bolde Cl PO13 ....181 B2
Boldens Rd PO12 ....181 B2
Bolderwood Arboretum
Ornamental Dr* BH24,
SO43 ....120 C2
Bolderwood Cl SO50 ....56 F2
Bolderwood Deer
Sanctuary* SO43 ....120 A4
Boldre Cl
Bournemouth BH10 ....189 E4
Southampton SO15 ....78 C1
Boldre La SO41 ....197 B8
Boldrewood Rd SO16 ....78 E4
Boleyn Cres BH9 ....190 D4
Bolhinton Ave SO41 ....101 D1
Bolton Cl BH6 ....206 F3
Bolton Ct BH23 ....166 A6
Bolton Cr 3 BH6 ....206 F3
Bolton Dr PO12 ....181 C8
Bolton La BH6 ....206 F3

Boltons The
Milford on S SO41 ....211 D4
Waterlooville PO7 ....134 E3
Bonchurch Cl SO16 ....79 C5
Bonchurch Rd PO4 ....183 A5
Bond Ave BH22 ....138 D4
Bond Cl SO41 ....172 B3
Bond Rd Poole BH15 ....202 F5
Southampton SO18 ....79 E1
Bond St SO14 ....103 C6
Bondfields Cres PO9 ....135 F6
Bones La GU31 ....65 D5
Bonfire Cnr PO1 ....182 A6
Bonham Rd BH9 ....204 F7
Boniface Cl SO40 ....100 D8
Boniface Cres SO16 ....77 E4
Bonington Cl BH23 ....207 E8
Bonner Cotts SP5 ....4 E7
Boothby Cl SO40 ....101 A6
Bordean La GU32 ....39 C6
Borden La GU32 ....54 A4
Border Cl GU33 ....21 B1
Border Dr BH16 ....201 C5
Border Rd BH16 ....201 C5
Bordon Rd PO9 ....135 F5
Boreham Rd BH6 ....206 D5
Borland Ho PO17 ....108 F1
Borough Gr GU32 ....40 E3
Borough Hill GU32 ....40 E3
Borough Rd GU32 ....40 D2
Borough The SP5 ....46 F8
Borrowdale Rd SO16 ....77 E1
Borthwick Rd BH1 ....205 E5
Boscobel Rd GU32 ....40 F3
Boscombe Cliff Rd BH5 ....205 F3
Boscombe Grove Rd
BH1 ....205 D5
Boscombe Overcliff Dr
BH5 ....205 D3
Boscombe Spa Rd BH5 ....205 A3
Bosham Rd PO12 ....182 F8
Bosham Wlk PO13 ....155 B2
Bosley Cl BH23 ....191 E2
Bosley Way PO13 ....191 E2
Bossley Ct SO19 ....106 D1
Bossington Cl SO16 ....77 F5
Bosmere Jun Sch PO9 .....159 F8
Bosmere Rd PO11 ....185 E1
Bossington Cl SO53 ....55 D7
Boston Ct SO53 ....55 D7
Boston Lo 51 BH4 ....204 C3
Boston Rd PO6 ....133 E1
Bosuns Cl PO16 ....157 F7
Bosuns Ct PO16 ....155 F6
Bosville SO50 ....56 A6
Boswell Cl Botley SO30 ....106 C6
Southampton SO19 ....104 C6
Bosworth Mews BH9 ....190 A4
Botany Bay Rd SO19 ....104 A3
Botany Ho PO7 ....129 D8
Botley CE Prim Sch
SO30 ....106 A7
Botley Dr PO9 ....135 C3
Botley Gdns SO19 ....104 E3
Botley Hill SO30 ....106 B7
Botley Mill Craft & Bsns Ctr
SO30 ....106 B7
Botley Rd
Bishop's Waltham SO32 ......83 B6
Curdridge SO32 ....82 F2
Fair Oak SO50 ....57 D1
Hedge End SO30 ....81 B1
Horton Heath SO50 ....81 C7
North Baddesley SO52 ....54 B4
Romsey SO51,SO52 ....53 D6
Southampton SO19 ....104 D3
Swanwick SO31 ....129 B7
Botley Sta SO30 ....106 C7
Bottings Est SO30 ....106 B7
Bottom La
West Wellow SO51 ....50 D4
West Wellow SO51 ....50 E4
Boughton Ct PO3 ....158 C4
Boulnois Ave BH14 ....203 E3
Boulou Cotts SO43 ....121 D5
Boulter La PO17 ....133 A7
Boulton Rd PO5 ....216 D1
Bound La PO11 ....185 A2
Boundary Acre SO31 ....105 B4
Boundary Cl SO15 ....101 F7
Boundary Dr BH21 ....163 D6
Boundary La PO4 ....183 C6
Boundary Oak Prep Sch
PO17 ....131 C5
Boundary Rd
Bournemouth BH10 ....189 D11
Bursledon SO31 ....127 F8
Boundary Rdbt BH3,
BH10 ....189 E4
Boundary Way
Bournemouth BH10 ....189 F4
Havant PO9 ....136 C2
Boundary Wlk 13 PO17 ...130 E7
Boundstone SO45 ....125 F3
Boundway SO41 ....171 E1
Bountys La BH12 ....203 E5
Bourne Ave
Bournemouth BH2 ....204 E3
Southampton SO15 ....78 C1
Bourne Ct
Bournemouth BH2 ....204 D3
Otterbourne SO21 ....31 C4
Waterlooville PO8 ....112 B6
West Wellow SO51 ....50 D3
Bourne Com Coll PO10 ...132 F5
Bourne Cotts SO41 ....44 E1
Bourne Ct
1 Bournemouth BH2 ....204 F3
Wimborne Minst BH21 ......163 D5

Bourne Fields S021 ....32 B7
Bourne La Bartley S040 ....99 D6
 Twyford S032 ....32 B6
Bourne Pines **4** BH2 ....204 F4
Bourne Rd Bartley S040 ....99 C6
 Cosham PO6 ....157 B8
 Southampton S015 ....102 D5
Bourne River Ct **9** BH4 .204 D4
Bourne Valley Bsns Pk
 BH12 ....204 A5
Bourne Valley Rd BH12 ....204 A5
Bourne View Cl PO10 ....137 D2
Bournemouth & Poole Coll
 (Constitution Hill Campus)
 The BH14 ....202 F5
Bournemouth & Poole Coll
 (North Road Campus) The
 BH14 ....202 F4
Bournemouth & Poole Coll
 Annexe The BH1 ....205 A3
Bournemouth & Poole Coll
 The BH1 ....205 B3
Bournemouth Ave PO12 ...181 A9
Bournemouth Aviation Mus*
 BH23 ....191 A8
Bournemouth Central Bsns
 Pk BH1 ....205 C5
Bournemouth Ho
 2 Bournemouth BH1 ...205 B3
 7 Havant PO9 ....136 A5
Bournemouth Int Ctr*
 BH2 ....204 F2
Bournemouth International
 Airport BH23 ....190 E8
Bournemouth Learning
 Support Centre PRU
 BH10 ....189 D1
Bournemouth Meml Homes
 BH8 ....190 F1
Bournemouth Nuffield
 Dervent Suite BH7 ....191 B1
Bournemouth Nuffield Hospl
 The BH8 ....205 A5
Bournemouth Rd
 Chandler's Ford S053 ....55 C4
 Lyndhurst S043 ....121 E5
 Poole BH14 ....203 D4
Bournemouth Sch for Girls
 BH8 ....190 C2
Bournemouth Sta BH8 .....205 B4
Bournemouth Station Rdbt
 BH8 ....205 B4
Bournemouth Univ
 (Lansdowne Campus)
 BH1 ....205 B3
Bournemouth Univ (Talbot
 Campus) BH12 ....204 C8
Bournemouth West Rdbt
 BH2 ....204 D3
Bournewood Dr BH4 ....204 C4
Bourton Gdns BH7 ....206 B8
Bouverie Cl **7** BH25 ....195 A1
Boveridge Gdns BH9 ......190 B4
Bovington Cl BH17 ....187 F1
Bowater Cl S040 ....76 C1
Bowater Way S040 ....76 C1
Bowcombe S031 ....127 C7
Bowden Ho **8** S017 .....79 C2
Bowden La S017 ....79 C2
Bowden Rd BH12 ....188 C2
Bowen La GU31 ....40 F3
Bower Cl Holbury S045 ...150 C3
 Southampton S019 ......103 F1
Bower Rd BH8 ....205 D8
Bowers Cl PO8 ....112 A4
Bowers Hill SP5 ....47 E7
Bowerwood Cotts SP6 .....93 C8
Bowerwood Rd SP6 ....93 D8
Bowes Hill PO9 ....113 C3
Bowes-Lyon Ct PO8 ....112 B7
Bowland Rise
 Chandler's Ford S053 ....55 A7
 New Milton BH25 ....195 C2
Bowland Way S045 ....177 E7
Bowler Ave PO1 ....182 F6
Bowler Ct PO1 ....182 F6
Bowman Ct S019 ....104 B3
Box Cl BH17 ....202 B7
Boxgrove Ho PO1 ....216 C4
Boxwood Cl
 Porchester PO16 ....132 B1
 Waterlooville PO7 ....134 E6
Boyatt Cres S050 ....56 A8
Boyatt La S050 ....56 A7
Boyatt Wood Sch Ctr
 S050 ....56 C5
Boyd Cl PO14 ....179 B6
Boyd Rd Gosport PO13 ...155 B4
 Poole BH12 ....203 F6
Boyes La S021 ....32 A1
Boyle Cres PO7 ....134 D5
Boyne Mead Rd S023 ....2 C7
Boyne Rise S023 ....2 B8
Boynton Cl S053 ....55 B8
Brabant Cl PO15 ....129 B7
Brabazon Dr BH23 ....208 B7
Brabazon Rd
 Locks Heath PO15 ....129 D5
 Merley BH21 ....163 F1
Brabourne Ave BH22 ......165 C4
Bracken Cl
 Lee-on-t-S PO13 ....180 A6
 North Baddesley S052 ....54 A3
 St Leonards BH24 ....139 D4
Bracken Cres S050 ....56 F2
Bracken Ct **10** BH4 ....204 D4
Bracken Glen BH15 ....202 E5

Bracken Hall S016 ....79 B8
Bracken Heath **8** PO7 .112 B1
Bracken La S016 ....78 A1
Bracken Lodge **3** BH6 .206 F4
Bracken Pl S016 ....79 A7
Bracken Rd
 Bournemouth BH6 ....206 C4
 Ferndown BH22 ....165 B7
 North Baddesley S052 ....54 A3
 Petersfield GU31 ....41 C2
Bracken Way BH23 ....194 B1
Brackendale Ct BH21 .....138 E8
Brackendale Rd BH8 ......205 D8
Brackenhill S031 ....204 A1
Brackenhill Rd BH21 ......164 A7
Brackens The
 Hythe S045 ....125 D3
 Locks Heath S031 ....129 B2
Brackens Way
 Lymington S041 ....197 F2
 2 Poole BH15 ....214 F8
Brackenway Rd S053 ......55 C8
Bracklesham Cl S019 .....103 F3
Bracklesham Pl BH25 ....209 F7
Bracklesham Rd
 Gosport PO13 ....180 D8
 South Hayling PO11 .....185 F2
Brackley Ave S050 ....57 B3
Brackley Cl BH23 ....191 A8
Brackley Way S040 ....100 D8
Bradburne Rd BH2 ....204 E3
Bradbury Ho BH22 ....165 D7
Bradford Ct **8** PO13 ...180 C6
Bradford Junc PO5 ....216 C2
Bradford Rd
 Bournemouth BH9 ....190 C4
 Portsmouth PO5 ....216 C2
Brading Ave
 Gosport PO13 ....155 C2
 Portsmouth PO4 ....183 A2
Brading Cl S016 ....79 C5
Bradley Cl **10** PO9 .....136 B6
Bradley Gn S016 ....78 B4
Bradley Peak S022 ....215 A7
Bradley Rd S022 ....1 C4
Bradly Rd PO15 ....130 C1
Bradpole Rd BH8 ....190 E1
Bradshaw Cl S050 ....57 E2
Bradstock Cl BH12 ....203 F8
Braehead S045 ....125 F2
Braemar Ave
 Bournemouth BH6 ....207 A4
 Cosham PO6 ....158 B7
Braemar Cl
 Bournemouth BH6 ....207 A4
 Fareham PO15 ....130 E3
Braemar Dr BH23 ....193 F1
Braemar Rd S053 ....155 C2
Braemore Cl S022 ....215 A5
Braeside Bsns Pk BH15 ..202 B4
Braeside Cl
 Southampton S019 ......103 E5
 Winchester S022 ....10 B4
Braeside Cres S019 ....103 E5
Braeside Rd
 Southampton S019 ......103 E5
 St Leonards BH24 ....139 E3
 West Moors BH22 ....138 E3
Braggers La BH23 ....169 B4
Braidley Rd BH2 ....204 E4
Brailswood Rd BH15 .....202 E4
Braintree Rd PO6 ....133 D1
Braishfield Cl S016 ....77 F1
Braishfield Gdns BH8 ....190 D2
Braishfield Prim Sch
 S051 ....28 D6
Braishfield Rd
 Havant PO9 ....136 A4
 Romsey S051 ....28 C4
Brake Ho PO9 ....135 D2
Bramar Ct **8** BH4 ......204 C2
Bramber Rd PO12 ....181 A6
Bramble Cl Alderholt SP6 .93 A5
 Eastleigh S050 ....56 B5
 Havant PO9 ....136 C3
 Holbury S045 ....150 C3
 Stubbington PO14 ....179 A6
Bramble Ct
 Petersfield GU31 ....41 C3
 West Moors BH22 ....138 E2
Bramble Dr S031 ....28 C1
Bramble Hill S053 ....55 A6
Bramble La Clanfield PO8 ..88 B7
 Sarisbury S031 ....128 E5
 Walkford BH23 ....194 E1
Bramble Mews **1** S018 .104 A8
Bramble Rd
 Petersfield GU31 ....41 C3
 Portsmouth PO4 ....182 E4
Bramble Way
 Bransgore BH23 ....169 B1
 Gosport PO13 ....155 A2
Bramble Wlk S041 ....197 C4
Bramblegate S050 ....57 E1
Brambles Bsns Ctr The
 PO7 ....111 C1
Brambles Cl S021 ....57 A8
Brambles Ent Ctr The
 PO7 ....111 C1
Brambles Farm Ind Est
 PO7 ....134 D8
Brambles Rd PO13 ....179 D4
Brambling Cl S016 ....78 B6
Brambling Rd PO13 ....111 B1
Bramblings The S040 ....100 C7
Brambridge S050 ....56 E8
Brambridge Ho S051 ....31 D1

Bramdean Dr PO9 ....135 D5
Bramdean Mews S019 ...103 E5
Bramdean Rd S018 ....104 D7
Bramham Moor PO14 ....179 B7
Bramley Cl
 Lymington S041 ....197 E2
 Waterlooville PO7 ....134 F8
Bramley Cres S019 ....104 B2
Bramley Ct BH22 ....165 C6
Bramley Gdns
 Emsworth PO10 ....161 B8
 Gosport PO12 ....181 B2
 Horton Heath S050 ....81 C6
Bramley Ho
 Gosport PO12 ....181 B2
 Hedge End S030 ....105 B6
 5 Portsmouth PO5 ...216 B2
Bramley Rd
 Bournemouth BH10 .....189 C5
 Ferndown BH22 ....165 D6
Bramleys The SP5 ....24 B3
Brampton La PO3 ....158 C4
Brampton Manor S016 ....78 F5
Brampton Rd BH15 ....202 D6
Brampton Twr S016 ....78 F5
Bramsdon Ct **5** PO4 ..182 F2
Bramshaw Cl S022 ....1 C3
Bramshaw Ct **18** PO9 .136 B5
Bramshaw Gdns BH8 ....190 D3
Bramshaw Way BH25 ....209 D8
Bramshott Rd
 Portsmouth PO4 ....182 F4
 Southampton S019 ......126 F8
Branksome Rd S015 .....102 C8
Branches La S051 ....25 F3
Branders Cl BH6 ....207 A4
Branders La BH6 ....207 B5
Brandon Ct
 6 Poole BH12 ....204 B4
 Portsmouth PO1 ....216 D1
Brandon Ho PO5 ....216 B1
Brandt Ho **8** PO17 .....130 E7
Brandwood Ct **4** BH14 .203 A3
Branewick Cl PO15 ....129 D3
Branksea Ave BH15 ......201 E1
Branksea Cl BH15 ....201 E1
Branksome Ave S015 .....78 C1
Branksome Cl
 New Milton BH25 ....195 B2
 Winchester S022 ....10 B6
Branksome Ct **4** BH13 .214 F8
Branksome Dene Rd
 BH4 ....204 B2
Branksome Heath Mid Sch
 BH12 ....203 D7
Branksome Hill Rd BH4 .204 B5
Branksome Sta BH12 ....203 F4
Branksome Twrs BH13 ..214 H8
Branksome Wood Gdns
 BH2 ....204 D4
Branksome Wood Rd
 BH2,BH4 ....204 C4
Bransbury Cl S016 ....78 C4
Bransbury Rd PO4 ....183 B3
Bransgore Ave PO9 ......136 D6
Bransgore CE Prim Sch
 BH23 ....193 D8
Bransgore Gdns BH23 ...169 C1
Bransley Cl S051 ....28 B1
Branwell Cl BH23 ....192 A1
Branwood Cl S041 ....196 E1
Brasenose Cl PO14 ....129 C1
Brasher Cl S050 ....57 A2
Brassey Cl BH9 ....190 A1
Brassey Rd
 Bournemouth BH9 ....190 A1
 Winchester S022 ....215 D7
Brassey Terr BH9 ....189 F1
Brasted Ct PO4 ....183 C5
Braunston Cl **4** PO4 ..133 A1
Braxall Lawn PO9 ....135 D6
Braxton Ctyd S041 ....211 E7
Braxton Ho **1** S023 ....11 C8
Breach Ave PO10 ....137 E2
Breach La S050 ....56 D5
Breamore CE Prim Sch
 SP6 ....70 B8
Breamore Cl
 Eastleigh S050 ....56 A4
 New Milton BH25 ....194 E3
Breamore Countryside Mus*
 SP6 ....46 A2
Breamore Ho* SP6 ....46 A2
Breamore Rd
 Downton SP5 ....46 E7
 Southampton S018 ......104 D7
Brean Cl S016 ....77 E2
Brearley Ch BH23 ....209 B8
Brecon Ave PO6 ....158 B8
Brecon Cl
 Bournemouth BH10 .....189 C6
 Chandler's Ford S053 ....55 B3
 Fareham PO14 ....154 B8
 Hythe S045 ....125 E3
 Southampton S019 ......195 C2
Brecon Ho **22** PO1 ....182 A4
Brecon Rd S019 ....104 C5
Bredenbury Cres PO6 ...133 C1
Bredon Wlk PO14 ....154 E8
Bredy Cl BH17 ....187 D1
Breech Cl **3** PO3 ......157 F4
Breeze Cl **3** PO4 ......182 B4
Brenchley Cl PO16 ....156 B7
Brendon Cl S045 ....125 D2
Brendon Gn S016 ....101 F6
Brendon Rd PO14 ....154 D8
Brent Ct PO10 ....160 E7

Brentwood Cres S018 ....80 A1
Breton Cl PO15 ....129 B7
Brewells La GU33 ....21 E5
Brewer Cl S031 ....129 B4
Brewer St PO1 ....216 B4
Brewers La
 Gosport PO13 ....155 D2
 Twyford S021 ....31 F5
 West Tisted S024 ....17 C7
Brewhouse Sq PO12 .....181 D7
Brewster Cl PO8 ....112 A3
Briar Cl
 Christchurch BH23 ....207 F6
 Gosport PO12 ....180 E3
 Poole BH15 ....202 E5
 Waterlooville PO8 ....112 B5
Briar Way Romsey S051 ...28 C1
 Wimborne Minst BH21 .164 B5
Briar Wood GU33 ....21 A7
Briardene Ct S040 ....100 E7
Briarfield **40** BH4 ....204 C3
Briarfield Gdns PO8 ....112 B6
Briars The S042 ....145 F1
Briarswood S016 ....78 B1
Briarswood Rd BH16 ....201 C7
Briarswood Rise S045 ...125 D2
Briarwood Cl PO10 ....155 B8
Briarwood Gdns PO11 ...184 F3
Briarwood Rd S040 ......100 C6
Brick Kiln La S024 ....17 B8
Brick La BH23 ....169 E4
Brickets Terr PO12 ....181 B3
Brickfield La
 Chandler's Ford S053 ....55 C5
 Lymington S041 ....197 F5
Brickfield Rd S017 ....79 C2
Brickfield Trad Est S053 ..55 C5
Brickmakers Rd S021 .....56 F8
Brickwoods Cl S051 ....53 B8
Bricky Lake La S051 ....24 A3
Bricky Lake La S051 ....75 C7
Brickyard La
 Corfe Mullen BH21 ......162 A1
 Ferndown BH22 ....165 A6
Brickyard Rd S032 ....84 A3
Brickyard The S040 ....99 B8
Brickyards Ind Est The
 GU32 ....20 A1
Bridefield Cl PO10 ....111 D3
Bridefield Cres PO8 ......111 D3
Bridge App BH15 ....202 B1
Bridge Cl S031 ....105 B1
 West Wellow S051 ....50 F4
Bridge Ct S051 ....52 E6
Bridge Education Ctr The
 S050 ....56 B3
Bridge Farm S030 ....106 D4
Bridge Ho Gosport PO13 .155 C4
 Southampton S015 ......102 C5
Bridge Industries PO16 ..131 C3
Bridge La S021 ....31 E7
Bridge Mdws GU33 ....20 E4
Bridge Mead S032 ....61 D5
Bridge Pl BH10 ....189 C4
Bridgefoot Dr PO16 ......131 C1
Bridgefoot Hill PO16 .....131 C1
Bridgefoot Path PO10 ...160 F8
Bridgemary Ave PO13 ...155 D3
Bridgemary Com Sch
 PO13 ....155 C2
Bridgemary Gr PO13 .....155 C5
Bridgemary Rd PO13 ....155 C5
Bridgers Cl S016 ....77 E5
Bridges Ave PO6 ....132 F1
Bridges Cl Eastleigh S050 .55 F3
 West Moors BH22 ....138 F3
Bridges The BH24 ....140 E7
Bridgeside Cl PO1 ....216 C3
Bridget Cl PO8 ....112 C7
Bridgewater Rd BH12 ...203 D6
Bridgeway St S040 ....101 A7
Bridgewater Ct S015 ....102 D5
Bridle Cl BH17 ....201 D7
Bridle Cres BH7 ....206 D7
Bridle Way BH21 ....164 C6
Bridlewood Rd S015 ....102 D8
Bridport Ct S015 ....102 C5
Bridport Rd Poole BH12 .203 F8
 Verwood BH31 ....114 F6
Bridport St PO1 ....216 B3
Brierley Ave BH10 ....165 E1
Brierley Cl BH10 ....189 E5
Brierley Rd BH10 ....189 E4
Brigantine Rd S031 ......128 E1

Brigham Cl **5** PO2 .....157 E3
Brighstone Cl S016 ....79 C5
Bright Rd BH15 ....202 E6
Bright Wire Cres S050 ....55 F2
Brightlands Ave BH6 .....206 F5
Brighton Ave PO12 ....180 F8
Brighton Rd
 Southampton S015 ......102 F7
 Sway S041 ....172 A3
Brights La PO11 ....184 F5
Brightside PO7 ....134 D6
Brightside Rd S016 ....77 F3
Brimsons Ct BH23 ....192 C3
Brinton La S045 ....103 A5
Brinton's Rd S014 ....103 B5
Brinton's Terr S014 ......103 A6
Brisbane Ho **14** PO1 ..182 D7
Brisbane Rd BH23 ....191 E1
Bristol Ct PO13 ....180 C6
Bristol Rd PO4 ....182 F2
Britain St PO1 ....182 A5
Britannia Cl Poole BH12 .203 B7
 Southampton,Bitterne Manor
 S014 ....103 C5
Britannia Gdns S030 ......81 B3
Britannia Pl S041 ....197 F4
Britannia Rd Poole BH14 .203 A3
 Portsmouth PO5 ....216 C2
 Southampton S014 .....103 B5
Britannia Rd N PO5 ......216 D2
Britannia St S041 ....41 A5
Britannia Way
 Christchurch BH23 ....208 B7
 Gosport PO12 ....181 C8
Britannic Ho **8** S014 .103 C5
Britnell Ho **8** GU31 .....40 F4
Briton St S014 ....103 A3
Britten Rd PO13 ....179 E3
Britten Way PO7 ....134 E4
Brittons Cotts S042 ......145 D1
Brixey Cl BH12 ....203 C7
Brixey Rd BH12 ....203 C7
Brixworth Cl **3** PO6 ...133 A1
Broad Ave BH8 ....205 D8
Broad Chalke Down
 S022 ....215 A2
Broad Croft PO9 ....113 C3
Broad Gdns PO6 ....158 E8
Broad Gn **2** S014 .....103 A4
Broad La Denmead PO7 ..110 B6
 Lymington S041 ....197 F2
 North Baddesley S052 ....53 E5
 Southampton S014 ......102 F3
 Swanmore S032 ....84 A5
Broad Mead Rd BH21 ...114 F1
Broad Oak S030 ....105 C7
Broad St PO1 ....181 F4
Broad View La S022 ....10 A3
Broad Way
 Froxfield Green GU32 ....39 E8
 Hamble-le-R S031 ....127 E7
Broad Woods La S051 .....51 A6
Broadbent Cl S016 ....77 E6
Broadcut PO16 ....131 C2
Broadfields Cl S041 ......211 D5
Broadhill La SP6 ....94 E8
Broadhurst Ave BH10 ....189 E4
Broadlands*
 Romsey S051 ....52 E5
 27 Bournemouth BH4 .204 C3
Broadlands Ave
 Bournemouth BH6 ....206 F4
 Eastleigh S050 ....56 A4
 Waterlooville PO7 ....134 E7
Broadlands Cl
 Bournemouth BH8 ....190 D3
 Walkford BH23 ....194 B2
Broadlands Cotts GU32 ...41 B6
Broadlands Rd
 Brockenhurst S042 ....145 E1
 Brockenhurst S042 ......145 E2
 Southampton S017 ....79 B2
Broadlaw Wlk **3** PO14 .154 E7
Broadley Cl S045 ....150 C4
Broadly Cl S041 ....197 B2
Broadmarsh Bsns &
 Innovation Ctr PO9 ....159 C8
Broadmayne Rd BH12 ...204 A8
Broadmead Cl **2** S041 .197 F2
Broadmead Flats S041 ...77 D5
Broadmead Rd S018 ......77 D5
Broadmeadow Cl S040 ..100 C7
Broadmeadows La **6**
 PO7 ....135 A2
Broadmere Ave PO9 .....135 F5
Broadmoor Rd BH21 ....186 C7
Broadoak Cl S045 ....150 C3
Broads The BH21 ....162 F6
Broadsands Dr PO12 ....180 D3
Broadsands Wlk PO12 ...180 E3
Broadshard La BH24 ....141 A8
Broadstone Fst Sch
 BH18 ....187 B4
Broadstone Mid Sch
 BH18 ....187 B4
Broadstone Way
 Bournemouth BH17 .....186 F1
 Poole BH17 ....202 B7
Broadwater Ave BH14 ...203 C2
Broadwater Rd
 Romsey S051 ....52 E6
 Southampton S018 ....79 F3
Broadway BH6 ....207 B3

Broadway Ct BH12 . . . . .204 A5
Broadway Gables BH14 . .203 E4
Broadway Gdns 🎵
 BH21 . . . . .163 C4
Broadway Ho BH18 . . . . .187 B4
Broadway La
 Bournemouth BH8 . . . . . . .190 C4
 Horndean PO8 . . . . .111 D7
Broadway Mews BH14 . . .202 F3
Broadway Pk
 Petersfield GU31 . . . . .40 F1
 🎵 Wimborne Minst BH21 . .163 C4
Broadway The
 🎵 Bitterne Pk SO18 . . . . . . .79 F1
 Bournemouth BH10 . . . . . . .189 D6
 🎵 Portswood SO17 . . . . . . .79 B1
 Southampton,Thornhill Pk
 SO18 . . . . .104 D7
 Winchester SO23 . . . . .215 E5
Brock Hill Forest Wlks*
 SO43 . . . . .144 F8
Brock Ho SO42 . . . . .145 F1
Brock Way BH31 . . . . .114 E7
Brockenhurst Ave PO9 . .135 C6
Brockenhurst CE Prim Sch
 SO42 . . . . .172 F8
Brockenhurst Coll SO42 .146 A2
Brockenhurst Rd BH9 . . . .190 B2
Brockenhurst Sta SO42 . .135 E1
Brockhampton La PO9 . . .135 C1
Brockhampton Rd
 Havant PO9 . . . . .135 D1
 Langstone PO9 . . . . .159 D8
Brockhills La BH25 . . . . . .195 C6
Brockhurst Ind Est
 PO12 . . . . .155 F1
Brockhurst Inf Sch
 PO12 . . . . .180 F7
Brockhurst Jun Sch
 PO12 . . . . .181 A8
Brockhurst Rd PO12 . . . . .180 F7
Brockishill Rd SO40 . . . . .99 A5
Brocklands PO9 . . . . .135 D1
Brockley Rd BH10 . . . . . .189 E4
Brocks Cl SO45 . . . . .125 D2
Brocks Pine BH24 . . . . . .139 F3
Brockwood Bottom SO24 .36 F8
Brockwood Park Sch
 SO24 . . . . .15 F1
Brodrick Ave PO12 . . . . . .181 A4
Brog St BH21 . . . . .162 C1
Brokenford Ave SO40 . . . .101 A7
Brokenford Bsns Ctr
 SO40 . . . . .100 F7
Brokenford Ct 🎵 SO40 . .100 F7
Brokenford La SO40 . . . . .100 F7
Brombys The 🎵 BH15 . . . .202 C2
Bromley Ho BH12 . . . . . . .204 B5
Bromley Rd SO18 . . . . .79 F1
Brompton Ct BH2 . . . . . . .204 E3
Brompton Rd PO4 . . . . . . .182 F3
Bromyard Cres PO6 . . . . .133 D1
Bronte Ave BH23 . . . . .192 A1
Bronte Cl SO40 . . . . .100 D6
Bronte Gdns PO15 . . . . . .129 C8
Bronte Way SO19 . . . . . . .103 E6
Bronwen Ct SO19 . . . . . . .104 A2
Brook Ave
 New Milton BH25 . . . . .195 B4
 Warsash SO31 . . . . .128 C3
Brook Ave N BH25 . . . . . .195 B4
Brook Cl
 Bournemouth BH10 . . . . . .189 C4
 North Baddesley SO52 . . . . .54 A3
 Sarisbury SO31 . . . . .128 E3
Brook Cnr SO43 . . . . .74 A1
Brook Cotts Compton SO20 . .6 C5
Brook Ct
 Chandler's Ford SO53 . . . . .55 C6
 Romsey SO51 . . . . .52 E6
 Southampton SO15 . . . . . .102 D5
Brook Dr BH31 . . . . .115 B4
Brook Farm Ave PO15 . . .130 F1
Brook Gdns PO10 . . . . . . .160 D8
Brook Hill SO41 . . . . .198 E2
Brook Ho
 Barton on S BH25 . . . . . . .209 E2
 Southampton SO19 . . . . . .104 A3
Brook La Botley SO30 . . . .105 F6
 Bransgore BH23 . . . . .193 B7
 Corfe Mullen BH21 . . . . . . .186 C6
 Hambledon PO7 . . . . .86 D5
 Lower Swanwick SO31 . . . .129 A5
 Warsash SO31 . . . . .128 D3
 Woodgreen SP6 . . . . .70 E2
Brook Mdw PO15 . . . . . . .130 F1
Brook Rd
 Bournemouth BH10 . . . . . .189 C4
 Fair Oak SO50 . . . . .57 C2
 Lymington SO41 . . . . .197 F2
 Poole BH12 . . . . .203 C5
 Southampton SO18 . . . . . .104 A7
 Wimborne Minst BH21 . . . .163 C4
Brook Road Depot
 BH21 . . . . .163 E3
Brook St SO32 . . . . .83 C8
Brook Terr SP6 . . . . .93 F8
Brook Valley SO16 . . . . . . .78 A2
Brook Way
 Christchurch BH23 . . . . . . .208 C7
 Romsey SO51 . . . . .28 A1
Brook Wlk SO40 . . . . .76 C1

Brookdale Cl
 Broadstone BH18 . . . . .187 A4
 Waterlooville PO7 . . . . .134 F8
Brookdale Farm BH18 . . .187 A4
Brooke Cl SO23 . . . . .2 B8
Brookers La PO13 . . . . . . .155 B3
Brookes Hill Ind Est
 SO40 . . . . .76 B4
Brookfield Cl 🎵 PO9 . . . .135 C2
Brookfield Com Sch &
 Language Coll SO31 . . . . .128 E4
Brookfield Gdns SO31 . . .128 F4
Brookfield Pl SO17 . . . . . . .79 B2
Brookfield Rd
 Fair Oak SO50 . . . . .57 B2
 Portsmouth PO1 . . . . .182 E6
Brookfields SO51 . . . . .50 D3
Brookland Cl SO41 . . . . . .197 C3
Brooklands
 Bournemouth BH4 . . . . . . .204 B3
 Lyndhurst SO43 . . . . .122 A4
Brooklands Rd
 Bishop's Waltham SO32 . . . .83 C8
 Havant PO9 . . . . .135 B2
Brooklyn Cl SO21 . . . . .31 C3
Brooklyn Ct
 New Milton BH25 . . . . .194 F3
 Otterbourne SO21 . . . . .31 C3
Brooklyn Dr PO7 . . . . .134 F8
Brooklynn Cl SO32 . . . . . . .83 E2
Brookman Ct SO18 . . . . . .104 A7
Brookmead Way PO9 . . . .159 F8
Brooks Cl BH24 . . . . .141 B6
Brooks Sh Ctr The SO23 .215 E6
Brookside Gosport PO13 . .155 B5
 Ibsley SP6 . . . . .94 C2
 Landford SP5 . . . . .49 D4
 Totton SO40 . . . . .100 F5
Brookside Ave SO15 . . . . .101 F7
Brookside Cl
 Bransgore BH23 . . . . .169 A1
 Denmead PO7 . . . . .110 F4
Brookside Ho SO18 . . . . . .79 E4
Brookside Park Homes
 BH21 . . . . .186 B4
Brookside Rd
 Bransgore BH23 . . . . .193 A8
 Brockenhurst SO42 . . . . . .145 F2
 Havant,Bedhampton PO9 . .135 C1
 Langstone PO9 . . . . .159 E8
 Wimborne Minst BH21 . . . .163 F4
Brookside Way
 Christchurch BH23 . . . . . . .193 E1
 Southampton SO18 . . . . . . .79 E4
 West End SO30 . . . . .80 E3
Brookvale Ct 🎵 SO17 . . . .79 A1
Brookvale Rd SO17 . . . . . .79 A1
Brookwood Ave SO50 . . . .55 F3
Brookwood Ind Est SO50 .56 A5
Brookwood Rd SO16 . . . . .101 D8
Broom Cl
 Portsmouth PO4 . . . . .183 D4
 Waterlooville PO7 . . . . .135 A5
Broom Hill SO41 . . . . .199 B7
Broom Hill Way SO50 . . . . .56 A7
Broom La BH6 . . . . .206 E3
Broom Rd
 Petersfield GU31 . . . . .41 C2
 Poole BH12 . . . . .188 C1
Broom Road Bsns Pk
 BH12 . . . . .188 C1
Broom Sq PO4 . . . . .183 D5
Broom Way
 Gosport PO13,PO14 . . . . . .155 A1
 Lee-on-t-S PO13 . . . . .179 F4
Broomfield Cres PO13 . . .180 B7
Broomfield Ct BH22 . . . . .165 E6
Broomfield Dr SP6 . . . . . . .93 A5
Broomfield La SO41 . . . . .197 E4
Broomhill SP5 . . . . .49 D2
Broomhill Cl SO41 . . . . . . .197 B2
Broom Gr SO19 . . . . .100 D3
Broomy Cl SO45 . . . . .125 C4
Brougham La PO12 . . . . . .181 A7
Brougham Rd PO5 . . . . . .216 B2
Brougham St PO12 . . . . . .181 A7
Broughton Ave BH10 . . . .189 E3
Broughton Cl
 Bournemouth BH10 . . . . . .189 E3
 🎵 Southampton SO19 . . . . .79 A1
Broughton Ho 🎵 SO18 . . .103 E8
Broughton Rd SO41 . . . . .121 F6
Brow Cvn Site The
 BH25 . . . . .171 E5
Brow The PO7 . . . . .134 C2
Browndown Rd PO13 . . . .180 C3
Brownen Rd BH9 . . . . .205 B8
Brownfield Ho 🎵 GU31 . . . .40 F3
Brownhill Cl SO53 . . . . . . .55 C7
Brownhill Ct SO16 . . . . . . .77 C3
Brownhill Gdns SO53 . . . . .55 D7
Brownhill Rd
 Chandler's Ford SO53 . . . . .55 D7
 New Milton BH25 . . . . .170 E3
 North Baddesley SO52 . . . . .54 A4
Brownhill Way SO16 . . . . . .77 D3
Browning Ave
 Bournemouth BH5 . . . . . . .206 A4
 Portchester PO6 . . . . .132 E1
 Southampton SO19 . . . . . .104 D6
Browning Cl
 Eastleigh SO50 . . . . .55 F3
 Swanwick PO15 . . . . .129 C8
 Totton SO40 . . . . .100 D7
Browning Dr SO22 . . . . . .215 B6
Browning Rd BH12 . . . . . .203 D6
Brownings Cl SO41 . . . . . .197 A4
Brownlow Ave SO19 . . . . .104 A6

Brownlow Cl PO1 . . . . . . .182 D7
Brownlow 🎵 BH4 . . . . . . .204 C3
Brownlow Gdns SO19 . . . .104 A6
Browns La Damerham SP6 .68 B5
 East End SO41 . . . . .199 C5
Brownsea Ave BH21 . . . . .186 D6
Brownsea Cl BH25 . . . . . .194 E3
Brownsea Ct BH14 . . . . . .214 B8
Brownsea Island (NT)*
 BH15 . . . . .213 D4
Brownsea Rd BH13 . . . . . .214 B3
Brownsea View Ave
 BH14 . . . . .203 C1
Brownsea View Cl BH14 .203 C1
Brownwich La PO14 . . . . .153 D5
Browsholme Cl SO50 . . . . .56 A6
Broxburn Cl SO53 . . . . .30 E1
Broxhead Rd PO9 . . . . . . .136 A6
Bruce Cl PO16 . . . . .131 A3
Bruce Rd PO4 . . . . .182 F2
Brudenell Ave BH13 . . . . .214 D7
Brudenell Rd BH13 . . . . . .214 D6
Bruce Cl SO53 . . . . .55 B7
Brune La PO13 . . . . .180 C8
Brune Park Com Coll
 PO12 . . . . .180 E8
Brune Way BH22 . . . . .165 D3
Brunei Ho SO16 . . . . .79 A5
Brunel Cl Hedge End SO30 .81 D1
 Verwood BH31 . . . . .115 C4
Brunel Rd
 Portsmouth PO2 . . . . .157 E3
 Southampton SO15 . . . . . .101 C8
 Totton SO40 . . . . .76 E3
Brunel Way SO15 . . . . . . .129 C4
Brunstead Pl 🎵 BH12 . . . .204 B4
Brunstead Rd BH12 . . . . . .204 B4
Brunswick Cl SO50 . . . . . . .57 B3
Brunswick Gdns PO9 . . . .135 D2
Brunswick Ho 🎵 SO15 . . . .103 A6
Brunswick Pl
 Lymington SO41 . . . . .197 E4
 Southampton SO15 . . . . . .103 A6
Brunswick Rd SO50 . . . . . .57 B3
Brunswick Sq SO41 . . . . .103 A3
Brunswick St PO5 . . . . . . .216 B2
Brushers BH23 . . . . .169 E4
Bruyn Cl SP6 . . . . .70 A2
Bruyn Rd SO19 . . . . .103 E5
Bryanstone Rd BH3 . . . . .204 E7
Bryant Rd BH12 . . . . .204 A8
Bryher Br PO6 . . . . .157 E5
Bryher Island PO6 . . . . . . .157 B7
Brympton Cl SP6 . . . . .69 D2
Bryony Cl
 Broadstone BH18 . . . . .186 F3
 Locks Heath SO31 . . . . . . .128 F2
Bryony Gdns SO50 . . . . . . .81 C6
Bryony Way PO7 . . . . .135 A7
Bryson Cl PO13 . . . . .180 A6
Bryson Rd PO6 . . . . .157 D8
Bub La BH23 . . . . .207 E6
Bubb La SO30 . . . . .81 C4
Buccaneers Cl BH23 . . . . .207 E6
Buccleuch Rd BH13 . . . . .204 A1
Bucehayes Cl BH23 . . . . .209 A8
Buchan Ave PO15 . . . . . . .129 C8
Buchan Ct SO45 . . . . .125 D2
Buchanan Ave BH7 . . . . . .205 E6
Buchanan Rd SO16 . . . . . .77 F5
Buckby La PO3 . . . . .158 C4
Bucketts Farm Ct SO32 . .84 B5
Buckingham Cl
 🎵 Christchurch BH23 . . . . .209 A7
 Fareham PO15 . . . . .130 E3
 Poole BH15 . . . . .202 D3
 🎵 Southampton SO17 . . . .103 A8
Buckingham Gn PO1 . . . .182 D7
Buckingham Mans 🎵
 BH1 . . . . .205 A3
Buckland Cl
 Eastleigh SO50 . . . . .56 A5
 Waterlooville PO7 . . . . .111 D2
Buckland Ct SO41 . . . . . . .197 E5
Buckland Dene SO41 . . . .197 D5
Buckland Gdns SO40 . . . . .76 E2
Buckland Gr BH23 . . . . . . .193 E2
Buckland Path PO2 . . . . . .182 B5
Buckland St PO2 . . . . .182 B5
Buckland Terr BH12 . . . . .203 C5
Buckland Way SO45 . . . . .125 E1
Bucklers Ct Havant PO9 . .135 D7
 Lymington SO41 . . . . .197 D3
 Portsmouth PO2 . . . . .157 D1
Bucklers Hard Maritime
 Mus* SO42 . . . . .176 D5
Bucklers Mews SO41 . . . .197 D3
Bucklers Rd PO12 . . . . . . .181 C9
Bucklers The SO41 . . . . . .211 A5
Bucklers Way BH8 . . . . . .190 D3
Buckley Ct SO16 . . . . .78 B7
Buckmore Ave GU32 . . . . . .40 D4
Bucks Head Hill SO32 . . . .61 C5
Bucksey Rd PO13 . . . . . . .180 C8
Buckstone Cl SO41 . . . . . .197 F2
Buckthorn Cl
 Christchurch BH23 . . . . . . .186 F1
 Totton SO40 . . . . .100 B8
Budden's La PO17 . . . . . . .108 E8
Buddens Mdw BH21 . . . . .186 C4
Buddens Rd PO17 . . . . . . .108 A4

Buddle Hill SP6 . . . . .94 C4
Budds La SO51 . . . . .27 E1
Budds Lane Trad Est
 SO51 . . . . .27 E1
Bude Cl PO6 . . . . .132 F1
Buffalo Mews BH15 . . . . .202 B2
Bugdens La BH31 . . . . . . .115 A6
Bugle St SO14 . . . . .102 F3
Bulbarrow Wlk PO14 . . . .154 E8
Bulbeck Rd PO9 . . . . .135 F1
Buldowne Wlk SO41 . . . . .172 B3
Bull Dro SO23 . . . . .215 F3
Bull Hill Boldre SO41 . . . .174 B1
 Rake GU33 . . . . .21 E4
Bull La Minstead SO43 . . . .98 C3
 Waltham Chase SO32 . . . . .83 D3
Bullar Rd SO18 . . . . .103 E8
Bullar St SO14 . . . . .103 B6
Bullfinch Cl
 Broadstone BH17 . . . . .186 F1
 Totton SO40 . . . . .100 C7
Bullfinch Ct PO13 . . . . . . .179 F4
Bullrush Cl SO45 . . . . .125 F1
Bulls Copse La PO8 . . . . .112 A6
Bulls Copse Rd SO40 . . . .101 A4
Bulls Dro SP5 . . . . .4 A6
Bulls Dro PO14 . . . . .179 B6
Bunkers Hill PO7 . . . . .110 D4
Bunns La PO7 . . . . .109 E5
Bunny La
 Michelmersh SO51 . . . . . . .27 E5
 Sherfield English SO51 . . . .25 A4
Bunstead La SO21 . . . . . . .30 D7
Bunting Gdns PO8 . . . . . . .111 F4
Bunting Rd BH22 . . . . .165 B8
Burbidge Gr PO4 . . . . .183 A2
Burbidge Cl BH11 . . . . . . .202 E8
Burbush Cl SO45 . . . . .150 C3
Burcombe Ave BH24 . . . . .117 F1
Burcombe Rd BH10 . . . . . .189 C5
Burcote Dr PO3 . . . . .158 B4
Burdale Dr PO11 . . . . .185 D3
Burdock Cl BH23 . . . . .193 B1
Bure Cl BH23 . . . . .208 B6
Bure Haven Dr BH23 . . . .208 A6
Bure Homage Gdns
 BH23 . . . . .208 B6
Bure Homage La BH23 . . .208 B6
Bure La BH23 . . . . .208 B6
Bure Rd BH23 . . . . .208 B6
Burford Cl BH23 . . . . .191 D1
Burford Ct 🎵 BH1 . . . . . . .205 B3
Burford La SO42 . . . . .146 A2
Burgate Cl PO9 . . . . .135 D3
Burgate Cross SP6 . . . . . . .70 A5
Burgate Ct SP6 . . . . .70 A4
Burgate Fields SP6 . . . . . . .70 A3
Burgate Sch & Sixth Form Ctr
 The SP6 . . . . .70 A3
Burgesmede Ho 🎵 GU32 . .40 F3
Burgess Cl
 Bournemouth BH11 . . . . . .188 F4
 South Hayling PO11 . . . . . .185 D1
Burgess Gdns SO16 . . . . . .79 B4
Burgess Fld BH21 . . . . . . .114 A6
Burgess Rd
 Southampton SO16 . . . . . . .79 B4
 Upper Shirley SO16 . . . . . . .78 D3
Burghclere Rd
 Havant PO9 . . . . .136 B6
 Southampton SO19 . . . . . .126 F8
Burgoyne Rd
 Portsmouth PO5 . . . . .182 D1
 Southampton SO19 . . . . . .104 E4
Burgundy Cl SO31 . . . . . .128 F2
Burgundy Terr 🎵 PO2 . . .157 E2
Buriton Cl PO16 . . . . .132 D1
Buriton Ho SO22 . . . . .1 D4
Buriton Rd PO9 . . . . .216 C4
Bure Dr SO19 . . . . .104 D5
Burleigh Rd
 Bournemouth BH6 . . . . . . .206 D5
 Portsmouth PO1 . . . . .182 F7
Burley Cl
 Barton on S BH25 . . . . . . .209 D8
 Chandler's Ford SO53 . . . . .55 B4
 🎵 Havant PO9 . . . . .136 B4
 Totton SO40 . . . . .100 B7
 Verwood BH31 . . . . .114 E5
Burley Ct 🎵 SO17 . . . . . . .79 A2
Burley Down SO53 . . . . . . .55 B4
Burley Ho 🎵 SO16 . . . . . .102 B8
Burley Lawn BH24 . . . . . .143 B4
Burley Prim Sch BH24 . . .143 A3
Burley Rd
 Bransgore BH23 . . . . .193 A8
 Bransgore,Thorney Hill
 BH23 . . . . .169 D3
 Brockenhurst SO42 . . . . . .172 C8
 Poole BH12 . . . . .203 C6
 Winchester SO22 . . . . .1 D1
 Winkton BH23 . . . . .192 D6
Burlington Arc 🎵 BH1 . . .204 F3
Burlington Ct SO19 . . . . . .104 E5
Burlington Mans 🎵
 SO15 . . . . .102 C7
Burlington Rd
 Portsmouth PO2 . . . . .157 E2
 Southampton SO15 . . . . . .102 C6
Burma Ho SO18 . . . . .79 E4
Burma Rd SO51 . . . . .29 F6
Burma Way SO40 . . . . . . .101 F1
Burmah Road N SO45 . . .151 C5

Burmah Road S SO45 . . .151 B5
Burmese Cl PO15 . . . . . . .129 C7
Burn Cl BH31 . . . . .115 B4
Burnaby Ct BH4 . . . . .204 C1
Burnaby Rd
 Bournemouth BH4 . . . . . . .204 C1
 Portsmouth PO1 . . . . .182 B4
Burnage Ct 🎵 BH13 . . . . .214 F7
Burnbake Rd BH31 . . . . . .115 A5
Burnbank Gdns SO40 . . . .100 C7
Burnbrae Rd BH22 . . . . . .165 E6
Burnett Ave BH23 . . . . . . .206 E8
Burnett Cl Hythe SO45 . . .126 B2
 Southampton SO18 . . . . . . .79 E1
 Winchester SO22 . . . . .215 A8
Burnett Rd
 Christchurch BH23 . . . . . . .206 F2
 Gosport PO12 . . . . .180 F6
Burnetts Fields SO50 . . . . .81 C7
Burnetts Gdns SO50 . . . . .81 D7
Burnetts La SO30 . . . . .81 C5
Burney Ho 🎵 PO12 . . . . . .181 D5
Burney Rd PO12 . . . . .180 E3
Burngate Rd BH15 . . . . . .201 E2
Burnham Beeches SO53 . .55 B6
Burnham Chase SO18 . . . .104 C7
Burnham Dr BH8 . . . . .205 C7
Burnham Rd
 Burton BH23 . . . . .192 C2
 Cosham PO6 . . . . .134 D1
 Fordingbridge SP6 . . . . . . .69 F3
Burnham Wood PO16 . . . .131 A3
Burnham's Wlk 🎵 PO12 . .181 D5
Burnleigh Gdns BH25 . . . .195 C4
Burns Cl SO50 . . . . .55 E1
Burns Pl SO16 . . . . .78 A2
Burns Rd
 Bournemouth BH6 . . . . . . .206 D7
 Eastleigh SO50 . . . . .55 F1
 Southampton SO19 . . . . . .104 D6
Burnside
 Christchurch BH23 . . . . . . .208 D8
 Gosport PO13 . . . . .155 B5
 Waterlooville PO7 . . . . .112 A1
Burnt House La
 Boldre SO41 . . . . .174 A1
 Bransgore BH23 . . . . .169 B1
 Stubbington PO14 . . . . . . .154 D4
Burr Cl SO21 . . . . .56 F8
Burrard Gr SO41 . . . . .197 F2
Burrfields Rd PO3 . . . . . . .158 B1
Burridge Rd SO31 . . . . . . .106 A2
Burrill Ave PO6 . . . . .158 A8
Burrow Hill Pl SO50 . . . . . .56 D5
Burrows Cl PO9 . . . . .136 A3
Burrows La BH31 . . . . .114 F8
Bursledon CE Inf Sch
 SO31 . . . . .128 A8
Bursledon Ho 🎵 BH25 . . .195 A2
Bursledon Hts SO31 . . . . .105 B1
Bursledon Jun Sch
 SO31 . . . . .128 A8
Bursledon Pl PO7 . . . . . . .134 D5
Bursledon Rd
 Hedge End SO30 . . . . .105 B5
 Southampton SO19,SO31 .104 C5
 Waterlooville PO7 . . . . .134 D5
Bursledon Sta SO31 . . . . .128 B8
Bursledon Windmill*
 SO31 . . . . .105 A2
Burt's Hill BH21 . . . . .163 D7
Burt's La BH21 . . . . .138 A7
Burtley Rd BH6 . . . . .206 F3
Burton CE Prim Sch
 BH23 . . . . .192 C3
Burton Cl Burton BH23 . . .192 C1
 St Leonards BH24 . . . . . . .139 E5
Burton Hall BH23 . . . . . . .192 C3
Burton Hall Pl BH23 . . . . .192 D3
Burton Ho BH23 . . . . .192 D1
Burton Rd
 Christchurch BH23 . . . . . . .207 E7
 Poole BH13 . . . . .204 A3
 Southampton SO19 . . . . . .102 E6
Burtoncroft BH23 . . . . . . .192 C3
Burwood Gr PO11 . . . . . . .185 A4
Bury Brickfield Park Cvn Site
 SO40 . . . . .101 C4
Bury Cl PO12 . . . . .181 B5
Bury Cres PO12 . . . . .181 B5
Bury Cross PO12 . . . . .181 A5
Bury Farm SO30 . . . . .106 C3
Bury Hall La PO12 . . . . . . .180 F3
Bury Ho PO12 . . . . .131 A1
Bury La SO40 . . . . .101 A3
Bury Rd Gosport PO12 . . .181 A5
 Marchwood SO40 . . . . . . .101 C3
 Poole BH13 . . . . .203 F1
 Poole BH13 . . . . .178 E8
Bus Dro SO45 . . . . .178 E8
Bush Ho PO5 . . . . .216 B1
Bush St E PO5 . . . . .216 B1
Bush St W PO5 . . . . .216 B1
Bushell Rd BH15 . . . . .202 C7
Bushells Farm SP6 . . . . . . .93 E8
Bushey Rd BH8 . . . . .190 C1
Bushmead Dr BH24 . . . . . .139 C5
Bushy Mead PO7 . . . . .134 C3
Busket La SO23 . . . . .215 E5
Busketts Way SO40 . . . . .100 A2
Butcher's Cnr SO41 . . . . . .73 E4
Butchers Bush SO43 . . . . . .98 B5
Bute Dr BH23 . . . . .209 B8
Butlers Cl SO51 . . . . .4 F1
Butlers La BH24 . . . . .117 C1
Butser Ancient Farm*
 PO8 . . . . .88 F6

Butser Ct P08 ....88 D3
Butser Wlk
  Fareham PO14 ....154 E8
  Petersfield GU31 ....41 B4
Butt La SP5 ....22 B8
Butt's Cl SO19 ....104 D4
Butt's Cres SO19 .....104 C4
Butt's Rd SO19 ....104 C3
Butt's Sq SO19 ....104 C4
Buttercup Cl
  Hedge End SO30 ......105 A6
  Hythe SO45 ....126 A1
Buttercup Dr BH23 ....193 B1
Buttercup Way SO31 ...118 D2
Butterfield Rd SO16 ....78 E3
Butterfly Dr PO6 ......133 A1
Butteridge Rise SO51 ...26 E6
Buttermere Cl SO21 ....77 E2
Buttermere Ho **16** PO6 .133 B1
Buttery The BH23 ......207 D7
Button's La SO51 ......50 F3
Butts Ash Gdns SO45 ..126 A1
Butts Ash La SO45 ....126 A1
Butts Bridge Hill SO45 .126 A2
Butts Cl SO22 ....215 B7
Butts Farm La SO32 ....83 D8
Butts Lawn SO42 ......145 F2
Butts The SO32 ....61 C6
Buttsash Ave SO45 ....126 A1
Buttsbridge Rd SO45 ..126 A1
By Pass Rd SO51 ......52 E6
By The Wood SO40 .....76 D2
Byams La SO40 ....102 A2
Bye Rd SO31 ....128 D8
Byerley Cl PO10 ......137 B5
Byerley Rd PO11 ......182 F5
Byeways SO45 ....125 F2
Byngs Bsns Pk PO7 ....111 F2
Byrd Cl PO7 ....134 E5
Byres The PO14 ....154 C4
Byron Ave SO22 ....215 B6
Byron Cl
  Bishop's Waltham SO32 ..83 E8
  Fareham PO16 ....131 A2
Byron Ct Ferndown BH22 .165 D5
  Southampton SO15 ....102 E6
Byron Ho **10** BH25 ...195 A2
Byway SO45 ....125 F2

C

  Barton on S BH25 .....209 E8
  Bournemouth BH5 .....205 F3
  Eastleigh SO50 ....56 B4
  Portsmouth PO2 ......182 F8
  Southampton SO19 ....104 D6
  Wimborne Minst BH21 .163 C6

C Ave SO45 ....150 D5
Cable St Eastleigh SO50 ..56 A2
  2 Southampton SO14 ..103 C5
Cabot Bsns Village
  BH17 ....202 A7
Cabot Dr SO45 ....150 C5
Cabot La BH17 ....202 B8
Cabot Way PO15 ......194 F3
Cadgwith Pl PO6 ......157 B7
Cadhay Cl BH25 ......194 C3
Cadington Ho **9** PO1 ..182 A5
Cadland Cl SO14 ......103 C2
Cadland Pk SO45 ......150 C6
Cadland Rd Fawley SO45 .151 B5
  Fawley,Buttsash SO45 ..150 D7
Cadnam Cl **8** PO12 ..180 D3
Cadnam La SO40 ......74 F2
Cadnam Lawn PO9 ....135 D6
Cadnam Rd PO4 ......183 B3
Cadogan Rd BH24 ....141 B7
Cador Dr PO16 ....156 B6
Caen Ho **7** PO14 ....154 E8
Caer Peris View PO16 ..132 C2
Caerleon Ave SO19 ...104 C6
Caerleon Dr SO19 ....104 C6
Caernarvon Gdns SO53 ..55 A4
Caesar's Way BH18 ...186 C4
Cains Cl PO14 ....179 C8
Caird Ave BH25 ......195 C2
Cairns Cl BH23 ....206 F8
Cairo Terr PO2 ....182 D7
Caister Cl PO12 ......165 C6
Caistor Cl SO16 ......78 A4
Calabrese SO31 ......129 B7
Calbourne SO31 ......127 C7
Calcot La SO32 ....82 E3
Caldecote Wlk **4** PO5 ..216 B2
Calder Cl SO15 ....101 E8
Calder Ho **6** PO1 ....182 A5
Calder Rd BH17 ......202 F8
Calderwood Dr SO19 ..104 A4
Caledon Rd BH14 ....203 E3
Caledonia Dr SO45 ...125 D3
Caledonian Cl BH23 ..208 B7
California Cl SO40 ....76 F2
Calkin Cl SO19 ....192 A1
Callowing Cl SO21 ....56 F8
Calluna Rd BH12 .....203 B8
Calmore Cl BH8 ......190 D3
Calmore Cres SO40 ...76 B1
Calmore Dr SO40 .....100 C8
Calmore Gdns SO40 ..100 D7
Calmore Inf Sch SO40 .76 C1
Calmore Inf Sch SO40 .76 C1
Calmore Jun Sch SO40 .76 C1
Calmore Rd SO40 .....100 C8
Calpe Ave SO43 ......121 F6

Calshot Activities Ctr
  SO45 ....152 B3
Calshot Castle* SO45 ..152 B3
Calshot Cl SO45 ......178 F8
Calshot Ct SO14 ......103 C2
Calshot Dr SO53 ......55 A4
Calshot Rd Fawley SO45 .151 B3
  Havant PO9 ....135 C7
Calshot Way PO13 ....155 B1
Calvin Rd BH9 ....204 F8
Camargue Cl PO15 ...129 B8
Camber Pl **3** PO1 ...182 A3
Cambria Dr SO45 .....125 D3
Cambrian Cl SO31 ....105 A2
Cambrian Terr PO5 ...216 C1
Cambrian Wlk PO14 ..154 F7
Cambridge Ct **17** SO14 .103 A8
Cambridge Dr SO53 ..55 C3
Cambridge Gdns BH23 .191 F2
Cambridge Gn
  Chandler's Ford SO53 ..55 C2
  Titchfield PO14 ......129 C2
Cambridge Junc PO1 ..182 B4
Cambridge Rd
  Bournemouth BH2 ....204 D3
  Gosport PO12 ....180 F6
  Lee-on-t-S PO13 .....179 F2
  Portsmouth PO1 .....182 B4
  Southampton SO14 ...103 A8
Camcross Cl **2** PO6 ..133 B1
Camden Cl BH9 ......190 B1
Camden Hurst **1** SO41 .211 B4
Camden St PO12 .....181 A7
Camden Terr **8** PO1 ..181 A7
Camel Green Rd SP6 ..93 A6
Camelia Cl PO9 ......136 C3
Camelia Gdns SO18 ...80 A2
Camelia Gr SO50 .....57 E2
Camellia Cl
  North Baddesley SO52 ..54 A5
  Three Legged Cross BH21 .114 E1
Camellia Ct SO18 .....79 E2
Camellia Gdns BH25 ..195 B8
Camelot Cres PO16 ...132 B1
Cameron Cl PO13 .....155 C3
Cameron Ct SO16 .....77 F5
Cameron Rd BH23 ...207 D7
Camilla Cl SO40 ......76 B1
Camilla Ct BH13 .....204 B2
Camley Cl SO19 ......103 E1
Cammel Rd BH24 ....165 D2
Camp Rd SO13 ....155 D3
Campbell Cres PO7 ...134 C5
Campbell Ct SO50 ....57 C2
Campbell Mews SO18 .104 D7
Campbell Rd
  Bournemouth BH1 ...205 E5
  Burton BH23 ....192 C3
  Eastleigh SO50 ......56 B1
  Portsmouth PO5 .....216 D1
Campbell St SO14 ....103 C6
Campbell Way SO50 ..57 C2
Campion Cl
  Horton Heath SO50 ...81 D6
  Locks Heath SO31 ...128 E2
  Waterlooville PO7 ...135 A6
Campion Cr SO11 .....28 C1
Campion Gr BH23 ....207 F6
Campion Rd SO19 ....104 D5
Campion Way
  Kings Worthy SO23 ....2 C7
  Lymington SO41 .....197 E5
Cams Bay Cl PO16 ....131 F1
Cams Hill Hambledon PO7 .86 B2
  Portchester PO16 ....131 E1
Cams Hill Sch PO16 ..155 E8
Canada Cl **9** PO12 ..181 C9
Canada Pl BH16 ....78 F4
Canada Rd
  Southampton SO19 ...103 E2
  West Wellow SO51 ...50 D1
Canal Cl SO51 ....28 A1
Canal Wlk
  Portsmouth PO1 .....216 C3
  Romsey SO51 ....52 F8
  Southampton SO14 ...103 A3
Canalside The PO1 ...182 A4
Canberra Cl PO12 ....180 F4
Canberra Ct **7** PO12 .180 F4
Canberra Ho PO1 ....216 B3
Canberra Rd
  Christchurch BH23 ...191 E1
  Nursling SO16 ....77 B4
  Thorney Island PO10 .161 A3
Canberra Twrs SO31 ..126 F8
Candlemas Pl **16** SO17 .103 A8
Candover Ct SO19 ....127 A8
Candy La SO14 ....104 E6
Candys Cl BH21 ......162 E2
Candys La BH21 ......162 E2
Canford Ave BH11 ...189 A2
Canford Cl BH21 .....164 C6
Canford Heath Fst & Mid
  Schs BH17 ....202 D7
Canford Heath Nature
  Reserve* BH11 ......188 B4
Canford Heath Rd BH17 .187 E1

Canford Park Events Arena &
  Sports Gd* BH21 .....188 B7
Canford Pl **2** BH13 ..214 F7
Canford Rd
  Bournemouth BH11 ...189 A1
  Poole BH15 ....202 D4
Canford Sch BH21 ....164 B2
Canford View Dr BH21 .164 B6
Canford Way BH12 ...188 C2
Canhouse La GU31,GU33 .21 F3
Cannock Wlk **8** PO14 .154 E7
Cannon Cl BH18 .....187 A1
Cannon Hill Gdns BH21 .164 B7
Cannon Hill Rd BH21 ..164 A7
Cannon Ho **1** SO14 ..197 E4
Cannon St
  Lymington SO41 .....197 E4
  Southampton SO15 ..102 C8
Canoe Cl SO31 ......128 F1
Canon Ct SO50 ......57 C2
Canon St SO23 ......215 E5
Canon's Barn Cl PO11 ..132 C1
Canons Wlk SO41 ....211 D5
Cantell Sch SO16 ....79 A4
Canterbury Ave SO19 .104 C3
Canterbury Cl
  Lee-on-t-S PO13 .....180 B4
  West Moors BH22 ....138 F1
Canterbury Dr SO45 ..125 D3
Canterbury Rd
  Portsmouth PO4 .....182 F3
  Stubbington PO14 ...154 C4
Canterton La SO43 ...98 B8
Canterton Manor SO43 .98 A8
Canton St SO15 ......102 F6
Cantue Ho **5** SO14 ..169 B1
Canute Ho **6** SO14 ..103 A3
Canute Rd
  Southampton SO14 ...103 B3
  5 Winchester SO23 ..215 E5
Canvey Cl SO16 ......77 E2
Capel Ley PO7 ....134 E4
Capella Ct BH4 ......204 F2
Capella Gdns SO45 ..125 D3
Capers End La SO32 ..82 E1
Capesthorne PO15 ...129 B8
Capital Ho **7** SO22 ..215 D6
Capon Cl SO18 ....79 E4
Capstan Gdns SO31 ..129 C3
Capstan Ho
  2 Cosham PO6 .....157 F7
  Warsash SO31 ....128 C1
Capstans The BH14 ..214 B8
Capstone Pl BH8 .....205 B6
Capstone Rd BH8 ....205 B6
Captain's Row SO41 ..197 F4
Captains Cl PO12 ....102 A8
Captains Cres PO15 ..201 E3
Captains Pl SO14 ....103 B3
Captains Row **9** PO1 .182 A3
Caradon Pl BH31 .....114 D7
Carberry Dr PO16 ...156 C7
Carbery Ave BH6 ....206 D5
Carbery Ct PO9 ......135 D7
Carbery Gdns BH6 ...206 C4
Carbery La BH6 ......206 C4
Carbery Row **2** BH6 .206 C4
Carbis Cl PO6 ....157 A7
Cardew Rd GU33 .....21 A3
Cardigan Rd
  Bournemouth BH9 ...204 F8
  Poole BH12 ....203 F4
Cardinal Dr PO7 .....112 B1
Cardinal Way SO31 ...129 B2
Cardington Ct SO16 ...77 F4
Carey Rd
  Bournemouth BH9 ...189 F3
  Southampton SO19 ..104 C5
Careys Cotts SO42 ...145 F2
Careys Rd BH9 ......190 D4
Carina Ct BH13 ......214 C2
Carisbrooke Netley SO31 .127 C7
  Poole BH15 ....214 E7
Carisbrooke Ave PO14 .179 B7
Carisbrooke Ct PO9 ..136 B2
Carisbrooke Cres
  Chandler's Ford SO53 ..55 E5
  Hamworthy BH15 ....201 D3
Carisbrooke Ct
  1 Christchurch BH23 .209 B7
  1 Knowle Village BH17 .130 E7
  New Milton BH25 ....194 F3
  Romsey SO51 ....28 A1
Carisbrooke Dr SO19 .103 F8
Carisbrooke Rd
  Gosport PO12 ....155 C2
  Portsmouth PO4 .....183 A4
Carisbrooke Way BH8 .193 E1
Carless Cl PO13 .....180 D7
Carlinford **5** BH5 ...205 F3
Carlisle Ct **3** SO16 ..102 E8
Carlisle Rd
  Portsmouth PO5 .....216 C3
  Southampton SO16 ..102 B8
  Southbourne BH25 ..209 D8
Carlton Commerce Ctr The
  SO14 ....103 B7
Carlton Cres SO15 ...103 A7
Carlton Ct **6** SO15 ..102 F8
Carlton Gr PO12 .....181 C8
Carlton Ho **4** SO41 ..197 E4
Carlton Mount PO2 ..182 C8
Carlton Pl SO15 .....102 F6
Carlton Rd
  Bournemouth BH1 ...205 C4
  Gosport PO12 ....181 C6
  Portchester PO16 ...132 E1
  Southampton SO15 ..102 F6

Carlton Way PO12 ....181 C6
Carlyle Rd
  Bournemouth BH6 ...206 D6
  Gosport PO12 ....181 B6
Carlyn Dr SO53 ......55 D7
Carmans La SO21 .....31 D8
Carmarthen Ave PO6 .158 B8
Carmel Cl BH15 ....201 D2
Carmine Cl **5** PO13 ..180 C6
Carnarvon Rd
  4 Bournemouth BH1 .205 E4
  Gosport PO12 ....181 A5
  Portsmouth PO2 .....182 F8
Carnation Rd SO16 ...79 C4
Carne Cl SO53 ....55 C8
Carne Pl PO6 ....157 A7
Caroline Gdns BH23 ..207 F6
Caroline Cl BH22 .....203 D5
Caroline Ct SO15 ....102 B7
Caroline Gdns PO15 ..130 C2
Caroline Pl PO12 .....181 B7
Caroline Rd BH11 ....189 B2
Carolyn Cl SO19 .....103 E2
Carpathia Cl SO18 ...80 A2
Carpenter Cl Hythe SO45 .126 A1
  Lymington SO41 ....197 D5
  4 Portsmouth PO4 .183 A3
Carradale BH23 .....208 B8
Carran Wlk PO14 ....154 E7
Carraway PO15 ......129 D7
Carrbridge Cl BH3 ...204 D7
Carrbridge Gdns BH3 .204 D7
Carrbridge Rd BH3 ..204 D7
Carrick Way SO41 ...195 C2
Carrington Cl SO40 ..201 A2
Carrington Cvn Pk SO41 .211 F3
Carrington Ho **26** SO7 .79 A1
Carrington La SO41 ..211 E4
Carrol Cl SO30 ......57 D1
Carroll Ave BH22 ....165 E5
Carroll Cl BH12 .....204 A6
Carronade Wlk PO13 .157 F5
Carronades The **3**
  SO14 ....103 A5
Carshalton Ave PO6 ..158 B8
Carsworth Way PO17 .188 A2
Carter Com Sch BH15 .201 F2
Carter Ho Gosport PO13 .155 B5
  5 Portsmouth PO1 .182 A5
Carter's Cl SO16 .....47 D3
Carter's Clay Rd SO51 .26 B5
Carter's Copse Nature Trail*
  PO13 ....180 C5
Carter's La **9** BH15 .202 C2
Carters Ave PO15 ...201 D4
Carthage Cl SO53 ...55 F8
Cartref Cl BH31 .....114 F6
Cartwright Cl BH17 ..189 C4
Cartwright Dr PO15 .129 F2
Carvers Ind Est BH24 .141 A7
Carvers La BH24 ....141 A7
Carysfort Rd BH1 ...205 D4
Cascades App PO1 ...216 B4
Cascades Sh Ctr PO1 .216 B4
Cases Bakery PO17 ..108 A4
Cashmoor Cl **4** BH12 .203 F7
Caslake Cl SO41 .....194 F1
Caspar John Cl PO14 .179 B6
Caspian Cl PO15 ....129 B7
Cassel Ave BH13 ....204 B1
Casselles Ct **6** BH25 .195 A2
Casterbridge Cl **5** BH4 .204 C3
Casterbridge Rd BH22 .165 C3
Castle Ave
  Christchurch BH23 ..208 E8
  Havant PO9 ....136 B1
  Winchester SO23 ...215 D6
Castle Cl
  Milford on S SO41 ..211 E3
  Netley SO31 ....107 E7
  Winchester SO23 ...215 D6
Castle Court Prep Sch
  BH21 ....186 B7
Castle Ct
  2 Bitterne Pk SO18 ..79 F1
  2 Christchurch BH23 .209 A7
  Southampton,Millbrook
    SO16 ....102 A6
Castle Farm La PO17 .108 B2
Castle Gate Cl BH8 ..190 C2
Castle Gdns GU32 ....40 E3
Castle Gr PO16 ......156 D7
Castle Hill Poole BH14 .203 B4
  Winchester SO23 ...215 D6
Castle Hill La
  Burley BH24 ....142 E3
  Ringwood BH24 .....91 A7
Castle Hts BH15 .....79 F1
Castle La Calshot SO45 .178 F7
  Chandler's Ford SO53 ..55 B4
  North Baddesley SO52 ..54 D4
  1 Southampton SO14 ..102 F3
Castle La W BH9 .....190 C2
Castle Lane E BH7 ...206 C8
Castle Malwood Lodge
  SO43 ....98 B5
Castle Marina PO1 ...179 F1
Castle Mdw SP5 .....46 F7
Castle Mews SO14 ...102 F3
Castle Par BH7 ......206 D7
Castle Prim Sch PO16 .156 D7
Castle Rd
  Bournemouth BH9 ...190 A1
  Netley SO31 ....127 B6
  Portsmouth PO5 ....216 B1
  Rowlands Castle PO9 .113 B1
  Southampton SO18 ...79 E2
  Southwick PO17 ....132 F6
  Southampton SO15 ..102 F3
Castle Sq **3** SO14 ..102 F3

Castle St
  Christchurch BH23 ..207 E6
  Poole BH15 ....202 C1
  Portchester PO16 ...156 D7
  Southampton SO14 ..103 A7
Castle Trad Est PO16 .156 E8
Castle View PO12 ....181 B9
Castle View Rd PO16 .156 E6
Castle Way SO14 ....102 F3
Castle Woods SP5 ....47 D6
Castledene Cres BH13 .203 A2
Castlemain Ave BH6 .206 C5
Castleman Cl BH22 ..203 D7
Castleman Way BH24 .141 A6
Castlemans La PO11 .160 A1
Castlemews BH24 ....140 C5
Castlepoint BH8 .....190 E2
Castleshaw Cl SO16 ..101 F8
Castleton Ave BH10 ..189 D6
Castleton Ct PO5 ....216 A1
Castleway PO9 ....136 B1
Castlewood BH24 ....140 D5
Catalina Cl BH23 ....208 A6
Catalina Dr BH15 ....202 E1
Catamaran Cl SO31 ..128 F1
Cateran Cl SO16 .....101 F8
Cathay Gdns SO45 ...125 C3
Cathedral View **4** SO23 .215 F4
Catherine Cl SO30 ...80 E2
Catherine Cres SP5 ..46 D7
Catherine Gdns SO30 .80 E2
Catherine Wheel Gdns
  BH23 ....191 E3
Catherington CE Inf Sch
  PO8 ....88 B1
Catherington La
  Horndean PO8 ......112 B7
  Horndean,Catherington PO8 .88 B1
Catherington Way PO9 .135 F3
Catisfield Ho **3** PO1 ..216 C4
Catisfield La PO15 ...130 B1
Catisfield Rd
  Fareham PO15 ......130 C1
  Portsmouth PO4 ....183 B4
Catmint Cl SO53 .....54 F7
Caton Cl BH12 ......204 B8
Cattistock Rd BH8 ...190 E2
Catways SO21 ......30 B7
Causeway End SO43 ..122 D5
Causeway Cres SO40 .101 A8
Causeway Ct **5** SO18 .103 E8
Causeway Farm PO8 ..112 B1
Causeway The
  Petersfield GU31 ....40 E1
  Portchester PO16 ...131 E1
Causton Gdns SO50 ..56 A3
Cavalier Cl SO45 ....125 D3
Cavalier Cl PO6 .....158 D8
Cavan Cres BH17 ....187 B1
Cavanna Cl PO13 ....155 B3
Cavell Dr PO6 ......133 E1
Cavendish Cl
  Romsey SO51 ....28 B2
  Waterlooville PO7 ...134 F8
Cavendish Corner Mobile
  Home Pk **5** BH24 ..141 B8
Cavendish Ct **3** BH4 .204 C3
Cavendish Dr PO7 ...134 F8
Cavendish Gr
  Southampton SO17 ..102 F8
  Winchester SO23 .....2 B3
Cavendish Hall BH1 ..205 A5
Cavendish Mews **3**
  SO15 ....102 F8
Cavendish Pl BH1 ....205 A5
Cavendish Rd
  Bournemouth BH1 ...205 A5
  Portsmouth PO5 ....216 C1
Caversham Cl
  Hamworthy BH15 ...201 E3
  Southampton SO19 ..104 A4
  West End SO30 ......80 D1
Cawdor Rd BH3 .....204 D7
Cawte Rd SO15 .....102 D6
Cawte's Pl PO16 .....131 C1
Caxton Ave SO19 ....104 B6
Caxton Cl BH23 .....208 A7
Cecil Ave Ashurst SO40 .100 C2
  Bournemouth BH8 ...205 C8
  Southampton SO16 ...78 B1
Cecil Cl BH21 ....186 E6
Cecil Ct BH8 ....205 B8
Cecil Hill BH8 ......205 A8
Cecil Pl Poole BH15 ..216 A1
Cecil Rd
  Bournemouth BH5 ...205 D8
  Poole BH12 ....203 D6
  Southampton SO19 ..103 F3
Cecil Vales SO17 .....79 C1
Cedar Ave
  Bournemouth BH10 ..189 D6
  Christchurch BH23 ..206 D8
  Southampton SO15 ..102 D8
  St Leonards BH24 ..139 E3
Cedar Cl Burstedon SO31 .127 F8
  Gosport PO12 ....156 A1
  Hedge End SO30 ....105 C7
  Kings Worthy SO23 ....2 B8
  Upton BH16 ....201 B8
  Waterlooville PO7 ...134 E6
Cedar Cres
  North Baddesley SO52 ..53 F5
  Waterlooville PO8 ...112 C5

Cedar Ct
Bishop's Waltham SO32 . . . . . .83 D8
Bournemouth BH4 . . . . .204 B2
🔟 Fareham PO16 . . . . . . .131 C1
Portsmouth PO5 . . . . .216 C1
Cedar Dr Hordle SO41 . . . .211 D8
Wimborne Minst BH21 . . . . .164 A5
Cedar Gdns Havant PO9 . .136 A2
Old Milton BH25 . . . . .194 F1
Southampton SO14 . . . . . . .103 A8
Cedar Gr PO3 . . . . .183 B7
Cedar Grange 🔞 BH13 . . .204 A4
Cedar Lawn SO51 . . . . . . .28 C1
Cedar Manor BH4 . . . . . . .204 C3
Cedar Pl BH23 . . . . .169 B1
Cedar Rd Eastleigh SO50 . . .55 E1
Hythe SO45 . . . . .150 A7
Southampton SO14 . . . . . . .103 A7
Cedar Sch The SO16 . . . . .77 E4
Cedar Trad Pk BH21 . . . . .164 F6
Cedar Way
Fareham PO14 . . . . .154 E8
Ferndown BH22 . . . . .165 C8
Cedar Wlk SO22 . . . . .215 C5
Cedar Wood Cl
Fair Oak SO50 . . . . .57 E2
Totton SO40 . . . . .100 C8
Cedarmount SO43 . . . . . . .121 F4
Cedars The
Bournemouth BH4 . . . . .204 C4
Fareham PO16 . . . . .130 F3
Cedars View SP5 . . . . .4 E7
Cedarwood SO23 . . . . .2 C7
Cedarwood Lodge 🔞
PO16 . . . . .131 B2
Ceder Ho SO14 . . . . .103 B3
Cedric Cl SO45 . . . . .177 F8
Celandine Ave
Locks Heath SO31 . . . . .128 F2
Waterlooville PO8 . . . . .112 B3
Celandine Cl
Chandler's Ford SO53 . . . . . .54 F5
Christchurch BH23 . . . . . . .208 B8
Celia Cl PO7 . . . . .135 B8
Cellars Farm Rd BH6 . . . .207 A3
Cement Terr 2 SO14 . . . .102 F3
Cemetery Ave SO51 . . . . . .52 F6
Cemetery Junc BH22 . . . .204 F5
Cemetery La
Denmead PO7 . . . . .110 F5
Westbourne PO10 . . . . .137 D3
Cemetery Rd
Southampton SO15 . . . . . . .102 F8
Wimborne Minst BH21 . . . . .163 B5
Centaur St PO2 . . . . .182 E6
Centaury Gdns SO50 . . . . .81 C7
Centenary Cl SO41 . . . . . .172 C2
Centenary Gdns PO9 . . . .135 F2
Centenary Ho BH23 . . . . .207 B7
Centenary Way BH1 . . . . .205 E5
Central Ave
Corfe Mullen BH21 . . . . . . .186 D7
Poole BH12 . . . . .203 E6
Central Bridge SO14 . . . .103 B3
Central Dr
Bournemouth BH2 . . . . . . .204 E5
West Moors BH24 . . . . .166 B8
Central Point PO3 . . . . . . .183 B6
Central Prec The SO15 . . .55 C5
Central Rd Cosham PO6 . . .158 C7
Portchester PO16 . . . . .156 B7
Southampton SO14 . . . . . . .103 A2
Central Sq PO1 . . . . .182 A4
Central St PO1 . . . . .216 C4
Central Station Bridge
SO15 . . . . .102 E5
Central Way N SO45 . . . . .151 E2
Centre La SO41 . . . . .196 E1
Centre Pl BH24 . . . . .140 F7
Centre Way SO31 . . . . . . .129 A3
Centurion Ct 2 PO1 . . . . .182 A4
Centurion Gate PO4 . . . . .183 D3
Centurion Ho SO18 . . . . . .103 C7
Centurion Ind Pk SO18 . .103 C7
Cerdic Mews SO31 . . . . . .128 A4
Cerne Abbas BH13 . . . . . .204 A1
Cerne Cl
Bournemouth BH9 . . . . . . .190 B4
North Baddesley SO52 . . . . . .53 F4
West End SO18 . . . . .80 B1
Cessac Ho PO12 . . . . .181 C2
Chadderton Gdns PO1 . . .182 B3
Chaddesley Glen BH13 . . .214 E6
Chaddesley Grange
BH13 . . . . .214 F6
Chaddesley Pines BH13 . .214 E6
Chaddesley Wood Rd
BH13 . . . . .214 E6
Chadswell Mdw PO9 . . . .135 D1
Chadwell Ave SO19 . . . . . .104 B4
Chadwick Rd SO50 . . . . . . .55 F2
Chadwick Way SO31 . . . . .127 F2
Chafen Rd SO18 . . . . .103 D7
Chaffey Cl PO14 . . . . .141 C8
Chaffinch Cl
Broadstone BH17 . . . . .186 F2
New Milton BH25 . . . . .194 F2
Totton SO40 . . . . .100 C8
Chaffinch Dr PO8 . . . . . . .111 E4
Chaffinch Way
Lee-on-t-S PO13 . . . . .179 F4
Portchester PO16 . . . . .155 F8
Chalbury Cl BH17 . . . . . . .188 A2
Chalbury Ct 2 BH14 . . . .203 B4

Chalcroft Distribution Pk
SO30 . . . . .81 B5
Chaldecott Gdns BH10 . . .189 C4
Chaldon Rd BH17 . . . . . . .187 F2
Chale Cl PO13 . . . . .155 C2
Chalewood Rd SO45 . . . . .177 E2
Chalfont Ave BH23 . . . . . .191 D3
Chalfont Ct 7 SO16 . . . . .78 A1
Chalice Cl BH14 . . . . .203 A4
Chalice Ct SO30 . . . . .105 B6
Chalk Hill Soberton SO32 . . .85 C5
West End SO18 . . . . .80 C1
Chalk Hill Rd PO8 . . . . . . .112 C8
Chalk Pit SO41 . . . . .131 B7
Chalk Pit Cotts PO17 . . . .131 B7
Chalk Ridge
Horndean PO8 . . . . .88 D3
Winchester SO23 . . . . .11 D7
Chalk's Cl SP5 . . . . .47 D7
Chalkpit Rd PO6 . . . . .133 B1
Chalkridge Rd PO6 . . . . . .134 A1
Chalky La SO32 . . . . .83 D8
Challenge Ent Ctr The
PO3 . . . . .158 B3
Challenger Dr PO12 . . . . .181 C8
Challenger Way SO45 . . . .125 D2
Challis Ct 🔟 SO14 . . . . . .103 A3
Chalmers Way SO31 . . . . .127 E3
Chaloner Cres SO45 . . . . .126 A1
Chalton Cres PO9 . . . . . . .135 D4
Chalton Ho PO1 . . . . .216 B4
Chalton La PO8 . . . . .88 D6
Chalvington Ct SO53 . . . . .55 C5
Chalvington Rd SO53 . . . . .55 C4
Chalwyn Ind Est BH15,
BH12 . . . . .203 A7
Chalybeate Cl SO16 . . . . . .78 B2
Chalybeate Hospl SO16 . . .78 B2
Chamberlain Gr PO14 . . . .155 A8
Chamberlain Hall SO16 . . .79 A4
Chamberlain Rd SO17 . . . .79 A3
Chamberlayne Ct SO32 . . . .54 B4
Chamberlayne Ho SO31 . .127 B6
Chamberlayne Park Sch
SO19 . . . . .104 A1
Chamberlayne Rd
Bursledon SO31 . . . . .127 F8
Eastleigh SO50 . . . . .56 A2
Netley SO31 . . . . .127 B6
Chambers Ave SO51 . . . . . .53 B7
Chambers Cl SO16 . . . . . . .77 C5
Champion Cl SO41 . . . . . .211 F4
Chancel Rd SO31 . . . . .129 B3
Chancellors La SO32 . . . . .81 F4
Chanctonbury Ho PO5 . . .216 B1
Chander Cl BH22 . . . . .165 E4
Chandler's Ford Ind Est
SO53 . . . . .55 B5
Chandler's Ford Inf Sch
SO53 . . . . .55 D6
Chandler's Ford Sta
SO53 . . . . .55 C6
Chandlers Cl
Bournemouth BH7 . . . . . . .206 B8
South Hayling PO11 . . . . . . .185 C2
Chandlers Cl 🔞 SO14 . . . .103 A3
Chandlers Pl SO31 . . . . . .127 B6
Chandlers Way SO31 . . . . .129 B6
Chandos Ave BH12 . . . . . .204 A8
Chandos Ho 🔞 SO14 . . . .103 A3
Chandos St 🔞 SO14 . . . . .103 A3
Channel Ct
Barton on S BH25 . . . . .209 E7
Bournemouth BH6 . . . . .206 D3
Channel Mouth Rd
SO45 . . . . .151 F1
Channel Way SO14 . . . . . .103 C3
Channs Farm Rd SO14 . . . .79 D5
Channon Ct 🔟 SO15 . . . . .102 E7
Channon Ret Pk SO50 . . . .55 E3
Chant Cl BH23 . . . . .207 D7
Chantrell Wlk PO15 . . . . .130 D3
Chantry Cl BH23 . . . . .193 F1
Chantry Mead SO22 . . . . .215 C2
Chantry Rd
Gosport PO12 . . . . .181 A8
Horndean PO8 . . . . .112 B7
Southampton SO14 . . . . . . .103 B3
Chantry The
Bournemouth BH1 . . . . . . .205 A4
Locks Heath PO14 . . . . .129 C3
Chapel Cl Brashfield SO51 . .28 C6
Corfe Mullen BH21 . . . . . . .186 C6
West End SO18 . . . . .80 D2
Chapel Cres SO19 . . . . . . .104 A4
Chapel Ct 🔟 PO1 . . . . . . .182 C7
Chapel Dro
Hedge End SO30 . . . . .105 B6
Horton Heath SO50 . . . . .81 C7
Chapel Gate BH23 . . . . . .190 C8
Chapel La Bishopstone SP5 . .22 B7
Blackfield SO45 . . . . .177 E8
Bransgore BH24 . . . . .193 A8
Burley BH24 . . . . .143 B3
East Boldre SO42 . . . . .175 B6
East Parley BH23 . . . . .190 C8
Fawley SO45 . . . . .151 A2
Lockerley SO51 . . . . .26 A5
Lyndhurst SO43 . . . . .121 F4
Michelmersh SO51 . . . . .27 D8
Nomansland SP5 . . . . .73 C7
Otterbourne SO21 . . . . .31 B1
Poole BH15 . . . . .202 C2
Redlynch SP5 . . . . .47 E6
Sway SO41 . . . . .172 D1
Totton SO40 . . . . .100 E5

Chapel La continued
5 Waterlooville PO7 . . . . .134 E7
Wimborne Minst BH21 . . . . .163 B5
Winchester SO23 . . . . .12 B8
Chapel Rd Droxford SO32 . .61 C3
Poole BH14 . . . . .203 A4
Sarisbury SO31 . . . . .128 E6
Soberton SO32 . . . . .85 B2
Southampton SO14 . . . . . . .103 B4
Swanmore SO32 . . . . .84 B5
West End SO18 . . . . .80 E2
Chapel Rise BH24 . . . . . . .140 D2
Chapel Sq PO12 . . . . .180 F7
Chapel St East Meon GU32 . .38 D1
Gosport PO12 . . . . .181 B9
Petersfield GU32 . . . . .40 F3
3 Portsmouth PO5 . . . . . .216 A1
Portsmouth,Buckland PO2 . .182 D8
Southampton SO14 . . . . . . .103 B4
Chapelside PO14 . . . . .154 A8
Chaplains Ave PO8 . . . . . .111 D3
Chaplains Cl PO8 . . . . . . .111 D3
Charborough Rd BH18 . . . .187 B3
Charden Ct SO18 . . . . .104 B7
Charden Rd
Bishopstoke SO50 . . . . .57 A2
Eastleigh SO50 . . . . .57 A2
Charfield Cl
Fareham PO14 . . . . .154 D8
Winchester SO22 . . . . .2 D3
Charing Cl BH24 . . . . .141 A6
Charity View PO17 . . . . . .130 E7
Chark La PO13 . . . . .179 F5
Charlcot Lawn PO9 . . . . . .135 D6
Charlecote Dr SO53 . . . . . .55 A8
Charlecote Ho SO15 . . . . .102 D5
Charlecote Mews 14
SO22 . . . . .215 D6
Charlemont Dr 2 PO16 . .131 D1
Charles Cl
Waterlooville PO7 . . . . .134 D6
Winchester SO23 . . . . .215 F8
Charles Cres BH25 . . . . . .195 B5
Charles Dickens Birthplace
Mus* PO1 . . . . .182 C7
Charles Dickens Inf Sch
PO1 . . . . .182 D7
Charles Dickens Jun Sch
PO1 . . . . .182 D7
Charles Dickens St PO1 . .216 B3
Charles Knott Gdns
SO15 . . . . .102 F7
Charles Ley Ct SO45 . . . . .151 B3
Charles Miller Ct 4
SO15 . . . . .102 F8
Charles Norton-Thomas Ct 4
PO1 . . . . .182 D7
Charles Rd
Christchurch BH23 . . . . . . .207 F8
Poole BH15 . . . . .202 D3
Charles St
Petersfield GU32 . . . . .40 E3
Portsmouth PO1 . . . . .216 C4
Charles Watts Way
SO30 . . . . .105 B8
Charles Wyatt Ho 3
SO14 . . . . .103 A7
Charles's La BH24 . . . . . . .141 A2
Charlesbury Ave PO12 . . .180 F4
Charleston Cl PO11 . . . . . .184 E4
Charleston Rd SO45 . . . . .150 D8
Charlesworth Dr PO7 . . . .111 D2
Charlesworth Gdns
PO7 . . . . .111 D1
Charlie Soar Ct 1 SO50 . . .56 A2
Charliejoy Gdns 1
SO14 . . . . .103 C6
Charlock Cl PO7 . . . . .216 B1
Charlotte Cl
Christchurch BH23 . . . . . . .208 A6
3 New Milton BH25 . . . . .195 A2
Poole BH12 . . . . .204 C7
Charlotte Ct
Chandler's Ford SO53 . . . . . .55 F2
Southampton SO19 . . . . . . .103 F2
Charlotte Mews PO12 . . . .181 A3
Charlotte Pl SO14 . . . . . . .103 A6
Charlotte St PO1 . . . . .216 B4
Charlton Cl
Bournemouth BH9 . . . . . . .190 C4
Hordle SO41 . . . . .195 F3
Charlton Dr GU31 . . . . . . .41 A5
Charlton Rd SO15 . . . . . . .102 D7
Charltons The BH2 . . . . . .204 F5
Charminster 6 PO5 . . . . .182 E2
Charminster Ave BH9 . . . .190 B1
Charminster Cl
Bournemouth BH8 . . . . . . .190 B2
Waterlooville PO7 . . . . .134 E8
Charminster Pl BH8 . . . . .190 C2
Charminster Rd BH8 . . . . .205 B7
Charmouth Gr BH14 . . . . .203 A4
Charmouth Terr 6 SO16 . .78 A1
Charmus Rd SO40 . . . . . . .76 B2
Charmwen Cres SO30 . . . . .80 C2
Charnock Cl SO41 . . . . . . .195 F3
Charnwood PO13 . . . . .155 D2
Charnwood Ave BH9 . . . . .190 B2
Charnwood Cl
Chandler's Ford SO53 . . . . . .30 C2
Totton SO40 . . . . .76 D1
West Moors BH22 . . . . .138 E2

Charnwood Cres SO53 . . . .30 C2
Charnwood Dr SP6 . . . . . . .69 E3
Charnwood Gdns SO53 . . . .30 C2
Charnwood Way SO45 . . . .177 E7
Chartcombe BH13 . . . . . . .214 E8
Charter Ho 2 PO5 . . . . . .216 A2
Charter Rd BH11 . . . . .188 D6
Chartergrove Ho 12
GU31 . . . . .40 F3
Charterhouse Way SO30 . .81 C1
Chartwell 6 BH13 . . . . . .204 B3
Chartwell Cl
Eastleigh SO50 . . . . .56 B6
Titchfield PO14 . . . . .129 C1
Chartwell Dr PO9 . . . . . . .136 C3
Chase Cl GU33 . . . . .21 A4
Chase Farm Cl SO32 . . . . . .83 E3
Chase Gr SO32 . . . . .83 E3
Chase Rd GU33 . . . . .21 A4
Chaseside Funtic Gr Poole BH12 . . .180 F4
St Leonards BH24 . . . . .140 D5
Titchfield PO14 . . . . .129 D2
Verwood BH31 . . . . .115 C5
Chaseside BH7 . . . . .206 A8
Chasewater Ave PO3 . . . . .183 A7
Chatburn Ave PO8 . . . . . . .111 F3
Chatfield Ave PO6 . . . . . . .182 A8
Chatfield Ho 16 PO1 . . . . .216 C4
Chatfield Rd PO13 . . . . . . .155 C4
Chatham Cl PO12 . . . . . . .181 C8
Chatham Dr PO1 . . . . .182 B3
Chatham Rd SO22 . . . . . . .215 A3
Chatsworth Ave
Cosham PO6 . . . . .158 A6
Portsmouth PO6 . . . . .157 F6
Chatsworth Ct PO15 . . . . .130 C1
Chatsworth Ct PO5 . . . . . .216 C1
Chatsworth Rd
Bournemouth BH8 . . . . . . .205 C6
Eastleigh SO50 . . . . .56 B6
Poole BH14 . . . . .203 B5
Chatsworth Way BH25 . . . .194 F3
Chaucer Ave PO6 . . . . .132 E1
Chaucer Bsns Pk SO23 . . . .2 C1
Chaucer Cl
Fareham PO14 . . . . .130 F2
Waterlooville PO7 . . . . .111 E2
Wimborne Minst BH21 . . . . .163 C6
Chaucer Dr SO41 . . . . .211 D5
Chaucer Rd BH18 . . . . . . .214 F8
Southampton SO19 . . . . . . .104 B1
Chaucombe Pl BH25 . . . . .194 F1
Chaundler Rd SO23 . . . . . .215 E8
Chaveney Cl SO45 . . . . . . .125 F1
Chavy Water SO51 . . . . . . .52 F8
Chawton Cl
Southampton SO18 . . . . . . .104 D8
Winchester SO22 . . . . .1 D4
Cheam Rd BH18 . . . . .186 F4
Cheam Way SO40 . . . . .76 D1
Cheater's La SP6 . . . . .92 C8
Cheddar Cl SO19 . . . . .103 F3
Cheddington Rd BH9 . . . . .190 A4
Cheddington Cl BH17 . . . . .187 E2
Chedworth Cres PO6 . . . . .133 A1
Cheerphile Ho SO42 . . . . .181 C8
Cheesecombe Farm La
GU33 . . . . .19 F6
Chellowdene SO53 . . . . . . .55 C5
Chelmsford Rd
Portsmouth PO2 . . . . .157 F2
Upton BH16 . . . . .201 A7
Chelsea Rd PO5 . . . . .216 C1
Cheltenham Cres PO13 . . .179 F4
Cheltenham Ct 10 SO17 . . .79 C3
Cheltenham Gdns SO30 . . .81 C3
Cheltenham Rd
Cosham PO6 . . . . .157 C8
Poole BH12 . . . . .203 C5
Chelveston Cres SO16 . . . . .78 A4
Chelwood Gate SO16 . . . . .77 E6
Chene Rd BH21 . . . . .163 D4
Cheping Gdns SO30 . . . . . .106 A6
Chepstow Cl
Chandler's Ford SO53 . . . . . .55 B6
Totton SO40 . . . . .100 C8
Chepstow Ct PO7 . . . . . . .134 E5
Cheqhers Ho 4 PO16 . . . .131 B1
Chequers Ct BH13 . . . . . . .214 E6
Chequers Quay 8 PO10 . .161 A8
Cherbourg Prim Sch
SO50 . . . . .56 A1
Cherbourg Rd SO50 . . . . . .56 A1
Cherford Rd BH11 . . . . . . .189 B2
Cherita Ct BH15 . . . . .202 F6
Cheriton 7 BH4 . . . . .204 C4
Cheriton Ave
Bournemouth BH7 . . . . . . .206 C8
Southampton SO18 . . . . . . .104 D8
Cheriton Cl Havant PO9 . . .135 D4
Horndean PO8 . . . . .112 D7
Winchester SO22 . . . . .215 B7
Cheriton Ct 5 SO15 . . . . .102 F5
Cheriton La
Bramdean SO24 . . . . .15 C8
Cheriton SO24 . . . . .14 C6
Cheriton Prim Sch SO24 . . .14 C6
Cheriton Rd
Eastleigh SO50 . . . . .55 F1
Gosport PO12 . . . . .181 C4
Portsmouth PO4 . . . . .183 C4
Winchester SO22 . . . . .215 B7
Cherque La PO13 . . . . .179 C1
Cherque Way PO13 . . . . . .180 A7
Cherrett Cl BH11 . . . . .188 F4

Cherries Dr BH9 . . . . .189 E2
Cherry Blossom Ct 19
PO1 . . . . .182 D7
Cherry Cl
Lee-on-t-S PO13 . . . . .179 F2
Poole BH14 . . . . .203 B4
Cherry Ct Poole BH14 . . . .203 B5
16 Southampton SO17 . . .103 A8
Cherry Dro SO50 . . . . .81 D6
Cherry Gdns SO32 . . . . . . .83 D7
Cherry Gr BH22 . . . . .165 C6
Cherry Hill Gdns BH16 . . .201 B6
Cherry Hill Gr BH16 . . . . .201 B6
Cherry Tree Ave
Fareham PO14 . . . . .154 D8
Waterlooville PO8 . . . . .112 B2
Cherry Tree Cl
Hordle SO41 . . . . .211 D8
St Leonards BH24 . . . . .139 D3
Cherry Tree Ct 4 BH25 . . .195 B1
Cherry Tree Dr PO15 . . . . .194 E5
Cherry Wlk SO15 . . . . .102 C8
Cherrygarth Rd PO15 . . . .130 C1
Cherryton Gdns SO45 . . . .150 B3
Cherrywood SO30 . . . . . . .105 B6
Cherrywood Gdns
South Hayling PO11 . . . . . . .185 A4
Southampton SO40 . . . . . . .100 C7
Chervil Cl
Chandler's Ford SO53 . . . . . .54 F6
Horndean PO8 . . . . .88 C1
Cherville Ct SO51 . . . . .52 E7
Cherville Mews SO51 . . . . .52 E8
Cherville St SO51 . . . . .52 E8
Cherwell Cres SO16 . . . . . .101 E8
Cherwell Gdns SO53 . . . . . .55 D5
Cherwell Ho SO16 . . . . . . .101 E8
Cheshire Cl PO15 . . . . .129 F5
Cheshire Dr BH8 . . . . .191 A2
Cheshire Way PO10 . . . . . .137 D2
Chesil Gdns BH12 . . . . . . .203 B8
Chesil St SO23 . . . . .215 F5
Chesil Terr SO23 . . . . .215 F5
Chesil Wood SO23 . . . . . . .11 C7
Chesilbourne Gr BH8 . . . .190 D3
Chesildene Ave BH8 . . . . .190 D3
Chesildene Dr BH8 . . . . . .190 D3
Chessel Ave
Bournemouth BH5 . . . . . . .205 F4
Southampton SO19 . . . . . . .103 E6
Chessel Cres SO19 . . . . . . .103 E6
Chester Cres PO13 . . . . . . .180 A4
Chester Ct SO16 . . . . .78 C2
Chester Cts 8 PO12 . . . . .181 C5
Chester Pl 7 PO5 . . . . . . .182 D2
Chester Rd Poole BH13 . . .204 A2
Southampton SO18 . . . . . . .80 A1
Winchester SO23 . . . . .215 F6
Chesterfield Ct BH13 . . . . .214 F8
Chesterfield Rd BH1 . . . . .205 C3
Chesterfield Rd PO3 . . . . . .183 A8
Chesterton Gdns PO8 . . . .111 E3
Chesterton Pl PO15 . . . . . .129 C8
Chestnut Ave
Barton on S BH25 . . . . .210 A8
Bournemouth BH6 . . . . .206 C4
Christchurch BH23 . . . . . . .206 D8
2 Colden Common SO21 . .31 F1
Eastleigh SO50 . . . . .55 F1
Ellingham BH24 . . . . .116 B6
Havant PO9 . . . . .135 B3
Littleton SO22 . . . . .1 C4
Portsmouth PO4 . . . . .182 F4
Waterlooville PO8 . . . . .112 C5
Chestnut Cl
Chandler's Ford SO53 . . . . . .55 C2
Denmead PO7 . . . . .110 F4
Romsey SO51 . . . . .53 D6
West End SO18 . . . . .80 D3
Chestnut Ct
Durrants PO9 . . . . .136 B8
Southampton SO17 . . . . . . .79 B2
Chestnut Dr
Ashurst SO40 . . . . .100 C3
Petersfield GU31 . . . . .40 F1
Chestnut Gr BH21 . . . . . . .164 E6
Chestnut Lodge 4 SO16 . .78 E3
Chestnut Rd
Brockenhurst SO42 . . . . . . .146 A1
Southampton SO16 . . . . . . .78 A2
Chestnut Rise
Droxford SO32 . . . . .61 B2
Eastleigh SO53 . . . . .55 D1
Chestnut Way
Burton BH23 . . . . .192 C3
Titchfield PO14 . . . . .129 C1
Chestnut Wlk
Botley SO30 . . . . .105 F8
Gosport PO12 . . . . .156 A1
Chestnuts The SO31 . . . . .129 A2
Chetnole Cl BH17 . . . . . . .188 A1
Chettle Rd SO19 . . . . .104 E5
Chetwode Way BH17 . . . . .187 B2
Chetwynd Dr SO16 . . . . . . .78 F4
Chetwynd Rd
Bournemouth PO4 . . . . .182 E3
Southampton SO16 . . . . . . .78 F5
Cheviot Court Flats
BH23 . . . . .207 F8
Cheviot Cres SO16 . . . . . . .101 E8
Cheviot Dr SO45 . . . . .125 D3
Cheviot Gn SO31 . . . . .152 D10
Cheviot Rd SO16 . . . . .101 E8
Cheviot Way BH31 . . . . . . .114 F5
Cheviot Wlk PO14 . . . . . . .154 F7
Cheviots The BH14 . . . . . .203 C3

Chevron Bsns Pk SO45 . . . . . **150** B6
Chewter Cl PO4 . . . . **182** E1
Chewton Common Rd
BH23 . . . . **209** B8
Chewton Farm Rd BH23 **194** C1
Chewton Lodge BH23 . . . **209** B8
Chewton Mews BH23 . . . . **194** B2
Chewton Way BH23 . . . . . **194** B1
Cheyne Gdns BH4 . . . . **204** C2
Cheyne Way PO13 . . . . **179** F2
Chichester Ave PO11 . . . . **185** A3
Chichester Cl
Gosport PO13 . . . . **155** B2
Hedge End SO30 . . . . **81** C1
Sarisbury SO31 . . . . **128** E3
West Wellow SO51 . . . . **51** B2
Chichester Ho PO4 . . . . . . **136** A3
Chichester Rd
North Hayling PO11 . . . . . . **160** C1
Portsmouth PO2 . . . . **182** E8
Havant PO21 . . . . **117** C1
Southampton SO18 . . . . . . **104** A7
Chichester Way BH23 . . . **208** A5
Chickenhall La SO50 . . . . . **56** C2
Chickerell Cl BH9 . . . . **190** B3
Chidden Cl GU32 . . . . **38** D1
Chidden Holt SO53 . . . . **55** A5
Chideock Cl BH12 . . . . **203** E6
Chidham Cl PO9 . . . . **135** E2
Chidham Dr PO9 . . . . **135** E2
Chidham Rd PO9 . . . . **134** A1
Chidham Sq PO9 . . . . **135** E2
Chidham Wlk 2 PO9 . . . . **135** E2
Chigwell Rd BH8 . . . . **190** B1
Chilbolton Ave SO22 . . . . **215** B6
Chilbolton Ct
11 Havant PO9 . . . . **136** B6
Winchester SO22 . . . . **215** A5
Chilcomb La
Chilcomb SO21 . . . . **11** E5
Winchester SO23 . . . . **11** C5
Chilcomb Rd SO18 . . . . . . **104** C8
Chilcombe Cl PO9 . . . . . . **135** F3
Chilcombe Hts SO23 . . . . **215** F5
Chilcombe Rd BH6 . . . . . . **206** B5
Chilcote Rd PO3 . . . . **183** A7
Childe Sq PO2 . . . . **157** C2
Chilfrome Cl BH17 . . . . . . **187** C1
Chilgrove Rd PO6 . . . . **158** C8
Chilham Cl SO50 . . . . **56** A4
Chillenden Ct SO40 . . . . . **100** C6
Chillerton SO31 . . . . **127** C7
Chilling La SO31 . . . . **152** F7
Chillington Gdns 5
SO53 . . . . **30** B1
Chilly Hill SP6 . . . . **94** F7
Chilmark Ct GU33 . . . . **20** E4
Chilsdown Way PO7 . . . . **134** E4
Chiltern Cl
Old Milton BH25 . . . . **194** F1
Poole BH4 . . . . **204** B5
Totton SO40 . . . . **100** D5
Chiltern Ct
5 Christchurch BH23 . . **207** F8
Gosport PO12 . . . . **181** B6
2 Portsmouth PO5 . . . . . **182** D1
Chiltern Dr
Barton on S BH25 . . . . **209** B8
Verwood BH31 . . . . **114** F6
Chiltern Gn SO16 . . . . **101** E8
Chiltern Wlk PO14 . . . . . . **154** F5
Chilworth Cl SO16 . . . . **54** D1
Chilworth Dro SO16 . . . . . **54** D1
Chilworth Gdns PO8 . . . . . **88** D4
Chilworth Gr PO12 . . . . . . **181** A6
Chilworth Old Village
SO16 . . . . **54** C2
Chilworth Rd SO16 . . . . . . **54** E1
Chimes The BH4 . . . . **204** B3
Chine Ave SO19 . . . . **103** E6
Chine Cl SO31 . . . . **129** A4
Chine Cres PO4 . . . . **204** D2
Chine Crescent Rd BH2 **204** D2
Chine The PO13 . . . . **155** E1
Chine Wlk BH22 . . . . **165** E1
Chinham Rd SO40 . . . . **99** C6
Chipstead Ho 9 PO6 . . . **157** F8
Chipstead Rd 3 PO6 . . . **157** F8
Chirk Pl SO51 . . . . **53** A7
Chisels La BH23 . . . . **193** B6
Chisholm Cl SO16 . . . . **77** F5
Chislehurst 8 BH4 . . . . . **204** C3
Chiswell Rd BH17 . . . . . . **187** D1
Chitty Rd PO4 . . . . **183** A2
Chivers Cl PO5 . . . . **216** B1
Chloe Gdns BH12 . . . . **203** D7
Chorley Cl BH15 . . . . **202** C6
Chris Cres BH16 . . . . **202** B6
Christ the King RC Prim Sch
BH11 . . . . **189** A5
Christ's Hospl 18 SO23 . **215** D5
Christchurch Bay Rd
BH25 . . . . **209** F7
Christchurch By-Pass
BH23 . . . . **207** D8
Christchurch Castle*
BH23 . . . . **207** B6
Christchurch Gdns
Cosham PO7 . . . . **134** B2
11 Winchester SO23 . . . . **215** D3
Christchurch Hospl
BH23 . . . . **206** F8
Christchurch Jun Sch
BH23 . . . . **207** A7
Christchurch Prim Sch
BH23 . . . . **207** A7

Christchurch Priory*
BH23 . . . . **207** C6
Christchurch Rd
Barton on S BH25 . . . . **209** D8
BH1,BH7 . . . . **205** D4
Bournemouth,Iford BH7 . . **206** B6
Ferndown BH22 . . . . **165** C1
Hordle SO41 . . . . **211** C8
Hurn BH23 . . . . **191** C5
Ringwood BH24 . . . . **140** F7
Ringwood,Moortown BH24 **141** A4
Winchester SO23 . . . . **215** D5
Christchurch Sta BH23 . **207** A7
Christie Ave PO15 . . . . . . **129** C8
Christine Ct 8 SO18 . . . . **103** E8
Christopher Cres BH15 . **202** C6
Christyne Ct PO7 . . . . **134** D4
Church Cl
Bishopstoke SO50 . . . . **56** D4
Clanfield PO8 . . . . **88** B6
Locks Heath SO31 . . . . . . **129** B3
Minstead SO43 . . . . **98** C2
North Baddesley SO52 . . . . **54** A4
Church End SO15 . . . . **102** C8
Church Farm SP6 . . . . **93** F8
Church Farm Cl SO45 . . . **125** B6
Church Hatch SP5 . . . . **47** A8
Church Hill
Milford on S SO41 . . . . . . **211** E4
Redlynch SP5 . . . . **47** F5
Verwood BH31 . . . . **114** E6
West End SO30 . . . . **80** C1
Church La Awbridge SO51 . **26** E3
Botley SO30 . . . . **106** A5
Braishfield SO51 . . . . **28** D7
Bramdean SO24 . . . . **15** C4
Brockenhurst SO42 . . . . . **173** B8
Burley BH24 . . . . **143** B3
Burseldon SO31 . . . . **128** B8
Christchurch BH23 . . . . . **207** B6
Colden Common SO21 . . . . **56** F8
Compton PO18 . . . . **90** F2
Curdridge SO32 . . . . **106** D8
Damerham SP6 . . . . **68** D4
Durley SO32 . . . . **81** F6
East Boldre SO42 . . . . **175** D5
Easton Down SO21 . . . . **2** F5
Fawley SO45 . . . . **151** A3
Ferndown BH22 . . . . **189** F7
Hambledon PO7 . . . . **86** D3
Havant PO9 . . . . **160** B8
Hedge End SO30 . . . . **105** B5
Highfield SO17 . . . . **79** B2
Kings Worthy SO23 . . . . **2** C6
Littleton SO22 . . . . **1** A6
Lymington SO41 . . . . **197** E3
Lyndhurst SO43 . . . . **121** F5
Meonstoke SO32 . . . . **61** C7
Mottisfont SO51 . . . . **5** F2
North Hayling PO11 . . . . . **160** C3
Nursling SO16 . . . . **76** F6
Old Milton BH25 . . . . **194** F1
Pilley SO41 . . . . **173** F2
Plaitford SO51 . . . . **50** B5
Romsey SO51 . . . . **52** E7
Sherfield English SO51 . . . **25** D3
12 Southampton SO14 . . **102** F3
Swanmore SO32 . . . . **84** C6
Sway SO41 . . . . **172** B1
Twyford SO21 . . . . **32** A7
West Meon GU32 . . . . **37** B5
Church Leat SP5 . . . . **47** E4
Church Mead 9 SO41 . . . **197** E2
Church Path
11 Emsworth PO10 . . . . . **160** F8
Fareham PO16 . . . . **131** C1
Gosport PO12 . . . . **181** D5
Horndean PO8 . . . . **112** D6
Titchfield PO14 . . . . **154** A8
Church Path N PO1 . . . . . **216** B4
Church Pl 7 Fareham PO16 **131** C2
Romsey SO51 . . . . **52** E7
Church Rd
Bishopstoke SO50 . . . . **56** D5
Bournemouth BH6 . . . . . . **206** F3
Ferndown BH22 . . . . **165** C5
Locks Heath SO31 . . . . . . **129** B3
Micheimersh SO51 . . . . **6** D2
Poole BH14 . . . . **203** A4
Portchester PO16 . . . . . . **156** E6
Portsmouth PO1 . . . . **216** C4
Privett GU31 . . . . **121** F5
Romsey SO51 . . . . **52** E7
Shedfield SO32 . . . . **107** C6
Soberton PO17 . . . . **109** C2
South Hayling PO11 . . . . . **185** A5
Southampton SO19 . . . . . **103** D2
Southbourne PO10 . . . . . **161** E8
Steep GU32 . . . . **40** E7
Swanmore SO32 . . . . **84** B5
Thorney Island PO10 . . . . **161** D1
Three Legged Cross BH21 **114** E1
Warsash SO31 . . . . **152** D10
Waterlooville PO10 . . . . . **137** B3
Church St
Christchurch BH23 . . . . . **207** B6
East Meon GU32 . . . . **38** E1
Fordingbridge SP6 . . . . **93** F8
Liss GU33 . . . . **20** E6
Poole BH15 . . . . **202** B1
Portsmouth PO1 . . . . **216** C4
Romsey SO51 . . . . **52** E7
Titchfield PO14 . . . . **154** A8

Church St continued
Upham SO32 . . . . **58** F6
6 Wimborne Minst BH21 **163** B5
Church View
Portsmouth PO4 . . . . **183** A5
Shedfield SO32 . . . . **107** F7
Southampton SO19 . . . . . **103** D2
Westbourne PO10 . . . . . . **137** B3
Church View Cl SO19 . . . **104** A3
Churcher Cl PO12 . . . . . . **180** D3
Churcher Rd PO10 . . . . . . **137** B4
Churcher Wlk 3 PO12 . . **180** D3
Churcher's Coll GU31 . . . **41** A4
Churcher's Coll Jun Sch
GU32 . . . . **40** E3
Churchfield BH31 . . . . . . **114** E6
Churchfield Cres BH15 . **202** E4
Churchfield Rd 2 BH15 . **202** E3
Churchill Ave SO32 . . . . . . **59** A8
Churchill Cl Alderholt SP6 **92** E5
Titchfield BH17 . . . . **129** C1
Churchill Cres SO17 . . . . **203** C6
Churchill Ct
Farlington PO6 . . . . **158** E8
New Milton BH25 . . . . **194** F2
Waterlooville PO8 . . . . . . **112** A6
Churchill Dr PO10 . . . . . . **136** F4
Churchill Dro PO11 . . . . . . **91** C7
Churchill Gdns BH12 . . . **203** C5
Churchill Ho SO18 . . . . . . **104** C8
Churchill Mews PO12 . . . **181** A7
Churchill Rd
Bournemouth BH1 . . . . . . **205** E5
Poole BH12 . . . . **203** D6
Wimborne Minst BH21 . . . **163** E3
Churchill Sq 3 PO4 . . . . **183** B2
Churchill Yard Ind Est
PO7 . . . . **111** E1
Churchmoor Rd BH21 . . . **164** A5
Churchward Gdns SO30 . **81** C2
Cinderford Cl 21 PO6 . . . **133** B1
Cinnamon Ct 3 SO15 . . **102** E6
Cinnamon La 11 BH15 . . **202** B1
Circle The
8 Bournemouth BH9 . . . **190** A4
Poole BH13 . . . . **214** F7
Portsmouth PO5 . . . . **182** D2
Wickham PO17 . . . . **108** A4
Circular Rd PO6 . . . . **182** C7
Circus The PO6 . . . . **133** A2
Cirrus Gdns SO31 . . . . . . **127** F2
City Bldgs PO1 . . . . **216** B4
City Bsns Ctr SO23 . . . . . **215** E6
City Commerce Ctr 6
SO14 . . . . **103** B3
City Ct 27 SO14 . . . . **103** A3
City Ind Pk SO15 . . . . **102** D4
City of Portsmouth Boys' Sch
PO7 . . . . **157** E4
City of Portsmouth Girls' Sch
PO1 . . . . **182** E6
City of Toronto Homes
SO16 . . . . **101** F8
City Rd SO23 . . . . **215** E6
Civic Centre Rd
Havant PO9 . . . . **135** F2
Southampton SO14 . . . . . **102** F5
Civic Way PO16 . . . . **131** C1
Clacton Rd PO6 . . . . **157** D8
Claire Ct 6 BH23 . . . . . . **209** A7
Claire Gdns PO8 . . . . **88** C2
Clamp Gn SO21 . . . . **56** F8
Clandon Dr SO50 . . . . **55** F5
Clanfield Cl SO53 . . . . **55** D6
Clanfield Dr SO53 . . . . **55** D6
Clanfield Ho 7 PO1 . . . . **216** C4
Clanfield Jun Sch PO8 . . . **88** B7
Clanfield Rd SO18 . . . . . . **104** C7
Clanfield Way SO53 . . . . . **55** D6
Clanwilliam Rd PO13 . . . **179** F3
Clare Cl PO14 . . . . **129** C2
Clare Gdns
Blackfield SO45 . . . . **177** F7
Petersfield GU31 . . . . **41** C3
Clare Ho PO14 . . . . **180** F7
Claremont Ave BH9 . . . . . **190** B2
Claremont Cl SO50 . . . . . . **56** A6
Claremont Cres SO15 . . **102** A7
Claremont Gdns PO7 . . . **134** E4
Claremont Rd
Bournemouth BH9 . . . . . . **190** B2
Portsmouth PO1 . . . . **216** D3
Southampton SO15 . . . . . **102** A7
Clarence Espl PO5 . . . . . **182** C1
Clarence Ho 5 SO14 . . . **103** C6
Clarence Par PO5 . . . . . . **182** C2
Clarence Park Rd BH7 . . **206** A6
Clarence Pl BH23 . . . . . . **206** F8
Clarence Rd
Gosport PO12 . . . . **181** D6
Lyndhurst SO43 . . . . **121** F5
3 Poole BH14 . . . . **203** A3
Portsmouth PO5 . . . . **182** D1
Clarence St PO1 . . . . **216** C4
Clarendon Cl
Broadstone BH18 . . . . . . **187** A4
Denmead PO7 . . . . **110** F5
10 Romsey SO51 . . . . **28** B1

Clarendon Cres PO14 . . . **129** C1
Clarendon Ct
3 Bournemouth BH2 . . . **204** D2
Portsmouth PO5 . . . . **182** D1
Clarendon Ho PO1 . . . . . . **216** C4
Clarendon Pl
1 Bournemouth BH7 . . . **216** B3
Portsmouth PO1 . . . . **216** C4
Clarendon Rd
Bournemouth BH4 . . . . . . **204** D3
Broadstone BH18 . . . . . . **186** F4
Christchurch BH23 . . . . . **207** A7
Havant PO9 . . . . **135** E1
Portsmouth,Southsea PO5 **182** D2
Southampton SO16 . . . . . **102** A8
Clarendon St PO1 . . . . . . **216** C4
Clark's Cl BH24 . . . . **141** A7
Clarkes Rd PO1 . . . . **182** F6
Claude Ashby Cl SO18 . . . **79** E5
Claudeen Cl SO18 . . . . **79** E5
Claudeen Ct SO19 . . . . . . **104** E6
Claudia Ct PO12 . . . . **180** F6
Claudius Cl SO53 . . . . **55** F7
Claudius Gdns SO53 . . . . . **55** F7
Clausen Way SO41 . . . . . **197** C1
Clausentum Cl SO53 . . . . . **55** F7
Clausentum Ho SO18 . . . **103** C7
Clausentum Rd
Southampton SO14 . . . . . **103** B7
Winchester SO23 . . . . **215** D3
Claxton St PO1 . . . . **216** C3
Clay Hill SO43 . . . . **122** A3
Clay St SP5 . . . . **24** A3
Claybank Rd PO3 . . . . . . **158** A1
Claybank Spur PO3 . . . . **158** A1
Claydon Ave PO4 . . . . . . **183** A4
Clayford Ave BH22 . . . . . **165** B7
Clayford Cl BH17 . . . . **187** D2
Clayhall Rd PO12 . . . . . . **181** B3
Clayhill Cl SO32 . . . . **83** D4
Claylake Dr BH31 . . . . . . **115** A5
Claylands Cl SO32 . . . . **83** B8
Claylands Rd SO32 . . . . . . **83** B8
Claylands Road Ind Est
SO32 . . . . **83** B8
Claypit Rd SO51 . . . . **29** C6
Claypits La SO45 . . . . **125** D4
Claypitt La GU32 . . . . **40** E8
Clearwater Apartments 5
PO4 . . . . **182** E1
Cleasby Cl SO16 . . . . **102** A4
Cleasby Grange 2 BH5 **205** F3
Clease Way SO21 . . . . **31** C7
Clee Ave PO14 . . . . **154** D8
Cleek Dr SO16 . . . . **78** F5
Cleethorpes Rd SO19 . . **104** B4
Cleeve Cl PO6 . . . . **133** B1
Cleeve Ho PO6 . . . . **209** F7
Cleeves Cl BH12 . . . . **188** D2
Cleeves The SO40 . . . . . . **100** C6
Clegg Rd PO4 . . . . **183** A3
Clem's Way SO51 . . . . **5** A1
Clematis Cl BH23 . . . . . . **208** C8
Clement Attlee Way
PO6 . . . . **157** B8
Clement Mews BH4 . . . . **204** B3
Cleric Ct PO14 . . . . **129** C3
Clerkenwell Cl BH25 . . . **209** D7
Cleveland Cl
4 Bournemouth BH2 . . . **204** D2
3 Southampton SO18 . . **80** A1
Cleveland Dr
Fareham PO14 . . . . **154** D8
Hythe SO45 . . . . **125** D2
Cleveland Gdns BH1 . . . **205** C5
Cleveland Rd
Gosport PO12 . . . . **181** B4
Portsmouth PO5 . . . . **216** D2
Southampton SO18 . . . . . . **79** F1
Clevelands Cl SO53 . . . . . **30** B1
Cleverley Ho 20 PO1 . . . **182** A5
Clewers Hill SO32 . . . . **83** D4
Clewers La SO32 . . . . **83** D4
Cliff Cres BH25 . . . . **209** F7
Cliff Dr
Christchurch BH23 . . . . . **208** C6
Poole BH13 . . . . **214** E6
Cliff Rd Milford on S SO41 **211** B4
Southampton SO15 . . . . . **102** D5
Swanage BH19 . . . . **2** D2
Cliff The SO13 . . . . **103** D3
Cliff Way SO21 . . . . **31** D7
Cliff Wlk 17 BH4 . . . . . . **204** C2
Cliffdale Gdns PO6 . . . . . **134** A1
Cliffdale Prim Sch PO2 . **157** F2
Cliffe Ave SO31 . . . . **127** E3
Cliffe Rd BH25 . . . . **203** A3
Clifford Dibben Mews 1
SO14 . . . . **103** A8
Clifford Pl SO50 . . . . **57** C2
Clifford Rd BH9 . . . . **190** A1
Clifford St SO14 . . . . **103** B5
Clifton Cres PO7 . . . . **111** B4
Clifton Ct
1 Bournemouth BH7 . . . **205** F4
Hamworthy BH15 . . . . . . **201** D4
3 New Milton BH25 . . . **195** A1
2 Southampton SO18 . **102** A8
Clifton Gdns
Ferndown BH22 . . . . **165** C4
1 Southampton SO18 . . **102** A8
West End SO18 . . . . **80** C1
Clifton Hill SO22 . . . . **215** D6
Clifton Lodge SO15 . . . . **102** A8
Clifton Lodge No 1 18
SO22 . . . . **215** D6

Clifton Lodge No 2 19
SO22 . . . . **215** D6
Clifton Rd
Bournemouth BH6 . . . . . . **206** D3
Lee-on-t-S PO13 . . . . **180** A4
Poole BH14 . . . . **203** E2
10 Portsmouth PO5 . . . . **182** C2
Southampton SO15 . . . . . **102** A8
Winchester SO22 . . . . **215** D6
Clifton St Gosport PO12 . . **180** F6
Portsmouth PO1 . . . . **216** D4
Clifton Terr
11 Portsmouth PO5 . . . . **182** C2
Winchester SO22 . . . . **215** D6
Clingan Rd BH6 . . . . **206** D7
Clinton Cl BH23 . . . . **194** B2
Clinton Rd
Lymington SO41 . . . . **197** E5
Waterlooville PO7 . . . . . . **111** C2
Clipper Cl SO31 . . . . **128** E1
Clitheroe Cotts SO42 . . . **148** F1
Clive Ct 28 BH4 . . . . **204** C3
Clive Gr PO16 . . . . **156** C7
Clive Rd
Christchurch BH23 . . . . . **189** F1
Christchurch BH23 . . . . . **193** C2
Portsmouth PO1 . . . . **182** E6
Cliveden Cl BH22 . . . . . . **165** C2
Clock Ho Rd PO7 . . . . . . **134** E7
Clock House The SO40 . . **76** A2
Clock St 7 PO1 . . . . **182** A2
Clocktower Dr 1 PO4 . . **183** B2
Cloisters The
8 Christchurch BH23 . . **207** B6
Fareham PO15 . . . . **130** C2
Lymington SO41 . . . . **197** E3
Ringwood BH24 . . . . **141** C6
3 Romsey SO51 . . . . **52** E8
Southampton SO16 . . . . . . **79** A3
Close Bellfield The
PO14 . . . . **153** F7
Close The
Barton on S BH25 . . . . . . **210** B8
Broadstone BH18 . . . . . . **186** E3
Colden Common SO50 . . . **31** D1
Cosham PO6 . . . . **158** A7
Fordingbridge SP6 . . . . **94** C7
Hedge End SO30 . . . . **128** A4
Hedge End SO30 . . . . **105** B6
Hobury SO45 . . . . **125** C4
Langrish GU32 . . . . **39** C3
Portchester PO16 . . . . . . **156** C8
Redlynch SP5 . . . . **47** D7
Ringwood BH24 . . . . **140** F7
Southampton SO18 . . . . . **104** D7
St Leonards,Avon Castle
BH24 . . . . **140** D4
St Leonards,St Ives SO41 **140** A4
Sway SO41 . . . . **172** A2
Whitsbury SP6 . . . . **45** B3
Closewood Rd PO7 . . . . . **111** A2
Clough La BH24 . . . . **142** F3
Clough's Rd BH24 . . . . . . **141** A3
Clovelly Rd breach PO10 **137** D1
Emsworth PO10 . . . . **160** E8
North Hayling PO11 . . . . **160** A4
Portsmouth PO4 . . . . **183** A4
Southampton SO14 . . . . . **103** B6
Clover Cl
Christchurch BH23 . . . . . **208** B8
Gosport PO13 . . . . **155** B3
Southampton SO31 . . . . . **128** E2
Clover Ct
New Milton BH25 . . . . **195** D4
Waterlooville PO7 . . . . . . **135** A6
Clover Dr BH17 . . . . **186** F1
Clover Nooke SO15 . . . . . **101** C8
Clover Way
Hedge End SO30 . . . . **105** A6
Romsey SO51 . . . . **53** C8
Clovers The BH12 . . . . . . **204** A8
Clowes Ave BH6 . . . . **207** B3
Clubhouse La SO32 . . . . . **83** D3
Clump Hill BH21 . . . . **114** B1
Cluster Ind Est PO4 . . . . **183** A5
Clyde Ct PO12 . . . . **180** F6
Clyde Ho 2 SO14 . . . . . . **103** C5
Clyde Rd Gosport PO12 . . **180** F6
Poole BH17 . . . . **187** B2
Clydebank Rd PO12 . . . . **182** D8
Clydes Dale Ct 5 SO17 . **79** B1
Clydesdale Rd PO15 . . . **129** B7
Clydesdale Way SO40 . . **100** B8
Coach Hill PO14 . . . . **153** F8
Coach Hill Cl SO53 . . . . . **55** B7
Coach Hill La BH24 . . . . . **142** C5
Coach Ho The SO22 . . . . . **1** B2
Coach House Mews
BH22 . . . . **165** F3
Coach House Pl BH1 . . . **205** A5
Coach Rd SO31 . . . . **127** E3
Coach-House Mews
PO4 . . . . **183** C4
Coachmakers Mews 6
SO51 . . . . **52** E7
Coachmans Copse SO18 . **80** A2
Coachmans Halt PO7 . . . **86** C2
Coal Park La SO31 . . . . . **128** D8
Coalville Rd SO19 . . . . . **104** B4
Coastguard Cl PO12 . . . . **181** B7
Coastguard Cotts
Barton on S BH25 . . . . . . **209** E8
Exbury SO45 . . . . **178** A2
Langstone PO9 . . . . **159** F6

Coastguard Cotts *continued*
Lymington SO41 . . . . .198 A2
Coastguard Way BH23 . . . .207 F5
Coat Gdns SO45 . . . . .126 A3
Coates Rd SO19 . . . . .104 D4
Coates Way PO7 . . . . .134 E5
Cobalt Ct 3 PO13 . . . . . . .180 C6
Cobb's Rd BH21 . . . . .163 E6
Cobbett Cl SO22 . . . . .215 A3
Cobbett Ct 3 SO18 . . . . . .103 E7
Cobbett Rd SO18 . . . . .103 E8
Cobbett Way SO30 . . . . . . .105 F7
Cobblers Cnr SO41 . . . . . . .173 B3
Cobblewood PO10 . . . . . . .136 F3
Cobbs La BH15 . . . . .202 E6
Cobden Ave
Portsmouth PO3 . . . . .183 A8
Southampton SO18 . . . . . . .103 E8
Cobden Cres SO18 . . . . . . .103 E8
Cobden Ct SO18 . . . . .103 E8
Cobden Dell 4 SO18 . . . . .103 E8
Cobden Gdns SO18 . . . . .79 E1
Cobden Hts SO18 . . . . .79 E1
Cobden Marine Ct
SO17 . . . . .103 D8
Cobden St SO18 . . . . .79 E1
Cobden St PO12 . . . . .181 B6
Cobham Gr PO15 . . . . .129 F5
Cobham Rd
Bournemouth BH9 . . . . .190 A3
Ferndown BH21 . . . . .165 A8
Cobham Way BH21 . . . . . . .163 E1
Coblands Ave SO40 . . . . . .100 D7
Coburg Ho 6 SO14 . . . . . .103 C6
Coburg St
Portsmouth PO1 . . . . .216 C3
Southampton SO14 . . . . . . .103 C6
Cochrane Cl PO13 . . . . .180 D6
Cochrane Ho 18 PO1 . . . . .182 A5
Cockerell Cl
Locks Heath PO15 . . . . .129 C5
Merley BH21 . . . . .163 F1
Cockleshell Cl SO31 . . . . . .128 E1
Cockleshell Gdns PO4 . . . .183 C3
Cockleshell Sq PO12 . . . . .181 D6
Cocklydown La SO40 . . . . .100 E5
Cockshott La GU32 . . . . .19 C2
Codogan Ct 3 BH1 . . . . . .205 B3
Cogdean Cl BH21 . . . . .186 E8
Cogdean Way BH21 . . . . . . .186 E8
Cogdean Wlk BH21 . . . . . . .186 E8
Cogdeane Rd BH17 . . . . . . .187 D2
Coghlan Cl PO16 . . . . .131 B2
Coker Cl SO22 . . . . .215 C6
Colborne Ave BH21 . . . . . .163 F6
Colborne Cl
Lymington SO41 . . . . .197 E5
Poole BH15 . . . . .202 D1
Colbourne Cl BH23 . . . . . . .193 A8
Colbourne Ct 7 SO23 . . . .215 E8
Colburn Cl SO16 . . . . .77 D2
Colbury Gr PO9 . . . . .135 C4
Colchester Ave SO50 . . . . . .56 E4
Colchester Rd PO6 . . . . . . .133 E1
Cold Harbour Cl PO17 . . . .107 F4
Coldeast Cl SO31 . . . . .128 D5
Coldeast Hospl SO31 . . . . .128 F5
Coldeast Way SO31 . . . . . .128 F5
Colden Common Prim Sch
SO21 . . . . .56 F8
Coldharbour Farm Rd
PO10 . . . . .136 F1
Coldharbour La SO16,
SO53 . . . . .77 B8
Coldhill La PO8 . . . . .111 F7
Cole Hill SO32 . . . . .85 C5
Colebrook Ave
Portsmouth PO3 . . . . .183 B7
Southampton SO15 . . . . .78 C1
Colebrook Pl SO23 . . . . . . .215 F5
Colebrook St SO23 . . . . . . .215 F5
Colehill Cres PO9 . . . . .190 B3
Colehill Fst Sch BH21 . . . . .164 A7
Colehill Gdns SO32 . . . . .83 A8
Colehill La Colehill BH21 . . .163 F8
Wimborne Minst BH21 . . . . . .164 A8
Coleman Rd BH11 . . . . .189 A3
Coleman St SO14 . . . . .103 B4
Colemere Gdns BH23 . . . . .208 F8
Colemore Rd BH7 . . . . .206 C7
Colemore Sq PO9 . . . . .135 F4
Colenso Rd PO16 . . . . .131 A2
Coleridge Cl SO31 . . . . . . .128 D1
Coleridge Ct SO19 . . . . . . .104 D5
Coleridge Gdns PO8 . . . . . .111 F4
Coleridge Gn BH23 . . . . . . .207 F8
Coleridge Rd PO6 . . . . .132 F1
Coles Ave BH15 . . . . .201 E2
Coles Cl SO21 . . . . .32 A7
Coles Gdns BH15 . . . . .201 E2
Coles Mede SO21 . . . . .31 B3
Coles's La SP5 . . . . .48 E5
Colesbourne Rd PO12 . . . . .133 B1
Coleson Rd SO18 . . . . .103 E8
Coleville Ave SO45 . . . . . . .151 B3
Colin Cl BH21 . . . . .186 D5
Colinton Ave PO16 . . . . . . .132 D1
Coll of Air Traffic Control
BH23 . . . . .190 F7
Collard Way 4 GU33 . . . . . .20 F4
College Cl
Hamble-le-R SO31 . . . . .127 F2
Rowlands Castle PO9 . . . . . .113 C1
College Keep SO14 . . . . . . .103 B3
College La 28 PO1 . . . . . . .182 A5

College Park Inf Sch
PO2 . . . . .157 E1
College Pl 9 SO15 . . . . . . .103 A6
College Rd
Bournemouth BH5 . . . . .206 A4
Portsmouth PO1 . . . . .182 A5
Ringwood BH24 . . . . .141 A7
Southampton SO19 . . . . . . .103 E2
Waterlooville PO7 . . . . .134 F3
College St
Petersfield GU32 . . . . .40 F3
Portsmouth PO1 . . . . .182 A5
Southampton SO14 . . . . . . .103 A3
Winchester SO23 . . . . .215 E5
College Wlk SO23 . . . . .215 E4
Collett Cl SO30 . . . . .81 B2
Colley Cl SO23 . . . . .2 A3
Collier Cl SO17 . . . . .103 D6
Collingbourne Ave BH6 . . . .206 D7
Collingbourne Dr SO53 . . . . .55 A6
Collington Cres PO6 . . . . . .133 B1
Collingwood Ho PO15 . . . . .130 D2
Collingwood Rd
Portsmouth PO5 . . . . .182 D2
West Moors BH31 . . . . .138 C6
Collingwood Ret Pk
PO14 . . . . .155 B6
Collingwood Way GU31 . . . . .41 A5
Collingworth Cl SO31 . . . . .129 B6
Collingworth Rise SO31 . . . .129 B6
Collins Cl SO53 . . . . .54 F6
Collins La Compton GU31 . . . .66 F7
Ringwood BH24 . . . . .141 A7
Collins Rd PO4 . . . . .183 A2
Collins' La SO21 . . . . .30 C7
Collis Rd PO3 . . . . .183 A8
Collwood Cl BH15 . . . . .202 C7
Collyers Rd SO42 . . . . .172 F7
Colman Ct BH1 . . . . .205 C3
Colne Ave SO16 . . . . .77 D2
Colne Ct SO16 . . . . .77 E2
Colonnade Rd 3 BH5 . . . . .206 A5
Colonnade Road W 2
BH5 . . . . .206 A5
Colonnade The SO19 . . . . . .103 D3
Colpoy St PO5 . . . . .216 A2
Colson Cl SO23 . . . . .215 F6
Colson Rd SO23 . . . . .215 F6
Colt Cl Rownhams SO16 . . . . .77 F5
Wimborne Minst BH21 . . . . . .164 B6
Colton Copse SO53 . . . . .54 F6
Colts Rd SO16 . . . . .77 E7
Coltsfoot Cl SO30 . . . . .105 B7
Coltsfoot Dr
Locks Heath SO31 . . . . .128 E2
3 Waterlooville PO7 . . . . . .134 F5
Coltsfoot Wlk SO51 . . . . . . .28 C1
Coltsmead PO6 . . . . .156 F8
Columbia Rd BH10 . . . . .189 C2
Columbia Trees La
BH10 . . . . .189 C1
Columbian Way BH10 . . . . . .189 C2
Columbine Cl BH23 . . . . . . .193 B1
Colvedene Cl SO21 . . . . .31 F1
Colville Cl 4 BH5 . . . . .206 A5
Colville Dr SO32 . . . . .83 D8
Colville Rd
6 Bournemouth BH5 . . . . . .206 A5
Cosham PO6 . . . . .158 A8
Colvin Gdns SO53 . . . . .55 B8
Colwell Cl SO16 . . . . .101 D8
Colwell Rd PO6 . . . . .157 F7
Combe Down SO41 . . . . .31 E2
Combe Rd GU33 . . . . .21 B1
Comber Rd 1 BH9 . . . . .190 A3
Comet Way SO31 . . . . .208 A6
Comfrey Cl Horndean PO8 . . . .88 C1
Romsey SO51 . . . . .28 C1
Comines Way SO30 . . . . . . .104 F7
Comley Ct 11 SO51 . . . . . . .52 E7
Comley Hill PO9 . . . . .136 D5
Comley Rd BH9 . . . . .189 F2
Commercial Pl PO1 . . . . . . .216 B4
Commercial Rd
Bournemouth BH2 . . . . .204 E3
Poole BH14 . . . . .203 A4
Portsmouth PO1 . . . . .216 B4
Southampton SO14 . . . . . . .102 F5
Southampton SO15 . . . . . . .102 E5
Totton SO40 . . . . .101 A7
Commercial St SO18 . . . . . .103 B7
Commodore Ct 11 SO14 . . .103 B3
Commodore Pl PO12 . . . . . .181 D7
Common Barn La
Lee-on-t-S PO13 . . . . .179 F4
Lee-on-t-S PO13 . . . . .180 A5
Common Cl SO53 . . . . .55 C8
Common Gdns SO53 . . . . . . .55 C8
Common Hill Rd SO51 . . . . . .28 D6
Common La
Southwick PO17 . . . . .132 E7
Titchfield PO14 . . . . .153 E8
Common Rd
Chandler's Ford SO53 . . . . . .55 C8
Emsworth PO10 . . . . .137 F5
Whiteparish SP5 . . . . .24 B2
Southampton SP1 . . . . .216 C4
Common The SP6 . . . . .68 D3
Commonside PO10 . . . . .137 B5
Compass Cl
Gosport PO13 . . . . .180 D6
Southampton SO19 . . . . . . .104 A4
Compass Ct 21 SO17 . . . . . .79 A1
Compass Point
Fareham PO16 . . . . .155 A8
Hamble-le-R SO31 . . . . .127 E2
Compass Rd PO16 . . . . .157 B8

Compton & Up Marden CE
Prim Sch PO18 . . . . .90 F2
Compton Acres Gdns★
BH13 . . . . .214 E7
Compton All Saints CE Prim
Sch SO21 . . . . .31 D8
Compton Ave BH14 . . . . . . .203 D1
Compton Beeches
BH24 . . . . .140 A5
Compton Cl
Eastleigh SO50 . . . . .55 F6
Havant PO9 . . . . .135 F3
9 Lee-on-t-S PO13 . . . . . .179 F3
Verwood BH31 . . . . .114 F6
Winchester SO22 . . . . .10 B3
Compton Cotts
Compton SO21 . . . . .6 D7
Minstead SO43 . . . . .98 C3
Compton Cres BH22 . . . . . .139 B1
Compton Ct
4 Bournemouth BH6 . . . . .206 F4
4 Havant PO9 . . . . .135 E2
Poole BH14 . . . . .203 D3
Compton Dr BH14 . . . . .203 C2
Compton Gdns BH14 . . . . . .203 C2
Compton Ho 6 SO16 . . . . .102 B8
Compton Lo 28 BH4 . . . . . .204 C3
Compton Rd
New Milton BH25 . . . . .195 A2
Portsmouth PO2 . . . . .157 F2
Totton SO40 . . . . .101 A8
Winchester SO23 . . . . .215 D5
Compton St SO21 . . . . .31 D8
Compton Way SO22 . . . . . . .10 B3
Compton Wlk 1 SO14 . . . . .103 A5
Compton's Dr SO51 . . . . .50 A6
Conan Rd PO2 . . . . .157 E4
Concorde Cl PO15 . . . . .129 D5
Concorde Way PO15 . . . . . .129 D5
Condor Ave PO16 . . . . .155 F8
Condor Cl
Southampton SO19 . . . . . . .103 D3
Three Legged Cross BH21 . . .139 B5
Coney Gn 6 SO23 . . . . .215 E8
Coneygar La BH22 . . . . .165 B3
Conference Dr SO31 . . . . . .129 B3
Conference Pl 3 SO41 . . . .197 F2
Conford Ct PO9 . . . . .135 D6
Congleton Cl SO43 . . . . .98 C3
Conifer Ave BH14 . . . . .203 B2
Conifer Cl
Christchurch BH23 . . . . .191 D3
Ferndown BH22 . . . . .165 F1
Hythe SO45 . . . . .125 F3
St Leonards BH24 . . . . .139 D4
Waterlooville PO8 . . . . .112 A2
Winchester SO22 . . . . .215 D7
Conifer Cres SO41 . . . . .197 B3
Conifer Gr PO13 . . . . .155 C4
Conifer Mews PO16 . . . . . . .132 D1
Conifer Rd SO16 . . . . .78 A4
Conifers 4 BH13 . . . . .204 B3
Conigar Rd PO10 . . . . .136 E5
Coniston Ave
Bournemouth BH11 . . . . . . .188 F6
4 Portsmouth PO3 . . . . . .183 A8
Coniston Cl BH31 . . . . .114 C5
Coniston Gdns SO30 . . . . . .105 B5
Coniston Ho 8 PO6 . . . . . . .133 B1
Coniston Rd
Eastleigh SO50 . . . . .56 B5
Ringwood BH24 . . . . .141 B6
Southampton SO16 . . . . . . .101 C8
Coniston Wlk PO14 . . . . . . .154 E7
Connaught Cl BH25 . . . . . . .194 E1
Connaught Cres BH12 . . . . .203 E6
Connaught Hall SO18 . . . . . .79 D4
Connaught La PO6 . . . . .156 F8
Connaught Pl 8 PO9 . . . . . .136 A1
Connaught Rd
Bournemouth BH5 . . . . .206 B5
Havant PO9 . . . . .136 A1
Portsmouth PO2 . . . . .157 D2
Connell Rd BH15 . . . . .202 C5
Connemara Cres PO15 . . . .129 B7
Connigar Cl PO13 . . . . .180 C7
Conqueror Way PO14 . . . . .179 D6
Conrad Gdns PO15 . . . . . . .129 C8
Conservatory The 6
SO23 . . . . .215 F5
Consort Cl Eastleigh SO50 . . .56 B5
Poole BH12 . . . . .203 C5
Consort Ct 5 PO16 . . . . . . .131 C1
Consort Ho
Ferndown BH22 . . . . .165 D6
3 Portsmouth PO1 . . . . . .182 D7
Consort Mews 7 PO17 . . . .130 E7
Consort Rd SO50 . . . . .56 B5
Constable Cl
Ferndown BH22 . . . . .165 C4
Gosport PO12 . . . . .181 C2
Constable's Gate 10
SO23 . . . . .215 D5
Constantine Ave SO53 . . . . .55 F6
Constantine Cl SO53 . . . . . . .55 F6
Constitution Hill Gdns
BH14 . . . . .203 A5
Constitution Hill Rd
BH14 . . . . .203 A5
Consulate Ho 4 SO31 . . . . .103 B3
Convent Ct PO10 . . . . .160 E8
Convent La PO10 . . . . .160 F8
Convent Meadow Mobile
Home Site BH23 . . . . .207 C5
Conway Cl
Chandler's Ford SO53 . . . . . .55 B3
New Milton BH25 . . . . .195 B3

Conway Ct 10 BH25 . . . . . .195 B3
Conways Dr BH14 . . . . .203 A4
Cook Cl BH24 . . . . .141 C8
Cook Row BH21 . . . . .163 B4
Cook St SO14 . . . . .103 A4
Cooke Gdns BH12 . . . . .203 F6
Cooke Rd BH12 . . . . .203 F6
Cooks La Axbridge SO51 . . . .27 A4
Breach PO10 . . . . .137 E1
Lockerley SO51 . . . . .25 E8
Totton SO40 . . . . .76 C2
Cooley Ho PO13 . . . . .155 B5
Coolhurst BH14 . . . . .214 C7
Coombe Ave BH10 . . . . .189 E3
Coombe Farm Ave
PO16 . . . . .155 A8
Coombe Gdns BH10 . . . . . . .189 E2
Coombe La Axbridge SO51 . . .26 F3
Sway SO41 . . . . .196 D8
West Meon GU32 . . . . .37 E4
Coombe Rd
Axbridge SO51 . . . . .26 F3
Gosport PO12 . . . . .181 B8
Coombe Road Terr GU32 . . . .63 D8
Coombedale SO31 . . . . .129 B2
Coombs Cl PO8 . . . . .88 C1
Cooper Dean Dr BH8 . . . . . .190 F1
Cooper Dean Rdbt The
BH7,BH8 . . . . .191 A1
Cooper Gr PO16 . . . . .156 D6
Cooper Rd Ashurst SO40 . . .100 C7
Portsmouth PO3 . . . . .183 B8
Cooper's Cl
West End SO18 . . . . .80 C1
West Wellow SO51 . . . . .51 B2
Cooper's La SO19 . . . . .103 D3
Coopers La SP6 . . . . .34 B1
Coopers Rise PO8 . . . . .114 F8
Copeland Dr BH14 . . . . .214 B8
Copeland Dr BH14 . . . . .203 B2
Copeland Rd SO16 . . . . .77 D1
Copenhagen Twrs SO19 . . . .126 F8
Copinger Cl SO40 . . . . .100 C6
Copnor Bridge Bsns Ctr
PO3 . . . . .183 A7
Copnor Inf & Jun Sch
PO3 . . . . .158 A1
Copnor Rd PO2 . . . . .157 F3
Copper Beech BH13 . . . . . . .204 A4
Copper Beech Dr PO6 . . . . .158 E8
Copper Beech Gdns
BH10 . . . . .189 D2
Copper Beeches
Blackfield SO45 . . . . .150 F2
Portsmouth PO2 . . . . .204 F4
Copper St 5 PO5 . . . . .216 A1
Coppercourt Leaze 6
BH21 . . . . .163 C4
Copperfield Ho 17 PO1 . . . .182 D7
Copperfield Rd SO16 . . . . . . .79 A5
Copperfields SO40 . . . . .100 B7
Coppers Cl SP6 . . . . .93 A6
Coppice Ave BH22 . . . . .165 B7
Coppice Cl
New Milton BH25 . . . . .195 A4
St Leonards BH24 . . . . .139 F4
Winchester SO22 . . . . .215 A7
Coppice Hill SO32 . . . . .83 D7
Coppice Rd SO40 . . . . .76 C2
Coppice The
Brockenhurst SO42 . . . . . . .145 D1
Christchurch BH23 . . . . .208 B6
Gosport PO13 . . . . .155 D2
Netley SO31 . . . . .127 C5
Waterlooville PO8 . . . . .112 A6
Coppice View
Bournemouth BH10 . . . . . . .189 E3
Whiteley PO15 . . . . .129 D7
Coppice Way PO15 . . . . .130 D3
Coppins Gr PO16 . . . . .156 C6
Copse Ave BH25 . . . . .195 B2
Copse Cl Liss GU33 . . . . .21 A4
North Baddesley SO52 . . . . . .53 F4
Otterbourne SO21 . . . . .31 C4
Petersfield GU31 . . . . .41 C4
Poole BH14 . . . . .202 F3
Totton SO40 . . . . .100 F6
Waterlooville PO7 . . . . .134 D2
Copse Cvn Pk The SO40 . . . .99 D5
Copse La Chilworth SO16 . . . .54 F1
Gosport PO13 . . . . .155 D1
Hamble-le-R SO31 . . . . .127 F2
North Hayling PO11 . . . . . . .185 A8
Copse Rd Burley BH24 . . . . .142 F2
New Milton BH25 . . . . .195 B2
Southampton SO18 . . . . . . .80 A3
Verwood BH31 . . . . .114 F6
Copse The
Chandler's Ford SO53 . . . . . .55 B5
Fareham PO15 . . . . .130 D4
Romsey SO51 . . . . .28 C1
West Moors BH24 . . . . .166 C8
Copse View SO19 . . . . .104 E5
Copse Way BH23 . . . . .208 E8
Copsewood Ave BH8 . . . . . .190 E1
Copsewood Rd
Ashurst SO40 . . . . .100 C3
Hythe SO45 . . . . .125 F3
Southampton SO18 . . . . . . .79 E2
Copsey Cl PO6 . . . . .158 D8
Copsey Gr PO6 . . . . .158 D8
Copthorne Cotts SO45 . . . . .151 C3
Copthorne La SO45 . . . . . . .151 B3
Copythorn Rd PO2 . . . . .157 F1
Copythorne CE Inf Sch
SO40 . . . . .74 E4
Copythorne Cl BH8 . . . . .190 D2
Copythorne Cres SO40 . . . . .75 C3

Coracle Cl SO31 . . . . .128 F1
Coral Cl PO16 . . . . .156 C6
Coral Ct 6 Gosport PO13 . . .180 C6
2 Poole BH13 . . . . .204 A4
Coralin Gr PO7 . . . . .112 B1
Coram Cl 3 SO23 . . . . .215 E8
Corbar Rd BH23 . . . . .206 E8
Corbett Rd PO7 . . . . .134 D5
Corbiere Ave BH12 . . . . . . .188 D1
Corbiere Cl SO16 . . . . .77 E3
Corbin Ave BH22 . . . . .166 A6
Corbin Cl SO41 . . . . .197 B2
Corbin Rd SO41 . . . . .197 B2
Corbould Rd SO45 . . . . .149 F8
Corby Cres PO3 . . . . .158 B4
Cordelia Cl SO45 . . . . .125 D3
Corfe Cl PO14 . . . . .179 A7
Corfe Hall Sch BH21 . . . . . .162 E1
Corfe Hills Sch BH18 . . . . . .186 F6
Corfe Lodge Rd BH18 . . . . .186 C6
Corfe Mews BH15 . . . . .202 D4
Corfe View Rd
Corfe Mullen BH21 . . . . .186 C5
Poole BH14 . . . . .203 C3
Corfe Way BH18 . . . . .186 E3
Corfu BH13 . . . . .214 E6
Corhampton Cres PO9 . . . . .135 D4
Corhampton Ho 11 PO1 . . .216 C4
Corhampton La
Droxford SO32 . . . . .60 D6
Meonstoke SO32 . . . . .61 A5
Corhampton Rd BH6 . . . . . .206 C6
Coriander Dr SO40 . . . . .100 C7
Coriander Way PO15 . . . . . .129 D8
Corinna Gdns SO45 . . . . . . .125 D3
Corinthian Rd SO53 . . . . .55 E7
Cork La SO40 . . . . .101 F2
Cormorant Cl PO16 . . . . . . .155 F8
Cormorant Dr SO45 . . . . . . .126 C2
Cormorant Wlk PO13 . . . . . .155 B2
Corn Mkt SO51 . . . . .52 E7
Cornaway La PO16 . . . . .156 B8
Cornbrook Gr PO7 . . . . .112 C1
Cornel Rd SO19 . . . . .103 F5
Cornelia Cres BH12 . . . . . . .204 A6
Cornelius Dr PO7 . . . . .112 B1
Corner Mead PO7 . . . . .110 F4
Corner The SO22 . . . . .11 C7
Cornerways Ct 3 BH25 . . . .195 B2
Cornes Cl SO22 . . . . .215 B5
Cornfield PO16 . . . . .131 B4
Cornfield Cl SO53 . . . . .54 F6
Cornfield Rd PO13 . . . . .179 F3
Cornflower Cl SO31 . . . . . . .128 D2
Cornflower Dr BH23 . . . . . . .208 C8
Cornford Way BH23 . . . . . . .208 B8
Cornforth Rd SO40 . . . . .76 C1
Cornish Gdns BH10 . . . . . . .189 D1
Cornmarket Cl 7 BH21 . . . .163 B5
Cornpits La SP6 . . . . .68 C3
Cornwall Cl 4 SO18 . . . . . . .80 A2
Cornwall Cres SO18 . . . . . . .79 F2
Cornwall Rd
Chandler's Ford SO53 . . . . . .55 C3
Portsmouth PO1 . . . . .182 E5
Southampton SO18 . . . . .79 F2
Cornwallis Cres PO1 . . . . . .216 C4
Cornwallis Ho PO1 . . . . .216 C4
Cornwallis Rd SO41 . . . . . . .211 B4
Cornwell Cl
Gosport PO13 . . . . .180 D7
Portsmouth PO2 . . . . .157 B2
Coronado Rd PO12 . . . . .181 B8
Coronation Ave
Bournemouth BH9 . . . . .189 F2
Upton BH16 . . . . .201 B4
Coronation Cl BH31 . . . . . . .114 F7
Coronation Eventide Homes
4 PO2 . . . . .157 E4
Coronation Homes
SO18 . . . . .104 D8
Coronation Par SO31 . . . . . .127 E3
Coronation Rd
South Hayling PO11 . . . . . . .185 E1
Swanmore SO32 . . . . .84 B5
Verwood BH31 . . . . .114 F7
Coronation Terr SP6 . . . . . . .69 A2
Coronation Rd BH1 . . . . .205 C5
Corpus Christi RC Prim Sch
Bournemouth BH5 . . . . .206 A5
Portsmouth PO2 . . . . .157 D2
Corsair Dr SO45 . . . . .125 D3
Corscombe Cl BH17 . . . . . . .187 E2
Cort Way PO15 . . . . .130 C4
Cortina Way SO30 . . . . .105 C5
Cortmerron 20 BH4 . . . . . . .204 A7
Cortry Cl BH12 . . . . .204 A7
Corvette Ave SO31 . . . . .128 F1
Corylus Ct SO40 . . . . .76 B1
Cosford Cl SO50 . . . . .57 A2
Cosham Park Ave PO6 . . . . .157 F7
Cosham St SO32 . . . . .84 E6
Cossack Gn 1 SO14 . . . . . . .103 A4
Cossack La SO23 . . . . .215 E6
Cossack Lane Ho 28
SO23 . . . . .215 E6
Cossworth Dr SO45 . . . . . . .125 D3
Cotes Ave BH14 . . . . .203 A5
Cotes Ct BH14 . . . . .203 A5
Cotlands Rd BH8 . . . . .205 C3
Cotsalls SO50 . . . . .57 D1
Cotswold Cl Havant PO9 . . . .135 F3
Hythe SO45 . . . . .125 D3
Verwood BH31 . . . . .114 F5
Cotswold Ct
6 Christchurch BH23 . . . . .207 F8
5 Southampton SO17 . . . . . .79 A1

Cotswold Ho 3 PO6 .....157 C8
Cotswold Rd SO16 .....101 F8
Cotswold Wlk 1 PO14 ..154 F7
Cott La BH24 ......143 B2
Cott St SO32 ......84 D4
Cott Street La SO32 ..84 E4
Cottage Cl PO7 ......110 F3
Cottage Gdns BH12 ..203 C5
Cottage Gr Gosport PO12 .181 B6
　Portsmouth PO5 ....216 B2
Cottage Grove Prim Sch
　PO5 ....216 B1
Cottage La GU32,GU33 ..19 F3
Cottage Mews SP6 ....69 E2
Cottage View PO 216 C3
Cottagers La SO41 ....196 A4
Cotteridge Ho 1 PO5 ..216 C2
Cottes Way PO14 ......179 B6
Cottesway E PO14 ....179 B6
Cotton Cl
　Bishopstoke SO50 ....56 E3
　Corfe Mullen BH18 ..186 F5
Cotton Dr PO10 ......136 E3
Cotwell Ave PO8 ......112 B4
Coulmere Rd PO12 ..181 A7
Coulsdon Rd SO30 ..105 C6
Coultas Rd SO13 ......30 E2
Council Hos
　Horton Heath BH21 ..114 A1
　Lockerley SO51 ......26 B5
　Sopley BH23 ....167 F2
Countess Cl BH7 ....187 E8
Countess Gdns BH7 ..205 F8
Country View
　Stubbington PO14 ..154 B4
　West Wellow SO51 ....50 E3
County Gates La 11 BH4 ..204 B4
County Gdns PO14 ..129 D2
Course Park Cres PO14 ..129 D2
Court Barn Cl PO13 ..179 F4
Court Barn La PO13 ..179 F4
Court Cl
　3 Christchurch BH23 ..207 E7
　Cosham PO6 ....158 B7
　Lymington SO41 ....197 D2
　Southampton SO18 ..104 A6
　Totton SO40 ....76 D2
Court Hill SP6 ......68 E5
Court House Cl SO45 ..126 A4
Court La PO6 ....158 B7
Court Lane Jun Sch
　PO6 ....158 A7
Court Mead PO6 ....158 B7
Court Rd
　Bournemouth BH9 ..190 B1
　Kings Worthy SO23 ....2 C5
　Lee-on-t-S PO13 ....179 E4
　Southampton SO15 ..102 F7
Court Royal Mews SO15 ..102 F8
Court The SO41 ......197 D2
Courtenay Dr BH21 ..163 C6
Courtenay Pl SO41 ..197 E3
Courtenay Rd
　Poole BH14 ....203 B4
　Winchester SO23 ....2 A3
Courthill Fst Sch BH14 ..203 D4
Courtier Rd BH14 ..203 C4
Courtier Cl SO45 ....125 C3
Courtland Gdns SO16 ..79 B5
Courtlands 3 SO41 ..197 E4
Courtlands Terr PO8 ..112 A4
Courtleigh Manor 6
　BH5 ....205 D4
Courtmount Gr PO6 ..158 A8
Courtnay Cl PO15 ....129 D3
Courtney Pl SO41 ....186 C5
Courtyard Cl SO42 ..145 F1
Courtyard Mews SO42 ..145 F1
Courtyard The
　Christchurch BH23 ..207 D6
　Finchdean PO8 ......113 B7
　11 Petersfield GU31 ..40 F3
　Poole BH12 ....188 C1
　4 Romsey SO51 ......52 E7
　Wimborne Minst BH21 ..164 A1
Cousins Gr PO4 ......182 F2
Cove Rd SO14 ......189 C2
Covena Rd BH6 ......206 E6
Coventry Cl BH21 ..186 C4
Coventry Cres BH17 ..187 A1
Coventry Ct
　Gosport PO13 ......180 A1
　8 Winchester SO23 ..215 E6
Coventry Rd SO15 ..102 F6
Coverack Way PO6 ..157 B7
Covert Gr PO7 ......135 A5
Covert The SO51 ......53 B6
Covindale Ho 2 PO4 ..183 A3
Coward Rd PO10 ....137 B5
Cow La Cosham PO6 ..156 D7
　Portchester PO16 ..156 D7
Cowan Rd PO7 ......134 D5
Coward Rd PO12 ....180 F2
Cowdown La PO18 ....90 D4
Cowdray Cl
　Bishopstoke SO50 ....56 F2
　Southampton SO16 ..78 B4
Cowdray Ho
　Portsmouth PO1 ....216 C3
　28 Winchester SO23 ..215 D6
Cowdray Pk PO14 ....179 A7
Cowdrey Gdns BH8 ..190 F2
Cowdrys Field 2 BH21 ..163 B6
Cowell Dr BH7 ......206 B8
Cowes La SO31 ......148 D4
Cowgrove Rd BH21 ..162 F5
Cowleas Cl SO51 ......26 E5

Cowleas Cotts SO51 ..26 E5
Cowley Cl SO16 ......77 E2
Cowley Rd
　Lymington SO41 ....197 C4
　Poole BH17 ....202 D8
Cowleys Rd BH23 ..192 C2
Cowper Ave BH25 ..195 A1
Cowper Rd
　Bournemouth BH9 ..189 F2
　Portsmouth PO1 ....182 E7
　Southampton SO19 ..104 D6
Cowpitts La BH24 ..117 D2
Cowplain Com Sch PO8 ..111 F2
Cowslip Cl Gosport PO13 ..155 C2
　Locks Heath SO31 ..128 E2
Cowslip Rd BH18 ..186 F2
Cowslip Way SO51 ..28 C1
Cox Ave BH9 ....190 B4
Cox Cl BH9 ....190 B4
Cox Dale PO14 ......129 C1
Cox Row SO53 ......55 D3
Cox's Dr SO19 ......104 B2
Cox's La SO19 ......103 D3
Coxes Mdw GU32 ....40 E5
Coxford Cl SO16 ....78 A2
Coxford Dro SO16 ....78 A3
Coxford Rd SO16 ....78 C4
Coxs Hill SO21 ......32 A8
Coxstone La 2 BH24 ..141 A6
Coy Pond Rd BH12 ..204 B5
Cozens Cl SO19 ......103 E1
Crab Orchard Way
　BH21 ....114 F2
Crabapple Cl SO40 ..100 C7
Crabbe Ct PO5 ......216 B2
Crabbs Way SO40 ..100 B7
Crabbswood La SO41 ..195 E8
Crabden La PO8 ......88 E1
Crableck La SO31 ..128 B5
Crabthorn Farm La
　PO14 ....129 B8
Crabton Close Rd BH5 ..205 F4
Crabtree SO16 ......77 F1
Crabtree Cl BH23 ..192 C2
Crabwood Cl SO16 ....77 F2
Crabwood Dr SO30 ..80 E1
Crabwood Rd SO16 ..77 E2
Cracknore Hard
　Marchwood SO40 ..102 A1
　Marchwood SO40 ..102 C2
Cracknore Hard La
　SO40 ....102 A1
Cracknore Rd SO15 ..102 D5
Craddock Ho
　11 Portsmouth PO1 ..182 A5
　2 Winchester SO23 ..11 C8
Crafts La GU31 ......41 A5
Craig Ho 3 PO5 ......182 D2
Craigmoor Ave BH8 ..190 F1
Craigmoor Cl BH8 ..190 F1
Craigmoor Way BH8 ..190 E2
Craigside Rd BH24 ..139 D4
Craigwell Rd PO7 ..134 E4
Craigwood Dr BH22 ..165 E4
Crammpour La SO51 ..28 E1
Cranberry Cl SO40 ..101 F1
Cranberry Cres BH12 ..203 E8
Cranborne Ct
　1 Bournemouth,Westbourne
　　BH4 ....204 B4
　Bournemouth,Winton BH9 ..205 B8
Cranborne Gdns 8 SO53 ..30 B1
Cranborne Pl BH21 ..194 E3
Cranborne Rd
　Alderholt SP6 ......92 A5
　Bournemouth BH2 ..204 E2
　Cosham PO6 ......134 A1
　Wimborne Minst BH21 ..163 C7
Cranborne Wlk PO14 ..154 F7
Cranbourne Cl SO15 ..78 D1
Cranbourne Ct BH17 ..188 A2
Cranbourne Dr SO21 ..31 B3
Cranbourne Pl SO15 ..78 D1
Cranbourne Rd PO12 ..181 C4
Cranbrook Mews BH12 ..203 B6
Cranbrook Rd BH12 ..203 B6
Cranbury Ave SO14 ..103 B6
Cranbury Cl Downton SP5 ..86 F6
　Otterbourne SO21 ..31 B3
Cranbury Ct SO19 ..103 F3
Cranbury Gdns SO31 ..104 F1
Cranbury Pl SO14 ..103 A6
Cranbury Rd
　Eastleigh SO50 ......56 A1
　Eastleigh SO50 ......56 A2
　Southampton SO19 ..103 F3
Cranbury Terr 5 SO14 ..103 A6
Cranbury The 4 SO14 ..103 A6
Cranbury Twrs 6 SO14 ..103 A6
Crane Cl Gosport PO13 ..155 B2
　Verwood BH31 ......114 E6
Crane Dr BH31 ......114 E6
Crane Way BH31 ......139 B6
Cranemoor Ave BH23 ..193 E2
Cranemoor Cl BH23 ..193 E2
Cranemoor Gdns BH23 ..193 E2
Cranes Mews BH15 ..202 D3
Craneswater Ave PO4 ..182 F2
Craneswater Gate 10
　PO4 ....182 F2
Craneswater Jun Sch
　..................182 F2
Craneswater Mews 5
　PO4 ....182 F2
Craneswater Pk PO4 ..182 E2
Cranfield Ave BH21 ..163 D5
Cranford Gdns SO53 ..55 B8

Cranford Ho 6 SO17 ..79 A2
Cranford Rd GU32 ....40 E2
Cranford Way SO17 ..79 A2
Cranleigh Ave PO1 ..182 E6
Cranleigh Ct BH6 ..206 E5
Cranleigh Gdns BH6 ..206 E5
Cranleigh Ho
　Hedge End SO30 ....81 C3
　Southampton SO17 ..103 A8
Cranleigh Paddock
　SO43 ....121 F6
Cranleigh Rd
　Bournemouth BH6 ..206 D5
　Hedge End SO30 ....105 C6
　Portchester PO16 ..156 A7
　Portsmouth PO1 ....182 E6
Cranmer Dr SO16 ....77 C5
Cranmer Rd BH9 ......204 F8
Cranmore SO31 ......127 C7
Cransley Ct
　Bournemouth BH4 ..204 C2
　Bournemouth BH4 ..204 C2
Crantock Gr BH8 ....190 F2
Cranwell Cl
　Bournemouth BH11 ..188 E4
　Bransgore BH23 ....169 B1
Cranwell Ct SO16 ....77 F5
Cranworth Rd SO22 ..215 B7
Craswell St PO1 ....216 C4
Craven Ct PO15 ....130 D3
Craven Rd SO53 ......55 D6
Craven St 9 SO14 ..103 A5
Crawford Cl SO16 ....77 D5
Crawford Dr PO16 ..130 F3
Crawley Ave PO9 ..136 A6
Crawley Hill SO51 ....50 D2
Crawshaw Rd BH14 ..203 B2
Crawte Ave SO45 ..150 D2
Crawters La 6 GU31 ..40 F3
Cray Ho PO12 ......181 D5
Creasey Rd BH11 ..189 A5
Credenhill Rd PO6 ..133 C1
Creech Rd BH12 ....203 C5
Creech View PO7 ..110 E4
Creech Wood Forest Sch *
　PO7 ....110 D3
Creedy Dr BH23 ....207 B5
Creedy Gdns SO18 ..80 A3
Creek End PO10 ....160 F7
Creek Rd Gosport PO12 ..181 D5
　South Hayling PO11 ..185 D1
Creekmoor La PO7 ..202 A8
Creighton Rd SO15 ..101 F6
Cremorne Pl 7 GU32 ..40 F4
Cremyll Cl PO14 ....179 C7
Crescent Cl SO22 ....10 B4
Crescent Ct
　Barton on S BH25 ..209 F7
　Poole BH12 ....203 F6
Crescent Dr BH25 ..209 F7
Crescent Ho SO50 ....56 B3
Crescent Prim Sch The
　SO50 ....56 A3
Crescent Rd
　Bournemouth BH4 ..204 B3
　Fareham PO16 ......131 A1
　Gosport PO12 ......181 A2
　Locks Heath SO31 ..53 F5
　North Baddesley SO52 ..53 B6
　Poole BH14 ....203 E4
　Verwood BH31 ......115 A6
　Wimborne Minst BH21 ..163 C4
Crescent The
　Barton on S BH25 ..209 D8
　3 Bournemouth BH1 ..205 E4
　Eastleigh SO50 ......56 A3
　Exbury SO45 ......127 A6
　Marchwood SO40 ..101 E1
　Netley SO31 ......127 C6
　Romsey SO51 ......53 B8
　Southampton SO19 ..104 A2
　Southbourne PO10 ..161 D8
　Twyford SO21 ......32 A6
　Upham SO32 ......35 C7
　West Moors BH24 ..166 B8
　West Moors BH24 ..166 B8
　Woodlands SO40 ....99 E3
Crescent Wlk BH22 ..165 E2
Cressey Rd SO51 ....52 F7
Cressy Rd PO2 ......182 D7
Crest Cl PO16 ......131 D1
Crest Rd BH12 ......203 C6
Crest The PO7 ......134 C2
Crest Way SO41 ....104 C4
Cresta Ct 6 PO4 ..182 F2
Cresta Gdns PO12 ..165 E2
Crestland Cl PO8 ..112 B3
Crestwood Coll for Bsns &
　Enterprise SO50 ....55 F5
Crete Cotts SO45 ..125 E1
Crete La SO45 ......125 F1
Crete Rd SO45 ......125 F1
Cribb Cl BH17 ......202 A5
Crichel Mount Rd BH14 ..214 C7
Crichel Rd BH9 ....205 A8
Crichton Ho SO31 ..127 B6
Cricket Chambers BH1 ..205 A4
Cricket Cl BH23 ....207 B6
Cricket Dr PO8 ......112 A5
Cricklemede SO32 ....83 D7
Cricklewood Cl SO32 ..83 D7
Crigdon Cl SO16 ....101 E8
Crimea Rd BH9 ......204 F7
Cringle Ave PH6 ....207 A4
Crinoline Gdns PO4 ..183 B2
Cripple Gate La SO42 ..145 F7
Crispin Cl
　Christchurch BH23 ..208 F8

Crispin Cl continued
　Horton Heath SO50 ..81 C6
　Locks Heath SO31 ..129 B4
Crispstead La SO23 ..215 D3
Crisspyn Cl PO8 ....112 B6
Criterion Arc 8 BH1 ..204 F3
Crittall Cl SO41 ....172 C2
Croad Ct 4 PO14 ..131 C1
Crockford Cl BH25 ..195 B5
Crockford Rd PO10 ..137 B4
Croft Cl BH21 ......186 D7
Croft Hts SP5 ......24 B3
Croft La PO11 ......159 F1
Croft Rd
　Bournemouth BH9 ..189 F2
　Bransgore BH23 ....193 B6
　Christchurch BH23 ..207 F7
　Poole BH12 ....203 B6
　Portsmouth PO2 ....157 D1
　Ringwood BH24 ....117 C1
Croft The Bishopstone SP5 ..22 B8
　Chandler's Ford SO53 ..55 C3
　Stubbington PO14 ..154 C5
　Totton SO40 ....76 C2
　7 Eastleigh SO50 ....56 A2
Croftlands Ave PO14 ..179 C8
Crofton Anne Dale Inf Sch
　PO14 ....179 C7
Crofton Anne Dale Jun Sch
　PO14 ....179 C7
Crofton Ave PO13 ..179 C5
Crofton Cl
　Christchurch BH23 ..191 E1
　Southampton SO17 ..79 A4
　Waterlooville PO7 ..134 D5
Crofton Ct PO14 ....179 C7
Crofton Hammond Inf Sch
　PO14 ....179 C7
Crofton Hammond Jun Sch
　PO14 ....179 C7
Crofton La PO14 ....179 B6
Crofton Rd
　Portsmouth,Milton PO4 ..183 B5
　Portsmouth,North End
　　PO2 ....157 C2
　Crofton South PO14 ..179 C7
Crofton Way
　Swanmore SO32 ....84 A5
　Warsash SO31 ......128 C1
Cromalt Cl SO45 ....125 D2
Cromarty Ave PO4 ..183 B4
Cromarty Cl PO14 ..154 B5
Cromarty Rd SO16 ..77 E5
Crombie Cl PO8 ....111 F4
Cromer Gdns BH12 ..203 F5
Cromer Rd
　Bournemouth BH8 ..205 D2
　Poole BH12 ....203 F5
　Poole BH12 ....133 E1
Cromhall Cl PO14 ..154 C8
Crompton Way PO15 ..129 C5
Cromwell Pl 2 BH5 ..206 B5
Cromwell Rd
　Bournemouth BH5 ..206 B5
　Poole BH12 ....203 D5
　Southampton SO15 ..102 F7
　4 Wimborne Minst BH21 ..163 D4
　Winchester SO22 ..215 C4
Crondall Ave PO9 ..135 E6
Crooked Hays Cl SO40 ..101 F1
Crooked Walk La PO17 ..132 F4
Crookham Cl PO9 ..135 C4
Crookham Rd SO19 ..126 F8
Crookhorn Coll of
　Technology PO7 ....134 F4
Crookhorn La
　Soberton SO32 ......85 C8
　Waterlooville PO7 ..134 E3
Crosby Rd BH4 ......204 C1
Crosfield Cl SO51 ....51 B2
Cross House Ctr SO14 ..103 C3
Cross Keys Pas 6 SO23 ..215 E5
Cross La
　Bishop's Waltham SO32 ..59 A2
　Waterlooville PO8 ..112 A5
Cross Lanes BH24 ..117 C7
Cross Rd Lee-on-t-S PO13 ..180 A4
　Southampton SO19 ..103 E7
Cross St
　1 Bishop's Waltham
　　SO32 ....83 C7
　Portsmouth PO5 ....216 C2
　Portsmouth,Portsea PO1 ..182 A6
　Winchester SO23 ..215 E5
Cross The Bishopstone SP5 ..22 B7
　Burley BH24 ......143 A3
　East Meon GU32 ....38 D1
　Gosport PO12 ......45 F1
Cross Trees SP6 ......45 F1
Cross Way
　Christchurch BH23 ..191 D1
　Compton SO21 ......31 D5
　Havant PO9 ....135 E2
Cross Ways BH23 ..169 D5
Crossbill Cl PO8 ....112 A7
Crossfell Wlk PO14 ..154 C8
Crosshouse Rd SO14 ..103 C3
Crossland Cl PO12 ..181 C4
Crossland Dr PO9 ..136 A3
Crossley Ct 2 SO15 ..102 C6
Crossley Pl 5 SO15 ..102 E6
Crossmead Ave BH25 ..195 A2
Crossway The PO16 ..156 C8
Crossways SO41 ....196 D1
Crossways SP5 ......24 F1
Crossways The
　Denmead PO7 ......111 B7

Crossways The continued
　Gosport PO12 ......181 B7
　Upton BH16 ....201 C7
Crosswell Cl SO19 ..104 C5
Crouch La PO8 ......112 A7
Croucher's Croft SO22 ..215 A1
Crow Arch La BH24 ..141 B6
Crow Arch Lane Ind Est
　BH24 ....141 B5
Crow Cotts BH24 ..141 D4
Crow Hill Top BH24 ..142 A4
Crow La BH24 ......141 C5
Crowder Terr SO22 ..215 D5
Crowders Gn SO21 ..56 F8
Crowe Hill Ct 2 BH15 ..202 E4
Crowlin Ho 1 PO17 ..130 E8
Crown Cl Poole BH12 ..203 C5
　Waterlooville PO7 ..134 C3
Crown Ct
　Portsmouth PO1 ....216 C4
　4 Wimborne Minst BH21 ..163 B5
Crown Mead BH21 ..163 B5
Crown Mews 1 PO12 ..181 D5
Crown St
　Portsmouth PO1 ....216 C4
　Southampton SO15 ..102 B8
Crows Nest La SO32 ..81 F1
Crowsbury Cl PO10 ..136 E3
Crowsport SO31 ......128 A3
Crowther Cl SO19 ..104 C4
Croxton Rd PO1 ....182 B3
Croydon Cl SO16 ....78 A4
Crummock Rd SO53 ..55 A8
Crundles GU31 ......41 B3
Crusader Ct
　3 Bournemouth BH4 ..204 B4
　4 Gosport PO12 ....181 C8
Crusader Rd
　Bournemouth BH11 ..188 D4
　Hedge End SO30 ..105 D6
　Squadrons Way SO53 ..54 F6
Cruse Cl SO41 ......172 B2
Cruxton Farm Ctyd
　BH21 ....163 D2
Crystal Way PO7 ..133 B8
Cucklington Gdns BH9 ..190 B4
Cucklington Gdns BH9 ..190 B4
Cuckmere La SO16 ..101 D8
Cuckmere La SO16 ..101 D8
Cuckoo Bushes La SO53 ..55 C8
Cuckoo Hill Rly* SP6 ..94 C1
Cuckoo Hill Way 3 BH23 ..169 C1
Cuckoo La
　17 Southampton SO14 ..102 F3
　Stubbington PO14 ..179 B8
Cuckoo Rd BH24 ..203 A8
Cudnell Ave BH11 ..189 A6
Cudworth Mead SO30 ..81 C1
Cuffnells Cl BH24 ..117 B8
Cul-De-Sac BH25 ..209 C8
Culford Ave SO40 ..100 C6
Culford Cl BH8 ......190 F2
Culford Ct 1 BH8 ..205 A5
Culford Way SO40 ..100 C6
Cull Cl BH12 ....204 A3
Cull La BH25 ......195 B5
Culliford Cres BH17 ..187 E2
Culloden Cl PO15 ..130 C2
Culloden Rd PO14 ..154 C8
Cullwood La BH25 ..195 A5
Cully Terr PO13 ....155 C4
Culver SO31 ....127 C7
Culver Cl SO16 ......77 D2
Culver Dr PO11 ....185 A6
Culver Mews SO23 ..215 E5
Culver Rd
　New Milton BH25 ..194 F2
　2 Portsmouth PO4 ..183 A2
　Winchester SO23 ..215 D4
Culverhayes Cl BH21 ..163 B6
Culverhayes Pl BH21 ..163 B6
Culverhayes Rd BH21 ..163 B6
Culverin Sq PO3 ....158 E4
Culverlands Bsns Pk
　SO32 ....107 C6
Culverlands Cl SO32 ..107 C7
Culverley Cl SO42 ..145 F1
Culverwell Gdns 6
　SO23 ....215 D5
Culvery Gdns SO16 ..80 B2
Cumber Rd SO31 ..128 C3
Cumberland Ave
　Chandler's Ford SO53 ..55 E6
　Emsworth PO10 ....136 F4
Cumberland Bsns Ctr
　PO1 ....216 C3
Cumberland Cl SO32 ..55 E6
Cumberland Ho PO1 ..182 A6
Cumberland Natural
　History Mus* PO4 ..182 F1
Cumberland Inf Sch
　PO4 ....183 A3
Cumberland Pl SO15 ..102 F5
Cumberland Rd PO5 ..216 D3
Cumberland St
　Portsmouth PO1 ....182 A6
　Southampton SO14 ..103 B4
Cumberland Way SO45 ..125 D3
Cumbrian Way SO16 ..101 F8
Cummins Gn SO31 ..105 A1
Cumnor Rd BH1 ....205 A3
Cunard Ave SO15 ..102 C8
Cunard Rd SO14 ..103 A2
Cundell Way SO23 ....2 B8
Cunningham Cl
　Bournemouth BH11 ..189 A3

Cunningham Cl *continued*
Christchurch BH23 ....208 A6
Portsmouth PO2 ....157 D4
Ringwood BH24 ....141 C8
Cunningham Cres
Bournemouth BH11 ....189 B3
Southampton SO19 ....104 B4
Cunningham Ct
New Milton BH25 ....194 F3
11 Portsmouth PO5 .....182 D2
Cunningham Dr
Gosport PO13 ....155 C4
Locks Heath SO31 ....155 C4
Cunningham Gdns SO31 .127 F8
Cunningham Ho SO32 .....83 B8
Cunningham Pl BH11 ...189 A3
Cunningham Rd
Horndean PO8 ....112 C7
Waterlooville PO7 ....134 D5
Cupernham Cl SO51 ......28 B1
Cupernham Inf Sch SO51 .28 B1
Cupernham Jun Sch
SO51 ....28 B1
Cupernham La SO51 ......28 A2
Curdridge Cl 2 PO9 ...136 A5
Curdridge La SO32 ......83 C3
Curdridge Prim Sch
SO32 ....106 D8
Curlew Cl
Emsworth PO10 ....160 E7
Ferndown BH22 ....165 B7
Hythe SO45 ....126 B2
Southampton SO16 ....78 B5
Curlew Dr Hythe SO45 ...126 B2
Portchester PO16 ....155 F8
Curlew Gdns PO8 ....111 F4
Curlew Path 3 PO4 ....183 B5
Curlew Rd
Bournemouth BH8 ....190 D2
Christchurch BH23 ....208 A6
Curlew Sq SO50 ....55 E2
Curlew Wlk
Gosport PO13 ....155 A3
Hythe SO45 ....126 B2
Curlews The BH31 ......115 A5
Curlieu Rd BH15 ....202 E6
Curtis Mead PO2 ....157 F4
Curtis Rd BH12 ....203 C5
Curtiss Gdns PO12 .....180 F4
Curve The Gosport PO13 .155 B2
Horndean PO8 ....111 F6
Curzon Ct
48 Bournemouth BH4 ...204 C3
Southampton SO16 ....78 D4
Curzon Howe Rd PO1 ....182 A5
Curzon Pl SO41 ....197 D2
Curzon Rd
Bournemouth BH1 ....205 D6
Poole BH14 ....203 A3
Waterlooville PO7 ....134 E7
Curzon Way BH23 ....208 D8
Custards Rd SO43 ......121 F6
Custards The SO43 .....122 A6
Cut Throat La
Droxford SO32 ....61 B2
Swanmore SO32 ....84 C6
Cutbush La
Southampton SO18 ....104 B8
West End SO18 ....80 A3
Cuthbert Rd PO1 ....182 F6
Cuthburga Rd BH21 .....163 C4
Cuthbury Cl BH21 ......163 A4
Cuthbury Gdns BH21 ....163 A5
Cutler Cl
New Milton BH25 ....195 C3
Poole BH12 ....204 C7
Cutlers La PO14 ....179 C8
Cutlers Pl BH21 ....164 A5
Cutter Ave SO31 ....128 E1
Cutts Arch SO32 ....85 B7
Cygnet Ct PO16 ....155 F8
Cygnet Ho PO12 ....181 B8
Cygnet Rd PO6 ....158 F7
Cygnus Gdns SO45 ......125 C3
Cynthia Cl BH12 ....203 B7
Cynthia Ho BH12 ....203 B7
Cynthia Rd BH12 ....203 B7
Cypress Ave SO19 ......103 F5
Cypress Cres PO8 ......112 A5
Cypress Gdns
Botley SO30 ....106 A7
Totton SO40 ....100 C7
Cypress Gr SO41 ....211 D8
Cyprus Rd
Portsmouth PO2 ....182 E8
Titchfield PO14 ....129 C1
Cyril Rd BH8 ....205 C6

D

D Ave SO45 ....150 E5
D-Day Mus* PO5 ....182 C1
Dacombe Cl BH16 ......201 C7
Dacombe Dr BH16 ......201 C7
Dacres Wlk 3 SO41 ....211 D5
Daffodil Rd SO16 ....79 C4
Daggons Rd SP6 ....92 D6
Dagmar Mews 24 PO5 ..182 C2
Dahlia Cl BH15 ....202 E6
Dahlia Rd SO16 ....79 A4
Daintree Cl SO19 ......104 D3
Dairy Cl
Christchurch BH23 ....207 D7
Corfe Mullen BH21 ....186 B4

Dairy Cl *continued*
Redlynch SP5 ....47 D6
Dairy La SO16 ....77 B5
Dairymoor PO17 ....108 A4
Daisy Cl BH15 ....202 D6
Daisy La Gosport PO12 .181 B5
Locks Heath SO31 ....129 C3
Daisy Mead PO7 ....135 A7
Daisy Rd SO16 ....79 B4
Dakota Cl BH23 ....208 B7
Dale Cl Littleton SO22 ..1 A5
Poole BH15 ....202 F6
Dale Dr PO13 ....155 B5
Dale Gn SO53 ....55 B8
Dale Park Ho 4 PO1 ...216 B3
Dale Rd Hythe SO45 ...125 F3
Poole BH15 ....202 F6
Southampton SO16 ....78 C2
Stubbington PO14 ....179 D8
Dale The PO7 ....134 D2
Dale Valley Cl SO16 ...78 C2
Dale Valley Gdns SO16 .78 C2
Dale Valley Rd
Poole BH15 ....202 F7
Southampton SO16 ....78 C2
Dales Cl BH21 ....164 C6
Dales Dr BH21 ....164 C6
Dales La BH23 ....190 E7
Dales Way SO40 ....100 B8
Dalewood Ave BH11 ....188 E5
Dalewood Rd PO15 .....130 D1
Dalkeith Ave BH1 .....204 F3
Dalkeith Rd
Corfe Mullen BH21 ....186 D4
Poole BH13 ....204 A1
Dalley Way 6 GU33 .....20 F4
Dalling Rd BH12 ......204 A5
Dallington Cl PO14 ....179 C6
Dalmally Gdns SO18 ...103 F8
Dalmeny Rd BH6 ....207 A3
Dalzell 13 SO23 ......215 E8
Damask Gdns PO7 ......112 B1
Dame Elizabeth Kelly Ct 3
PO2 ....157 E4
Damson Cl SO30 ....105 B5
Damerham Rd 8 BH8 ...190 D3
Damerham Trout Lakes*
SP6 ....68 D2
Dampier Cl PO13 ......180 C7
Damson Cres SO50 ......57 B1
Damson Hill SO32 ....60 B1
Danbury Ct PO10 ......137 A2
Dances Way PO11 ......184 E4
Dandelion Cl PO13 ....155 B2
Dando Rd PO7 ....111 A4
Dandy's Ford La SO51 ..25 F1
Dane Cl SO45 ....150 F1
Dane Ct BH14 ....203 A4
Dane Dr BH22 ....165 E3
Dane Rd SO41 ....211 A6
Danebury Cl PO9 ......135 E6
Danebury Gdns SO53 ....55 A4
Danebury Way SO16 .....77 D3
Danecourt Cl BH14 ....202 F4
Danecourt Rd BH14 ....202 F4
Danecrest Rd SO41 ....195 F3
Danehurst SO41 ....211 A6
Danehurst New Rd
SO41 ....195 C8
Danehurst Pl SO31 ....129 A2
Danemark Ct 18 SO23 ..215 E6
Danes Cl BH25 ....210 A7
Danes Rd Awbridge SO51 .26 D3
Portchester PO16 ....132 B1
4 Winchester SO23 .....215 E7
Danesbrook La PO7 ....135 A7
Danesbury Ave BH6 ....206 D4
Danesbury Mdws BH25 ..195 C5
Danestead Ho 3 BH25 ..195 A3
Danestream Cl SO41 ...211 D4
Danestream Ct SO41 ...211 E4
Daneswood Rd BH25 ....195 C3
Daniel Gdns 2 BH15 ...202 C1
Daniell's Cl SO41 .....197 F3
Daniell's Wlk SO41 ....197 E3
Daniels Wlk SO41 ......76 B1
Dansie Cl BH14 ....203 B4
Dapple Pl SO40 ....102 A1
Darby's Cl BH15 ......202 D6
Darby's Cnr BH17 .....187 C2
Darby's La BH15 ......202 D8
Darby's La N BH17 ....202 D8
Dark La Blackfield SO45 .150 F1
Cheriton SO24 ....14 D5
Hinton BH23 ....194 A4
Darley Rd BH23 ....165 C3
Darlington Gdns SO15 ..78 D1
Darlington Rd PO4 ....182 E3
Darnan Rd 6 SO14 ....103 A7
Darracott Rd BH5 .....206 B5
Darren Cl PO14 ....154 D4
Darren Ct 8 SO14 ....131 B2
Darrian Ct BH16 ......201 B7
Dart Ho SO18 ....103 F8
Dart Rd SO18 ....80 B3
Dartington Rd SO50 ....56 D5
Dartmouth Bldgs 5
PO14 ....155 A6
Dartmouth Cl 6 PO14 ..181 C8
Dartmouth Mews PO5 ..216 A1
Dartmouth Rd PO3 .....158 B8
Darwin Ave BH23 ......191 E1
Darwin Cl PO13 ....179 F4
Darwin Ct 4 BH13 ....204 A4
Darwin Ho PO1 ....216 C4
Darwin Rd Eastleigh SO50 .56 B4
Southampton SO15 ....102 E7

Darwin Way PO13 .....180 D6
Daubney Gdns PO9 ....135 C6
Daulston Rd PO1 ......182 F7
Davenport Cl
Gosport PO13 ....180 C6
Upton BH16 ....201 C7
Daventry La PO3 ......158 C4
David Cowan Ho 23
SO23 ....215 D6
David Ct SO51 ....53 A6
David Hart Bsns Ctr SP5 .46 E8
David Newberry Dr
PO13 ....180 A6
David Way BH15 ......201 D2
David's La BH24 ......140 D5
Davidia Ct PO7 ....135 A6
Davidson Cl SO45 .....126 B4
Davidson Ct 12 PO1 ...182 A5
Davis Cl PO13 ....180 C8
Davis Ct BH12 ....203 E5
Davis Field BH25 .....194 F2
Davis Rd BH12 ....203 E5
Davis Way PO14 ......155 A6
Daw La PO11 ....184 F8
Dawkins Bsns Ctr BH15 .201 D3
Dawkins Rd BH15 .....201 D3
Dawkins Way BH25 ....195 A2
Dawlish Ave SO15 ....102 D8
Dawn Cl BH10 ....189 C2
Dawn Gdns SO22 ......215 A4
Davnay Cl SO16 ....79 D5
Daws Ave BH11 ....189 B2
Dawson Rd SO19 ......104 C2
Day La PO8 ....111 E7
Day's Ct BH21 ....163 D4
Daylesford Cl BH14 ...203 A2
Dayrell Cl SO40 ....76 B1
Dayshes Cl PO13 .....155 B3
Dayslondon Rd PO7 ...134 D5
Daytona PO15 ....214 C7
De Courtenai Cl BH11 ..188 A5
De Grouchy La SO17 ...79 A1
De Haviland Cl BH21 ..163 F2
De Havilland Ho BH23 .208 A6
De Havilland Way BH23 .208 A6
De La Warr Rd SO41 ...211 F4
De Lisle Cl PO2 ......157 F4
De Lisle Rd BH3 ......204 F7
De Lunn Bldgs 8 SO23 .215 E6
De Mauley Ct BH13 ...214 D8
De Mauley Rd BH13 ...214 E8
De Montfort Rd BH21 ..163 D1
De Mowbray Way SO41 .197 D2
De Port Hts SO32 ......61 C6
De Redvers Rd BH14 ..203 C2
Deacon Cl SO19 ......104 A5
Deacon Cres SO19 ....104 A6
Deacon Gdns BH11 ....189 A5
Deacon Rd
Bournemouth BH11 ....189 A5
Locks Heath SO31 ....129 B2
Southampton SO19 ....104 A6
Deacon Trad Est SO50 ..56 C2
Deadman Hill SP6 ......71 D5
Deakin Cl SO53 ....55 C5
Deal Cl PO14 ....154 C4
Deal Rd PO6 ....133 E1
Dean Cl Hamworthy BH15 .201 E3
3 Winchester SO22 .....215 A8
Dean Court (Bournemouth
FC) BH7 ....205 F6
Dean Ct Hedge End SO30 .105 C7
3 Southampton SO18 ...104 A8
Dean Farm PO17 ......131 A5
Dean La
Bishop's Waltham SO32 ...59 E3
Finchdean PO8,PO9 ......113 D5
Whiteparish SP5 ....24 B4
Winchester SO22 ....1 B2
Dean Park Cres BH1 ...204 F3
Dean Park Rd BH1 ....204 F4
Dean Rd Cosham PO6 ..157 F8
Fair Oak SO50 ....57 C1
Southampton SO18 ....104 A7
West Dean SP5 ....3 B2
West Tytherley SP5 ......3 E5
Dean St SO1 ....182 A5
Dean Sta SP5 ....3 D3
Dean Swift Cres BH14 .214 C8
Dean Villas PO17 .....130 C8
Dean's Rd 6 BH5 .....206 B5
Deane Ct 22 PO9 ......136 B5
Deane Down Dro SO22 ..1 B4
Deane Gdns 5 PO13 ...179 F3
Deane's Park Rd PO16 .131 C1
Deanery The SO53 ......55 B8
Deanfield Cl SO31 ....129 C2
Deanfields Ct SO18 ...104 B8
Deans Court La BH21 ..163 C4
Deans Ct SO41 ....211 D5
Deans Dell GU32 ......18 E1
Deans Gate PO14 .....179 C6
Deans Gr BH21 ....163 D7
Deans The BH1 ....204 F4
Deanscroft Rd BH10 ...189 E4
Deansfield Cl SO51 .....53 B8
Deansleigh Rd BH7 ....191 B1
Deanswood Dr PO7 ....111 E1
Dear Hay La BH15 .....202 B2
Dearing Cl SO43 ......121 F4
Debney Lodge PO7 ....136 B2
Decies Rd BH14 ....203 B5
Dee Cl SO53 ....55 A5
Dee Way BH15 ....202 B1
Deep Dell PO8 ....112 B5

Deepdene SO18 ....103 E8
Deepdene La BH11 ....188 E5
Deeping Cl SO19 ......103 F1
Deeping Gate PO7 .....135 A7
Deer Leap PO15 ....130 D5
Deer Park Cl BH25 ....194 F4
Deer Park Farm Ind Est
SO50 ....57 E1
Deer Wlk SO30 ....105 D8
Deerhurst Cl SO40 ....100 D6
Deerhurst Cres PO6 ...133 A1
Deerhurst Ho 3 PO6 ...133 A1
Deerleap Cl SO45 .....126 A3
Deerleap La SO40 .....100 D2
Deerleap Way
Hythe SO45 ....126 A3
New Milton BH25 ....195 B5
Defender Rd SO19 .....103 D3
Defender Wlk SO19 ....103 D3
Defoe Cl PO15 ....129 C8
Delamere Gdns BH10 ..189 E3
Delamere Rd PO4 .....182 F3
Delaval Ho 2 PO1 .....182 B5
Delft Cl SO31 ....128 F3
Delft Gdns PO8 ....111 D2
Delft Mews BH23 ......207 D6
Delhi Cl BH14 ....203 D3
Delhi Rd BH9 ....190 B3
Delilah Rd PO1 ....201 D2
Delius Ave SO19 ......104 D3
Delius Wlk PO7 ....134 E5
Dell Cl Broadstone BH18 .186 E4
Cosham PO7 ....134 B2
Fair Oak SO50 ....57 C1
Dell Cotts SO24 ....15 F1
Dell Piece E PO8 .....112 D5
Dell Piece W PO8 .....112 C5
Dell Quay Cl PO13 ....155 B2
Dell Rd Southampton SO18 .79 F2
Dellcrest Path PO6 ....134 B2
Dellfield GU32 ....18 E2
Dellfield Cl 11 PO6 ...133 A1
Delme Ct 4 PO16 .....131 A1
Delme Dr PO16 ....131 D2
Delme Sq 7 PO16 .....131 A1
Delph Rd BH21 ....187 D8
Delph Woods Woodland
Trail* BH18,BH21 ....187 C7
Delphi Way PO7 ......134 F2
Delta Bsns Pk PO16 ...155 B7
Delta Cl BH23 ....208 A7
Dempsey Cl SO19 .....104 A5
Denbigh Cl Eastleigh SO50 .55 F1
Totton SO40 ....100 D5
Denbigh Dr PO16 ......130 F2
Denbigh Gdns SO16 ....78 F4
Denby Rd BH15 ....202 D4
Dene Cl Chilworth SO16 ..78 F7
Ringwood BH24 ....117 C1
Sarisbury SO31 ....128 E4
Dene Hollow PO6 ......158 D8
Dene Rd SO40 ....100 C2
Dene The BH14 ....204 A2
Dene Way SO40 ....100 C3
Dene Wlk SO41 ....165 E1
Denecote Lodge BH13 ..214 H8
Deneside Copse SO41 ..197 B1
Deneve Ave BH17 .....187 C1
Denewood Copse BH22 .138 D3
Denewood Rd
Bournemouth BH4 ....204 B3
West Moors BH22 ....138 D4
Denewulf Cl 2 SO32 ...83 C8
Denham Cl Poole BH17 ..187 E3
Stubbington PO14 ....179 B7
Winchester SO23 ....215 D8
Denham Dr BH23 ......193 F1
Denham Fields SO50 ....57 B5
Denham Gdns SO31 ....127 B5
Denham's Cnr SO32 ....81 D5
Denhill Cl PO11 ......184 E5
Denholm Cl BH24 .....117 D1
Denison Rd PO1 ......187 C1
Denham La BH15 ......202 D3
Denmark Rd
Bournemouth BH9 ....189 F1
Poole BH15 ....202 D3
Denmark Terr BH11 ...205 E6
Dennead BH25 ....195 D4
Dennead Ho PO16 .....216 C4
Denmead Inf Sch PO7 ..111 A4
Denmead Jun Sch PO7 ..111 A4
Denmead Rd
Bournemouth BH6 ....206 D7
Southampton SO18 ......104 C8
Dennet Ho SO23 ....2 D1
Denning Mews PO5 ....216 B3
Dennis Rd BH21 ......186 D5
Dennis Way GU33 ......21 A3
Denny Cl SO45 ....126 B2
Denniston Ave BH23 ..207 F7
Denny Cl SO45 ....151 B3
Densome Cnr SP6 ....71 A6
Denville Ave PO16 ....156 D6
Denville Cl PO6 ......158 F8
Denvilles Cl PO9 .....136 B2
Denzil Ave Netley SO31 .127 C6
Southampton SO14 ......103 B6
Depden Gdns SO45 ....125 D1
Depedene Cl SO45 ....150 B4

Derby Ct 12 PO13 ....180 C6
Derby Ho SO50 ....56 A1
Derby Rd
Bournemouth BH1 ....205 C8
Eastleigh SO50 ....55 F2
Portsmouth PO2 ....157 D1
Southampton SO14 ......103 B6
Dereham Way BH12 ....203 F6
Deridene Ct SO40 .....100 C6
Derlyn Rd PO16 ....131 A1
Derritt La BH23 ......192 D8
Derrybrian Gdns BH25 .195 A2
Dersingham Ct PO6 ....133 E1
Derwent Cl
Bournemouth BH9 ....190 A2
Ferndown BH22 ....166 A6
Horndean PO8 ....88 C2
Stubbington PO14 ....154 D4
West End SO18 ....80 B1
Derwent Dr SO40 .....100 B8
Derwent Rd
Lee-on-t-S PO13 ....179 F3
New Milton BH25 ....195 B5
Southampton SO16 ....77 C1
Derwentwater Rd BH21 .163 C2
Desborough Cl 6 PO6 ..133 A1
Desborough Rd SO50 ...56 A2
Devenish Rd SO22 ......1 D3
Deverel Cl BH23 ......207 A8
Deverell Pl PO7 ......134 C3
Deverel Gdns SO50 .....56 E2
Devon Cl SO53 ....55 C3
Devon Dr SO53 ....55 C3
Devon Mews 6 SO15 ...102 E5
Devon Rd
Christchurch BH23 ......206 E8
Poole BH15 ....202 E5
Portsmouth PO3 ....158 A3
Devonshire Ave PO4 ...183 A3
Devonshire Gdns
Burslodon SO31 ....105 A2
Hythe SO45 ....150 A8
Devonshire Inf Sch PO4 .182 F4
Devonshire Mans 16
SO15 ....102 F6
Devonshire Rd SO15 ...102 F6
Devonshire Sq PO4 ....182 F4
Devonshire Way PO14 ..154 C8
Dew La SO50 ....55 F3
Dewar Cl PO15 ....129 C5
Deweys La BH24 ....140 F7
Dewlands Pk BH31 ....114 D6
Dewlands Rd BH31 ....114 E6
Dewlands Way BH31 ...114 E6
Dewlish Cl BH17 ......188 A2
Dewsbury Ct 3 SO18 ...80 A2
Dhekelia Ct PO1 ......216 C4
Dial Cl BH23 ....169 D2
Diamond Cl SP6 ....93 E8
Diamond Ct
Fordingbridge SP6 ....93 E8
7 Waterlooville PO7 ...134 E8
Diamond St 2 PO5 ....216 A1
Diana Cl Emsworth PO10 .136 E4
Ferndown BH22 ....165 B6
Gosport PO12 ....180 E4
Diana Ct 7 BH23 .....209 A7
Diana Way BH21 ......186 E7
Dibben Wlk SO51 ......28 C1
Dibbe Dr SO52 ....53 F3
Dibden Cl
Bournemouth BH8 ....190 D3
Havant PO9 ....135 C4
Dibden Lodge Cl SO45 .125 F5
Dibles Pk SO31 ....128 E1
Dibles Rd
Locks Heath SO31 ....128 D1
Locks Heath SO31 ....128 E1
Dickens Cl PO2 ....182 D7
Dickens Dell SO40 ....100 B7
Dickens Dr PO15 .....106 C1
Dickens Ho PO4 ......183 B4
Dickens Rd BH6 ......206 D7
Dickson Cl GU31 ....41 A5
Dickinson Rd PO4 ....182 F5
Dickson Pk PO17 .....108 A4
Didcot Rd Poole BH17 ..202 D7
Southampton SO15 ....78 C1
Dieppe Cres PO2 ......157 E4
Dieppe Rd PO12 ......180 F4
Dight Rd PO12 ....181 C3
Diligence Cl SO31 ....105 A1
Dillington Ho 8 PO7 ..134 E8
Dilly La BH25 ....210 A7
Dimond Cl SO18 ....79 E1
Dimond Hill SO18 ......79 E1
Dimond Rd SO18 ....79 E2
Dingle Rd BH5 ....206 B4
Dingle Way SO31 .....129 A4
Dingley Rd BH15 .....202 D6
Dinham Ct BH25 ......195 D4
Dinham Rd BH25 ......195 D4
Diprose Rd BH12 .....186 E7
Disa Ho SO15 ....102 E6
Discovery Cl PO14 ....154 C5
Discovery Court Bsns Ctr
BH12 ....188 E2
Disraeli Rd BH23 .....207 D6
Ditcham Cres PO9 .....135 E4
Ditcham Park Sch GU31 .89 F8
Ditchbury SO41 ......197 D6
Ditton Cl PO14 ....154 C4
Ditton Cotts SO42 ....148 F1
Dock La SO42 ....149 A1
Dock Mill Cotts 18 PO5 .182 D2
Dockens Rd PO12 .....181 C5
Dockenfield Cl PO9 ...135 C4
Doctor's Hill SO51 ....26 A3

Doctors La GU32 . . . . .37 C5
Dodds La SO32 . . . . .84 C5
Dodgson Cl SP6 . . . . .70 E8
Dodwell La SO31 . . . . .105 B3
Dodwell Terr SO31 . . . . .105 B1
Doe Copse Way BH25 . . . .194 E4
Doe Wlk SO30 . . . . .105 D8
Dogdean BH21 . . . . .163 C8
Dogkennel La PO7 . . . . .86 F4
Dogwood Dell **1** PO7 . . . .134 F5
Dogwood Rd BH18 . . . . . . .186 E2
Dolbery Rd N BH12 . . . . . . .188 D2
Dolbery Rd S BH12 . . . . . . .188 C1
Dolman Rd PO12 . . . . .181 C4
Dolphin Ave BH10 . . . . .189 E5
Dolphin Cl SO50 . . . . .56 F2
Dolphin Cres PO12 . . . . . . .181 C4
Dolphin Ct Poole BH13 . . . . .204 B7
11 Portsmouth PO5 . . . . . . .182 E1
Dolphin Ct PO14 . . . . .154 B4
Stubbington PO14 . . . . .55 C5
Dolphin Dr **3** BH15 . . . . . .202 C2
Dolphin Hill SO21 . . . . .32 A6
Dolphin Mans BH25 . . . . . . .210 A6
Dolphin PI BH25 . . . . .210 A7
Dolphin Quays **10** BH15 . . .202 C1
Dolphin Way PO12 . . . . .181 D2
Dolton Rd SO16 . . . . .77 F3
Dombey Ct **8** PO1 . . . . . . .182 D7
Dome Alley SO23 . . . . .215 E5
Dominie Wlk **1** PO13 . . . . .179 F3
Dominion Cir BH11 . . . . .188 E3
Dominion Rd BH11 . . . . .188 E3
Dominy Cl SO45 . . . . .126 B4
Domum Rd
  Portsmouth PO2 . . . . .157 F2
  Winchester SO23 . . . . . . .215 C5
Domvilles App PO2 . . . . . . .157 B1
Donaldson Rd PO6 . . . . .157 F6
Doncaster Rd SO50 . . . . .80 A8
Donigers Cl SO32 . . . . .84 A6
Donigers Dell SO32 . . . . .84 A6
Donkey La SO30 . . . . .106 A7
Donnelly Rd BH6 . . . . .206 F5
Donnelly St PO12 . . . . .181 A4
Donnington Ct **3** SO23 . . .215 E7
Donnington Dr
  Chandler's Ford SO53 . . . . .55 B3
  Christchurch BH23 . . . . . . .207 C4
Donnington Rd **1**
  BH1 . . . . .205 E4
Dorcas Cl PO7 . . . . .112 A2
Dorchester Ct SO15 . . . . . . .102 F8
Dorchester Gdns BH15 . . . .202 E5
Dorchester Mans BH1 . . . . .205 D3
Dorchester Rd
  Poole BH15 . . . . .202 E6
  Upton BH16 . . . . .201 A4
Dore Ave PO16 . . . . .132 C1
Dores La SO51 . . . . .29 B7
Doric Cl SO53 . . . . .55 F7
Dorking Cres PO6 . . . . .157 F7
Dorland Gdns SO40 . . . . . . .100 D6
Dormers The BH25 . . . . .194 F1
Dormington Rd PO6 . . . . . . .133 C1
Dormy Cl SO31 . . . . .128 D3
Dormy Way PO13 . . . . .155 B1
Dorney Ct **8** PO6 . . . . .158 A7
Dornie Rd BH13 . . . . .214 E7
Dornmere La PO7 . . . . .135 A7
Dorothy Ct PO5 . . . . .216 C1
Dorothy Dymond St
  PO1 . . . . .216 B3
Dorrick Ct **10** SO15 . . . . . .102 F7
Dorrien Rd PO12 . . . . .181 B8
Dorrita Ave PO8 . . . . .112 A4
Dorrita Cl PO4 . . . . .182 F2
Dorrits The SO40 . . . . .100 B7
Dorset Ave BH22 . . . . .165 D3
Dorset Cl PO8 . . . . .112 B6
Dorset Grange BH23 . . . . . .206 F7
Dorset Heavy Horse & Animal
  Ctr* BH21 . . . . .91 D2
Dorset Lake Ave BH14 . . . . .214 B8
Dorset Lake Manor
  BH14 . . . . .203 A2
Dorset Rd
  Bournemouth BH4 . . . . . . .204 C5
  Chandler's Ford SO53 . . . . .55 C3
  Christchurch BH23 . . . . . . .207 F8
Dorset St SO14 . . . . .103 A6
Dorset Way BH17 . . . . .202 E7
Dorstone Rd PO6 . . . . .133 C1
Dorval Ho **6** SO15 . . . . . . .102 E7
Dorval Manor **7** SO15 . . .102 E7
Douglas Ave BH23 . . . . .207 A6
Douglas Cl BH16 . . . . .201 C7
Douglas Cres SO19 . . . . . . .104 D6
Douglas Gdns
  Havant PO9 . . . . .136 A4
  Poole BH12 . . . . .203 E5
Douglas Mews
  Bournemouth BH6 . . . . . . .206 C5
  Upton BH16 . . . . .201 C8
Douglas Rd
  Bournemouth BH6 . . . . . . .206 C4
  Poole BH12 . . . . .203 E5
  Portsmouth PO3 . . . . .182 E7
Douglas Way SO45 . . . . .125 F4
Doulton Gdns BH14 . . . . . . .203 B2
Doussie Cl BH14 . . . . .201 B8
Dove Cl PO8 . . . . .111 F4
Dove Dale SO50 . . . . .55 D2
Dove Gdns **3** SO31 . . . . . .129 B5
Dove La SO51 . . . . .9 B7
Dover Cl Poole BH13 . . . . . .204 A3
  Stubbington PO14 . . . . . . .179 B8

Dover Ct PO11 . . . . .184 E5
Dover Rd Poole BH13 . . . . . .204 A3
  Portsmouth PO3 . . . . .183 A8
Dover St SO14 . . . . .103 A7
Dovercourt Rd PO6 . . . . . . .158 A6
Doveshill Cres BH10 . . . . . . .189 D3
Doveshill Gdns BH10 . . . . . .189 D3
Doveshill Mobile Home Pk
  BH10 . . . . .189 D3
Doveys Cl BH24 . . . . .143 A3
Dowds Cl SO30 . . . . .105 B8
Dowell Ho **10** PO4 . . . . . . .183 B2
Dowlands Cl BH10 . . . . .189 D4
Dowlands Rd BH10 . . . . .189 D4
Down End PO6 . . . . .134 C1
Down End Rd PO6 . . . . .134 C1
Down Farm Cotts SP6 . . . . . .44 C4
Down Farm La SO22 . . . . .1 E7
Down Farm Pl PO8 . . . . .88 C1
Down Lodge Cl SP6 . . . . .93 A6
Down Rd Horndean PO8 . . . .112 C8
  Horndean PO8 . . . . .88 B1
Down's Park Ave SO40 . . . . .101 A6
Down's Park Cres SO40 . . . .101 A5
Down's Park Rd SO40 . . . . . .101 A6
Downend Rd PO16 . . . . .131 F1
Downey Cl BH11 . . . . .188 F2
Downham Cl PO8 . . . . .111 F3
Downhouse Rd PO8 . . . . .88 A4
Downing Ct PO14 . . . . .129 C1
Downland Cl
  Botley SO30 . . . . .105 F7
  Locks Heath SO31 . . . . . . .129 A4
Downland Pl SO30 . . . . .105 B5
Downlands Cl SP5 . . . . .46 F6
Downlands Pk BH17 . . . . . . .202 F8
Downlands Rd SO22 . . . . . . .10 B4
Downley Point PO9 . . . . .136 B4
Downley Rd PO9 . . . . .136 B4
Downs Cl PO17 . . . . .134 F3
Downscroft Gdns SO30 . . . .105 B7
Downside PO13 . . . . .155 D2
Downside Ave SO19 . . . . . . .104 A6
Downside Rd
  Waterlooville PO7 . . . . . . .134 C3
  Winchester SO22 . . . . .1 B2
Downsway The PO16 . . . . . .156 C8
Downton CE Prim Sch
  SP5 . . . . .46 E8
Downton Cl BH8 . . . . .190 D3
Downton Cvn Pk SO41 . . . . .211 A6
Downton Hill SP5 . . . . .47 D7
Downton Ho **2** PO6 . . . . . .157 C8
Downton La SO41 . . . . .210 E7
Downton Rd SO18 . . . . .79 F2
Downton Sch SP5 . . . . .46 E7
Downview Rd PO4 . . . . .43 A4
Downwood Cl
  Fordingbridge SP6 . . . . . . .69 D2
  Hythe SO45 . . . . .125 C2
Downwood Way PO8 . . . . . . .88 C1
Doyle Ave PO2 . . . . .157 E3
Doyle Cl PO12 . . . . .157 E4
Doyle Ct
  1 Portsmouth PO2 . . . . . .157 F2
  Southampton SO19 . . . . . .103 F1
Doyle Ho PO9 . . . . .135 B3
Dradfield La SO32 . . . . .109 C8
Dragon Est PO6 . . . . .158 E7
Dragon La BH23 . . . . .168 B7
Dragoon Cl SO19 . . . . .104 C4
Dragoon Way BH23 . . . . . . .206 F7
Drake Cl
  Christchurch BH23 . . . . . . .207 F6
  Locks Heath SO31 . . . . . . .129 B5
  Marchwood SO40 . . . . . . .102 A2
  New Milton BH25 . . . . . . .194 F3
  Ringwood BH24 . . . . .117 D1
Drake Ct Lee-on-t-S PO13 . .179 D4
  5 Poole BH15 . . . . .202 C1
Drake Ho **3** PO1 . . . . .182 A5
Drake Rd
  Bishopstoke SO50 . . . . . . .56 E4
  Lee-on-t-S PO13 . . . . .179 D4
  Poole BH15 . . . . .202 C1
Drakes Cl SO45 . . . . .125 F2
Drakes Cl SO40 . . . . .102 A3
Drakes Rd BH22 . . . . .165 F3
Draper Rd
  Bournemouth BH11 . . . . . .189 A4
  Christchurch BH23 . . . . . . .207 A5
Drapers Copse Mobile Home
  Pk SO45 . . . . .125 D4
Draycote Rd PO8 . . . . .88 C3
Draycott Rd BH10 . . . . .189 D2
Drayton Cl SO19 . . . . .126 F8
Drayton La PO6 . . . . .134 B1
Drayton Pl SO40 . . . . .100 D7
Drayton Rd PO2 . . . . .157 E1
Drayton St SO22 . . . . .137 B3
Dreadnought Rd PO14 . . . . .154 F5
Dresden Dr PO8 . . . . .111 E3
Dreswick Cl BH23 . . . . .191 D4
Drew Cl BH12 . . . . .204 C7
Drew Grange BH15 . . . . . . .201 E4
Drewitt Ind Est BH11 . . . . . .188 E3
Drift Rd Clanfield PO8 . . . . . .88 E6
  Fareham PO16 . . . . .131 D2
Drift The PO9 . . . . .113 B1
Driftwood Gdns
  Portsmouth PO4 . . . . .183 C2
  Totton SO40 . . . . .100 C4
Drill Shed Rd PO2 . . . . .157 B1
Drinkwater Cl SO50 . . . . .55 F3
Drive The Fareham PO16 . . . .131 A1

Drive The continued
  Gosport PO13 . . . . .155 A2
  Havant PO9 . . . . .135 F3
  Poole,Lilliput BH13 . . . . . .214 D7
  Poole,Upper Parkstone
  BH12 . . . . .203 D5
  Sherfield English SO51 . . . .25 B1
  Southbourne PO10 . . . . . . .161 D8
  Totton SO40 . . . . .100 F5
  West End SO18 . . . . .80 B3
  West Wellow SO51 . . . . . . .51 B2
Droffatts Ho SO15 . . . . .102 D7
Drove Cl SO21 . . . . .31 F5
Drove Rd
  Southampton SO19 . . . . . .104 B4
  Southwick PO17 . . . . .133 A4
Drove The
  Blackfield SO45 . . . . .150 L1
  Durley SO32 . . . . .82 D8
  Horton Heath SO50 . . . . . . .81 D6
  Redlynch SP5 . . . . .47 D6
  Southampton SO18 . . . . . .104 B7
  Swanmore SO32 . . . . .84 B5
  Totton SO40 . . . . .76 B1
  Twyford SO21 . . . . .31 F5
  West End SO30 . . . . .80 F3
  West Wellow SO51 . . . . . . .50 E3
Droxford Cl **2** PO12 . . . . .180 F4
Droxford Jun Sch SO32 . . . .61 A1
Droxford Rd
  Bournemouth BH6 . . . . . . .206 B6
  East Meon GU32 . . . . .63 D3
  Swanmore SO32 . . . . .84 D5
Druids Cl BH22 . . . . .165 D2
Druitt Rd BH23 . . . . .207 F8
Drum La GU32 . . . . .40 F3
Drum Mead GU32 . . . . .40 E3
Drummond Rd SO50 . . . . . . .55 F2
Drumlanrig Terr **4**
  PO 181 C9
Drummond Cl SO22 . . . . . . .215 C3
Drummond Ct
  Eastleigh SO50 . . . . .56 B5
  Hythe SO45 . . . . .126 A5
  Southampton SO19 . . . . . .103 E3
Drummond Dr SO14 . . . . . . .103 C8
Drummond Rd
  Bournemouth BH1 . . . . . . .205 D4
  Hedge End SO30 . . . . .81 C1
  Hythe SO45 . . . . .126 A4
  Portsmouth PO1 . . . . .216 C4
  Titchfield PO15 . . . . .129 D4
Drummond Way SO53 . . . . . .55 B8
Drury Rd BH4 . . . . .204 B2
Dryden Ave PO6 . . . . .132 E1
Dryden Cl Fareham PO16 . . .131 A1
  St Leonards BH24 . . . . . . .139 E5
  Waterlooville PO7 . . . . . . .111 E2
Dryden Pl **4** SO41 . . . . . . .211 D5
Dryden Rd SO19 . . . . .104 E5
Drysdale Mews **5** PO7 . . .134 D3
Duart Ct BH25 . . . . .195 C3
Duck Island La **5** BH24 . . .141 A6
Duck La BH11 . . . . .188 C2
Ducking Stool La BH23 . . . .207 B6
Duckmead La SO32 . . . . .21 B5
Duckworth Ho **34** PO1 . . .182 A5
Duddon Cl SO18 . . . . .80 B2
Dudleston Heath Dr
  PO8 . . . . .112 B2
Dudley Ave
  Fordingbridge SP6 . . . . . . .69 F3
  Hordle SO41 . . . . .195 F3
Dudley Gdns BH10 . . . . .189 D5
  Portsmouth PO3 . . . . .183 A7
Dudley Rd BH10 . . . . .189 D5
Dudley Terr GU33 . . . . .21 A5
Dudmoor Farm Rd
  BH23 . . . . .191 F4
Dudmoor La BH23 . . . . .191 F3
Dudsbury Ave BH22 . . . . . . .165 E4
Dudsbury Cres BH22 . . . . . .165 E4
Dudsbury Gdns BH22 . . . . . .165 D1
Dudsbury Rd BH22 . . . . .165 D1
Dudsway Ct BH22 . . . . .165 D4
Duffield La PO10 . . . . .137 D3
Dugald Drummond St
  PO1 . . . . .216 B3
Dugdell Cl BH22 . . . . .165 F6
Duisburg Way PO5 . . . . .182 B2
Duke Cres PO1 . . . . .182 B6
Duke of Edinburgh Ho
  PO1 . . . . .182 A6
Duke Rd SO30 . . . . .105 D5
Duke St SO14 . . . . .103 B3
Duke Terr PO9 . . . . .135 D4
Dukes Cl
  Bournemouth BH6 . . . . . . .206 D6
  Petersfield GU32 . . . . .40 D4
  Westbourne PO10 . . . . . . .137 B3
Dukes Ct
  Bournemouth BH6 . . . . . . .206 D6
  4 Bishop's Waltham
  SO32 . . . . .83 C8
  Verwood BH31 . . . . .114 F7
Dukes Dr BH11 . . . . .188 E5
Dukes Mill **12** SO51 . . . . . .52 E7
Dukes Rd Gosport PO12 . . . .180 D4
  Southampton SO14 . . . . . .103 B7
Dukes Wlk **7** PO7 . . . . . . .134 C7
Dukes Wlk Service Rd **6**
  PO7 . . . . .134 C7
Dukesfield BH23 . . . . .191 D2
Dukeswood Dr SO45 . . . . . .126 A1
Dulsie Rd BH3 . . . . .204 C7
Dumbarton Cl PO2 . . . . .182 D8
Dumbleton Cl SO19 . . . . . . .104 F5

Dumbleton's Twrs SO19 . . . .104 E4
Dummer Ct PO9 . . . . .135 D6
Dummer Mews **5** SO23 . . .215 D5
Dummers Rd SO51 . . . . .28 D7
Dumpers Dro SO50 . . . . .81 D7
Dumpton Sch BH21 . . . . . . .163 D8
Dunbar Cl SO16 . . . . .77 F5
Dunbar Cres BH23 . . . . .193 F2
Dunbar Rd
  Bournemouth BH3 . . . . . . .204 E6
  Portsmouth PO4 . . . . .183 B4
Dunbridge La SO51 . . . . .26 F7
  Dunbridge Sta SO51 . . . . . .5 O1
Duncan Cl SO19 . . . . .103 E1
Duncan Cooper Ho PO7 . . .134 D7
Duncan Ct SO19 . . . . .104 C4
Duncan Rd
  Locks Heath SO31 . . . . . . .129 B6
  New Milton BH25 . . . . . . .195 D4
  Portsmouth PO5 . . . . .182 D2
Duncans Dr PO14 . . . . .154 B8
Duncliff Rd BH6 . . . . .207 A4
Duncombe Dr BH24 . . . . . . .116 C3
Duncton Rd PO8 . . . . .88 D5
Duncton Way PO13 . . . . . . .155 C3
Dundas La PO3 . . . . .158 B2
Dundas La PO3 . . . . .158 B1
Dundas Rd BH17 . . . . .202 E8
Dundas Spur PO3 . . . . .158 B2
Dundee Cl PO15 . . . . .130 E3
Dundee St SO14 . . . . .79 C1
Dundonald Cl
  South Hayling PO11 . . . . . .185 A5
  Southampton SO19 . . . . . .103 D1
Dundridge La SO32 . . . . .60 C2
Dundry Way SO30 . . . . .105 D7
Dune Crest BH13 . . . . .214 C3
Dunedin Cl BH22 . . . . .165 B3
Dunedin Dr BH22 . . . . .165 B3
Dunedin Gdns BH22 . . . . . . .165 B3
Dunedin Gr BH23 . . . . .208 C7
Dunfield Way SO45 . . . . .150 F2
Dunford Cl
  Barton on S BH25 . . . . . . .209 E8
  Old Milton BH25 . . . . .194 E1
Dunford Rd BH12 . . . . .203 D5
Dunhurst Cl PO9 . . . . .136 A3
Dunhurst Sch (Bedales Jun
  Sch) GU32 . . . . .40 E6
Dunkeld Rd
  Bournemouth BH3 . . . . . . .204 E6
  Gosport PO12 . . . . .181 A8
Dunkirk Cl SO16 . . . . .78 D4
Dunkirk Rd SO16 . . . . .78 D4
Dunlin Cl
  Christchurch BH23 . . . . . . .208 B5
  Portsmouth PO4 . . . . .183 D5
Dunn Cl PO4 . . . . .183 B3
Dunnings La SO52 . . . . .53 F5
Dunnock Cl
  Ferndown BH22 . . . . .165 B8
  Rowlands Castle PO9 . . . . .113 B1
Dunsbury Way PO9 . . . . . . .135 E5
Dunsmore Cl PO5 . . . . .216 B2
Dunstable Wlk PO14 . . . . . .154 D7
Dunstans La BH15 . . . . .203 A6
Dunster Cl SO16 . . . . .78 C5
Dunvegan Dr SO16 . . . . .78 C5
Dunyeats Rd BH18 . . . . .187 B4
Dunyeats Rdbt BH18 . . . . . .187 D5
Duplock Ho PO8 . . . . .195 A3
Dupree Dr PO4 . . . . .183 A3
Durban Cl SO51 . . . . .28 A1
Durban Ho PO1 . . . . .216 C4
Durban Rd PO1 . . . . .182 E6
Durdells Ave BH11 . . . . .189 A5
Durdells Gdns BH11 . . . . . . .189 A5
Durford Ct PO9 . . . . .135 D6
Durford Rd GU31 . . . . .41 C3
Durham Gdns PO7 . . . . .134 F5
Durham St Gosport PO12 . . .181 A7
  Portsmouth PO1 . . . . .216 B3
Durland Cl BH25 . . . . .195 B1
Durlands Rd PO8 . . . . .112 C8
Durley Brook Rd SO32 . . . . . .82 A6
Durley CE Prim Sch
  SO32 . . . . .82 A6
Durley Chine Ct **12** BH2 . .204 D2
Durley Chine Rd BH2 . . . . . .204 D2
Durley Chine Rd S BH2 . . . .204 D2
Durley Cres SO40 . . . . .100 D5
Durley Gdns BH2 . . . . .204 D2
Durley Hall La SO32 . . . . .58 C1
Durley Rd
  Bournemouth BH2 . . . . . . .204 E2
  Durley SO32,SO50 . . . . . . .81 E7
  Gosport PO12 . . . . .181 A7
  Poole BH12 . . . . .204 E2
Durley St SO32 . . . . .82 C7
Durlston Court Sch
  BH25 . . . . .210 A8
Durlston Cres BH23 . . . . . . .191 D4
Durlston Rd Poole BH14 . . . .203 C2
  Southampton SO16 . . . . . . .77 D1
Durnford Rd SO14 . . . . .103 B6
Durngate Ho SO23 . . . . .215 F6
Durngate Terr **3** SO23 . . . .215 F6
Durnstown SO41 . . . . .172 C2
Durrant Rd
  Bournemouth BH2 . . . . . . .204 E4
  Poole BH14 . . . . .203 C3
Durrant Way SO41 . . . . .172 B2
Durrants Gdns PO9 . . . . . . .136 B8
  Durrants PRU PO9 . . . . . . .136 B8
Durrants Rd PO9 . . . . .136 B7

Durrington Pl BH7 . . . . .206 B6
Durrington Rd BH7 . . . . .206 B7
Dursley Cres PO6 . . . . .157 D8
Durweston Cl BH9 . . . . .190 B3
Dutton La SO50 . . . . .56 B3
Dutton's Rd SO51 . . . . .52 E8
Dyer Rd SO15 . . . . .102 C7
Dymchurch Ho **3** PO6 . . . .157 E8
Dymewood Rd BH21 . . . . . .138 C2
Dymoke St PO10 . . . . .136 E4
Dymott Cl SO15 . . . . .102 D5
Dyneley Gn SO18 . . . . .80 A1
Dyram Cl SO50 . . . . .56 C6
Dysart Ave PO6 . . . . .158 B7
Dyserth Cl SO19 . . . . .104 B1
Dyson Dr SO23 . . . . .215 E8

E

E Ave SO45 . . . . .150 F5
Eadens La SO40 . . . . .99 D7
Eagle Ave PO8 . . . . .111 E4
Eagle Cl
  Chandler's Ford SO53 . . . . .55 B4
  Portchester PO16 . . . . . . .155 F8
Eagle Cl **8** SO23 . . . . .215 D6
Eagle Rd Lee-on-t-S PO13 . .179 D4
  Poole BH13 . . . . .204 A4
Eagle Rise 190 D1
Eaglhurst **5** BH13 . . . . . . .204 A4
Eame's Cotts GU32 . . . . .38 E1
Eames La GU33 . . . . .19 F8
Earle Ho **8** SO23 . . . . .11 D8
Earle Rd BH4 . . . . .204 C1
Earley Ct SO41 . . . . .197 F4
Earlham Dr BH14 . . . . .203 C4
Earls Cl SO50 . . . . .57 A2
Earls Rd Fareham PO16 . . . .155 B7
  Southampton SO14 . . . . . .103 A7
Earlsdon St PO5 . . . . .216 B2
Earlsferry Way BH23 . . . . . .208 F8
Earlsdown **1** BH4 . . . . . . .204 C2
Earlswood Dr SP6 . . . . .92 F5
Earlswood Pk BH25 . . . . . . .195 C4
Earnley Rd PO11 . . . . .185 F2
Earthpits La SP5 . . . . .42 B1
East Ave
  Barton on S BH25 . . . . . . .209 C7
  Ferndown BH22 . . . . .204 D6
East Avenue Rdbt BH3 . . . .204 E6
East Bank Rd SO42 . . . . . . .173 A8
East Bargate **6** SO14 . . . .103 A5
East Bldg PO1 . . . . .182 A5
East Boldre Rd SO42 . . . . . .175 C6
East Borough BH21 . . . . . . .159 D1
East Cl SO45 . . . . .126 C1
East Cliff BH25 . . . . .209 D8
East Cliff BH2 . . . . .204 F4
East Cliff Way BH23 . . . . . . .208 C7
East Cosham Rd PO6 . . . . . .158 B8
East Ct Cosham PO6 . . . . . .158 B8
  Portsmouth PO1 . . . . .182 E7
East Dean Rd SO51 . . . . .4 E2
East Dorset Trade Pk
  BH21 . . . . .164 F6
East Dr Bishopstoke SO50 . . .56 E3
  West Moors BH24 . . . . . . .166 B7
East Field Cl PO10 . . . . .137 D7
East Hayling Light Rly*
  PO11 . . . . .185 A2
East Hill Lymington SO41 . . .197 E4
  Winchester SO23 . . . . . . .215 F4
East Hill Cl PO16 . . . . .131 D2
East Hill Dr GU33 . . . . .21 A3
East Hoe Rd PO7 . . . . .86 A4
East House Ave PO14 . . . . .179 D7
East La Fareham BH10 . . . . .189 C4
East La SO41 . . . . .196 E1
East Links SO53 . . . . .55 C2
East Lodge
  Fareham PO15 . . . . .130 C3
  Lee-on-t-S PO13 . . . . .179 E2
East Lodge Pk PO6 . . . . . . .158 F8
East Meon CE Prim Sch
  GU32 . . . . .38 D1
East Meon Rd PO8 . . . . .88 B6
East Mews **8** PO17 . . . . . .134 C1
East Overcliff Dr BH1 . . . . . .205 A4
East Park Terr SO14 . . . . . . .103 A5
East Quay **11** BH15 . . . . . .202 C1
East Quay Rd BH15 . . . . . . .202 C1
East St PO17 . . . . .133 A6
East Shore Sch PO4 . . . . . . .183 B6
East St Fareham PO16 . . . . .131 C1
  Hambledon PO7 . . . . .86 D3
  Havant PO9 . . . . .135 F1
  Poole BH15 . . . . .202 C1
  Portchester PO16 . . . . . . .156 E8
  Portsmouth PO1 . . . . .182 A4
  Southampton SO14 . . . . . .154 A8
  Titchfield PO14 . . . . .154 A8
  Westbourne PO10 . . . . . . .137 B3
  Wimborne Minst BH21 . . . .163 C4
East Street Ctr **3** SO14 . .103 A4
East Surrey St PO1 . . . . . . .216 B3
East View Ind Est PO4 . . . . .141 A1
East View Terr **2** PO9 . . . .135 F1
East Way
  Bournemouth BH8 . . . . . . .190 C1
  Corfe Mullen BH21 . . . . . .186 D5
East Woodhay Rd SO22 . . . .1 D4
Eastacre SO22 . . . . .215 C2

Eastbourne Ave
Gosport PO12 . . . . .180 F8
Southampton SO15 . . . . . .102 D8
Eastbourne Rd PO3 . . . .183 A8
Eastbrook Cl
Gosport PO12 . . . . .180 F8
Locks Heath SO31 . . . . . . .129 A5
Eastbrook Row BH21 . .163 C4
Eastbury Ct BH23 . . . . .207 F4
Eastchurch Cl SO16 . . . . .77 F4
Eastcliff Cl PO13 . . . . . .179 E4
Eastcot Cl SO45 . . . . . . .150 C3
Eastcott Cl BH7 . . . . . . .206 A8
Eastcroft Rd PO12 . . . . .180 F5
Easter Rd BH9 . . . . .190 A2
Eastern Ave PO4 . . . . . .183 B6
Eastern Ind Ctr PO6 . . .158 C6
Eastern Par
Fareham PO16 . . . . .155 B7
Portsmouth PO4 . . . . .182 F2
Eastern Rd Fawley SO45 .151 E2
Havant PO9 . . . . .136 A2
Lymington SO41 . . . . .197 D4
Portsmouth,Anchorage Park
PO6 . . . . .158 C4
Portsmouth,Baffins PO3 . .183 C7
Portsmouth,Whale Island
PO2 . . . . .157 B1
West End SO30 . . . . .80 D1
Eastern Terr ❹ PO4 . . . .183 A2
Eastern Villas Rd PO4 . .182 D1
Eastern Way
Fareham PO16 . . . . .131 C1
Milford on S SO41 . . . . . . .211 F4
Eastfield Ave PO14 . . . .154 F7
Eastfield Ct BH24 . . . . .141 C7
Eastfield La
Ringwood,Hightown BH24 .141 C7
Ringwood,Poulner BH24 . .141 C8
Eastfield Rd
Portsmouth,Eastney PO4 .183 A3
Portsmouth,Ports Down
PO6 . . . . .133 C2
Southampton SO17 . . . . . .103 C8
Eastfields PO5 . . . . .216 C1
Eastgate St
Southampton SO14 . . . . . .103 A3
Winchester SO23 . . . . .215 F5
Eastlake Ave BH21 . . . . .203 C6
Eastlake Cl GU31 . . . . . . .41 C3
Eastlake Hts PO4 . . . . . .183 D3
Eastlands PO35 . . . . . . .195 B1
Eastleigh Coll SO50 . . . . .56 A2
Eastleigh Coll of F Ed
SO50 . . . . .56 A2
Eastleigh Lakeside Rly*
SO50 . . . . .79 F8
Eastleigh Rd
Fair Oak SO50 . . . . .57 C1
Havant PO9 . . . . .136 D4
Eastleigh Sta SO50 . . . . .56 B3
Eastleigh Town Mus*
SO50 . . . . .56 A2
Eastman Cl SP5 . . . . .47 A6
Eastmeare Ct SO40 . . . .100 C6
Eastney Farm Rd PO4 . .183 C3
Eastney Rd PO4 . . . . . . .183 B3
Eastney St ❻ PO4 . . . . .183 A2
Eastoke Ave PO11 . . . . .185 B2
Eastoke Corner Sta*
PO11 . . . . .185 B2
Easton La
Easton Down SO21 . . . . .2 E3
Winchester SO23 . . . . .2 E3
Easton Lane Bsns Ctr
SO23 . . . . .215 F6
Eastover Ct PO9 . . . . . . .135 D6
Eastville Rd SO50 . . . . . .57 C1
Eastways SO32 . . . . .83 C7
Eastwood SO51 . . . . .25 C1
Eastwood Ave BH22 . . . .165 E6
Eastwood Cl PO11 . . . . .185 B5
Eastwood Rd ❺ PO2 . . .157 E4
Eastworth Rd BH31 . . . .114 E7
Eaton Rd BH13 . . . . .204 A2
Ebblake Cl BH31 . . . . . . .115 C3
Ebblake Ent Pk BH31 . . .115 C5
Ebblake Ind Est BH31 . .115 C4
Ebden Rd SO23 . . . . .215 F6
Ebenezer La BH24 . . . . .140 F7
Ebery Gr PO3 . . . . .183 C7
Ebor Cl BH22 . . . . .165 E2
Ebor Rd BH12 . . . . .204 C3
Ebury Ct ❼ BH4 . . . . . .204 C3
Eccles Rd BH15 . . . . . . .202 A2
Ecton La PO3 . . . . .158 C3
Eddystone Rd SO40 . . . . .76 D2
Edelvale Rd SO18 . . . . . . .80 B1
Eden Ct
❾ Bournemouth BH1 . . .205 B3
❶ Bournemouth,Westbourne
BH4 . . . . .204 C2
Eden Gr BH21 . . . . .163 D3
Eden Grange ❺ SO14 . . .103 A7
Eden Rd SO18 . . . . .80 B2
Eden Rise PO16 . . . . .155 B8
Eden St PO1 . . . . .216 B4
Eden Terr ❶ PO2 . . . . . .157 D2
Eden Wlk SO53 . . . . .55 A5
Edenbridge Rd PO4 . . . .183 C5
Edenbridge Way SO31 . .128 E6
Edenhurst ❷ BH4 . . . . .204 C3
Edgar Cres PO16 . . . . . . .130 C6
Edgar Rd SO23 . . . . .215 D4
Edgar Villas SO23 . . . . .215 D4
Edgarton Rd BH17 . . . . .187 D3
Edgbaston Ho PO5 . . . . .216 B2
Edgecombe Cres BH23 . .180 C8
Edgefield Gr PO7 . . . . . .112 C1
Edgehill Rd
Bournemouth BH9 . . . . . .189 F1
Southampton SO18 . . . . . . .79 F1
Edgell Rd PO10 . . . . .137 B4
Edgemoor Rd BH22 . . . .139 B1
Edgerly Gdns PO6 . . . . . .157 F6
Edgeware Rd PO4 . . . . . .183 B5
Edgewood Ct GU33 . . . . . .21 B2
Edifred Rd BH9 . . . . .190 A4
Edinburgh Cl ❷ SO15 . .102 A6
Edinburgh Ho ❹ SO22 . .215 D6
Edinburgh Rd PO1 . . . . .216 A3
Edington Cl SO32 . . . . . . .83 B8
Edington Rd SO23 . . . . .215 E7
Edith Haisman Cl SO15 .102 D5
Edmondsham Ho ❶❻
BH2 . . . . .204 E3
Edmondsham House Gdns*
BH21 . . . . .91 A4
Edmondsham Rd BH31 . .114 E8
Edmund Rd PO4 . . . . . . .182 F3
Edmunds Cl
Hedge End SO30 . . . . .105 D5
❽ Old Milton BH25 . . . . .195 A4
Edneys La PO7 . . . . .111 B6
Edward Ave SO50 . . . . . . .56 D4
Edward Cl SO45 . . . . . . .150 E1
Edward Gdns PO9 . . . . . .135 C1
Edward Rd PO10 . . . . . . .132 E1
Edward May Ct BH11 . . .189 A4
Edward Rd
Bournemouth BH11 . . . . . .189 B3
Christchurch BH23 . . . . . .207 F8
Hythe SO45 . . . . .126 A4
Poole BH15 . . . . .203 C5
Southampton SO15 . . . . . .102 C7
Winchester SO23 . . . . .215 D3
Edward's Cl ❶❺ PO6 . . .133 B1
Edwards Cl
Lymington SO41 . . . . .197 B3
Waterlooville PO8 . . . . . . .111 F2
Edwards Rd BH23 . . . . . .209 A8
Edwin Jones Gn SO15 . .102 E8
Edwina Cl
North Baddesley SO52 . . . .54 B4
Ringwood BH24 . . . . .117 C1
Edwina Dr BH17 . . . . . . .187 B2
Edwina Ho SO19 . . . . .79 E4
Effingham Gdns SO19 . .104 C4
Efford Ct SO41 . . . . .197 B2
Efford Farm Cotts SO41 .197 A1
Efford Way SO41 . . . . . . .197 B2
Egan Cl PO2 . . . . .157 F3
Egbert Rd SO23 . . . . . . .215 E7
Egdon Cl BH22 . . . . .165 B3
Egdon Dr BH16 . . . . .201 B7
Egdon Dr BH21 . . . . .187 E8
Egerton Ct BH8 . . . . . . .205 D6
Egerton Gdns BH8 . . . . .205 D6
Egerton Rd BH8 . . . . . . .205 D6
Eglantine Cl BH24 . . . . .140 D2
Eglantine Wlk PO8 . . . . .112 C4
Egmont Cl BH24 . . . . . . .140 D2
Egmont Dr BH24 . . . . . . .140 D2
Egmont Gdns BH24 . . . .140 D2
Egmont Rd BH16 . . . . . . .201 B4
Eight Acres SO51 . . . . . . .53 B7
Eileen Beard Ho ❶ PO9 .136 A8
Elaine Gdns PO8 . . . . . . .112 A5
Elan Cl SO18 . . . . .80 B1
Elcombes Cl SO43 . . . . . .121 F5
Elder Cl
Locks Heath SO31 . . . . . . .128 F2
Marchwood SO40 . . . . . . .102 A1
Winchester SO22 . . . . .215 A2
Elder Gn SO21 . . . . .57 A8
Elder Rd PO9 . . . . .136 B3
Elderberry Cl
Clanfield PO8 . . . . .88 D4
Fair Oak SO50 . . . . .57 B1
Elderberry La BH23 . . . .207 F6
Elderberry Way PO8 . . . .112 C4
Elderfield Cl PO10 . . . . .137 A3
Elderfield Rd PO9 . . . . . .135 D7
Eldon Ave BH25 . . . . . . .209 E8
Eldon Cl BH25 . . . . .209 E8
Eldon Ct ❺ Poole BH14 .203 A4
Portsmouth PO5 . . . . .216 B2
Eldon Ho ❾ SO14 . . . . . .103 A3
Eldon Pl BH4 . . . . .204 B3
Eldon Rd
Bournemouth BH9 . . . . . .189 E1
Compton SO20 . . . . .7 A5
Eldon St PO5 . . . . .216 B2
Eldridge Gdns SO51 . . . . .52 F8
Eleanor Cl SP5 . . . . .194 F1
Eleanor Dr BH11 . . . . . . .188 D5
Eleanor Gdns BH23 . . . .206 E8
Eleanor Way SO45 . . . . . .55 C5
Electra Ave PO7 . . . . . . .134 C8
Eleven Cross SP6 . . . . . . .68 B5
Elfin Ct ❶❶ SO17 . . . . . .103 A8
Elfin Dr BH22 . . . . .165 C7
Elgar Cl Gosport PO12 . . .181 A3
Portchester PO16 . . . . .156 E8
Southampton SO19 . . . . . .104 C3
Elgar Ct SO41 . . . . .197 F4
Elgar Rd
Bournemouth BH10 . . . . . .189 D4
Southampton SO19 . . . . . .104 C3
Elgar Wlk PO7 . . . . .134 F5
Elgin Cl Fareham PO15 . .130 F2
Hythe SO45 . . . . .126 A3

Elgin Rd
Bournemouth BH4 . . . . . .204 D6
Cosham PO6 . . . . .157 F6
Poole BH14 . . . . .203 C2
Southampton SO15 . . . . . .102 D5
Elijah Cl BH15 . . . . .201 E2
Eling Cl PO9 . . . . .135 D6
Eling Hill SO40 . . . . .101 B5
Eling Inf Sch SO40 . . . . .101 A6
Eling La SO40 . . . . .101 A6
Eling Tide Mill* SO40 . .101 A6
Eling View SO15 . . . . . . .101 C7
Eling Wharf SO40 . . . . . .101 B6
Elingfield Ct SO40 . . . . .101 A7
Eliot Ho
❽ New Milton BH25 . . . . .195 A4
Southampton SO17 . . . . . . .79 C2
Elise Cl BH7 . . . . .206 B8
Eliza Pl ❻ PO12 . . . . . . .181 C6
Elizabeth Ave BH23 . . . .206 F8
Elizabeth Cl Downton SP5 .46 D7
West End SO30 . . . . .80 D1
Elizabeth Ct PO17 . . . . .107 F4
Elizabeth Cres SO41 . . . .196 B2
Elizabeth Ct
Aldermoor SO16 . . . . .78 A3
❶ Bournemouth BH1 . . . .205 B3
❸ Cosham PO6 . . . . .157 F8
Eastleigh SO50 . . . . .56 A4
Fareham PO14 . . . . .154 F7
❹ Gosport PO12 . . . . . . .181 A2
❽ New Milton BH25 . . . . .195 B2
Portswood SO17 . . . . .79 C1
West End SO30 . . . . .80 D1
Elizabeth Gdns
Christchurch BH23 . . . . . .208 D7
Hythe SO45 . . . . .126 A1
Portsmouth PO4 . . . . .182 F2
Elizabeth Ho SO40 . . . . . .76 B2
Elizabeth Rd Poole BH15 .202 D3
Stubbington PO14 . . . . . . .179 D7
Upton BH16 . . . . .201 C7
Waterlooville PO7 . . . . . . .134 E5
Wickham PO17 . . . . .108 A4
Wimborne Minst BH21 . . .163 C5
Elizabeth Way
Bishop's Waltham SO32 . . .83 B7
Eastleigh SO50 . . . . .56 B5
Elkhams Cl SO41 . . . . . . .196 D1
Elkstone Rd PO6 . . . . . . .133 B1
Ellachie Gdns PO12 . . . .181 B2
Ellachie Mews PO12 . . . .181 B2
Ellachie Rd PO12 . . . . . .181 B2
Elland Cl SO50 . . . . .57 C2
Ellardene Ct SO40 . . . . .100 E5
Ellen Gdns SO53 . . . . .55 A5
Ellen Wren Ho SO18 . . . . .79 E4
Ellerslie Cl PO14 . . . . . . .179 A6
Ellery Gr SO41 . . . . .197 E5
Ellesfield Dr BH22 . . . . .165 D2
Ellesmere Orch PO10 . . .137 B5
Ellingham Cross BH24 . .116 F5
Ellingham Dr BH24 . . . . .116 D5
Ellingham Dro BH24 . . . .117 B5
Ellingham Rd BH25 . . . .209 D8
Elliot Cl SO40 . . . . .100 D7
Elliot Rise SO30 . . . . .81 C2
Elliott Rd BH11 . . . . .188 F3
Ellis Rd SO19 . . . . .104 E5
Ellisfield Rd PO9 . . . . . . .135 E4
Ellwood Ave SO19 . . . . .104 E6
Ellwood Cl SO19 . . . . . . .104 E6
Elm Ave
Christchurch BH23 . . . . . .191 E1
Lymington SO41 . . . . .197 C1
New Milton BH25 . . . . . . .195 A2
Elm Cl
South Hayling PO11 . . . . . .185 A3
Southampton SO16 . . . . . . .78 F4
Elm Close Est PO11 . . . .184 F3
Elm Cotts Hythe SO45 . .150 A7
Upham SO32 . . . . .58 E5
Elm Ct
Chandler's Ford SO53 . . . . .30 C1
❷ New Milton BH25 . . . . .195 A2
Southampton,Sholing
SO19 . . . . .103 F3
❷❹ Westwood Park SO17 . .79 A1
Winchester SO22 . . . . .215 C6
Elm Dr GU31 . . . . .40 E1
Elm Gdns
Bournemouth BH4 . . . . . .204 C5
West End SO30 . . . . .80 D3
Elm Gr Eastleigh SO50 . . .55 F2
Gosport PO12 . . . . .181 B6
Portsmouth PO5 . . . . .216 B1
South Hayling PO11 . . . . . .185 A3
Elm La PO9 . . . . .135 F1
Elm Lodge PO5 . . . . .216 C1
Elm Park Rd PO9 . . . . . . .135 F2
Elm Rd
Bishop's Waltham SO32 . . .83 E8
Havant PO9 . . . . .160 A8
Portsmouth PO2 . . . . .157 E1
Southampton SO15 . . . . . .102 B8
Thorney Island PO10 . . . . .161 B2
Wimborne Minst BH21 . . .163 C5
Elm St Portsmouth PO5 . .216 A1
Southampton SO14 . . . . . .103 B4
Elm Terr Liss GU33 . . . . . .20 E5
Southampton SO14 . . . . . .103 B3
Elm Tree Cl SO40 . . . . . .100 B2
Elm Tree Wlk SO40 . . . . .100 B2
Elmdale GU31 . . . . .41 A4
Elmdale Cl SO31 . . . . . . .152 D10
Elmdale Gr SO51 . . . . .51 B1
Elmers Way BH23 . . . . . .169 B1
Elmes Dr SO15 . . . . .101 F7

Elmes Rd BH9 . . . . .189 F2
Elmeswelle Rd PO8 . . . . .112 A6
Elmfield Cl SP5 . . . . .47 D5
Elmfield La SO45 . . . . . . .178 E7
Elmfield North Block
SO15 . . . . .102 D5
Elmfield West Block
SO15 . . . . .102 D5
Elmgate Dr BH7 . . . . . . .206 A7
Elmhurst Rd
Bournemouth BH11 . . . . . .189 A5
Fareham PO16 . . . . .155 B8
Gosport PO12 . . . . .181 C5
West Moors BH22 . . . . . . .138 F2
Elmhurst Way BH22 . . . .138 F1
Elmleigh Rd PO9 . . . . . . .135 F2
Elmore Ave PO13 . . . . . .180 A5
Elmore Cl PO13 . . . . .179 F2
Elmore Dr BH24 . . . . . . .139 E6
Elmore Rd PO13 . . . . . . .179 F2
Elmrise Prim Sch BH11 .189 A4
Elms Ave BH14 . . . . .203 A1
Elms Cl Fordingbridge SP6 . .69 B2
Poole BH14 . . . . .203 A1
Elms Rd PO16 . . . . .155 B7
Elms Way BH6 . . . . .206 E4
Elmsdown Ct BH24 . . . . .140 F7
Elmsleigh Ct SO17 . . . . . .79 A4
Elmsleigh Gdns SO16 . . . .79 A4
Elmslie Gdns SO31 . . . . .104 F1
Elmstead Rd BH13 . . . . .214 F8
Elmtree Gdns SO51 . . . . .53 C6
Elmtree Rd PO6 . . . . .158 E8
Elmwood Ave
Fordingbridge SP6 . . . . . . .69 D2
Waterlooville PO7 . . . . . . .134 E6
Elmwood Ct SO16 . . . . . . .78 B2
Elmwood Lodge ❽
PO16 . . . . .131 B2
Elmwood Rd PO2 . . . . . . .157 E4
Elmwood Way BH24 . . . .209 A7
Elphinstone Rd
Portsmouth PO5 . . . . .182 C2
Walkford BH23 . . . . .194 B1
Elsfred Rd PO14 . . . . . . .179 A6
Elson Inf Sch PO12 . . . . .181 A9
Elson Jun Sch PO12 . . . .181 A9
Elson La PO12 . . . . .181 A9
Elson Rd PO12 . . . . .181 A9
Elstead Gdns PO7 . . . . . .134 C8
Elstree Rd SO19 . . . . . . .103 E5
Eltham Cl BH7 . . . . .206 B8
Elvin Cl SO41 . . . . .195 F3
Elwell Gn PO11 . . . . .184 F3
Elwyn Rd BH1,BH8 . . . . .205 C5
Ely Ct ❸ PO13 . . . . .180 D5
Elysium Ct BH22 . . . . . . .165 E3
Emanuel St PO2 . . . . . . .182 D7
Embankment Way BH24 .141 B6
Embassy Ct PO4 . . . . . . .216 D2
Emberley Cl BH22 . . . . . .166 A6
Embley Cl SO40 . . . . .176 D2
Embley La SO51 . . . . .51 E7
Embley Park Ind Est
SO51 . . . . .51 E7
Embley Park Jun Sch
SO51 . . . . .52 E7
Embsay Rd SO31 . . . . . . .128 D8
Emer Cl SO22 . . . . .54 A5
Emerald Cl
Southampton SO19 . . . . . .104 B6
St Leonards BH24 . . . . . . .139 E6
Waterlooville PO7 . . . . . . .135 A7
Emerald Cres SO45 . . . . .126 B4
Emerson Cl ❶❷ BH15 . . .202 C2
Emerson Rd BH15 . . . . . .202 D2
Emily Cl BH23 . . . . .192 A1
Emily Ct BH14 . . . . .203 D2
Emmadale Cl ❼ SO45 . . .126 A4
Emmanuel CE Mid Sch
BH31 . . . . .114 E5
Emmanuel Cl PO14 . . . . .129 C2
Emmett Rd SO16 . . . . .77 F5
Emmons Cl SO31 . . . . . . .128 A1
Emperor Ho SO18 . . . . . . .82 A4
Empire Ct ❽ PO9 . . . . . .135 F1
Empress Pk SO14 . . . . . .103 B7
Empress Rd
Lyndhurst SO43 . . . . .121 F5
Southampton,Bevois Valley
SO14 . . . . .103 B7
Empshott Rd PO4 . . . . . .183 A3
Empson Wlk PO13 . . . . . .179 F4
Emsbrook Dr PO10 . . . . .136 F2
Emsworth Common Rd
PO10 . . . . .136 F6
Emsworth House Cl
PO10 . . . . .136 E1
Emsworth Mus* PO10 . .160 F8
Emsworth Prim Sch
PO10 . . . . .136 E1
Emsworth Rd
Havant PO9 . . . . .136 B1
Lymington SO41 . . . . .197 E4
Portsmouth PO2 . . . . .157 E1
Southampton SO15 . . . . . .102 B8
Emsworth Sta PO10 . . . .136 D2
Encombe Cl BH12 . . . . . .203 F8
Endeavour Bsns Pk PO9 .157 E2
Endeavour Cl
Gosport PO12 . . . . .181 D5
Southampton SO19 . . . . . .103 B7
Endeavour Ct ❺ SO14 . .103 B3
Endeavour Pk BH24 . . . .141 B6
Endeavour Way SO45 . . .126 A5
Enderleigh Ho PO9 . . . . .135 E1

Enderwood Cl SO40 . . . .100 B8
Endfield Cl BH23 . . . . . . .191 F1
Endfield Rd
Bournemouth BH9 . . . . . .190 A2
Christchurch BH23 . . . . . .191 E1
Endle St SO14 . . . . .103 C3
Endofield Ct PO14 . . . . .154 F6
Enfield Ave BH15 . . . . . .202 E6
Enfield Cres BH15 . . . . . .202 E6
Enfield Gr SO19 . . . . .103 E3
Enfield Rd BH15 . . . . .202 E6
Englands Way BH11 . . . .188 D4
Englefield Ct SO31 . . . . .127 A6
Englefield Rd SO18 . . . . .103 D7
English Cl
❺ Bournemouth BH2 . . . .204 D4
❼ Romsey SO51 . . . . .52 F7
English Rd SO15 . . . . . . .102 B7
Enmill La SO22 . . . . .9 E5
Ennel Copse SO52 . . . . . . .54 A4
Ennerdale Cl PO8 . . . . . . .88 C2
Ennerdale Gdns SO18 . . . .80 B1
Ennerdale Rd
Southampton SO16 . . . . . . .77 E2
Stubbington PO14 . . . . . . .154 D4
Ensbury Ave BH10 . . . . .189 D1
Ensbury Cl BH10 . . . . . . .189 D1
Ensbury Ct BH10 . . . . . . .189 E2
Ensbury Park Rd BH9 . . .189 E2
Ensign Dr PO13 . . . . .180 B6
Ensign Rd BH25 . . . . .195 A4
Ensign Way SO31 . . . . . .127 E2
Enterprise Cl SO31 . . . . .128 E1
Enterprise Ind Est PO8 .112 C8
Enterprise Pk SO16 . . . . .131 E2
Enterprise Rd
Chilworth SO16 . . . . .54 C1
Horndean PO8 . . . . .112 C8
Enterprise Way BH24 . . .190 C8
Eperston Rd PO8 . . . . . . .112 B4
Epiphany CE Prim Sch The
BH9 . . . . .190 B4
Epping Cl SO18 . . . . .80 B1
Epsom Cl SO30 . . . . .81 D7
Epsom Ct PO15 . . . . .129 C8
Epworth Rd PO2 . . . . . . .157 F1
Erasmus Park Student Village
SO23 . . . . .2 C1
Erica Cl Locks Heath SO31 .128 F3
Waterlooville PO8 . . . . . . .112 B3
Erica Dr BH21 . . . . .186 D6
Erica Way PO8 . . . . .112 B3
Ericksen Rd BH11 . . . . . .189 C3
Erinbank Mans BH1 . . . .205 C3
Ernest Cl PO10 . . . . .136 F1
Ernest Rd Havant PO9 . . .135 C3
Portsmouth PO1 . . . . .182 E7
Erpingham Rd BH12 . . . .204 A1
Errington Ho ❸ SO50 . . . .56 A2
Erskine Ct SO16 . . . . .78 F5
Erskine Rd SO22 . . . . . . .215 C5
Escombe Rd SO50 . . . . . . .56 D3
Escur Cl PO12 . . . . .157 F4
Esdaile La BH24 . . . . .142 F3
Esher Gr PO7 . . . . .111 C2
Eskdale Cl PO8 . . . . .88 C2
Eskdale Ho ❺ PO6 . . . . .133 B1
Esmond Cl PO10 . . . . . . .160 F8
Esmonde Cl PO13 . . . . . .179 F3
Esmonde Way BH17 . . . .202 F8
Esplanade Poole BH13 . . .214 F7
Esplanade The PO12 . . . .181 C5
Essex Ave BH23 . . . . .191 F1
Essex Gn SO53 . . . . .55 C2
Essex Rd PO4 . . . . .183 A4
Esslemont Rd PO4 . . . . . .183 B2
Estancia Cl PO13 . . . . . . .179 F4
Estella Rd PO2 . . . . .182 D8
Estridge Cl SO21 . . . . . . .105 A1
Ethel Rd PO1 . . . . .182 E6
Ethelbert Rd BH21 . . . . .163 D2
Ethelburt Ave SO16 . . . . .79 C5
Ethelred Gdns SO40 . . . .100 C6
Eton Gdns BH4 . . . . .204 C4
Eton Mans ❷ BH4 . . . . . .206 E3
Eton Rd PO5 . . . . .182 E6
Ettrick Rd BH13 . . . . . . .204 A1
Eucalyptus Ave BH24 . . .140 A2
European Way SO14 . . . .103 B2
Euryalus Rd PO14 . . . . . .154 E6
Euston Gr BH24 . . . . .141 A6
Euston Rd BH24 . . . . .141 A6
Eva Allaway Ct ❷ PO1 . .182 A5
Evans Cl
Bournemouth BH11 . . . . . .188 F1
Portsmouth PO2 . . . . .157 B2
St Leonards BH24 . . . . . . .139 E6
Evans Rd PO4 . . . . .183 A4
Evans St SO14 . . . . .103 A4
Evelegh Rd PO6 . . . . .158 D8
Evelyn Cl SO32 . . . . .83 C8
Evelyn Cres SO15 . . . . . .102 A7
Evelyn Mews ❶ BH9 . . . .189 F1
Evelyn Rd BH9 . . . . .189 F2
Evening Glade BH22 . . . .165 E4
Evenlode Rd SO16 . . . . . . .77 E1
Eventide Homes BH8 . . .190 E2
Everdene CI BH22 . . . . . .165 C2
Everdon La PO3 . . . . .158 C4
Everest Rd BH23 . . . . . . .207 E8
Everglades Ave PO8 . . . .112 A7
Everglades Cl BH22 . . . . .165 D7
Evergreen Cl
Marchwood SO40 . . . . . . .101 F1
Three Legged Cross BH21 .138 E8

Evergreen Cl continued
Waterlooville PO7 ....134 D7
Evergreens
St Leonards BH24 ....139 E5
Totton SO40 ....101 A6
Evering Ave BH12 ....188 D1
Evering Gdns BH12 ....188 C1
Everlea Cl SO41 ....196 D1
Everon Gdns BH25 ....195 B1
Evershot Rd BH8 ....190 E2
Eversleigh 10 BH2 ....204 D2
Eversley Cres PO9 ....135 E4
Eversley Pl SO22 ....215 B3
Everton Rd SO41 ....196 B2
Evesham Cl
Bournemouth BH7 ....206 B8
Southampton SO16 ....79 B5
Evesham Ct BH13 ....204 A4
Ewart Cl SO45 ....126 A5
Ewart Rd PO1 ....182 E7
Ewell Way SO40 ....76 D1
Ewer Comm PO12 ....181 B3
Exbury Cl PO9 ....135 D4
Exbourne Manor BH1 ....205 C3
Exbury Central Sta
SO45 ....177 A6
Exbury Cl SO50 ....56 F2
Exbury Dr BH11 ....188 F5
Exbury Gdns* SO45 ......177 A5
Exbury Rd Beaulieu SO42 149 D2
Blackfield SO45 ....150 E1
Havant PO9 ....136 A5
Excellent Rd PO14 ......154 F5
Excelsior Rd BH14 ......203 E3
Exchange Ho PO2 ....157 D1
Exchange Rd PO1 ....216 A3
Exchange The 3 PO4 ....182 E2
Exeter Cl Eastleigh SO50 ..55 F5
Emsworth PO10 ....136 F2
Locks Heath SO31 ....128 F3
Southampton SO18 ....80 A1
Exeter Cres BH2 ....204 F3
Exeter Ct
5 Christchurch BH23 ....209 B7
Portsmouth PO13 ....180 C6
Exeter La BH2 ....204 F2
Exeter Park Mans BH2 ..204 F2
Exeter Park Rd BH2 ......204 F2
Exeter Rd
Bournemouth BH2 ......204 F2
Portsmouth PO4 ....182 F2
Southampton SO18 ....104 A8
Exford Ave SO18 ....104 A4
Exford Dr SO18 ....104 C7
Exleigh Cl SO18 ....104 B6
Exmoor Cl
Swanwick PO15 ....129 B7
Totton SO40 ....100 B7
Exmoor Rd SO14 ....103 B6
Exmouth Gdns SO50 ......81 C7
Exmouth Rd
Gosport PO12 ....181 A9
Portsmouth PO5 ....182 D2
Exmouth St SO14 ....103 A5
Explosion Mus of Naval
Firepower* PO12 ....181 D8
Exton Gdns PO16 ....132 C2
Exton Rd
Bournemouth BH6 ......206 D7
Havant PO9 ....136 B5
Eyebright Cl SO50 ....81 C6
Eyeworth Wlk SO45 ......125 C4
Eynham Ave SO19 ....104 C6
Eynham Cl SO19 ....104 B6
Eynon Mews BH24 ......140 F6
Eyre Cl SO40 ....106 D6

F

F Ave SO45 ....150 F6
Faber Cl PO9 ....136 A4
Faber Mews SO51 ....53 B8
Fabers Yd 12 SO22 ......215 D6
Fabian Cl PO7 ....135 A8
Factory Rd Eastleigh SO50 ..56 A2
Upton BH16 ....201 C6
Fair Field SO51 ....28 A1
Fair Gn SO19 ....104 B5
Fair Isle Cl PO14 ....179 B8
Fair La SO21 ....11 F8
Fair Lea BH2 ....204 F3
Fair Oak Cl Fair Oak SO50 57 D2
8 Gosport PO12 ....180 D3
Fair Oak Dr PO9 ....135 F3
Fair Oak Inf Sch SO50 ....57 D1
Fair Oak Jun Sch SO50 ....57 C1
Fair Oak Rd PO4 ....183 C4
Fair View 2 SO50 ....56 A3
Fairacre Rise PO14 ......154 B8
Fairacre Wlk PO14 ......154 B8
Fairbairn Wlk SO53 ......54 F6
Fairbourne Cl PO8 ......111 E2
Fairclose Dr SO22 ....1 B5
Faircourt 8 BH25 ....195 B3
Faircross Cl SO45 ....150 C3
Fairdown Cl SO23 ....11 C7
Fairfax Cl SO22 ....10 B5
Fairfax Ct SO19 ....104 E6
Fairfax Mews SO19 ......104 E6
Fairfield
Christchurch BH23 ......207 B7
Denmead PO7 ....110 F5
Fairfield Ave PO14 ......154 F7
Fairfield Cl
Christchurch BH23 ......207 B7
Emsworth PO10 ....136 F2
Hythe SO45 ....125 F4

Fairfield Cl continued
Lymington SO41 ....197 E3
Wimborne Minst BH21 ..163 F5
Fairfield Inf Sch PO9 ..136 A1
Fairfield Rd
Barton on S BH25 ......209 E3
Compton SO21 ....31 D5
Havant PO9 ....135 F1
Wimborne Minst BH21 ..163 D4
Winchester SO22 ....215 D7
Fairfield Sq PO6 ....157 E8
Fairfield Terr 7 PO9 ....135 F1
Fairgate Ctr The SP6 ....70 A4
Fairhaven Ct 3 BH5 ....205 E4
Fairholme Ct 1 SO50 ....56 A3
Fairhome Cl PO12 ......181 B8
Fairies Dr BH22 ....165 F3
Fairisle Inf Sch SO16 ....77 E4
Fairisle Jun Sch SO16 ....77 E4
Fairisle Rd SO16 ....77 E4
Fairlands Montessori Sch
SO32 ....107 E7
Fairlawn BH22 ....165 D5
Fairlawn Cl SO16 ....77 F6
Fairlawn Ho 9 SO22 ....215 D5
Fairlea Grange 3 SO16 ..78 F4
Fairlea Rd
Emsworth PO10 ....136 F3
Lymington SO41 ....197 E5
Fairlead Dr PO13 ......180 D6
Fairlie BH24 ....117 C1
Fairlie Cl SO30 ....81 C3
Fairlie Pk BH24 ....117 B1
Fairlight Holiday Chalets
PO11 ....185 C2
Fairlight La SO41 ......195 D8
Fairmead Ct
Locks Heath SO31 ......128 E1
South Hayling PO11 ....184 E3
Fairmead Way SO40 ....100 E5
Fairmead Wlk PO8 ......112 B3
Fairmile Par BH23 ......191 F1
Fairmile Rd BH23 ......191 F1
Fairoak Rd
Bishopstoke SO50 ......56 E2
Bishopstoke SO50 ......56 E4
Fair Oak SO50 ....57 B2
Fairthorn Ct 3 BH2 ....204 F4
Fairthorne Gdns PO12 ..181 A5
Fairview Cl Hythe SO45 ..126 A3
Romsey SO51 ....28 B1
Fairview Cres BH18 ....187 A5
Fairview Ct PO12 ....180 E4
Fairview Dr
Broadstone BH18 ......187 A5
Hythe SO45 ....126 A3
Romsey SO51 ....28 B1
Fairview Par 1 SO45 ..126 A2
Fairview Pk BH14 ......203 C3
Fairview Rd BH18 ......187 A5
Fairwater Cl PO13 ......155 B1
Fairway Bsns Ctr PO13 158 C2
Fairway Dr BH23 ......206 F6
Fairway Gdns SO16 ......77 E5
Fairway Rd Hythe SO45 ..125 F4
Poole BH14 ....214 C8
Fairway The
Barton on S BH25 ......210 B7
Gosport PO13 ....155 C1
Locks Heath SO31 ......128 F1
Portchester PO16 ......156 C8
Rowlands Castle PO9 ..113 C2
Fairways BH23 ....165 F6
Fairwinds BH13 ....214 B3
Fairwood Rd BH11 ......115 C5
Fairy Cross Way PO8 ..112 B2
Falaise Cl SO16 ....78 C4
Falcon Cl
2 Gosport PO12 ....181 A8
Portchester PO16 ......155 F8
Falcon Ct PO7 ....110 F3
Falcon Dr BH23 ....208 A5
Falcon Fields SO45 ....151 B3
Falcon Gn PO6 ....158 F7
Falcon Rd PO8 ....112 A7
Falcon Sq SO50 ....55 E1
Falcon View SO22 ......215 A2
Falcon Way SO32 ....81 F1
Falconer Ct SO45 ......150 C6
Falconer Dr BH15 ......201 E4
Falconwood Cl SP6 ......69 F1
Falkland Cl SO53 ....55 C3
Falkland Rd
Chandler's Ford SO53 ..55 C3
1 Portsmouth PO2 ....157 E4
Southampton SO15 ....102 A8
Falkland Sq 2 BH15 ....202 C2
Falklands Cl PO13 ......179 F4
Fallow Cres SO30 ......105 D8
Fallow Field SO22 ......215 B2
Fallows The PO15 ......195 B5
Falmouth Rd PO6 ......132 F1
Falstaff Way SO40 ......100 E5
Fancy Rd BH12 ....203 B8
Fanshawe St SO14 ......103 A6
Far Ends 4 BH14 ......203 B4
Far Meadow Way PO10 160 D8
Farcroft Rd BH12 ......203 B5
Fareham Cl PO14 ......130 C1
Fareham Ent Ctr 3
PO14 ....155 A6
Fareham Hts PO16 ......131 B3
Fareham Ind Pk PO16 ..131 C3
Fareham Park Rd PO15 130 C3
Fareham Rd
Gosport PO13 ....155 D4
Southwick PO17 ......132 E6

Fareham Rd continued
Wickham PO17 ....108 A3
Fareham Sta PO15 ......130 F1
Faringdon Ct 17 SO23 ..215 E8
Faringdon Rd SO18 ......104 D7
Farleigh Cl PO9 ....135 D5
Farley Cl Fair Oak SO50 ..57 D1
Winchester SO22 ....10 B4
Farley Ct SO16 ....78 D2
Farley La SO51 ....7 C1
Farley Mount Ctry Pk*
SO21 ....9 B8
Farley Mount Rd SO21 ..9 A4
Farlington Ave PO6 ....134 D1
Farlington Marshes (Nature
Reserve)* PO6 ....158 F5
Farlington Rd PO2 ......182 E8
Farm Cl
Hamble-le-R SO31 ......128 A2
Ringwood BH24 ....141 A8
Farm Ct BH21 ....164 A4
Farm Edge Rd PO14 ....179 C6
Farm House Cl PO14 ..154 C5
Farm La
Christchurch BH23 ......208 A5
Southbourne PO18 ......161 F7
Farm La N BH25 ....210 A8
Farm La S BH25 ....210 A8
Farm Rd BH25 ....210 A8
Farm View Ave PO8 ......88 B5
Farm View Rd PO10 ....136 F1
Farmdene Cl BH23 ......208 D8
Farmers Wlk
Hordle SO41 ....211 D8
1 Wimborne Minst BH21 163 B6
Farmery Cl SO18 ....79 D4
Farmhouse Way PO8 ..112 A5
Farmlea Rd PO6 ....157 A8
Farmside Gdns PO3 ....157 F4
Farnham Rd Liss GU33 ..52 E4
Poole BH12 ....204 A7
Steep GU32 ....204 A7
Farnleys Mead SO41 ..197 E2
Faroes Cl PO14 ....179 B8
Farrier Way PO16 ......155 B6
Farriers Cl BH21 ......164 B6
Farriers Ct 4 PO5 ......182 D2
Farriers Way PO7 ......112 C1
Farriers Wlk PO12 ......181 D6
Farringdon Rd PO9 ....136 A4
Farrington Way SO50 ..104 D5
Farrington 2 BH4 ......204 C2
Farthing Cl PO12 ......181 A6
Farthing La PO1 ....182 A3
Farthingale Terr 11
PO1 ....182 A3
Farthings Ct The 13
Farthings Gate PO7 ....134 E3
Farthings The PO14 ....153 C8
Farwell Cl BH23 ....192 C3
Farwell Rd BH12 ......188 C2
Fastnet Cl SO16 ....77 E5
Fastnet Ho 9 PO5 ......182 D1
Fastnet Way PO14 ......154 B4
Fathersfield SO42 ......145 F2
Fathoms Reach PO11 ..184 F4
Faulkton Cotts SP5 ......22 D8
Faversham 9 BH2 ......204 D2
Fawcett Rd
New Milton BH25 ......194 F2
Portsmouth PO4 ....216 D2
Fawley Bsns Ctr SO45 ..151 A3
Fawley By Pass SO45 ..151 B3
Fawley Ct 24 PO9 ......136 B5
Fawley Gn BH8 ....190 D3
Fawley Inf Sch SO45 ..151 A3
Fawley La Owslebury SO21 33 A8
Privett GU34 ....17 B4
Fawley Rd Fawley SO45 ..150 F5
Hythe SO45 ....126 A2
Hythe,Buttsash SO45 ..150 B8
Southampton SO15 ....102 A6
Fawn Cres SO30 ....105 D8
Fawn Gdns BH25 ......194 F4
Fay Cl PO14 ....179 C7
Fayre Rd PO16 ....155 A8
Fayrewood Ct BH31 ....114 F7
Fearon Rd PO1 ....182 B8
Felix Rd PO12 ....181 B8
Fell Cl SO31 ....129 A4
Fell Dr PO13 ....179 F3
Felmer Dr SO23 ....2 C7
Feltham Cl SO51 ....53 C8
Felton Cres BH23 ......208 F8
Felton Ct BH14 ....202 F5
Felton Rd BH14 ....202 F5
Feltons Pl PO14 ....154 F5
Fen Ave PO16 ....155 B7
Fenleigh Cl BH25 ......194 F5
Fennel Gdns SO41 ......197 E5
Fennell Cl PO7 ....111 D1
Fenton Rd BH6 ....206 C5
Fenwick Ct BH4 ....204 B4
Fenwick Hosp SO43 ..121 E6
Fern Bank
5 Bournemouth BH2 ..204 D3
Three Legged Cross BH21 138 C7
Fern Barrow BH12 ......188 E1
Fern Cl Alderholt SP6 ....93 A5
Burton BH23 ....192 C2
Petersfield GU31 ....41 C3
Fern Cotts 2 PO16 ....131 C2
Fern Ct SO18 ....103 E7
Fern Dr PO9 ....136 A2

Fern Hill La SO51 ....28 E8
Fern Rd Hythe SO45 ....125 F3
Southampton SO19 ....103 F2
Fern Way PO15 ....129 D3
Fernacre Bsns Pk SO51 ..27 E1
Ferncroft Ct PO14 ......179 C6
Ferncroft Gdns BH10 ..189 D5
Ferncroft Rd BH10 ......189 D5
Ferndale
Hedge End SO30 ......105 D5
Waterlooville PO7 ......135 A8
Ferndale Mews PO13 ..155 B4
Ferndale Rd
Marchwood SO40 ......101 F1
New Milton BH25 ......195 B4
Ferndene Way SO18 ....103 F8
Ferndown Cl SP6 ....69 D1
Ferndown Fst Sch BH22 165 C5
Ferndown Ind Est BH21 164 F7
Ferndown Mid Sch
BH22 ....165 C5
Ferndown Upper Sch
BH22 ....165 B6
Ferneham Rd PO15 ....130 C2
Fernglade BH25 ....195 A3
Fernheath Cl BH11 ....189 A3
Fernheath Rd BH11 ....189 A3
Fernhill SO53 ....55 E6
Fernhill Cl BH17 ....188 A2
Fernhill Flats 6 BH2 ..204 F3
Fernhill Gate BH25 ....195 A5
Fernhill La BH25 ......195 A4
Fernhill Rd BH25 ......195 A3
Fernhill Sch BH25 ......126 B1
Fernhurst Cl PO11 ......184 D3
Fernhurst Jun Sch PO4 182 F4
Fernhurst Rd PO4 ......182 F4
Fernlea BH23 ....207 D6
Fernlea Ave BH22 ......165 D4
Fernlea Cl
Ferndown BH22 ....165 D4
St Leonards BH24 ......139 E4
Fernlea Gdns
Ferndown BH22 ....165 D4
Southampton SO16 ......78 E3
Fernlea Way SO45 ......125 D3
Fernside Ave SO19 ....104 B3
Fernside Bsns Pk BH21 165 A7
Fernside Cl
Holbury SO45 ....150 C3
Southampton SO16 ....101 F8
Locks Heath SO31 ......202 E4
Fernside Rd
Bournemouth BH9 ......204 D8
Poole BH15 ....202 E4
West Moors BH22 ......138 E2
Fernside Way SO50 ......57 E2
Fernside Wlk SO50 ......57 E2
Fernway Cl PO21 ......164 B4
Fernwood Cl BH24 ......140 B5
Fernwood Cres SO18 ..103 F8
Fernwood Ho PO8 ......112 A2
Fernyhurst Ave SO16 ....77 F6
Ferris Ave BH8 ....190 D2
Ferris Pl BH8 ....190 D2
Ferrol Rd PO12 ....181 C7
Ferry Rd
Bournemouth BH6 ......206 F3
Poole BH15 ....125 F3
Poole,Lower Hamworthy
BH15 ....202 B1
Portsmouth PO4 ....183 D3
Portsmouth PO4 ....183 A4
Ferry Way BH13 ....214 B3
Ferrybridge Gn 4 SO30 105 C6
Ferrymans Quay SO31 ..127 B5
Ferrypoint SO41 ....198 A4
Festing Bldgs 1 PO4 ..182 F2
Festing Gr PO4 ....183 A2
Festing Mews 2 PO4 ..182 F2
Festing Rd PO4 ....182 F2
Feversham Ave BH8 ..190 E1
Fey Rd PO12 ....181 C6
Fibbards Rd SO42 ......145 F1
Field Cl Compton SO21 ..31 C6
Gosport PO13 ....155 B5
Locks Heath SO31 ......129 A2
Romsey SO51 ....29 C5
Southampton SO16 ......79 C5
Field End SO23 ....2 C7
Field Pl Barton on S BH25 209 D8
Verwood BH31 ....114 E7
Field View SO53 ....54 F6
Field Way
Christchurch BH23 ....193 D1
Compton SO21 ....31 C6
Cowplain,Blue BH21 ..106 E8
Denmead PO7 ....110 F4
Godshill SP6 ....70 D2
Field Wlk SO41 ....197 D5
Fielden Cl SO52 ....53 F4
Fielder Dr 1 PO14 ......155 A6
Fielders Ct
Waterlooville PO7 ......134 C4
West End SO30 ....80 E1
Fielders' Way SO51 ....51 B2
Fieldfare Cl PO8 ....88 C4
Fieldhouse Dr PO13 ..179 F4
Fieldmore Rd PO12 ....181 B8
Fields Cl SO45 ....150 E1
Fields The BH31 ....114 F7
Fieldway BH24 ....141 B8
Fifth Ave Cosham PO6 ..157 E8

Fifth Ave continued
Havant PO9 ....136 B2
Fifth St PO1 ....182 F6
Filmer Cl PO13 ....180 D8
Filmorehill La GU34 ....17 B3
Filton Cl SO40 ....76 C1
Filton Rd SO41 ....197 D4
Finch Ho 11 PO4 ......183 B3
Finch Rd PO4 ....183 D3
Finch's La SO21 ....31 F6
Finchdean Rd
Havant PO9 ....135 D4
Rowlands Castle PO9 ..113 D3
Finches The SO17 ......79 B2
Finchfield Ave BH11 ..188 F6
Finchmead La GU32 ....40 B4
Finchwood Farm Ind Units
PO11 ....160 B1
Findon Rd PO12 ......181 B9
Fineshade 7 BH13 ....214 F7
Finisterre Cl PO14 ....154 B4
Finlay Cl SO19 ....104 C4
Finley Cl SO40 ....76 B1
Finzi Cl SO19 ....104 C3
Fiona Cl SO23 ....11 F8
Fir Ave BH25 ....195 B2
Fir Cl Lyndhurst SO43 ..121 F4
West Moors BH22 ......138 E3
Fir Copse Rd PO7 ......134 D4
Fir Croft Dr SO53 ......55 D5
Fir Rd SO40 ....100 B2
Fir Tree Cl
Horton Heath SO50 ......81 C7
St Leonards BH24 ......139 D2
Fir Tree Cotts GU33 ....21 E4
Fir Tree Ct SO18 ......104 B8
Fir Tree Gdns PO8 ....112 C5
Fir Tree Hill SP6 ......93 D1
Fir Tree La
Christchurch BH23 ....193 D1
Horton Heath SO50 ......81 B7
Fir Tree Rd Bartley SO40 99 A7
South Hayling PO11 ..185 A3
Fir Vale Rd BH1 ....204 F3
Firbank Rd BH9 ....205 B8
Firecrest Cl SO16 ......78 B6
Firefly Cl PO13 ....180 A5
Firgrove Cl SO52 ....53 F4
Firgrove Cres PO3 ....157 F5
Firgrove Ct SO15 ......102 C7
Firgrove La PO17 ......108 F2
Firgrove Rd
North Baddesley SO52 ..54 A5
Southampton SO15 ....102 C7
Firlands Rise PO9 ......135 A1
Firmain Rd BH11 ......188 D1
Firmount Cl SO41 ....196 E1
Firmstone Rd SO23 ....11 C8
Firs Ave PO8 ....111 F2
Firs Cres SO23 ....2 B8
Firs Dr SO30 ....105 A5
Firs Glen Rd
Bournemouth BH9 ....204 E8
Verwood BH31 ....115 A4
West Moors BH22 ......138 E2
Firs La SO41 ....214 B8
Firs Pk Rd SO31 ......41 C3
Firs The
Bournemouth BH1 ....205 A4
Chandler's Ford SO53 ..55 C3
Gosport PO13 ....155 D1
Southampton SO16 ......78 F4
Winchester SO22 ......10 F8
Firshill BH23 ....208 E8
Firside Rd BH21 ......186 C4
First Ave Cosham PO6 ..157 F8
Farlington PO6 ....158 E8
Havant PO9 ....136 B2
Horndean PO8 ....88 C3
Southampton SO15 ....101 D7
Southbourne PO10 ....161 F7
First Marine Ave BH25 209 F7
First St SO45 ....150 E8
Firsway BH16 ....201 C7
Firtree Cres SO41 ......195 F3
Firtree Gdns PO8 ......112 C5
Firtree Way SO19 ......104 B5
Firwood Cl SO53 ....55 D8
Fisgard Rd PO12 ......181 E8
Fisher Cl PO14 ....179 B8
Fisher Rd PO13 ....155 C3
Fisher's Rd SO40 ......101 A6
Fisherman's Ave BH5 ..206 B4
Fisherman's Bank BH23 207 E5
Fisherman's Wlk BH5 ..206 B4
Fishermans The PO10 ..161 A8
Fishermans Wlk BH15 ..185 E2
Fishers Gr PO6 ....158 E7
Fishers Hill PO15 ......130 B2
Fishery La PO11 ......185 C2
Fishlake Mdws SO51 ....27 F1
Fitzgerald Cl PO15 ....129 C8
Fitzharris Ave BH9 ....205 A7
Fitzherbert Rd PO6 ..158 D7
Fitzherbert Spur PO6 ..158 E7
Fitzherbert St PO1 ....216 B4
Fitzhugh Ho 8 SO15 ..102 E6
Fitzhugh Pl SO15 ......102 F7
Fitzhugh St 3 SO15 ..102 F5
Fitzmaurice Rd BH23 ..206 E8
Fitzpain Cl BH22 ......165 D2
Fitzpain Rd BH22 ......165 D2
Fitzpatrick Ct PO6 ....133 D1
Fitzroy Cl SO16 ....78 F7

Fitzroy Dr PO13 . . . . .180 A7
Fitzroy Wlk PO1 . . . . .216 C4
Fitzwilliam Ave PO14 . . . .179 A7
Fitzwilliam Cl BH11 . . . . . .188 E5
Fitzworth Ave BH16 . . . . . .201 C4
Fitzwygram Cres PO9 . . . .135 F3
Five Bridges Rd SO23 . . . .215 C1
Five Elms Dr SO51 . . . . . . .53 C6
Five Heads Rd PO8 . . . . . .112 C8
Five Post La PO12 . . . . . . .181 B7
Fivefields Cl SO23 . . . . . . .11 C6
Fivefields Rd SO23 . . . . . .11 C7
Flag Wlk PO8 . . . . .111 F5
Flaghead BH13 . . . . .214 E6
Flaghead Chine Rd
BH13 . . . . .214 E6
Flaghead Rd BH13 . . . . . .214 E7
Flagstaff Gn PO12 . . . . . .181 D7
Flambard Ave BH23 . . . . .192 A1
Flambard Rd BH14 . . . . . .203 C2
Flamborough Cl SO16 . . . .77 D3
Flamingo Ct PO16 . . . . . . .155 F8
Flamstone St SP5 . . . . . . .22 B8
Flanders Ho ⓵ PO14 . . . .154 E8
Flanders Ind Pk SO30 . . . .105 B8
Flanders Rd SO30 . . . . . . .105 B8
Flathouse Rd PO1 . . . . . . .182 C7
Flaxfields End SP6 . . . . . .69 E1
Flazen Cl BH11 . . . . .188 D3
Fleet Cl PO13 . . . . .155 D1
Fleet End Bottom
SO31 . . . . .152 F10
Fleet End Rd
Locks Heath SO31 . . . . . .128 F1
Warsash SO31 . . . . .152 F10
Fleet Farm Cvn & Camping
Ctr PO11 . . . . .185 A8
Fleet Terr SO21 . . . . .31 B1
Fleet Way PO1 . . . . .182 B6
Fleet's Cnr BH17 . . . . .202 B7
Fleetend Cl PO9 . . . . .135 C6
Fleets Est BH15 . . . . .202 B6
Fleets La BH15 . . . . .202 C6
Fleetsbridge Bsns Ctr
BH17 . . . . .202 B7
Fleetspoint Bsns Ctr
BH15 . . . . .202 B5
Fleetwood Ct BH15 . . . . . .202 C7
Fleming Ave SO52 . . . . . . .54 B4
Fleming Cl SO15 . . . . .129 D4
Fleming Ct
North Baddesley SO52 . . . .54 B4
Southampton SO19 . . . . . .103 D2
Fleming Pl
Colden Common SO21 . . . .31 F1
⓵ Romsey SO51 . . . . . . .52 F7
Fleming Rd
Southampton SO16 . . . . . .79 D4
Winchester SO22 . . . . .1 C3
Fletcher Cl
Bournemouth BH10 . . . . . .189 D3
Hythe SO45 . . . . .125 D3
Fletcher Rd BH10 . . . . . . .189 D3
Fletchwood La
Totton SO40 . . . . .100 B4
Woodlands SO40 . . . . . . .99 F2
Fleur de Lys Mobile Home Pk
SO14 . . . . .173 F1
Fleuret Cl SO45 . . . . .126 A1
Flexford Cl SO33 . . . . .30 A1
Flexford Gdns PO9 . . . . . .136 A3
Flexford La SO41 . . . . .196 C6
Flexford Rd SO52,SO53 . . .54 E7
Flinders Cl ⓴ PO4 . . . . . .183 B2
Flint Cl SO19 . . . . .104 E4
Flint St PO5 . . . . .216 A1
Floating Bridge Rd
SO14 . . . . .103 C3
Floral Farm BH21 . . . . . . .164 A2
Florence Cl SO51 . . . . .51 B2
Florence Ct ⓾ SO18 . . . . .103 E8
Florence Rd
Bournemouth BH5 . . . . . .205 F4
Poole BH14 . . . . .203 D4
Portsmouth PO5 . . . . .182 D1
Southampton SO19 . . . . . .103 D2
Florentine Way PO7 . . . . .135 A8
Florins The
Locks Heath PO47 . . . . . .129 A1
Waterlooville PO7 . . . . . . .134 E3
Floriston Gdns BH25 . . . . .195 D3
Floud La GU32 . . . . .37 B5
Flower Bldgs PO13 . . . . . .179 E2
Flower Ct BH21 . . . . .163 D3
Flowerdown Cl SO40 . . . . .100 C8
Flowerdown Ho SO22 . . . . .1 C4
Flowerdown Mobile Home Pk
SO22 . . . . .1 C5
Flowers Cl SO31 . . . . .127 E3
Flowers La SO51 . . . . .50 D6
Flume Rd SO45 . . . . .151 C4
Flushards SO41 . . . . .197 F3
Flying Bull Cl ⓷ PO2 . . . .182 D8
Flying Bull La PO2 . . . . . . .182 D8
Flying Bull l'rim Sch
PO2 . . . . .182 D8
Foldsgate Cl SO43 . . . . . . .121 F6
Foley Ho PO1 . . . . .216 B4
Folkestone Rd PO3 . . . . . .183 A8
Folland Cl SO52 . . . . .54 A4
Folly Farm La BH24 . . . . . .140 C6
Folly Field SO32 . . . . .83 D7
Folly La GU32 . . . . .40 F3
Folly Mkt �7 GU31 . . . . . . .40 F3
Font Cl PO14 . . . . .129 C3

Fontley Rd PO15 . . . . .130 A5
Fontmell Rd BH18 . . . . . . .187 C3
Fontwell Cl SO40 . . . . .76 C1
Fontwell Gdns SO50 . . . . .81 D7
Fontwell Mews ⓹ PO7 . . .112 B1
Fontwell Rd ⓸ PO5 . . . . . .182 D2
Foord Rd SO30 . . . . .105 B5
Football Gn SO43 . . . . .98 D3
Footner Cl SO51 . . . . .28 C2
Footners La BH23 . . . . . . .192 C2
Forbes Almshouses
GU32 . . . . .38 E1
Forbes Cl SO16 . . . . .77 F6
Forbes Rd SO23 . . . . .2 B8
Forbury Rd ⓶ PO5 . . . . . .216 C2
Ford Ave SO53 . . . . .55 D4
Ford Cl BH22 . . . . .165 F7
Ford La BH22 . . . . .166 A7
Ford Rd PO12 . . . . .180 F6
Fordingbridge Bsns Pk
SP6 . . . . .69 D1
Fordingbridge Hospl SP6 . .69 D1
Fordingbridge Inf Sch
SP6 . . . . .69 F3
Fordingbridge Jun Sch
SP6 . . . . .69 F3
Fordingbridge Rd
Alderholt SP6 . . . . .93 B7
Portsmouth PO4 . . . . .183 B3
Fordington Ave SO22 . . . .215 C6
Fordington Rd SO22 . . . . .215 C7
Fore Bridge GU31 . . . . .40 F2
Foreland Cl BH23 . . . . . . .191 D4
Foreland Ct PO11 . . . . . . .185 C2
Foreland Rd BH16 . . . . . . .201 C4
Forelle Ctr The BH31 . . . . .115 C4
Foremans Cotts PO12 . . . .181 B7
Foreshore N SO45 . . . . . . .151 B6
Foreshore S SO45 . . . . . . .151 B6
Forest Ave PO8 . . . . .111 F3
Forest Cnr GU33 . . . . .21 A7
Forest Cl
Fordingbridge SP6 . . . . . .69 F1
Lymington SO41 . . . . .197 B2
New Milton BH25 . . . . . . .195 B2
Forest Edge
Fawley SO45 . . . . .151 B3
New Milton BH25 . . . . . . .195 C4
Forest Edge Cl
St Leonards BH24 . . . . . .139 D5
Sway SO41 . . . . .172 A3
Forest Edge Dr BH24 . . . . .139 D6
Forest Edge Rd BH24 . . . .141 E5
Forest Edge Sch SO40 . . . .100 C6
Forest End PO7 . . . . .134 D7
Forest Front SO45 . . . . . . .150 A8
Forest Gate SO45 . . . . . . .177 F7
Forest Gate Gdns SO41 . . .197 D1
Forest Gdns
Lyndhurst SO43 . . . . .121 F5
Waltham Chase SO32 . . . .83 E3
Forest Glade Cl SO42 . . . .145 D1
Forest Hall SO42 . . . . .146 A1
Forest Hill Way SO45 . . . . .125 F2
Forest Hills Ctr BH24 . . . . .141 D6
Forest Hills Dr SO18 . . . . .79 F3
Forest Ho ⓮ BH1 . . . . . . .205 A3
Forest La Fareham PO17 . .131 B8
Hardley SO45 . . . . .150 B6
Ringwood BH24 . . . . .141 F6
Verwood BH31 . . . . .114 E7
Forest Links Rd BH22 . . . .138 B1
Forest Mdw SO45 . . . . . . .150 A8
Forest Oak Dr BH25 . . . . .195 A5
Forest Park Rd SO42 . . . . .145 E2
Forest Pines BH25 . . . . . . .195 A4
Forest Rd
Bransgore BH23 . . . . .169 F4
Burley Street BH24 . . . . . .142 F5
Chandler's Ford SO53 . . . .55 D8
Denmead PO7 . . . . .110 D4
Liss GU33 . . . . .21 A6
Nomansland SP5 . . . . . . .73 C7
Poole BH13 . . . . .204 A2
Waltham Chase SO32 . . . .83 E3
West Moors PO22 . . . . . . .138 F3
Woodgreen SP6 . . . . .47 E3
Forest Rise
Christchurch BH23 . . . . . .193 D2
Liss GU33 . . . . .21 A6
Forest Side Gdns BH24 . . .117 C1
Forest View
Beckley BH25 . . . . .194 D5
Brockenhurst SO42 . . . . . .145 D1
⓸ Southampton SO14 . . . .102 F4
Forest View Cl BH9 . . . . . .190 A2
Forest View Dr BH21 . . . . .165 A5
Forest View Rd BH9 . . . . . .190 A3
Forest Way
Christchurch BH23 . . . . . .193 D1
Everton BH25 . . . . .196 D1
Fareham PO10 . . . . .165 A5
Gosport PO13 . . . . .155 E1
Totton SO40 . . . . .76 A2
Forest Wlks (Blackwater)*
SO42 . . . . .144 E6
Forester Rd SO32 . . . . .85 B1
Foresters Gate SO45 . . . . .177 D7
Foresters Rd SO23 . . . . . . .2 A4
Foresters Rd SO45 . . . . . .150 F2

Forestlake Ave BH24 . . . . .141 D6
Forestside Ave PO9 . . . . . .136 A5
Forestside The BH31 . . . . .115 D5
Forge Cl SO31 . . . . .105 A1
Forge La SO45 . . . . .151 B3
Forge Rd SO45 . . . . .177 F7
Forneth Gdns PO15 . . . . . .154 B8
Forres Sandle Manor
SP6 . . . . .69 D2
Forster Rd SO14 . . . . .103 B7
Forsyth Gdns BH10 . . . . . .189 C1
Forsythia Cl Havant PO9 . .136 C4
Hedge End SO30 . . . . . . .105 B8
Hythe SO45 . . . . .150 A7
Forsythia Pl SO19 . . . . . . .103 F5
Fort Brockhurst* PO12 . . .155 E5
Fort Cumberland* PO4 . . .183 E3
Fort Cumberland Cl
BH15 . . . . .201 D2
Fort Cumberland Rd
PO4 . . . . .183 D3
Fort Fareham Ind Est
PO14 . . . . .155 A6
Fort Fareham Rd PO14 . . .154 F6
Fort Nelson* PO17 . . . . . . .132 B3
Fort Rd Gosport PO12 . . . .181 B2
Southampton SO19 . . . . . .103 C3
Fort Wallington Ind Est
PO6 . . . . .131 D2
Fort Widley Married Quarters
PO6 . . . . .133 F1
Fortescue Rd
Bournemouth BH3 . . . . . .205 A6
Poole BH12 . . . . .203 D6
Forth Cl
Chandler's Ford SO53 . . . .55 B5
Stubbington PO14 . . . . . . .179 B8
Forth Ho ⓶ SO14 . . . . . . .103 C6
Forties Cl PO14 . . . . .154 B4
Forton Cl BH10 . . . . .189 E4
Forton Lodge ⓷ PO12 . . .181 C6
Forton Rd Gosport PO12 . .181 B6
Portsmouth PO1 . . . . .182 E6
Fortune Cl SO53 . . . . .55 C6
Fortune Ho PO12 . . . . .181 A6
Fortunes Way PO9 . . . . . . .134 F1
Forty Acre La GU31 . . . . . .66 D3
Forum The ⓶ PO9 . . . . . . .135 E2
Forward Dr SO41 . . . . .197 C2
Foster Cl PO14 . . . . .154 C4
Foster Rd Gosport PO12 . .181 B4
Portsmouth PO1 . . . . .216 C4
Founders Way PO13 . . . . .155 D2
Foundry Cres SO31 . . . . . .127 F8
Foundry Ct ⓺ PO5 . . . . . .182 A5
Foundry La SO15 . . . . . . .102 B7
Foundry Lane Prim Sch
SO15 . . . . .102 B7
Foundry Rd SP5 . . . . .47 D7
Fountain Ct
⓸ Colden Common SO21 . .31 F1
Hedge End SO30 . . . . . . .105 B6
Poole BH13 . . . . .204 B2
Fountain Rdbt BH23 . . . . .207 B6
Fountain Sq PO14 . . . . . . .184 E4
Fountain St PO1 . . . . .216 B3
Fountain Way PO7 . . . . . . .207 B6
Fountains Pk SO31 . . . . . .127 A7
Four Acres SO41 . . . . .66 A6
Four Cnrs SP5 . . . . .68 A4
Four Marks Gn ⓷ PO9 . . .136 B6
Four Wells Rd BH21 . . . . . .164 A7
Fourposts Hill ⓷ SO15 . . .102 E5
Fourshells Cl SO45 . . . . . .150 F2
Fourth Ave Cosham PO6 . .157 E8
Havant PO9 . . . . .136 B2
Fourth Cl PO14 . . . . .182 F6
Fowey Cl SO53 . . . . .55 B6
Fowey The SO45 . . . . .150 E2
Fowlers Rd SO30 . . . . .105 B8
Fowlers Wlk SO54 . . . . . . .54 D2
Fox Cl SO50 . . . . .56 F2
Fox Field SO41 . . . . .196 D1
Fox La
Wimborne Minst BH21 . . .164 C5
Winchester SO22 . . . . . . .215 A3
Fox Pond La SO41 . . . . . . .197 D1
Fox's Wlk SO45 . . . . .177 F7
Foxbury Cl SO45 . . . . .126 A2
Foxbury Gr PO16 . . . . .156 B7
Foxbury La
Gosport PO13 . . . . .155 C4
Westbourne PO10 . . . . . . .137 D4
Foxbury Rd BH24 . . . . .166 F8
Foxcombe Cl SO32 . . . . . . .84 A5
Foxcote Gdns BH25 . . . . . .194 F3
Foxcote Ho ⓺ PO6 . . . . . .132 F2
Foxcott Cl SO19 . . . . .126 F8
Foxcott Gr PO9 . . . . .135 F5
Foxcroft Dr
Holbury SO45 . . . . .150 B3
Wimborne Minst BH21 . . .164 B5
Foxdale Cl ⓷ PO4 . . . . . . .204 E3
Foxes Cl Verwood BH31 . . .114 F5
Waterlooville PO7 . . . . . . .134 E6
Foxes La SO51 . . . . .50 F5
Foxglade SO45 . . . . .177 F7
Foxglove Cl BH23 . . . . . . .208 C8
Foxglove Pl BH25 . . . . . . .195 D4
Foxgloves Fareham PO16 . .131 C3
Upton BH16 . . . . .201 B7
Foxgloves The SO30 . . . . .105 D5
Foxhayes La SO45 . . . . . . .177 D7
Foxhills Ashurst SO40 . . . .140 D4
Verwood BH31 . . . . .115 B6
Foxhills Cl SO40 . . . . .100 C4
Foxhills Inf Sch SO40 . . . .100 D4
Foxhills Jun Sch SO40 . . . .100 D4

Foxholes ⓵ BH6 . . . . .206 F4
Foxholes Rd
Bournemouth BH6 . . . . . .206 F4
Poole BH15 . . . . .202 F6
Foxlands SO45 . . . . .177 F7
Foxlea ⓷ SO15 . . . . .102 E7
Foxlea Gdns PO12 . . . . . . .181 B8
Foxlease Terr SO43 . . . . . .121 F7
Foxley Dr PO3 . . . . .158 B4
Foxtail Dr SO45 . . . . .125 F1
Foxwood Ave BH23 . . . . . .207 F5
Foxy Paddock SO45 . . . . . .177 F7
Foyes Cl SO31 . . . . .128 C1
Foyes Ct SO15 . . . . .102 D6
Foyle Rd SO53 . . . . .55 B6
Frampton Cl
⓵ Colden Common SO21 . .31 F1
New Milton BH25 . . . . . . .195 C5
Frampton Pl BH24 . . . . . . .141 A7
Frampton Rd BH9 . . . . . . .205 A8
Frampton Way
Totton SO40 . . . . .2 C7
Totton SO40 . . . . .100 F6
Frances Ct �7 BH23 . . . . . .209 B7
Frances Rd
Bournemouth BH1 . . . . . .205 C4
Waterlooville PO7 . . . . . . .134 E1
Frances Sheldon Ct
SO22 . . . . .215 C5
Francesca Ct ⓹ BH23 . . . .207 E7
Francesca Grange ⓸
BH23 . . . . .207 E7
Francesca Lo ⓵ BH23 . . . .207 E6
Francis Ave
Bournemouth BH11 . . . . . .188 D3
Portsmouth PO4 . . . . .182 F3
Francis Avenue Ind Est
BH11 . . . . .188 D3
Francis Cl PO13 . . . . .180 A5
Francis Gdns SO23 . . . . . . .2 B3
Francis Pl PO14 . . . . .179 D7
Francis Rd Horndean PO8 . .88 C3
Poole BH12 . . . . .203 E5
Franconia Dr SO16 . . . . . . .77 B3
Frank Judd Ct ⓶ PO1 . . .182 A5
Frank Miles Ho ⓸ PO5 . . .216 B2
Frank Wareham Cottage
Homes The BH9 . . . . .190 E3
Frankland Cres BH14 . . . . .203 E3
Frankland Terr ⓸ PO10 . . .161 A8
Franklin Rd
Bournemouth BH9 . . . . . .190 A3
Gosport PO13 . . . . .180 C7
New Milton BH25 . . . . . . .195 C4
Twyford SO21 . . . . .32 A7
Franklyn Ave SO19 . . . . . .104 A4
Franklyn Cl BH10 . . . . .201 B7
Franks Way BH12 . . . . . . .203 B7
Frankston Rd BH6 . . . . . . .206 C4
Frankton Way PO12 . . . . . .181 D6
Frarydene PO10 . . . . .161 D8
Fraser Cl SO16 . . . . .77 F6
Fraser Ct BH25 . . . . .194 F3
Fraser Gdns PO10 . . . . . . .161 D8
Fraser Rd Gosport PO13 . . .155 C4
Havant PO9 . . . . .135 D2
Kings Worthy SO23 . . . . . .2 C8
Poole BH12 . . . . .203 F8
Portsmouth PO5 . . . . .216 C2
Portsmouth,Whale Island
PO2 . . . . .157 B2
Frater La PO12 . . . . .156 A1
Fratton Ct PO1 . . . . .216 D3
Fratton Park (Portsmouth
FC) PO4 . . . . .183 A5
Fratton Rd PO1 . . . . .216 D4
Fratton Sta PO1 . . . . .182 E5
Fratton Way
Fair Oak SO50 . . . . .57 C1
Portsmouth PO4 . . . . .182 F5
Frattton Ind Est PO4 . . . . .183 A5
Frayslea ⓸ SO45 . . . . .150 A3
Freda Rd BH23 . . . . .206 F6
Freda Rundle Gdns SO50 . .57 D2
Frederica Rd BH9 . . . . . . .204 E8
Frederick St
Portsmouth PO1 . . . . .216 B4
Southampton SO14 . . . . . .103 B6
Free St SO32 . . . . .83 D8
Freedom Cl SO45 . . . . . . .126 A3
Freefolk Gn ⓵ PO9 . . . . . .136 C5
Freegrounds Ave SO30 . . .105 C6
Freegrounds Cl ⓵
SO30 . . . . .105 C6
Freegrounds Inf Sch
SO30 . . . . .105 C6
Freegrounds Jun Sch
SO30 . . . . .105 C6
Freegrounds Rd SO30 . . . .105 C6
Freemans Cl BH21 . . . . . . .164 B6
Freemans La BH21 . . . . . . .164 B5
Freemantle Bsns Ctr
SO15 . . . . .102 C5
Freemantle CE Inf Sch
SO15 . . . . .102 C5
Freemantle Cl SO19 . . . . .103 F5
Freemantle Common Rd
SO19 . . . . .103 F6
Freemantle Rd PO12 . . . . .181 B8
Freestone Rd ⓾ PO5 . . . .182 D2
Fremington Ct ⓶ BH25 . . .195 B3
French Rd BH17 . . . . .187 B1
French St
⓼ Portsmouth PO1 . . . . .182 A3
Southampton SO14 . . . . . .102 F3
French's Farm Rd BH16 . . .201 A7
Frenches La SO51 . . . . .51 C8
Frenches View PO7 . . . . . .110 E4

Frenchmans Rd GU32 . . . . .40 E4
Frenchmoor La
East Dean SP5 . . . . .3 F2
West Tytherley SP5 . . . . . . .3 F4
Frendstaple Rd PO7 . . . . .135 A6
Frensham Cl
Bournemouth BH10 . . . . . .189 E3
Hedge End SO30 . . . . . . .105 C6
Frensham Ct
Hedge End SO30 . . . . . . .105 C6
Portsmouth PO4 . . . . .182 F4
Frensham Rd PO4 . . . . . . .182 F4
Freshfield Rd SO17 . . . . . .134 E8
Freshfield Sq SO15 . . . . . .102 B7
Freshwater Cl
Chandler's Ford SO53 . . . .30 E1
Lee-on-t-S PO13 . . . . .179 E3
Freshwater Dr BH15 . . . . .201 D3
Freshwater Rd
Christchurch BH23 . . . . . .208 C6
Cosham PO6 . . . . .157 E7
Freneen Liby PO1 . . . . . . .182 B4
Friars Croft SO40 . . . . .76 C2
Friars Gate BH23 . . . . .208 C6
Friars Pond Rd PO15 . . . . .130 C1
Friars Rd
Christchurch BH23 . . . . . .208 B6
Eastleigh SO50 . . . . .55 F1
Friars Way SO18 . . . . .79 D8
Friars Wlk BH25 . . . . .210 A8
Friarscroft SO31 . . . . .127 B7
Friarsgate SO23 . . . . .215 E6
Friary Cl ⓺ PO5 . . . . .182 C2
Friary Gdns �7 SO23 . . . . .215 D5
Friary The ⓺ PO5 . . . . . . .182 C2
Friday's Ct BH24 . . . . .140 F7
Friendly Societies' Homes
PO4 . . . . .183 B3
Friends Provident St Mary's
Stadium (Southampton FC)
The SO14 . . . . .103 B5
Friendship Ho PO5 . . . . . .216 B1
Frinton Ct ⓶ BH14 . . . . . .203 A4
Frith La PO17 . . . . .108 B7
Frith Lane End PO12 . . . . .180 B8
Fritham Cl SO40 . . . . .100 C7
Fritham Gdns BH8 . . . . . . .190 D3
Fritham Rd SO18 . . . . .104 D8
Frobisher Ave BH12 . . . . . .188 F1
Frobisher Cl
Christchurch BH23 . . . . . .207 F6
Gosport PO13 . . . . .180 C6
Ringwood BH24 . . . . .117 C1
Frobisher Ct SO40 . . . . . . .102 A3
Frobisher Gdns
⓺ Emsworth PO10 . . . . .160 F8
Southampton SO19 . . . . . .104 C4
Frobisher Gr PO16 . . . . . . .156 C7
Frobisher Ho ⓺ PO1 . . . . .182 A5
Frobisher Ind Ctr SO51 . . .27 E1
Froddington Rd PO5 . . . . .216 C2
Froghall La Fordingbridge SP6 .93 E7
Titchfield PO14 . . . . .154 A8
Froghall SO45 . . . . .126 A1
Frogham Cross SP6 . . . . . .94 E6
Frogham Gn PO9 . . . . .135 D6
Frogham Hill SP6 . . . . .94 D6
Frogmore PO14 . . . . .154 C8
Frogmore La
Nursling SO16 . . . . .77 D3
Waterlooville PO8 . . . . . . .112 A6
Frome Cl SO40 . . . . .102 A1
Frome Rd SO18 . . . . .80 A3
Fromond Cl SO41 . . . . .197 C5
Fromond Rd SO22 . . . . .1 D3
Front Lawn Jun Sch PO9 . .135 F5
Front Lawn Jun Sch
PO9 . . . . .135 F5
Frost La SO45 . . . . .135 F5
Frost Rd BH11 . . . . .188 F3
Frosthole Cl PO15 . . . . . . .130 C3
Frosthole Cres PO15 . . . . .130 E3
Froud Way BH21 . . . . .186 C4
Froude Ave PO12 . . . . .181 C3
Froude Rd PO12 . . . . .181 D3
Froxfield CE Inf Sch
GU32 . . . . .18 E2
Froxfield Cl SO22 . . . . .215 C6
Froxfield Gdns PO16 . . . . .132 C1
Froxfield Ho PO1 . . . . .216 C4
Froxfield Rd PO9 . . . . .136 B5
Froyle Ct ⓾ PO9 . . . . .136 B5
Fry Cl Blackfield SO45 . . . .150 F2
Hamble-le-R SO31 . . . . . .128 A4
Fry's La SO32 . . . . .61 D4
Fryer Cl BH11 . . . . .189 B5
Fryer Cl SO53 . . . . .55 E7
Fryern Court Rd SP6 . . . . . .69 E5
Fryern Cl SO53 . . . . .55 E7
Fryern Inf Sch SO53 . . . . . .55 E6
Fryern Jun Sch SO53 . . . . .55 E6
Fryers Cl SO23 . . . . .2 C8
Fryers Copse BH21 . . . . . .164 C6
Fryers Rd BH21 . . . . .138 D8
Frys La SO41 . . . . .196 D1
Fuchsia Gdns SO15 . . . . . .78 D2
Fulflood Ctr The PO12 . . . .188 C2
Fulfoot Ct ⓷ SO22 . . . . . . .215 C6
Fullflood Rd PO9 . . . . .135 E5
Fullegar Cotts SO32 . . . . . .84 B6
Fullerton Cl
⓷ Havant PO9 . . . . .136 B5
Fullerton Rd SO19 . . . . . . .126 F8
Fullerton Rd SO41 . . . . . . .197 C4
Fulmar Cl SO16 . . . . .78 B5
Fulmar Dr SO45 . . . . .126 B2

Fulmar Rd BH23 . . . . 208 A5
Fulmar Rd PO13 . . . . 155 A3
Fulmer Wlk PO8 . . . . 111 E4
Fulwood Ave PO11 . . . . 188 E5
Funtington Rd PO2 . . . . 182 E8
Furley Ct PO16 . . . . 130 E4
Funtley Hill PO16 . . . . 130 E5
Funtley La PO17 . . . . 130 E5
Funtley Rd PO17 . . . . 130 E5
Furdies PO7 . . . . 110 E4
Furley Cl 8 SO23 . . . . 215 F6
Furlong Mews BH24 . . . . 140 F7
Furlong The BH24 . . . . 140 F7
Furlong Ho PO10 . . . . 136 E1
Furneaux Gdns PO16 . . . . . . 131 B3
Furnell Rd SO15 . . . . 102 D1
Furness Rd 10 PO5 . . . . 182 D1
Furniss Way PO11 . . . . 184 D4
Furnston Gr PO10 . . . . 137 E1
Fury Way PO14 . . . . 179 B8
Furze Cl SO19 . . . . 104 A5
Furze Croft BH25 . . . . 195 A2
Furze Hall PO16 . . . . 131 B4
Furze Hill Dr BH14 . . . . 203 C1
Furze La PO4 . . . . 183 D4
Furze Rd SO19 . . . . 104 A5
Furze Way PO8 . . . . 112 B4
Furzebrook Cl BH17 . . . . 187 E3
Furzedale Gdns SO45 . . . . . . 126 B1
Furzedale Pk SO45 . . . . 126 B2
Furzedown Cotts SO20 . . . . . . 7 B7
Furzedown Cres 4 PO9 . . . . 136 A5
Furzedown Ho SO20 . . . . 7 B6
Furzedown Mews 2
SO45 . . . . 126 B1
Furzedown Rd
Compton SO20 . . . . 2 B8
Southampton SO17 . . . . 79 A2
Furzehall Ave PO16 . . . . 131 B3
Furzehill BH21 . . . . 163 C8
Furzelands Rd BH21 . . . . 138 E8
Furzeley Rd PO7 . . . . 110 F2
Furzey Ave SO45 . . . . 126 B1
Furzey Cl SO45 . . . . 150 F1
Furzey Gdns* SO43 . . . . 98 A3
Furzey La SO42 . . . . 148 B1
Furzey Rd BH16 . . . . 201 B6
Furzley Ct PO9 . . . . 135 C6
Furzley La SO43 . . . . 74 D6
Furzley Rd SO40 . . . . 74 E3
Furzy Whistlers Cl
BH23 . . . . 169 B1
Fushia Cl PO9 . . . . 136 C4
Futcher Sch The PO6 . . . . . . 158 C8
Fyeford Cl SO16 . . . . 77 F6
Fyfield Cl PO15 . . . . 129 C8
Fyfield Way SO22 . . . . 1 B5
Fyning St PO1 . . . . 216 C4

G

G Ave SO45 . . . . 150 F6
Gable Mews PO11 . . . . 185 A4
Gablehurst BH16 . . . . 201 C7
Gables Ct SO16 . . . . 78 F5
Gadbridge Ct 12 BH4 . . . . . . 204 C2
Gage Cl SO40 . . . . 102 A2
Gain's Rd PO4 . . . . 182 E2
Gainsborough Ave
BH25 . . . . 195 B5
Gainsborough Cl SO19 . . . . . 104 C2
Gainsborough Ho
4 Bournemouth BH5 . . . . . . 206 B5
Lymington SO41 . . . . 197 D2
North Baddesley SO52 . . . . . 54 B4
Gainsborough Ho
Barton on S BH25 . . . . 210 A6
2 Portsmouth PO4 . . . . 182 E1
Gainsborough Mews
PO14 . . . . 153 F8
Gainsborough Rd
Bournemouth BH7 . . . . 205 F7
St Leonards BH24 . . . . 139 F5
Gainsford Rd SO19 . . . . 103 E5
Galaxie Rd PO8 . . . . 112 B4
Gale Moor Ave PO12 . . . . . . 180 D4
Galleon Cl SO31 . . . . 128 F1
Gallia Ct SO17 . . . . 79 B8
Gallop Way BH12 . . . . 204 C7
Gallops The PO14 . . . . 129 D2
Galloway Rd BH15 . . . . 201 D4
Galsworthy Rd BH24 . . . . . . 165 E1
Galsworthy Rd SO40 . . . . . . 100 D7
Galt Rd PO6 . . . . 158 B8
Galton Ave BH23 . . . . 206 F6
Gamble Cl SO19 . . . . 103 F4
Gamble Rd PO2 . . . . 182 D8
Gambledon La SO51 . . . . 25 F5
Gamblins La SO32 . . . . 107 F8
Ganger Farm La SO51 . . . . . 28 C2
Ganger Rd SO51 . . . . 28 C2
Gannet Cl Hythe SO45 . . . . . 126 B2
Southampton SO16 . . . . 78 B5
Gannets The PO14 . . . . 179 B8
Gar St SO23 . . . . 215 D5
Garage Cotts GU32 . . . . 40 E4
Garbett Rd SO23 . . . . 11 C8
Garden City SO45 . . . . 125 A6
Garden Cl
Lyndhurst SO43 . . . . 121 E5
New Milton BH25 . . . . 195 A1
South Hayling PO11 . . . . . . 184 F3
Garden Court Cotts
BH22 . . . . 138 D3
Garden Ct
Bournemouth BH1 . . . . 205 D6
Portchester PO16 . . . . 156 D8

Garden Ho 6 BH1 . . . . 205 B3
Garden La
Portsmouth PO5 . . . . 216 B1
2 Winchester SO23 . . . . . . 215 E6
Garden Mews
10 Petersfield GU32 . . . . . . 40 F3
Warsash SO31 . . . . 128 C1
Garden Rd BH24 . . . . 142 F3
Garden Terr 12 PO5 . . . . 182 D2
Garden Wlk BH24 . . . . 165 E7
Garden-La BH24 . . . . 139 E3
Gardeners Cotts BH24 . . . . . 141 A4
Gardeners La SO51 . . . . 52 A4
Gardenia Dr PO15 . . . . 129 E3
Gardens Cres BH14 . . . . 214 B8
Gardens Ct 5 BH15 . . . . 202 E3
Gardens Rd BH14 . . . . 214 B8
Gardens The
Fareham PO16 . . . . 131 C3
Hambledon PO7 . . . . 86 C3
Havant PO9 . . . . 136 B1
Gardiner Cl SO40 . . . . 102 A2
Gardiners Cnr SO51 . . . . 28 D6
Gardner Ct BH23 . . . . 206 E8
Gardner Rd
Christchurch BH23 . . . . 206 E8
Ringwood BH24 . . . . 141 B6
Titchfield PO14 . . . . 153 F7
Gardner Way SO50 . . . . 55 B8
Garendon Ct SP6 . . . . 69 E2
Garfield Ave BH1 . . . . 205 D5
Garfield Cl SO32 . . . . 83 C8
Garfield Rd
Bishop's Waltham SO32 . . . . 83 C8
Netley SO31 . . . . 127 A6
Portsmouth PO2 . . . . 182 D8
Southampton SO19 . . . . 103 F7
Garland Ave PO10 . . . . 136 F3
Garland Ct 5 PO12 . . . . 181 B6
Garland Rd BH15 . . . . 202 D4
Garland Way SO40 . . . . 100 B8
Garnett Cl PO14 . . . . 154 C4
Garnier Pk PO17 . . . . 108 A4
Garnier Rd SO23 . . . . 215 E3
Garnier St PO1 . . . . 216 D3
Garnock Rd SO19 . . . . 103 D2
Garratt Cl SO30 . . . . 81 D2
Garrett Cl SO19 . . . . 104 A1
Garrick Gdns SO19 . . . . 104 B2
Garrick Ho 4 PO2 . . . . 157 F4
Garrison Hill SO32 . . . . 61 B2
Garrow Dr SO41 . . . . 197 E5
Garsdale Cl BH11 . . . . 189 A6
Garsons Rd PO10 . . . . 161 D8
Garston Cl GU32 . . . . 63 D8
Garstons Cl PO14 . . . . 153 F8
Garstons Rd PO14 . . . . 153 F8
Garth Cl BH24 . . . . 139 D4
Garth Rd BH9 . . . . 190 A1
Garth The SO45 . . . . 125 F2
Garth View SO19 . . . . 103 D3
Gashouse Hill SO31 . . . . 127 C5
Gaston Gdns SO51 . . . . 52 F8
Gatcombe SO31 . . . . 127 C7
Gatcombe Ave PO3 . . . . 158 A2
Gatcombe Dr PO2 . . . . 157 F3
Gatcombe Gdns
Fareham PO14 . . . . 154 B8
West End SO18 . . . . 80 A2
Gatcombe Park Prim Sch
PO2 . . . . 157 F4
Gate House Rd PO16 . . . . . . 156 A7
Gatehouse The
11 Southampton SO18 . . . . . 103 E8
West End SO30 . . . . 80 C2
Gatekeeper Cl 7 SO23 . . . . 11 C8
Gateway The BH14 . . . . 203 F4
Gatwick Cl SO16 . . . . 78 A4
Gaulter Cl PO9 . . . . 136 A3
Gavan St SO19 . . . . 104 D5
Gawn Pl PO12 . . . . 181 D3
Gaydon Rise BH11 . . . . 188 E4
Gaylyn Way PO14 . . . . 154 B8
Gaza Ave SO42 . . . . 175 C6
Gaza Ho PO15 . . . . 130 D3
Gazelle Cl PO13 . . . . 180 D5
Gazing La SO51 . . . . 50 E3
Gazings The SO51 . . . . 50 D4
Geddes Way SO41 . . . . 41 C4
Gemini Cl SO16 . . . . 77 F4
General Johnson Ct 4
SO22 . . . . 215 A4
Geneva Ave BH6 . . . . 206 D5
Genoa Cl SO41 . . . . 197 D2
Genoa Ho PO14 . . . . 157 A7
Gento Cl SO30 . . . . 105 E6
Geoffrey Ave PO7 . . . . 134 B2
Geoffrey Cres PO16 . . . . 157 E4
George Byng Way PO2 . . . . . 182 C8
George Ct PO5 . . . . 182 D2
George Ct The 16 PO1 . . . . . 182 A3
George Curl Way SO18 . . . . . 79 F6
George Eyston Dr SO41 . . . . 197 F6
George Mews The BH24 . . . . 140 F7
George Rd SO41 . . . . 197 A5
George Rdbt The BH15 . . . . . 202 C3
George St Eastleigh SO50 . . . 56 B3
Gosport PO12 . . . . 181 C6
Portsmouth PO1,PO2 . . . . . . 182 F7
George Wright Cl SO50 . . . . 55 F2
Georges Mews BH24 . . . . . . 186 D7
Georgia Cl Havant PO9 . . . . . 135 E3
Lee-on-t-S PO13 . . . . 179 F4
Georgian Cl BH24 . . . . 141 A8
Georgian Way BH10 . . . . . . 189 F4
Georgina Cl Poole BH12 . . . . 204 C8
Totton SO40 . . . . 76 B1

Georgina Talbot Ho
BH12 . . . . 204 B8
Gerald Rd BH3 . . . . 205 A6
Gerard Cres SO19 . . . . 104 D6
Gerard Ho 8 PO2 . . . . 157 E4
Germaine Cl BH23 . . . . 208 F8
Gervis Cres BH14 . . . . 203 A4
Gervis Pl BH1 . . . . 204 F3
Gervis Rd BH1 . . . . 205 B3
Gibbs Cl SO45 . . . . 150 A8
Gibbs Rd SO14 . . . . 102 F5
Giblet Ore PO14 . . . . 179 A6
Gibraltar Cl PO15 . . . . 130 D2
Gibraltar Rd
Fareham PO14 . . . . 154 F6
Portsmouth PO4 . . . . 183 D3
Gibson Cl
Lee-on-t-S PO13 . . . . 179 F4
Whiteley PO15 . . . . 129 E5
Gibson Rd BH17 . . . . 202 E7
Giddylake PO11 . . . . 163 D6
Gifford Cl PO15 . . . . 130 E3
Gilbert Cl Alderholt SP6 . . . . 93 B6
Gosport PO13 . . . . 180 D8
Lymington SO41 . . . . 197 D2
Gilbert Mead PO11 . . . . 184 E4
Gilbert Rd BH8 . . . . 205 D6
Gilbert Way PO7 . . . . 134 E5
Gilbury Cl SO18 . . . . 79 F4
Gilchrist Gdns SO31 . . . . 152 C9
Giles Cl Fareham PO16 . . . . . 131 B3
Gosport PO12 . . . . 181 A7
Hedge End SO30 . . . . 81 D1
Giles La SP5 . . . . 50 A4
Gilkicker Rd PO12 . . . . 181 C2
Gillam Rd BH10 . . . . 189 D5
Gillcrest PO14 . . . . 129 C4
Gillett Rd BH12 . . . . 204 B6
Gillies The 6 PO16 . . . . 131 A1
Gillingham Cl
Bournemouth BH9 . . . . 190 C4
Kings Worthy SO23 . . . . 2 C7
Gillingham Rd SO41 . . . . 211 D4
Gillion Ct 2 BH23 . . . . 207 E6
Gilpin Cl Poole BH12 . . . . . . 204 B8
Southampton SO19 . . . . 104 E5
Gilpin Hill SO41 . . . . 172 B2
Gilpins Folly SO41 . . . . 172 A3
Gins La SO42 . . . . 176 E1
Girton Cl PO14 . . . . 129 C1
Gisors Rd PO4 . . . . 183 B4
Gisham Gdns PO7 . . . . 134 C3
Gladdis Rd BH11 . . . . 188 F3
Glade The
Blackfield SO45 . . . . 177 E7
Chandler's Ford SO53 . . . . . 30 F1
Christchurch BH23 . . . . 191 E1
Fareham PO15 . . . . 130 D4
Gosport Sch SO30 . . . . 189 D1
South Hayling PO11 . . . . . . 185 C1
Waterlooville PO7 . . . . 135 A8
Gladelands Cl BH18 . . . . 186 E4
Gladelands Pk BH22 . . . . . . 165 F7
Glades The SO31 . . . . 129 A4
Gladstone Cl BH23 . . . . 207 D6
Gladstone Gdns PO16 . . . . . 156 C7
Gladstone Pl 11 PO2 . . . . . . 182 D8
Gladstone Rd
Bournemouth BH7 . . . . 205 F5
Gosport PO12 . . . . 181 A8
Poole BH12 . . . . 203 C5
Southampton SO19 . . . . 104 B5
Gladstone Rd E BH7 . . . . . . 205 F5
Gladstone Rd W BH1 . . . . . . 205 E5
Gladys Ave
Portsmouth PO2 . . . . 157 D2
Waterlooville PO8 . . . . 112 A4
Glamis Ave BH10 . . . . 189 E5
Glamis Ct PO14 . . . . 179 C8
Glamorgan Rd PO8 . . . . 88 B3
Glasford Way PO4 . . . . 183 B3
Glasslaw Rd SO18 . . . . 104 A8
Glasspool PO7 . . . . 110 E5
Gleadowe Ave BH23 . . . . . . 207 A6
Glebe Cl PO11 . . . . 184 E5
Glebe Cnr PO17 . . . . 108 B3
Glebe Ct Botley SO30 . . . . . . 106 A8
Fair Oak SO50 . . . . 57 D2
Portsmouth PO4 . . . . 183 B2
Glebe Dr PO13 . . . . 155 C1
Glebe La SP5 . . . . 49 D4
Glebe Mdw SP5 . . . . 4 A2
Glebe Park Ave PO9 . . . . . . 135 A1
Glebe Rd Buriton GU31 . . . . . 65 D5
Southampton SO14 . . . . 103 A3
Glebe The PO14 . . . . 179 C6
Glebefield Gdns 1 PO4 . . . . 183 B2
Glebefields 6 SO41 . . . . . . 211 D5
Glen Cl BH25 . . . . 209 D8
Glen Dale PO9 . . . . 113 C1
Glen Eyre Cl SO16 . . . . 79 A4
Glen Eyre Dr SO16 . . . . 79 A5
Glen Eyre Hall SO16 . . . . 79 A5
Glen Eyre Rd SO16 . . . . 78 F5
Glen Eyre Way SO16 . . . . . . 79 A4
Glen Fern Rd BH1 . . . . 205 A3
Glen Ho PO12 . . . . 180 F3
Glen Park Mobile Home Pk
SP5 . . . . 57 B8
Glen Rd
Bournemouth BH5 . . . . 205 D4
Poole BH14 . . . . 203 B4
Sarisbury SO31 . . . . 128 F6
Southampton SO19 . . . . 103 D2

Glen Spey BH25 . . . . 195 D2
Glen The Gosport PO13 . . . . . 155 E1
Poole BH12 . . . . 203 D6
Poole,Canford Cliffs BH13 . . 214 E8
Glenair Ave BH14 . . . . 203 A3
Glenair Cres BH14 . . . . 203 A3
Glenair Rd BH14 . . . . 203 A3
Glenavon BH25 . . . . 195 C2
Glenavon Rd BH23 . . . . 193 F1
Glenbrook Wlk PO14 . . . . . . 154 C8
Glencarron Way 3 SO16 . . . 78 E3
Glencoe Rd
Bournemouth BH7 . . . . 205 F7
Poole BH12 . . . . 203 D5
Portsmouth PO1 . . . . 182 F7
Glencoyne Gdns SO16 . . . . . 77 F2
Glenda Cl SO31 . . . . 152 D10
Glendale
Locks Heath SO31 . . . . 129 B2
Swanmore SO32 . . . . 84 B4
Glendale Ave BH22 . . . . 165 E6
Glendale Cl
Christchurch BH23 . . . . 191 D3
Wimborne Minst BH21 . . . . . 163 C5
Glendale Ct BH23 . . . . 191 D3
Glendale Rd BH6 . . . . 207 A4
Glendeep Cl SO23 . . . . 2 B6
Glendon Ave BH10 . . . . 189 C6
Glendowan Rd SO53 . . . . . . 55 A7
Glendrive BH6 . . . . 209 C8
Gleneagles
Christchurch BH23 . . . . 206 F6
Poole BH13 . . . . 204 B2
Gleneagles Ave PO14 . . . . . 203 D2
Gleneagles Cl BH22 . . . . 165 F6
Gleneagles Dr PO7 . . . . 112 B2
Glenelg PO15 . . . . 130 F2
Glenesha Gdns PO15 . . . . . 130 D2
Glenferness Ave BH4 . . . . . . 204 D5
Glenfield Ave SO18 . . . . 103 F7
Glenfield Cres SO18 . . . . . . 103 F7
Glenfield Way SO18 . . . . 103 F7
Glengariff Rd BH14 . . . . 203 D2
Glengarry BH25 . . . . 195 C2
Glengarry Way PO13 . . . . . . 208 C6
Glenhurst Sch PO9 . . . . 136 A1
Glenives Cl BH24 . . . . 140 A4
Glenlea Cl SO30 . . . . 80 D1
Glenlea Dr SO30 . . . . 80 D1
Glenleigh Ave 6 PO6 . . . . . 157 F7
Glenleigh Ct 5 PO6 . . . . . . 157 F7
Glenleigh Pk PO9 . . . . 136 B2
Glenmeadows Dr BH10 . . . . 189 B5
Glenmoor Cl BH10 . . . . 189 D1
Glenmoor Rd
Bournemouth BH9 . . . . 204 E8
Ferndown BH22 . . . . 165 C4
Glenmoor Sch BH10 . . . . . . 189 D1
Glenmore Cl SO17 . . . . 103 A8
Glenmore Gdns PO8 . . . . . . 111 C2
Glenmount Dr BH14 . . . . 203 B4
Glenn Rd SO30 . . . . 80 D2
Glenny Cl PO13 . . . . 180 A6
Glenroyd Gdns BH6 . . . . 206 E4
Glenside
Barton on S BH23,BH25 . . . 209 B7
Hythe SO45 . . . . 125 F3
Glenside Ave SO19 . . . . 104 D3
Glenthorne Cl PO14 . . . . 179 D6
Glenthorne Mdw GU32 . . . . . 38 E1
Glenthorne Rd PO3 . . . . 158 A1
Glenville Cl BH23 . . . . 194 B2
Glenville Gdns BH10 . . . . . . 189 C2
Glenville Rd
Bournemouth BH10 . . . . 189 C2
Walkford BH23 . . . . 194 B2
Glenwood Cl SO30 . . . . 79 A5
Glenwood Cl BH22 . . . . 138 E2
Glenwood Gdns PO8 . . . . . . 111 F3
Glenwood La BH22 . . . . 138 E2
Glenwood Rd
Breach PO10 . . . . 137 E1
Verwood BH31 . . . . 114 F5
Glenwood Rise SO53 . . . . . . 138 E2
Glenwood Way BH22 . . . . . . 138 E2
Glidden Cl PO1 . . . . 216 C3
Glidden La PO7 . . . . 86 E3
Glissons PO3 . . . . 165 A2
Globe La BH15 . . . . 202 C2
Gloster Ct PO15 . . . . 129 C5
Gloucester Cl GU32 . . . . 40 D3
Gloucester Ct 3 GU32 . . . . . 40 F4
Gloucester Ho 1 PO2 . . . . . 181 C5
Gloucester Mews PO15 . . . . 216 B2
Gloucester Pl PO5 . . . . 216 B2
Gloucester Rd
Bournemouth BH7 . . . . 205 F5
Poole BH12 . . . . 203 E5
Portsmouth PO5 . . . . 182 A6
Waterlooville PO7 . . . . 134 F6
Gloucester Sq 23 SO14 . . . . 103 A3
Gloucester Terr PO5 . . . . 216 B1
Gloucester View PO5 . . . . . . 216 B2
Glyn Dr PO14 . . . . 179 C7
Glyn Jones Cl SO45 . . . . 150 F2
Glyn Way PO14 . . . . 179 C7
Glynville Cl BH21 . . . . 164 A7
Glynville Ct BH21 . . . . 164 A7
Glynville Rd BH21 . . . . 164 A7
Goathorn Cl BH16 . . . . 201 D4
Goathouse La PO17 . . . . 109 B4
Goddard Cl SO51 . . . . 50 E3
Godfrey Olson Ho SO50 . . . . 54 D3
Godfrey Pink Way SO32 . . . . 83 D7
Godiva Lawn PO4 . . . . 183 C3

Godmanston Cl BH17 . . . . . . 188 A1
Godshill Cl BH8 . . . . 190 D3
Godson Ho 9 SO23 . . . . 215 E6
Godwin Cl
Emsworth PO10 . . . . 136 A3
Winchester SO22 . . . . 1 C3
Godwin Cres PO8 . . . . 88 C3
Godwins Field SO21 . . . . . . 31 F8
Godwit Cl PO12 . . . . 181 B9
Godwit Rd PO4 . . . . 158 E7
Gofton Ave PO6 . . . . 158 B7
Gogg's La SP5 . . . . 47 F6
Gold Mead Cl 5 SO41 . . . . . 197 E2
Gold Oak SP6 . . . . 91 F7
Gold St PO5 . . . . 216 A1
Goldcrest Cl
Fareham PO16 . . . . 155 E8
Horndean PO8 . . . . 112 A7
Goldcrest Gdns SO16 . . . . . . 78 A5
Goldcrest La SO40 . . . . 100 C7
Golden Cres SO41 . . . . 196 D5
Golden Ct
Waterlooville PO7 . . . . 134 E7
West End SO30 . . . . 80 F3
Golden Gates BH13 . . . . 214 B3
Golden Gr SO14 . . . . 103 B5
Golden Hind Pk SO45 . . . . . 125 F2
Golden Sands BH13 . . . . . . 214 B3
Goldenleas Ct BH11 . . . . 188 D3
Goldenleas Dr BH11 . . . . . . 188 D3
Goldfinch Cl BH25 . . . . 194 F2
Goldfinch Rd PO13 . . . . 179 F4
Goldfinch Rd BH17 . . . . 201 E8
Goldsmith Ave PO4 . . . . 182 F4
Goldsmith Cl SO40 . . . . 100 D7
Goldsmith Inf Sch PO4 . . . . 182 E4
Goldsmith Rd SO50 . . . . 55 F1
Goldwire Dr SO53 . . . . 54 F5
Golf Course Rd SO16 . . . . . . 78 E6
Golf Links Rd
Broadstone BH18 . . . . 187 B5
Ferndown BH22 . . . . 165 E4
Goliath Rd BH15 . . . . 201 D2
Gomer Ct PO12 . . . . 180 E3
Gomer Inf Sch PO12 . . . . . . 180 E3
Gomer Jun Sch PO12 . . . . . 180 E3
Gomer La PO12 . . . . 180 E3
Good Rd BH12 . . . . 203 C7
Goodacre Dr SO53 . . . . 54 F5
Goodall Ct 15 PO16 . . . . 131 B1
Goodens The SO24 . . . . 14 C5
Goodison Cl SO50 . . . . 57 B1
Goodlands Vale SO30 . . . . . 105 A3
Goodsell Ct PO14 . . . . 179 B7
Goodwin Cl SO16 . . . . 77 D2
Goodwood Cl
Gosport PO12 . . . . 181 B9
Titchfield PO14 . . . . 129 D2
Waterlooville PO8 . . . . 112 B1
Goodwood Ct PO10 . . . . 161 E8
Goodwood Gdns SO40 . . . . . 100 C8
Goodwood Rd
Eastleigh SO50 . . . . 55 E4
Gosport PO12 . . . . 181 B9
Portsmouth PO5 . . . . 216 D1
Gooseberry La PO14 . . . . . . 140 F7
Gordleton Ind Pk SO41 . . . . 196 F5
Gordon Ave
Southampton SO14 . . . . 103 A8
Winchester SO23 . . . . 11 C7
Winchester SO23 . . . . 102 C8
Gordon Cl 1 BH4 . . . . 204 C4
Gordon Mount 3 . . . . 209 B8
Gordon Rd
Bournemouth BH1 . . . . 205 D4
Chandler's Ford SO53 . . . . . 30 D1
Christchurch BH23 . . . . 209 A8
Curdridge SO32 . . . . 83 A1
Emsworth PO10 . . . . 161 B8
Gosport PO12 . . . . 181 A5
Lymington SO41 . . . . 197 C3
Poole BH12 . . . . 204 A8
Portsmouth PO1 . . . . 182 B3
Waterlooville PO7 . . . . 134 F6
Wimborne Minst BH21 . . . . . 163 E4
Gordon Rd S BH12 . . . . 204 A5
Gordon Terr SO19 . . . . 104 A2
Gordon Watson Ho
SO23 . . . . 215 D3
Gordon Way BH23 . . . . 192 D1
Gore Grange BH25 . . . . 194 F2
Gore Rd BH25 . . . . 194 F2
Gore Rd Ind Est BH25 . . . . . 194 F2
Gorey Rd BH12 . . . . 188 D1
Goring Ave PO8 . . . . 112 A6
Goring Field SO22 . . . . 215 A7
Gorleston Rd BH12 . . . . 203 F5
Gorley Cross SP6 . . . . 94 B4
Gorley Ct PO9 . . . . 135 C5
Gorley Lynch SP5 . . . . 94 D4
Gorran Ave PO13 . . . . 155 C1
Gorse Cl
Locks Heath SO31 . . . . 128 F2
New Milton BH25 . . . . 195 D4
St Leonards BH24 . . . . 123 B4
Gorse Down SO21 . . . . 33 B4
Gorse Hill Cl BH15 . . . . 202 E5
Gorse Hill Cres BH15 . . . . . 202 E5
Gorse Hill Rd BH15 . . . . 202 E5

Gorse Knoll Dr BH31 .....114 E7
Gorse La BH16 ....201 D7
Gorse Rd
 Corfe Mullen BH21 ......186 C5
 Petersfield GU31 ....41 C3
Gorsecliff Ct 7 BH5 ....205 D4
Gorsecliff Rd BH10 .....189 D1
Gorsefield Rd BH25 .....195 B4
Gorseland Ct BH22 ......165 E3
Gorselands Rd SO18 .....80 B1
Gorselands Way PO13 ..180 D8
Gorseway PO11 ....184 D3
Gorseway The PO11 ....184 D3
Gort Cres SO19 ....104 B4
Gort Rd
 Bournemouth BH11 ....189 B3
 Poole BH17 ....187 A1
Gosling Cl BH17 ....202 F7
Gosport Ho 20 PO9 ....136 B5
Gosport La SO43 ....122 A4
Gosport Mus* PO12 ....181 D5
Gosport Rd
 Fareham PO16 ....155 B7
 Lee-on-t-S PO13 ....179 F2
 Stubbington PO14 ....179 E7
Gosport Sh Prec 6
 PO12 ....181 D5
Gosport St SO41 ....197 F4
Gough Cres BH17 ......187 B2
Gover Rd SO16 ....101 C8
Goyda Ho PO12 ....180 F6
Grace Ct 15 PO5 ......182 C2
Grace Darling Ho BH15 .202 D1
Grace Dieu Gdns SO31 .104 F1
Grace La SP6 ....70 E8
Gracefields PO15 ......154 B8
Graddidge Way SO40 ..100 D6
Graemar Cotts SO51 ...25 C3
Graemar La SO51 ....25 C2
Grafton Cl
 Bournemouth BH3 ....205 A7
 Christchurch BH23 ....207 D6
 Gosport PO12 ....181 C8
Grafton Gdns
 Lymington SO41 ....197 C1
 Southampton SO16 ....78 C5
Grafton Rd
 Bournemouth BH3 ....205 A6
 Winchester SO23 ....215 D4
Grafton St PO2 ....182 D7
Graham Ct SO19 ....104 B6
Graham Ho 4 SO14 ....103 C6
Graham Norris Bsns Ctr The
 SO45 ....150 E1
Graham Rd
 Gosport PO12 ....181 A8
 Portsmouth PO4 ....182 E3
 Southampton SO14 ......103 B6
 Graham St SO14 ....103 C6
Grainger Gdns SO19 ...104 C3
Grammar School La
 BH21 ....163 B4
Granada Cl PO8 ....112 A4
Granada Rd
 Hedge End SO30 ....105 B6
 Portsmouth PO4 ....182 E1
Granary Mews BH24 ...140 F7
Granary The BH24 .....140 F7
Granby Gr SO17 ....79 B3
Granby Rd BH9 ....190 A4
Grand Ave BH6 ....206 C4
Grand Division Row 1
 PO4 ....183 B3
Grand Par 8 Poole BH15 .202 B1
 Portsmouth PO1 ....182 A3
 South Hayling PO11 .....185 A2
Grange Cl Gosport PO12 .180 F6
 Havant PO9 ....136 B2
 Hordle SO41 ....211 E8
 Southampton SO18 ......79 E4
 Winchester SO23 ....215 C1
Grange Cotts SO30 .....105 E7
Grange Cres PO12 .....180 F6
Grange Ct
 5 Bournemouth BH1 ..205 B3
 Netley SO31 ....127 B7
Grange Dr SO30 ....105 D8
Grange Gdns BH12 .....203 E8
Grange Inf Sch PO13 ..180 C7
Grange Jun Sch PO13 .180 C7
Grange La PO13 ....180 C7
Grange Mews SO51 .....28 C1
Grange Park Mobile Homes
 SO30 ....81 C1
Grange Rd
 Bournemouth BH6 ....206 D3
 Broadstone BH18 ....187 A4
 Christchurch BH23 ......208 B7
 Gosport PO13 ....180 D6
 Hedge End SO30 ....105 C8
 Netley SO31 ....127 B7
 Petersfield GU32 ....40 E2
 Portsmouth PO2 ....157 D1
 2 Southampton SO16 ..78 B1
 St Leonards BH24 ......139 E1
 Winchester SO23 ....215 C1
Grange Road Bsns Ctr
 BH23 ....208 A7
Grange Sch The BH23 ..207 E7
Grange The Hordle SO41 .211 E8
 1 Southampton SO16 ..78 B1
Grangewood Ct BH31 ...57 B2
Grangewood Gdns SO50 .57 B2
Grangewood Hall BH23 .163 D5
Grant Rd PO6 ....158 D8

Grant's Ave BH11 ....205 D6
Grantham Ave SO31 ...127 E3
Grantham Ct 9 SO50 ...56 A2
Grantham Rd
 Bournemouth BH1 ....205 E5
 Eastleigh SO50 ....55 F2
 Southampton SO19 ......103 F6
Grantley Rd 3 BH5 ....205 F4
Grants Cl BH1 ....205 E6
Granville Cl PO9 ....160 A8
Granville Ct SO15 .....102 E7
Granville Pl
 8 Bournemouth BH1 ..204 F3
 Winchester SO23 ....215 F4
Granville Rd
 Bournemouth BH5 ......206 A5
 Poole BH12 ....203 B5
Granville St SO14 .....103 B4
Grasdean Cl **1** SO18 ...80 A1
Grasmere SO50 ....55 F2
Grasmere Cl
 Christchurch BH23 ......191 D3
 West End SO18 ....80 B1
Grasmere Ct SO16 ......77 E2
Grasmere Gdns BH25 ..195 B5
Grasmere Ho 7 PO6 ...133 B1
Grasmere Rd
 Bournemouth BH5 ......206 A4
 Poole BH13 ....214 B3
Grasmere Way PO14 ...154 D4
Grassmere Way PO7 ...112 C1
Grassymead PO14 .....129 C4
Grateley Cl SO19 ......126 F8
Grateley Cres PO9 ....135 C4
Gravel Cl SP5 ....46 E8
Gravel Hill
 Broadstone BH17,BH18,
 BH21 ....187 D5
 Swanmore SO32 ....84 B3
Gravel La BH24 ....140 F8
Gray Cl Locks Heath SO31 .128 F2
 Poole BH17 ....202 F8
Gray's Yd 4 BH15 .....202 C1
Graycot Cl BH10 ....189 D1
Grayland Cl PO11 .....184 E4
Grayling Mead SO51 ....27 F1
Grays Ave SO45 ....126 B3
Grays Cl
 Colden Common SO21 ....56 F8
 Gosport PO12 ....180 E3
 Romsey SO51 ....53 A7
Grays Ct PO1 ....182 A4
Grayshott Cl SO22 ....1 C4
Grayshott Rd
 Gosport PO12 ....180 F4
 Portsmouth PO4 ....182 F4
Grayson Cl PO13 ......180 A6
Great Copse Dr PO9 ...135 E6
Great Elms Cl SO45 ....150 B3
Great Farm Rd SO50 ...55 F3
Great Field Rd SO22 ....1 D3
Great Gays PO14 ....153 F1
Great Hanger GU31 .....41 B3
Great Mead
 Denmead PO7 ....111 A3
 Lyndhurst SO43 ....121 F4
Great Minster St 2
 SO23 ....215 E5
Great Posbrook Cotts
 PO14 ....153 E6
Great Southsea St PO5 .216 B1
Great Well Dr SO51 ....53 A8
Greatbridge Rd SO51 ...27 E1
Greater Horseshoe Way 3
 PO17 ....130 E8
Greatfield Way PO9 ...118 E3
Greatwood Cl SO45 ....126 A2
Greaves Cl BH10 ......189 C3
Grebe Cl
 Broadstone BH17 ....201 E8
 Christchurch BH23 ......208 A6
 Milford on S SO41 ......211 E4
 Portchester PO16 ......155 F8
 Waterlooville PO8 ......118 A6
 Westbourne PO10 ....137 B4
Green Acres BH23 .....207 F7
Green Acres Cl BH24 ..140 D5
Green Bottom BH21 ....164 A7
Green Cl Hythe SO45 ..126 A4
 Kings Worthy SO23 ......2 A5
 Poole BH15 ....202 D1
 Whiteparish SP5 ....24 B4
 Woodlands SO40 ....99 F4
Green Cres PO13 ....155 C1
Green Dr SP6 ....93 B6
Green Hollow Cl PO14 ..130 F4
Green Jacket Cl SO22 ..215 C3
Green La Ampfield SO51 .53 E8
 Barton on S BH25 ....210 B8
 Bishop's Waltham SO32 ..83 D7
 Blackfield SO45 ....177 F8
 Bournemouth BH10 .....189 D3
 Burridge SO31 ....104 F1
 Chilworth SO16 ....78 C5
 Clanfield PO8 ....88 D5
 Denmead PO7 ....110 E4
 Downton SP5 ....46 F8
 Ferndown BH22 ....165 A1
 Fordingbridge SP6 ....69 F2
 Gosport,Alverstoke PO12 .181 A5
 Gosport,Elson PO12 .....181 C9
 Hamble-le-R SO31 ......128 A2
 Hambledon PO7 ....86 B4
 High Cross GU32 ....18 F5
 Locks Heath SO31 ......128 F1

Green La continued
 Lower Swanwick SO31 ..128 D8
 Ossemsley BH25 ....194 E8
 Portsmouth PO3 ....158 A3
 Ringwood BH24 ....141 A7
 Ringwood,Upper Kingston
 BH24 ....141 C4
 Soberton BH7 ....86 C7
 South Hayling PO11 ....184 E3
 Southampton SO16 ......77 E2
 Swanmore SO32 ....84 D7
 Totton SO40 ....76 B4
 Whitsbury SP6 ....69 C7
Green Loaning BH23 ...207 F5
Green Park Cl SO23 ...215 F8
Green Park Rd SO16 ..101 E7
Green Pastures Cvn Site
 SO51 ....75 E4
Green Pk BH1 ....205 D3
Green Pond Cnr 2 PO9 .136 B1
Green Pond La SO51 ....29 C3
Green Rd
 Bournemouth BH9 ......205 A8
 Gosport PO12 ....181 A3
 Poole BH15 ....202 D1
 Portsmouth PO5 ....216 B2
 Stubbington PO14 ......154 C4
Green The Burton BH23 .192 D2
 East Meon GU32 ....38 D1
 Liss GU33 ....20 E5
 Romsey SO51 ....28 C1
 Rowlands Castle PO9 ...113 C2
 Sarisbury SO31 ....128 E6
 Whiteparish SP5 ....24 B4
Green Wlk PO15 ....130 E3
Green's Cl SO50 ....57 A1
Greenacre BH25 ....210 A8
Greenacre Cl BH16 ....201 C6
Greenacre Gdns PO7 ..134 D4
Greenacres
 32 Bournemouth BH4 ..204 C3
 Downton SP5 ....46 D8
Greenacres Cl BH10 ...189 E6
Greenacres Dr SO21 ....31 C3
Greenaway La
 Locks Heath SO31 ......128 E2
 Warsash SO31 ....128 D2
Greenbank Cres SO16 ..78 F5
Greenbanks Cl SO41 ...211 D5
Greenbanks Gdns PO16 .131 D2
Greenclose La BH21 ...163 D4
Greendale Cl
 Chandler's Ford SO53 ....55 E6
 Fareham PO15 ....130 D4
Greendale The PO15 ...130 D4
Greenfield Cres PO8 ...112 C4
Greenfield Gdns BH25 ..210 B8
Greenfield Rd BH15 ....202 E7
Greenfield Rise PO8 ....112 B3
Greenfields Liss GU33 ...21 A4
 1 Poole BH12 ....203 F7
Greenfields Ave SO40 ..76 F1
Greenfields Cl SO40 ....76 F1
Greenfinch Cl
 Broadstone BH17 ....186 F1
 Eastleigh SO50 ....56 F1
Greenfinch Wlk BH24 ..141 C6
Greenhayes BH18 ......187 C2
Greenhays Rise BH21 ..163 C5
Greenhill Ave SO22 ....215 C3
Greenhill Cl
 Wimborne Minst BH21 ..163 D6
 Winchester SO22 ....215 C6
Greenhill La
 Rownhams SO16 ....77 E8
 Winchester SO22 ....163 D6
Greenhill Rd
 Wimborne Minst BH21 ..163 D6
 Winchester SO22 ....215 C6
Greenhill Terr SO22 ...215 C6
Greenidge Ct 8 SO15 ..102 F8
Greenlea Cl PO7 ....134 B2
Greenlea Cres SO16 ....79 D5
Greenlea Rd PO12 .....180 F7
Greenmead Ave SO41 ..196 D1
Greens Cl SO32 ....83 B8
Greens Meade SP5 .....47 D6
Greenside Ct BH25 ....210 B8
Greensleeves Ave BH18 .187 B6
Greensome Dr BH22 ...165 F6
Greenway GU32 ....38 F1
Greenway Cl SO41 .....197 C3
Greenway Cres SO16 ..101 C3
Greenway La GU31 .....65 C6
Greenway Rd PO13 ....181 B7
Greenway The PO10 ...136 F4
Greenways
 Chandler's Ford SO53 ....55 E6
 Christchurch BH23 ......208 E8
 Milford on S SO41 ......211 C5
 Southampton SO32 ......79 D5
 Swanmore SO32 ....84 B5
Greenways Ave BH8 ...190 C3
Greenways Ct 2 BH22 ..165 E3
Greenways Rd SO42 ...146 A1
Greenwich The
 Blackfield SO45 ....177 F8
 24 Southampton SO14 ..103 A3
Greenwood Ave
 Cosham PO6 ....157 C8
 Ferndown BH22 ....165 C6
 Poole BH14 ....214 C7
 Rownhams SO16 ....77 D6
Greenwood Cl
 Eastleigh SO50 ....55 F1
 Fareham PO16 ....131 A4
 Romsey SO51 ....53 A8

Greenwood Copse
 BH24 ....140 A4
Greenwood La SO32 ....82 A4
Greenwood Rd BH9 ....204 E8
Greenwood Way BH24 .140 A4
Greenwoods 8 BH25 ...195 B1
Greetham St PO5 ......216 B3
Gregg Sch The SO18 ...80 A3
Gregory Gdns SO40 ....76 C1
Gregory La SO32 ....82 C5
Gregson Ave PO13 .....155 C4
Gregson Cl PO13 ....155 C3
Grenadier Cl SO30 .....129 B2
Grendon Cl SO16 ....79 B5
Grenehurst Way GU31 ..40 F4
Grenfell Rd BH9 ....189 F3
Grenfield Ct PO10 ......136 F3
Grenville Cl BH24 ......117 D1
Grenville Ct
 Bitterne Pk SO18 ....79 F3
 4 Bournemouth BH4 ..204 C2
 10 Poole BH15 ....202 C2
Grenville Gdns SO45 ...126 A1
Grenville Ho 32 PO12 ..182 A5
Grenville Rd
 Portsmouth PO4 ....216 D1
 Wimborne Minst BH21 ..163 D4
Gresham Rd BH9 ....190 B1
Gresley Gdns SO30 .....81 C2
Greville Gn PO10 ....136 E3
Greville Rd SO15 ....102 D7
Grevillea Ave PO15 ....129 E3
Greycot Cl BH21 ....138 E8
Greyfriars **2** PO5 .....216 B1
Greyfriars Ct PO5 ......216 B1
Greyfriars Rd PO15 ....130 C2
Greyhound Cl SO30 .....81 B3
Greyladyes SO31 ....128 B7
Greys Farm Cl SO24 ....14 B4
Greyshott Ave PO14 ...154 C8
Greystoke Ave BH11 ..188 F5
Greywell Ave SO16 .....78 C4
Greywell Ct SO16 ....78 C4
Greywell Sq PO9 ......135 F5
Griffen Cl SO50 ....56 C2
Griffin Ct
 Southampton SO17 .....103 C8
 Wimborne Minst BH21 ..163 D4
Griffin Ind Pk SO40 ....76 E2
Griffin Wlk PO13 ......180 C6
Griffiths Gdns BH10 ...189 B5
Griffon Cl SO31 ....105 A2
Grigg La SO42 ....146 A1
Grindle Cl PO16 ....132 C1
Gritanwood Rd PO4 ...183 B3
Grosvenor Cl
 Southampton SO17 ......79 C2
 St Leonards BH24 ......139 D5
Grosvenor Ct
 8 Bournemouth BH1 ..205 B3
 2 Bournemouth,Springbourne
 BH1 ....205 C3
 Christchurch BH23 ......209 B8
 Farlington PO6 ....158 F8
 Romsey SO51 ....53 C7
 1 Southampton SO17 ..79 C1
 Stubbington PO14 ......179 D7
 Grosvenor Dr SO23 .....215 E6
Grosvenor Gdns
 Bournemouth BH1 ......205 C4
 Southampton SO17 ......79 C2
 West End SO30 ....104 D8
Grosvenor Ho
 4 Portsmouth PO5 ....216 B1
 12 Southampton SO15 ..102 D6
 4 Southampton BH4 ...204 C3
Grosvenor Lodge 5
 SO17 ....79 C2
Grosvenor Mews
 5 Gosport PO12 ......181 C6
 7 Highfield SO17 ......79 C1
 Lymington SO41 ....197 D5
 2 Southampton SO17 ..79 C1
Grosvenor Pines 13
 BH4 ....204 C3
Grosvenor Rd
 Bournemouth BH4 ......204 C3
 Chandler's Ford SO53 ...30 E1
 Southampton SO17 ......79 C2
Grosvenor Sq SO15 ....102 D6
 Southampton SO17 ......79 C2
Grosvenor Sq SO15 ....102 D6
 Portchester PO16 ......156 C6
Grove Bldgs 7 PO13 ...181 C5
Grove Ct **5** PO9 ......135 F1
Grove Gdns
 Barton on S BH25 ......210 A7
 Southampton SO19 .....104 B2
Grove Ho
 Portsmouth PO6 ....216 B1
 Portsmouth PO6 ....216 C1
Grove La SP5 ....47 F7
Grove Mans 10 BH2 ...204 C3
Grove Mews SO19 .....104 B2
Grove Pastures SO41 ..197 E3
Grove Pl Lymington SO41 .197 F3
 Southampton SO19 .....104 B2
Grove Rd
 Barton on S BH25 ......210 A7
 Bournemouth BH1 ......205 B3
 Compton SO21 ....31 D1
 Cosham PO6 ....158 C7
 Fareham PO16 ....131 B4
 Gosport PO13 ....181 B8
 Havant PO9 ....136 A3
 Lee-on-t-S PO13 ....179 E3
 Lymington SO41 ....197 F3

Grove Rd continued
 Poole BH12 ....203 B6
 Southampton SO15 .....102 C7
 Wimborne Minst BH21 ..163 D4
Grove N PO5 ....216 B1
Grove Rd S PO5 ....216 B1
Grove Road E BH23 ....207 A8
Grove Road W BH23 ...206 F8
Grove St SO14 ....103 B4
Grove The
 Bournemouth BH9 ......189 F3
 Burseldon SO31 ....105 A1
 Christchurch BH23 ......191 E1
 Ferndown BH22 ....165 C4
 Netley SO31 ....127 D7
 Southampton SO19 .....104 B1
 Stubbington PO14 ......179 B7
 Verwood BH31 ....115 A5
 Westbourne PO10 ......137 B3
Grovebury SO31 ....129 A2
Grovelands Rd SO22 .....1 B1
Groveley Bsns Ctr BH23 .207 E6
Groveley Rd
 Bournemouth BH4 ......204 B2
 Christchurch BH23 ......207 E6
Groveley Way SO51 .....28 C1
Grovely Ave BH5 ....205 F3
Groves Down SO51 ......50 E4
Groves La BH25 ....189 A4
Grunelsen Rd PO2 ......157 C2
Guardhouse Rd PO1 ...182 B7
Guardian Ct 25 SO17 ...79 A1
Guardroom Rd PO2 ....157 B1
Gudge Heath La PO15 ..130 D2
Guelders The PO7 .....134 E3
Guernsey Cl SO16 ....77 E3
Guernsey Rd PO12 .....188 D1
Guessens La PO14 .....153 F8
Guest Ave BH12 ....204 A6
Guest Cl BH12 ....204 A6
Guest Rd
 Bishopstoke SO50 ....56 B3
 Upton BH16 ....201 B7
Guild Ho 18 SO14 .....103 A3
Guildford Cl PO10 .....137 E1
Guildford Ct
 2 Bournemouth BH4 ..204 C4
 15 Gosport PO13 ......180 D5
Guildford Dr SO53 ......55 B3
Guildford Rd PO1 ......182 E6
Guildford St **1** SO14 ..103 C5
Guildhall Ct BH15 .....202 B2
Guildhall Mus* BH15 ..202 B2
Guildhall Sq PO1 ......216 B3
Guildhall Wlk PO1 .....216 A3
Guildhill Rd BH6 ......206 A4
Guillemot Cl SO45 .....126 B2
Guillemot Gdns PO13 ..155 B3
Gull Cl PO13 ....155 B2
Gulliver Cl BH14 ......214 C8
Gulliver Cl 1 SO45 .....57 B5
Gulls The SO40 ....101 F2
Gullycroft Mead SO30 .105 B7
Gunners Bldgs PO3 ....157 F4
Gunners Mews SO32 ...83 E8
Gunners Pk SO32 ......83 E7
Gunners Row PO4 .....183 B2
Gunners Way PO12 ....155 F1
Gunstore Rd PO3 ......158 C8
Gunville Cres BH9 .....190 B3
Gunwharf Quays PO1 ..181 F6
Gunwharf Quays (Sh Ctr)
 PO1 ....182 A4
Gunwharf Rd PO1 .....182 A4
Gurjun Cl PO13 ....201 A8
Gurkha Mus The*
 SO23 ....215 D5
Gurnard Rd PO6 ....157 E7
Gurnays Mead SO51 ....50 E3
Gurney Rd
 Corfe Mullen BH21 ......186 C6
 Portsmouth PO4 ....183 B4
 Southampton SO15 .....102 C8
Gussage Rd PO12 .....203 F8
Guttar La PO11 ....160 C1
Guttridge Dro SO51 ....27 B7
Guy's Cl BH24 ....141 B6
Gwatkin Cl PO9 ....135 C3
Gwen-Rhian Ct 4 SO15 .102 F7
Gwenlyn Rd BH16 .....201 C6
Gwessin Terr 6 PO12 ..181 C5
Gwynne Rd PO12 ......203 E5
Gypsy La Ringwood BH24 .141 B8
 Waterlooville PO8 ......111 F5

H

H Ave SO45 ....150 F6
Ha'penny Dell PO7 ....134 E3
Hacken Mews BH21 ....207 D7
Haccups La SO51 ......50 C3
Hack Dr SO21 ....56 F8
Hackett Way 2 PO14 ..155 A6
Hacketts La SO32 ......60 F2
Hackleys La SO51 ......51 B5
Hackworth Gdns SO30 ..81 C2
Hadden Rd BH8 ....205 D8
Haddon Cl PO14 ......130 C1
Haddon Dr SO50 ....56 A5
Haddons Dr BH21 .....139 D7
Hadleigh Gdns SO50 ...56 A5
Hadleigh Rd 3 PO6 ....158 C7
Hadley Field SO45 .....150 B5
Hadley Way BH18 .....186 E6
Hadow Rd BH10 ......189 C3
Hadrian Cl BH22 ......165 D2

Hadrian Way
  Chilworth SO16 ....78 E7
  Corfe Mullen BH21 .....186 E8
Hadrians Cl SO53 ....55 E7
Haflinger Dr PO15 ......129 B8
Haglane Copse SO41 ....197 C2
Hahnemann Rd BH2 ....204 E2
Haig Ave BH13 ....203 E1
Haig Ct 6 PO2 ....157 E3
Haig Rd SO50 ....57 A1
Haileybury Gdns SO30 ..81 C1
Hainault Dr BH11 ....115 A6
Haking Rd BH23 ....207 D7
Halcyon Ct BH15 ....202 C6
Halden Cl 2 SO51 ......28 B1
Hale Ave BH25 ....195 B2
Hale Ct PO1 ....182 E7
Hale Gdns BH25 ....195 B2
Hale La SP6 ....47 B3
Hale Prim Sch SP6 .....47 C3
Hale Rd SP6 ....70 E8
Hale St N PO1 ....216 C4
Hale St S PO1 ....216 C4
Hales Dr SO30 ....105 A5
Halesowen Ho 4 PO5 ...216 A2
Halewood Way BH23 ....206 F8
Half Moon St 1 PO1 ...182 A5
Halfpenny La PO1 ......182 A5
Halfway Rd SO45 ......151 E1
Halifax Cl SO30 ....80 C2
Halifax Rise PO7 ......134 F7
Halifax Way BH23 .....208 B7
Hall Cl SO32 ....83 D8
Hall Ct SO32 ....107 A7
Hall Lands La SO50 ....57 D2
Hall of Aviation (Mus)*
  SO14 ....103 B3
Hall Rd BH11 ....188 F3
Hall Way The SO22 ....1 B5
Hallet Cl SO18 ....80 A2
Hallett Rd PO9 ....136 B2
Halletts Cl PO14 ......179 C8
Halliards The PO16 ....155 B7
Halliday Cl PO12 ......181 B6
Halliday Cres PO4 .....183 C3
Halliday Ho 12 PO4 ....183 B2
Hallowell Ho PO7 ......216 B4
Halls Farm Cl SO22 ....1 E3
Halsey Cl PO12 ....180 F3
Halstead Rd
  Cosham PO6 ....157 D8
  Southampton SO18 ....79 F2
Halstock Cres BH17 ...187 D2
Halter Path BH15 .....201 E3
Halter Rise BH21 .....164 C6
Halterworth Cl SO51 ..53 B7
Halterworth Com Prim Sch
  SO51 ....53 C7
Halterworth La SO51 ..53 C7
Halton Cl BH23 ....193 B8
Haltons Cl SO40 ......76 D1
Halyard Cl PO13 ......180 D7
Halyards SO31 ....128 A4
Ham La Gosport PO12 ..156 A1
  Hampreston BH21 .....164 E3
  Horndean PO8 ....112 A8
  Southbourne PO10 ....161 D7
  Wimborne Minst BH21 .164 C5
Hambert Way SO40 ....100 E5
Hamble Cl SO31 ....128 C1
Hamble Com Sports Coll
  SO31 ....127 E5
Hamble Court Bsns Pk
  SO31 ....127 E3
Hamble Ct
  Chandler's Cford SO53 ..55 D5
  Stubbington PO14 .....179 B8
  3 Waterlooville PO8 ..111 F4
Hamble Ho PO16 ......155 A7
Hamble House Gdns
  SO31 ....128 A2
Hamble La
  Burslom SO31 ....104 F2
  Burslodon SO31 ....127 F8
  Hamble-le-R SO31 ....127 F2
  Waterlooville PO7 ....134 E5
Hamble Manor SO31 ...128 A2
Hamble Pk SO31 ......128 F1
Hamble Prim Sch SO31 .127 E4
Hamble Rd Gosport PO12 127 C3
  Poole BH15 ....203 A6
Hamble Springs SO32 ..83 D7
Hamble Sta SO31 ......127 E5
Hamblecliff Ho SO31 ..127 D3
Hambledon Cl SO22 ....1 D4
Hambledon Gdns BH6 .206 D6
Hambledon Inf Sch PO7 .86 D3
Hambledon La PO7,SO32 ..85 E3
Hambledon Par PO7 ...111 C2
Hambledon Rd
  Bournemouth BH7 .....206 B7
  Bournemouth,West Southbourne
  BH6 ....206 C6
  Clanfield PO8 ....88 B6
  Denmead PO7 ....111 B3
  Hambledon PO7 ....110 D8
  Waterlooville PO7 ....134 E7
Hambleside Ct SO31 ..127 F2
Hambleswood SO30 ...106 A6
Hambleswood Cl SO30 .106 A6
Hamblin Way BH8 ....190 E2
Hambrook Rd 1 PO4 ..181 A7
Hambrook St PO5 .....216 A1
Hamdown Cres SO51 ..51 B2
Hameldon Cl SO16 ....101 E7
Hamfield Dr PO11 ....184 E4
Hamilton Bsns Pk BH23 .194 E2

Hamilton Cl
  Bournemouth BH1 .....205 D5
  Christchurch BH23 ....207 F4
  Hamworthy BH15 ......201 E2
  Langstone PO9 ....159 F8
Hamilton Cres BH15 ..201 E2
Hamilton Ct
  1 Bournemouth BH8 ..205 B5
  Milford on S SO41 ....211 C4
  16 Portsmouth PO5 ...182 C2
  5 Southampton SO17 ..79 A1
  1 Wimborne Minst BH21 163 E5
Hamilton Gr PO13 ....155 B2
Hamilton Ho PO1 .....216 D4
Hamilton Mews
  Bransgore BH23 ......193 B8
  4 Hythe SO45 ....126 B1
  Lymington SO41 ......197 F4
Hamilton Pl SO41 .....197 D3
Hamilton Rd SO45 .....47 A8
Hamilton Rd
  Bishopstoke SO50 .....56 D3
  Bournemouth BH1 ....205 D4
  Corfe Mullen BH21 ...186 E5
  Hamworthy BH15 .....201 E2
  4 Hythe SO45 ....150 B8
  Portchester PO6 ......156 E8
  Portsmouth PO5 ......182 D2
Hamilton Way BH25 ..194 E2
Hamlet Ct SO45 ......151 B3
Hamlet Way PO12 ....156 A1
Hammond Cl PO15 ....129 A1
Hammond Ho 9 PO12 .181 E5
Hammond Ind Pk PO14 179 D6
Hammond Rd PO15 ....130 E2
Hammond's Gn SO40 ..100 C8
Hammonds Cl SO40 ...100 E8
Hammonds La SO40 ...100 E8
Hammonds Way SO40 .100 E8
Hampage Gn PO9 .....135 D7
Hampden La BH6 .....206 B5
Hampshire CE Fst Sch
  BH21 ....164 E3
Hampshire Cl BH23 ...191 F2
Hampshire Corporate Pk
  SO53 ....55 B2
Hampshire Ct
  3 Bournemouth BH2 ..204 F3
  Chandler's Cford SO53 ..55 C3
Hampshire Hatches La
  BH24 ....141 A4
Hampshire Ho 2 PO2 .204 D4
Hampshire St PO1 ....182 E7
Hampshire Terr 1 PO1 216 A2
Hampton Cl
  Blackfield SO45 ......177 E8
  Waterlooville PO7 ....135 A7
Hampton Dr 8 BH2 ...204 D4
Hampton Dr BH24 ....117 B1
Hampton Farm La SO32 .84 A6
Hampton Gdns SO45 ..177 E8
Hampton Gr PO15 ....130 B1
Hampton Hill SO32 ...84 B6
Hampton La
  Blackfield SO45 ......150 E1
  Waterlooville SO22 ...215 A7
Hampton Twrs SO19 ..59 C4
Hamptworth Rd SP5 ..48 D4
Hamtun Cres SO40 ....76 E1
Hamtun Gdns SO40 ...76 E1
Hamtun Rd SO19 .....104 C3
Hamtun St 6 SO14 ...102 F3
Hamwic Ho 3 SO14 ...102 F3
Hamworthy Fst Sch
  BH15 ....201 F1
Hamworthy LODGE
  BH15 ....201 F2
Hamworthy Mid Sch
  BH15 ....201 F1
Hamworthy Sta BH15 .201 D4
Hanbidge Cres PO13 ..155 C4
Hanbidge Wlk PO13 ..155 C4
Hanbury Sq GU31 .....41 A5
Handel Rd SO15 ......102 F5
Handel Terr SO15 ....102 F6
Handford Pl 2 SO15 ..102 F6
Handley Ct BH24 .....140 F7
Handley Lodge 2 BH12 203 F7
Handley Rd PO12 .....180 F6
Handsworth Ho PO5 ..216 C2
Handy Villas 8 SO23 .215 E6
Hanger Way GU31 ....41 A5
Hangers The SO32 ....59 E2
Hanham Ct BH12 .....204 B8
Hanham Rd
  Corfe Mullen BH21 ...186 D5
  Wimborne Minst BH21 .163 C5
Hankinson Rd BH9 ...205 A8
Hanley Rd SO15 ......102 D8
Hanlon Cl BH11 ......189 B4
Hann Rd SO16 ....77 F6
Hannah Gdns PO7 ....134 F8
Hannah Way SO41 ....196 F5
Hannay Rise SO19 ....104 D5
Hannington Pl BH7 ...206 A6
Hannington Rd
  Bournemouth BH7 ....206 A5
  Havant PO9 ....135 D7
Hanns Way SO50 .....56 A2
Hanover Bldgs SO14 ..103 A4
Hanover Cotts SO32 ..36 E3
Hanover Ct Hythe SO45 .126 A4
  7 Portsmouth PO1 ...182 A4
Hanover Ho
  Gosport PO13 ....155 B5
  Poole BH15 ....202 D3

Hanover Ho continued
  7 Southampton SO14 .103 A4
  Totton SO40 ....101 A8
Hanover Lodge SO23 ..215 D6
Hanover St PO1 ....182 A5
Hanoverian Way PO15 ..129 C7
Hanway Rd PO1,PO2 ..182 E7
Harbeck Rd BH8 ......190 C3
Harborough Rd SO15 ..102 F6
Harbour Cl
  Marchwood SO40 .....102 C2
  Poole BH15 ....214 D6
Harbour Cres BH23 ...207 E5
Harbour Ct
  Barton on Sea BH25 ..209 E7
  Christchurch BH23 ...207 E6
  8 Emsworth PO10 ....160 F8
  Poole BH13 ....214 E6
Harbour Hill Cres BH15 202 E5
Harbour Hill Rd BH15 .202 E5
Harbour Hospl The
  BH15 ....202 D3
Harbour Lights BH15 ..202 E4
Harbour Par SO15 ....102 F4
Harbour Prospect BH14 .214 C8
Harbour Rd
  Bournemouth BH6 .....207 A3
  Gosport PO1 ....181 E6
  South Hayling PO11 ..184 C4
Harbour Side Cvn & Camping
  Site PO3 ....158 D1
Harbour Twr 10 PO12 ..181 C5
Harbour View 8 BH21 .156 C6
Harbour View Cl BH14 .203 A5
Harbour View Ct BH14 .203 A5
Harbour View Rd BH14 .203 A5
Harbour Watch BH14 ..214 C7
Harbour Way
  Emsworth PO10 ......161 A8
  Portsmouth PO2 ......157 C2
Harbourgate Bsns Pk
  PO6 ....157 B8
Harbourne Gdns SO18 ..80 B2
Harbourside PO9 .....159 F6
Harbridge Ct
  Havant PO9 ....135 D7
  Verwood BH24 ....115 F6
Harbridge Dro BH24 ..137 A5
Harbridge Dro BH24 ..137 E3
Harcourt Cl PO8 .....112 A4
Harcourt Mews 6 BH5 .206 A5
Harcourt Rd
  Bournemouth BH5 ....206 A5
  Fareham PO14 ....154 B7
  Gosport PO12 ....181 A6
  Portsmouth PO3 ......103 E8
  Waterlooville PO7 ....135 A7
Hard The PO1 ....182 A5
Harding La SO50 .....57 B3
Harding Rd PO12 .....180 F6
Hardley Ind Est SO45 ..150 B6
Hardley La SO45 .....150 B4
Hardley Rdbt SO45 ...150 B6
Hardley Sch & 6th Form
  SO45 ....150 B7
Hardman Ct 2 PO3 ...158 B4
Hardwick Rd SO53 ....55 D6
Hardwicke Cl SO16 ..77 F2
Hardwicke Way SO31 ..127 E3
Hardy Ave GU31 .....41 A5
Hardy Cl
  Locks Heath SO31 ....129 B4
  New Milton BH25 ....194 F3
  Southampton SO15 ..102 B6
  West Moors BH22 ....138 C1
Hardy Cres BH21 .....163 D4
Hardy Dr SO45 ....126 B1
Hardy Rd Eastleigh SO50 .56 A1
  Farlington PO6 ......158 C7
  Poole BH14 ....203 D4
  West Moors BH22 ....138 F1
Harebell Cl PO15 ....130 C3
Harefield Ct SO51 ...53 B8
Harefield Ind Est SO18 ..79 D8
Harefield Jun Sch SO18 104 B8
Harefield Rd SO17 ...79 C3
Hares Gn BH7 ....206 A8
Harestock Cl SO22 ...1 C1
Harestock Cnr SO22 ..1 D3
Harestock Prim Sch SO22 .1 D3
Harestock Rd
  Havant PO9 ....135 D3
  Winchester SO22 .....1 C2
Harewood Ave PO7 ...206 A6
Harewood Cl SO50 ...56 A5
Harewood Cres BH7 ..205 F8
Harewood Gdns BH7 ..205 F7
Harewood Gn SO41 ..212 A4
Harewood Pl BH7 ....206 B6
Harford Cl SO41 .....197 C1
Harford Rd BH12 .....203 C8
Harewood Dr BH15 ..201 E4
Harland Cres BH15 ..78 D1
Harland Rd BH6 ......207 B6
Harlaxton Cl SO50 ...55 F5
Harlech Dr SO53 .....55 B2
Harlequin Gr PO15 ..130 F1
Harleston Rd PO9 ...135 F1
Harlestone Villas 5
  BH21 ....163 D4
Harley Ct SO31 ......128 C1
Harley Wlk PO1 .....216 C4
Harlyn Rd SO16 .....77 F1
Harman Rd PO13 ....155 C3

Harness Cl BH21 .....164 B6
Harold Cl SO40 ......100 C6
Harold Rd
  Portsmouth PO4 .....182 E3
  South Hayling PO11 ..185 B2
  Southampton SO15 ..102 C7
  Stubbington PO14 ...179 D8
  Westbourne PO10 ...137 B4
Harold Terr PO10 ....136 F1
Harper Way 15 PO16 .131 B1
Harpway La BH23 ....192 C6
Harraby Gn BH18 ....187 A3
Harrage The SO51 ...52 F7
Harrier Cl Horndean PO8 .112 A7
  Lee-on-t-S PO13 .....78 B6
Harrier Dr BH21 .....163 D2
Harrier Gn SO45 .....150 B6
Harrier Mews SO31 ..127 E3
Harrier Way
  Hardley SO45 ....150 B6
  Petersfield GU31 .....41 C2
Harriers Cl BH24 ....140 E6
Harriet Cl PO14 .....179 B7
Harrington Ct BH23 ..208 F7
Harris Ave SO30 .....105 C8
Harris La PO8 ....89 E5
Harris Rd PO13 ......155 C3
Harris Way
  New Milton BH25 ....195 B6
  North Baddesley SO52 ..54 A4
Harrison Cl BH23 ....203 C3
Harrison Ho 8 PO2 ..157 D2
Harrison Prim Sch
  PO16 ....131 B2
Harrison Rd
  Fareham PO16 ....131 B2
  Southampton SO17 ..79 C3
Harrison Way BH22 ..138 E3
Harrison's Cut SO14 ..103 A4
Harrow Cl BH23 .....193 B7
Harrow Down SO22 ..215 B2
Harrow La GU32 .....40 F6
Harrow Rd
  Bransgore BH23 .....193 B6
  Portsmouth PO5 .....216 D2
Harrowgate La PO7,PO8 ..87 B1
Harry Barrow Cl 1
  BH24 ....141 A6
Harry Law Hall PO1 ..216 B3
Hart Cl BH25 ....194 F4
Hart Ct SO19 ....103 F3
Hart Hill SO45 ....126 C2
Hart Plain Ave
  Waterlooville PO8 ....111 D3
  Waterlooville PO8 ....111 F2
Hart Plain Jun & Inf Schs
  PO7,PO8 ....111 E2
Hartford Ho PO1 .....216 A1
Harthill Dro SP5 .....47 E6
Harting Cl PO8 ......88 D4
Harting Down GU31 ..41 B4
Harting Rd BH6 .....206 D7
Hartington Rd
  Gosport PO12 ....180 F6
  Portsmouth PO1 .....137 D1
Hartland's Rd PO16 ..131 B1
Hartley Ave SO17 ....79 B3
Hartley Cl
  Bishopstoke SO50 ...57 A1
  Hythe SO45 ....126 A1
Hartley Ct 5 SO17 ...103 A8
Hartley Gr SO16 .....79 A4
Hartley Rd
  Bishopstoke SO50 ...57 A1
  Portsmouth PO1 .....157 E3
Hartley Wlk 1 SO45 ..126 A1
Hartnell Ct BH21 ....186 D5
Harts Farm Way PO9 ..159 C8
Harts Way SO41 .....196 D1
Hartsbourne Dr BH7 ..206 B8
Hartsgrove Ave SO45 .150 E1
Hartsgrove Cl SO45 ..150 E1
Hartwell Rd PO3 .....158 C4
Hartwood Gdns PO8 ..111 E2
Harvard Cl BH13 .....180 A5
Harvest Cl SO22 .....215 B2
Harvest La SP5 ......22 C8
Harvest Rd
  Chandler's Cford SO53 ..54 F7
  Denmead PO7 ....110 E4
Harvester Dr PO16 ...131 B5
Harvester Way SO41 ..197 D6
Harvestgate Wlk PO9 .135 C6
Harvesting La GU32 ..64 C5
Harvey Brown Ho PO11 .185 A5
Harvey Cres SO31 ...128 F2
Harvey Ct SO45 .....150 E2
Harvey Gdns SO45 ..126 B3
Harvey Rd Eastleigh SO50 .56 A2
  Poole BH14 ....183 B2
Harvey Rd
  Bishopstoke SO50 ...56 B2
  Bournemouth BH5 ...206 A5
  Oakley BH21 ....187 E8
Harwell Rd PO13 ....202 D3
Harwich Rd PO6 .....133 D1
Harwood Cl
  Gosport PO13 ....155 C4
  Totton SO40 ....100 D8
Harwood Ct SO15 ...194 F3
Harwood Pl SO23 ....2 C8
Harwood Rd PO12 ...155 C4
Haselbury Rd SO40 ..100 F1
Haselfoot Gdns SO30 ..104 E7
Haselworth Dr PO12 ..181 B2

Haselworth Prim Sch
  PO12 ....181 B4
Haskells Cl SO43 ....121 E4
Haskells Rd BH12 ...203 B7
Haslar Cres PO7 .....111 D2
Haslar Marina PO11 ..181 E4
Haslar Rd
  Gosport,Clayhall PO12 ..181 D3
  Gosport,Newtown PO12 .181 E5
Haslar Terr PO11 ....181 D3
Haslegrave Ho 6 PO2 .182 D8
Haslemere Ave BH23 .209 A8
Haslemere Gdns PO11 .185 F2
Haslemere Pl BH23 ..209 A8
Haslemere Rd
  Breach PO10 ....137 D2
  Portsmouth PO4 .....182 F3
Hasler Rd BH17 .....187 B2
Haslop Rd PO12 .....164 A7
Hassocks The 7 PO2 .135 A7
Hastings Ave PO12 ..180 F8
Hastings Ho 3 PO2 ..157 C2
Hastings Rd
  Bournemouth BH8 ...190 F2
  Poole BH17 ....187 B2
Hatch Cl PO9 ....135 C7
Hatch La GU33 ......21 C4
Hatch Mead SO30 ...80 C2
Hatch Pond Rd BH17 ..202 C8
Hatchers La SO21 ...33 A5
Hatchet Cl SP6 ......47 D3
Hatchet La SO42 ....175 D8
Hatchley La SO32 ...58 B5
Hatfield Ct BH25 ....194 E3
Hatfield Gdns BH7 ..206 B8
Hatfield Rd 1 PO4 ..183 A3
Hathaway Cl SO50 ..56 A4
Hathaway Gdns PO7 ..112 B1
Hathaway Rd BH6 ...206 D4
Hatherden Ave BH14 .202 F5
Hatherell Cl SO30 ...80 D1
Hatherley Cres PO16 .156 B8
Hatherley Dr PO16 ..156 B8
Hatherley Mans 4
  SO15 ....102 C7
Hatherley Rd
  Portsmouth PO6 .....133 A1
  Winchester SO22 ....215 D7
Hatley Rd SO18 .....104 B8
Hatt La SO51 ....5 E2
Havant Bsns Ctr PO9 .159 D8
Havant Coll PO9 ....135 E2
Havant Education PRU
  PO8 ....111 F2
Havant Farm Cl PO9 .135 F3
Havant Mus & Arts Ctr*
  PO9 ....136 A1
Havant Rd Cosham PO6 .157 F8
  Emsworth PO10 .....160 D8
  Farlington PO6 ......158 D8
  Horndean PO8 ......112 D6
  North Hayling PO11 ..160 A5
  North Hayling,Fleet PO11 .185 A7
  Portsmouth PO2 .....157 C1
  Stoke PO11 ....159 F2
Havant Ret Pk PO9 ..135 E5
Havant St PO1 ....182 A5
Havant War Meml Hospl
  PO9 ....135 E2
Havant-by-pass PO9 ..160 A8
Havelock Cl SO23 ...128 C1
Havelock Mans PO5 ..216 D2
Havelock Rd Poole BH12 .204 A5
  Portsmouth PO5 .....216 C2
  Southampton SO14 ..128 C1
  Warsash SO31 ....102 F5
Havelock Way BH23 ..193 D2
Haven Cotts BH14 ...208 A4
Haven Cres PO14 ...153 F1
Haven Ct
  4 Milford on S SO41 .211 C4
  Poole BH13 ....214 B3
  Poole BH23 ....195 B2
Haven Rd
  Corfe Mullen BH21 ..186 C6
  Poole BH13 ....214 E7
  South Hayling PO11 ..185 E1
Haven The Eastleigh SO50 .56 B5
  Gosport PO12 ....181 B3
  Locks Heath SO31 ...183 B5
  Southampton SO19 ..103 E4
Havendale SO30 .....105 D5
Havenhurst BH13 ....214 E6
Havenstone Way SO18 ..79 E4
Haverstock Rd BH9 ..190 B2
Haviland Mews BH7 ..205 F5
Haviland Rd
  Bournemouth BH7 ...205 F5
  Ferndown BH21 .....165 A7
Haviland Rd E BH7 ..205 F5
Haviland Rd W BH1 ..205 F5
Havisham Rd PO2 ...182 C7
Havre Twrs SO19 ....126 E8
Hawden Rd BH11 ....189 A1
Haweswater Cl SO16 .77 F1
Hawk Cl BH23 ....78 B6
Hawk Ct
  Stubbington PO14 ...179 B7
  Wimborne Minst BH21 .164 A7
Hawkchurch Gdns BH17 .187 E2
Hawke St PO1 ....182 A5
Hawker Cl BH21 .....163 F1
Hawkers Cl SO40 ....76 E1

Hawkeswood Rd SO18 103 C7
Hawkewood Ave PO7 111 D2
Hawkhill SO45 125 C3
Hawkhurst CI SO19 104 A1
Hawkins CI BH24 117 C1
Hawkins Ct SO40 101 F3
Hawkins Rd
  Gosport PO13 155 D2
  Poole BH12 188 F1
Hawkley CI PO9 135 E6
Hawkley Gn SO19 126 F8
Hawkley Rd GU33 20 C5
Hawks Mead GU33 20 E5
Hawkwell PO16 185 F8
Hawkwood Rd BH1,BH5 205 F4
Haworth CI BH23 192 A1
Hawstead Gn PO9 135 D6
Hawthorn CI
  Colden Common SO21 57 A8
  Fair Oak SO50 57 C2
  Hedge End SO30 105 D6
  New Milton BH25 195 C4
  Portchester PO16 132 B1
Hawthorn Cres PO6 158 B6
Hawthorn Ct GU31 41 C3
Hawthorn Dr
  Broadstone BH17 186 F1
  Sway SO41 172 B2
Hawthorn La SO31 128 E5
Hawthorn Rd
  Bournemouth BH9 204 F8
  Burton BH23 192 E4
  Denmead PO7 110 E4
  Horndean PO8 88 C2
  Hythe SO45 125 F3
  Southampton SO17 79 A2
Hawthorn Wlk 8 PO13 179 F3
Hawthorne Gr PO11 185 B4
Hawthorns The SO40 100 D8
Hawthorns The
  Bishop's Waltham SO32 83 A8
  Christchurch BH23 207 F6
  Eastleigh SO50 55 E1
  Marchwood SO40 102 A1
Hawthorns The Urban
  Wildlife Ctr* SO15 102 F8
Hayburn Rd SO16 77 D2
Haydens Ct SO41 197 F4
Haydn CI SO23 2 B8
Haydock CI SO40 100 C8
Haydock Mews PO7 112 B1
Haydon Rd BH13 204 B1
Hayes Ave BH7 205 E6
Hayes CI Fareham PO15 130 D3
  Wimborne Minst BH21 164 A4
Hayes La BH21 164 B5
Hayes Mead SO45 150 B6
Hayeswood Fst Sch
  BH21 164 B6
Hayeswood Rd BH21 164 A6
Hayle Rd SO18 80 B2
Hayley CI SO45 149 F8
Hayling Ave PO3 183 B7
Hayling Billy Bsns Ctr
  PO11 184 D4
Hayling CI
  Fareham PO14 154 D8
  Gosport PO12 181 C9
Hayling Sch The PO11 185 A5
Haymoor Mid Sch BH17 187 E1
Haymoor Rd BH15 203 A7
Haynes Ave BH15 202 D4
Haynes Way SO45 125 E1
Hays Cotts GU32 40 D7
Haysoms CI BH25 195 B1
Hayter Gdns SO51 53 A8
Hayters Way SP6 92 A3
Hayton Ct 2 SO40 100 F7
Hayward Bsns Ctr PO9 136 B3
Hayward CI SO40 100 D7
Hayward Cres BH31 114 E5
Hayward Ct SO45 150 C4
Hayward Way BH31 114 E5
Haywards Ct 11 PO1 182 A4
Haywards Farm CI
  BH31 114 E5
Haywards La BH31 186 C7
Hazel CI Alderholt SP6 93 A5
  Christchurch BH23 193 C1
  Colden Common SO21 57 A8
Hazel Ct
  Bournemouth BH9 190 C4
  1 New Milton BH25 195 B1
  Portsmouth PO4 182 F4
  Winchester SO22 215 A8
Hazel Dr BH22 165 D8
Hazel Farm Rd SO40 100 C7
Hazel Gr
  Locks Heath SO31 129 B2
  Winchester SO22 215 B3
  Woodlands SO40 99 F3
Hazel Rd Clanfield PO8 88 C5
  Lymington SO41 197 A4
  Southampton SO19 103 D3
Hazel Wlk GU31 40 F1
Hazel Wood Inf Sch
  SO40 100 C2
Hazelbank CI GU31 41 B4
Hazeldale Villas SO45 126 A5
Hazeldean Ct PO9 113 B1
Hazeldean Rd PO9 113 B1
Hazeldown Rd SO16 77 E5
Hazeleigh Ave SO19 103 E2
Hazeley Farm Cotts SO21 32 E7

Hazeley Gn PO9 136 B5
Hazeley Rd SO21 32 D6
Hazelgrove PO8 88 C5
Hazelholt Dr PO9 135 D3
Hazell Ave BH10 189 B2
Hazelton CI BH7 206 A8
Hazelwood PO14 154 B5
Hazelwood Ave
  Hazel PO9 135 B3
  New Milton BH25 194 F4
Hazelwood Dr BH31 115 B4
Hazelwood Rd SO18 80 A1
Hazlebury Rd BH17 202 A7
Hazlemere Dr PO14 139 E3
Hazleton Way PO8 112 B4
Head Down GU31 41 B3
Head's La BH10 189 E5
Headbourne Worthy Ho
  SO23 2 B5
Headinglea 9 BH13 204 B3
Headland BH31 129 A4
Headlands Bsns Pk
  BH24 117 A2
Headlands The SP5 46 E7
Headless Cross BH10 189 D5
Headley CI PO13 179 F3
Headon View GU32 37 C5
Headswell Ave BH10 189 E5
Headswell Cres BH10 189 E4
Headswell Gdns BH10 189 E4
Heanor CI BH10 189 C2
Hearne Gdns SO32 84 A1
Hearts of Oak Mews
  SO41 197 D4
Heath Ave BH15 202 D6
Heath CI Fair Oak SO50 57 D1
  Horndean PO8 112 B7
  Wimborne Minst BH21 164 B7
Heath Ct GU31 40 F2
Heath Farm CI BH22 165 C3
Heath Farm Rd BH22 165 C3
Heath Farm Way BH22 165 C3
Heath House CI SO30 105 B4
Heath House GU31 127 D7
Heath House Gdns
  SO30 105 B4
Heath House La SO30 105 B4
Heath La SO42 175 C2
Heath Lawns PO15 130 D1
Heath Lodge GU31 40 F2
Heath Rd Hordle SO41 195 F3
  Locks Heath SO31 129 A3
  North Baddesley SO52 54 A3
  Petersfield GU31 41 A3
  Soberton SO32 85 A1
  Southampton SO19 104 A5
  St Leonards BH24 139 D4
  Walkford BH23 194 B1
Heath Rd E GU31 41 B2
Heath Rd N GU31 128 F3
Heath Rd S GU31 128 F3
Heath Rd W GU31 41 A2
Heath The PO7 111 A4
Heathcote Ct 2 BH7 205 F4
Heathcote Pt SO21 30 B7
Heathcote Rd
  Bournemouth BH5,BH7 205 F4
  Chandler's Ford SO53 55 D6
  Portsmouth PO2 157 F1
Heather Chase SO50 57 A2
Heather CI
  Bournemouth BH8 190 D4
  Corfe Mullen BH21 186 E6
  Gosport PO13 155 B2
  Hordle SO41 196 A3
  St Leonards BH24 139 E3
  Totton SO40 100 E7
  Walkford BH23 194 A2
  Waterlooville PO7 134 F6
Heather Ct SO18 104 D7
Heather Dr BH22 165 D7
Heather Gdns PO15 130 D3
Heather Lo 1 BH25 195 A3
Heather Rd
  Blackfield SO45 150 F2
  Bournemouth BH10 189 D3
  Petersfield GU31 41 C3
Heather View Rd BH12 203 F7
Heather Way BH22 165 D7
Heatherbank BH4 204 C3
Heatherbrae Gdns SO52 53 F4
Heatherbrae La BH16 201 B6
Heatherdeane Rd SO17 79 A2
Heatherdell BH16 201 B6
Heatherdene Rd SO53 30 E1
Heatherdown Rd BH22 139 A1
Heatherdown Way
  BH22 139 A1
Heatherfield GU31 65 D5
Heatherlands Fst Sch
  BH12 203 E5
Heatherlands Rd SO16 78 F8
Heatherlands Rise
  BH12 203 D5
Heatherlea Rd BH6 206 D4
Heatherley Ct PO5 216 C1
Heatherstone Ave
  Dibden Purlieu SO45 125 F1
  Hythe SO45 126 A1
Heatherton Mews PO10 136 F2
Heatherwood SO52 53 F5
Heathfield SO45 125 C3
Heathfield Ave
  Fareham PO15 130 D1
  Poole BH12 204 A8

Heathfield CI
  Chandler's Ford SO53 30 C2
  Southampton SO19 104 B3
Heathfield Cvn Pk BH23 169 F2
Heathfield Ho BH23 169 F1
Heathfield Jun Sch
  SO19 104 C3
Heathfield Rd
  Chandler's Ford SO53 30 C2
  Petersfield GU31 41 C3
  Portsmouth PO2 157 D1
  Southampton SO19 104 B3
  West Moors BH22 139 A1
Heathfield Specl Sch
  PO14 154 C8
Heathfield Way BH22 138 F1
Heathlands SO32 107 E7
Heathlands Ave BH22 165 D2
Heathlands CI
  Burton BH23 192 C3
  Chandler's Ford SO53 55 D8
  Verwood BH31 115 A6
Heathlands Ct SO45 149 E8
Heathlands Prim Sch
  BH11 189 A3
Heathlands Rd SO53 55 C8
Heathwood Ave BH25 209 E8
Heathwood Rd BH9 204 E8
Heathy CI BH25 209 F8
Heaton Rd
  Bournemouth BH10 189 B2
  Gosport PO12 181 A8
Heavytree Rd BH14 203 B4
Hebrides CI PO14 179 B8
Heckfield CI 10 PO9 136 B5
Heckford La BH23 202 D3
Heckford Rd
  Corfe Mullen BH21 186 C5
  Poole BH15 202 D4
Hector CI PO7 134 E2
Hector Rd PO14 155 A6
Hedera Rd SO31 128 F3
Hedge End Bsns Ctr
  SO30 81 B1
Hedge End Ret Pk SO30 105 A7
Hedge End Sta SO30 81 D3
Hedge End Trad Pk SO30 81 A1
Hedge End Wlk 7 PO9 136 B6
Hedgerley PO25 210 B8
Hedgerow CI SO16 77 E7
Hedgerow Dr SO18 80 B1
Hedgerow Gdns PO10 136 F3
Hedley CI SO45 150 F1
Hedley Gdns SO30 81 B2
Heidelberg Rd PO4 182 F4
Heights App BH16 201 C9
Heights Rd BH16 201 C8
Heights The
  Fareham PO16 131 D2
  Hedge End SO30 105 A6
Heinz Burt CI SO50 55 F3
Helena Rd PO4 182 F2
Helford Gdns PO18 80 B2
Helic Ho 2 BH21 163 C5
Helge Rd PO4 183 A3
Helm CI PO13 155 D8
Helsby CI PO14 154 E8
Helsted CI PO12 180 E4
Helston Dr PO10 112 A4
Helston Rd PO6 132 F1
Helvellyn Rd SO16 77 E5
Helyar Rd BH8 190 F2
Hemdean Gdns SO30 80 D1
Hemlock Rd PO8 111 E4
Hemlock Way SO53 54 F5
Hemming CI SO40 100 E6
Hemmingway Gdns
  PO15 129 C8
Hempland La GU34 17 C4
Hempsted Rd PO6 133 B1
Hemsley Wlk PO8 112 A4
Henbest CI BH21 164 C5
Henbury CI
  Corfe Mullen BH21 186 D6
  Poole BH17 188 A2
Henbury Rise BH21 186 D6
Henbury View Fst Sch
  BH21 186 C6
Henbury View Rd BH21 186 D6
Henchard CI PO22 165 C2
Henderson Pk PO4 183 C3
Henderson Rd PO4 183 C3
Hendford Gdns BH10 189 D3
Hendford Rd BH10 189 D3
Hendy CI PO5 216 B1
Henery St 10 PO12 181 C5
Hengist Cvn Pk BH6 207 B4
Hengist Rd BH1 205 D4
Hengistbury Head Nature
  Reserve* BH6 207 C2
Hengistbury Head Nature
  Trail* BH6 207 C3
Hengistbury Rd
  Barton on S BH25 209 E8
  Bournemouth BH6 207 A3
Henley Ct SO41 211 E3
Henley Gdns
  Bournemouth BH7 206 C4
  Fareham PO15 130 D4
Henley Rd PO4 182 F3
Henning's Park Rd
  BH15 202 E5
Henry Beaufort Sch SO22 1 E3
Henry CI SO45 150 B8
Henry Cort Com Coll The
  PO15 130 C3
Henry Cort Dr PO15 130 C3
Henry Player Ave PO12 181 D7

Henry Rd
  Bishopstoke SO50 56 D4
  Southampton SO15 102 C7
Henry St SO15 102 F6
Henstead Ct 9 SO15 102 F6
Henstead Rd SO15 102 F6
Hensting La SO50 32 E2
Henty Rd SO16 102 B8
Henville CI PO13 180 F5
Henville Rd 4 BH8 205 C5
Henwood Down GU31 41 A3
Hepworth CI SO19 104 C2
Herald Ind Est SO30 81 B1
Herald Rd SO30 81 B1
Herbert Ave BH12 203 D7
Herbert Ct BH12 203 D7
Herbert Hospl BH4 204 B2
Herbert Rd Gosport PO12 180 F5
  New Milton BH25 195 B3
  Poole BH4 204 B2
  Portsmouth PO4 182 E2
  Redlynch SP5 47 D6
Herbert St PO1 182 E2
Herbert Walker Ave
  Southampton SO15 102 C4
  Southampton SO15 102 E3
Herberton Rd BH6 206 C5
Hercules Rd BH15 201 D3
Hercules St PO12 182 D8
Hereford Ct
  10 Gosport PO13 180 C6
  Portsmouth PO5 216 C1
Hereford Rd PO5 216 C1
Hereward Ct SO51 53 B7
Heritage Bsns Pk PO12 155 F1
Heritage Ct BH13 214 F7
Heritage Gdns PO16 156 A2
Heritage Way PO12 155 F1
Heritage Way,Priddy's Hard
  PO12 181 C9
Herm Rd BH12 188 D1
Hermes Ct 8 PO12 181 C9
Hermes Rd PO13 179 D4
Hermitage CI
  Bishop's Waltham SO32 83 A8
  Havant PO9 135 E5
  Three Legged Cross BH21 138 E8
Hermitage Gdns PO7 134 F8
Hermitage Rd BH14 203 A5
Hermitage The BH14 203 A5
Hern La SP6 94 B6
Herne Jun Sch GU31 41 A4
Herne Rd Cosham PO6 157 E8
  Petersfield GU31 41 A3
Heron Court Rd BH3,
  BH9 205 A7
Heron Dr BH21 164 A8
Heron Ho 1 PO5 182 E2
Heron La SO41 27 D6
Heron Quay PO10 161 A7
Heron Sq PO10 55 E2
Heron Way PO13 155 B3
Herons CI PO14 154 C4
Herons Rd PO11 185 B5
Heronswood SO40 76 D2
Herrick CI SO19 104 D4
Herriot Ho PO8 112 A2
Herriott CI PO8 112 A5
Herstone CI BH17 187 F1
Hertford CI SP6 69 F3
Hertford Ct 6 BH23 209 B7
Hertford Pt PO1 182 D7
Hertsfield PO14 154 D8
Hesketh CI BH24 140 A5
Hesketh Rd 4 SO15 102 C5
Hestan CI BH23 191 D4
Hester Rd PO4 183 B4
Hestia CI SO51 53 B8
Heston Way BH22 138 D3
Heston Wlk PO12 180 E3
Hewett CI PO14 153 F7
Hewett Ho PO14 153 F7
Hewett Rd
  Portsmouth PO2 157 E2
  Titchfield PO14 153 F7
Hewetts Rise SO31 152 C10
Hewitt CI PO12 181 A8
Hewitt Rd BH15 201 E4
Hewitt's Rd SO15 102 A3
Heyes Dr SO19 104 C3
Heysham Rd
  Broadstone BH18 187 D4
  Southampton SO15 102 B7
Heyshott Gdns PO8 88 D4
Heyshott Rd PO4 182 F4
Heytesbury Rd BH6 206 D4
Heyward Rd PO4 182 E4
Heywood Gdns PO9 135 D6
Heywood Gn SO19 104 C3
Hibberd Ct BH10 189 D1
Hibberd Way BH10 189 C1
Hibberds Field BH21 91 A7
Hibbs CI SO31 126 E8
Hickes CI BH11 188 E6
Hickory CI BH16 201 A8
Hickory Dr SO22 214 B3
Hickory Gdns SO30 80 D3
High Barn Cotts SO32 36 F2
High Brow PO4 165 D5
High Cross GU32 18 D1
High Cross La GU32 18 C1
High Dr PO4 183 A3
High Dr PO13 155 C1
High Firs Gdns SO51 53 C7
High Firs Rd Romsey SO51 53 C7
  Southampton SO19 104 C5

High Howe CI BH11 188 E4
High Howe Gdns BH11 188 E4
High Howe La BH11 188 D4
High Lawn Way PO9 135 F5
High Marryats BH25 210 A7
High Mdw SO19 104 C6
High Mead
  Fareham PO15 130 E4
  Ferndown BH22 165 A2
High Mead La PO22 165 A1
High Oaks CI SO31 129 A3
High Oaks Gdns BH11 188 E4
High Park Rd BH18 186 E4
High Pines BH23 208 D7
High Point SO18 103 E8
High Rd Bishopstone SP5 22 B8
  Southampton SO16 79 D4
High Ridge Cres BH25 195 C2
High St Beaulieu SO42 148 F1
  Bishop's Waltham SO32 83 C7
  Botley SO30 106 A7
  Buriton GU31 65 D5
  Bursledon SO31 128 B7
  Christchurch BH23 207 B6
  Cosham PO6 157 F7
  Damerham SP6 68 C5
  Downton SP5 47 D8
  Droxford SO32 61 B1
  East Meon GU32 38 E1
  Eastleigh SO50 56 A2
  Emsworth PO10 160 F8
  Fareham PO16 131 C1
  Fordingbridge SP6 69 F1
  Gosport PO12 181 D5
  Hamble-le-R SO31 128 A2
  Hambledon PO7 86 D3
  Hythe SO45 126 A5
  Lee-on-t-S PO13 179 E2
  Lymington SO41 197 E4
  Lyndhurst SO43 121 F5
  Meonstoke SO32 61 C4
  Milford on S SO41 211 D4
  Petersfield GU32 40 F3
  Poole BH15 202 C2
  Portsmouth PO1 182 A3
  Ringwood BH24 140 F7
  Shedfield SO32 107 F7
  Soberton SO32 85 B4
  10 Southampton SO14 103 A3
  Southwick PO17 132 F6
  St Leonards BH24 139 F8
  Titchfield PO14 153 F8
  Totton SO40 101 A7
  Twyford SO21 32 A5
  Twyford,Northfields SO21 32 A7
  West End SO30 80 D1
  West Meon GU32 37 C5
  Wimborne Minst BH21 163 B4
  West Moors BH22 138 A8
  Winchester SO23 215 E5
  Winchester SO23 215 E5
  Wonston SP6 70 E7
High St N BH15 202 D3
High Trees Fair Oak SO50 57 F4
  Waterlooville PO7 134 F8
High Trees CI SO22 214 C8
High Trees Wlk BH22 188 C8
High View Ho PO16 132 C1
High View Way SO18 103 F8
High Walls PO16 131 C1
High Wlk PO15 130 E3
Highbank Ave PO7 134 C3
Highbank Rd BH22 89 F1
Highbridge Rd
  Colden Common,Highbridge
  SO50 56 D7
  Colden Common,Twyford
  SO21 31 F2
  Poole BH14 203 C3
Highbury Bldgs PO6 157 A6
Highbury CI Fair Oak SO50 57 C1
  New Milton BH25 195 B2
Highbury Coll PO6 158 A6
Highbury Gr
  Cosham PO6 158 A6
  Portsmouth PO6 157 F6
Highbury Prim Sch PO6 158 A6
Highbury St 6 PO1 182 A4
Highbury Way PO6 157 F6
Highclere Ave PO9 135 E4
Highclere Rd SO16 78 D3
Highclere Way SO53 55 B3
Highcliff Ave SO14 103 A8
Highcliffe Castle* BH23 208 B3
Highcliffe Cnr BH23 209 B8
Highcliffe Dr SO50 56 A7
Highcliffe Rd
  Christchurch BH23 208 C7
  Gosport PO12 180 F4
  Winchester SO23 215 F4
Highcliffe St Mark's Prim
  Sch BH23 193 F1
Highcroft Ind Est PO8 112 C8
Highcroft La PO8 112 C7
Highcrown Mews SO17 79 A2
Highcrown St SO17 79 A2
Higher Blandford Rd
  BH18,BH21 186 F6
Higher Merley La BH21 186 E8
Highfield
  Lymington SO41 197 D3
  Twyford SO21 32 A5
Highfield Ave
  Fareham PO14 154 A8

Highfield Ave *continued*
Lymington SO41 . . . . .197 C3
Ringwood BH24 . . . . .141 A8
Southampton SO17 . . . . .79 F3
Twyford SO21 . . . . .32 A5
Waterlooville PO7 . . . . .111 F1
Highfield Campus (Univ of Southampton) SO17 . . . . . .79 A3
Highfield CE Prim Sch (Inf) SO17 . . . . .79 B2
Highfield CE Prim Sch (Jun) SO17 . . . . .79 A2
Highfield Cl
Chandler's Ford SO53 . . . . .55 E6
Corfe Mullen BH21 . . . . .186 E5
Southampton SO17 . . . . .79 A2
Sway SO41 . . . . .172 B2
Waterlooville PO7 . . . . .111 F1
Highfield Cres SO17 . . . . .79 B2
Highfield Ct SO32 . . . . .83 B8
Highfield Dr BH24 . . . . .141 A8
Highfield Gdns Liss GU33 . . . .21 B4
Sway SO41 . . . . .172 B2
Highfield Hall SO17 . . . . .79 A2
Highfield Ho 3 BH14 . . . . . . .203 B4
Highfield La Redlynch SP5 . . .47 D5
Southampton SO17 . . . . .79 A2
Highfield Lodge 3 SO17 . . . . .79 A2
Highfield Par PO7 . . . . .112 A1
Highfield Rd
Bournemouth BH9 . . . . .189 E2
Chandler's Ford SO53 . . . . .55 E6
Corfe Mullen BH21 . . . . .186 E5
Gosport PO12 . . . . .180 F6
Lymington SO41 . . . . .197 C3
Petersfield GU32 . . . . .40 F4
Portsmouth PO1 . . . . .216 C3
Ringwood BH24 . . . . .141 A8
Southampton SO17 . . . . .79 A2
West Moors BH22 . . . . .138 E4
Highfield Terr 1 SO22 . . . . .215 D5
Highfields SO31 . . . . .128 F1
Highgate Rd PO13 . . . . .158 C4
Highgrove Cl SO40 . . . . .100 D5
Highgrove Ind Pk PO3 . . . . .158 B3
Highgrove Rd PO3 . . . . .183 B8
Highland Ave BH21 . . . . .194 B1
Highland Cl PO10 . . . . .160 E8
Highland Rd
Emsworth PO10 . . . . .136 E1
Poole BH14 . . . . .203 B5
Portsmouth PO4 . . . . .183 A3
Wimborne Minst BH21 . . . . . .163 D6
Highland St 4 PO4 . . . . .183 A2
Highland Terr PO4 . . . . .182 F3
Highland View Cl BH21 . . . . .163 D5
Highlands Cl Hythe SO45 . . .126 A2
North Baddesley SO52 . . . . . . .53 E5
Highlands Cres BH10 . . . . . .189 C4
Highlands Ho SO19 . . . . .103 D3
Highlands Rd
Barton on S BH25 . . . . .210 A8
Fareham PO15,PO16 . . . . .130 D3
Farlington PO6 . . . . .158 D8
Highlands Way
Hythe SO45 . . . . .125 F2
Whiteparish SP5 . . . . .24 B4
Highmoor Cl
Corfe Mullen BH21 . . . . .186 D5
Poole BH14 . . . . .203 B3
Highmoor Rd
Bournemouth BH11 . . . . .189 A1
Corfe Mullen BH21 . . . . .186 D5
Poole BH14 . . . . .203 B3
Highmount Cl SO23 . . . . .11 C7
Highnam Gdns SO31 . . . . . . .128 F4
Hightown Gdns BH24 . . . . . .141 C6
Hightown Hill BH24 . . . . . . .141 F7
Hightown Ind Est BH24 . . . .141 B6
Hightown Prim Sch SO19 . . . . .104 E4
Hightown Rd
Ringwood,Hightown BH24 . . . .141 C6
Ringwood,Moortown BH24 . . .141 A6
Hightown Twrs SO19 . . . . . .104 E4
Hightrees Ave BH8 . . . . .190 F1
Highview Cl BH23 . . . . .191 E3
Highview Gdns BH12 . . . . . .203 C7
Highways Rd SO21 . . . . .31 C5
Highwood Cl SP6 . . . . .92 D6
Highwood La
North Baddesley SO51 . . . . . . .53 D7
Ringwood BH24 . . . . .117 E3
Highwood Lawn PO9 . . . . . .135 D7
Highwood Rd
Brockenhurst SO42 . . . . .172 E8
Gosport PO13 . . . . .180 C7
Poole BH14 . . . . .203 E4
Higworth Cvn Site PO11 . . .184 F5
Higworth La PO11 . . . . .184 F5
Hilary Ave PO6 . . . . .158 A7
Hilary Ct PO13 . . . . .180 D6
Hilary Rd BH17 . . . . .187 C1
Hilda Cl 1 SO15 . . . . .102 F7
Hilda Gdns PO7 . . . . .111 A4
Hilda Pl 3 SO14 . . . . .103 C5
Hilda Rd BH12 . . . . .203 E7
Hilden Ct PO11 . . . . .184 E3
Hilden Way SO22 . . . . .1 B5
Hiley Rd BH15 . . . . .202 C6
Hill Brow Cl PO9 . . . . .113 B1
Hill Brow Rd GU33 . . . . .21 B2
Hill Cl Bransgore BH23 . . . . .193 A8
Fair Oak SO50 . . . . .57 C5
Hill Close Est SP6 . . . . .70 E8
Hill Croft PO15 . . . . .129 E3
Hill Dr PO15 . . . . .130 D3
Hill Farm Rd SO15 . . . . .102 E6

Hill Grove La SO32 . . . . .84 C5
Hill Head Rd PO14 . . . . .179 A6
Hill House Sch SO41 . . . . . .173 D1
Hill Houses La SO24 . . . . . . .14 B6
Hill La Bransgore BH23 . . . . .193 A8
Burton BH23 . . . . .192 F2
Colden Common SO21 . . . . . . .31 F1
Southampton SO15 . . . . .78 E2
Hill Park Rd
Fareham PO15 . . . . .130 D4
Gosport PO12 . . . . .180 F6
Hill Pl SO31 . . . . .128 B8
Hill Rd PO16 . . . . .132 D1
Hill Rise Meonstoke SO32 . . .61 C5
Twyford SO21 . . . . .32 A5
Hill St Poole BH15 . . . . .202 C2
Totton SO40 . . . . .76 C5
Hill Terr Fair Oak SO50 . . . . .57 C5
Wimborne Minst BH21 . . . . . .164 A2
Hill View GU32 . . . . .38 D1
Hill View Cvn Pk SO50 . . . . .57 B5
Hill View Prim Sch BH10 . . . . .189 E3
Hill View Rd
Braishfield SO51 . . . . .28 C6
Ferndown BH22 . . . . .165 C7
Michelmersh SO51 . . . . .27 C8
Porchester PO16 . . . . .132 D1
Hill Way BH24 . . . . .139 F5
Hill Wlk PO15 . . . . .130 D3
Hillary Cl Fareham PO16 . . .130 F2
Lyndhurst SO43 . . . . .122 A3
Hillary Rd BH23 . . . . .207 E8
Hillborough Cres 2 PO5 . . . . .216 C1
Hillborough Ct 1 PO5 . . . . .216 C1
Hillburne Com Fst & Mid Schs BH17 . . . . .187 B2
Hillburne Rd BH17 . . . . .187 A2
Hillbrow Cl PO15 . . . . .130 D3
Hillbrow Rd BH6 . . . . .206 B6
Hillbury Pk SP6 . . . . .93 B5
Hillbury Rd SP6 . . . . .93 B5
Hillcrest Ave
Chandler's Ford SO53 . . . . .55 E6
Ferndown BH22 . . . . .165 C8
Hillcrest Cl
Bournemouth BH9 . . . . .190 A3
North Baddesley SO52 . . . . . . .53 F5
Hillcrest Dr SO53 . . . . .55 D6
Hillcrest Gdns SO32 . . . . . . .83 E4
Hillcrest Hospl BH10 . . . . . .189 E1
Hillcrest Rd
Bournemouth BH9 . . . . .190 A3
Corfe Mullen BH21 . . . . .186 C5
Poole BH12 . . . . .203 A5
Hillcroft SP5 . . . . .47 D6
Hillcroft Cl SO41 . . . . .197 E4
Hilldene Way SO30 . . . . .80 E1
Hilditch SO41 . . . . .197 D6
Hilldown Rd SO17 . . . . .79 B2
Hilldowns Ave PO2 . . . . .157 C2
Hiller Wlk 2 PO13 . . . . .179 F3
Hillgrove Rd SO18 . . . . .79 F3
Hillier Way SO23 . . . . .215 E8
Hillman Rd BH14 . . . . .203 D5
Hillmead Gdns PO9 . . . . . . .135 B2
Hillmeadow BH31 . . . . .115 A4
Hillsea Mkt PO2 . . . . .157 E5
Hillside Curdridge SO32 . . . .106 F8
Littleton SO22 . . . . .1 D7
Hillside Ave Romsey SO51 . . .53 A7
Southampton SO18 . . . . .79 E1
Waterlooville PO7 . . . . .134 B2
Hillside Cl
Chandler's Ford SO53 . . . . .55 D6
Horndean PO8 . . . . .88 C3
West Dean SP5 . . . . .3 D2
Winchester SO22 . . . . .215 A8
Hillside Cotts SO33 . . . . .21 B2
Hillside Cres PO6 . . . . .132 F1
Hillside Dr BH23 . . . . .191 F4
Hillside Fst Sch BH31 . . . . .114 F7
Hillside Gdns PO7 . . . . .186 C4
Hillside Ind Est PO8 . . . . .112 C8
Hillside Ind Est PO8 . . . . .112 C8
Hillside Mews BH31 . . . . . . .186 C4
Hillside Rd
Corfe Mullen BH21 . . . . .186 C5
Lymington SO41 . . . . .197 C3
Poole BH12 . . . . .188 F1
Verwood BH31 . . . . .114 F7
Winchester SO22 . . . . .215 A7
Woodlands Common BH21 . . .114 A6
Hillside Wlk BH21 . . . . .164 A8
Hillsley Rd PO6 . . . . .132 F2
Hillson Dr PO15 . . . . .130 D3
Hillson Ho PO15 . . . . .130 D3
Hillsons Rd SO30 . . . . .106 B8
Hilltop SO22 . . . . .1 C5
Hilltop Cl PO12 . . . . .165 B7
Hilltop Cres PO6 . . . . .134 C2
Hilltop Dr SO19 . . . . .104 D4
Hilltop Gdns PO8 . . . . .88 E2
Hilltop Rd
Corfe Mullen BH21 . . . . .186 E5
Ferndown BH22 . . . . .165 B7
Portsmouth PO6 . . . . .133 A2
Hillview PO8 . . . . .112 C5
Hillview Rd
Bournemouth BH10 . . . . .189 D3
Hythe SO45 . . . . .125 F3
Hillway The
Chandler's Ford SO53 . . . . .55 D7
Portchester PO16 . . . . .156 C8
Hilly Cl SO21 . . . . .33 B4
Hillyfields SO18 . . . . .104 C8
Hilsea Cres PO2 . . . . .157 E5
Hilsea Mkt PO2 . . . . .157 E5

Hilsea Sta PO3 . . . . .158 A4
Hiltingbury Cl SO53 . . . . . . .30 D1
Hiltingbury Ct 4 SO53 . . . . .30 B1
Hiltingbury Inf Sch SO53 . .30 C1
Hiltingbury Jun Sch SO53 . . . . .30 C1
Hiltingbury Rd
Chandler's Ford SO53 . . . . .30 D1
3 Havant PO9 . . . . .136 A5
Hiltom Rd BH24 . . . . .141 B7
Hilton Cl BH15 . . . . .203 A6
Hilton Rd Gosport PO12 . . . .181 C4
Hedge End SO30 . . . . .105 C7
New Milton BH25 . . . . .195 B4
Hinchliffe Cl BH15 . . . . .201 F2
Hinchliffe Rd BH15 . . . . .201 F2
Hinkler Cl SO19 . . . . .104 D4
Hinkler Rd SO19 . . . . .104 E5
Hinton Admiral Mews BH23 . . . . .193 C2
Hinton Admiral Sta BH23 . . . . .193 C2
Hinton Ampner Ho* SO24 .14 E3
Hinton Cl PO9 . . . . .135 C4
Hinton Cres SO19 . . . . .104 E4
Hinton Fields SO23 . . . . .2 D3
Hinton Hill SO24 . . . . .14 F4
Hinton Ho 3 PO7 . . . . .134 E8
Hinton House Dr SO23 . . . . . .2 C6
Hinton Manor La PO8 . . . . . .87 F2
Hinton Rd BH1 . . . . .204 F3
Hinton Wood Ave BH23 . . . .193 A8
Hintonwood La BH23 . . . . . .193 E2
Hipley Rd PO9 . . . . .136 A3
Hirst Rd SO45 . . . . .126 B3
Hispano Ave PO15 . . . . .129 C7
Hither Gn PO10 . . . . .137 E2
Hitherwood Cl 9 PO7 . . . . .112 B1
Hive Gdns BH13 . . . . .214 D6
Hives Way SO41 . . . . .197 D6
**HMS Victory* PO1 . . . . .181 F7
**HMS Warrior* PO1 . . . . . . .181 F6
Hoad's Hill PO17 . . . . .108 B2
Hoadlands GU31 . . . . .41 B4
Hobart Dr SO45 . . . . .126 B3
Hobart Rd BH25 . . . . .194 F2
Hobb La SO30 . . . . .105 D6
Hobbs Cl 2 PO12 . . . . .181 E5
Hobbs Pk BH24 . . . . .139 F4
Hobbs Rd BH12 . . . . .203 C8
Hobby Cl
Portsmouth PO3 . . . . .158 A4
Waterlooville PO8 . . . . .111 E4
Hobson Way SO45 . . . . .150 D3
Hoburne Cvn Pk BH23 . . . . .208 C8
Hoburne Gdns BH23 . . . . . .193 C1
Hoburne La BH23 . . . . .208 C8
Hockham Ct PO9 . . . . .135 C7
Hockley Cl 4 PO4 . . . . .157 D8
Hockley Cotts
Cheriton SO24 . . . . .13 E3
Twyford SO21 . . . . .32 A8
Hockley Link SO21 . . . . .10 E1
Hocombe Dr SO53 . . . . .30 B2
Hocombe Park Cl SO53 . . . . .30 B2
Hocombe Rd SO53 . . . . .30 B2
Hocombe Wood Rd SO53 . . .30 A2
Hodder Cl SO53 . . . . .55 B5
Hodges Cl Havant PO9 . . . . .136 A3
Poole BH17 . . . . .202 F7
Hoe La SO51,SO52 . . . . .53 D3
Hoe Rd SO32 . . . . .83 E7
Hoe St PO7 . . . . .109 F7
Hoe The PO13 . . . . .155 E1
Hoeford Cl PO16 . . . . .155 B6
Hogarth Cl
7 Romsey SO51 . . . . .28 B1
Southampton SO19 . . . . .104 C2
Hogarth Way BH8 . . . . .191 A2
Hogarth Cl GU31 . . . . .41 A4
Hogg Lodge La PO8 . . . . .88 E8
Hogue Ave BH10 . . . . .189 D5
Hogwood La SO30 . . . . .80 E6
Holbeach Cl PO6 . . . . .133 E1
Holbein Lodge SO41 . . . . . .198 B3
Holbrook Pl 3 SO51 . . . . . . .52 E7
Holbrook Prim Sch PO13 . . . . .155 C3
Holbrook Rd
Fareham PO16 . . . . .155 B8
Portsmouth PO1 . . . . .216 C3
Holburne Naish BH25 . . . . . .209 D8
Holbury Cl BH8 . . . . .190 E3
Holbury Ct 6 PO9 . . . . .136 B5
Holbury Dro SO45 . . . . .150 C4
Holbury La SO51 . . . . .4 D3
Holbury Prim Sch SO45 . . . .150 C3
Holcombe Rd BH16 . . . . .201 B6
Holcot La PO3 . . . . .158 C4
Holcroft Rd SO19 . . . . .104 E5
Holdaway Cl SO23 . . . . .2 C1
Holden La SO24 . . . . .34 F7
Holdenbury Ct PO3 . . . . .158 C5
Holdenhurst Ave BH7 . . . . .206 C7
Holdenhurst Ct 5 BH8 . . . . .88 C1
Holdenhurst Rd
Bournemouth BH8 . . . . .205 C6
Bournemouth,Holdenhurst BH8 .191 B3
Holdings The BH24 . . . . .141 B5
Hole La Curdridge SO32 . . . . .83 A1
Soberton PO17 . . . . .110 A8
Holes Bay North Rdbt BH17 . . . . .202 A4
Holes Bay Pk BH15 . . . . .202 B4

Holes Bay Rd BH15 . . . . .202 B4
Holes Bay Rd BH15 . . . . .202 B5
Holes Cl SO41 . . . . .195 F4
Holkham Cl SO16 . . . . .77 E3
Hollam Cl PO14 . . . . .154 B8
Hollam Cres PO14 . . . . .154 B8
Hollam Dr PO14 . . . . .154 B8
Hollam Rd PO4 . . . . .183 B4
Holland Cl SO53 . . . . .55 C3
Holland Pl SO31 . . . . .128 F3
Holland Pl Gosport PO13 . . .155 D2
Southampton SO16 . . . . .78 B1
Holland Rd
Portsmouth PO4 . . . . .216 D2
Southampton SO19 . . . . .103 D2
Totton SO40 . . . . .100 C7
Holland Way BH11 . . . . .186 F5
Hollands Cl SO22 . . . . .1 B5
Hollands Wood Cvn & Camping Site SO42 . . . . . .146 A4
Hollands Wood Dr BH25 . . . . .195 B5
Hollenden 1 BH13 . . . . .204 A4
Hollies Cl SO41 . . . . .172 B1
Hollies The Horndean PO8 . . .88 C2
West Wellow SO51 . . . . .50 D2
Hollingbourne Cl SO18 . . . .103 D8
Holliman Dr SO51 . . . . .52 D7
Hollow La PO11 . . . . .184 F3
Holloway Ave BH11 . . . . . . .188 F5
Holly Bank Cl PO8 . . . . .112 C5
Holly Cl Hythe SO45 . . . . . . .150 A7
Sarisbury SO31 . . . . .128 E3
St Leonards BH24 . . . . .139 B4
Upton BH16 . . . . .201 A7
West Moors BH22 . . . . .138 D2
Holly Ct Lymington SO41 . . .197 B2
Poole BH15 . . . . .202 D4
West Moors BH22 . . . . .138 D2
Holly Dell SO16 . . . . .78 E5
Holly Dr PO7 . . . . .135 A6
Holly Gdns Burton BH23 . . . .192 D4
Milford on S SO41 . . . . .211 C5
West End SO30 . . . . .80 D3
Holly Gr Fareham PO16 . . . . .130 E4
Verwood BH31 . . . . .114 E5
Holly Green Rise BH11 . . . . .188 E4
Holly Hatch Rd SO40 . . . . . .100 E6
Holly Hedge La BH17 . . . . . .202 C8
Holly Hill SO16 . . . . .78 E6
Holly Hill Cl SO16 . . . . .78 E5
Holly Hill La SO31 . . . . .128 C4
Holly Hill Mans SO31 . . . . . .128 E4
Holly Hill Woodland Pk* SO31 . . . . .128 C4
Holly Ho SO19 . . . . .103 E2
Holly La Boldre SO41 . . . . . . .174 B1
New Milton BH25 . . . . .195 C4
Southampton SO19 . . . . .103 E2
Holly Lo 18 BH13 . . . . .204 A4
Holly Lodge
Chandler's Ford SO53 . . . . .55 C3
Southampton SO17 . . . . .79 B1
Holly Mdws SO22 . . . . .215 A8
Holly Oak Cl SO16 . . . . .78 A4
Holly Oak Rd SO16 . . . . .78 A4
Holly Rd Ashurst SO40 . . . . .100 B2
Blackfield SO45 . . . . .177 E8
Holly St PO12 . . . . .181 C5
Hollybank PO13 . . . . .179 F2
Hollybank Cl SO45 . . . . .126 A3
Hollybank Cres SO45 . . . . . .125 F3
Hollybank La PO10 . . . . .136 F4
Hollybank Rd SO45 . . . . .125 F4
Hollybrook Appartments PO16 . . . . .156 B8
Hollybrook Ave SO16 . . . . . . .78 C3
Hollybrook Cl SO16 . . . . .78 B2
Hollybrook Gdns SO31 . . . .129 A5
Hollybrook Jun Sch SO16 .78 B3
Hollybrook Rd SO16 . . . . . . .78 C2
Hollybrook Villas SO45 . . . .126 A4
Hollywell Dr PO6 . . . . .157 B7
Hollywood Cl SO52 . . . . .53 F4
Hollywood Cl SO41 . . . . .197 D5
Hollywood La SO41 . . . . . . .197 D5
Holm Cl BH24 . . . . .117 C1
Holm Hill La BH23 . . . . .194 B7
Holm Oak Cl Littleton SO22 . .1 B5
Verwood BH31 . . . . .114 E8
Holman Cl PO8 . . . . .112 A2
Holmbush Ct PO5 . . . . .216 B1
Holmdale Rd PO12 . . . . .180 F7
Holme Rd BH23 . . . . .209 B8
Holmefield Ave PO14 . . . . . .154 F7
Holmes Cl SO31 . . . . .127 B6
Holmesland Dr SO30 . . . . . .105 F7
Holmesland La SO30 . . . . . .105 F8
Holmesland Wlk SO30 . . . . .105 F7
Holmfield Ave BH7 . . . . .206 C7
Holmgrove PO4 . . . . .129 C3
Holmhurst Ave BH23 . . . . . .193 F1
Holmsley Cl
Lymington SO41 . . . . .197 B2
Southampton SO18 . . . . .104 C2
Holmsley Ct 8 SO40 . . . . . .100 B8
Holmsley Pas BH24 . . . . . . .170 C7
Holmsley Rd BH25 . . . . .170 E2
Holmsley Ct SO16 . . . . .79 A4
Holmwood Garth BH7 . . . . .141 D6
Holne Ct PO4 . . . . .183 C3
Holnest Rd BH17 . . . . .186 F1
Holst Way PO7 . . . . .134 E5
Holt Cl Lee-on-t-S PO13 . . . .180 A6
Wickham PO17 . . . . .107 F4

Holt Ct SO19 . . . . .126 E8
Holt Down SO31 . . . . .41 B3
Holt Gdns PO9 . . . . .113 B3
Holt Ho BH8 . . . . .205 D5
Holt Pl BH22 . . . . .165 F7
Holt Rd Poole BH12 . . . . .203 F6
Southampton SO15 . . . . .102 F6
Three Legged Cross BH21 . . . .138 D8
Holt View SO50 . . . . .56 F2
Holworth Cl BH11 . . . . .188 C3
Holy Family RC Prim Sch SO16 . . . . .77 D2
Holy Rood Est SO14 . . . . . . .103 A3
Holy Rood Pl 1 SO14 . . . . .103 A3
Holyborne Rd SO51 . . . . .53 B7
Holybourne Rd PO9 . . . . . . .135 F3
Holyrood Ave SO17 . . . . .79 B2
Holyrood Cl Poole BH17 . . . .202 A8
2 Waterlooville PO7 . . . . . . .135 A7
Holyrood Ho 5 SO14 . . . . . .103 A3
Holywell Cl PO14 . . . . .187 D3
Home Farm BH21 . . . . .114 E4
Home Farm Bsns Ctr SO51 . . .4 E5
Home Farm Cl SO45 . . . . . . .126 B3
Home Farm Office Village PO16 . . . . .155 D8
Home Farm Rd BH31 . . . . . .114 E7
Home Field Dr SO16 . . . . . . .77 C7
Home Mead PO7 . . . . .110 F4
Home Rd BH11 . . . . .189 B6
Home Rule Rd SO31 . . . . . . .129 B4
Home Way GU31 . . . . .41 C3
Homeborough Ho SO45 . . . .126 A5
Homebridge Ho 2 SP6 . . . . .69 F2
Homecliffe Ho BH23 . . . . . . .209 B8
Homecorfe Ho BH18 . . . . . . .187 B5
Homedale Ho BH2 . . . . .204 F5
Homedene Ho BH15 . . . . . . .202 D3
Homefayre Ho 3 PO16 . . . .131 B1
Homefield SO51 . . . . .28 A1
Homefield Cotts
Hawkley GU33 . . . . .19 E7
Liss GU33 . . . . .20 E5
Homefield Ho 5 BH25 . . . . .195 A2
Homefield Ind Prep Sch BH6 .206 F5
Homefield Rd
Cosham PO6 . . . . .158 C7
Westbourne PO10 . . . . .137 B4
Homeforde Ho SO42 . . . . . . .146 A1
Homefort Ho 2 PO12 . . . . . .181 B5
Homegrange Ho SO41 . . . . .211 D3
Homegrove Ho PO5 . . . . . . .216 C1
Homeheights 3 PO5 . . . . . .182 C2
Homelake Ho BH14 . . . . . . .203 B3
Homelands Est BH23 . . . . . .206 F6
Homelands Rd BH23 . . . . . . .165 D5
Homelife Ho BH8 . . . . .205 B4
Homemead Ho SO51 . . . . . . .52 E6
Homeoaks Ho BH2 . . . . .204 F5
Homepoint Ho SO18 . . . . . .104 A7
Homer Cl Gosport PO13 . . . .180 B8
Waterlooville PO7 . . . . .111 E2
Homer Farm La SO45 . . . . . .177 E6
Homer Mobile Home Pk SO45 . . . . .177 E6
Homerise Ho 1 SO22 . . . . .215 E6
Homerose Ho PO5 . . . . .216 B2
Homeryde Ho PO13 . . . . . . .179 E2
Homesea Ho PO5 . . . . .216 B2
Homeside Rd BH9 . . . . .190 A2
Homespinney Ho SO18 . . . . .79 D1
Homestour Ho 1 BH23 . . . .207 A6
Hometide Ho PO13 . . . . .179 E2
Homeview Ho BH15 . . . . . . .202 C3
Homewater Ho 8 PO7 . . . . .134 E8
Homeway Cotts SO40 . . . . .101 B5
Homewell PO9 . . . . .135 F1
Homewood Cl BH25 . . . . . . .195 C3
Homewood Ho SO41 . . . . . .197 C2
Homington Rd SP5 . . . . .23 F8
Honey La Burley BH24 . . . . . .142 E2
Fareham PO15 . . . . .130 D5
Honeybourne Cres BH6 . . . .207 A4
Honeycritch La GU32 . . . . . . .19 C3
Honeysuckle Cl
Gosport PO13 . . . . .155 B3
Locks Heath SO31 . . . . .129 A5
Winchester SO22 . . . . .215 C2
Honeysuckle Ct
Locks Heath SO31 . . . . .129 A5
3 Southampton SO18 . . . . . .104 B7
Waterlooville PO7 . . . . .135 A5
Winchester SO22 . . . . .1 C3
Honeysuckle Gdns SO41 . . . . .196 C1
Honeysuckle La BH17 . . . . . .186 F1
Honeysuckle Rd SO16 . . . . . .79 B4
Honeysuckle Way
Chandler's Ford SO53 . . . . .55 A6
Christchurch BH23 . . . . .208 B8
Honeywood Cl
Portsmouth PO3 . . . . .157 F4
Totton SO40 . . . . .76 D1
Honister Cl SO16 . . . . .101 E8
Hood Cl
Bournemouth BH10 . . . . .189 B1
Locks Heath SO31 . . . . .129 B4
Hood Cres BH10 . . . . .189 B1
Hood Rd SO18 . . . . .104 A8

Hook Cl SO51 . . . . .30 A2
Hook Cotts SO31 . . . . . .152 F9
Hook Cres SO51 . . . . .30 A2
Hook La PO14,SO31 . . . .153 B8
Hook Park Rd SO31 . . . .152 E8
Hook Rd SO51 . . . . .29 F2
Hook Water Cl SO53 . . . . .30 B2
Hook Water Rd SO53 . . . .30 B2
Hook with Warsash CE Prim
  Sch SO31 . . . . .152 D10
Hook's Farm Way PO9 . .135 D3
Hook's La PO9 . . . . .135 D3
Hooke Cl BH17 . . . . .188 A2
Hookpit Farm La SO23 . . . .2 B8
Hookwood La SO51 . . . . .29 F2
Hop Cl BH16 . . . . .201 A7
Hop Gdns The SP5 . . . . . . .24 A3
Hope Lodge Sch SO18 . .103 E7
Hope Rd SO30 . . . . .80 E2
Hope St PO1 . . . . .216 B4
Hopfield Cl PO7 . . . . . . .134 E7
Hopfield Ho PO7 . . . . . .134 C6
Hopfield Mews PO7 . . . .134 E6
Hopkins Cl
  Bournemouth BH8 . . . . .191 A2
  Portchester PO6 . . . . . .156 E8
Hopkins Ct PO4 . . . . . . .183 B2
Hopwood Ct PO16 . . . . .130 F3
Horace Rd **7** BH5 . . . . .205 E4
Horder Ct SO16 . . . . .78 F3
Hordle CE Prim Sch
  SO41 . . . . .196 A3
Hordle La SO41 . . . . . . .196 A2
Hordle Rd PO9 . . . . .135 C2
Hordle Walhampton Sch
  SO41 . . . . .198 A6
Horlock Rd SO42 . . . . . .146 A2
Hornbeam Cl **2** SO30 . .105 D6
Hornbeam Gdns SO30 . . .80 D3
Hornbeam Rd
  Chandler's Ford SO53 . . . .54 F6
  Havant PO9 . . . . .136 B3
Hornbeam Sq BH15 . . . .202 D2
Hornbeam Way BH21 . . .163 E5
Hornby Cl SO31 . . . . . . .152 D10
Hornby Halt* PO11 . . . . .185 A2
Hornchurch Rd SO16 . . . .77 F4
Horndean CE Jun Sch
  PO8 . . . . .112 C7
Horndean Ho **6** PO1 . . .216 C4
Horndean Inf Sch PO8 . .112 C7
Horndean Prec PO8 . . . .112 D7
Horndean Rd PO9 . . . . . .136 E3
Horndean Tech Coll
  PO8 . . . . .112 B7
Hornet Cl Fareham PO15 .130 D2
  Gosport PO12 . . . . .181 C4
Hornet Rd Fareham PO14 .154 F5
  Thorney Island PO10 . . . .161 A3
Horning Rd BH12 . . . . . .203 F5
Horns Dro SO16 . . . . .77 F2
Horns Hill Nursling SO16 .77 F2
  Soberton SO32 . . . . .85 B2
Horns Hill Cl SO16 . . . . . .77 D6
Horsa Cl BH6 . . . . .206 E4
Horsa Ct BH6 . . . . .206 E4
Horsa Rd BH6 . . . . .206 E4
Horse Sands Cl PO4 . . . .183 D3
Horsea La PO2 . . . . .157 E4
Horsea Rd PO2 . . . . .157 E5
Horsebridge Rd PO9 . . . .136 A4
Horsebridge Way SO16 . . .77 E6
Horsecroft SO51 . . . . .52 F8
Horsefair Mews SO51 . . . .52 E7
Horsefair The SO51 . . . . .52 E7
Horsepost La PO7,PO8 . . .87 B2
Horseshoe Bridge SO14 .103 C8
Horseshoe Cl
  Titchfield PO14 . . . . . . .129 D2
  Wimborne Minst BH21 . . .164 B6
Horseshoe Common Rdbt
  BH1 . . . . .204 F3
Horseshoe Ct
  5 Bournemouth BH1 . .204 F4
  Downton SP5 . . . . .46 F7
Horseshoe Dr
  Romsey SO51 . . . . .28 B2
  Totton SO40 . . . . .76 A2
Horseshoe Lodge SO31 . .128 F1
Horseshoe Paddocks Bsns
  Ctr PO15 . . . . .130 B6
Horseshoe The BH13 . . .214 C4
Horsham Ave BH10 . . . . .189 C6
Horton Cl BH9 . . . . .190 C2
Horton Ho PO2 . . . . .165 F7
Horton Rd Horndean PO10 .155 C4
  Horton Heath BH21 . . . .114 B1
  Ringwood BH24 . . . . . . .140 C6
  St Leonards BH24 . . . . .139 C6
Horton Way
  Bishopstoke SO50 . . . . . .56 F1
  Verwood BH31 . . . . .114 D5
Hosker Rd BH5 . . . . .206 B5
Hoskins Ho PO1 . . . . . . .182 B6
Hospital La PO16 . . . . . .156 E6
Hospital Rd PO17,SO32 . .108 B8
Hotspur Cl SO45 . . . . . . .125 F5
Houchin St SO32 . . . . .83 C7
Houghton Cl **1** PO9 . . .136 B6
Houlton Rd BH15 . . . . . .202 E4
Hound Cl SO31 . . . . .127 C6
Hound Farm SO31 . . . . .127 E6
Hound Manor SO31 . . . . .127 C6
Hound Rd SO31 . . . . .127 D6
Hound Road Gdns SO31 .127 D6

Hound Way SO31 . . . . . .127 D6
Hounds Way BH21 . . . . .164 B5
Houndwell Pl SO14 . . . . .103 A4
Hounsdown Ave SO40 . . .100 F5
Hounsdown Bsns Pk
  SO40 . . . . .101 A3
Hounsdown Cl SO40 . . . .100 F5
Hounsdown Sch SO40 . . .100 F4
Hounslow Cl BH15 . . . . .201 F1
House Farm Rd PO12 . . .180 E4
Hove Ct PO13 . . . . .179 E3
Hoverfly Cl PO13 . . . . . .180 A5
Hoveton Gr SO53 . . . . . . .55 B8
Howard Cl Burley BH24 . .143 A3
  Chandler's Ford SO53 . . . .55 C4
  Christchurch BH23 . . . . .207 F6
  Fair Oak SO50 . . . . .57 C2
  Lee-on-t-S PO13 . . . . . . .180 A7
  Southampton SO18 . . . . . .79 E4
Howard Lo **20** PO5 . . . .182 C2
Howard Oliver Ho SO45 . .126 B3
Howard Rd
  Bournemouth BH8 . . . . .205 C8
  Portsmouth PO2 . . . . . . .157 E4
  Southampton SO15 . . . . .102 D6
  Verwood BH31 . . . . .114 F6
Howard's Gr SO15 . . . . . .102 C8
Howards Mead SO41 . . . .197 B2
Howe Cl
  Christchurch BH23 . . . . .207 F5
  New Milton BH25 . . . . . .194 F3
Howe La BH31 . . . . .114 F5
Howe Rd PO13 . . . . .180 C5
Howell Cl SO14 . . . . .103 C5
Howell Ho PO1 . . . . .163 F7
Howerts Cl SO31 . . . . . .152 D10
Howeth Rd BH10 . . . . . . .189 D3
Howeth Rd BH10 . . . . . . .189 D3
Howlett Cl SO41 . . . . . . .197 C4
Howton Cl BH10 . . . . . . .189 C5
Howton Rd BH10 . . . . . . .189 C5
Hoxley Rd BH10 . . . . . . .189 D4
Hoyal Rd BH15 . . . . .201 D3
Hoylake Cl PO13 . . . . . . .155 C1
Hoylake Rd PO6 . . . . . . .134 C1
Hoyle Cl SO32 . . . . .58 D3
Hoylecroft Cl PO15 . . . . .130 E3
Hubert Rd SO23 . . . . . . .215 C2
Hudson La
  Poole BH12 . . . . .188 C2
  Ringwood BH24 . . . . . . .141 C8
Hudson Ct SO40 . . . . . . .100 D6
Hudson Davies Cl SO41 . .173 F1
Hudson Rd PO5 . . . . .216 C2
Hughes Bsns Ctr BH23 . .208 A7
Hughes Cl SO45 . . . . . . .150 E1
Hulbert Jun Sch PO7 . . . .134 F6
Hulbert Rd Havant PO9 . .135 B4
  Waterlooville PO7 . . . . . .134 F7
Hull Cres BH11 . . . . .188 D4
Hull Rd BH11 . . . . .188 E4
Hulles Way SO52 . . . . . . .53 F4
Hulse Lodge **5** SO15 . .102 F8
Hulse Rd SO15 . . . . .102 F8
Hulton Cl SO19 . . . . .103 D3
Humber Cl PO14 . . . . . . .179 B8
Humber Gdns SO31 . . . . .105 A1
Humber Rd PO22 . . . . . .166 A6
Hummicks The SO42 . . . .176 C8
Hundred Acres PO17 . . . .108 F4
Hundred Acres Rd
  PO17 . . . . .108 E4
Hundred La SO41 . . . . . .198 A7
Hundred The
  5 Fordingbridge SP6 . . .69 F1
  Romsey SO51 . . . . .52 E7
  Waterlooville PO7 . . . . . .111 D1
Hunger Hill SO15 . . . . . .202 C2
Hungerfield Cl BH23 . . . .169 A1
Hungerford SO21 . . . . .2 B6
Hungerford Hill SP6 . . . . .94 D5
Hungerford Rd BH8 . . . . .190 D3
Hunt Ave SO31 . . . . .127 C6
Hunt Rd
  Christchurch BH23 . . . . .207 F8
  Poole BH15 . . . . .202 E4
Hunter Cl
  Christchurch BH23 . . . . .208 A7
  Gosport PO13 . . . . .180 D7
  Hardley SO45 . . . . .150 B6
  Wimborne Minst BH21 . . .164 C6
Hunter Ct **4** SO16 . . . . .78 B1
Hunter Rd
  Portsmouth PO4 . . . . . . .182 F3
  Thorney Island PO10 . . . .161 A3
Hunter's Ride SO21 . . . . . .29 E4
Hunters Chase SO32 . . . . .84 C3
Hunters Cl SO31 . . . . . . .135 C5
Hunters Cres
  Romsey SO51 . . . . .28 C1
  Totton SO40 . . . . .100 B6
Hunters Ct SO31 . . . . . . .105 B3
Hunters Hill SO40 . . . . . .100 D3
Hunters Lodge PO15 . . . .130 B1
Hunters Ride PO7 . . . . . .134 E6
Hunters Way SO17 . . . . . .57 A2
Huntfield Rd BH9 . . . . . . .190 B2
Huntingdon Cl
  Titchfield PO14 . . . . . . .129 C1
  Totton SO40 . . . . .76 E1
Huntingdon Dr BH21 . . . .163 E1
Huntingdon Gdns
  Christchurch BH23 . . . . .192 A2
  Horton Heath SO50 . . . . .81 D7
Huntley Cl **19** PO6 . . . .133 B1
Huntly Rd BH3 . . . . .204 D7
Huntly Way SO18 . . . . . .103 F7

Hunton Cl SO16 . . . . .78 D3
Hunts Pond Rd SO31 . . . .129 C3
Huntsbottom La GU33 . . .21 B3
Huntsman Cl PO8 . . . . . .111 F5
Huntvale Rd BH9 . . . . . . .190 B3
Hurdle Way SO21 . . . . . . .31 C7
Hurdles Mead SO41 . . . .211 D3
Hurdles The
  Christchurch BH23 . . . . .206 E8
  Titchfield PO14 . . . . . . .129 D2
Hurlingham Gdns SO16 . .79 A5
Hurn Cl BH24 . . . . .140 D6
Hurn Court La BH23 . . . .190 F6
Hurn Ct
  Bournemouth BH8 . . . . .191 A4
  12 Havant PO9 . . . . . .136 B6
Hurn La BH24 . . . . .140 D6
Hurn Rd
  Christchurch BH23 . . . . .191 D3
  St Leonards BH24 . . . . .140 C3
Hurn Way BH23 . . . . . . .191 D1
Hurricane Dr SO16 . . . . . .77 E6
Hursley Cl BH7 . . . . .206 C8
Hursley Ct **2** SO53 . . . . .30 B1
Hursley Park Rd SO21 . . .30 A6
Hursley Rd
  Chandler's Ford SO53 . . . .55 C7
  Havant PO9 . . . . .135 D5
Hurst Castle* SO41 . . . . .212 D1
Hurst Cl
  Barton on S BH25 . . . . .209 D8
  Chandler's Ford SO53 . . . .55 A4
  Stubbington PO14 . . . . . .179 A6
  Totton SO40 . . . . .100 F8
  Walkford BH23 . . . . .194 C2
Hurst Ct
  4 Christchurch BH23 . .209 A7
  5 Milton on S SO41 . . .211 C4
Hurst Gn PO13 . . . . .155 B2
Hurst Green Cl
  Southampton SO19 . . . . .104 A1
  Waterlooville PO8 . . . . . .112 B2
Hurst Hill BH14 . . . . .214 C8
Hurst La
  Colden Common SO21,SO50 .58 A7
  High Cross GU34 . . . . . . .18 B3
Hurst Rd
  Milford on S SO41 . . . . .211 E3
  Ringwood BH24 . . . . . . .117 A1
Hurstbourne Ave PO23 . .193 E1
Hurstbourne Pl SO19 . . .135 D5
Hurstbourne Pl SO19 . . .126 F8
Hurstdene Rd BH8 . . . . . .190 C2
Hurstly La SO41 . . . . . . .173 B4
Hurstville Dr PO7 . . . . . .134 F6
Hurstwood Ave PO10 . . .137 E1
Hussar Cl BH23 . . . . .206 F7
Hussar Ct PO7 . . . . .111 C1
Hussey Cl **2** SO23 . . . .215 E8
Hutfield Ct **1** PO12 . . .181 B6
Hutwood Rd SO16 . . . . . .79 A8
Huxley Cl SO31 . . . . .129 B2
Huxley Ct SO45 . . . . .125 C2
Hyacinth Cl BH17 . . . . . .186 F1
Hyde Abbey Rd SO23 . . .215 E6
Hyde CE Prim Sch SP6 . . .94 D5
Hyde Church La SO23 . . .215 E7
Hyde Church Path **6**
  SO23 . . . . .215 E7
Hyde Cl Southampton SO15 .78 C1
  Sway SO41 . . . . .172 B2
  Totton SO40 . . . . .100 B7
  Winchester SO23 . . . . . .215 E7
Hyde Gate SO23 . . . . . . .215 E7
Hyde House Gdns **5**
  SO23 . . . . .215 E7
Hyde La SP6 . . . . .94 C6
Hyde Lodge SO23 . . . . . .215 E7
Hyde Park Ho PO5 . . . . .216 B2
Hyde Park Rd PO5 . . . . .216 B3
Hyde Rd BH10 . . . . .189 C5
Hyde St Portsmouth PO5 .216 B2
  Winchester SO23 . . . . . .215 E7
Hyde The BH25 . . . . .194 E4
Hyden Cross GU32 . . . . . .63 E2
Hyden Farm La
  East Meon GU32 . . . . . . .63 D1
  Hambledon PO8 . . . . . . .87 D7
Hyden Wood GU32 . . . . . .63 F2
Hylton Rd GU32 . . . . .64 F3
Hymans Way SO40 . . . . .100 C7
Hynes Ct **1** SO17 . . . . .103 B8
Hynesbury Rd BH23 . . . .208 C6
Hyssop Cl PO15 . . . . . . .129 D7
Hythe By Pass SO45 . . . .149 E8
Hythe Hospl SO45 . . . . . .126 A2
Hythe Prim Sch SO45 . . .126 A4
Hythe Rd Cosham PO6 . . .157 E8
  Marchwood SO40 . . . . . .124 F8
  Poole BH15 . . . . .203 A7

I

I O Ctr The PO15 . . . . . .129 E2
Ibbertson Cl BH8 . . . . . .190 F1
Ibbertson Rd BH8 . . . . . .190 F1
Ibbertson Way BH8 . . . . .190 F2
Ibbett Rd BH10 . . . . .189 C3
Ibbotson Way SO40 . . . . .100 D5
Ibsen Cl PO15 . . . . .188 A5
Ibsley Cl BH8 . . . . .205 C6
Ibsley Dro BH24 . . . . . . .115 A4
Ibsley Gr PO9 . . . . .135 D3
Icarus Pl PO7 . . . . .134 F2
Iddesleigh Rd BH3 . . . . .205 A6

Ideal Park Homes Cvn Pk
  SO50 . . . . .56 E6
Idsworth Cl PO8 . . . . . . .112 E6
Idsworth Ho PO1 . . . . . .216 B4
Idsworth Rd
  Portsmouth PO3 . . . . . . .183 A8
  Waterlooville PO8 . . . . . .112 B2
Iford Bridge Home Pk
  BH6 . . . . .206 D7
Iford Cl **15** BH6 . . . . . .206 D7
Iford Gdns BH7 . . . . .206 C7
Iford La BH6 . . . . .206 C6
Ilex Cl SO23 . . . . .2 B8
Ilex Cres SO31 . . . . .129 A3
Ilex Wlk PO11 . . . . .185 C2
Ilford Cl BH6 . . . . .206 F8
Illustrious Rd PO14 . . . . .179 B6
Imber Cl BH23 . . . . .208 F8
Imber Rd SO23 . . . . .11 C8
Imber Way SO19 . . . . . . .104 A3
Imbrecourt BH13 . . . . . . .214 E7
Imperial Appartments **8**
  SO14 . . . . .103 B3
Imperial Ave SO15 . . . . .102 B7
Imperial Ct **4** BH13 . . .214 F7
Imperial Pk SO14 . . . . . .103 B3
Imperial Rd SO14 . . . . . .103 B7
Imperial Way SO15 . . . . .102 B2
Implacable Rd PO13 . . . .179 E4
Ingarth **7** BH6 . . . . . . .206 E4
Ingersley Rise SO30 . . . . .80 D1
Ingle Glen SO45 . . . . . . .150 E2
Ingle Gn SO40 . . . . .76 B1
Inglenne Cl
  Gosport PO12 . . . . .181 B5
  Havant PO9 . . . . .135 D2
Inglegreen Cl BH25 . . . . .194 F1
Inglesham Way BH15 . . .201 E4
Ingleside SO31 . . . . .127 C7
Ingleside Cl PO14 . . . . . .154 B8
Ingleton Rd SO16 . . . . . . .78 D2
Inglewood Ave BH8 . . . . .190 F1
Inglewood Dr BH25 . . . . .195 B2
Inglewood Gdns SO50 . . .57 C3
Inglis Rd PO5 . . . . .216 D1
Ingoldfield La PO17,
  SO32 . . . . .109 C7
Ingram Ct SO17 . . . . . . .103 C8
Ingram St BH2 . . . . .163 D4
Ingworth Rd BH12 . . . . .204 A5
Inhams La PO7 . . . . .110 D5
Inhurst Ave PO2 . . . . . . .135 A8
Inhurst Rd PO2 . . . . .157 E2
Inkerman Rd SO19 . . . . .103 D3
Inkpen Wlk PO9 . . . . . . .135 C2
Inlands Rd PO18 . . . . . . .161 F8
Inmans La GU32 . . . . .41 B5
Insley Cres BH18 . . . . . . .186 E5
Interch* SO21 . . . . .12 B7
International Pk SO18 . . . .79 F6
International Way SO19 . .126 F8
Inveravon BH23 . . . . .210 A7
Inverclyde Rd BH14 . . . . .203 B4
Inverclyde Rd BH14 . . . . .203 B4
Invergordon Ave PO6 . . .158 B7
Inverkip Cl PO13 . . . . . . .179 E4
Inverleigh Rd BH6 . . . . . .206 C6
Inverness Ave PO15 . . . .130 E3
Inverness Rd
  Gosport PO12 . . . . .181 A3
  Poole BH13 . . . . .214 E7
  Portsmouth PO1 . . . . . . .182 E7
Invincible Rd PO14 . . . . .179 B6
Inwood Rd GU33 . . . . . . .23 A4
Iolanthe Dr BH8 . . . . . . .191 A2
Iping Ave PO9 . . . . .135 E4
Ipley Way SO45 . . . . . . .126 A2
Ipswich Rd BH12 . . . . . .204 B4
Ireland Way PO7 . . . . . . .134 E5
Irene Ct SO16 . . . . .78 B2
Irequois St SO14 . . . . . . .103 B7
Iris Rd Bournemouth BH9 .189 F1
  Southampton SO16 . . . . .79 B4
Iron Mill Cl PO13 . . . . . .130 C3
Ironbridge Cres SO31 . . .129 A6
Ironbridge La PO4 . . . . . .183 C4
Ironmill La PO15 . . . . . . .130 B5
Ironside Ct **7** SO14 . . .102 F3
Irvine Cl PO16 . . . . .131 A3
Irvine Way BH23 . . . . . . .207 E8
Irving La BH6 . . . . .206 D5
Irving Rd
  Bournemouth BH6 . . . . .206 D5
  Southampton SO16 . . . . .77 F1
Irwell Cl SO53 . . . . .55 A5
Irwin Hts PO12 . . . . .181 A9
Isaacs Cl BH11 . . . . .204 B7
Isambard Brunel Jun Sch
  PO1 . . . . .182 A8
Isambard Brunel Rd
  PO1 . . . . .182 B6
Isis Cl SO16 . . . . .101 E8
Island Cl PO11 . . . . .185 A5
Island Point SO41 . . . . . .197 F4
Island View Ave BH23 . . .210 F4
Island View Cl SO41 . . . .211 E3
Island View Rd BH23 . . . .211 E3
Island View Rd BH25 . . . .209 C2
Island View Terr PO2 . . .157 E5
Island View Wlk PO16 . . .132 C1
Islay Gdns PO3 . . . . .133 C5
Itchen Ave SO50 . . . . .56 F2
Itchen Cl Petersfield GU31 .40 E2
  West Wellow SO51 . . . . . .50 D3
Itchen Coll SO19 . . . . . . .104 A5
Itchen Ct
  4 Waterlooville PO8 . .111 F4

Itchen Ct continued
  9 Winchester SO23 . . .215 F6
Itchen Rd PO9 . . . . .136 B6
Itchen Valley Ctry Pk*
  SO30 . . . . .80 C5
Itchen Valley Ctry Pk Visitor
  Ctr* SO30 . . . . .80 C5
Itchen View SO18 . . . . . . .79 E4
Itchenor Rd PO11 . . . . . .185 F2
Itchenside Cl SO18 . . . . . .79 F4
Itchin Cl SO40 . . . . .100 D6
Ithica Cl PO11 . . . . .185 A4
Ivamy Pl BH11 . . . . .188 F2
Ivanhoe Rd SO15 . . . . . . .78 D1
Ivor Cl SO45 . . . . .150 C4
Ivor Rd
  Corfe Mullen BH21 . . . . .186 D4
  Poole BH15 . . . . .202 A1
Ivy Cl St Leonards BH24 . .139 D8
  Totton SO40 . . . . .76 E2
  Winchester SO22 . . . . . .215 C3
Ivy Cotts SO21 . . . . .31 A1
Ivy Ct Southampton SO16 .78 D3
  Waterlooville PO7 . . . . . .134 D4
7 Whiteley PO15 . . . . .129 D8
Ivy Dene SO19 . . . . .104 B2
Ivy Ho PO12 . . . . .181 C5
Ivy La Portsmouth PO12 . .182 A6
  Ringwood BH24 . . . . . . .117 B4
  West End SO30 . . . . .80 C2
Ivy Orch PO8 . . . . .88 B6
Ivy Rd Oakley BH21 . . . .187 D8
  Southampton SO17 . . . . .103 C8
Ivydene Gdns PO8 . . . . .112 A4
Ivyhouse La GU32 . . . . . .18 E3
Iwerne Cl BH9 . . . . .190 B4

J

J Ave SO45 . . . . .151 A2
Jacaranda Cl PO15 . . . . .129 E3
Jacey Ho **8** BH1 . . . . . .205 A3
Jack Cl SO53 . . . . .54 E6
Jack Cockerill Way **8**
  PO5 . . . . .182 D1
Jackdaw Cl PO8 . . . . . . .111 E4
Jackdaw Rise SO50 . . . . . .55 D1
Jackie Wigg Gdns SO40 .101 A7
Jacklin Cl BH18 . . . . .187 B5
Jacklin Ct BH18 . . . . . . .187 B5
Jackman's Hill SO21 . . . .33 A6
Jackmans Cl SO19 . . . . .103 D3
Jackson Cl PO6 . . . . .158 C6
Jackson Gdns BH12 . . . .203 C6
Jackson Rd BH12 . . . . . .203 C6
Jacmar Ct **4** BH25 . . . .195 B2
Jacob's Gutter La SO40 . .101 A4
Jacob's St PO1 . . . . .216 B4
Jacobean Cl BH23 . . . . . .194 B1
Jacobs Cl Clanfield PO8 . .88 C5
  Romsey SO51 . . . . .53 A7
Jacobs Ct PO9 . . . . .135 E1
Jacobs Gn BH15 . . . . . . .201 E2
Jacobs Wlk SO40 . . . . . .100 E5
Jacomb Pl PO12 . . . . . . .155 C2
Jacqueline Ave PO7 . . . .134 D4
Jacqueline Rd BH12 . . . .203 C7
Jade Ct **8** PO12 . . . . . .181 C4
Jaffrey Rd PO13 . . . . . . .180 D7
7 Waterlooville PO7 . . .134 E8
Jago Rd PO1 . . . . .181 F7
Jamaica Pl PO12 . . . . . . .181 C5
Jamaica Rd PO12 . . . . . .181 D6
James Butcher Ct **11**
  PO5 . . . . .182 D1
James Callaghan Dr
  PO6 . . . . .133 B2
James Cl Gosport PO13 . .155 C4
  South Hayling PO11 . . . .184 E4
James Copse Rd PO8 . . .111 F5
James Ct SO51 . . . . .53 A6
James Grieve Ave SO31 . .129 B2
James Howell Ct PO7 . . .110 F4
James Rd Gosport PO13 . .180 A6
  Havant PO9 . . . . .135 E2
Poole BH12 . . . . .204 A5
James St SO14 . . . . .103 B4
Jameson Rd
  Bournemouth BH9 . . . . .189 F1
  Southampton SO19 . . . . .103 F3
Janaway Gdns SO17 . . . .103 D8
Jane Cl BH12 . . . . .188 E1
Janred Ct PO5 . . . . .229 E7
Janson Rd SO15 . . . . . . .102 D8
Japonica Way PO9 . . . . .136 C4
Jardyce Wlk PO2 . . . . . . .182 D7
Jarvis Fields SO31 . . . . .128 B8
Jasmine Ct
  2 Gosport PO13 . . . .180 C6
  Lymington SO41 . . . . . . .197 C4
  1 Southampton SO15 .102 B6
  Whiteley PO15 . . . . .106 D1
Jasmine Gr PO7 . . . . . . .135 A6
Jasmine Rd SO30 . . . . . .105 B8
Jasmine Way PO8 . . . . . . .88 C5
Jasmine Wlk **5** PO14 . .154 E6
Jasmond Rd PO6 . . . . . . .157 F6
Jason Pl PO12 . . . . .180 B8
Jason Way PO12 . . . . . . .180 F8
Jaundrells Cl BH25 . . . . .195 C3
Java Dr PO15 . . . . .129 C7
Javelin Rd PO13 . . . . . . .161 A3
Jay Cl Horndean PO8 . . . .112 A7
  Stubbington PO14 . . . . . .154 B5
Jay's Ct BH23 . . . . .209 B8
Jealous La SO41 . . . . . . .173 A2
Jefferson Ave BH1 . . . . . .205 D6
Jeffries Cl SO16 . . . . .77 E5
Jellicoe Ave PO12 . . . . . .180 F3

Jellicoe Cl BH14 ... 202 F5
Jellicoe Dr BH23 ... 207 F6
Jellicoe Ho 8 PO1 ... 216 C4
Jenkins Gr PO3 ... 183 B7
Jenkyns Cl SO30 ... 106 A7
Jenner Cl BH31 ... 114 E7
Jenner Way SO51 ... 53 C8
Jennings Rd Poole BH14 ... 203 C2
 Totton SO40 ... 101 A8
Jensen Ct SO15 ... 102 F7
Jephcote Rd BH11 ... 188 F4
Jermyns La SO51 ... 28 E4
Jerome Ct SO19 ... 104 D6
Jerram Cl PO12 ... 180 F3
Jerrett's La SO16 ... 77 D3
Jersey Cl Poole BH12 ... 188 D1
 Southampton SO16 ... 77 E3
 Stubbington PO14 ... 179 D6
Jersey Rd Poole BH12 ... 188 D1
 Portsmouth PO2 ... 182 E8
Jervis Court La SO32 ... 84 A7
Jervis Dr PO12 ... 181 B7
Jervis Rd PO2 ... 157 C2
Jesmond Ave BH23 ... 208 F8
Jesmond Gr SO31 ... 129 A1
Jessamine Rd SO16 ... 78 B2
Jessica Ave BH31 ... 114 D7
Jessica Cl 1 PO7 ... 112 B1
Jessica Cres SO40 ... 76 B1
Jessie Rd Gosport PO12 ... 181 A5
 Havant PO9 ... 135 C3
 Portsmouth PO4 ... 182 E4
Jessie Terr 23 SO14 ... 103 A3
Jessop Cl SO45 ... 125 F5
Jessop Wlk SO45 ... 125 F5
Jessopp Cl BH10 ... 189 F4
Jessopp Ho 6 BH21 ... 163 C5
Jessopp Rd BH21 ... 164 B6
Jetty Rd SO45 ... 151 C5
Jewell Rd BH8 ... 191 A2
Jewry St SO23 ... 215 E6
Jex Blake Cl SO16 ... 78 B4
Jimmy Brown Ave BH21 ... 138 F5
Jinny La SO51 ... 27 E5
Jo Benson Ct 3 PO4 ... 182 F2
Joanna Cl SP5 ... 46 D7
Jockey La SO50 ... 56 E5
Jodrell Cl PO8 ... 112 C7
Joe Bigwood Cl SO16 ... 77 D5
John Bunyan Cl PO15 ... 129 C8
John Darling Mall SO50 ... 56 A4
John Keble CE Prim Sch
 SO21 ... 30 B6
John King Shipyard 10
 PO10 ... 161 A8
John St SO14 ... 103 A3
John's Rd SO19 ... 103 D3
Johns Rd PO16 ... 155 B7
Johnson Rd BH21 ... 165 A8
Johnson St 4 SO14 ... 103 A4
Johnson View PO15 ... 129 E6
Johnston Rd BH15 ... 202 D7
Johnstone Rd BH23 ... 207 E6
Jolliffe Ave BH15 ... 202 D4
Jolliffe Ct 13 GU32 ... 40 F3
Jolliffe Rd BH15 ... 202 D4
Jonas Nichols Sq SO14 ... 103 B4
Jonathan Cl SO41 ... 197 E5
Jonathan Rd PO15 ... 130 E1
Jones La SO45 ... 126 A5
Jopps Cnr BH23 ... 192 C4
Jordan Ho SO15 ... 102 C5
Jordans La
 Portmore SO41 ... 198 B8
 Sway SO41 ... 172 C2
Joseph Nye Ct 41 PO1 ... 182 A5
Joseph St 9 PO12 ... 181 C5
Joshua Cl BH15 ... 201 E2
Josian Wlk SO14 ... 103 B5
Jowitt Dr BH25 ... 194 F2
Joyce Dickson Cl BH24 ... 141 B6
Joys La SO41 ... 198 E8
Joys Rd BH21 ... 138 E8
Jubilee Ave PO6 ... 156 E8
Jubilee Bsns Ctr PO7 ... 134 E8
Jubilee Cl
 Corfe Mullen BH21 ... 186 E7
 Eastleigh SO50 ... 55 F1
 Fordingbridge SP6 ... 69 C1
 Ringwood BH24 ... 141 C8
Jubilee Cotts GU32 ... 37 C4
Jubilee Cres BH12 ... 203 D5
Jubilee Ct Alderholt SP6 ... 92 E5
 Fareham PO14 ... 155 A7
 Sway SO41 ... 172 B1
Jubilee Gdns
 Bournemouth BH10 ... 189 D2
 Southampton SO18 ... 104 B7
Jubilee Ho PO10 ... 136 E1
Jubilee Mews PO10 ... 161 C8
Jubilee Rd
 Corfe Mullen BH21 ... 186 E7
 Fordingbridge SP6 ... 69 C1
 Gosport PO12 ... 181 B6
 Poole BH12 ... 203 D5
 Portchester PO16 ... 156 D7
 Portsmouth PO4 ... 182 F3
 Romsey SO51 ... 52 E8
 Waterlooville PO7 ... 111 E1
Jubilee Terr
 Portsmouth PO5 ... 216 A1
 Westbourne PO10 ... 137 B3
Jukes Wlk SO30 ... 80 F2
Julia Cl BH23 ... 208 F8
Julian Cl SO16 ... 78 F6
Julian Ct SO18 ... 79 E2
Julian Rd SO19 ... 104 B3
Julian's Rd BH21 ... 163 A4
Julie Ave PO15 ... 130 E1
Juliet Ct PO7 ... 135 A8
Julius Cl SO53 ... 55 E6
Julyan Ave BH12 ... 204 A8
Jumar Cl SO31 ... 152 D9
Jumpers Ave BH23 ... 206 E8
Jumpers Rd BH23 ... 206 F8
Junction Rd
 Bournemouth BH9 ... 204 F8
 Hamworthy BH16 ... 201 D4
 Totton SO40 ... 101 A7
Juniper Cl
 Ferndown BH22 ... 165 C8
 Lymington SO41 ... 197 B2
 North Baddesley SO52 ... 53 F5
 Three Legged Cross BH21 ... 138 E8
 Winchester SO22 ... 215 B3
Juniper Ct 5 SO18 ... 103 E7
Juniper Flats BH23 ... 206 E8
Juniper Rd Horndean PO8 ... 88 C1
 Southampton SO18 ... 103 F7
Juniper Sq PO9 ... 159 F8
Jupiter Cl SO16 ... 77 E3
Jupiter Ct PO1 ... 182 A4
Jupiter Way BH21 ... 186 E8
Jura Cl PO6 ... 134 A1
Jurd Way SO31 ... 104 F1
Jurds Lake Way SO19 ... 103 E1
Justin Cl Fareham PO14 ... 154 E8
 Gosport PO12 ... 181 D7
Justin Gdns BH10 ... 189 E4
Justine Ct 2 SO18 ... 104 B7
Justinian Cl SO53 ... 55 F7
Jute Cl PO16 ... 132 B1
Jutland Cl PO15 ... 129 B7
Juventu Cl PO9 ... 136 A3

K

K&B Est BH17 ... 202 B8
Kamptee Copse BH25 ... 195 B6
Kanes Hill SO19 ... 104 F5
Kanes Hill Cvn Site
 SO19 ... 104 F4
Kanes Hill Prim Sch
 SO19 ... 104 E6
Kangaw Pl BH15 ... 201 D2
Karen Ave PO6 ... 158 C6
Kassassin St PO4 ... 183 A2
Kassel Cl PO7 ... 135 B8
Katherine Chance Cl
 BH23 ... 192 C3
Kathleen Rd SO19 ... 104 B4
Kathryn Cl SO40 ... 76 B1
Katrina Gdns PO11 ... 185 A5
Katrine Cres SO53 ... 55 A8
Katterns Cl BH23 ... 191 E2
Kay Cl BH23 ... 207 E6
Kayak Cl SO31 ... 128 E1
Kayleigh Cl SO40 ... 100 D6
Kealy Rd PO12 ... 181 A7
Kearsney Ave PO2 ... 157 E2
Keast Wlk PO13 ... 155 D4
Keats Ave
 Milford on S SO41 ... 211 D5
 Portchester PO6 ... 132 E1
Keats Cl Swanwick PO15 ... 106 B1
 Waterlooville PO8 ... 111 F4
 Winchester SO22 ... 215 A2
Keats Ho Havant PO9 ... 135 F4
 1 New Milton BH25 ... 195 A1
Keats Rd SO19 ... 104 C6
Keble Cl
 Chandler's Ford SO53 ... 55 C4
 Hursley SO21 ... 30 B8
Keble Rd SO53 ... 55 C4
Keble St SO22 ... 215 A4
Keeble Cl BH10 ... 189 D6
Keeble Cres BH10 ... 189 D6
Keeble Rd BH10 ... 189 D6
Keel Cl Gosport PO13 ... 180 D7
 Portsmouth PO3 ... 158 C3
Keelan Ct PO5 ... 182 D2
Keenans Cotts GU33 ... 20 E5
Keep The PO16 ... 156 D7
Keepers Cl SO53 ... 55 B6
Keepers La Dunbridge SO51 ... 5 C2
 Wimborne Minst BH21 ... 164 F4
Kefford Cl PO8 ... 112 B6
Keighley Ave BH18 ... 186 F1
Keith Cl PO12 ... 181 B7
Keith Ho 24 PO1 ... 182 A5
Keith Rd BH3 ... 204 D7
Kelburn Cl SO53 ... 55 B7
Kellaway Rd BH17 ... 202 F8
Kellett Rd SO15 ... 102 E8
Kelly Cl BH17 ... 202 F8
Kelly Ct
 10 Fareham PO16 ... 131 B2
 Southampton SO16 ... 78 C5
 1 Southampton,Bitterne
 SO18 ... 103 E8
Kelly Ho SO18 ... 79 E4
Kelly Rd PO7 ... 134 E5
Kelmscott Gdns SO53 ... 30 B1
Kelsall Gdns BH25 ... 195 A3
Kelsey Ave PO10 ... 137 E1
Kelsey Cl Liss GU33 ... 21 A5
 Locks Heath PO14 ... 129 B1
Kelsey Head PO6 ... 157 A7
Kelston Cl SO15 ... 102 A7
Kelvin Cl SO45 ... 126 A3
Kelvin Gr Netley SO31 ... 127 C6
 Portchester PO16 ... 156 D8
Kelvin Rd SO50 ... 55 F2
Kemp Rd BH9 ... 204 F8
Kemp Welch Ct BH12 ... 204 B8
Kempfelt Ho 20 PO1 ... 182 A5
Kemps Quay Ind Pk
 SO18 ... 103 D7
Kempton Ct PO15 ... 129 C8
Kempton Pk 3 PO7 ... 112 B1
Kemshott Ct PO9 ... 135 D6
Ken Berry Ct PO9 ... 136 B6
Ken Rd BH6 ... 206 E4
Kench The PO11 ... 183 F4
Kendal Ave
 Portsmouth PO3 ... 158 A1
 Southampton SO16 ... 101 D8
Kendal Cl
 Chandler's Ford SO53 ... 55 E7
 Waterlooville PO8 ... 112 A4
Kendal Ct SO16 ... 77 D1
Kenilworth Cl
 Lee-on-t-S PO13 ... 179 F4
 New Milton BH25 ... 195 B3
Kenilworth Ct
 2 Christchurch BH23 ... 207 A7
 1 Poole BH13 ... 214 F8
 9 Winchester SO23 ... 215 E8
Kenilworth Dr SO50 ... 56 A6
Kenilworth Gdns SO30 ... 80 E1
Kenilworth Ho 15 SO14 ... 103 C6
Kenilworth Rd
 Portsmouth PO5 ... 182 D1
 Southampton SO15 ... 102 F6
Kenmore Cl SO40 ... 100 E5
Kennard Ct BH25 ... 194 F3
Kennard Rd BH25 ... 194 F3
Kennart Rd BH17 ... 202 B7
Kennedy Ave PO15 ... 130 E3
Kennedy Cl PO7 ... 134 E4
Kennedy Cres PO12 ... 180 F2
Kennedy Rd SO16 ... 77 F3
Kennel La SO22 ... 1 C4
Kennet Cl Gosport PO12 ... 181 B2
 West End SO18 ... 80 B3
Kennet Rd GU31 ... 40 E2
Kenneth Ct 9 BH23 ... 209 B7
Kennett Cl SO51 ... 53 C7
Kennett Rd SO51 ... 53 C7
Kennington La SO40 ... 99 B7
Kennington Rd BH17 ... 202 D8
Kensington Cl SO50 ... 56 D5
Kensington Ct
 14 Gosport PO12 ... 181 C9
 14 Poole BH13 ... 204 B3
 3 Southampton SO17 ... 79 C2
Kensington Dr 1 BH2 ... 204 D4
Kensington Fields SO45 ... 125 D2
Kensington Gdns PO14 ... 129 C2
Kensington Pk SO41 ... 211 C4
Kensington Rd
 Gosport PO12 ... 181 C4
 Portsmouth PO2 ... 157 F1
Kenson Gdns SO19 ... 104 A4
Kent Gdns SO40 ... 100 D5
Kent Gr PO16 ... 156 C6
Kent Ho
 28 Bournemouth BH4 ... 204 C3
 4 Southampton SO14 ... 103 C5
Kent La BH24 ... 93 D1
Kent Rd
 Chandler's Ford SO53 ... 55 C3
 Gosport PO13 ... 155 B4
 Poole BH12 ... 203 E6
 Portsmouth PO5 ... 216 B1
 Southampton SO17 ... 79 C1
Kent St Portsmouth PO1 ... 182 A5
 Southampton SO14 ... 103 C6
Kentidge Rd PO7 ... 134 D5
Kentish Rd SO15 ... 102 C7
Kenwood Bsns Pk PO9 ... 136 A2
Kenwood Rd PO16 ... 156 D6
Kenwyn Cl SO18 ... 80 B2
Kenya Rd PO16 ... 156 B7
Kenyon Cl BH15 ... 202 E7
Kenyon Rd Poole BH15 ... 202 E7
 Portsmouth PO2 ... 157 F2
Keppel Cl BH24 ... 141 B7
Kerley Rd BH2 ... 204 E2
Kern Cl SO16 ... 77 F3
Kernells Ct 2 BH4 ... 204 B4
Kerrfield SO22 ... 215 B5
Kerrfield Mews SO22 ... 215 B5
Kerrigan Ct SO17 ... 103 A7
Kerry Cl
 Chandler's Ford SO53 ... 55 C6
 Lymington SO41 ... 197 C3
Kerry Gdns SP6 ... 69 B2
Kersley Gdns SO19 ... 104 A4
Kesteven Way SO18 ... 80 B1
Kestrel Cl
 Bishop's Waltham SO32 ... 83 A8
 Botley SO32 ... 81 F1
 Clanfield PO8 ... 88 C4
 Ferndown BH22 ... 165 B7
 Marchwood SO40 ... 101 E1
 Southampton SO16 ... 78 B5
 Stubbington PO14 ... 154 B4
 Upton BH16 ... 201 B8
 Winchester SO22 ... 215 B2
Kestrel Ct BH24 ... 141 A8
Kestrel Dr BH23 ... 208 A6
Kestrel Pl PO6 ... 158 F7
Kestrel Rd Eastleigh SO50 ... 55 E2
 Portsmouth PO3 ... 158 A4
Kestrel Way SP6 ... 93 B5
Kestrels The SO31 ... 127 F8
Keswick Ave PO3 ... 183 A8
Keswick Ct BH25 ... 195 B5
Keswick Rd
 Bournemouth BH5 ... 205 F4
 New Milton BH25 ... 195 B5
 Southampton SO19 ... 103 D2
Keswick Way BH31 ... 114 E5
Kettering Terr PO2 ... 182 C8
Keverstone Ct BH1 ... 205 D3
Kevlyn Cres SO31 ... 104 F1
Kew La SO31 ... 128 A7
Kewlake La SO40 ... 74 D1
Keydell Ave PO8 ... 112 A5
Keydell Cl PO8 ... 112 A5
Keyes Cl
 Christchurch BH23 ... 207 F6
 Gosport PO13 ... 155 C3
 Poole BH12 ... 188 F1
Keyes Ct 4 PO5 ... 216 C1
Keyes Rd PO13 ... 155 C3
Keyhaven Cl PO13 ... 155 A2
Keyhaven Dr PO9 ... 135 C5
Keyhaven Rd SO41 ... 212 A4
Keynsham Rd SO19 ... 104 B6
Keysworth Ave BH25 ... 209 F8
Keysworth Rd BH16 ... 201 C4
Khandala Gdns PO7 ... 134 F4
Khartoum Rd SO17 ... 79 A2
Khyber Rd BH12 ... 203 D5
Kidmore La PO7 ... 110 F6
Kidson Ct PO2 ... 182 D8
Kielder Cl SO53 ... 55 A7
Kielder Gr PO13 ... 155 D2
Kilbride Path 5 PO2 ... 182 D8
Kilderkin Dr PO8 ... 112 D7
Kilford Ct SO30 ... 106 A6
Kilham La SO22 ... 10 B6
Killarney Cl SO19 ... 104 E3
Killock 6 BH13 ... 214 F7
Kilmarnock Rd BH9 ... 189 F1
Kilmeston Cl PO9 ... 135 F6
Kilmeston Rd
 Cheriton SO24 ... 14 D4
 Kilmeston SO24 ... 14 D2
Kilmington Way BH23 ... 208 F8
Kilmiston Cl PO1 ... 182 E7
Kilmiston Dr PO16 ... 132 C1
Kiln Acre PO16 ... 131 B3
Kiln Cl Corfe Mullen BH21 ... 186 C4
 Hythe SO45 ... 125 E3
Kiln Field GU33 ... 20 E5
Kiln Gn SO21 ... 57 A8
Kiln Hill SO32 ... 109 B8
Kiln La Braishfield SO51 ... 28 C6
 Buriton GU31 ... 65 D5
 Otterbourne SO21 ... 31 C2
 Redlynch SP5 ... 47 E7
 Southwick PO7 ... 109 D4
Kiln Rd Fareham PO16 ... 131 A3
 Portsmouth PO3 ... 158 A1
Kiln Way BH31 ... 115 C3
Kilnside PO7 ... 110 F3
Kilnyard Cl SO40 ... 76 D1
Kilpatrick Cl 6 PO2 ... 182 D8
Kilwich Way PO16 ... 156 B6
Kimber Rd BH11 ... 188 F3
Kimberley Cl
 Christchurch BH23 ... 206 F8
 Fair Oak SO50 ... 57 D2
 Hedge End SO30 ... 105 B5
Kimberley Ct SO19 ... 103 E2
Kimberley Rd
 Bournemouth BH6 ... 206 C5
 Poole BH14 ... 203 B3
 Portsmouth PO4 ... 183 A2
Kimbers GU32 ... 40 E4
Kimbolton Rd PO3 ... 183 A6
Kimbridge Cnr SO51 ... 27 B8
Kimbridge Cres PO9 ... 136 A6
Kimbridge La SO51 ... 26 F7
Kimmeridge Ave BH12 ... 203 C8
Kimpton Cl PO13 ... 179 F3
Kimpton Ct 9 PO9 ... 136 B6
Kineton Rd SO15 ... 78 E1
King Albert Ct PO1 ... 216 C4
King Albert St PO1 ... 216 C4
King Alfred Pl SO23 ... 215 E7
King Alfred Terr 13
 SO23 ... 215 E7
King Arthur's Ct PO6 ... 158 D8
King Charles St 9 PO1 ... 182 A4
King Cl BH24 ... 139 F4
King Cup Ave SO31 ... 128 F3
King Edward Ave
 Bournemouth BH9 ... 190 A2
 Southampton SO16 ... 102 A8
King Edward Cres PO2 ... 157 D2
King Edward Ct BH9 ... 189 F2
King Edward Cvn Pk The
 SO52 ... 30 A1
King Edward Pk (Cvn Pk)
 SO52 ... 55 A8
King Edward VI Sch
 SO15 ... 102 E8
King George Ave
 Bournemouth BH9 ... 189 F2
 Petersfield GU32 ... 40 F4
King George Mews 4
 GU32 ... 40 F4
King George Mobile Home Pk
 BH25 ... 194 F1
King George Rd PO16 ... 156 D7
King George's Ave SO15 ... 101 F7
King Harold Ct SO23 ... 215 D4
King Henry 1 St PO1 ... 216 A3
King James Terr 2
 PO1 ... 182 A3
King John Ave
 Bournemouth BH11 ... 188 D5
 Portchester PO16 ... 156 B7
King John Cl BH11 ... 188 D6
King La GU32 ... 39 F8
King Richard 1 Rd PO1 ... 216 A3
King Richard Cl PO6 ... 157 D8
King Richard Dr BH11 ... 188 D5
King Richard Sec Sch
 PO6 ... 156 F8
King St Emsworth PO10 ... 161 A8
 Gosport PO12 ... 181 D6
 Portsmouth PO5 ... 216 B2
 Southampton SO14 ... 103 A3
 Westbourne PO10 ... 137 B3
 Wimborne Minst BH21 ... 163 B4
King William St PO1 ... 182 A6
King's Ave BH23 ... 206 F6
King's Cl SO53 ... 55 D7
King's Copse Rd SO45 ... 177 D8
King's Cres BH14 ... 203 E2
King's Croft La PO9 ... 135 C2
King's Ho 6 SO14 ... 103 A3
King's La GU32 ... 18 D4
King's Park Dr BH7,BH1 ... 205 E6
King's Park Prim Sch
 BH1 ... 205 E5
King's Park Rd BH7 ... 205 E6
King's Prim Sch The
 SO30 ... 80 E3
King's Rd
 Bournemouth BH3 ... 205 A7
 Emsworth PO10 ... 160 E8
 Fareham PO16 ... 131 B1
 Lee-on-t-S PO13 ... 179 E4
 Portsmouth PO5 ... 216 B1
 Waterlooville PO8 ... 111 F3
King's Royal Hussars Mus
 The* SO23 ... 215 D5
King's Saltern Rd SO41 ... 198 A2
King's Terr
 4 Emsworth PO10 ... 160 F8
 Portsmouth PO1,PO5 ... 216 A1
King's Wlk 8 SO23 ... 215 E5
Kingcome Ho PO1 ... 216 B4
Kingcup Cl BH18 ... 186 E2
Kingdom Cl PO15 ... 129 D5
Kingfisher Cl
 Bournemouth BH6 ... 206 E6
 Hamble-le-R SO31 ... 128 A4
 Rowlands Castle PO9 ... 113 B1
 South Hayling PO11 ... 185 C2
 Waterlooville PO8 ... 111 E4
 West Moors BH22 ... 138 F2
Kingfisher Copse SO31 ... 129 B3
Kingfisher Ct
 Bournemouth BH8 ... 205 D6
 Havant PO9 ... 136 B2
 Portsmouth PO3 ... 158 A4
 1 Southampton SO17 ... 79 A2
Kingfisher Cvn Pk PO13 ... 180 C3
Kingfisher Dr PO10 ... 137 B4
Kingfisher Park Homes 3
 BH10 ... 189 F4
Kingfisher Pk BH21 ... 138 E6
Kingfisher Rd SO50 ... 55 E2
Kingfisher Way
 Christchurch BH23 ... 208 A5
 Marchwood SO40 ... 101 E1
 Ringwood BH24 ... 117 B1
 Romsey SO51 ... 52 F8
Kingfishers
 4 Christchurch BH23 ... 207 A5
 Portchester PO16 ... 155 F8
Kingfishers The BH31 ... 115 A5
Kingland Cres 4 BH15 ... 202 C2
Kingland Rd BH15 ... 202 D2
Kings Arms La BH24 ... 140 F7
Kings Arms Row BH24 ... 140 F7
Kings Ave
 Hamble-le-R SO31 ... 127 E3
 Poole BH14 ... 203 D2
 Winchester SO22 ... 215 C3
Kings Bench Alley 19
 PO1 ... 182 A5
Kings Cl Lymington SO41 ... 197 D4
 Lyndhurst SO43 ... 121 F5
 Poole BH15 ... 202 D5
 Rowlands Castle PO9 ... 113 A1
 Twyford SO21 ... 32 A7
 West Moors BH22 ... 138 E1
Kings Copse Ave SO30 ... 105 D5
Kings Copse Prim Sch
 SO30 ... 105 C5
Kings Copse Rd SO30 ... 105 D5
Kings Cote Villas 3
 PO5 ... 182 E1
Kings Court Sch PO8 ... 88 A1
Kings Cres SO41 ... 197 D4
Kings Ct SP6 ... 69 F1
Kings Field SO31 ... 105 A1
Kings Field Gdns SO31 ... 105 A1
Kings Grange 11 BH4 ... 204 D2
Kings Head Yd 1 SO23 ... 215 E5
Kings High Sch BH10 ... 189 C3
Kings Huts SO41 ... 197 A3
Kings La Chilcomb SO21 ... 11 F6
 Sway SO41 ... 196 E8
Kings Mede PO8 ... 112 B5
Kings Mews PO5 ... 182 D2
Kings Park Com Hospl
 BH7 ... 205 F5
Kings Park Rd SO15 ... 103 A6
Kings Rd
 Chandler's Ford SO53 ... 55 D6
 Gosport PO12 ... 181 B6
 Lymington SO41 ... 197 D4
 New Milton BH25 ... 195 C3
 Petersfield GU32 ... 40 D4
 South Hayling PO11 ... 185 A5
 Winchester SO22 ... 215 A4
Kings Ride SO45 ... 177 E7

Kings Row **3** SO22 ....215 D6
Kings Sch The SO50 .....57 B1
Kings Somborne Rd SO51 .7 D2
Kings Way PO9 ....113 A1
Kings Worthy Prim Sch
SO23 ....2 C6
Kings' Sch SO22 ....10 B7
Kingsbere Ave BH10 ...189 B2
Kingsbere Gdns BH23 ..209 A8
Kingsbere Rd BH15 .....202 E5
Kingsbridge Rd BH14 ...203 C3
Kingsbury Ct PO8 ....88 B6
Kingsbury Rd SO14 ....103 B7
Kingsbury's La BH24 ...140 F2
Kingsclere Ave
Havant PO9 ....135 D5
Southampton SO19 ....126 F8
Kingsclere CI SO19 ....103 F1
Kingscote Ho **7** PO6 .132 F2
Kingscote Rd
Portchester PO6 ......132 F2
Waterlooville PO8 ....111 D3
Kingscroft Ct PO9 ....135 D1
Kingsdale Ct **3** SO22 .215 D6
Kingsdown PI PO1 ....216 D3
Kingsdown Rd PO7 ....111 C2
Kingsdown Way SO18 ...80 A2
Kingsey Ave PO10 ....160 E8
Kingsfernsden La GU31,
GU32 ....41 A5
Kingsfield
Lymington SO41 ......198 A2
Ringwood BH24 ......141 A7
Kingsfold Ave SO18 ....79 F3
Kingsford CI SP5 ......47 D5
Kingsgate **10** BH13 ..204 B3
Kingsgate Rd SO23 ....215 D4
Kingsgate St SO23 ....215 E4
Kingsland CI PO6 .....133 C1
Kingsland Ct Poole BH12 .214 F7
3 Southampton SO14 .103 A5
Kingsland Ho **4** SO14 .103 A5
Kingsland Mkt SO14 ...103 A4
Kingsland Sq **5** SO14 .103 A4
Kingsleigh Prim Sch
BH10 ....189 C3
Kingsley Ave BH6 .....207 A4
Kingsley CI BH6 ......207 A4
Kingsley Gdns SO40 ..100 B7
Kingsley Gn PO9 .....135 E6
Kingsley PI SO22 .....215 C3
Kingsley Rd
Gosport PO12 ....180 F7
Portsmouth PO4 .....183 C4
Southampton SO15 ...102 B7
Kingsmead PO17 .....108 D8
Kingsmead Ave PO14 .179 D6
Kingsmead Cotts PO17 .108 C7
Kingsmead Ct
7 Southampton SO15 ..78 B1
5 Wimborne Minst BH21 .163 B5
Kingsmill CI PO12 ....180 F4
Kingsmill CI SO31 ....182 E7
Kingston SO31 ....127 C7
Kingston Cres PO2 ...182 D8
Kingston Cross PO2 ..182 D8
Kingston Ct SO16 .....77 F2
Kingston Gdns PO15 .130 D4
Kingston Lacy Ho*
BH21 ....162 B7
Kingston Pk
Lymington SO41 ......197 D2
West Wellow SO51 ....74 E8
Kingston Rd
Gosport PO12 ....180 F5
Poole BH15 ....202 D4
Portsmouth PO1,PO2 ..182 E8
Southampton SO15 ...102 D2
Kingsway
Chandler's Ford SO53 ..55 D6
Chandler's Ford SO53 ..55 E8
Ferndown BH22 ......165 B8
North Hayling PO11 ...160 A3
Southampton SO14 ...103 A5
Kingsway CI BH23 ....191 F1
Kingsway Ct SO53 .....55 F8
Kingsway Gdns SO53 ..55 F8
Kingsway The PO16 ..156 C8
Kingswell CI BH10 ....189 D2
Kingswell Gdns BH10 .189 D2
Kingswell Gr BH10 ...189 B2
Kingswell Path PO1 ..216 B4
Kingswell Rd BH10 ...189 C2
Kingswell St PO1 .....216 B3
Kingswood
Marchwood SO40 ....102 A1
15 Bournemouth BH4 .204 C2
Kingswood CI PO15 ..129 D8
Kingswood CI **3** PO15 .129 D8
Kingswood PI PO17 ..130 E7
Kingsworthy Rd PO9 .135 F3
Kinloss Ct SO16 ......78 A5
Kinloss Ct PO10 .....160 F8
Kinross Cres PO6 ....158 B7
Kinross Rd
Bournemouth BH3 ...204 E6
Totton SO40 ....100 F7
Kinsbourne Ave BH10 .189 D6
Kinsbourne CI SO19 .104 E6
Kinsbourne Rise SO19 .104 F5
Kinsbourne Way SO19 .104 E6
Kinsford Ct SO42 ....145 F1
Kinson Ave BH15 ....203 A7
Kinson Gr BH10 .....189 C6
Kinson Park Rd BH10 .189 D6

Kinson Pottery Ind Est
BH14 ....203 A6
Kinson Prim Sch BH11 .189 B5
Kinson Rd BH10 ......189 C3
Kinterbury Ct **10** SO17 .103 A8
Kintyre Rd PO6 ......133 F1
Kinver CI SO51 ....28 B1
Kiosks The **9** BH15 .202 C1
Kipling Bldgs **3** PO2 .157 E3
Kipling CI PO15 .....106 B1
Kipling Ct SO19 .....103 F1
Kipling Rd Eastleigh SO50 .55 F3
Poole BH14 ....203 B5
Portsmouth PO2 .....157 E3
Kirby CI BH15 ....202 F6
Kirby Ct **4** PO2 ....157 E2
Kirby Rd PO2 ....157 F2
Kirby Way BH6 .....206 D4
Kirk Gdns SO40 .....100 F5
Kirkham Ave BH23 ..192 C3
Kirkstall Rd PO4 ....182 E1
Kirkway BH18 ....187 B4
Kirpal Rd PO3 ....183 B6
Kirtley CI PO6 ....158 C6
Kitchen Ct PO6 .....158 C7
Kitchener Cres BH17 .187 B2
Kitchener Rd SO17 ...79 C2
Kitchers CI SO41 ....172 B2
Kite CI PO8 ....111 E4
Kites Croft Bsns Pk
SO31 ....129 E2
Kites Croft CI PO14 .129 C1
Kitnocks Hill SO32 ..106 F8
Kitscroft Rd BH10 ...189 C5
Kitt's La GU32,SO24 ..16 C2
Kittiwake CI
Bournemouth BH6 ...206 D6
Gosport PO13 ....155 B2
Kitwalls La SO41 ....211 D5
Kitwood Gn **28** PO9 .136 B5
Kivernell Pl SO41 ...211 C4
Kivernell Rd SO41 ..211 C4
Kiwi CI BH15 ....202 E3
Kleves Ct SO19 .....104 B6
Knapp CI BH23 .....207 A8
Knapp La SO51 ......29 D4
Knapp Mill Ave BH23 .207 A8
Knapps Hard GU32 ...37 B5
Knatchbull CI SO51 ..52 F7
Knellers La SO40 ...100 D4
Knight Gdns PO6 ...158 E7
Knightcrest Pk SO41 .196 E1
Knighton Cnr PO8 ..112 C7
Knighton Cvn Pk SO41 .196 E1
Knighton Heath CI
BH11 ....188 E4
Knighton Heath Ind Est
BH11 ....188 E4
Knighton Heath Rd
BH11 ....188 E4
Knighton La PO7 ....188 D7
Knighton Pk BH25 ..209 E8
Knighton Rd SO19 ..103 F4
Knights Bank Rd PO14 .153 F1
Knights CI SO31 ....128 E1
Knights Rd BH11 ...188 B6
Knightsbridge Ct BH22 .204 E2
Knightsfield GU32 ....40 E3
Knightstone Ct **3** PO2 .157 F4
Knightstone Gr BH22 .204 E2
Knightstone Grange **2**
SO45 ....126 A2
Knightwood Ave
Havant PO9 ....136 A5
Lyndhurst SO43 .....121 F5
Knightwood CI
Ashurst SO40 ....100 B2
Christchurch BH23 ...208 D8
Lyndhurst SO43 .....121 F5
Knightwood Glade SO51 .54 F7
Knightwood Oak*
SO41 ....120 F1
Knightwood Prim Sch
SO53 ....54 F7
Knightwood Rd
Chandler's Ford SO53 ..55 A6
Hythe SO45 ....126 B3
Knightwood View SO53 .55 C5
Knobcrook Rd **8** BH21 .163 B6
Knole CI **6** BH1 ....205 D4
Knole Gdns BH1 ....205 D4
Knole Rd BH1 ....205 D4
Knoll Gdns*
Ferndown BH22 .....164 F4
St Leonards BH24 ..139 F4
Knoll La BH21 ......186 B7
Knoll Manor BH2 ...204 F5
Knotgrass Rd SO31 .128 E2
Knowland Dr SO41 .211 D5
Knowle Ave PO17 ..130 E8
Knowle Hill SO50 ....56 B7
Knowle La SO50 .....57 E1
Knowle Rd
Brockenhurst SO42 .145 E2
Fareham PO17 ......131 A7
Knowle Village BH21 .130 F7
Knowle Village Bsns Pk
PO17 ....130 D8
Knowles CI
Christchurch BH23 ...207 E7
Nursling SO16 ....77 D5
Knowles Mdw GU33 ..21 B1
Knowlton Gdns BH10 .189 D6
Knowlton Rd BH17 ..187 F2
Knowsley Cres BH10 .189 D6
Knowsley Rd PO6 ...157 F7
Knox Rd Havant PO9 .135 D1

Knox Rd continued
Portsmouth PO2 .....157 C1
Knyght CI SO51 ......53 A6
Knyveton Ho BH1 ...205 B4
Knyveton Rd BH1 ...205 C4
Kootenay Ave SO18 .104 E7
Kooyong CI SO51 ....51 B2
Kornwestheim Way SO50 .55 E3
Kynegils Rd SO22 ...215 B8
Kynon CI **2** PO12 .181 C9
Kyoto WIk PO9 .....136 A3
Kyrchil La BH21 ....163 F6
Kyrchil Way BH21 ..163 F7
Kytes La SO32 ....82 C6

L

Labrador Dr BH15 ...202 D1
Laburnum Ave PO6 .158 C7
Laburnum CI
Ferndown BH22 .....165 B6
North Baddesley SO52 .54 A5
Verwood BH31 ......115 C5
Laburnum Cres SO45 .150 B8
Laburnum Ct SO19 ..103 D3
Laburnum Dr
Everton SO41 ....211 D8
Kings Worthy SO23 ...2 B8
Laburnum Gr
Eastleigh SO50 ......56 A3
Portsmouth PO2 .....157 E1
South Hayling PO11 .185 B4
Laburnum Ho
8 Bournemouth BH10 .189 F4
Hedge End SO30 ....105 D6
Laburnum Rd
Fareham PO16 ......155 B6
Hedge End SO30 ....105 D6
Southampton SO16 ..79 C4
Waterlooville PO7 ...134 D6
Lacey Cres BH15 ...203 A6
Lackford Ave SO40 .100 C6
Lacon CI SO18 ......103 E8
Lacy CI BH21 ....163 C6
Lacy Dr BH21 ......163 C6
Ladram Rd PO12 ...180 E4
Lady Betty's Dr PO15 .129 E5
Ladybridge Rd PO7 .134 C4
Ladycross Rd SO45 .126 A2
Ladysmith CI BH23 .207 E7
Ladysmith Terr SO32 .83 A7
Ladywood SO16 ......55 F6
Ladywood Ho PO6 ..216 B2
Lagado CI BH14 ....214 C8
Lagland CI BH14 ...202 C2
Lagland St BH15 ...214 B8
Lagoon CI BH14 ....214 B8
Laidlaw CI BH12 ...204 B8
Laidlaw Gdns SO31 ..30 B1
Lainston CI SO22 ...215 A3
Lake Ave BH15 .....201 D1
Lake Cres BH15 ....201 E3
Lake Dr Hamworthy BH15 .201 E3
Poole BH15 ....201 E3
Lake Farm CI
Ferndown BH22 .....189 B8
Hedge End SO30 ....105 C8
Lake Grove Rd BH25 .195 A4
Lake Ho SO15 ......102 C6
Lake Rd
Bournemouth BH11 .189 C6
Chandler's Ford SO53 .55 E8
Curdridge SO32 ....106 F8
Hamworthy BH15 ..201 E2
Portsmouth PO1 ...216 C4
Southampton SO19 .103 D2
Verwood BH31 .....115 A5
Lake View Manor BH25 .195 A3
Lakeland Gdns SO40 .101 E1
Lakelands Dr SO15 .102 C6
Laker Ho SO15 .....102 C6
Lakes The SO32 ....106 A4
Lakeside Fareham PO17 .130 E5
Lee-on-t-S PO13 ...179 F1
Ower SO51 ....75 D6
Ringwood BH24 ....141 D6
Lakeside Ave
Portsmouth PO3 ...183 B7
Rowlands SO16 .....77 E5
Lakeside CI PO4 ...182 F2
Lakeside Ctry Pk* SO50 .79 F8
Lakeside Gdns SO30 .136 A2
Lakeside Pines BH25 .195 A4
Lakeside Rd BH13 ..204 A1
Lakeview Dr BH24 .141 D6
Lakewood Rd
Ashurst SO40 ....100 C3
Chandler's Ford SO53 .55 D8
Christchurch BH23 ..193 F1
Lamбert CI SO19 ...104 D8
Lambert CI PO7 ....134 E5
Lambourn CI PO14 .154 D8
Lamburn Sq SO15 ...55 B6
Lambs CI BH21 .....125 F1
Lambs Green La BH21 .124 D1
Lambscombe La GU33 .21 A2
Lambsh Lease GU33 .23 A1
Lambsgreen La BH21 .162 F2
Lammas Rd SO45 ...126 B2

Lampeter Ave PO6 ..158 B8
Lampton Gdns **5** BH9 .189 F1
Lamward Mans **1** SO14 .103 A7
Lanark Ct BH15 ....201 E2
Lancaster CI
Bursledon SO31 ....105 A1
Christchurch BH23 ..208 C7
Corfe Mullen BH18 .186 F5
Lee-on-t-S PO13 ...180 B4
Portchester PO16 ..132 B1
Lancaster Ct SO30 ...80 C2
Lancaster Dr
Corfe Mullen BH18 .186 F5
Verwood BH31 .....114 E6
Lancaster Rd
Ferndown BH21 ....165 A8
Southampton SO16 ..77 F3
Lancaster Way PO7 .134 F4
Lance's Hill SO18 ..103 F7
Lancer CI BH23 ....206 F7
Lancer Ho PO7 .....111 C1
Lander CI BH15 ....202 D1
Landford CE Prim Sch
SP5 ....49 D4
Landford Common Farm
SP5 ....49 E2
Landford Gdns BH8 .190 D2
Landford Way BH8 .190 D2
Landguard Rd
Portsmouth PO4 ...183 A3
Southampton SO15 .102 D6
Landon Ct PO12 ...181 A3
Landon Rd PO13 ...155 D1
Landport St
Portsmouth PO1 ...216 C4
Portsmouth,Southsea PO5 .216 A2
Landport Terr PO1 .216 B4
Landport View PO1 .216 B4
Lands End Rd SO31 .128 C7
Landsdowne St PO5 .216 A2
Landseer Rd
1 Bournemouth BH4 .204 C3
Southampton SO19 .104 C3
Lane End CI SO41 ...17 C8
Lane End Cotts SP5 .49 D3
Lane End Dr PO10 .160 F8
Lane Lowther Gdns The **4**
BH8 ....205 C5
Lane The Fawley SO45 .151 B3
Gosport PO12 ......181 A2
Portsmouth PO4 ...182 F2
Lanehays Rd SO45 .125 F3
Lanes End PO14 ...179 C2
Lanes The BH25 ...195 A5
Lanesbridge CI SO40 .99 F2
Langbar CI SO19 ..103 E6
Langbrook CI PO9 .136 B5
Langdale CI SO16 ..101 D6
Langdale Ct BH14 .203 D4
Langdon Rd BH14 .203 C3
Langdown Firs SO45 .126 C3
Langdown Lawn SO45 .126 B3
Langdown Lawn CI
SO45 ....126 A2
Langdown Rd SO45 .126 C3
Langford CI **12** PO16 .131 B1
Langford La SP5 .....47 E8
Langford Rd PO1 ..182 F7
Langham CI SO52 ...53 F4
Langham Rd BH23 .191 F1
Langhorn Rd SO16 ..79 C4
Langley Chase BH24 .140 F4
Langley Gdns SP6 ...70 A3
Langley Lodge Gdns
SO45 ....177 F7
Langley Rd
Christchurch BH23 ..193 E1
Poole BH14 ....203 F4
Southampton SO15 .102 A6
Langrish CI PO9 ...136 A4
Langrish Prim Sch GU32 .40 A3
Langside Ave BH12 .203 B8
Langslade Rd BH12 .204 A8
Langside Sch BH12 .204 A8
Langstone Ave PO9 .159 F7
Langstone High St PO9 .159 F6
Langstone Ho PO1 ..80 C6
Langstone Harbour Nature
Reserve* PO9 ......159 A3
Langstone Inf Sch PO9 .135 A1
Langstone Jun Sch PO9 .135 A1
Langstone Marina Hts
PO4 ....183 D3
Langstone WIk
Fareham PO14 ......154 C8
Gosport PO13 ......155 B2
Langton CI
Barton on S BH25 ..210 B8
Lee-on-t-S PO13 ...180 A6
Winchester SO22 ..215 C8
Langton Farm Gdns
PO1 ....182 E7
Langton Rd
Bishop's Waltham SO32 .83 C8
Bournemouth BH7 ..205 F5
Lanham La SO22 .....1 B1
Lankhills Rd SO23 .215 B8
Lansdell Ct **4** BH15 .202 E3
Lansdown Ave PO16 .131 C1
Lansdown Terr PO10 .137 B5

Lansdowne PO7 .....134 B2
Waterlooville PO7 ...134 B2
Winchester SO23 ...215 D3
Lansdowne CI **2** SO51 .52 E8
Lansdowne Cres BH1 .205 B3
Lansdowne Ct
1 Romsey SO51 .....52 E8
3 Winchester SO23 .215 D3
Lansdowne Gdns
Bournemouth BH1 ..205 A4
Romsey SO51 ....52 E8
Lansdowne Hill **4** SO14 .102 F3
Lansdowne Ho **3** PO12 .181 A7
Lansdowne Rd
Bournemouth BH1 ..205 A5
Southampton SO16 .102 A7
Lansdowne Rdbt The
BH1 ....205 A3
Lantana CI PO7 ....134 F6
Lanvalley Rd SO23 .215 C4
Lanyard Dr PO13 ..180 D6
Lapthorn CI PO13 .155 B1
Lapwing CI Gosport PO12 .181 B8
Hordean PO8 ....112 A7
Lapwing Dr SO40 ..100 C8
Lapwing Gr PO16 ..155 F8
Lapwing Rd
Portsmouth PO4 ...183 C5
Wimborne Minst BH21 .164 A7
Lara CI BH8 ....190 D3
Larch CI
Broadstone BH17 ..186 E1
Hordle SO41 ....195 F3
Kings Worthy SO23 ..2 B8
St Leonards BH24 .140 A4
West End SO30 ....80 D2
Larch Ct SO16 .....78 A3
Larch Row SP6 ....70 D2
Larch Way
Bursledon SO31 ...127 F8
Ferndown BH22 ...165 C7
Larchdale CI SO31 .152 D10
Larches Gdns PO15 .130 C1
Larchfield Way PO8 .112 C5
Larchwood Ave PO9 .135 B4
Larchwood Rd SO40 .100 C4
Larcombe Rd GU32 .40 D2
Larg Dr SO22 ....1 C4
Lark Hill Rise SO22 .215 B2
Lark Rd BH23 .....196 E5
Lark Way PO10 ...137 C4
Larkhill Rd PO3 ...157 F4
Larks Rise BH22 ..165 B7
Larksfield Ave BH9 .190 C3
Larkshill Ct BH25 .194 C5
Larkspur Chase SO19 .104 C5
Larkspur CI
Locks Heath SO31 .128 F2
Swanmore SO32 ....84 A5
Larkspur Dr
Chandler's Ford SO53 .54 F6
Marchwood SO40 ..124 F8
Larkspur Gdns
7 Hedge End SO30 .105 C6
Southampton SO45 .150 B4
Larkwhistle Wlk PO9 .135 C2
Lascelles Ct **1** BH7 .206 B6
Lascelles Rd BH7 ..206 B6
Laser CI SO31 .....128 E1
Lasham Gn **28** PO9 .136 B5
Lasham Ho **5** SO16 .102 B8
Lasham Wlk PO14 .154 D7
Lashly Mdw PO7 ..134 C6
Latch Farm Ave BH23 .207 A8
Latchmore Dr SO45 .125 C6
Latchmore Forest Gr
PO8 ....112 A3
Latchmore Gdns PO8 .111 F3
Latelie CI SO31 ...127 C5
Latham CI SO50 ...57 B2
Latham Rd Eastleigh SO50 .57 B2
Latham Rd Fair Oak SO50 .57 B2
Romsey SO51 ....53 A8
Latimer Ct
Portsmouth PO3 ...158 B4
4 Southampton SO17 .79 A1
Latimer Gdns **2** SO24 .103 A3
Latimer Ho **5** SO15 .102 F5
Latimer St Romsey SO51 .52 E7
Southampton SO14 .103 A3
Lauder CI PO10 ...160 F7
Launceston CI **3** SO51 .53 F3
Launceston Dr SO53 .55 C5
Laundry La SO41 ..211 E4
Laundry Rd BH10 .189 D6
Laurel CI
Christchurch BH23 ..193 D1
Corfe Mullen BH21 .186 D6
8 Gosport PO12 ...181 C8
Hordle SO41 ....195 E4
Hythe SO45 ....125 F3
Langley SO45 .....150 A2
St Leonards BH24 .139 E3
Laurel Gdns
Broadstone BH18 ..187 C4
1 Hamworthy BH15 .201 E2
Laurel La PO8 .....89 B4
Laurel Rd
Locks Heath SO31 .128 F2

Laurel Rd *continued*
Waterlooville PO8 . . . . .112 C4
Laurels The
Broadstone BH18 . . . . .187 B4
Brockenhurst SO42 . . . . .172 F8
Ferndown BH22 . . . . .165 C7
Lauren Mews PO11 . . . . .184 E2
Lauren Way SO40 . . . . .76 B1
Laurence Ct SO50 . . . . .57 C2
Laurence Gn PO10 . . . . .136 F4
Laurence Mews SO51 . . . . . .52 F8
Lauriston Dr 7 SO53 . . . . . . .30 B1
Laurus Cl PO7 . . . . .135 A5
Laurus Wlk 4 PO13 . . . . .179 F3
Lavant Cl PO8 . . . . .112 B1
Lavant Ct GU32 . . . . .40 E4
Lavant Dr PO9 . . . . .136 A3
Lavant St GU32 . . . . .40 E3
Lavender Cl
Southampton SO19 . . . . .103 F5
Verwood BH31 . . . . .115 C5
Lavender Rd
Bournemouth BH8 . . . . .190 D4
Hordle SO41 . . . . .195 E3
Waterlooville PO7 . . . . .135 A6
Lavender Villas BH23 . . . . . .209 A8
Lavender Way BH11 . . . . . . .188 D3
Lavender Wlk BH8 . . . . .190 D4
Laverock Lea PO16 . . . . .132 C1
Laverstock 3 BH5 . . . . .205 F3
Laverstoke Cl SO16 . . . . .77 E6
Lavey's La PO15 . . . . .130 B6
Lavington Gdns SO52 . . . . . .53 F3
Lavinia Rd Gosport PO12 . . .181 A6
Poole BH12 . . . . .203 C7
Lawford Rd BH9 . . . . .190 A4
Lawford Way SO40 . . . . .100 E7
Lawn Cl Gosport PO13 . . . . . .180 D8
Milford on S SO41 . . . . .211 E4
Lawn Ct
18 Bournemouth BH2 . . . . . .204 D4
Southampton SO17 . . . . .103 A7
Lawn Dr SO31 . . . . .129 A2
Lawn Ho 24 SO23 . . . . .215 E6
Lawn Rd Eastleigh SO50 . . . .56 B5
Littleton SO22 . . . . .1 C5
Lymington SO41 . . . . .197 B3
Southampton SO17 . . . . .103 B8
Lawn St SO23 . . . . .215 E6
Lawn View BH25 . . . . .194 D5
Lawns Cl BH21 . . . . .164 C6
Lawns Rd BH21 . . . . .164 B6
Lawns The BH23 . . . . .209 B8
Lawnside Rd SO15 . . . . .102 A8
Lawnswood SO50 . . . . .57 D1
Lawnswood Cl
Dibden Purlieu SO45 . . . . . . .125 E1
Waterlooville PO8 . . . . .111 F2
Lawrence Ave PO8 . . . . .111 E2
Lawrence Cl
Bournemouth BH8 . . . . .205 C6
Southampton SO19 . . . . .103 F2
Lawrence Dr BH13 . . . . .203 E1
Lawrence Gr SO19 . . . . .103 F2
Lawrence Ho SO45 . . . . .126 B4
Lawrence La SP6 . . . . .94 B4
Lawrence Mans PO5 . . . . . . .216 D1
Lawrence Rd
Fareham PO15 . . . . .130 F2
Portsmouth PO5 . . . . .216 D1
Ringwood BH24 . . . . .117 D2
Lawrence Sq 3 PO12 . . . . . .181 D5
Lawrence Way 4 SO23 . . . . .215 E8
Lawrence Wlk PO13 . . . . .180 D6
Lawson Cl SO31 . . . . .128 D8
Lawson Ct 3 SO41 . . . . .78 B1
Lawson Rd Poole BH12 . . . . .203 B6
Portsmouth PO5 . . . . .216 D2
Laxton Cl
Locks Heath SO31 . . . . .129 B3
Southampton SO19 . . . . .104 A2
Layard Dr BH21 . . . . .163 D1
Laymoor La BH21 . . . . .164 C6
Layton Cl BH12 . . . . .203 D5
Layton Rd Gosport PO13 . . .155 C3
Poole BH12 . . . . .203 D5
Lazy Acre PO10 . . . . .161 D8
Le Patourel Cl BH23 . . . . . . .207 D7
Le Tissier Ct 6 SO15 . . . . . .102 E6
Lea Rd SO45 . . . . .177 E7
Lea The BH31 . . . . .115 A5
Lea Way BH11 . . . . .188 B5
Lea-Oak Gdns PO15 . . . . . . .130 D3
Leabrook SO31 . . . . .129 A5
Leacock Cl SO32 . . . . .84 B5
Leafy La PO15 . . . . .129 E6
Lealand Gr PO6 . . . . .158 D8
Lealand Rd PO6 . . . . .158 D7
Leamington Cres PO13 . . . .179 F3
Leamington Ho 9 PO5 . . . .216 B2
Leamington Rd BH9 . . . . . . .205 A7
Leander Cl SO50 . . . . .56 A5
Leander Dr 7 PO12 . . . . .181 C8
Leaphill Rd BH7 . . . . .206 B6
Lear Rd PO12 . . . . .181 B6
Learoyd Rd BH17 . . . . .202 E7
Leaside Way SO16 . . . . .79 C5
Leatham Cl BH13 . . . . .204 D5
Leaway The PO16 . . . . .156 D8
Lebanon Rd SO15 . . . . .101 D7
Lebern Ho SO30 . . . . .105 D7
Lechlade Gdns
Bournemouth BH7 . . . . .206 B8
Fareham PO15 . . . . .130 E4
Leckford Cl
Portchester PO16 . . . . .132 B2
Southampton SO18 . . . . .104 D8

Leckford Rd PO9 . . . . .136 B6
Ledbury Rd
Christchurch BH23 . . . . .207 F5
Portsmouth PO6 . . . . .133 C1
Lederle La PO13 . . . . .155 C5
Ledgard Cl BH14 . . . . .203 B4
Ledwell Ct PO12 . . . . .181 D7
Lee Church La SO51 . . . . . . .76 F8
Lee Ct BH22 . . . . .165 D4
Lee Dro SO51 . . . . .53 B1
Lee Ground PO15 . . . . .129 F5
Lee La SO16,SO51 . . . . .53 A2
Lee Lands SO41 . . . . .197 D1
Lee Rd PO12 . . . . .181 A7
Lee-on-the-Solent Inf Sch
PO13 .179 F2
Lee-on-the-Solent Jun Sch
PO13 .179 F2
Leedam Rd BH10 . . . . .189 D4
Leep La PO12 . . . . .181 B3
Lees Cl BH23 . . . . .191 D4
Lees La PO12 . . . . .181 B6
Lees Lane N 9 PO12 . . . . . . .181 B6
Leesland CE Inf Sch
PO12 .181 A5
Leesland CE Jun Sch
PO12 .181 B5
Leesland Rd PO12 . . . . .181 A6
Leeson Dr BH22 . . . . .165 B8
Leeson Rd BH7 . . . . .205 E7
Legg La BH21 . . . . .163 D4
Legion Cl
Hamworthy BH15 . . . . .201 E2
Southampton SO16 . . . . .79 C4
Legion La SO23 . . . . .2 C7
Legion Rd
Hamworthy BH15 . . . . .201 E2
South Hayling PO11 . . . . .185 A4
Leicester Ct 11 PO11 . . . . . .180 D5
Leicester Gdns BH13 . . . . . .203 F3
Southampton SO15 . . . . .78 D2
Leicester Way SO23 . . . . .2 C1
Leigh Cl BH21 . . . . .163 E4
Leigh Comm BH21 . . . . .163 E5
Leigh Cres PO9 . . . . .136 A4
Leigh Ct SO50 . . . . .55 E3
Leigh Gdns BH21 . . . . .163 D4
Leigh House Hospl SO21 . . .11 E7
Leigh La BH21 . . . . .163 F5
Leigh Mans 2 SO17 . . . . . . .79 A1
Leigh Pk SO41 . . . . .197 C3
Leigh Rd Eastleigh SO50 . . . .55 E3
Fareham PO16 . . . . .131 A2
Havant PO9 . . . . .135 F2
New Milton BH25 . . . . .195 A3
Southampton SO17 . . . . .79 A1
Wimborne Minst BH21 . . . . . .163 E4
Leigham Vale Rd BH6 . . . . . .206 D4
Leighton Ave 8 SO15 . . . . .102 B8
Leighton Lo 3 BH21 . . . . . .204 D4
Leighton Rd SO19 . . . . .103 F3
Leisure The PO13 . . . . .155 D4
Leith Ave PO16 . . . . .132 E1
Lemon Rd SO15 . . . . .102 B7
Len Williams Terr PO12 . . . .182 E7
Lendorber Ave PO6 . . . . . . .158 A8
Lennox Cl
Chandler's Ford SO53 . . . . . . .55 E7
Gosport PO12 . . . . .181 C2
Southampton SO16 . . . . .77 F5
Lennox Ct 9 PO5 . . . . .182 D1
Lennox Mans PO5 . . . . .182 D1
Lennox Rd N PO5 . . . . .182 D1
Lennox Rd S PO5 . . . . .182 D2
Lensyd Gdns PO8 . . . . .111 F6
Lent Hill Ct SO22 . . . . .215 B4
Lentham Cl BH17 . . . . .187 D1
Lentune Way SO41 . . . . .197 D2
Ledric Ct PO4 . . . . .183 C3
Leominster Ho BH8 . . . . .204 F7
Leominster Rd PO6 . . . . .133 B1
Leonard Rd PO12 . . . . .181 C6
Leonards Ct SO16 . . . . .101 C8
Leopold Dr SO32 . . . . .83 B7
Leopold Rd PO4 . . . . .182 E2
Lepe Ctry Pk* SO45 . . . . . . .178 B2
Lepe Rd SO45 . . . . .178 A3
Leroux Cl SO15 . . . . .102 F5
Lerryn Rd PO13 . . . . .180 C6
Leslie Loader Ct SO50 . . . . . .56 A4
Leslie Loader Ho SO19 . . . . .103 E5
Leslie Rd
Bournemouth BH9 . . . . .204 F7
Poole BH14 . . . . .203 A3
Lesser Horseshoe Cl 2
PO17 .130 E8
Lester Ave PO9 . . . . .135 C2
Lester Rd PO12 . . . . .181 C5
Lester Sq BH24 . . . . .143 C3
Leven Ave BH4 . . . . .204 D5
Leven Cl
Bournemouth BH4 . . . . .204 D4
Chandler's Ford SO53 . . . . . . .55 A7
Leventhorpe Ct PO12 . . . . . .181 C5
Leveret Cl PO12 . . . . .181 F8
Leveson Cl PO12 . . . . .180 F3
Levet's La 4 BH25 . . . . .202 B1
Leviathan Cl PO14 . . . . .179 D7
Lewins Cl SO16 . . . . .101 C4
Lewens La BH21 . . . . .163 C4
Lewes Cl SO50 . . . . .56 A6
Lewesdon Dr BH18 . . . . .186 F4
Lewin Cl SO21 . . . . .56 F8
Lewins Wlk SO16 . . . . .104 F1
Lewis Cl SO45 . . . . .125 C2
Lewis Ho 5 SO40 . . . . .4 A8
Lewis Rd PO10 . . . . .137 A3
Lewis Silkin Way SO16 . . . . .78 A4

Lewry Cl SO30 . . . . .105 C7
Lexby Rd SO40 . . . . .101 A6
Lexden Gdns PO11 . . . . .184 E4
Leybourne Ave
Bournemouth BH10 . . . . .189 D4
Southampton SO18 . . . . .104 A8
Leybourne Cl BH10 . . . . .189 D4
Leybourne Ct BH10 . . . . .189 C5
Leydene Ave BH8 . . . . .190 F1
Leydene Cl BH8 . . . . .190 F1
Leydene Pk GU32 . . . . .63 E3
Leyland Cl PO12 . . . . .181 B4
Leyland Rd BH12 . . . . .188 E2
Leyside BH23 . . . . .207 F6
Leyton Conyers 11 BH13 . . .214 F7
Leyton Rd SO14 . . . . .103 C6
Liam Cl PO9 . . . . .136 A4
Liberty Cl BH21 . . . . .139 B6
Liberty Ct BH23 . . . . .206 F7
Liberty Rd PO17 . . . . .109 A8
Liberty Row SO31 . . . . .128 A2
Liberty The PO7 . . . . .110 E3
Library Gdns PO9 . . . . .135 E3
Library Mews BH12 . . . . .203 D5
Library Rd
Bournemouth BH9 . . . . .189 F1
Ferndown BH22 . . . . .165 D5
Poole BH12 . . . . .203 E5
Totton SO40 . . . . .101 A7
Lichen Way SO40 . . . . .100 F2
Lichfield Ct 4 BH13 . . . . .180 D5
Lichfield Dr PO12 . . . . .181 C8
Lichfield Rd
Locks Heath PO14 . . . . .129 C3
Portsmouth PO3 . . . . .183 A6
Liddel Way SO53 . . . . .55 B5
Liddiard Gdns PO4 . . . . .183 B2
Liddiards Way PO7 . . . . .134 E3
Liddied Gdns PO4 . . . . .183 B2
Lieberkror Dr BH1 . . . . .115 C4
Lightfoot Lawn PO4 . . . . . . .183 C3
Lighthouse The 16 PO1 . . . .182 A4
Lightning Cl SO45 . . . . .150 F2
Lights Cl BH23 . . . . .207 B7
Lilac Cl Havant PO9 . . . . .136 C3
Southampton SO40 . . . . .101 B8
Lilac Rd SO16 . . . . .79 B4
Lilley Cl SO40 . . . . .101 F2
Lillies The SO50 . . . . .81 D7
Lilliput CE Fst Sch
BH14 .214 C8
Lilliput Cl BH14 . . . . .203 B3
Lilliput Rd BH14 . . . . .214 D8
Lily Ave PO7 . . . . .134 B2
Limberline Rd PO3 . . . . .158 A4
Limberline Spur PO3 . . . . . .158 A5
Lime Ave SO19 . . . . .104 A5
Lime Cl
Colden Common SO21 . . . . . . .57 A8
Hythe SO45 . . . . .125 E2
Poole BH15 . . . . .202 F6
Lime Gdns SO30 . . . . .80 D3
Lime Gr Hordle SO41 . . . . . . .211 D8
Portsmouth PO6 . . . . .133 B1
South Hayling PO11 . . . . .184 C3
Lime Kiln Lane Estate Mobile
Home Pk SO45 . . . . .150 B5
Lime St SO14 . . . . .103 A3
Lime Tree Cl SP6 . . . . .92 F6
Lime Tree Ho 1 SO41 . . . . .197 E4
Lime Wlk Botley SO30 . . . . . .105 F7
Hythe SO45 . . . . .125 E2
Limekiln La
Bishop's Waltham SO32 . . . . . .59 F4
East Meon GU32 . . . . .64 D6
Limes La GU33 . . . . .20 F4
Limes The Gosport PO13 . . .155 D1
Langstone PO9 . . . . .159 F8
Marchwood SO40 . . . . .102 A1
Waterlooville PO7 . . . . .134 D3
Limetree Wlk 3 SO23 . . . . .11 E8
Limited Rd BH9 . . . . .190 A1
Lin Brook Dr BH24 . . . . .117 C2
Linacre Rd SO19 . . . . .104 D5
Linbrook Ct BH24 . . . . .117 A1
Lincoln Ave
Bournemouth BH1 . . . . .205 D5
Christchurch BH23 . . . . .191 F2
Lincoln Cl
Locks Heath PO14 . . . . .129 C3
Romsey SO51 . . . . .28 B1
Lincoln Ct
9 Bournemouth BH1 . . . . . .205 D5
Southampton SO15 . . . . .78 E2
West End SO30 . . . . .80 C2
Lincoln Pl SO53 . . . . .55 D4
Lincoln Rd Poole BH12 . . . . .203 C5
Portsmouth PO1 . . . . .182 E5
Lincoln Rise SO30 . . . . .112 B4
Lincolns Rise SO50 . . . . .81 B1
Lind Cl PO7 . . . . .134 F3
Lind Rd PO12 . . . . .181 E6
Linda Gr PO8 . . . . .111 F3
Linda Rd SO45 . . . . .151 A4
Lindal Cl SO30 . . . . .105 C7
Lindbergh Cl PO13 . . . . .180 F6
Lindbergh Rd SO15 . . . . .101 F8
Lindbergh Rise PO13 . . . . . .180 F6
Linden Cl
Ferndown BH22 . . . . .165 D1
Waltham Chase SO32 . . . . .83 E3
Linden Ct
Locks Heath SO31 . . . . .129 C3
Ringwood BH24 . . . . .140 F8
6 Romsey SO51 . . . . .28 D1
West End SO18 . . . . .80 B3
Linden Dr GU33 . . . . .20 F4

Linden Gdns
Hedge End SO30 . . . . .105 D5
Ringwood BH24 . . . . .140 F8
Linden Gr
Chandler's Ford SO53 . . . . . . .55 C8
Gosport PO12 . . . . .181 B4
South Hayling PO11 . . . . .185 A3
Linden Lea PO16 . . . . .132 C1
Linden Rd
Bournemouth BH9 . . . . .190 A3
Ferndown BH22 . . . . .165 D1
Poole BH12 . . . . .203 C6
Linden Way Havant PO9 . . . .135 F3
Lymington SO41 . . . . .197 C4
Waterlooville PO8 . . . . .112 C5
Linden Wlk SO52 . . . . .53 F5
Lindens Cl PO10 . . . . .136 F2
Lindens The BH23 . . . . .192 D3
Lindford Rd BH24 . . . . .117 D1
Lindisfarne Cl PO6 . . . . .158 A7
Lindley Ave PO4 . . . . .183 A2
Lindon Ct PO4 . . . . .182 F4
Lindsay Ct 19 BH13 . . . . .204 A4
Lindsay Ho 3 PO5 . . . . .182 D2
Lindsay Manor 11 BH13 . . . .204 A4
Lindsay Pk 18 BH13 . . . . .204 A4
Lindsay Rd BH13 . . . . .204 A4
Southampton SO19 . . . . .104 E6
Lindum Ct 3 BH23 . . . . .204 A4
Lindway SO31 . . . . .129 A5
Liners Ind Est SO15 . . . . . . .102 C6
Lineside BH23 . . . . .207 C8
Linford Cl BH25 . . . . .195 B4
Linford Cres SO16 . . . . .78 D3
Linford Cr Fair Oak SO50 . . . .57 C2
Havant PO9 . . . . .135 D7
Linford Ho BH24 . . . . .117 F3
Linford Rd BH24 . . . . .117 D1
Ling Dale SO16 . . . . .78 F7
Ling Rd BH12 . . . . .188 B1
Lingdale Pl 3 SO17 . . . . .103 A8
Lingdale Rd BH6 . . . . .206 D6
Lingfield Cr PO1 . . . . .182 B3
Lingfield Gdns SO18 . . . . . . .79 F2
Lingfield Grange 11
BH13 .204 B3
Lingwood Ave BH23 . . . . . . .207 F6
Lingwood Cl SO16 . . . . .78 F7
Lingwood Wlk SO16 . . . . . . .78 F7
Linhorns La BH25 . . . . .195 A5
Link Ho PO3 . . . . .183 A6
Link Rd Portsmouth PO6 . . .133 B2
Ringwood BH24 . . . . .141 C8
Southampton SO16 . . . . .77 F3
Link Rise BH21 . . . . .186 E6
Link The PO7 . . . . .112 A1
Linkenholt Way PO9 . . . . . . .135 C4
Linklater Path PO1 . . . . .182 D7
Links Cl PO9 . . . . .113 B1
Links Dr BH23 . . . . .191 D1
Links La
Rowlands Castle PO9 . . . . . . .113 B2
South Hayling PO11 . . . . .184 C3
Links Rd Poole BH14 . . . . . . .203 D2
Portsmouth PO5 . . . . .155 C1
Links View Ave PO14 . . . . . .129 C3
Links View Way SO16 . . . . . .78 F6
Linkside Ave BH7 . . . . .205 F8
Linkway PO14 . . . . .179 C6
Linmead Dr BH11 . . . . .188 A6
Linnet Cl Petersfield GU31 . . .41 C2
Ringwood BH24 . . . . .141 C6
Linnet Cr Gosport PO12 . . . .180 B2
New Milton BH25 . . . . .194 F3
Linnet Rd BH17 . . . . .201 F8
Linnet Sq SO50 . . . . .55 D1
Linnets The
Portchester PO16 . . . . .155 F8
Totton SO40 . . . . .100 C8
Linnies La SO41 . . . . .196 E1
Linthorpe Rd BH15 . . . . .202 E4
Linton Lawns BH22 . . . . .165 E3
Linwood Cl SO45 . . . . .126 A2
Linwood Rd BH9 . . . . .205 B7
Lion Brewery The 1
PO2 . . . . .182 D8
Lion Ho PO17 . . . . .108 A4
Lion Rd PO14 . . . . .181 F8
Lion St PO1 . . . . .182 B5
Lion Terr PO1 . . . . .182 B5
Lionheart Cl BH11 . . . . .188 D5
Lionheart Way SO31 . . . . . . .105 A1
Lions Hall 4 SO22 . . . . .215 D5
Lions La BH24 . . . . .139 D5
Lions Wood PO9 . . . . .136 B5
Liphook Ho GU32 . . . . .136 F5
Lipizzaner Fields PO15 . . . . .129 B8
Lippen Cl SO32 . . . . .36 F4
Lisbon Rd SO15 . . . . .102 D6
Lisle Cl Lymington SO41 . . . .197 D3
Winchester SO22 . . . . .10 A3
Lisle Court Rd SO41 . . . . . . .198 C3
Lisle Ct SO22 . . . . .215 C4
Lisle Gr SO32 . . . . .83 D6
Lisle Rd & Inf Schs GU33 . . .21 A3
Liss Rd PO4 . . . . .182 F4
Liss Sta GU33 . . . . .21 B3
Lissenden 1 BH13 . . . . .204 B3
Litchfield Cres SO18 . . . . . . .79 F1
Litchfield Rd
Southampton SO18 . . . . .79 F1
Winchester SO22 . . . . .1 D4
Litchford Rd BH25 . . . . .195 C3

Lith Ave SO16 . . . . .112 C8
Lith La PO9 . . . . .88 C1
Little Abshot Rd PO14 . . . . .153 B8
Little Anglesey PO12 . . . . . .181 B3
Little Anglesey Rd
PO12 .181 A3
Little Arthur St PO2 . . . . . . .182 E7
Little Ashton La SO32 . . . . . . .59 E3
Little Barn Pl GU33 . . . . .21 B4
Little Barrs Dr BH25 . . . . . . .195 B4
Little Bull La SO32 . . . . .83 D2
Little Burn SO41 . . . . .172 B2
Little Cnr PO7 . . . . .111 A3
Little Coburg St PO1 . . . . . .216 C3
Little Croft Rd BH12 . . . . . . .203 B6
Little Ct Poole BH14 . . . . . . .214 C7
Poole,Canford Cliffs BH13 . . .214 F8
Little Dene Copse SO41 . . . .197 B2
Little Dewlands BH31 . . . . . .114 D6
Little Dro SP6 . . . . .70 E7
Little Forest Mans 12
BH1 . . . . .205 A3
Little Forest Rd BH4 . . . . . . .204 E5
Little Fosters BH13 . . . . .214 E6
Little Fox Dr 2 SO31 . . . . . . .129 B5
Little Gays PO14 . . . . .129 C7
Little George St PO1 . . . . . . .182 E7
Little Gn PO12 . . . . .181 A3
Little Green Orch PO12 . . . .181 A3
Little Hambrook St 6
PO5 . . . . .216 A1
Little Holbury Park Homes
Mobile Home Pk SO45 . . . .150 B5
Little Hyden La PO8 . . . . .88 B7
Little Kimble Wlk 3
SO30 .105 C6
Little La PO12 . . . . .181 A3
Little Lance's Hill SO19 . . . .103 F6
Little Lonnen
Colehill BH21 . . . . .163 F8
Wimborne Minst BH21 . . . . . .164 A8
Little Mead PO7 . . . . .111 A3
Little Minster St SO23 . . . . .215 E5
Little Oak Rd SO16 . . . . .78 F4
Little Park Cl SO30 . . . . .105 B6
Little Park Farm Rd
PO15 .129 C5
Little Park Mans PO17 . . . . .107 E4
Little Quob La SO30 . . . . .80 E2
Little Reynolds SO40 . . . . . .100 D5
Little Shore La SO32 . . . . .83 D7
Little Southsea St PO5 . . . . .216 A1
Little Stodham Ho GU33 . . . .20 D2
Little Toller SO19 . . . . .104 A2
Little Woodfalls Dr SP5 . . . .47 D4
Little Woodham La
PO13 .180 C5
Littledown Ave BH7 . . . . . . .190 B3
Littledown Dr BH7 . . . . .205 F7
Littlefield Cres SO53 . . . . . . .54 E6
Littlegreen Ave PO9 . . . . . . .136 B4
Littlegreen Sch PO18 . . . . . . .90 E4
Littlemead Cl BH17 . . . . .202 A7
Littlemeads SO51 . . . . .52 D7
Littlemill La SP6 . . . . .68 C6
Littlemoor Ave BH11 . . . . . .188 D4
Littlepark Ave PO9 . . . . .135 B3
Littleton Cl PO9 . . . . .135 F4
Littleton La SO21,SO22 . . . . . .1 A5
Littleton Rd SO22 . . . . .1 B4
Littlewood SO51 . . . . .50 F3
Littlewood Gdns
Sarisbury SO31 . . . . .128 E3
West End SO30 . . . . .80 D1
Liverpool Ct 2 PO13 . . . . . . .180 D5
Liverpool Rd
Fareham PO14 . . . . .154 F6
Portsmouth PO1 . . . . .182 E5
Liverpool St SO14 . . . . .103 A7
Livesay Gdns PO1 . . . . .182 F6
Livingstone Ct PO13 . . . . . . .180 D6
Livingstone Rd
Bournemouth BH5 . . . . .206 B5
Christchurch BH23 . . . . .207 D7
Poole BH12 . . . . .203 C6
Portsmouth PO5 . . . . .216 C1
Southampton SO14 . . . . .103 A8
Wimborne Minst BH21 . . . . . .163 E4
Llewellin Cl BH21 . . . . .186 C7
Llewelyn Cl BH16 . . . . .201 C7
Lloyd Ave SO40 . . . . .101 E1
Loader Cl SO23 . . . . .2 C7
Loaders Cl BH9 . . . . .205 A8
Loane Rd SO19 . . . . .103 F3
Lobelia Ct PO7 . . . . .135 A6
Lobelia Rd SO16 . . . . .79 C5
Locarno Rd PO12 . . . . .158 A2
Loch Rd BH14 . . . . .203 E5
Lock App PO6 . . . . .157 A7
Lock View PO6 . . . . .157 A7
Lock's Cotts SO45 . . . . .125 D5
Locke Rd SO30 . . . . .105 C8
Lockerley CE Prim Sch
SO51 . . . . .5 A1
Lockerley Cl SO41 . . . . .197 E2
Lockerley Cres SO16 . . . . . . .77 F1
Lockerley Rd
Awbridge SO51 . . . . .26 D5
Dunbridge SO51 . . . . .26 C8
Havant PO9 . . . . .136 A3
Lockhams Rd SO32 . . . . .106 F8
Locks Heath Jun & Inf Schs
SO31 .129 A1

Locks Rd SO31 . . . . .129 A3
Locksheath Cl PO9 . . . . .135 D6
Locksheath Park Rd
SO31 . . . . .129 B2
Locksley Cl SO15 . . . . .102 F7
Locksley Dr BO22 . . . . .165 C3
Locksley Rd SO50 . . . . .55 E1
Locksway Rd PO4 . . . . .183 C4
Lockswood Keep SO31 . . . . .129 A4
Lockswood Rd SO31 . . . . . . .128 F3
Lockyer Ct GU32 . . . . .41 B5
Lockyer's Mid Sch
BH21 . . . . .186 D8
Lockyers Dr BH22 . . . . .165 F6
Lockyers Rd BH21 . . . . .186 E8
Lode Hill SP5 . . . . .47 B8
Loders Cl PO17 . . . . .187 D3
Lodge Ave PO6 . . . . .158 A8
Lodge Cl BH14 . . . . .203 E4
Lodge Ct BH14 . . . . .203 E4
Lodge Dr SO45 . . . . .126 A1
Lodge Dro SP5 . . . . .47 D4
Lodge Gdns PO12 . . . . .181 A4
Lodge Hill PO17 . . . . .109 B6
Lodge Rd
Christchurch BH23 . . . . .206 D4
Havant PO9 . . . . .135 B1
Locks Heath SO31 . . . . .129 B3
Lymington SO41 . . . . .197 B3
Southampton SO14 . . . . .103 A7
Lodge The
Bournemouth BH2 . . . . .204 C4
Southampton SO15 . . . . .102 F7
Waterlooville PO7 . . . . .135 A6
Lodge Vale SO51 . . . . .51 B1
Lodgebury Cl PO10 . . . . .161 E8
Lodsworth Cl PO8 . . . . .88 D4
Lodsworth Ho PO1 . . . . .216 C4
Loewy Cres BH12 . . . . .188 D2
Lofting Cl SO50 . . . . .56 E2
Logan Cl SO16 . . . . .77 F5
Lomax Cl SO30 . . . . .81 C1
Lombard Ave BH6 . . . . .206 D5
Lombard Ct PO1 . . . . .182 A4
Lombard St PO1 . . . . .182 A3
Lombardy Cl
Gosport PO13 . . . . .155 E2
Verwood BH31 . . . . .115 B5
Lombardy Rise PO7 . . . . .134 F5
Lomer La BH24 . . . . .93 C3
Lomond Cl PO2 . . . . .182 D3
Londesborough Rd PO4 . . . .182 E3
London Ave PO2 . . . . .157 D2
London La BH23 . . . . .167 F2
London Rd
Blendworth PO8 . . . . .112 D8
Clanfield PO8 . . . . .88 D4
Clanfield PO8 . . . . .88 E5
Cosham PO6 . . . . .157 F8
Hill Brow GU33 . . . . .21 B1
Horndean PO8 . . . . .88 D2
Kings Worthy SO23 . . . . .2 B5
Petersfield GU31 . . . . .41 D6
Portsmouth PO2 . . . . .157 E3
Southampton SO15 . . . . .103 A6
Waterlooville PO7,PO8 . . . . . .111 F1
Waterlooville,Purbrook
PO7 . . . . .134 C4
London Tavern Cvn Pk The
BH24 . . . . .141 C8
Lone Barn La SO32 . . . . .60 E7
Lone Pine Dr BH22 . . . . .165 E3
Lone Pine Pk BH22 . . . . .165 F3
Lone Pine Way BH22 . . . . . .165 F2
Lone Valley PO7 . . . . .134 C3
Long Acre Ct PO1 . . . . .182 E7
Long Beech Dr SO40 . . . . . . .100 D6
Long Cl SO23 . . . . .215 C3
Long Cl W SP5 . . . . .46 E8
Long Copse SO45 . . . . .150 E3
Long Copse Ct PO10 . . . . . . .137 A4
Long Copse La PO10 . . . . . . .137 A4
Long Curtain Rd PO5 . . . . . .182 A2
Long Down GU31 . . . . .41 B4
Long Dr Gosport PO13 . . . . . .155 C1
West End SO30 . . . . .80 E2
Long La Bursledon SO31 . . . . .105 A1
Colehill BH21 . . . . .163 E8
Holbury SO45 . . . . .150 C5
Marchwood SO40 . . . . .101 D1
Ringwood BH24 . . . . .141 B4
Long Lane Cl SO45 . . . . .150 D3
Long Meadow Ind Est
BH21 . . . . .138 E2
Long Priors GU32 . . . . .37 B5
Long Rd
Bournemouth BH10 . . . . .189 C5
Petersfield GU32 . . . . .41 A5
Soberton SO32 . . . . .85 D2
Long Steeple La SP6 . . . . .45 D2
Long Water Dr PO12 . . . . . . .181 C2
Long Wlk SO17 . . . . .45 C2
Longacre Cl GU33 . . . . .21 A4
Longacre Dr PO12 . . . . .155 C2
Longacres PO14 . . . . .129 C4
Longbarrow Cl BH8 . . . . .191 A1
Longbridge Cl SO40 . . . . .76 D2
Longbridge Ho PO5 . . . . .216 B2
Longbridge Ind Pk
SO14 . . . . .103 C3
Longclose Rd SO30 . . . . .105 D2
Longcroft PO9 . . . . .135 E1
Longdean Cl PO6 . . . . .133 A1
Longdon Dr PO13 . . . . .179 F4

Longdown Activity Farm*
SO40 . . . . .100 D2
Longespee Rd BH21 . . . . . . .187 E8
Longfield Ave PO14 . . . . .154 E7
Longfield Cl PO4 . . . . .183 C5
Longfield Dr
Bournemouth BH11 . . . . .189 A6
Ferndown BH22 . . . . .189 E8
Longfield Rd
Emsworth PO10 . . . . .136 E3
Fair Oak SO50 . . . . .57 D1
Hordle SO41 . . . . .196 B2
Winchester SO23 . . . . .11 D8
Longfleet CE Comb Sch
BH15 . . . . .202 D4
Longfleet Rd BH15 . . . . .202 E4
Longford Pl SO41 . . . . .197 D1
Longham Bsns Ctr
BH22 . . . . .165 B2
Longhouse Gn 6 SO23 . . . . .11 C8
Longlands Rd PO10 . . . . .161 D8
Longleat Gdns
New Milton BH25 . . . . .194 E3
Southampton SO16 . . . . .78 B4
Longman Ct 22 PO5 . . . . . . .182 C2
Longmead GU33 . . . . .20 F4
Longmead Ave SO50 . . . . . . .56 D4
Longmead Ct PO9 . . . . .159 F7
Longmead Dro PO9 . . . . .159 F7
Longmead Rd
Burley Street BH24 . . . . .142 F4
1 Southampton SO18 . . . . . . .80 A2
Longmeadow Gdns
BH18 . . . . .187 B5
Longmeadow La BH17 . . . . .201 E6
Longmore Ave SO19 . . . . . . .103 D2
Longmore Cres SO19 . . . . . .103 D2
Longmynd Dr PO14 . . . . .154 D8
Longridge Rd SO30 . . . . .105 C6
Longs La PO14 . . . . .179 C8
Longs Wlk PO1 . . . . .182 D7
Longshore Way PO4 . . . . . . .183 D4
Longspee Sch BH17 . . . . . . .202 D7
Longstaff Gdns PO16 . . . . . .130 F3
Longstock Ct SO19 . . . . .127 A8
Longstock Cres SO40 . . . . . .100 D7
Longstock Rd PO9 . . . . .136 B6
Longwood Ave PO8 . . . . .111 F3
Longwood Dean La 34 B5
Longworthy 3 SO45 . . . . . . .125 E1
Lonnen Rd BH21 . . . . .164 A8
Lonnen Wood Cl BH21 . . . . .164 A8
Lonsdale Ave
Cosham PO6 . . . . .158 A7
Portchester PO16 . . . . .156 C6
Lonsdale Rd BH3 . . . . .204 F6
Loosehanger SP5,SP6 . . . . . . .47 F3
Loperwood SO40 . . . . .76 A2
Loperwood La SO40 . . . . .76 A3
Loraine Ave BH23 . . . . .209 C8
Lord Cl BH17 . . . . .202 F7
Lord Montgomery Way 1
PO1 . . . . .216 A2
Lord Mountbatten Cl
SO18 . . . . .79 E4
Lord Wilson Sch SO31 . . . . .128 F4
Lord's Hill Ctr E SO16 . . . . . .77 F4
Lord's Hill Ctr W SO16 . . . . . .77 F4
Lord's Hill District Ctr
SO16 . . . . .77 E4
Lord's Hill Way SO16 . . . . . . .78 B5
Lordington Cl PO6 . . . . .158 B8
Lords Ct PO1 . . . . .216 C4
Lords St PO1 . . . . .216 C4
Lordshill Rdbt SO16 . . . . .77 E4
Lordswood SO50 . . . . .56 E7
Lordswood Cl SO16 . . . . .78 A4
Lordswood Ct SO16 . . . . .78 D4
Lordswood Gdns SO16 . . . . .78 D4
Lordswood Rd SO16 . . . . .78 C4
Loreille Gdns SO16 . . . . .77 E7
Loring Ho 7 PO2 . . . . .157 E4
Lorne Park Rd BH1 . . . . .205 A3
Lorne Pl SO18 . . . . .104 A7
Lorne Rd PO5 . . . . .216 D1
Lortemore Pl 4 SO51 . . . . . .52 F7
Loughwood Cl SO50 . . . . . . .56 A6
Louis Flagg Ho 2 PO5 . . . . .216 B2
Lovage Gdns SO40 . . . . .100 C7
Lovage Rd PO15 . . . . .129 D7
Lovage Way PO8 . . . . .88 C1
Lovatt Gr PO15 . . . . .130 D3
Love La
Milford on S SO41 . . . . .211 D5
Petersfield GU31 . . . . .41 A4
Romsey SO51 . . . . .52 E7
Twyford SO21 . . . . .32 B5
Upham SO24,SO32 . . . . .35 B4
West Meon GU32 . . . . .37 C4
Woodgreen SP6 . . . . .70 E8
Lovedean La
Horndean PO8 . . . . .111 F6
Waterlooville PO8 . . . . .112 A4
Lovedon La SO23 . . . . .2 C7
Lovelock Terr 16 PO13 . . . . .180 C6
Loveridge Way SO50 . . . . . . .56 A3
Lovett Rd PO3 . . . . .158 A3
Lovett Wlk SO22 . . . . .1 E5
Lovcay Rd PO5 . . . . .182 E2
Lowden Cl SO22 . . . . .215 B2
Lower Alfred St SO14 . . . . . .103 B6
Lower Ashley Rd BH25 . . . . .195 D2
Lower Banister St 7
SO15 . . . . .102 F6
Lower Bartons SP6 . . . . .69 F1

Lower Baybridge La 33 C2
Lower Bellfield PO14 . . . . . . .153 F7
Lower Bere Wood PO7 . . . . .134 F7
Lower Blandford Rd
BH18 . . . . .187 B3
Lower Brook St SO23 . . . . . .215 E6
Lower Brookfield Rd
PO1 . . . . .182 E6
Lower Brownhill Rd
SO16 . . . . .77 D3
Lower Buckland Rd
SO41 . . . . .197 D5
Lower Canal Wlk SO14 . . . .103 A3
Lower Chase Rd SO32 . . . . . .83 F4
Lower Church Path
PO1 . . . . .216 B3
Lower Church Rd PO14 . . . . .129 C3
Lower Common La
BH21 . . . . .139 A7
Lower Common Rd SO51 . . . .50 E3
Lower Crabbick La PO7 . . . . .110 B5
Lower Densome Wood
SP6 .70 E8
Lower Derby Rd PO2 . . . . . . .157 C1
Lower Drayton La PO6 . . . . .158 C7
Lower Duncan Rd SO31 . . . .129 B5
Lower Farlington Rd
PO6 . . . . .158 E8
Lower Farm Dr PO6 . . . . .157 E7
Lower Farm La SO51 . . . . .29 B3
Lower Forbury Rd PO5 . . . . .216 C2
Lower Golf Links Rd
BH18 . . . . .187 B5
Lower Gr SP6 . . . . .45 B2
Lower Grove Rd PO9 . . . . . . .160 A8
Lower Heyshott GU31 . . . . . .41 A3
Lower La SO32 . . . . .83 C8
Lower Lamborough La
SO24 . . . . .14 D5
Lower Mead SO41 . . . . .41 B4
Lower Mead End Rd
SO41 . . . . .171 F1
Lower Moors Rd SO21 . . . . . .31 F1
Lower Mortimer Rd
SO19 . . . . .103 D3
Lower Mullin's La SO45 . . . .125 E4
Lower New Rd SO30 . . . . .80 D2
Lower Northam Rd
SO30 . . . . .105 C7
Lower Pennington La
SO41 . . . . .212 D7
Lower Preshaw La SO32 . . . . .59 F8
Lower Quay Cl PO16 . . . . . . .155 B8
Lower Quay Ct PO16 . . . . . . .155 B8
Lower Quay Rd PO16 . . . . . .155 B8
Lower Rd PO9 . . . . .135 C1
Lower Sandy Down La
SO41 . . . . .173 C3
Lower Spinney SO31 . . . . . . .152 C9
Lower St St Helens Rd
SO31 . . . . .105 C5
Lower Stanmore La
SO23 . . . . .215 C3
Lower Swanwick Rd
SO31 . . . . .128 D8
Lower Tye Cvn & Camping
Ctr PO11 . . . . .160 C1
Lower Vicarage Rd
SO19 . . . . .103 D3
Lower Wardown GU31 . . . . . .41 B4
Lower William St SO14 . . . . .103 D6
Lower William St Ind Est
SO14 . . . . .103 D6
Lower Wingfield St
PO1 . . . . .216 C4
Lower Woodside SO41 . . . . .212 E8
Lower York St SO14 . . . . . . .103 D6
Lowesmore Ct BH14 . . . . . . .203 C4
Lowestoft Rd PO6 . . . . .133 D1
Loweswater Ho 10 PO6 . . . .133 B1
Lowford Hill Cl SO31 . . . . . . .105 A1
Lowland Rd PO7 . . . . .110 E4
Lowry Gdns SO19 . . . . .104 C2
Lowther Gdns 3 BH8 . . . . . .205 C5
Lowther Rd BH8 . . . . .205 B6
Loxwood Rd PO8 . . . . .111 F6
Loyd-Lindsay Sq SO22 . . . . .215 B8
Luard Ct 4 PO9 . . . . .136 B1
Lucas Cl SO16 . . . . .77 F5
Lucas Rd Poole BH15 . . . . . .202 B1
Poole,Upper Parkstone
BH12 . . . . .203 C6
Luccombe Pl SO15 . . . . .78 D2
Luccombe Rd SO15 . . . . .78 D2
Lucerne Ave
Bournemouth BH6 . . . . .206 D5
Waterlooville PO7 . . . . .111 D2
Lucerne Gdns SO30 . . . . . . .105 B7
Lucerne Rd SO41 . . . . .211 D4
Lucia Foster Welch Coll
Student Village 7
SO14 . . . . .103 B3
Luckham Cl BH9 . . . . .190 B2
Luckham Gdns BH9 . . . . . . .190 C2
Luckham Pl BH9 . . . . .190 B2
Luckham Rd BH9 . . . . .190 B2
Luckham Rd E BH9 . . . . .190 B2
Lucknow St PO1 . . . . .216 D3
Lucky La SO41 . . . . .174 A1
Ludcombe PO7 . . . . .110 F5
Ludlow Inf Sch SO19 . . . . . . .103 E4
Ludlow Jun Sch SO19 . . . . . .103 E4
Ludlow Rd
Portsmouth PO1 . . . . .133 C1
Southampton SO19 . . . . .103 E4
Ludwell's La SO32 . . . . .83 F4

Lugano Cl PO7 . . . . .111 D1
Lukes Cl SO31 . . . . .128 A2
Lukin Dr SO16 . . . . .77 C6
Lulworth Ave SO15 . . . . .201 E1
Lulworth Bsns Ctr SO40 . . . .76 E2
Lulworth Cl
Chandler's Ford SO53 . . . . .55 B3
Hamworthy BH15 . . . . .201 E1
South Hayling PO11 . . . . .185 A5
Southampton SO16 . . . . .77 C2
Lulworth Cres BH15 . . . . . . .201 E1
Lulworth Ct BH15 . . . . .201 E2
Lulworth Gn SO16 . . . . .77 E2
Lulworth Rd PO13 . . . . .179 E2
Lumby Drive Mobile Home Pk
2 BH24 . . . . .141 B8
Lumley Gdns PO10 . . . . .161 A8
Lumley Path 7 PO10 . . . . . .161 A8
Lumley Rd PO10 . . . . .137 A1
Lumley Terr PO10 . . . . .137 A1
Lumsden Ave SO15 . . . . .102 D7
Lumsden Mans 8 SO15 . . . .102 C7
Lumsden Rd PO4 . . . . .183 D3
Lundy Cl SO16 . . . . .77 E5
Lundy Wlk PO14 . . . . .179 B8
Lunedale Rd SO45 . . . . .149 E8
Lupin Gdns SO22 . . . . .1 B2
Lupin Rd SO16 . . . . .79 C5
Luscombe Rd BH14 . . . . .203 C2
Luther Rd BH9 . . . . .204 F8
Lutman St PO10 . . . . .136 E4
Luton Rd SO19 . . . . .104 B4
Luxor Pk PO9 . . . . .159 E2
Luxton Cl SO30 . . . . .105 F8
Luzborough La SO51 . . . . .53 D6
Lyburn Cl SO16 . . . . .78 C4
Lyburn Ct SO16 . . . . .78 C4
Lyburn Ho SP5 . . . . .73 B7
Lyburn Rd
Nomansland SP5 . . . . .73 B8
Redlynch SP5 . . . . .48 F1
Lych Gate Ct BH24 . . . . .141 C6
Lychgate Dr PO8 . . . . .112 B7
Lychgate Gn PO14 . . . . .154 C5
Lydden Ct PO13 . . . . .155 D2
Lydford Gdns BH11 . . . . .189 A2
Lydford Rd BH11 . . . . .189 A2
Lydgate
Milford on S SO41 . . . . .211 A5
Totton SO40 . . . . .100 A5
Lydgate Cl SO19 . . . . .104 D4
Lydgate Gn SO19 . . . . .104 D4
Lydgate Rd SO19 . . . . .104 D4
Lydiard Cl SO50 . . . . .56 A5
Lydlinch Cl BH22 . . . . .165 D1
Lydlynch Inf Sch SO40 . . . . .100 F7
Lydlynch Rd SO40 . . . . .100 F7
Lydney Cl PO6 . . . . .157 C8
Lydney Rd SO31 . . . . .128 F3
Lydwell Cl BH11 . . . . .188 F5
Lyell Rd BH12 . . . . .203 C6
Lymbourne Rd PO9 . . . . .136 A4
Lyme Cl SO50 . . . . .55 F5
Lyme Cres BH23 . . . . .208 F8
Lymefields SO41 . . . . .211 E6
Lymer La SO16 . . . . .77 C6
Lymer Villas SO16 . . . . .77 C6
Lymington CE Inf Sch
SO41 . . . . .197 D4
Lymington Hospl SO41 . . . . .197 D4
Lymington Jun Sch
SO41 . . . . .197 D4
Lymington Pier Sta
SO41 . . . . .198 A3
Lymington Rd
Brockenhurst SO42 . . . . .166 A1
Christchurch BH23 . . . . .208 F7
East End SO41 . . . . .199 B7
Milford on S SO41 . . . . .211 E6
New Milton BH25 . . . . .195 C1
Lymington Rehabilitation
Unit SO41 . . . . .197 E4
Lymington Town Sta
SO41 . . . . .197 F4
Lymington Vineyard*
SO41 . . . . .197 B2
Lymore La SO41 . . . . .211 F6
Lymore Valley SO41 . . . . . . .211 E6
Lynch Cl SO22 . . . . .215 C8
Lynch La SO32 . . . . .37 C4
Lyndale Cl SO41 . . . . .211 E5
Lyndale Rd SO31 . . . . .129 C4
Lynden Cl PO14 . . . . .154 B8
Lynden Gate SO19 . . . . .104 A3
Lyndhurst Cl
South Hayling PO11 . . . . .185 A3
Winchester SO22 . . . . .1 D4
Lyndhurst Ho PO9 . . . . .135 C6
Lyndhurst Jun Sch PO2 . . . .157 F1
Lyndhurst Rd
Ashurst SO40 . . . . .100 A2
Bransgore BH24 . . . . .193 D6
Brockenhurst SO42 . . . . .146 A2
Burley BH24 . . . . .143 C5
Cadnam SO40 . . . . .98 E7
Christchurch BH23 . . . . .193 D8
Gosport PO12 . . . . .181 A5
Landford SP5 . . . . .49 D3
Portsmouth PO2 . . . . .157 F1
Lyndock Cl SO14 . . . . .103 C4
Lyndock Pl SO19 . . . . .103 C4
Lyndon Ct BH23 . . . . .191 F1
Lyndum Cl GU32 . . . . .40 F4
Lyne Pl PO8 . . . . .112 B6
Lynes La BH24 . . . . .140 F2
Lynford Ave SO22 . . . . .215 C8
Lynford Way SO22 . . . . .215 C8

Lynn Cl SO18 . . . . .80 B3
Lynn Rd Poole BH17 . . . . . . .187 F1
Portsmouth PO2 . . . . .182 F8
Lynn Way SO23 . . . . .2 C7
Lynric Cl BH25 . . . . .210 A7
Lynton Cres BH23 . . . . .191 D3
Lynton Ct SO40 . . . . .100 E6
Lynton Gdns PO16 . . . . .130 F3
Lynton Gr PO3 . . . . .183 A8
Lynton Rd
Hedge End SO30 . . . . .105 C7
Petersfield GU32 . . . . .40 F4
Lynwood Ave PO8 . . . . .111 D3
Lynwood Ct BH22 . . . . .165 D7
Lynwood Cr
Lymington SO41 . . . . .197 D3
Winchester SO22 . . . . .215 D8
Lynwood Dr BH21 . . . . .187 E8
Lynx Cl SO50 . . . . .56 F2
Lyon Ave PO25 . . . . .195 B3
Lyon Cl SO14 . . . . .103 A6
Lyons Pl SO30 . . . . .105 B5
Lysander Cl BH23 . . . . .208 C7
Lysander Ct 21 PO1 . . . . . . .182 A4
Lysander Way PO7 . . . . .135 A8
Lyse Cl SO33 . . . . .20 F4
Lysses Ct PO16 . . . . .131 C1
Lyster Rd SP6 . . . . .70 A2
Lystra Rd BH9 . . . . .190 A3
Lytchett Dr BH18 . . . . .186 F2
Lytchett Way BH16 . . . . .201 B6
Lyteltane Rd SO41 . . . . .197 D2
Lytham Rd
Broadstone BH18 . . . . .187 A3
Southampton SO18 . . . . .80 A1
Lythe La GU32 . . . . .40 A5
Lytton Rd
Bournemouth BH1,BH8 . . . . . .205 C5
Hythe SO45 . . . . .126 B2

M

Mabey Ave BH10 . . . . .189 D2
Mabey Cl PO12 . . . . .181 C3
Mablethorpe Rd PO6 . . . . . .133 E1
Macandrew Rd BH13 . . . . . . .214 F7
Macarthur Cres SO18 . . . . . .104 A8
Macaulay Ave PO6 . . . . .132 F1
Macaulay Rd BH18 . . . . .187 A4
Macklin Ho 21 SO22 . . . . . .215 D6
Maclaren Rd BH9 . . . . .189 F3
Maclean Rd BH11 . . . . .188 F3
Macnaghten Rd SO18 . . . . . .103 D8
Madden Cl PO12 . . . . .180 F3
Maddison St 5 SO14 . . . . . .102 F6
Maddoxford La SO32 . . . . . . .82 A1
Maddoxford Way SO32 . . . . . .81 F2
Madeira Rd
Bournemouth BH1 . . . . .205 A4
Poole BH14 . . . . .203 D5
Portsmouth PO2 . . . . .157 F3
Madeline Cl BH12 . . . . .203 B7
Madeline Cres BH12 . . . . . . .203 B7
Madeline Rd GU31 . . . . .40 F4
Madison Ave BH1 . . . . .205 D6
Madison Cl PO13 . . . . .180 E8
Madison Ct 8 PO16 . . . . . . .131 C1
Madrisa Ct SO41 . . . . .197 E4
Mafeking Rd PO4 . . . . .182 F3
Maffey Cl SO30 . . . . .106 A7
Mag's Barrow BH20 . . . . . . .165 E2
Magazine La SO40 . . . . .102 A3
Magdala Rd Cosham PO6 . . .157 F7
South Hayling PO11 . . . . .184 C3
Magdalen Ct 4 PO2 . . . . . . .157 E3
Magdalen Hill SO23 . . . . . . .215 F5
Magdalen Rd BH23 . . . . .207 A6
Magdalen Mews 8
SO23 . . . . .215 F5
Magdalen Rd PO14 . . . . .129 C2
Magennis Cl PO13 . . . . .180 D7
Magenta Ct 4 PO13 . . . . . . .180 A5
Maggie Dr PO13 . . . . .180 A5
Magna Cl BH11 . . . . .188 F6
Magna Gdns BH11 . . . . .188 F6
Magna Rd BH21 . . . . .188 C7
Magnolia Cl
Bournemouth BH6 . . . . .207 A5
Fareham PO14 . . . . .154 E8
Hythe SO45 . . . . .125 C4
Verwood BH31 . . . . .115 C4
Magnolia Gr SO50 . . . . .57 E2
Magnolia Ho 6 BH10 . . . . . .189 F4
Magnolia Rd SO19 . . . . .103 F5
Magnolia Terr PO7 . . . . .134 E6
Magnolia Way PO8 . . . . .112 C4
Magpie Cl
Bournemouth BH8 . . . . .190 C3
Fareham PO14 . . . . .154 E6
Magpie Cotts PO8 . . . . .113 C4
Magpie Dr SO40 . . . . .100 C7
Magpie Gdns SO19 . . . . .104 E2
Magpie Gr BH25 . . . . .194 F2
Magpie La Eastleigh SO50 . . . .55 F1
Lee-on-t-S PO13 . . . . .179 F4
Magpie Rd PO8 . . . . .113 C5
Magpie Wlk PO8 . . . . .113 D4
Maiden La SO41 . . . . .197 F1
Maidford Gr PO3 . . . . .158 C4
Maidment Cl BH11 . . . . .188 E4
Maidstone Cres PO6 . . . . . . .133 E1
Main Dr PO17 . . . . .133 A6
Main Rd
Colden Common SO21 . . . . . . .32 A1
East End SO41 . . . . .199 B8

Main Rd continued
Gosport PO13 . . . . .155 D5
Hardley SO45 . . . . .150 C6
Hermitage PO10,PO18 . .161 D8
Hythe SO45 . . . . .125 C5
Littleton SO22 . . . . .1 B5
Marchwood SO40 . . . . . . .101 F1
Marchwood SO40,SO45 . .125 A6
Otterbourne SO21 . . . . . . .31 C3
Owslebury SO21 . . . . .33 B3
Portmore SO41 . . . . .198 B7
Portsmouth PO1 . . . . .181 F7
Totton SO40 . . . . .100 E4
Twyford SO21 . . . . .31 F2
Mainsail Dr PO16 . . . . . . .155 B8
Mainstone SO51 . . . . .52 D6
Mainstream Ct SO50 . . . . .56 D3
Maisemore Gdns PO9 . . . .160 D8
Maitland Ct SO41 . . . . . . .197 D3
Maitland St PO1 . . . . .182 D7
Maitlands The **2** SO42 . . .204 C2
Maizemore Wlk **7**
  PO13 . . . . .179 F3
Majestic Rd SO16 . . . . .77 B4
Major Ct PO12 . . . . .181 B8
Majoram Way PO15 . . . . .129 D7
Majorca Mans **4** PO4 . . .204 E3
Malan Cl BH17 . . . . .202 E8
Malcolm Cl
  Chandler's Ford SO53 . . . .30 E1
  Locks Heath SO31 . . . . . .129 B3
Malcolm Rd SO53 . . . . .30 E1
Malcomb Cl BH6 . . . . . . .207 E3
Malcroft Mews SO40 . . . .102 A1
Maldon Cl SO50 . . . . .56 D3
Maldon Rd
  2 Bournemouth PO6 . . . .157 D8
  Southampton SO19 . . . . .103 C4
Malibres Rd SO53 . . . . .55 F8
Malin Cl
  Southampton SO16 . . . . . .77 E4
  Stubbington PO14 . . . . . .179 B8
Malins Rd PO2 . . . . .182 D8
Malins Road Apts **18**
  PO2 . . . . .182 D7
Mall The Burley BH24 . . . .143 A3
  Chandler's Ford SO53 . . . . .55 F7
  Portsmouth PO2 . . . . . . .157 D1
Mallard Bldgs **8** BH25 . .195 A3
Mallard Cl
  Bishop's Waltham SO32 . . .83 A8
  Bournemouth BH8 . . . . . .190 C1
  Christchurch BH23 . . . . . .208 A6
  Romsey SO51 . . . . .52 F8
Mallard Gdns
  Gosport PO13 . . . . .155 B2
  Hedge End SO30 . . . . .81 C2
Mallard Rd
  Bournemouth BH8 . . . . . .190 D1
  Portsmouth PO4 . . . . . . .183 B5
  Rowlands Castle PO9 . . . .113 B1
  Wimborne Minst BH21 . . .164 A7
Mallard Way PO10 . . . . . .137 C4
Mallards Rd SO31 . . . . . . .127 F8
Mallards The
  Fareham PO16 . . . . .131 A3
  Langstone PO9 . . . . .159 F7
Mallett Cl SO30 . . . . .81 E2
Mallory Cl BH23 . . . . .207 F8
Mallory Cres PO16 . . . . . .131 A3
Mallow Cl
  Broadstone BH18 . . . . . . .186 E3
  Christchurch BH23 . . . . . .208 C8
  2 Cosham PO6 . . . . .157 F8
  Locks Heath SO31 . . . . . .128 F2
  Waterlooville PO7 . . . . . . .134 F6
Mallow Rd SO30 . . . . .105 A6
Mallows The BH25 . . . . . .195 D4
Malmesbury Cl SO50 . . . . .57 C2
Malmesbury Ct BH8 . . . . .205 C6
Malmesbury Gdns SO22 . .215 B8
Malmesbury Park Pl 7
  BH8 . . . . .205 C5
Malmesbury Park Prim Sch
  BH8 . . . . .205 B5
Malmesbury Park Rd
  BH8 . . . . .205 C6
Malmesbury Pl SO15 . . . .102 D7
Malmesbury Rd
  Romsey SO51 . . . . .52 E8
  Southampton SO15 . . . . .102 D7
  St Leonards BH24 . . . . . .139 C3
Malmesbury Ct **12** BH23 .207 A5
Maloney Mews PO11 . . . .185 E1
Maloren Way BH22 . . . . . .139 A1
Malory Cl SO19 . . . . .104 D6
Malt La SO32 . . . . .83 C7
Malta Rd PO2 . . . . .182 C2
Malthouse 7 BH15 . . . . . .202 C2
Malthouse Cl
  Easton Down SO21 . . . . .2 F4
  Romsey SO51 . . . . .52 E8
Malthouse Cotts SO51 . . . .77 A8
Malthouse Gdns SO40 . . .101 F1
Malthouse La PO16 . . . . .131 B1
Malthouse Rd PO2 . . . . . .182 D8
Maltings The
  Bournemouth BH11 . . . . .188 F6
  Fareham PO16 . . . . .131 D2
  Petersfield GU31 . . . . .40 F3
  3 Poole BH15 . . . . .202 E3
Malus Cl PO14 . . . . .154 F7
Malvern Ave PO14 . . . . . .154 E8
Malvern Bsns Ctr SO15 . . .78 D2
Malvern Cl
  Bishop's Waltham SO32 . . .83 D7

Malvern Cl continued
  Bournemouth BH9 . . . . . .190 A3
Malvern Ct
  4 Bournemouth BH9 . . .190 A2
  2 Christchurch BH23 . . .207 F8
Malvern Dr SO45 . . . . . . .125 D3
Malvern Gdns SO30 . . . . . .81 D2
Malvern Mews PO10 . . . .136 F1
Malvern Rd
  Bournemouth BH9 . . . . . .190 A2
  Gosport PO12 . . . . .180 F5
  Hill Brow GU33 . . . . .21 B2
  Portsmouth PO5 . . . . . . .182 D1
  Southampton SO16 . . . . . .78 C2
Malvern Terr SO16 . . . . . . .78 D2
Malwood Ave SO16 . . . . . .78 D3
Malwood Cl PO9 . . . . .136 A6
Malwood Gdns SO40 . . . .100 C8
Malwood Rd SO45 . . . . . .126 A4
Malwood Rd W SO45 . . . .125 F4
Manaton Way SO30 . . . . . .81 B1
Manchester Ct **10** PO13 .180 C1
Manchester Rd
  Netley SO31 . . . . .127 A5
  Portsmouth PO1 . . . . . . .182 E5
  Sway SO41 . . . . .172 B3
Manchester Terr PO10 . . .137 B4
Mancroft Ave PO14 . . . . .179 C7
Mandalay Cl BH31 . . . . . .114 E5
Mandale Cl BH11 . . . . . . .189 A4
Mandale Rd BH11 . . . . . . .188 F3
Mandarin Way PO13 . . . .180 C6
Mandela Way SO15 . . . . .102 E5
Manderley SO41 . . . . .211 E3
Manington Hall **5** BH4 . .204 C2
Manley Rd SO31 . . . . .104 F1
Manners La PO4 . . . . .182 E4
Manners Rd PO4 . . . . .182 E4
Manning Ave PO13 . . . . . .193 C1
Manningford Cl SO23 . . . . .2 A3
Mannings Heath Rd
  BH12 . . . . .188 B1
Mannings Heath Rdbt
  BH17 . . . . .188 B2
Mannings Heath Ret Pk
  PO3 . . . . .183 A8
Mannington Pl **2** BH2 . .204 E3
Mannington Way BH22 . . .138 D2
Manns Cl SO18 . . . . .80 C2
Mannyngham Way SO51 . .27 D7
Manor Cl Burseldon SO31 .104 F1
  Ferndown BH22 . . . . .165 E5
  Fordingbridge SP6 . . . . . . .69 F1
  8 Havant PO9 . . . . .135 F1
  Milford on S SO41 . . . . . .211 D6
  Totton SO40 . . . . .100 E6
  Wickham SO23 . . . . .215 F6
Manor Cres
  Burseldon SO31 . . . . .104 F1
  Cosham PO6 . . . . .158 B7
Manor Ct Havant PO9 . . . .135 D1
  Ringwood BH24 . . . . .140 F8
  Titchfield PO15 . . . . .129 D4
  Verwood BH31 . . . . .114 F6
Manor Farm SO24 . . . . . . .14 D1
Manor Farm Cl
  Bishopstoke SO50 . . . . . . .56 E2
  Old Milton BH25 . . . . . . .194 F1
Manor Farm Cotts
  Exton SO32 . . . . .61 C7
  Rockbourne SP6 . . . . .44 E2
  South Hayling PO11 . . . . .185 A6
  Whitsbury SP6 . . . . .45 A5
Manor Farm Ctry Pk*
  SO31 . . . . .105 D3
Manor Farm Gn SO21 . . . .31 F5
Manor Farm Gr SO50 . . . . .56 E2
Manor Farm La SO51 . . . . . .6 E1
Manor Farm Mus*
  SO30 . . . . .105 F4
Manor Farm Rd
  Bournemouth BH10 . . . . .189 C7
  Fordingbridge SP6 . . . . . . .69 C1
  Southampton SO18 . . . . . .79 D2
Manor Farmyard BH8 . . . .191 B3
Manor Flats SO21 . . . . . . .31 F5
Manor Gdns
  Breach PO10 . . . . .137 D2
  Ringwood BH24 . . . . .140 F8
  Verwood BH31 . . . . .114 F6
Manor Ho BH18 . . . . .187 A4
Manor House Ave SO15 . .101 E6
Manor Inf Sch
  Holbury SO45 . . . . .150 B4
  Portsmouth PO1 . . . . . . .182 E7
Manor La BH11 . . . . .189 A4
Manor Lodge Rd PO9 . . . .113 A1
Manor Mews PO6 . . . . . . .158 C8
Manor Park Ave **5** PO3 .183 A8
Manor Park Inf Sch
  8 Havant PO9 . . . . .135 F1
  Poole BH15 . . . . .202 B5
Manor Quay SO18 . . . . . .103 D7
Manor Rd
  Bishopstoke SO50 . . . . . . .56 E2
  Bournemouth BH1 . . . . . .205 C3
  Breach PO10 . . . . .137 D1
  Chilworth SO16 . . . . .54 D1
  Christchurch BH23 . . . . . .207 A6
  Durley SO32 . . . . .82 D7
  East Tytherley SP5 . . . . .4 E7
  Holbury SO45 . . . . .150 C4
  Hythe SO45 . . . . .125 A4
  Milford on S SO41 . . . . . .211 D6
  New Milton BH25 . . . . . . .195 B3
  Portsmouth PO1 . . . . . . .182 E7
  Ringwood BH24 . . . . .141 B7

Manor Rd continued
  South Hayling PO11 . . . . .184 F5
  Twyford SO21 . . . . .31 F5
  Verwood BH31 . . . . .114 F6
Manor Rd N SO19 . . . . . . .103 E4
Manor Rd S SO19 . . . . . . .103 E3
Manor Terr
  Burseldon SO31 . . . . .104 F1
  Durley SO32 . . . . .82 E7
Manor Villas PO17 . . . . . .108 A3
Manor Way Breach PO10 .137 D1
  Lee-on-t-S PO13 . . . . . . .179 E3
  South Hayling PO11 . . . . .185 A2
  Verwood BH31 . . . . .114 F7
Manor Wharf SO18 . . . . . .103 E7
Manor Wks SO40 . . . . . . .101 B7
Manorside Comb Sch
  BH12 . . . . .188 D1
Mansard Ct BH13 . . . . . . .214 B3
Mansbridge Cotts SO18 . . .79 F4
Mansbridge Prim Sch
  SO18 . . . . .79 E4
Mansbridge Rd
  Eastleigh SO50 . . . . .56 A1
  Southampton SO18 . . . . . .79 F4
Mansel Cl BH12 . . . . .204 C2
Mansel Ct SO16 . . . . .77 E2
Mansel Inf Sch SO16 . . . . .77 D1
Mansel Jun Sch SO16 . . . .77 D2
Mansel Rd E SO16 . . . . . . .77 E2
Mansel Rd W SO16 . . . . . .77 D2
Mansel Cl SO45 . . . . .125 E1
Mansergh Wlk SO40 . . . . .100 B8
Mansfield Ave BH14 . . . . .203 C4
Mansfield Cl
  Ferndown BH22 . . . . .165 D2
  Poole BH14 . . . . .203 C4
Mansfield La SO32 . . . . . .107 B4
Mansfield Rd
  Bournemouth BH9 . . . . . .189 E1
  Gosport PO13 . . . . .180 C8
  Poole BH14 . . . . .203 C4
  Ringwood BH24 . . . . .140 F7
Mansion Ct **6** PO4 . . . . .182 E1
Mansion Rd
  Portsmouth PO4 . . . . . . .182 E1
  Southampton SO15 . . . . .102 D6
Manston Cl SO16 . . . . .77 F4
Mansvid Ave PO6 . . . . . . .158 B7
Mantle Cl PO13 . . . . .180 D7
Mantle Sq PO2 . . . . .157 B2
Manton Cl BH15 . . . . .201 E3
Manton Rd PO3 . . . . .183 A6
Manwell Dr SO41 . . . . . . .199 D1
Maple Cl
  Barton on S BH25 . . . . . .210 B7
  Burseldon SO31 . . . . .127 F8
  Christchurch BH23 . . . . . .208 F7
  Emsworth PO10 . . . . .136 F2
  Fareham PO15 . . . . .130 C1
  Lee-on-t-S PO13 . . . . . . .179 F2
  Romsey SO51 . . . . .53 C6
Maple Cres PO6 . . . . .88 D6
Maple Ct Lymington SO41 .197 B2
  Southampton,Sholing
    SO19 . . . . .104 B4
  Southampton,Woolston
    SO19 . . . . .103 C2
Maple Dr Denmead PO7 . .111 A4
Maple Ho Havant PO9 . . .136 A2
  Southampton SO15 . . . . . .78 F7
Maple Lo BH16 . . . . .201 C7
Maple Rd
  Bournemouth BH9 . . . . . .204 F8
  Hythe SO45 . . . . .150 B8
  Poole BH15 . . . . .202 D3
  Portsmouth PO5 . . . . . . .182 D2
  Southampton SO18 . . . . .103 E7
Maple Sq SO50 . . . . .55 E1
Maple Wlk GU31 . . . . .40 F1
Maple Wood PO9 . . . . . . .135 E5
Mapleleaf Gdns **5** SO50 . .56 A2
Maples The SO53 . . . . .55 C8
Mapleton Rd SO30 . . . . . .105 D6
Mapletree Ave PO8 . . . . .112 C4
Maplewood Cl SO40 . . . . .100 C6
Maplin Rd SO16 . . . . .77 D2
Mapperton Cl BH17 . . . . .187 F2
Marabout Cl BH23 . . . . . .207 D7
Maralyn Ave PO7 . . . . . . .134 E6
Maratham Pl SO50 . . . . . . .57 B2
Marazan Rd PO13 . . . . . .180 B2
Marchesi Ct PO14 . . . . . .154 C4
Marchwood By Pass
  SO40 . . . . .124 E8
  Totton SO40 . . . . .101 B3
Marchwood CE Inf Sch
  SO40 . . . . .124 E8
Marchwood Cl **8** PO12 . .180 D3
Marchwood Ind Pk
  SO40 . . . . .102 A3
Marchwood Jun Sch
  SO40 . . . . .124 E8
Marchwood Priory Hospl
  SO40 . . . . .125 A7
Marchwood Rd
  Bournemouth BH10 . . . . .189 C3
  Havant PO9 . . . . .135 E6
  Southampton SO15 . . . . .102 B6
  Totton SO40 . . . . .101 F2
Marchwood Terr SO40 . . .101 F2
Marcus Cl SO50 . . . . .57 B2
Mardale Rd SO16 . . . . . . .101 D8
Mardale Wlk SO16 . . . . . .101 D8

Marden Paddock SO42 . .145 F1
Marden Way GU31 . . . . . . .41 A3
Mardon Ct SO18 . . . . .79 E5
Mare La SO21 . . . . .32 F6
Margam Ave SO19 . . . . . .103 F5
Margards La BH31 . . . . . .114 E5
Margaret Ct PO7 . . . . .111 D1
Margaret Rule Hall **5**
  PO1 . . . . .216 B3
Margarita Rd PO15 . . . . . .130 E2
Margate Rd PO5 . . . . .216 C2
Margery's Ct **31** PO1 . . . .182 A5
Marian Cl BH21 . . . . .186 C4
Marian Rd BH21 . . . . .186 C4
Marianne Cl SO15 . . . . . .101 F6
Marianne Rd Poole BH12 .204 C8
  Wimborne Minst BH21 . . .164 A7
Marie Ave SP5 . . . . .46 D7
Marie Cl BH12 . . . . .203 D7
Marie Ct **6** PO7 . . . . . . .134 E8
Marie Rd SO19 . . . . .104 C3
Marigold Cl PO15 . . . . . . .130 E2
Marina Bldgs **8** PO12 . .181 B5
Marina Cl PO10 . . . . .161 A7
Marina Ct
  2 Bournemouth BH5 . . .205 E3
  Christchurch BH23 . . . . . .209 A7
Marina Dr
  Hamble-le-R SO31 . . . . . .128 A2
  Poole BH14 . . . . .203 B1
Marina Gr
  Portchester PO16 . . . . . . .156 C6
  Portsmouth PO3 . . . . . . .183 B7
Marina Keep PO6 . . . . . . .157 A6
Marina The BH5 . . . . .205 E3
Marina Twrs **5** BH5 . . . .205 E3
Marina View
  Christchurch BH23 . . . . . .207 A5
  Netley SO31 . . . . .126 F7
Marine Cotts **7** PO12 . . .181 B6
Marine Ct
  Barton on S BH25 . . . . . .209 D7
  Portsmouth PO4 . . . . . . .183 A2
Marine Dr BH25 . . . . .209 E7
Marine Dr E BH25 . . . . . .210 A6
Marine Drive W BH25 . . .209 E7
Marine Par SO14 . . . . . . .103 B4
Marine Par E PO13 . . . . . .179 F2
Marine Par W PO13 . . . . .179 D4
Marine Point BH25 . . . . . .209 F7
Marine Prospect BH25 . . .209 F7
Marine Rd BH6 . . . . .206 D3
Marine Wlk PO11 . . . . . . .185 D3
Mariner's Cl SO31 . . . . . .128 A4
Mariners Ct
  Christchurch BH23 . . . . . .208 A6
  Lymington SO41 . . . . . . .197 F2
  South Hayling PO11 . . . . .185 D1
Mariners Mews SO45 . . . .126 A4
Mariners Reach BH25 . . . .210 A6
Mariners The SO31 . . . . .127 B6
Mariners Way
  Gosport PO12 . . . . .181 D4
  Warsash SO31 . . . . .128 C1
Mariners Wlk PO4 . . . . . .183 B5
Marion Rd PO4 . . . . .182 E2
Maritime Ave SO40 . . . . . .102 A3
Maritime Chambers
  SO14 . . . . .103 B2
Maritime Wlk SO14 . . . . .103 A2
Maritime Wlk SO14 . . . . .103 B2
Marjoram Cres PO8 . . . . .112 B3
Mark Anthony Ct PO11 . .184 F3
  Southampton SO15 . . . . .102 A7
Mark Ct PO7 . . . . .134 E8
Mark Way SO51 . . . . .4 D3
Mark's La BH25 . . . . .194 F4
Mark's Rd PO14 . . . . .179 E7
Markall Cl SO31 . . . . .14 D5
Marken Cl SO31 . . . . .128 E3
Market Bldgs SO16 . . . . . .79 D4
Market Cl BH15 . . . . .202 C2
Market La SO23 . . . . .215 E5
Market Par PO9 . . . . .135 F1
Market Pl
  Fordingbridge SP6 . . . . . . .69 F1
  Ringwood BH24 . . . . .140 F7
  Romsey SO51 . . . . .52 E7
  10 Southampton SO14 . .103 A3
Market St Eastleigh SO50 . .56 B2
  Eastleigh SO50 . . . . .56 B2
  Lee-on-t-S PO13 . . . . . . .179 F2
  Winchester SO23 . . . . . . .215 E5
Market Way BH21 . . . . . . .163 D4
Marketway PO1 . . . . .216 B4
Markham Ave BH10 . . . . .189 D6
Markham Cl BH10 . . . . . .189 D6
Markham Rd BH9 . . . . . . .205 A8
Marks Rd BH9 . . . . .189 F3
Marks Terr SO32 . . . . .83 B1
Marks Tey Rd PO14 . . . . .154 C5
Markway Cl PO10 . . . . . . .136 D1
Marl La SP6 . . . . .69 D2
Marlands Lawn PO9 . . . . .135 C6
Marlands Sh Ctr SO14 . . .102 F4
Marlborough Cl PO7 . . . . .134 D5
Marlborough Ct
  8 Bournemouth BH4 . . .204 C3
  Chandler's Ford SO53 . . . .55 A4
  3 Gosport PO12 . . . . . .181 C9
  Hythe SO45 . . . . .126 A1
  3 Wimborne Minst BH21 .163 C5
Marlborough Gdns SO30 .81 C1
Marlborough Gr PO16 . . .156 C2
Marlborough Ho
  3 Highfield SO17 . . . . . .79 A1
  Southampton SO15 . . . . .102 F8

Marlborough Mans **2**
  BH7 . . . . .206 B6
Marlborough Pines **25**
  BH4 . . . . .204 C3
Marlborough Pk PO9 . . . .136 C3
Marlborough Pl
  Lymington SO41 . . . . . . .197 D5
  Wimborne Minst BH21 . . .163 D5
Marlborough Rd
  Bournemouth BH4 . . . . . .204 C3
  Chandler's Ford SO53 . . . .30 F1
  Gosport PO12 . . . . .180 F6
  Poole BH14 . . . . .203 C4
  Southampton SO15,SO16 .102 B8
Marlborough Row PO1 . . .182 A6
Mardell Cl PO9 . . . . .136 A5
Marler Ho **8** BH4 . . . . . .204 B4
Marles Cl PO13 . . . . .180 D8
Marley Ave BH25 . . . . . . .194 E3
Marley Cl BH25 . . . . .194 F3
Marley Ct BH25 . . . . .194 E3
Marley Mount SO41 . . . . .171 E1
Marlhill Cl SO18 . . . . .79 F2
Marlin Cl PO13 . . . . .180 D6
Marline Rd BH12 . . . . . . .203 D6
Marlott Rd BH15 . . . . . . .202 C5
Marlow Cl PO13 . . . . .180 D6
Marlow Dr BH23 . . . . .191 E3
Marlow Rd SO32 . . . . .83 A8
Marlowe Ct
  Southampton SO19 . . . . .103 F1
  Waterlooville PO7 . . . . . . .111 D1
Marlpit Dr BH23 . . . . .194 A2
Marlpit La BH25 . . . . .195 A8
Marls Rd SO30 . . . . .105 E7
Marmion Ave PO5 . . . . . .182 D2
Marmion Gn BH23 . . . . . .207 F7
Marmion Rd PO5 . . . . . . .182 D2
Marne Ho **8** PO14 . . . . .154 E8
Marne Rd SO18 . . . . .104 A7
Marnhull Rd PO15 . . . . . .202 C4
Marnhull Rise SO22 . . . . .215 A5
Marpet Ct BH11 . . . . .188 F6
Marpigs Way PO9 . . . . . . .135 D1
Marquis Way BH11 . . . . . .188 D5
Marram Cl SO41 . . . . .197 E5
Marrelswood Gdns PO7 . .134 C4
Marryat Ct
  Christchurch BH23 . . . . . .209 B7
  New Milton BH25 . . . . . . .194 F3
Marryat Rd BH25 . . . . . . .194 F3
Marsden Rd PO6 . . . . .157 B8
Marsh Cl PO6 . . . . .158 C6
Marsh Gdns SO30 . . . . . . .81 C2
Marsh Ho BH14 . . . . .103 A3
Marsh La Breamore SP6 . . .70 A8
  Christchurch BH23 . . . . . . .91 A4
  Fawley SO45 . . . . .151 B4
  Lymington SO41 . . . . . . .197 E5
  Southampton SO19 . . . . .103 B3
  Upton BH16 . . . . .201 A7
Marsh Par SO45 . . . . .126 A4
Marshal Rd BH17 . . . . . . .187 B1
Marshall Cl SO15 . . . . . . .102 F8
Marshall Dr SO30 . . . . . . .80 F1
Marshall Pl **1** SO16 . . . . .78 E3
Marshall Rd PO13 . . . . . . .185 C2
Marshall Sq SO15 . . . . . .102 F8
Marshfield BH21 . . . . .163 F7
Marshfield Cl SO40 . . . . .101 D1
Marshfield Ho PO6 . . . . . .158 C7
Marshlands Cl BH23 . . . . .207 D6
Marshlands Rd PO6 . . . . .158 D7
Marshlands Spur PO6 . . . .158 E7
Marshwood Ave
  Poole BH17 . . . . .187 F3
  Waterlooville PO7 . . . . . . .135 A7
Marston Cl BH25 . . . . . . .195 B5
Marston Gate **6** SO23 . .215 E6
Marston Gn BH23 . . . . . . .193 E1
Marston La PO13 . . . . . . .193 C1
Marston Rd
  New Milton BH25 . . . . . . .195 B5
  Poole BH15 . . . . .202 B2
  Southampton SO19 . . . . .104 C5
Martello Cl PO12 . . . . . . .180 D3
Martello Ho **5** BH13 . . .214 F7
Martello Pk BH13 . . . . . . .214 F7
Martello Rd BH13 . . . . . . .203 F1
Martello Rd S BH13 . . . . .214 F8
Martello Twrs BH13 . . . . .214 F7
Martells Ct **1** PO1 . . . . .182 A4
Martells The BH25 . . . . . .210 B7
Martin Ave
  Denmead PO7 . . . . .111 A4
  Stubbington PO14 . . . . . .179 D7
Martin Cl
  Broadstone BH17 . . . . . . .201 F8
  Lee-on-t-S PO13 . . . . . . .179 F4
  Swanmore SO32 . . . . .84 B4
**Martin Down National Nature
  Reserve* SP5,SP6 . . . . . .42 C3
Martin Rd Havant PO9 . . .136 A4
  Portsmouth PO3 . . . . . . .183 A8
  Stubbington PO14 . . . . . .179 D7
Martin St SO32 . . . . .83 B7
Martin's Rd SO42 . . . . . . .146 A2
Martindale Ave BH21 . . . .164 B5
Martindale Terr **1**
  SO16 . . . . .101 E7
Martingale Cl SO18 . . . . .201 D7
Martins Cl BH22 . . . . .165 D7
Martins Dr BH22 . . . . . . .165 E7
Martins Fields SO21 . . . . . .10 C1
Martins Hill Cl BH23 . . . .192 C3

Martins Hill La BH23 ....192 C1
Martins Rise SP5 ......24 A3
Martins The SO50 ......57 D1
Martins Way BH22 ....165 E7
Martlet Cl PO13 ....180 A5
Martley Gdns SO30 ....81 D2
Marvic Ct PO9 ....135 E6
Marvin Cl SO30 ....105 D7
Marvin Way
  Hedge End SO30 ......105 D7
  Southampton SO18 ....104 C6
Marwell Cl BH7 ....206 A7
Marwell Zoological Pk*
  SO21 ....57 E8
Mary Coombs Ct PO11 .185 A3
Mary La BH22 ....138 D2
Mary Mitchell Cl BH24 .140 F7
Mary Rose* PO1 ......181 F7
Mary Rose Cl PO15 ...130 E3
Mary Rose St The PO1 .216 B3
Marybridge Cl SO40 ..100 E6
Marycourt Sch PO12 ..181 A2
Maryfield SO14 ....103 B4
Maryland Cl SO18 .....79 F3
Maryland Ct 1 SO41 ..211 B4
Maryland Gdns SO41 ..211 B4
Maryland Rd BH16 ...201 C4
Masefield Ave PO6 ...132 F1
Masefield Cl SO50 ....55 F3
Masefield Cres PO8 ..111 F4
Masefield Gn SO19 ..104 C6
Mason Moor Prim Sch
  SO16 ....101 E8
Masseys La SO42 .....175 C7
Masten Cres PO13 ...180 C8
Masters Ct BH4 ......204 D3
Masterson Cl BH23 ..207 D7
Matapan Rd PO2 ....157 E4
Matchams Cl BH24 ..167 B7
Matchams La BH23 ..167 B4
Matheson Rd SO16 ..78 A5
Matilda Pl 4 SO23 ..215 E6
Matley Gdns SO40 ..100 B7
Matlock Rd BH22 ...165 C3
Matrix Pk pO15 ......129 E3
Matthews Cl PO9 ....135 C3
Matthews La SO42 ..175 C6
Matthews Pl PO7 ...134 E6
Maturin Cl SO41 ....197 D3
Maundeville Cres BH23 206 E8
Maundeville Rd BH23 .206 E8
Maunsell Way SO30 ..81 D2
Maureen Cl BH12 ...203 B8
Maurepas Way PO7 ..134 D7
Mauretania Ho 18 SO41 .103 C6
Mauretania Rd SO16 ..77 B4
Maurice Rd
  Bournemouth BH8 ...205 D8
  Portsmouth PO4 ....183 C4
Maury's La SO51 ....50 D4
Mavis Cres PO9 .....135 F2
Mavis Rd BH9 ......190 B1
Maxstoke Cl PO5 ...216 C3
Maxwell Rd
  Boscombe BH5 .....205 A7
  Broadstone BH18 ...186 E3
  Poole BH13 ....214 F7
  Portsmouth PO4 ....183 A3
  Southampton SO19 ..104 A3
May Ave SO41 ......197 D5
May Bush La SO32 ..85 B1
May Cl SO45 ....150 D3
May Copse SO45 ...150 D3
May Cres SO45 ....150 D3
May Gdns
  Bournemouth BH11 .188 E4
  Walkford BH23 .....194 B2
May La SO41 ......174 A1
May Rd SO15 ......102 C7
May Tree Cl SO22 ..215 A2
Maybray King Way
  SO18,SO19 ....104 A7
Maybush Ct 2 SO16 ..78 A1
Maybush Rd SO16 ...77 F2
Maycroft Cl 4 SO15 ..102 F8
Mayday Ct SO40 ...101 A7
Maydman Sq PO3 ..183 A6
Mayfair BH4 ....204 C2
Mayfair Ct Botley SO30 .106 A7
  Poole BH13 ....204 B2
Mayfair Gdns
  Bournemouth BH11 .189 A4
  Southampton SO15 .102 F7
Mayfield PO13 .....179 E2
Mayfield Ave Poole BH14 203 E3
  Totton SO40 ......100 F8
Mayfield Cl
  Ferndown BH22 ...165 C6
  Stubbington PO14 ..179 D8
Mayfield Dr BH22 ..165 C6
Mayfield Rd
  Bournemouth BH9 ..190 A2
  Fordingbridge SP6 ..69 C2
  Gosport PO12 .....181 C4
  Portsmouth PO2 ...157 F2
  Southampton SO17 .79 C3
Mayfield Way BH22 .165 C6
Mayflower Cl
  Chandler's Ford SO53 .55 B5
  Lymington SO41 ....198 A2
  Stubbington PO14 ..179 C6
Mayflower Ct
  10 Southampton SO16 .102 B8

Mayflower Ct continued
  7 Southampton,Banister's Park
  SO15 ....102 F7
Mayflower Dr PO4 ..183 C5
Mayflower Rd SO15 .102 B8
Mayflowers The SO16 .79 A4
Mayfly Cl SP6 ......69 F2
Mayford Rd BH12 ..204 B6
Mayhall Rd PO3 ....158 A1
Mayhill La SO32 ...84 E8
Maylands Ave PO4 .183 A5
Maylands Rd PO9 ..135 B2
Mayles Cl PO17 ....108 A3
Mayles Cnr PO17 ..130 D8
Mayles La
  Knowle Village PO17 .130 E8
  Wickham PO17 .....107 F1
Mayles Rd PO4 ....183 A4
Maylings Farm Rd PO16 130 F3
Maylyn Rd BH16 ...186 A4
Maynard Cl PO13 ..155 C4
Maynard Pl PO8 ...112 B7
Maynard Rd SO40 ..100 F7
Mayo Cl PO1 ......182 D7
Maypole Villas SO50 .56 B8
Mayridge PO14 ....129 C3
Mays Firs SP6 .....47 F2
Mays La PO14 .....154 C4
Mays Yd PO8 ......112 C8
Maytree Cl Fair Oak SO50 57 D2
  Locks Heath SO31 ..129 A3
Maytree Gdns PO8 .111 E3
Maytree Inf Sch SO14 103 B6
Maytree Rd
  Chandler's Ford SO53 .30 D2
  5 Fareham PO16 ....31 A1
  Southampton SO18 .104 A6
  Waterlooville PO8 ..111 E3
Mayvale Cl SO40 ...101 F1
Mayville High Sch PO5 182 D2
McGovern Mews SO41 152 D10
McIntyre Rd BH23 .191 A8
McKinley Rd BH4 ..204 C2
McWilliam Cl BH12 204 C8
McWilliam Rd 20 BH9 190 A2
Meacher Cl SO40 ..100 E8
Mead Cl
  Broadstone BH18 ..187 A1
  Romsey SO51 ......53 B7
Mead Ct
  Chandler's Ford SO53 .55 C6
  Southampton SO16 ..78 A3
Mead End Rd
  Denmead PO7 ......111 A3
  Sway SO41 ....171 F2
Mead Rd
  Chandler's Ford SO53 .55 C6
  Lymington SO41 ...197 B2
  Winchester SO23 ..215 C2
Mead The Gosport PO13 155 B3
  Hythe SO45 ....125 F3
  Liss GU33 ....20 F4
  Petersfield GU32 ..40 D2
Mead Way PO16 ...131 B3
Meadbrook Gdns SO53 55 C6
Meadcrest Wood SO42 145 D1
Meadcroft Cl SO31 .152 D10
Meadend Cl PO9 ...136 B5
Meadow Ave
  Fordingbridge SP6 ..69 C2
  Locks Heath SO31 ..129 A4
Meadow Cl
  2 Bournemouth BH9 190 A3
  2 Emsworth PO10 .160 F8
  Fordingbridge SP6 .69 C2
  Verwood BH31 .....115 A4
  Whiteparish SP5 ....24 C4
  8 Wimborne Minst BH21 164 D4
Meadow Edge PO1 .134 B2
Meadow Farm La BH21 186 D8
Meadow Gdns SO32 .83 E4
Meadow Gr
  Chandler's Ford SO53 .55 C4
  Verwood BH31 .....115 B5
Meadow La Burton BH23 192 C2
  Eastleigh SO50 .....56 A2
  Hamble-le-R SO31 ..128 A2
Meadow Rd
  Lymington SO41 ...197 C2
  New Milton BH25 ..195 B4
  Ringwood BH24 ...141 B8
Meadow Rise
  Corfe Mullen BH18 .186 F5
  Waterlooville PO8 .112 B3
Meadow St PO5 ....216 A2
Meadow Terr 10 PO16 131 A1
Meadow The
  Portsmouth PO4 ...110 F4
  Romsey SO51 ......27 F1
Meadow View Rd BH11 188 E4
Meadow Way
  Barton on S BH25 ..210 A7
  Fawley SO45 ......151 B3
  Ringwood BH24 ...141 B8

Meadow Way continued
  Verwood BH31 .....115 B5
  Winchester SO22 ..215 A2
Meadow Wlk
  Gosport PO13 .....155 B5
  11 Liss GU33 ......20 F4
  Portsmouth PO1 ..216 B4
Meadowbank BH16 .201 C8
Meadowbank Rd PO15 130 D1
Meadowcroft Cl SO21 .31 C3
Meadowhead Rd SO16 78 F3
Meadowland
  Christchurch BH23 .207 F6
  Kings Worthy SO23 ..2 B7
Meadowlands
  Havant PO9 ....136 A1
  Lymington SO41 ...197 C4
  Ringwood BH24 ....141 A4
  Rowlands Castle PO9 113 C3
Meadowlands Jun & Inf Schs
  PO8 ....111 E5
Meadowmead Ave
  SO15 ....102 A7
Meadows Cl BH16 ..201 C7
Meadows Dr BH16 .201 C7
Meadows The
  Fareham PO16 ....131 C3
  Lyndhurst SO43 ...122 A4
  Waterlooville PO8 .118 C8
Meadowside Cl SO18 .79 E4
Meadowsweet PO7 .112 C1
Meadowsweet Rd PO17 201 E8
Meadowsweet Way
  Horton Heath SO50 .81 C6
  Portsmouth PO6 ...133 D1
Meads The
  Chandler's Ford SO53 .55 A5
  Romsey SO51 ......52 D7
Meadway PO7 .....112 A1
Meadway The BH23 193 D2
Mears Rd SO50 ....57 D1
Meath Cl PO11 ....185 C1
Medina Cl SO53 ...55 E5
Medina Ct PO13 ..179 D4
Medina Ho PO16 ..155 A7
Medina Prim Sch PO6 157 E7
Medina Rd Cosham PO6 157 E8
  Southampton SO15 .78 B1
Medina Way SO41 .208 C6
Medlar Cl Burton BH23 192 D1
  1 Hedge End SO30 .105 D6
Medley Pl SO15 ...102 A7
Medlicott Way SO32 .84 B4
Medstead Rd PO9 .135 F3
Medwall Gn SO19 .104 D5
Medway Dr SO53 ..55 A8
Medway Rd BH22 .166 A6
Meerut Rd SO42 ..145 F2
Meeting House La BH24 140 F7
Megan Cl 7 PO6 ..157 F7
Megan Rd SO30 ...80 D2
Megana Way SO51 .28 C5
Meggeson Ave SO18 .80 A2
Megson Dr PO13 ..180 A6
Melbourne Gdns 6
  SO30 ....105 C6
Melbourne Ho PO1 216 B3
Melbourne Pl PO5 .216 B2
Melbourne Rd
  Bournemouth BH8 .205 C6
  Christchurch BH23 .191 E1
  5 Hedge End SO30 .105 C6
Melbourne St SO14 103 B4
Melbury Ave PO4 ..203 E7
Melbury Cl
  Ferndown BH22 ...165 D4
  Lymington SO41 ...197 D3
Melbury Ct 13 SO17 .79 A1
Melchet Cl SO51 ...25 B1
Melchet Rd SO18 .104 C8
Melford Ct BH1 ...205 A3
Melick Cl SO40 ...101 F2
Mellor Cl 1 PO6 ..157 D8
Mellstock Rd PO15 202 D5
Melrose Cl PO4 ...183 B4
Melrose Ct
  New Milton BH25 ..195 C3
  Totton SO40 ......76 C1
Melrose Gdns PO12 180 F7
Melrose Rd SO15 ..78 D2
Melton Ct BH13 ...203 F4
Melverley Gdns BH21 163 D5
Melville Cl SO15 ...78 C5
Melville Rd
  Bournemouth BH9 .204 E8
  Gosport PO12 .....181 B8
  Portsmouth PO4 ..183 D3
Melvin Jones Ho PO14 154 C4
Mendip Cl
  New Milton BH25 .195 B2
  Verwood BH31 ....114 F5
Mendip Ct 6 BH24 207 F8
Mendip Gdns SO45 125 D2
Mendip Rd
  Southampton SO16 101 F8
  Verwood BH31 ....114 F6
Mendips Rd PO14 .154 D8
Mendips Wlk PO14 154 D8
Mengham Inf Sch PO11 185 A3
Mengham Jun Sch
  PO11 ....185 A4
Mengham La PO11 .185 A3
Mengham Rd PO11 185 A3
Menin Ho PO11 ....130 C2
Menslands La
  Hambledon PO7 ....86 B1

Menslands La continued
  Soberton PO7 ......109 F8
Mentone Rd 2 BH14 203 A3
Menzies Cl SO16 ..77 F5
Meon Cl Clanfield PO8 88 D4
  Gosport PO13 .....155 B2
  Petersfield GU32 ..40 E4
  Romsey SO51 .....53 C7
Meon Cres SO53 ..55 D5
Meon Ct SO18 ....104 D8
Meon Gdns SO32 .84 B5
Meon Ho Fareham PO16 155 A7
  Winchester SO23 .215 E7
Meon Jun & Inf Schs
  PO4 ....183 B4
Meon Rd
  Bournemouth BH7 .206 B7
  Portsmouth PO4 ..183 B5
  Romsey SO51 .....53 C7
Meon Shore Chalets
  PO14 ....153 D2
Meonceos Sch PO14 154 D4
Meonside Ct PO17 .108 A3
Meonstoke CE Inf Sch
  SO32 ....61 C4
Meonwara Cres GU32 37 D5
Mercer Way SO51 .53 A8
Merchants Pl 14 SO23 215 E6
Merchants Row 5 PO1 182 A3
Merchants Wlk 10 SO30 102 F3
Merchistoun Rd PO8 112 D7
Mercury Cl SO16 ...77 F4
Mercury Gdns SO31 128 A4
Mercury Pl PO7 ...134 E2
Merdon Ave SO53 .55 D8
Merdon Cl SO53 ..55 D8
Merdon Ct SO53 ..55 D7
Merdon Jun Sch SO53 55 D7
Mere Croft PO15 ..129 D3
Meredith Cl BH23 .207 D7
Meredith Gdns SO40 100 D6
Meredith Inf Sch PO2 182 E8
Meredith Lodge 5 PO7 135 E3
Meredith Rd PO2 ..157 E3
Meredith Twrs SO19 104 E4
Meredun Cl SO21 ..30 B7
Merepond La GU32 17 F3
Merganser Cl PO12 181 B8
Meriden Cl BH13 ..214 F7
Meriden Ct 11 SO23 215 E8
Meriden Rd PO5 ..216 A2
Meridian Ctr 12 PO9 135 F7
Meridians The BH23 206 F6
Merino Way BH22 .138 F1
Merlewood Cl BH2 204 F4
Merlewood Ct 9 BH25 195 B3
Merley Court Touring Pk
  BH21 ....163 C1
Merley Dr BH23 ...209 A8
Merley Fst Sch BH21 163 D1
Merley Gdns BH21 .163 C1
Merley Ho BH21 ...163 B1
Merley House Holiday Pk
  BH21 ....163 B1
Merley House La BH21 163 C1
Merley La BH21 ...163 C1
Merley Park Rd
  Ashington BH21 ...187 B8
  Corfe Mullen BH21 186 F8
Merley Ways BH21 163 C1
Merlin Cl
  Bishop's Waltham SO32 83 B8
  Ringwood BH24 ...141 C6
  Waterlooville PO8 .111 E4
Merlin Cotts SO45 .151 B3
Merlin Dr PO3 ....158 A4
Merlin Gdns
  Hedge End SO30 ...105 B7
  Portchester PO16 .132 B1
Merlin Lodge SO19 103 D3
Merlin Mews 14 SO32 83 C7
Merlin Way
  Chandler's Ford SO53 54 F7
  Christchurch BH23 .208 A5
Mermaid Ct 12 BH5 205 D3
Mermaid Rd PO14 .154 F8
Mermaid Way PO14 103 B2
Merrick Way SO53 .55 A8
Merridale Rd SO19 103 E5
Merriefield Ave BH18 187 B7
Merrifield Cl BH18 .187 B6
Merrifield Dr BH18 187 B6
Merrieleas Cl SO53 55 C7
Merrieleas Dr SO53 55 C7
Merriemeade Cl 2
  SO45 ....125 E1
Merriemeade Par 1
  SO45 ....125 E1
Merrifield BH11 ...189 A4
Merritown La BH23 190 D7
Merritt St SO53 ...55 C3
Merrivale Ave BH6 206 E5
Merrivale Cl SO45 .125 E3
Merrivale Ct PO2 ..157 D1
Merrivale Rd PO2 .157 F7
Merrow Ave BH12 .204 B7
Merrow Chase 1 BH13 214 F7
Merrow Cl PO16 ..156 A8
Merry Gdns SO52 ..54 A5
Merryfield PO14 ..129 C4
Merryfield Ave SO19 135 C5
Merryfield Cl
  Bransgore BH23 ..193 A8
  Verwood BH31 ....114 F6
Merryfield Ct BH10 189 C4
Merryfield La BH10 189 C4
Merryfield Rd GU31 41 A4

Merryoak Gn SO19 .103 F5
Merryoak Rd SO19 .103 F5
Merrytree Cl SO51 ..50 E3
Merryweather Est BH24 141 C8
Mersea Gdns SO18 .104 A4
Mersham Gdns SO18 104 A7
Merstone Rd PO13 .155 C2
Merthyr Ave PO14 .158 B8
Merton Ave PO16 .156 D6
Merton Cl SP6 .....69 F3
Merton Cres PO16 156 D6
Merton Ct
  2 Christchurch BH23 209 B7
  3 Poole BH15 ......202 E4
  3 Portsmouth PO5 .216 C1
Merton Gr BH24 ...140 F8
Merton Rd
  Portsmouth PO5 ..216 C1
  Southampton SO17 79 B3
Merville Gdns BH9 204 F8
Meryl Rd PO4 .....183 C4
Mesh Pond SP5 ...46 D7
Mesh Rd SO51 ....41 B2
Metcalfe Ave PO14 179 D8
Meteor Rd PO10 ..161 A3
Methuen Cl 2 BH8 205 C5
Methuen Rd
  Bournemouth BH8 205 B5
  Poole BH17 ....187 B2
  Southampton SO14 183 A3
Methuen St SO14 .103 A7
Metuchen Way SO30 105 C4
Mews Ct SO21 ....31 B3
Mews La SO22 ...215 D5
Mews The
  Blackfield SO45 ..177 F7
  Bournemouth BH2 204 D3
  Chandler's Ford SO53 55 C3
  7 Gosport PO12 ..181 E5
  Havant PO9 ....135 E4
  Petersfield GU31 ..41 A4
  Rownhams SO16 ..77 F6
  Southampton SO16 104 D4
  Verwood BH31 ....115 A4
Mewsey Ct PO9 ...135 D7
Mey Cl PO7 ....135 A7
Meynell Cl SO53 ..55 F3
Meyrick Cl BH23 ..193 A7
Meyrick Park Cres BH2 204 F4
Meyrick Park Mans 7
  BH2 ....204 F4
Meyrick Rd
  Bournemouth BH1 205 B3
  Havant PO9 ....135 D1
  Portsmouth PO2 ..157 C1
Micawber Ho PO2 28 157 C1
Michael Crook Cl PO9 135 C3
Michael's Way SO45 125 F4
Michaels Way SO51 57 D2
Michelgrove Rd PO5 183 A5
Michelmersh Fst Sch
  SO51 ....51 A7
Michelmersh Gn BH8 190 D2
Michigan Way SO40 100 B8
Mickleham Cl BH12 204 B8
Midanbury Cres SO18 79 F1
Midanbury Ct 9 SO18 103 E8
Midanbury La SO18 79 F1
Midanbury Wlk SO18 103 E8
Midas Cl PO7 .....134 F4
Middle Brook BH11 189 A6
Middle Brook St SO23 215 E6
Middle Common Rd
  SO41 ....197 A3
Middle Ct PO1 ....182 E7
Middle La BH24 ...141 A7
Middle Mdw GU33 21 A4
Middle Mead PO14 154 B8
Middle Rd
  Bournemouth BH10 189 C5
  Locks Heath SO31 129 B5
  Lymington SO41 ..197 D3
  North Baddesley SO52 54 A4
  Poole BH15 ....202 E6
  Southampton SO19 104 A4
  Sway SO41 ....172 B2
  Tiptoe SO41 ......195 E8
  Winchester SO22 .215 C6
Middle St
  Portsmouth PO5 ..216 B2
  Southampton SO14 103 A7
Middlebere Cres BH16 201 C4
Middlebridge St SO51 52 E6
Middlebrook 8 SO23 83 C8
Middlecroft La PO12 181 D8
Middlehill Dr BH21 164 B6
Middlehill Rd BH21 164 A6
Middlesex Rd PO4 183 B3
Middleton Cl
  Fareham PO14 ....154 C7
  Southampton SO18 80 A1
Middleton Mews
  Locks Heath SO31 129 B5
  Old Milton BH25 ..194 F1
Middleton Rd
  Bournemouth BH9 189 F2
  Ringwood BH24 ..141 A8
Middleton Rise PO8 88 C4
Middleton Wlk 11 SO14 154 F7
Midfield Cl PO14 .154 C7
Midgham Farm Cotts
  SP6 ....93 B6
Midhurst Ho PO1 .216 C4
Midland Rd BH9 ..189 F1
Midlands Est SO32 85 A7
Midlington Barns SO32 85 A7
Midlington Hill SO32 85 A7

Midlingham Ho SO32 ....85 A7
Midlingham Rd SO32 ....85 B8
Midway SO45 ....125 F3
Midway Path BH13 ....214 C3
Midway Rd PO2 ....157 E5
Midways PO14 ....179 C6
Midwood Ave BH8 .....190 F1
Milbeck Cl PO8 ....112 A3
Milborne Cres BH12 ...203 E8
Milbourne Rd BH22 ...165 C6
Milburn Cl **3** BH4 ....204 C4
Milburn Rd BH4 ......204 B4
Milburns The SO51 .....27 D7
Milbury Cres SO18 ...104 A6
Milbury Ho PO6 ......133 A2
Mildenhall **8** BH2 ...204 C4
Mildmay Ct **2** SO23 ..215 F5
Mildmay St SO22 .....215 B3
Mile End Rd PO2 .....182 C7
Milebush Rd PO4 .....183 C5
Miles Ct PO11 ....185 D1
Miles's La SP5 ....24 C5
Milestone Point **1** PO9 135 F1
Milestone Rd BH15 ...202 D5
Milford Cl Havant PO9 .135 D3
West Moors BH22 .....138 F2
Milford Cres SO41 ...211 E4
Milford Ct
1 Gosport PO12 ....180 D3
Milford on S SO41 ...211 E4
4 Portsmouth PO4 ..183 B4
Milford Dr BH11 .....164 A6
Milford Gdns SO53 ....55 E6
Milford Ho
Milford on S SO41 ...211 E5
Southampton SO19 ...104 B6
Winchester SO23 .....215 D3
Milford on Sea CE Prim Sch
SO41 ....211 E6
Milford Rd
Barton on S BH25 ....210 C7
Lymington SO41 .....197 C1
Portsmouth PO1 .....182 E5
Milford Trad Est SO41 .211 E4
Military Rd
Fareham PO16 ....131 D2
Gosport,Alverstoke PO12 .181 A2
Gosport,Alverstoke PO12 ..87 B1
Gosport,Brockhurst PO12 .180 E6
Gosport,Clayhall PO12 ..181 A3
Portsmouth,Hilsea PO3 .157 F5
Portsmouth,Landport PO1 .182 B7
Milkwood Ct SO40 ....100 C7
Milky Down Back La
BH24 ....141 E7
Mill Cl Denmead PO7 ..111 B4
Nursling SO16 ....77 D5
Stoke PO11 ....159 F2
Mill Cross PO7 ....111 A4
Mill Ct Fordingbridge SP6 ..69 E1
4 Southampton SO17 ..79 C2
Mill End Damerham SP6 ..68 D4
Emsworth PO10 ....161 B8
Mill Gate Ho **30** PO1 ..182 A5
Mill Hill SO30 ....106 B6
Mill Hill Cl BH14 .....203 B3
Mill Ho SO18 ....80 A4
Mill House Bsns Ctr
SO19 ....103 D4
Mill House Ctr SO40 ..101 A7
Mill House Lodge SO50 ..56 C3
Mill La Bishopstone SP5 ..22 C8
Brockbridge SO32 .....61 C2
Brockenhurst SO42 ..146 B1
Burley BH4 ....143 C4
Christchurch BH23 ...209 B8
Droxford SO32 ....61 B1
Durley SO32 ....82 D3
Emsworth PO10 ....137 B2
Gosport PO12 ....181 A2
Havant,Bedhampton PO9 .135 C1
Hawkley GU33 ....19 F8
Hurn BH23 ....191 B6
Kings Worthy SO21 .....2 D6
Langstone PO9 ....159 F6
Lymington SO41 .....197 F4
Minstead SO43 ....98 E2
Nursling SO16 ....76 F4
Petersfield GU32 .....41 A6
Poole BH14 ....203 B3
Portsmouth,Landport PO1 .182 C7
Portsmouth,Wymering
PO6,PO7 ....133 F3
Romsey SO51 ....133 F3
Sherfield English SO51 ..25 E1
South Baddesley SO41 .198 F4
Steep Marsh GU32 .....19 F1
Sway SO41 ....196 F2
Titchfield PO15 ......130 A2
Wickham PO17 ....108 A5
Wimborne Minst BH21 .163 C5
Mill Mdw SO41 ....211 D5
Mill Pond Rd PO12 ...181 B7
Mill Pond The SO45 ..150 B6
Mill Quay PO10 ......161 A7
Mill Race View SP5 ....46 F8
Mill Rd
Christchurch BH23 ...207 A8
Denmead PO7 ....111 A4
Fareham PO16 ....155 A8
Gosport PO12 ....181 A7
Liss SO51 ....21 A5
Southampton SO15 ..102 A7
Totton SO40 ....101 A7
Waterlooville PO7 ...134 C6
Westbourne PO10 ....137 B4
Mill Rd N BH8 ....190 C4
Mill Rd S BH8 ....190 D2

Mill Rise SO51 ....5 D1
Mill Rythe Inf Sch PO11 .185 B6
Mill Rythe Jun Sch
PO11 ....185 B6
Mill Rythe La PO11 ...185 A7
Mill St Corfe Mullen BH21 .162 A1
Eastleigh SO50 ....56 B4
Mill Way SO40 ....100 E5
Mill Yd The SO16 ......77 C5
Millais Rd SO19 ......103 E3
Milland Rd SO23 .....215 F4
Millbank Ho
14 Southampton SO14 .103 C6
8 Wimborne Minst BH21 .163 C5
Millbank St SO14 ....103 C5
Millbridge Gdns SO19 .104 B4
Millbrook Cl
Chandler's Ford SO53 ..55 B5
Liss GU33 ....21 A4
Millbrook Com Sch SO16 .77 E3
Millbrook Dr PO9 ....136 A6
Millbrook Flyover SO15 .101 E7
Millbrook Point Rd
SO15 ....102 A6
Millbrook Rd W SO15 .101 F6
Millbrook Road E SO15 .102 B6
Millbrook Road W SO15 .102 A6
Millbrook Sta SO15 ..102 B6
Millbrook Trad Est
SO15 ....101 D7
Millcourt SO50 ....57 D2
Millennium Ct PO7 ...134 E5
Millennium Sq **1** PO16 .131 B1
Miller Cl BH25 ....195 C4
Miller Dr PO16 ....130 F3
Miller Rd BH23 ....207 D7
Miller's Pond Gdns
SO19 ....103 F3
Millers La SO22 ....9 F3
Millers Quay Ho PO16 .155 B8
Millers Way SO45 ....125 F2
Millfield
New Milton BH25 .....194 E3
Poole BH17 ....202 A7
Milhams Cl BH10 ....189 B6
Milhams Dr BH10 ....189 B6
Milhams Rd BH10 ....189 B6
Milhams St BH23 ....207 B6
Milhams Street N 2
BH23 ....207 B6
Milliken Cl SO45 .....150 F2
Mills Rd PO2 ....157 D1
Mills The BH12 ......203 E7
Millstream Cl
Poole BH17 ....202 A7
Wimborne Minst BH21 .163 C4
Millstream Rise SO51 ..52 F7
Millstream Trad Est
BH24 ....141 A5
Millverton Ct **1** SO18 .104 B7
Millvina Cl SO40 ......99 F4
Millway SO32 ....82 B5
Millyford Cl BH25 ....209 D8
Milman Ct **12** SO23 ..215 E6
Milne Cl SO45 ....125 C2
Milne Rd BH17 ....187 B1
Milner Ct SO15 ......102 C8
Milner Pl SO22 ....215 C4
Milner Rd BH4 ....204 C1
Milnthorpe La SO22 .215 C5
Milton Bsns Ctr BH25 .194 F3
Milton Cl BH14 ......203 D3
Milton Ct
Ferndown BH22 ......165 D5
3 Portsmouth PO4 ..183 A5
Milton Gr
Locks Heath SO31 ...129 B2
New Milton BH25 ....195 D7
Milton La PO4 ....183 A5
Milton Mead BH25 ..194 F2
Milton Par PO8 ......111 E2
Milton Park **1** BH8 ..189 A4
Milton Rd
Bournemouth BH8 ...205 A6
Eastleigh SO50 ....56 B5
Poole BH14 ....203 D3
Portsmouth PO4 .....183 A5
Southampton SO15 ..102 F6
Waterlooville PO7,PO8 .111 E1
Wimborne Minst BH21 .163 C6
Milton Villas BH8 ....205 A6
Miltoncross Sch PO3 .183 A6
Milverton Cl
Christchurch BH23 ...193 E1
Totton SO40 ....101 A6
Milverton Ho PO5 ...216 B2
Milverton Rd
Totton SO40 ....101 A6
Winchester SO22 ....215 C6
Milvil Ct PO13 ....179 C3
Milvil Rd PO13 ....179 C3
Mimosa Ave BH21 ...187 E8
Mimosa Cl PO15 .....130 C4
Mimosa Dr SO50 ......57 C2
Mincingfield La SO32 ..82 B7
Mincingfield Terr SO32 ..82 D5
Minden Ho
Fareham PO14 ....154 F8
Romsey SO51 ....53 B7
Minden Way SO22 ...215 A3
Minerva Cl PO7 ......134 C2
Minerva Cres **20** PO1 .182 A4
Minerva Ct **2** PO1 ...182 E1
Minerva Dr **9** PO7 ...134 C2
Minley Ct **18** PO9 ....136 B5
Minnitt Rd PO12 .....181 E5

Minstead Ave SO18 ..104 D8
Minstead Cl SO22 ......1 D1
Minstead Ct **4** SO17 .103 A8
Minstead Rd
Bournemouth BH10 ..189 C3
Portsmouth PO3 .....183 B3
Minster Cl PO15 .....130 C2
Minster Ct **9** SO15 ..102 C6
Minster La **3** SO23 ..215 E5
Minster Pk BH21 ....138 E5
Minster The BH21 ...163 B4
Minster View BH21 ..163 C5
Minster Way BH16 ..201 B7
Mint Rd GU33 ....21 A5
Mint The GU31,GU32 ..40 F2
Minter's Lepe PO7 ...134 E3
Mintern Cl SO50 .....56 D5
Minterne Grange BH14 .214 C7
Minterne Rd
3 Bournemouth BH9 .190 A2
Christchurch BH23 ..207 E5
Portsmouth PO3 ....214 C7
Minters Ct **2** SO23 ..215 D6
Minton Mews PO7 ...204 F5
Mintys Hill SP6 ....68 F8
Mintys Yd **4** BH24 ...141 A6
Mirabella Cl SO19 ...103 D2
Mirror Cl SO31 ......128 F1
Mislingford Rd SO32 ..84 D3
Missenden Acres SO30 .105 C8
Missenden Pl SO50 ....56 A1
Mission La
Broadstone BH18 ....187 A2
Waterlooville PO8 ...112 A3
Mission Rd BH18 ....187 A2
Misslebrook La SO16,
SO52 ....54 D3
Mistletoe Gdns SO31 .128 E6
Mistral **11** SO14 .....103 B3
Mitchell Cl
Barton on S BH25 ...210 A7
Locks Heath PO15 ...129 D5
Mitchell Dr SO50 .....57 C3
Mitchell Point SO31 .127 F2
Mitchell Rd
Eastleigh SO50 ....80 A8
Ferndown BH21 .....165 A7
Havant PO9 ....135 B3
Poole BH17 ....202 F8
Mitchell Way
Eastleigh SO18,SO50 ..80 A8
Portsmouth PO3 .....158 B3
Mitchells Cl Redlynch SP5 .47 D6
Romsey SO51 ....52 F7
Mitre Copse SO50 .....56 F2
Mitre Ct
5 Christchurch BH23 .207 A7
5 Fareham PO14 ....154 E7
Mizen Ho PO6 ....157 A7
Mizen Way SO31 .....180 D6
Miztah Villas SO32 ...83 E3
Moat Cl SO45 ....150 B3
Moat Ct
Bournemouth BH4 ...204 C5
Gosport PO12 ....180 D4
Moat Dr PO12 ....180 D3
Moat Hill SO18 ....79 F3
Moat La BH25 ....209 F8
Mockbeggar La BH24 .117 A7
Moffat Rd BH23 .....207 D7
Moggs Mead GU31 ...41 A3
Mole Hill PO7 ....134 F5
Molefields SO41 .....211 E5
Molesworth Rd PO12 .181 C4
Mollison Rise PO15 ..129 D6
Momford Rd SO22 ....16 A5
Mon Cres SO18 .....104 C7
Monaco Ct BH4 .....205 B8
Monarch Cl
Locks Heath SO31 ...129 A2
3 Waterlooville PO7 .135 A7
Monarch Way
West End SO18 ....80 F2
Winchester SO22 ....215 A4
Monastery Rd SO18 .103 E7
Monckton Rd
Gosport PO12 ....181 B2
Portsmouth PO3 ....158 A2
Moneyfield Ave PO3 .158 B1
Moneyfield La **3** PO3 .183 A8
Moneyfield Prim Sch
Moneyfly Rd BH31 ...115 B5
Monk's Hill PO12 ....137 B5
Monks Brook Cl SO50 ..55 E1
Monks Brook Ind Pk
SO53 ....54 E1
Monks Cl BH22 ......166 A8
Monks Ct **3** SO41 ...197 F2
Monks Hill PO13 ....179 C5
Monks Orch GU32 ....40 F6
Monks Pl SO40 .....100 D6
Monks Rd Netley SO31 .127 B6
Winchester SO23 ....215 B7
Monks Way
Bournemouth BH11 .188 D5
Eastleigh SO50 ....55 F1
Monks Wlk SO45 ....149 E8
Monks Wood GU32 ..79 B6
Monkshood Cl BH23 .193 B1
Monkswell Gn BH23 .207 D6
Monkton Cl BH22 ...165 F8
Monkton Cres BH22 .203 D8
Monkton La SO40 ...100 C6

Monkwood Cl PO9 ...135 D5
Monkworthy Dr BH24 .139 F5
Monmouth Cl
Chandler's Ford SO53 ..55 B6
Verwood BH31 ......115 B4
Monmouth Ct
Lymington SO41 ....197 E3
Ringwood BH24 .....140 F7
Monmouth Dr BH31 .115 B4
Monmouth Gdns SO40 .100 D5
Monmouth Rd PO12 .157 D1
Monmouth Sq SO22 ..10 B5
Monnow Gdns SO18 ..80 B1
Monroe Cl PO12 .....180 E3
Mons The PO7 ....215 D6
Monsal Ave BH22 ...165 C3
Montacute Sch BH17 .187 C2
Montacute Way BH21 .187 E8
Montagu Cl PO12 ...181 C9
Montagu Pk BH23 ...209 A7
Montagu Rd BH23 ..209 B8
Montague Ave SO19 .104 C6
Montague Cl SO45 ..103 D3
Montague Ct SO45 .149 E8
Montague Gdns GU31 ..41 B3
Montague Rd
Bishopstoke SO50 ....56 D3
Bournemouth BH5 ..206 B4
Portsmouth PO2 ....157 F2
Montague Wallis Ct 40
PO1 ....182 A5
Montana Ct PO7 ....135 A6
Montefiore Ho SO18 ..79 D4
Monteray Dr SO41 ..195 F4
Monterey Dr Havant PO9 .136 A4
Locks Heath SO31 ...129 A2
Montfort Cl SO51 ....53 C7
Montfort Coll SO51 ..53 C7
Montfort Ct SO45 ...149 E8
Montfort Rd SO51 ...53 C6
Montgomerie Rd PO5 .216 C2
Montgomery Ave
Bournemouth BH11 .189 B3
Totton SO40 ....100 D8
Montgomery Ct SO22 .215 A3
Montgomery Rd
Gosport PO13 ....155 C3
Havant PO9 ....136 A1
Southampton SO18 .104 A8
Montgomery Way SO53 ..55 B3
Montpelier Cl SO31 .129 C3
Montrose Ave PO16 .132 E1
Montrose Cl
Hedge End SO30 ....105 E6
Verwood BH31 ......114 F6
Montrose Dr BH10 ..189 B2
Montserrat Rd SO31 .179 E3
Montxton La SO24 ..103 A2
Monument La
Portchester PO17 ...132 B4
Southampton SO40 .198 A5
Woodmancote PO17 .137 F7
Monxton Gn **18** PO9 .136 B6
Moody Rd PO14 .....179 C6
Moody's Hill SP5 ......3 C2
Moon Cl SO40 ....101 E1
Moonhills La SO42 ..149 B2
Moonrakers Way BH23 .193 E1
Mooncross Ave SO40 .100 F6
Moor Cl BH25 ....48 C8
Moor Pk PO7 ....112 B1
Moor Rd BH18 ......187 B5
Moor Side BH24 ....166 B8
Moor View Rd BH15 .202 E6
Moorcroft Ave BH10 .192 C2
Moordown St John's CE Prim
Sch BH9 ....189 F1
Moore Ave BH11 ....189 A4
Moore Cl BH25 ......194 F1
Moore Cres SO31 ...127 C7
Moore Gdns PO12 ..180 F4
Moorfield Gr BH9 ...189 F2
Moorfield Rd BH13 .214 F8
Moorgreen Hospl SO30 ..80 E1
Moorgreen Rd
Havant PO9 ....136 A5
West End SO30 ....80 F2
Moorhaven Cl BH25 .165 D6
Moorhead Ct SO14 .103 C2
Moorhill Gdns SO18 .104 E7
Moorhill Rd SO30 ...105 D4
Moorland Ave PO9 ..136 A5
Moorland Cl Hythe SO45 .125 D3
Locks Heath SO31 ...129 A4
Moorland Cres SO31 .201 B7
Moorland Gate BH24 .141 A5
Moorland Par BH16 ..201 D6
Moorland Rd
Bournemouth BH11 .205 D4
Portsmouth PO1 ....182 E6
Moorlands Cl BH16 .201 B7
Moorlands Coll SO42 .145 D1
Moorlands Cres SO18 .192 B6
Moorlands Inf Sch SO18 ..80 B1
Moorland Rd
Christchurch BH23 ..207 D6
Poole BH17 ....202 A7
Moorings **2** SO31 ...104 D8
Moorings The
2 Christchurch BH23 .207 A5
Fareham PO16 ......155 B7
Moorings Way Inf Sch
PO4 ....183 C6

Moorlands Rd
Swanmore SO32 ......84 A7
Verwood BH31 ......114 F7
West Moors BH22 ....138 F3
Moorlands Rise BH22 .138 F3
Moorlea **2** BH8 ......205 B6
Moors Cl
Colden Common SO21 .31 F1
Hurn BH23 ....191 B7
Moors Valley Ctry Park
Visitor Ctr* BH24 ...139 D8
Moors Valley Ctry Pk*
BH24 ....115 E1
Moors Valley Rly*
BH24 ....115 C1
Moortown Ave PO6 .134 C7
Moortown Dr
Bournemouth BH21 .188 B8
Wimborne Minst BH21 .188 B8
Moortown Farm BH21 .188 B8
Moortown Ho BH24 .141 A5
Moortown La BH24 ..141 A4
Moorvale Rd BH9 ...190 A2
Moot Cl SP5 ....47 A7
Moot Gardens The* SP5 ..47 A7
Moot Gdns SP5 ....46 F5
Moot La SP5 ....46 F5
Mopley SO45 ....177 F7
Mopley Cl SO45 ....177 F7
Morant Cl **4** BH25 ..195 B3
Morant Rd BH24 ....141 A4
Moraunt Cl **1** PO12 .181 C9
Moraunt Dr PO16 ...156 B6
Moray Ct **11** BH21 ..163 B5
Moray Rd SO14 .....103 A7
Morden Ave BH22 ..165 C4
Morden Rd BH9 ....189 E1
Morecombe Ct **4** PO5 .216 C2
Moreland Cl SO31 ..181 B6
Morelands Ct PO7 ..134 F4
Morelands Prim Sch
PO7 ....134 E2
Morelands Rd PO7 ..134 E4
Moresby Ct **5** PO13 .131 B1
Morestead Rd
Winchester SO23 ....11 E3
Winchester SO23 ....16 E3
Moreton Rd BH9 ....190 B4
Morgan Le Fay Dr SO53 ..54 F7
Morgan Rd
Hedge End SO30 ....105 C5
Portsmouth PO4 ....183 C4
Morgan's La SP5 .....42 A1
Morgan's Vale & Woodfalls
CE Prim Sch SP5 ....47 D7
Morgans Dr PO14 ...154 C5
Morgans Rise Rd SP5 .47 D7
Morgans Vale Rd SP5 .47 D6
Moriconium Quay BH15 .201 D1
Morington Ct **3** BH25 .205 A5
Morland Rd SO15 .....78 C1
Morley Cl
Bournemouth BH5 ..206 A5
Burton BH23 ....192 C3
Southampton SO19 .103 F6
Morley Cres PO8 ....112 A3
Morley Dr SO32 ......83 C8
Morley Gdns SO53 ...55 C8
Morley Rd
Bournemouth BH5 ..206 A5
Portsmouth PO4 ....183 A2
Morleys La SO51 ....29 C3
Morningside Ave PO16 .132 E1
Mornington Dr SO22 .215 A4
Mornish Rd BH13 ...203 F2
Morpeth Ave SO40 ..100 F8
Morris Cl Gosport PO13 .155 B5
Hythe SO45 ....125 E3
Morris Rd Poole BH17 .202 D8
Southampton SO15 .102 F6
Morrison Ave PO4 ..183 F6
Morse Ct SO31 ......127 A6
Morshead Cres PO16 .130 F3
Mortimer Cl
Christchurch BH23 ..208 A6
Kings Worthy SO23 ...2 C6
Netley SO31 ....127 B6
Totton SO40 ....76 D1
Mortimer Lawn PO9 .135 F7
Mortimer Rd
Botley SO30 ....106 A6
Bournemouth BH8 ..190 B1
Portsmouth PO6 ....133 C1
Southampton SO19 .103 E4
Mortimer Way SO52 ..53 F3
Mortimer's Ind Units
SO51 ....75 E5
Mortimers Dr SO50 ..57 D2
Mortimers La SO50 ..57 E2
Mortimore Rd PO12 .180 F6
Mosaic Cl SO19 .....104 F4
Mosdell Rd PO10 ...161 A8
Mosedale Wlk **2** SO16 .101 E7
Moselle Ct SO15 ....102 C5
Moss Cl GU33 ....21 A4
Moss Dr SO40 ......101 F2
Moss Rd SO23 ......215 G6

Mossleigh Ave SO16 ...... .77 F5
Mossley Ave Poole BH12 .189 A1
  Poole BH12 .... .204 A8
Motcombe Rd BH13 ...... .204 A2
Mottisfont Abbey (NT)*
  SO51 .... .5 F3
Mottisfont Abbey Gdns*
  SO51 .... .5 F3
Mottisfont Cl **1** SO15 ..102 A6
Mottisfont Lodge **5**
  SO51 .... .52 F7
Mottisfont Rd SO50 ...... .56 A4
Moulin Ave PO5 .... .182 E2
Mound Cl PO12 .... .181 A4
Mount Ave BH25 .... .195 A1
Mount Cl
  New Milton BH25 .... .195 A1
  Winchester SO22 .... .1 E3
Mount Dr
  Chandler's Ford SO53 .... .55 E4
  Fareham PO15 .... .154 B8
Mount Grace Dr BH14 ...214 D7
Mount Heatherbank **7**
  BH1 .... .204 F3
Mount Hospl The SO50 ....56 D5
Mount House Cl SO45 ...126 A5
Mount La SO51 .... .25 F7
Mount Pleasant
  Christchurch BH23 ...... .208 A5
  Denmead PO7 .... .110 F2
  Kings Worthy SO23 ...... .2 C6
  Ringwood BH24 .... .141 A7
  Romsey SO51 .... .52 E6
Mount Pleasant Dr
  Bournemouth BH8 ...... .190 F1
  Bransgore BH23 .... .169 C1
Mount Pleasant Ind Pk
  SO14 .... .103 B7
Mount Pleasant Jun Sch
  SO14 .... .103 B7
Mount Pleasant La
  SO41 .... .197 A7
Mount Pleasant Rd
  Gosport PO12 .... .181 B4
  Poole BH14 .... .202 D3
  Southampton SO14 ...... .103 B6
Mount The
  5 Bassett SO16 ...... .78 F4
  Gosport PO13 .... .155 E1
  9 Old Shirley SO16 ....78 A1
  Ringwood BH24 .... .141 D8
Mount View SO50 ...... .56 B4
Mount View Rd SO22 ....10 B4
Mountain Ash Cl SO18 ..104 C7
Mountbatten Ave SO51 ..52 F7
Mountbatten Bsns Ctr
  SO15 .... .102 E5
Mountbatten Bsns Pk
  PO6 .... .158 C6
Mountbatten Cl
  Christchurch BH23 ...... .208 A5
  Gosport PO13 .... .155 C4
Mountbatten Ct
  New Milton BH25 ...... .194 F3
  Winchester SO22 ...... .1 E3
Mountbatten Dr
  Ferndown BH22 .... .165 C5
  Waterlooville PO7 ...... .134 D6
Mountbatten Gdns BH8 .190 F2
Mountbatten Pl SO23 ....2 C8
Mountbatten Rd
  Eastleigh SO50 .... .56 A5
  Poole BH13 .... .204 B1
  Totton SO40 .... .100 D8
Mountbatten Sch & Language
  Coll The SO51 .... .53 C6
Mountbatten Sq **4** PO4 .183 B2
Mountbatten Way
  Portsmouth PO1 .... .182 B7
  Southampton SO15 ...... .102 C5
Mountfield SO45 .... .125 E4
Mountjoy Cl PO21 ...... .163 F2
Mountjoy Cl **4** PO1 ..182 A3
Mountview Ave PO16 ....132 E1
Mountwood Rd PO10 ....137 D1
Mousehole La
  Hythe SO45 .... .126 A3
  Southampton SO18 ...... .103 F8
Mousehole Rd PO6 ...... .132 F1
Moxhams SP6 .... .69 F1
Moyles Court Sch BH24 ..117 C5
Muccleshell Cl PO9 ...... .136 A4
Muddyford Rd SP5 ...... .47 D8
Mude Gdns BH23 .... .208 A5
Mudeford Com Inf Sch
  BH23 .... .207 E6
Mudeford Green Cl
  BH23 .... .207 F5
Mudeford Jun Sch
  BH23 .... .207 F6
Mudeford La BH23 ...... .207 F6
Muir Ho SO45 .... .125 E1
Muira Est SO14 .... .103 C5
Mulberry Ave
  Cosham PO6 .... .158 A4
  Stubbington PO14 ...... .179 C6
Mulberry Cl PO12 ...... .181 B5
Mulberry Ct **4** BH23 ..207 A7
Mulberry Gdns SP6 ...... .93 E8
Mulberry Gr SO41 ...... .211 D6

Mulberry La
  Cosham PO6 .... .158 A7
  Sarisbury SO31 .... .128 E5
Mulberry Mews SP6 ...... .93 E8
Mulberry Rd SO40 ...... .101 F1
Mulberry Wlk SO15 ...... .102 C8
Mullen Cl SO19 .... .103 E4
Mullins Cl BH12 .... .204 C8
Mullion Cl PO4 .... .157 B7
Mumby Rd PO12 .... .181 D6
Mundys Row PO8 .... .88 C1
Munro Cres SO15 ...... .101 F7
Munster Rd Poole BH14 ..203 D3
  Portsmouth PO2 .... .157 D2
Murefield Rd PO1 ...... .216 C3
Muriel Rd PO7 .... .134 E8
Murley Rd BH9 .... .205 A8
Murray Cl Fareham PO15 .130 E2
  Southampton SO19 ...... .104 E6
Murray Cotts SO32 ...... .107 D7
Murray Rd PO8 .... .112 B6
Murray's La PO1 .... .181 F7
Murrills Est PO16 ...... .156 E8
Mus of Electricity*
  BH23 .... .207 B7
Muscliff Prim Sch BH9 ..190 C4
Muscliffe Ct **8** BH9 ..136 B5
Muscliffe La BH9 .... .190 B5
Muscliffe Rd BH9 ...... .189 F1
Museum of Archaeology*
  SO14 .... .103 A2
Museum Rd PO1 .... .182 B4
Mussett Cl SO40 .... .100 A7
Mustang Ave PO15 ...... .129 C7
My Lords La PO11 ...... .185 B3
Myers Cl SO32 .... .84 B5
Myrtle Ave
  Portchester PO16 ...... .156 D7
  Totton SO40 .... .100 D6
Myrtle Cl Gosport PO13 ..155 B3
  Hordle SO41 .... .195 F4
Myrtle Gr PO3 .... .183 B7
Myrtle Rd
  Bournemouth BH8 ...... .205 C6
  Southampton SO16 ...... .78 B4
Myvern Cl SO45 .... .150 D3

N

Nada Rd BH23 .... .193 D1
Nailsworth Rd PO6 ...... .133 B1
Nairn Cl BH3 .... .204 E7
Nairn Rd
  Bournemouth BH3 ...... .204 E6
  Poole BH13 .... .214 E7
Naish Ct PO9 .... .135 C7
Naish Dr PO12 .... .156 A1
Naish Rd BH25 .... .209 E7
Namu Rd BH9 .... .189 E1
Nancy Rd PO1 .... .216 D3
Nansen Ave BH15 ...... .202 D5
Napier Cl SO13 .... .180 D5
Napier Cres PO15 ...... .130 C1
Napier Rd
  Hamworthy BH15 ...... .201 C3
  Horndean PO8 .... .112 C6
  Portsmouth PO2 .... .182 D2
  Southampton SO19 ...... .104 E5
Narrow La
  Ringwood,North Poulner
    BH24 .... .117 D1
  Ringwood,Poulner BH24 .141 D8
  9 Romsey SO51 ...... .52 E7
Narvik Rd PO2 .... .157 D4
Naseby Cl **5** PO6 ...... .133 A1
Naseby Rd BH9 .... .190 A2
Nash Cl SO45 .... .125 D1
Nash Rd SO45 .... .125 D2
Nashe Cl PO15 .... .130 D3
Nashe Ho PO15 .... .130 C3
Nashe Way PO15 ...... .130 C3
Nasmith Cl PO12 ...... .180 D4
Nat Gonella Sq **4** PO12 .181 D5
Natanbury SP5 .... .47 A7
Nathen Gdns BH15 ...... .201 D3
National Air Traffic Services
  Hq PO15 .... .129 F8
National Motor Mus The*
  SO42 .... .148 E2
Nations Hill SO23 ...... .2 B6
Navarac Ct BH14 ...... .203 C3
Navigator's Way SO30 ..105 C8
Navy Rd PO1 .... .182 A6
Nea Cl BH23 .... .208 D8
Nea Dr BH24 .... .116 B5
Nea Rd BH23 .... .208 D8
Neacroft Cl BH25 ...... .209 D8
Neath Way SO53 ...... .55 A5
Needles Cl **11** SO41 ..211 C4
Needles Ho PO16 ...... .155 A7
Needles Point SO41 .... .211 D3
Neelands Gr PO6 ...... .156 E8
Neighbourhood Ctr
  BH17 .... .187 E2
Neilson Cl SO53 .... .55 C7
Nelson Ave
  Portchester PO16 ...... .156 B8
  Portsmouth PO2 .... .157 D2
Nelson Cl Holbury SO45 ..150 C3
  New Milton BH25 ...... .194 F3
  Romsey SO51 .... .52 F8
Nelson Cres PO8 ...... .112 C7
Nelson Ct Fareham PO14 .154 F6
  11 Hythe SO45 ...... .126 B1
  15 Poole BH15 ...... .202 C2
  8 Portsmouth PO1 ..182 D7
Nelson Ctr The PO3 ...... .158 B2

Nelson Dr BH23 .... .207 F6
Nelson Ho **3** PO2 ...... .181 E5
Nelson Ind Pk SO30 .... .81 B1
Nelson La PO17 .... .132 C2
Nelson Pl SO41 .... .197 F3
Nelson Rd
  Bishopstoke SO50 ...... .56 D4
  Gosport PO12 .... .181 B5
  Poole BH4,BH12 .... .204 B4
  Portsmouth PO5 .... .216 C1
  Portsmouth,Landport PO1 .182 D7
  Southampton SO15 ...... .102 C6
  Winchester SO23 ...... .11 C6
Nelsons Gdns SO30 .... .81 C3
Nepean Cl PO17 .... .132 C2
Neptune Ct
  4 Portsmouth PO1 ..182 A4
  Southampton SO16 ...... .77 F4
Neptune Ho
  1 Cosham PO6 ...... .157 F8
  Southampton SO14 ...... .103 B2
Neptune Way
  Fareham,Hill Park PO15 .130 C2
  Fareham,West End PO14 .154 F5
  Netley Abbey SO14 .... .103 B2
Nerissa Cl PO7 .... .135 B8
Nerquis Cl SO31 .... .53 B8
Nesbitt Cl PO13 .... .155 B3
Nessus St PO2 .... .182 D8
Nest Bsns Pk PO9 ...... .136 B4
Nethercliffe Sch SO22 ..215 C7
Netherfield Cl PO9 ...... .136 A1
Netherhall Gdns BH4 ....204 C3
Netherhill SO32 .... .82 C3
Netherhill La SO32 ...... .82 B2
Netherton Rd PO12 .... .180 F7
Netherwood Pl BH21 ....163 A5
Netley Abbey* SO31 ....127 A7
Netley Abbey Inf Sch
  SO31 .... .127 B7
Netley Abbey Jun Sch
  SO31 .... .127 B7
Netley Cl
  Chandler's Ford SO53 .... .55 B3
  Poole BH15 .... .203 A7
Netley Cliff SO31 ...... .127 B5
Netley Court Sch SO31 ..127 B5
Netley Ct **8** PO12 .... .181 C9
Netley Firs Rd
  Hedge End SO30 ...... .104 F4
  Southampton SO19 ...... .105 A6
Netley Hill Est SO19 ....104 F4
Netley Lodge Cl SO31 ..127 C5
Netley Mews **10** PO5 ..182 D1
Netley Marsh CE Inf Sch
  SO40 .... .100 A7
Netley Marsh Workshops
  SO40 .... .100 A7
Netley Rd
  13 Portsmouth PO5 ..182 C2
  Titchfield PO14 ...... .129 C1
  Netley Sta SO31 ...... .127 C6
Netley Terr **14** PO5 ..182 C2
Nettlecombe Ave PO4 ..182 E1
Nettlestone SO31 ...... .127 C2
Nettlestone Rd **1** PO4 .183 A2
Nettleton Cl BH17 ...... .202 E7
Netton Cl SP5 .... .22 B8
Netton St SP5 .... .22 C8
Neva Rd SO18 .... .103 F8
Neville Ave PO16 ...... .156 D6
Neville Dr SO51 .... .27 F7
Neville Gdns PO10 .... .136 E3
Neville Lovett Com Sch The
  PO14 .... .154 F8
Neville Rd PO3 .... .183 A7
Neville Shute Rd PO3 ..158 A3
New Borough Rd BH21 ..163 D3
New Brighton Rd PO10 ..136 F2
New Cliff Ho SO19 ...... .103 E1
New Coll (Univ of
  Southampton) SO15 ..102 F7
New Cotts Ashurst SO40 .123 F7
  Exbury SO45 .... .177 B5
  Fareham PO16 .... .155 A8
  Hampreston BH21 ...... .164 E2
  Nursling SO16 .... .77 F8
  South Baddesley SO41 ..199 A5
New Ct BH24 .... .140 E7
New Cut PO11 .... .159 F3
New Down La PO6,PO7 ..134 A2
New Fields Bsns Pk
  BH17 .... .202 D8
New Forest Dr SO42 ....145 D1
New Forest Ent Ctr
  SO40 .... .100 E5
New Forest Mus & Visitor
  Ctr* SO43 .... .122 A5
New Forest Otter, Owl &
  Wildlife Pk* SO43 .... .123 E8
New Forest Reptile Ctr*
  SO43 .... .121 A3
New Harbour Rd BH15 ..202 B2
New Harbour Rd S
  BH15 .... .213 B8
New Harbour Road W
  BH15 .... .202 A1
New Inn Cotts SO42 .... .175 C5
New Inn La Bartley SO40 .99 B6
  East Boldre SO42 ...... .172 B1
New Inn Rd SO40 ...... .99 B7
New Leaze BH21 ...... .163 D2
New Merridale* BH21 ..163 F7

New Milton Inf Sch
  BH25 .... .195 A1
New Milton Jun Sch
  BH25 .... .195 A1
New Milton Sta BH25 ..195 A3
New Orch BH15 .... .202 B2
New Par
  Bournemouth BH10 .... .189 E3
  Portchester PO16 ...... .156 D8
New Park Rd BH6 ...... .206 C4
New Quay Rd BH15 .... .202 B1
New Rd Ashurst SO40 ..100 C2
  Bishop's Waltham SO32 ..59 D2
  Blackfield SO45 ...... .150 E1
  Bournemouth BH10 .... .189 E7
  Clanfield PO8 .... .88 C5
  Colden Common SO21 ..31 F1
  Fair Oak SO50 .... .57 B2
  Fareham PO16 .... .131 A1
  Ferndown BH22 ...... .165 E3
  Havant PO9 .... .135 E2
  Holbury SO45 .... .150 C7
  Horndean PO8 .... .111 E6
  Hythe SO45 .... .126 A4
  Hythe,Buttsash SO45 ..150 B7
  Ibsley BH24 .... .117 B8
  Landford SP5 .... .49 F2
  Littleton SO22 .... .1 B6
  Meonstoke SO32 ...... .61 D3
  Michelmersh SO51 .... .27 D8
  Milford on S SO41 ...... .212 A4
  Netley SO31 .... .127 B6
  Poole BH12 .... .203 D6
  Portsmouth PO2 ...... .182 F7
  Ringwood BH24 ...... .141 A4
  Rockbourne SP6 ...... .44 E1
  Romsey SO51 .... .53 A8
  Southampton SO14 .... .103 A5
  Southbourne PO10 .... .161 E8
  Swanmore SO32 ...... .84 A5
  Swanwick SO31 ...... .128 F8
  Warsash SO31 .... .152 C10
  Westbourne PO10 .... .137 B3
  Woodlands Common BH24 .114 A6
New B E PO2 .... .182 F8
New St Lymington SO41 .197 E4
  Poole BH15 .... .202 B1
  Ringwood BH24 ...... .141 A6
New Street Mews SO41 ..197 E4
New Town PO16 ...... .156 D8
New Valley Rd SO41 ....211 C5
Newbarn La PO18 ...... .137 F8
Newbarn Rd Buriton GU31 .65 C2
  Havant PO9 .... .135 C3
Newbolt Cl PO8 .... .111 E3
Newbolt Rd PO6 ...... .132 F1
Newbridge SO31 ...... .127 C6
Newbridge Jun Sch
  PO2 .... .182 F7
Newbridge Rd
  Cadnam SO40 .... .75 A1
  Newbridge SO40 ...... .74 F3
Newbridge Way SO41 ..197 C1
Newbroke Rd PO13 .... .180 E8
Newburgh St SO23 .... .215 D6
Newbury Cl SO50 ...... .57 B2
Newbury Dr BH10 ...... .189 D1
Newbury Pl SO31 ...... .128 F2
Newbury Rd SO15 ...... .78 C1
Newcombe Rd
  Bournemouth BH6 ...... .206 C5
  Southampton SO15 ...... .102 E6
  West Moors BH22 ...... .138 D3
Newcome Rd PO1 ...... .182 E6
Newcomen Ct **8** PO2 ..157 C2
Newcomen Rd PO2 .... .157 C2
Newcroft Gdns BH23 ....207 A8
Newenham Rd SO41 ....197 E2
Newfield Rd SO23 ...... .21 A6
Newfoundland Dr BH15 .202 D2
Newfoundland Drive Rdbt
  BH15 .... .202 D1
Newgate La PO14 ...... .155 A4
Newgate Lane Ind Est
  PO14 .... .155 B6
Newitt Pl SO16 .... .78 F6
Newland Pl SO16 ...... .181 A5
Newlands BH25 .... .195 A4
Newlands Ave SO15 ....102 D7
Newlands Cl
  Blackfield SO45 ...... .150 E1
  Chandler's Ford SO53 .... .54 E5
Newlands Copse SO45 ..150 F1
Newlands La
  Denmead PO7 .... .111 A1
  Waterlooville PO7 .... .134 A6
Newlands Manor SO41 ..211 D7
  Newlands Prim Sch SO16 .77 E1
Newlands Rd
  Blackfield SO45 ...... .150 E2
  Bournemouth BH7 ...... .206 A6
  Christchurch BH23 .... .207 A8
  New Milton BH25 ...... .195 B1
  Waterlooville PO7 .... .134 A6
Newlands The **2** SO17 .79 C2
Newlands Way BH18 ....186 D3
Newlease Rd PO7 ...... .134 F6
Newlyn Way Poole BH12 .203 E7
  Portsmouth PO6 ...... .157 F7
Newlyn Wlk SO51 ...... .28 A1
Newman St **2** SO16 ..102 B8
Newman's La BH22 .... .138 C4
Newmans Cl
  West Moors BH21 ...... .138 D6
  Wimborne Minst BH21 ..163 D3
Newmans Copse Rd
  SO40 .... .101 A4
Newmans Hill PO17 .... .84 D1

Newmarket Cl SO50 .... .81 D7
Newmer Ct PO9 .... .135 C6
Newmorton Rd BH9 .... .190 A4
Newney Cl PO2 .... .157 F4
Newnham Ct PO9 ...... .136 B5
Newport Cl PO12 ...... .180 F5
Newport La SO51 ...... .28 C5
Newport Rd PO2 .... .157 E3
Newstead Rd BH6 ...... .206 D4
Newton Bglws SP5 ...... .24 A3
Newton Cl
  Stubbington PO14 ...... .154 C4
  Whiteparish SP5 ...... .24 A3
Newton La Romsey SO51 .52 E6
  Whiteparish SP5 ...... .24 A3
Newton Morrell BH14 ..203 D3
Newton Pl PO13 .... .179 E4
Newton Rd
  Barton on S BH25 ...... .210 B8
  Poole BH13 .... .214 F8
  Southampton SO18 ...... .79 E1
  Twyford SO21 .... .32 A7
Newton Rise
  4 Cosham PO6 ...... .158 B8
  Southampton SO16 ...... .78 A4
  Westbourne PO10 .... .137 B4
Nightingale Cl SO40 ....100 C8
Nightingale Gr SO15 ....102 C7
Nightingale Ho SO51 ..53 A8
Nightingale Mews
  Locks Heath SO31 ...... .129 A3
  Netley SO31 .... .127 C5
Nightingale Pk **1** BH31 .136 B1
Nightingale Prim Sch
  SO50 .... .55 D1
Nightingale Rd
  Petersfield GU32 ...... .40 A3
  Portsmouth PO5 ...... .182 B2
  Southampton SO15 .... .102 C7
Nightingale Wlk SO31 ..127 C4
Nightingale Ct **3**
  SO15 .... .102 C6
Nightjar Cl
  Broadstone BH17 ...... .201 F8
  Waterlooville PO8 .... .112 A6
Nile Rd SO17 .... .79 A2
Nile St PO10 .... .137 B6
Nimrod Dr PO13 ...... .180 D6
Nimrod Way PO6 ...... .164 F6
Nine Acres GU32 ...... .20 E3
Nine Elms La PO17 .... .131 E4
Ninian Cl SO50 .... .57 C1
Ninian Park Rd PO3 .... .158 A2
Nirvana Mans **17** PO5 .182 C1
Niton Cl PO13 .... .155 C2
Nizells Ave PO14 ...... .155 F2
Noads Cl SO45 .... .125 F2
Noads Way SO45 ...... .125 F2
Noadswood Sec Sch
  SO45 .... .125 E2
Nob's Crook SO50 ...... .57 A7
Nobbs La PO1 .... .182 A4
Nobes Ave PO13 ...... .155 D5
Nobes Cl PO13 .... .155 D2
Noble Cl SO40 .... .100 A4
Noble Rd SO30 .... .105 D6
Noctule Ct PO17 ...... .130 D2
Noel Cl SO42 .... .146 A1
Noel Rd BH10 .... .189 B2

Noel The BH25 ....195 C3
Nomad Cl SO18 ....80 B1
Nomansland & Hamptworth
 CE Prim Sch SP5 ......73 C8
Nook The Eastleigh SO50 ..56 B5
Noon Gdns BH31 ......115 B6
Noon Hill Dr BH31 ....115 B6
Noon Hill Rd BH31 ....115 B6
Norbury Cl SO53 ......55 B7
Norbury Gdns SO31 ...127 E2
Norcliffe Cl BH11 ....189 B3
Norcliffe Rd SO17 ....103 A8
Norcroft Ct SO15 ......78 C2
Nordik Gdns SO30 ....105 C5
Nore Cres PO10 ......136 D1
Nore Farm Ave PO10 ..136 D1
Noreuil Rd GU32 ......40 D3
Norfolk Ave BH23 ....191 F2
Norfolk Cres PO11 ...184 E2
Norfolk Ct SO53 ......55 C3
Norfolk Ho **6** PO9 ...136 A1
Norfolk Mews PO11 ..184 E2
Norfolk Rd Gosport PO12 ..188 F7
 Southampton SO15 ...102 D7
Norfolk St PO5 ......216 B2
Norgett Way PO16 ...156 B8
Norham Ave SO16 ....78 C2
Norham Cl SO16 ......78 C2
Norland Rd PO4 ......216 D1
Norlands Dr SO21 ....31 C4
Norley Cl PO9 ....135 E5
Norleywood BH23 ....208 E8
Norleywood Rd SO41 ..198 E8
Norman Ave BH12 ....204 A6
Norman Cl PO16 .....156 D6
Norman Ct **4** PO4 ...182 E2
Norman Gdns
 Hedge End SO30 .....105 A5
 Poole BH12 ....204 A6
Norman Ho **16** SO14 ..103 C6
Norman Rd
 Blackfield SO45 .....177 F8
 Gosport PO12 ....181 A6
 Portsmouth PO4 .....182 E3
 South Hayling PO11 ..185 B2
 Southampton SO15 ...102 D5
 Winchester SO23 ....215 D4
Norman Way PO9 ....135 C2
Normandy Cl
 Rownhams SO16 .....77 E6
 Sway SO41 ....172 A2
Normandy Ct
 Warsash SO31 ......128 C1
 Portsmouth PO7 ....108 B4
Normandy Dr BH23 ..207 D7
Normandy Gdns **1**
 PO12 ....180 F4
Normandy Ho SO51 ..53 B7
Normandy La SO41 ...198 A1
Normandy Rd PO2 ...157 E4
Normandy Way
 Fordingbridge SP6 ...69 E1
 Hamworthy BH15 ....201 D2
 Marchwood SO40 ....102 A1
Normanhurst Ave BH8 ..190 E1
Normans SO23 ......215 D4
Normanton Cl BH23 ..191 F1
Norris Cl Romsey SO51 ..28 C2
 St Leonards SO41 ....139 E4
Norris Gdns Havant PO9 ..160 A8
 New Milton BH25 ....195 A1
Norris Hill SO18 .....79 F8
Norrish Ct PO2 ......182 E7
Norrish Rd PO12 ....203 C5
Norset Rd PO15 .....130 D2
North Ave
 Bournemouth BH10 ..189 D6
 Portsmouth PO2 .....157 C5
North Baddesley Inf Sch
 SO52 ....54 B4
North Baddesley Jun Sch
 SO52 ....54 B4
North Battery Rd PO2 ..157 B2
North Bay PO10 .....161 A3
North Cl Gosport PO12 ..180 F4
 Havant PO9 ....160 A8
 Lymington SO41 .....197 E4
 Romsey SO51 ....28 C1
North Common La
 Landford SP5 ....49 B6
 Sway SO41 ....196 F7
North Cres PO11 .....185 B3
North Cross St PO12 ..181 D5
North Ct PO1 ....182 E7
North Dr Littleton SO22 ..1 B5
 Ossemsley BH25 .....194 E8
 Southwick PO17 .....132 F6
 West Moors BH21 ...166 B8
North East Cl SO19 ..104 C5
North East Rd SO19 ..104 B4
North End Ave PO2 ...157 C2
North End Cl SO53 ...55 C4
North End Farm Cotts
 SO24 ....14 C7
North End Gr PO2 ...157 D2
North End La
 Cheriton SO24 ......14 D7
 Ibsley BH24,SP6 ....93 D4
North Fields Cotts SO21 ..32 A7
North Greenlands SO41 ..197 C2
North Head SO41 ....211 A5
North Hill Fareham PO16 ..131 B3
 Portsmouth PO6 .....133 B2
North Hill Cl SO22 ...215 D8
North Hill Dr SO21 ...215 D8
North La Beaulieu SO42 ..148 E5
 Buriton GU31 ....65 E5

North La *continued*
 Clanfield PO8 ....88 C7
 East Meon PO8 ......64 C2
 Nomansland SP5 ....73 C7
North Lodge Rd BH14 ..203 E4
North Millers Dale SO53 ..55 B8
North Park Bsns Ctr
 PO17 ....130 D8
North Poulner Rd BH24 ..117 B2
North Rd
 Bournemouth BH7 ...205 E5
 Brockenhurst SO42 ..146 A1
 Dibden Purlieu SO45 ..125 E1
 Horndean PO8 ......88 C2
 Kings Worthy SO23 ..2 B8
 Petersfield GU32 ....40 F4
 Poole BH14 ....203 A4
 Portsmouth PO6 .....133 A2
 Southampton SO17 ..103 C8
North Road E PO17 ..133 A6
North Road W PO17 ..133 A6
North Shore Rd PO11 ..184 D4
North Sq **2** PO17 ...130 E7
North St Emsworth PO10 ..136 F1
 Gosport PO12 ....181 D6
 Havant PO9 ....135 F1
 Havant,Bedhampton PO9 ..135 D2
 Lymington SO41 .....197 C2
 Poole BH15 ....202 C2
 Portsmouth PO1 .....216 C4
 Portsmouth,Portsea PO1 ..182 A5
 Westbourne PO10 ...137 B4
North Street Arc **11**
 PO9 ....135 E1
North Stroud La GU32 ..39 E3
North Trestle Rd SO45 ..151 C6
North View SO22 ....215 C6
North Wallington PO16 ..131 C3
North Walls SO23 ...215 E6
North Way PO9 .....135 E1
North Weirs SO42 ...145 D1

North Bsns Ctr **21**
 SO14 ....103 C6
Northam Mews PO1 ..216 C3
Northam Rd SO14 ...103 B5
Northam St PO1 .....216 C3
Northampton La SO45 ..177 E8
Northarbour Rd PO6 ..157 D7
Northarbour Spur PO6 ..157 D8
Northbourne Ave BH10 ..189 D5
Northbourne Cl **5**
 SO45 ....126 A1
Northbourne Gdns
 BH10 ....189 C5
Northbourne Pl **3**
 BH10 ....189 D5
Northbourne Rdbt BH10 ..189 C5
Northbrook Ave SO23 ..11 C7
Northbrook Bower SO32 ..83 D8
Northbrook Cl
 Portsmouth PO1 .....182 D7
 Winchester SO23 ...11 C7
Northbrook Ho SO32 ..83 D8
Northbrook Ind Est SO16 ..78 C2
Northbrook Rd
 Broadstone BH18 ...187 A2
 Southampton SO14 ..103 B5
Northbrook Springs
 Vineyard* SO32 .....59 C5
Northcliffe Gdns SO23 ..11 C7
Northcote Gdns PO10 ..161 E8
Northcote Rd
 Bournemouth BH1 ...205 C4
 Portsmouth PO4 .....182 E3
 Southampton SO17 ..79 C2
Northcott Cl PO12 ...180 F3
Northcroft Rd PO12 ..180 F6
Northdene Rd SO53 ..55 C5
Northend La SO32 ...61 A2
Northern Access Rd
 SO45 ....151 D2
Northern Anchorage
 SO19 ....103 D3
Northern Bldgs **10** PO6 ..157 F8
Northern Galleries **4**
 PO14 ....155 A6
Northern Inf Sch PO16 ..132 C1
Northern Jun Com Sch
 PO16 ....132 C1
Northern Par PO2 ...157 E3
Northern Parade Inf Sch
 PO2 ....157 E3
Northern Parade Jun Sch
 PO2 ....157 E3
Northern Rd
 Cosham PO6 ....157 F7
 Cosham PO6 ....157 F8
 Fawley SO45 ....151 E2
Northern Way PO1 ...181 F8
Northerwood Ave SO43 ..121 A5
Northerwood Cl SO52 ..53 F4
Northerwood Ho SO43 ..121 E6
Northesk Ho PO1 ...216 C4
Northey Rd BH6 ....206 E6
Northfield Ave PO14 ..154 F7
Northfield Cl
 Bishop's Waltham SO32 ..59 A1
 Horndean PO8 ......88 C2
Northfield Pk PO16 ..132 B1
Northfield Rd
 Milford on S SO41 ...211 F4
 Ringwood BH24 .....117 B1
 Southampton SO18 ..79 F2
Northfields Farm La
 PO17 ....108 B5
Northgate Ave PO2 ..182 F8
Northgate Chambers **10**
 SO23 ....215 E6

Northgate Lodge **2**
 SO23 ....215 E6
Northlands Cl SO40 ..100 D8
Northlands Dr SO23 ..215 E8
Northlands Gdns SO15 ..102 E7
Northlea Rd
 Eastleigh SO50 ......56 A3
 Romsey SO51 ....53 C6
 Southampton SO15 ..102 E8
 Totton SO40 ....100 E8
Northleigh Cnr SO18 ..79 E5
Northleigh La BH21 ..163 E6
Northmead Dr BH17 ..201 F8
Northmere Dr BH17 ..203 F7
Northmere Rd BH12 ..203 F7
Northmore Cl SO31 ..129 B5
Northmore Rd SO31 ..129 B5
Northney La PO11 ...160 C4
Northney Rd PO11 ...160 B4
Northolt Gdns SO16 ..78 A5
Northover BH3 ......204 F6
Northover Rd PO11 ..160 C4
Northover Rd
 Lymington SO41 .....197 A4
 Portsmouth PO3 .....183 B8
Northshore BH13 ....214 C4
Northumberland Ct
 BH24 ....140 F7
Northumberland Rd
 Portsmouth PO5 .....216 D3
 Southampton SO14 ..103 B6
Northway Gosport PO13 ..155 C4
 Titchfield PO15 .....129 E3
Northways PO14 ....179 D7
Northwood Cl SO10 ..79 A6
Northwood La PO11 ..160 A1
Northwood Rd PO2 ..157 E4
Northwood Sq **8** PO16 ..131 B2
Norton Cl
 Christchurch BH23 ...207 D7
 Southampton SO19 ..103 E3
 Southwick PO17 .....132 F6
 Waterlooville PO7 ...134 D7
Norton Dr PO16 .....131 A3
Norton Gdns BH9 ...189 E1
Norton Rd
 Bournemouth BH9 ...204 E8
 Southwick PO17 .....132 F6
Norton Way BH15 ...202 A1
Norton Welch Cl SO52 ..54 B4
Norway Cl **3** BH9 ...189 F1
Norway Rd PO3 .....158 A4
Norwich Ave BH2 ...204 D3
Norwich Ave W PH2 ..204 D3
Norwich Cl SO31 ....128 C4
Norwich Ct **5** BH2 ..204 E3
Norwich Mans BH2 ..204 D3
Norwich Pl PO13 ....179 E4
Norwich Rd
 Bournemouth BH2 ...204 E3
 Portsmouth PO6 .....133 D1
 Southampton SO18 ..79 F2
Norwood Pl BH5 ....206 B6
Norwood Prim Sch SO50 ..56 A3
Nottingham Pl PO13 ..179 E4
Nouale La BH24 .....141 D7
Novello Gdns PO7 ...134 E6
Noyce Dr SO50 .....57 D1
Noyce Gdns BH9 ...191 B2
Nuffield Ind Est BH17 ..202 D8
Nuffield Rd BH17 ...202 D7
Nugent Rd BH6 .....207 A4
Nunns Pk SP5 ......24 B4
Nuns Rd SO23 ......215 E2
Nuns Wlk SO23 ....215 F8
Nurse's Path SO21 ..32 A5
Nursery Cl
 Emsworth PO10 ....136 F3
 Gosport PO13 ......155 B3
Nursery Cotts SP6 ..46 E1
Nursery Field GU33 ..20 E2
Nursery Gdns
 Chandler's Ford SO53 ..55 C3
 Romsey SO51 ....53 A7
 Southampton SO19 ..104 B6
 Waterlooville PO8 ...112 A5
 Winchester SO22 ....215 B6
Nursery Gr SO30 ...105 C5
Nursery Ho SO31 ...105 C6
Nursery La PO14 ...179 C6
Nursery Rd
 Bournemouth BH9 ...190 A3
 Havant PO9 ....135 C2
 Ringwood BH24 .....141 A6
 Southampton SO18 ..79 D1
Nursling CE Prim Sch
 SO16 ....77 C5
Nursling Cres PO9 ..136 A5
Nursling Gn BH9 ....190 D2
Nursling Ind Est SO16 ..77 B4
Nursling St SO16 ...77 C4
Nutash PO14 ....129 C4
Nutbeem Rd SO50 ..56 A2
Nutbourne Ho PO6 ..158 D7
Nutbourne Pk PO18 ..161 F7
Nutbourne Rd
 Farlington PO6 .....158 D7
 South Hayling PO11 ..185 E1
Nutburn Rd SO52 ...54 B5
Nutfield Ct SO16 ...77 E3
Nutfield Pl PO1 ....216 C4
Nutfield Rd SO16 ...77 D6
Nuthatch Cl
 Broadstone BH17 ...201 F8
 Ferndown BH22 ....165 B8
 Rowlands Castle PO9 ..113 B1
Nutley Cl BH11 .....188 F4

Nutley Rd PO9 .....135 D5
Nutley Way BH11 ...188 F4
Nutsey Ave SO40 ...76 D2
Nutsey Cl SO40 ....76 D2
Nutsey La SO40 ....76 E2
Nutshalling Ave SO16 ..77 E5
Nutshalling Cl SO40 ..76 C2
Nutwick Rd PO9 ...136 B3
Nutwood Way SO40 ..76 E2
Nyewood Ave PO16 ..132 D1
Nyria Way PO12 ...181 D5

O

O' Jays Ind Pk PO3 ..158 A2
O'connell Rd SO50 ..55 F2
Oak Ave BH23 .....206 D8
Oak Cl Corfe Mullen BH21 ..186 C5
 Dibden Purlieu SO45 ..125 E1
 Ferndown BH22 ....165 E1
 Lyndhurst SO43 ....121 D2
 Southampton SO15 ..101 C8
 Upham SO32 ....58 F5
 Waterlooville PO8 ..111 E2
Oak Coppice Cl SO50 ..57 A2
Oak Coppice Rd PO15 ..129 D8
Oak Ct Fareham PO15 ..130 C2
 Lymington SO41 ....197 C2
Oak Dr Fair Oak SO50 ..57 C1
 Petersfield GU31 ...40 E1
 Poole BH15 ....202 D2
Oak Gdns
 Bournemouth BH11 ..189 B1
 Hordle SO41 ....211 D8
Oak Green Way SO18 ..104 A8
Oak La BH24 ....141 B8
Oak Leaf Cl SO40 ..124 E8
Oak Lodge **4** PO2 ..157 C2
Oak Lodge Specl Sch
 SO45 ....125 C3
Oak Meadow CE Prim Sch
 PO15 ....130 C3
Oak Mews BH12 ...203 C5
Oak Park Dr PO9 ...136 A3
Oak Park Ind Est PO6 ..157 D8
Oak Rd Alderholt SP6 ..92 F5
 Bishop's Waltham SO32 ..83 E8
 Bournemouth BH8 ...205 C6
 Bursledon SO31 ...127 F8
 Clanfield PO8 ......88 C5
 Dibden Purlieu SO45 ..125 E1
 Fareham PO15 ....130 D2
 Southampton SO19 ..103 E2
 Upton BH16 ....201 C6
Oak St PO12 ....181 C5
Oak Tree Cl SO21 ..56 F8
Oak Tree Dr
 Emsworth PO10 ....136 F4
 Liss GU33 ....22 A4
Oak Tree Gdns SO30 ..105 B6
Oak Tree Way SO50 ..56 A5
Oak Vale SO18 .....80 B3
Oak Wlk SO50 .....57 C1
Oakapple Gdns PO6 ..158 E8
Oakbank Rd
 Bursledon SO31 ...127 F8
 Southampton SO19 ..103 D3
Oakcroft La PO14 ..154 C5
Oakdale Rd BH15 ..202 A2
Oakdale South Road Mid Sch
 BH15 ....202 C5
Oakdean Rd PO14 ..183 C4
Oakdene Gosport PO13 ..155 D1
 Southampton SO17 ..79 B2
 Totton SO40 ....100 C8
Oakdene Gdns SO50 ..57 C2
Oakdown Rd PO14 ..179 D8
Oaken Botton Cvn Site
 BH25 ....171 E5
Oakenbrow Hythe SO45 ..125 D2
 Sway SO41 ....172 A2
Oakes The PO14 ...136 B5
Oakfield Ct **12** PO9 ..136 B5
Oakfield Prim Sch SO40 ..76 C2
Oakfield Rd Bartley SO40 ..99 B7
 Poole BH15 ....202 C6
 Totton SO40 ....100 F7
Oakfields SO50 ....56 A7
Oakford Ct BH8 ....207 A3
Oakgrove Gdns SO50 ..56 E2
Oakgrove Rd SO50 ..56 E2
Oakham Grange PO15 ..165 E5
Oakhill SO31 ......105 B1
Oakhill Cl
 Bursledon SO31 ...105 B1
 Chandler's Ford SO53 ..55 E5
Oakhill Ct SO53 ...55 E5
Oakhill Terr SO31 ..105 B1
Oakhurst BH23 ....207 F7
Oakhurst CE Netley SO31 ..127 C6
 West Moors BH22 ..138 F2
Oakhurst Com Fst Sch
 BH22 ....138 F2
Oakhurst Dr PO7 ...135 A8
Oakhurst Gdns PO7 ..134 B2
Oakhurst La LS27 ..22 A2
Oakhurst Rd
 Southampton SO17 ..79 A3
 West Moors BH22 ..138 F2
Oakhurst Way SO31 ..127 C6
Oakland Dr SO40 ..101 F1
Oakland Wlk PO14 ..165 F1
Oaklands
 14 Chandler's Ford SO53 ..30 B1
 Lymington SO41 ....197 F2

Oaklands *continued*
 Waterlooville PO7 ..135 A6
Oaklands Ave SO40 ..100 F8
Oaklands Cl
 Fordingbridge SP6 ..69 E2
 Verwood BH31 ....114 E6
 6 Winchester SO22 ..215 A4
Oaklands Com Sch SO16 ..77 F5
Oaklands Gdns PO14 ..129 C1
Oaklands Gr PO8 ...111 E3
Oaklands Ho **9** PO6 ..132 F2
Oaklands RC Sch PO7 ..134 F5
Oaklands Rd Havant PO9 ..136 A1
 Petersfield GU32 ...40 E4
Oaklands The SO53 ..55 C5
Oaklands Way
 Hythe SO45 ....125 D2
 Southampton SO16 ..78 F4
 Winchester SO22 ...129 C1
Oaklea Cl PO7 .....134 B2
Oakleaf Pl SO53 ...55 C6
Oakleigh Cres SO40 ..100 E6
Oakleigh Dr SP5 ...73 D8
Oakleigh Gdns SO51 ..53 A7
Oakleigh Way BH23 ..208 F2
Oakley Cl SO45 ....150 C4
Oakley Ct **13** SO16 ..102 B8
Oakley Hill BH21 ...163 D2
Oakley Ho
 Portsmouth PO5 ....216 F4
 12 Southampton SO15 ..102 B8
 3 Southampton,Banister's Pk
  SO15 ....102 F7
Oakley La Merley BH21 ..163 E1
 Mottisfont SO51 ....5 F4
 Wimborne Minst BH21 ..164 A2
Oakley Pl Havant PO9 ..135 D5
 Mottisfont SO51 ....5 E3
 Southampton,Shirley SO16 ..102 A8
 Southampton,Wimpson
  SO16 ....101 F8
 Wimborne Minst BH21 ..163 D2
Oakley Sh Ctr BH21 ..163 E1
Oakley Straight BH21 ..163 E1
Oakmead Coll of Tech
 BH11 ....188 F4
Oakmead Gdns BH11 ..188 F4
Oakmead Rd BH17 ..201 F7
Oakmeadow Cl PO10 ..137 A3
Oakmoor Dr PO8 ...111 F2
Oakmount Ave
 Chandler's Ford SO53 ..55 D4
 Southampton SO17 ..79 A1
 Totton SO40 ....100 F8
Oakmount Mans SO17 ..78 F1
Oakmount Rd SO53 ..55 E5
Oakridge Rd SO15 ..101 D8
Oaks Coppice PO8 ..112 A6
Oaks Dr BH24 .....139 D3
Oaks Mead BH31 ..114 A5
Oaks The Burseldon SO31 ..127 F8
 Southampton SO19 ..103 F5
 Verwood BH31 ....114 E7
 Waterlooville PO8 ..112 A2
Oakshott Dr PO9 ...136 A5
Oakthorn Cl PO13 ..180 C6
Oaktree Ct
 Milford on S SO41 ...211 C4
 Southampton SO16 ..77 F6
Oaktree Par BH23 ..169 B1
Oaktree Pk SO30 ...80 C4
Oaktree Rd SO18 ...79 F2
Oakville Mans **11** SO15 ..102 F6
Oakwood BH1 .....204 F4
Oakwood Ave
 Havant PO9 ....135 B3
 New Milton BH25 ...195 C4
 Otterbourne SO21 ..31 C3
Oakwood Cl
 Bournemouth BH9 ...190 B2
 Christchurch BH23 ..30 D1
 Otterbourne SO21 ..31 C4
 Romsey SO51 ......28 C1
 Warsash BH21 ....152 D10
Oakwood Ct
 Chandler's Ford SO53 ..30 D1
 New Milton BH25 ...195 B3
 West End SO30 ....80 E2
Oakwood Ctr The PO9 ..136 B3
Oakwood Dr SO16 ..78 C5
Oakwood Ho SO21 ..31 C4
Oakwood Inf Sch SO16 ..78 B5
Oakwood Jun Sch SO16 ..78 B5
Oakwood Lodge SO21 ..31 C4
Oakwood Rd
 Bournemouth BH9 ...190 B2
 Chandler's Ford SO53 ..30 D1
 Christchurch BH23 ..193 E1
 Portsmouth PO2 ....157 E4
 South Hayling PO11 ..184 F3
Oakwood Way SO31 ..128 A3
Oasis Mews BH16 ..201 C6
Oasis The **12** BH13 ..204 A4
Oates Rd BH9 .....189 F3
Oatfield Gdns SO40 ..76 C1
Oatlands SO51 ....52 F8
Oatlands Cl SO32 ..81 F1
Oatlands Ho SO32 ..81 F1
Oban Rd BH3 .....204 E7
Obelisk Ct SO19 ...103 D3
Obelisk Rd SO19 ..103 C3
Ober Rd SO42 .....145 E2
Oberfield Rd SO42 ..145 D1

Oberland Ct SO41 .... **197** D4
Oberon Cl PO7 .... **135** A8
Occupation La PO14 .... **153** E7
Ocean Cl PO15 .... **130** D2
Ocean Ct PO11 .... **184** E3
Ocean Hts 4 BH5 .... **205** F3
Ocean Pk PO3 .... **158** B1
Ocean Rd Fareham PO14 . **154** F5
Southampton SO14 .... **103** A1
Ocean Way SO14 .... **103** B2
Oceanarium* BH2 .... **102** E5
Oceanarium* BH2 .... **204** F2
Ockendon Cl PO5 .... **216** B2
Ocknell Camping Site
SO43 .... **97** B6
Ocknell Gr SO45 .... **125** C3
Octavia Gdns SO53 .... **55** F7
Octavia Hill SO22 .... **215** B4
Octavia Rd SO18 .... **79** E4
Octavius Ct 2 PO7 ...... **112** B1
Odell Cl PO16 .... **130** F3
Odeon Bldgs 7 PO6 ..... **157** F8
Odiham Cl
Chandler's Ford SO53 ... **55** B3
Southampton SO16 .... **77** F4
Officers Quarters The
PO12 .... **181** D6
Oglander Rd SO23 .... **215** E8
Ogle Rd SO14 .... **102** F4
OK Mobile Home Pk
BH23 .... **208** B8
Okeford Rd BH18 .... **187** C2
Okement Cl SO18 .... **80** B2
Olave Cl PO13 .... **179** E3
Old Agwi Rd SO45 ...... **151** C5
Old Auction Ho 13 PO12 **181** E5
Old Barn Cl
Christchurch BH23 .... **191** D2
Ringwood BH24 .... **141** C7
Old Barn Cres PO7 .... **86** C2
Old Barn Farm Rd BH21 **139** B6
Old Barn Gdns PO8 ..... **111** F6
Old Barn Rd BH23 .... **191** D2
Old Bound Rd BH16 ..... **201** C6
Old Brewery The 10
BH15 .... **202** C2
Old Brickyard Rd SP6 .. **69** B2
Old Bridge Cl SO31 ..... **128** B8
Old Bridge House Rd
SO31 .... **128** B8
Old Bridge Rd
Bournemouth BH6 .... **206** D7
Portsmouth PO4 .... **182** E2
Old Canal 3 PO4 .... **183** B4
Old Christchurch La 12
BH1 .... **204** F3
Old Christchurch Rd
Bournemouth BH1 .... **204** F3
Everton SO41 .... **196** D1
Old Coach Mews BH14 . **203** A4
Old Coastguard Cotts
SO41 .... **212** A3
Old Coastguard Rd
BH13 .... **214** B4
Old Comm SO31 .... **129** A4
Old Commercial Rd
PO1 .... **182** C7
Old Common Gdns
SO31 .... **129** A4
Old Copse Rd PO9 .... **136** A3
Old Cottage Cl SO51 .... **50** E3
Old Cracknore Cl SO40 **101** F2
Old Cricket Mews SO15 **102** F8
Old Farm Cl BH24 .... **117** C2
Old Farm Copse SO51 .. **50** F3
Old Farm Dr SO18 .... **79** F3
Old Farm La
Stubbington PO14 .... **179** C6
Westbourne PO10 .... **137** D3
Old Farm Rd BH15 .... **202** E6
Old Farm Way PO6 ...... **158** E2
Old Farm Wlk SO41 ..... **197** D3
Old Farmhouse Mews
SO41 .... **197** E5
Old Forge Cl SP6 .... **92** F6
Old Forge Ct SO41 ...... **197** D2
Old Forge Rd BH21 ...... **164** F6
Old Forge The SO32 ..... **107** D7
Old Garden Cl SO31 .... **129** C2
Old Gdns SO22 .... **215** D8
Old Generator Ho The
BH12 .... **204** A5
Old Gosport Rd PO16 ... **155** B8
Old Granary The SP5 .... **46** F8
Old Ham La BH21 .... **164** D4
Old Highway Mews
BH21 .... **163** D4
Old Hillside Rd SO22 ... **215** A8
Old Infirmary Ho 13
PO1 .... **182** A4
Old Ivy La SO30 .... **80** B2
Old Kennels Cl SO22 ... **10** A3
Old Kennels La SO22 .... **10** B3
Old Kiln Rd BH14 .... **201** D6
Old Laundry The SO21 . **32** A5
Old Lifeboat Ho* BH15 **202** C1
Old Litten La GU32 ...... **119** D3
Old London Rd PO2 ...... **157** F4
Old Lyndhurst Rd SO40 **98** F8
Old Magazine Cl SO40 **101** F2
Old Maltings The SO41 **197** D3
Old Manor Cl BH21 ...... **163** D4
Old Manor Farm PO9 ... **135** B1
Old Manor Way PO6 .... **158** B7

Old Market Rd
Corfe Mullen BH21 .... **186** A8
Cosham PO6 .... **157** F8
Old Mill Ho BH24 .... **140** F6
Old Mill La
Denmead PO7,PO8 .... **111** B8
Hambledon PO8 .... **87** D3
Petersfield GU31 .... **41** C5
Old Mill Way SO16 .... **78** A1
Old Milton Gn BH25 .... **194** F1
Old Milton Rd BH25 .... **195** A2
Old Mulberry Cl BH10 . **189** A1
Old Orch BH15 .... **202** C1
Old Orchards SO41 ...... **197** E2
Old Park Rd SO24 .... **15** F8
Old Parsonage Ct SO21 **31** C3
Old Pines Cl BH22 .... **165** E4
Old Priory Cl SO31 ...... **128** A2
Old Priory Rd BH6 .... **206** F4
Old Rd Gosport PO12 ... **181** C4
Romsey SO51 .... **53** A7
Southampton SO14 .... **103** B2
Wimborne Minst BH21 . **163** B5
Old Rd The PO6 .... **157** F7
Old Rectory Cl
Corfe Mullen BH21 .... **186** D8
Westbourne PO10 .... **137** B3
Old Rectory Ct SO40 ... **101** B5
Old Rectory Gdns SO21 **2** D6
Old Rectory La SO21 .... **32** A6
Old Rectory Rd PO6 ..... **158** F8
Old Redbridge Rd SO15 **101** C8
Old Reservoir Rd PO6 .. **158** D7
Old River PO7 .... **110** F3
Old Romsey Rd SO40 ... **98** E8
Old Rope Wlk The BH15 **201** F1
Old Ropewalk BH15 ..... **202** A1
Old Salisbury La SO51 .. **27** B2
Old Salisbury Rd SO51 . **75** F7
Old Sandpit La BH16 ... **186** A2
Old Sawmill Cl BH31 ... **114** E7
Old School Cl
Ferndown BH22 .... **165** C5
Hardley SO45 .... **150** B6
Netley SO31 .... **127** D7
Poole BH14 .... **203** A4
Old School Dr PO11 ..... **185** B2
Old School Gdns SO30 **80** E2
Old School Rd GU33 .... **20** F4
Old Shamblehurst La
SO30 .... **81** C2
Old Spring La SO32 ...... **84** A5
Old St Stubbington PO14 **154** B4
Stubbington,Hill Head
PO14 .... **179** A7
Old St John's Mews
BH9 .... **189** F3
Old Stacks Gdns BH24 . **141** C6
Old Star Pl 2 PO1 .... **182** A5
Old Station App SO23 .. **215** F5
Old Swanwick La SO31 **128** D8
Old Tannery The SP5 .... **47** A8
Old Timbers PO11 .... **184** F3
Old Town Mews 8
BH15 .... **202** C2
Old Turnpike PO16 ...... **131** B3
Old Van Diemans Rd
PO7 .... **134** C5
Old Vicarage Cl BH10 . **189** E6
Old Vicarage La SO41 .. **196** C8
Old Vineries The SP6 ... **69** D1
Old Wareham Rd
Corfe Mullen BH16,BH21 **186** A3
Poole BH12 .... **203** A7
Old Well Cl The SO19 ... **104** C3
Old Winchester Hill La
Warnford SO32 .... **37** B2
West Meon GU32 .... **37** D2
Old Winchester Hill Nature
Reserve* SO32 .... **62** C6
Old Winchester Hill Nature
Trail* GU32 .... **62** D6
Old Wymering La PO6 .. **157** E8
Oldbarn Cl SO40 .... **76** C2
Oldbury Ct SO16 .... **77** D2
Oldbury Ho 9 PO5 .... **216** B2
Oldbury Way PO14 ...... **154** C8
Oldenburg PO15 .... **129** B8
Oldgate Gdns 1 PO2 ... **157** F4
Oldhouse La SO40 .... **50** E7
Oleander Cl SO31 .... **129** A5
Oleander Dr SO40 .... **100** B8
Olinda St PO1 .... **182** E6
Olive Cres PO16 .... **156** D6
Olive Rd SO16 .... **78** A3
Oliver Rd
Lymington SO41 .... **197** C3
Portsmouth PO4 .... **183** A3
Southampton SO18 .... **79** D3
Oliver's Battery Cres
SO22 .... **10** B4
Oliver's Battery Gdns
SO22 .... **10** B3
Oliver's Battery Prim Sch
SO22 .... **215** A1
Oliver's Battery Rd N
SO22 .... **10** B4
Oliver's Battery Rd S
SO22 .... **10** B4
Olivers Cl SO40 .... **100** B7
Olivers Ct PO2 .... **182** E8
Olivers Rd BH21 .... **164** A6
Olivers Way BH21 .... **164** A6
Olivia Cl PO7 .... **112** A1
Olympic Way SO50 ...... **57** B2
Omdurman Ct 2 SO17 . **79** A2
Omdurman Rd SO17 .... **79** A2
Omega Ho PO5 .... **216** C3

Omega St PO5 .... **216** C3
Onibury Cl SO18 .... **80** A1
Onibury Rd SO18 .... **80** A1
Onslow Gdns BH21 ...... **163** D6
Onslow Ho BH21 .... **163** D6
Onslow Rd
4 Portsmouth PO5 ...... **182** D1
Southampton SO14 .... **103** A6
Ophir Gdns 1 BH8 ...... **205** C5
Ophir Rd
Bournemouth BH8 .... **205** B5
Portsmouth PO2 .... **157** E3
Oracle Dr PO7 .... **134** E3
Orange Gr PO13 .... **155** D1
Orange Row PO10 .... **160** F8
Oratory Gdns BH13 ..... **214** F8
Orchard Ave
Bishopstoke SO50 .... **56** F1
Poole BH14 .... **202** F2
Orchard Bglws PO17 ... **109** A2
Orchard Cl
Christchurch BH23 .... **207** A6
Colden Common SO21 .. **31** F1
Corfe Mullen BH21 .... **186** D7
Edmondsham BH21 ...... **91** A4
Fawley SO45 .... **151** B3
Ferndown BH22 .... **165** E5
Fordingbridge SP6 .... **69** F2
Gosport PO12 .... **156** A1
Hordle PO8 .... **112** C6
North Baddesley SO52 . **53** F5
Ringwood BH24 .... **141** A8
South Hayling PO11 ..... **184** F2
Totton SO40 .... **100** F5
Orchard Ct Cadnam SO40 **98** F8
Hedge End SO30 .... **105** E7
Verwood BH31 .... **115** A5
Orchard Cvn Pk The
SO40 .... **99** D5
Orchard Gdns 1 SP6 ... **69** F1
Orchard Gr
New Milton BH25 .... **195** A4
Portchester PO16 .... **156** B7
Waterlooville PO8 .... **111** F3
Orchard Ho
4 Southampton SO14 . **103** A3
Winchester SO22 .... **215** C5
Orchard Inf Sch SO45 .. **125** C3
Orchard Jun Sch SO45 **125** C3
Orchard La
Corfe Mullen BH21 .... **186** D7
Emsworth PO10 .... **161** A8
Romsey SO51 .... **52** E7
Southampton SO14 .... **103** A3
Orchard Lea Inf Sch
PO15 .... **130** E4
Orchard Lea Jun Sch
PO15 .... **130** E4
Orchard Leigh 2 BH25 **195** B2
Orchard Mead 2 BH21 **141** A8
Orchard Mews 2 PO21 **207** A6
Orchard Mount 3 BH24 **141** A8
Orchard Pl SO14 .... **103** A3
Orchard Rd Fair Oak SO50 **57** C2
Gosport PO12 .... **181** D7
Havant PO9 .... **159** F8
Locks Heath SO31 .... **128** F2
Portsmouth PO4 .... **182** E4
Redlynch SP5 .... **47** D6
South Hayling PO11 ..... **185** A2
Orchard St BH2 .... **204** E3
Orchard The
Bournemouth BH8 .... **188** D6
Bransgore BH23 .... **193** C8
Chilworth SO16 .... **54** E1
Cosham PO6 .... **157** F7
Denmead PO7 .... **110** F4
Milford on S SO41 .... **211** D4
Southampton SO16 .... **79** B5
Orchard Way SO45 ...... **125** F2
Orchard Wlk
13 Bournemouth BH2 .. **204** E3
Winchester SO22 .... **215** B8
Orchardlea SO32 .... **84** C3
Orchards Way
Southampton SO17 .... **79** A2
West End SO30 .... **80** D1
Orcheston Rd BH8 .... **205** C6
Orchid Way BH23 .... **207** C7
Ordnance Ct PO3 .... **158** A5
Ordnance Rd
Gosport PO12 .... **181** D5
Southampton SO15 .... **103** A6
Ordnance Row PO1 ...... **182** A5
Ordnance Way SO40 ... **102** A3
Oregon Cl SO19 .... **104** A2
Orestes Gate BH23 ...... **208** A5
Orford Cl BH23 .... **191** D4
Orford Ct 4 PO6 .... **157** F7
Oriana Way SO16 .... **77** F5
Oriel Dr PO14 .... **129** B1
Oriel Rd PO2 .... **157** D2
Orient Dr SO22 .... **1** C3
Orion Ave PO12 .... **181** C8
Orion Cl
Southampton SO16 .... **77** F4
Stubbington PO14 .... **154** B7
Orion Ind Ctr SO18 ..... **79** E5
Orkney Cl SO16 .... **77** F4
Orkney Rd PO6 .... **133** F1
Ormesby Dr SO53 .... **55** B8
Ormond Cl SO30 .... **57** B2
Ormonde Rd BH13 ...... **204** A2
Ormsby Rd PO7 .... **135** A5
Orpen Rd SO19 .... **104** C4
Orpine Cl PO15 .... **129** F3
Orsmond Cl PO7 .... **134** F6
Orwell Cl Gosport PO12 **181** C8

Orwell Cl continued
Southampton SO16 .... **77** E1
Orwell Cres PO14 .... **129** C2
Orwell Rd GU31 .... **40** E2
Osborn Cres PO13 .... **155** B4
Osborn Rd PO16 .... **158** B4
Osborn Mall 3 PO16 ... **131** C1
Osborn Rd PO16 .... **131** B1
Osborn Rd PO16 .... **131** B1
Osborn Sq 2 PO16 ...... **131** C1
Osborne Cl Netley SO31 **127** C5
1 Waterlooville PO7 ... **135** A7
Osborne Ct
7 Milford on S SO41 .. **211** C4
Southampton SO17 .... **79** C1
Osborne Dr SO53 .... **55** E5
Osborne Gdns
Fair Oak SO50 .... **57** E1
Southampton SO17 .... **79** C1
Osborne Ho
Southampton SO14 .... **103** B3
West Wellow SO51 .... **50** E3
Osborne Rd
Bournemouth BH9 .... **204** E8
Gosport PO12 .... **181** D6
Lee-on-t-S PO13 .... **179** E3
New Milton BH25 .... **195** B3
Petersfield GU32 .... **40** F4
Poole BH14 .... **203** B3
Portsmouth PO5 .... **182** C2
Totton SO40 .... **101** A7
Osborne Rd N SO17 .... **79** C1
Osborne Rd S SO17 ..... **103** C1
Osborne Sch SO23 ...... **215** D7
Osborne View Rd PO13 **179** A6
Osbourne Ho 4 BH25 .. **195** B3
Oscier Cl PO2 .... **157** C3
Osier Rd GU31 .... **40** D1
Oslands La SO31 .... **128** D7
Oslo Twrs SO19 .... **126** E8
Osprey Cl
Christchurch BH23 .... **208** A5
Farlington PO6 .... **158** E7
Marchwood SO40 .... **101** C1
Southampton SO16 .... **78** B5
Osprey Ct PO16 .... **155** F8
Osprey Dr PO11 .... **185** B3
Osprey Gdns BH23 ...... **209** F3
Osprey Quay PO10 ...... **161** B7
Ossemsley Manor Ho
BH23 .... **194** D6
Ossemsley South Dr
BH25 .... **194** D6
Osterley Cl SO30 .... **105** E6
Osterley Ct BH23 .... **207** A8
Osterley Rd SO19 .... **103** E5
Ostlers The SO41 .... **196** A3
Oswald Cl PO7 .... **189** E2
Oswald Rd BH9 .... **189** F2
Othello Dr PO7 .... **135** A8
Otter Cl Bishopstoke SO50 **57** A2
3 Gosport PO13 .... **180** D5
Upton BH16 .... **201** B6
Verwood BH31 .... **115** A5
Otter Rd BH15 .... **202** F6
Otterbourne 14 BH2 ... **204** D4
Otterbourne CE Prim Sch
SO21 .... **31** B2
Otterbourne Cres PO9 **135** D5
Otterbourne Hill SO21 **31** B2
Otterbourne Ho SO21 . **31** B2
Otterbourne House Gdns
SO21 .... **31** B2
Otterbourne Rd SO21 . **31** D6
Otters Wlk BH25 .... **195** C6
Our Lady & St Joseph RC
Prim Sch SO41 .... **197** A4
Ouse Cl SO23 .... **55** A8
Outer Circ SO16 .... **78** A4
Outlands La SO30 .... **106** D7
Outram Rd PO6 .... **216** C1
Outwick Cross SP6 ...... **69** F8
Oval Gdns PO12 .... **180** F4
Oval Rd SO51 .... **5** A1
Oval The GU33 .... **20** F7
Oven Camping Site The
PO11 .... **184** F5
Over Links Dr BH14 ..... **203** D2
Overbrook SO45 .... **125** F2
Overbrook Way SO52 .. **53** E5
Overbury Manor BH12 **204** B5
Overcliff Rd BH14 .... **203** C3
Overcliff Rise SO16 ..... **78** E4
Overcliffe Mans BH1 ... **205** C3
Overcombe Cl BH17 .... **187** E2
Overdell Ct 8 SO15 .... **102** E7
Overstand Cres SO41 .. **211** D3
Overton Cres PO9 .... **135** D5
Overton Rd PO10 .... **137** E1
Oviat Cl SO40 .... **100** B8
Ovington Ave BH7 .... **206** C7
Ovington Ct SO18 .... **104** D8
Ovington Gdns BH7 .... **206** C7
Ovington Rd SO50 ...... **56** A1
Owen Cl PO13 .... **180** C7
Owen Rd SO50 .... **55** F2
Owen St SO14 .... **103** A4
Owen's Rd SO22 .... **215** D7
Owen St SO14 .... **178** E8
Owls Rd
Bournemouth BH5 .... **205** B5
Verwood BH31 .... **115** A5
Owlshotts BH13 .... **214** F7
Owslebury Bottom SO21 **33** A5
Owslebury Gr PO9 ...... **135** F5

Owslebury Prim Sch
SO21 .... **33** A4
Oxburgh Cl SO50 .... **55** F5
Oxendown SO32 .... **61** C4
Oxenwood Gn PO9 ..... **135** D6
Oxey Cl BH25 .... **195** A1
Oxford Ave
Bournemouth BH6 .... **206** B5
Southampton SO14 .... **103** B6
Oxford Cl PO16 .... **131** A2
Oxford La
Bournemouth BH8 .... **205** B4
Gosport PO12 .... **180** F5
Portsmouth PO5 .... **216** D1
Southampton SO14 .... **103** A7
Oxford St SO14 .... **103** A3
Oxford Terr SO41 .... **172** C2
Oxlease Cl SO51 .... **28** A1
Oxted Ct 8 PO4 .... **183** B5
Oyster Ct PO13 .... **179** D4
Oyster Est The PO6 ..... **158** C6
Oyster Mews
5 Emsworth PO10 ...... **160** F8
7 Portsmouth PO1 ..... **182** A3
Oyster Quay PO6 .... **157** B7
Oyster St PO1 .... **182** A3
Ozier Rd SO18 .... **80** A2

P

Pacific Cl SO14 .... **103** C2
Packridge La SO51,SO52 **53** F1
Padbury Cl PO2 .... **157** F4
Paddington Cl BH11 .... **188** D4
Paddington Gr BH11 ... **188** D3
Paddington Rd PO2 .... **157** F1
Paddock Cl
Ferndown BH22 .... **165** A5
Poole BH12 .... **203** B7
St Leonards BH24 .... **139** F4
Paddock End PO7 .... **112** B4
Paddock Gdns SO41 .... **197** D5
Paddock Gr BH31 .... **115** A5
Paddock The
Brockenhurst SO42 ...... **145** F1
Eastleigh SO50 .... **56** B6
Fordingbridge SP6 ...... **94** E6
Gosport PO12 .... **181** A4
Kings Worthy SO23 ...... **2** C5
Stubbington PO14 .... **154** C4
Totton SO40 .... **76** C2
West Moors BH24 .... **166** C8
Paddock Way GU32 .... **40** D2
Paddock Wlk PO6 .... **157** A8
Paddocks The
Bournemouth BH10 ...... **189** D4
Fawley SO45 .... **151** B3
Padfield Cl BH6 .... **206** E6
Padget Rd BH24 .... **117** C1
Padnell Ave PO8 .... **112** A2
Padnell Inf Sch PO8 ... **112** A3
Padnell Jun Sch PO8 .. **112** B3
Padnell Pl PO8 .... **112** B2
Padnell Rd PO8 .... **112** B2
Padstow Pl SP6 .... **93** E8
Padwell Rd SO14 .... **103** A7
Padwick Ave PO6 .... **158** A8
Padwick Ct PO11 .... **184** E3
Paffard Cl PO13 .... **180** C7
Page Cl SO45 .... **150** D2
Pages La SO42 .... **175** C6
Paget Cl BH21 .... **164** A7
Paget Rd
Bournemouth BH11 ..... **189** A4
Gosport PO12 .... **181** A3
Paget St SO14 .... **103** B4
Pagham Cl PO10 .... **161** A8
Pagham Gdns PO11 .... **185** F2
Paignton Ave PO3 .... **183** A8
Paignton Rd SO16 .... **77** F1
Paimpol Pl SO51 .... **52** E6
Pain's Rd PO5 .... **216** C2
Painswick Cl
Cosham PO6 .... **157** C8
Sarisbury SO31 .... **128** F6
Painter Cl PO3 .... **158** B3
Painters Field SO23 ..... **215** C2
Paisley Rd BH6 .... **206** C5
Palace Ho* SO42 .... **148** F1
Palace La SO42 .... **148** F1
Palace Mews SO32 ..... **83** C7
Palfrey Rd BH10 .... **189** D5
Paling Bsns Pk SO30 .. **105** B4
Palk Rd PO9 .... **135** D1
Pallant Gdns PO16 ..... **131** D2
Pallant The PO9 .... **135** F1
Pallot Cl SO21 .... **56** F8
Pallot Cl SO31 .... **104** F1
Palm Cl 17 PO5 .... **182** C2
Palm Hall Cl SO23 ...... **215** F5
Palm Rd SO16 .... **78** A3
Palma Ct BH23 .... **209** A7
Palmer Rd BH11 .... **189** A5
Palmer Rd BH15 .... **202** C5
Palmer's Rd PO10 .... **136** F1
Palmers Cl SO30 .... **57** D1
Palmerston Ave
Christchurch BH23 .... **207** D6
Fareham PO16 .... **131** B1
Palmerston Bsns Pk
SO51 .... **155** B7
Palmerston Cl BH16 ... **201** D7

Palmerston Ct
[28] Portsmouth PO5 ....182 C2
2 Winchester SO23 ....215 D3
Palmerston Dr PO14 ...155 A7
Palmerston Mans [3]
  PO5 ....182 C2
Palmerston Rd
Bournemouth BH1 ....205 E5
Poole BH14 ....203 D4
Portsmouth PO5 ....182 C2
South Hayling PO11 ....185 A4
Southampton SO14 ....103 A4
Upton BH16 ....201 C7
Palmerston Road Prec [4]
  PO5 ....182 C2
Palmerston St SO51 ...52 F7
Palmerston Way PO12 ..180 F2
Palmyra Rd PO12 ....181 A8
Palomino Dr PO15 ....129 B7
Pamela Ave PO6 ....132 F1
Pamphill CE Fst Sch
  BH21 ....162 E5
Pamplyn Cl SO41 ....197 C4
Pan St PO1 ....216 B4
Pangbourne Ave PO6 ...158 B7
Pangbourne Cl SO19 ...104 A4
Pannall Rd PO12 ....181 A8
Panorama Ct PO13 ....179 E3
Panorama Rd BH13 ....214 B3
Pans Cnr BH22 ....165 F3
Pansy Rd SO16 ....79 A4
Pantheon Rd SO53 ....55 F7
Pantiles The SP6 ....69 C1
Panton Cl PO10 ....136 E3
Panwell Rd SO18 ....104 A7
Parade Ct PO2 ....157 E5
Parade The
[4] Bournemouth BH6 ..206 E3
Cadnam SO40 ....98 F8
New Milton BH25 ....195 D3
Old Milton BH25 ....194 F1
Poole BH17 ....187 B1
Portsmouth PO1 ....182 A4
Paradise La Bartley SO40 ..99 D6
Bishop's Waltham SO32 ...83 F6
Fareham PO16 ....131 E2
Portsmouth PO1 ....137 B4
Paradise St
[14] Poole BH15 ....202 B1
Portsmouth PO1 ....216 B4
Parchment St SO23 ....215 E6
Parchment The PO9 ...135 F1
Pardoe Cl SO30 ....105 C5
Pardys Hill BH21 ....186 D8
Parham Cl BH25 ....194 E3
Parham Dr SO50 ....55 F4
Parham Rd
Bournemouth BH10 ....189 C2
Gosport PO12 ....181 C7
Parish Cl SO41 ....197 E4
Parish Rd BH15 ....202 E3
Park App PO17 ....130 E7
Park Ave
Bournemouth BH10 ....189 C6
Lymington SO41 ....197 D4
Waterlooville PO7 ....134 C3
Winchester SO23 ....215 E6
Park Cl
Brockenhurst SO42 ....146 A2
Burton BH23 ....192 C3
Gosport PO12 ....180 F6
Hythe SO45 ....126 B4
Lyndhurst SO43 ....122 A3
Marchwood SO40 ....101 D1
Milford on S SO41 ....211 E4
New Milton BH25 ....195 C5
Winchester SO23 ....215 E8
Park Com Sch PO9 ....135 C5
Park Court Flats [7]
  SO15 ....102 C6
Park Cres PO10 ....136 E3
Park Ct
[14] Milford on S SO41 ...211 C4
[1] Petersfield GU32 ....40 F3
[12] Poole BH13 ....204 B3
Portsmouth PO5 ....216 B1
Romsey SO51 ....53 D5
[1] Southampton SO23 ...215 E8
Park Dr BH31 ....114 E7
Park Farm Ave PO15 ...130 D3
Park Farm Cl PO15 ....130 D3
Park Farm Rd PO7 ....134 D4
Park Gate BH25 ....195 A2
Park Gate Bsns Ctr
  SO31 ....129 B6
Park Gate Mews [7] BH7 ..204 E3
Park Gate Prim Sch
  SO31 ....129 B4
Park Gdns BH31 ....207 E7
Park Glen SO31 ....129 C4
Park Gr PO6 ....157 F7
Park Heritage Ctr The*
  SO31 ....127 C4
Park Hill Cl SO45 ....150 C3
Park Ho
[9] Portsmouth PO5 ....182 C2
Winchester SO23 ....215 E6
Park Homer Dr BH21 ...164 A6
Park Homer Rd BH21 ...166 A7
Park La Alderholt SP6 ...92 F6
Bournemouth BH1 ....189 F4
Bucklers Hard SO42 ...200 D4
Cosham PO6 ....158 A7
Droxford SO32 ....61 B1
Fareham PO16 ....131 A2
Havant PO9 ....135 C2
Havant,Bedhampton PO9 ..135 C3

Park La _continued_
Holbury SO45 ....150 B4
Kings Worthy SO21 ....2 D6
Marchwood SO40 ....101 C1
Milford on S SO41 ....211 D4
Otterbourne SO21 ....56 B8
Rowland's Castle PO10 ..137 C8
[1] Southampton SO15 ...102 F5
Stubbington PO14 ....179 C8
Swanmore SO32 ....60 D1
Swanmore SO32 ....84 B8
Twyford SO21 ....32 A5
Waterlooville PO8 ....112 A2
West Dean SP5 ....3 B8
Wimborne Minst BH21 ..163 C4
Park Lake Rd BH15 ....202 E2
Park Mans [2] PO6 ....158 A7
Park Par PO9 ....135 F4
Park Pl BH14 ....202 F4
Park Rd
Bishop's Waltham SO32 ...83 A8
Bournemouth BH8 ....205 A5
Breach PO10 ....137 D1
Chandler's Ford SO53 ...55 C7
Denmead PO7 ....110 F5
Fordingbridge SP6 ....69 F2
Gosport PO12 ....181 B4
Lymington SO41 ....197 D4
Milford on S SO41 ....211 E4
New Milton BH25 ....195 C5
Old Milton BH25 ....194 F1
[2] Petersfield GU32 ....40 F3
Poole BH15,BH14 ....202 F3
Portsmouth PO1 ....182 B5
South Hayling PO11 ....184 C4
Southampton SO15 ....102 D6
Waterlooville PO7 ....134 C4
Winchester SO22,SO23 ..215 D8
Park Rd N PO9 ....135 E2
Park Rd S PO9 ....135 F1
Park Royal [2] PO2 ....157 E3
Park St Gosport PO12 ...181 B6
Portsmouth PO5 ....216 A2
Southampton SO15,SO16 ..102 D6
Park Terrs [11] PO12 ...181 C5
Park The
Barton on S BH25 ....209 C7
Droxford SO32 ....61 A1
Wimborne Minst BH21 ..164 A1
Park View Botley SO30 ..106 A7
Compton SO21 ....31 E6
Durrants PO9 ....136 B8
Hedge End SO30 ....105 B7
Lockerley SO51 ....4 E3
New Milton BH25 ....195 A2
Otterbourne SO21 ....31 A1
[7] Poole BH15 ....202 E3
Portsmouth PO2 ....157 D3
Winchester SO22 ....215 A8
Park View Ct BH8 ....205 C7
Park View Mews BH25 ..195 A2
Park Villas SO32 ....61 B1
Park Vista SO30 ....38 D1
Park Way Fair Oak SO50 ..57 E2
Havant PO9 ....135 E1
West Moors BH22 ....138 C8
Park Wlk Fareham PO15 ..130 D3
Southampton SO14 ....103 A5
Parker Cl PO12 ....156 A1
Parker Gdns PO7 ....202 C4
Parker Rd BH9 ....204 F7
Parkers Cl BH24 ....117 C1
Parkfield Ho [5] PO16 ...132 F2
Parkhouse Farm Way
  PO9 ....135 C5
Parkland Cl BH31 ....115 D4
Parkland Dr BH25 ....209 F8
Parkland Pl
New Milton BH25 ....195 A2
[18] Southampton SO17 ..103 A8
Parklands
Locks Heath SO31 ....129 A4
Southampton SO18 ....79 E1
Totton SO40 ....101 A8
[1] Bournemouth BH4 ..204 C3
Parklands Ave PO8 ....112 A5
Parklands Bsns Pk PO17 ..110 F3
Parklands Cl
Chandler's Ford SO53 ...55 C7
Gosport PO12 ....181 B7
Parkside
Christchurch BH23 ....193 D1
Havant PO9 ....135 C2
[4] Highfield SO17 ....79 A2
Ringwood BH24 ....141 A6
Totton SO40 ....100 F5
Parkside Ave SO16 ....101 D8
Parkside Gdns
Bournemouth BH10 ....189 C2
Winchester SO22 ....215 A8
Parkside Rd BH14 ....203 C4
Parkside Wlk SO16 ....102 A8
Parkstone Ave
Poole BH14 ....203 D4
Portsmouth PO4 ....182 E2
Parkstone Gram Sch
  BH17 ....187 B1
Parkstone Hts
Poole BH14 ....202 F5
Poole BH14 ....203 A5
Parkstone Rd BH15 ....202 E3
Parkstone Sta BH14 ....203 B3
Parkview BH24 ....204 E4
Parkville Rd SO16 ....79 D4
Parkwater Rd SP5 ....24 D2
Parkway PO15 ....129 F7
Parkway Dr BH8 ....205 E8
Parkway Gdns SO53 ....55 C7

Parkway S Rdbt PO15 ...129 D7
Parkway The
Gosport PO13 ....155 B2
Southampton SO16 ....79 B5
Parkwood Cl SO30 ....105 C7
Parkwood Ctr PO7 ....134 E8
Parkwood La [7] BH5 ...206 B5
Parkwood Rd
Bournemouth BH5 ....206 A4
Wimborne Minst BH21 ..163 C4
Parley Cl BH22 ....165 F1
Parley Cross BH22 ....189 E8
Parley Fst Sch BH22 ...165 D3
Parley Green La BH23 ..190 B7
Parley La BH23 ....190 D7
Parley Rd BH9 ....190 A2
Parliament Pl SO22 ...215 A2
Parmiter Dr BH21 ....163 E4
Parmiter Ho [6] SO23 ...215 F6
Parmiter Rd BH21 ....163 E4
Parmiter Way BH21 ....163 E4
Parnell Rd SO50 ....55 F2
Parr Ho [1] BH14 ....203 A4
Parr Rd PO6 ....157 D8
Parr St BH14 ....203 A4
Parry Cl PO6 ....156 E8
Parry Rd SO19 ....104 D4
Parsonage Barn La
  BH24 ....141 B7
Parsonage Cl
Fordingbridge SP6 ....69 F2
Petersfield GU32 ....41 B5
Parsonage Ct [5] BH8 ...205 A5
Parsonage La SO32 ....82 B5
Parsonage Park Dr SP6 ..69 E2
Parsonage Rd
Bournemouth BH1 ....205 A3
Southampton SO14 ....103 C6
Parsons Cl PO14 ....157 F5
Partridge Cl
Christchurch BH23 ....208 A5
Fareham PO16 ....155 E8
Partridge Down SO22 ...10 B3
Partridge Dr BH14 ....203 C1
Partridge Gdns PO8 ...111 D4
Partridge Gn PO15 ....195 B6
Partridge Hill SP5 ....50 A3
Partridge Rd
Brockenhurst SO42 ....172 F8
Dibden Purlieu SO45 ...125 F1
Partridge Wlk PO14 ...203 B1
Partry Cl SO53 ....55 A8
Pascoe Cl BH14 ....203 A4
Passage La SO31 ....128 B1
Passfield Ave SO50 ....55 E2
Passfield Cl SO50 ....55 E2
Passfield Wlk [21] PO9 ..136 B5
Passingham Wlk PO8 ...112 A4
Paston Ho [9] PO17 ....130 E7
Pastures The
Cheriton SO24 ....14 C6
Denmead PO7 ....110 E3
[6] Eastleigh SO50 ....56 A2
Locks Heath PO14 ....129 C4
Pat Bear Cl SO15 ....101 C8
Patchins Rd BH16 ....201 B4
Patchins The BH14 ....214 C8
Pathway Dr PO14 ....154 D8
Paternoster Ho [4] SO23 ..215 E5
Paternoster Row [5]
  SO23 ....215 E5
Patricia Cl SO30 ....80 C2
Patricia Dr SO30 ....105 D7
Patrick Howard-Dobson Ct
[6] PO8 ....111 F4
Patrick's Cl GU33 ....21 A4
Patrick's Copse Rd GU33 ..21 A4
Patterdale Ho [6] PO6 ...157 C1
Paulet Cl SO18 ....80 A1
Paulet Lacave Ave SO16 ..77 D6
Paulet Pl SO23 ....215 C3
Pauletts La SO40 ....76 B3
Pauls La SO41 ....196 E6
Paulsgrove Ent Ctr PO6 ..157 B8
Paulsgrove Inf Ctr PO6 ..157 B8
Paulsgrove Prim Sch
  PO6 ....157 C8
Paulsgrove Rd PO2 ....182 F8
Paulson Cl SO33 ....55 C8
Paultons Pk* SO51 ....75 C6
Pauncefoot Hill SO51 ...52 C5
Pauncefote Rd BH5 ....206 A5
Pauntley Rd BH23 ....207 E5
Pavan Gdns BH10 ....189 C2
Pavilion Cl SO50 ....81 D8
Pavilion Ct [4] SO15 ...102 E7
Pavilion Dr SO50 ....105 D8
Pavilion The [28] BH4 ..204 C2
Pavilion Way PO12 ....181 D6
Paxton Cl SO30 ....105 D5
Paxton Cl SO51 ....129 A2
Paxton Rd PO14 ....155 A8
Payne Cl PO12 ....156 E5
Payne's La SO50 ....57 C3
Payne's Rd SO15 ....102 C6
Paynes Hay Rd SO51 ...28 C8
Peach Rd SO16 ....78 A4
Peacock Cl PO16 ....155 E8
Peacock La PO1 ....216 B3
Peacock Pl [4] SO23 ....11 C8
Peak Cl SO16 ....101 F8
Peak Dr PO14 ....154 D8
Peak La Fareham PO14 ...154 D7
Upham SO32 ....59 B4
Peak Rd PO9 ....88 A5
Peak The PO9 ....113 C2
Peake New Rd SO32 ....61 F8

Penk Ridge PO9 ....158 F8
Penn Cl BH25 ....194 E1
Penn Ct BH22 ....138 D2
Penn Hill Ave BH14 ...203 D3
Penn Way PO12 ....180 E3
Pennant Hills PO9 ....135 B2
Pennant Way BH23 ...207 F7
Pennard Way SO53 ....55 A4
Pennefathers Rd PO9 ...159 E7
Pennerly Ct PO9 ....135 D7
Pennine Cl [8] BH23 ...207 F8
Pennine Gdns SO45 ...125 D2
Pennine Ho SO16 ....101 F7
Pennine Rd SO16 ....101 F8
Pennine Way
Chandler's Ford SO53 ...55 D4
Lee-on-t-S PO13 ....180 A1
Verwood BH31 ....114 F5
Pennine Wlk PO14 ....154 E7
Pennings Dro SP5 ....23 E8
Pennington CE Jun Sch
  SO41 ....197 C3
Pennington Cl
Colden Common SO21 ...56 F8
Lymington SO41 ....197 C2
West Moors BH22 ....138 C1
Pennington Cres BH22 ..138 D2
Pennington Cross SO41 ..197 D2
Pennington Ho [6] BH4 ..204 C2
Pennington Inf Sch
  SO41 ....197 C3
Pennington Oval SO41 ..197 C2
Pennington Rd BH22 ...138 D2
Pennington Way PO15 ..130 D3
Penns Pl GU31 ....41 D3
Penns Rd GU32 ....40 E4
Penny Ct
[2] Gosport PO12 ....181 C6
[5] Petersfield GU31 ...40 F3
Penny Hedge BH25 ....210 B8
Penny La PO10 ....161 B8
Penny Pl PO7 ....134 E3
Penny St PO1 ....182 A3
Penny Way BH23 ....208 C6
Penny's Cl SP6 ....69 F3
Penny's Cnr SO41 ....195 F4
Penny's Cres SP6 ....69 F3
Penny's Ct BH22 ....165 D5
Penny's Wlk BH22 ....165 D5
Pennycress SO31 ....128 E2
Pennys La SP6 ....69 F3
Pennywell Gdns BH25 ..195 D4
Penrhyn Ave PO6 ....158 B8
Penrhyn Cl SO50 ....55 F5
Penrith Cl BH31 ....114 F5
Penrith Ct SO16 ....101 E7
Penrith Rd BH5 ....206 A4
Penrose Cl [1] PO2 ....157 D2
Penrose Rd PO12 ....165 D6
Penshurst Way SO50 ....56 A6
Pentagon The SO45 ...151 A2
Pentere Rd PO8 ....112 A6
Pentire Ave SO15 ....78 D2
Pentire Way SO15 ....78 D2
Pentland Cl SO45 ....125 D2
Pentland Rise PO16 ...132 D1
Penton Cl PO9 ....136 B6
Penton Pl [8] SO23 ....215 F4
Penton Rd SO21 ....32 A7
Pentons Hill SP6 ....94 D6
Pentridge Way SO40 ...100 E5
Penwood Gn [15] PO9 ..136 B5
Peper Harow PO8 ....112 A6
Peppard Cl SO18 ....104 A7
Pepper Cl PO11 ....185 A5
Peppercorn Cl BH23 ...207 E8
Peppercorn Way SO30 ...81 B3
Pepys Ave SO19 ....104 D5
Pepys Cl Gosport PO12 ...181 C5
Portsmouth PO4 ....182 F3
Percival Rd PO2 ....182 F8
Percivale Rd SO53 ....54 F4
Percy Chandler St PO1 ..216 C4
Percy Cl SO45 ....125 F5
Percy Rd
Bournemouth BH5 ....205 F4
Gosport PO12 ....181 B4
Portsmouth PO4 ....182 E4
Southampton SO16 ....102 A8
Peregrine Cl SO40 ....100 C6
Peregrine Rd BH23 ....208 A5
Peregrines The PO16 ...155 F8
Pergin Cres BH17 ....202 B7
Pergin Way BH17 ....202 B7
Perkins Ho [3] PO1 ....182 B5
Pern Dr SO30 ....106 A7
Peronne Ct PO3 ....157 F5
Peronne Rd PO3 ....157 F5
Perran Rd SO16 ....77 D1
Perry Gdns BH15 ....202 C1
Perryfield Gdns BH7 ...206 B8
Perrywood Cl SO45 ...150 C3
Perrywood Gdns SO40 ..100 B8
Perseus Pl PO7 ....134 E3
Perseus Terr [3] PO1 ...182 A4
Pershore Cl SO31 ....129 B3
Persian Dr PO15 ....129 B7
Persley Rd BH10 ....189 C4
Perth Cl BH23 ....191 E1
Perth Ho PO1 ....182 A4
Perth Rd Gosport PO13 ..155 D3
Portsmouth PO4 ....183 B4
Pervin Rd PO6 ....157 F8
Pest Hos GU32 ....16 C1

Peststead La SO32 ....85 C4
Peter Ashley Activity Ctr
  PO6 ....134 D1
Peter Ashley Rd PO6 ...134 D1
Peter Grant Way BH22 ..165 C5
Peter Symonds Coll
  SO22 ....215 D7
Peterborough Ct 12
  PO13 ....180 D5
Peterborough Rd
  Portsmouth PO6 ....133 E1
  Southampton SO14 .....103 A7
Peters Cl Sarisbury SO31 128 E3
  Upton BH16 ....201 C6
Peters Rd
  Ferndown BH22 ....165 F3
  Locks Heath SO31 .....128 F3
Peterscroft Ave SO40 ...100 B2
Petersfield Bsns Pk
  GU32 ....40 D3
Petersfield Ho PO1 .....216 C4
Petersfield Hospl GU32 .40 E3
Petersfield Inf Sch GU32 40 F3
Petersfield La PO8 .....88 C6
Petersfield Mus* GU32 .40 E3
Petersfield Pl BH7 .....206 B7
Petersfield Rd
  Bournemouth BH7 ......206 B7
  Bramdean SO24 ....15 B5
  Buriton GU31 ....65 D6
  Cheriton SO24 ....14 D4
  Chilcomb SO21 ....11 D7
  Clanfield PO8 ....88 D7
  Havant PO9 ....136 A6
  Winchester SO23 ......11 C7
Petersfield Sch The
  GU32 ....40 E2
Petersfield Sta GU32 ...40 A4
Petersgate Inf Sch PO8 .88 C4
Petersham Cl PO7 ......111 D1
Petersham Ho 5 PO5 ...182 D1
Petersham Rd BH17 ....202 A8
Petit Rd BH9 ....190 A3
Petrel Wlk PO13 ....155 B2
Petrie Rd PO13 ....179 F3
Petticoat La SP5 ....47 E7
Pettinger Gdns SO17 ...103 D8
Petty Cl SO51 ....53 A6
Pettycot Cres PO13 ....155 B3
Petworth Gdns
  Eastleigh SO50 ....56 A5
  Southampton SO16 ....78 B5
Petworth Rd PO3 ....183 B6
Petwyn Cl BH22 ....166 A6
Pevensey Cl SO16 ......77 D1
Peverell Rd BH16 ......201 B4
Peverells Rd SO53 .....55 E7
Peverells Wood Ave
  SO53 ....55 E7
Peverells Wood Cl SO53 55 F6
Peveril Cl BH24 ....139 F6
Peveril Rd SO19 ....103 E4
Pewsey Pl SO15 ....78 D2
Phelipps Rd BH21 ......186 E6
Phoenix Way PO13 .....155 C1
Philip Green Meml Sch
  BH21 ....67 B2
Philip Rd PO7 ....134 F5
Phillimore Rd SO16 ....79 D4
Phillips Cl SO16 ....77 E6
Philpott Dr SO40 ......101 F1
Phoenix Bldgs PO3 ....158 A2
Phoenix Cl SO31 ....105 A2
Phoenix Ctr The SO40 ..76 D2
Phoenix Pk SO50 ......56 C2
Phoenix Sq PO2 ....157 E4
Phyldon Cl BH12 ......203 B5
Phyldon Rd BH12 ......203 B6
Pickard Rd BH22 ....165 F7
Pickering Cl BH18 .....187 A2
Picket Cl SP6 ....69 F2
Pickford Rd BH9 ....189 E1
Pickwick Cl SO40 ......100 B7
Pickwick Ho 10 PO1 ...182 D7
Picton Ho
  10 Portsmouth PO5 ....216 B2
  Waterlooville PO7 ......111 C1
Pier Head Rd PO2 .....157 B1
Pier Rd PO1 ....182 B3
Pier St PO13 ....179 E3
Pig Shoot La BH23 .....190 F5
Pigeon House La PO7 ..133 D4
Pikes Hill SO43 ....121 F6
Pikes Hill Ave SO43 ...121 E6
Pilbrow Ct 8 PO12 .....180 F4
Pilchards Ave SO50 ....57 B3
Pilford Heath Rd BH21 .164 B7
Pilgrim Park Homes
  BH24 ....141 C8
Pilgrim Pl
  Lymington SO41 ....197 E3
  Southampton SO18 ....79 E4
Pilgrim's Cl BH25 ......195 C3
Pilgrims Cl SO53 ....55 A4
Pilgrims Way
  Poole BH17 ....202 A7
  Stubbington PO14 ......179 B6
Pill Hill SP5 ....24 A4
Pilley Bailey SO41 .....174 A2
Pilley Gn SO41 ....174 A1
Pilley Hill SO41 ....173 E1

Pilley St SO41 ....174 A1
Pilning Cl PO14 ....154 C8
Pilot Hight Rd BH11 ...189 A4
Pilsdon Dr BH17 ....187 E3
Pimpern Cl BH17 ......187 F2
Pimpernel Cl SO31 ....128 E2
Pine Ave
  Bournemouth BH6 .....206 C4
  Poole BH12 ....203 F6
Pine Cl Ashurst SO40 ..100 C3
  Barton on S BH25 .....209 E8
  Ferndown BH22 ....165 C2
  Hythe SO45 ....125 F2
  Landford SP5 ....49 D2
  North Baddesley SO52 ..53 F5
  Winchester SO22 ......10 B3
Pine Cotts GU33 ....21 A7
Pine Cres
  Chandler's Ford SO53 ..30 C1
  Christchurch BH23 ....208 E8
Pine Ct PO10 ....136 F4
Pine Dr Clanfield PO8 ..88 C5
  Poole BH13 ....203 E8
  Southampton SO18 ....104 D7
  St Leonards BH24 ....139 F4
Pine Dr E SO18 ....104 E7
Pine End BH22 ....165 F3
Pine Glen Ave BH22 ...165 C8
Pine Gr PO9 ....136 A1
Pine Grange 4 BH1 ...205 A3
Pine Ho New Milton BH25 195 A3
  Southampton SO16 ....78 F7
Pine Lodge 10 BH13 ..214 F7
Pine Manor Rd BH24 ...139 D5
Pine Mans 3 BH1 .....205 D4
Pine Park Mans 16
  BH13 ....204 A4
Pine Rd Alderholt SP6 ..92 F5
  Bishop's Waltham SO32 .83 D8
  Bournemouth BH9 .....205 A8
  Chandler's Ford SO53 ..55 C8
  East End BH21 ....162 F1
  Romsey SO51 ....53 C6
Pine Top Cvn Site BH25 171 F5
Pine Tree Cl BH21 .....163 D5
Pine Tree Gdns PO8 ...112 A2
Pine Tree Glen BH4 ...204 A3
Pine Trees Cl PO14 ...154 D8
Pine Vale Cres BH10 ..189 F3
Pine View Cl
  Redlynch SP5 ....47 D4
  Upton BH16 ....201 C6
Verwood BH31 ....114 D7
Pine View Rd BH31 ...114 D7
Pine Way SO16 ....78 F7
Pine Wlk Chilworth SO16 78 F7
  Liss GU33 ....21 A6
  Locks Heath SO31 ....129 A5
  West Moors BH31 .....115 B5
  West Moors BH22 .....138 E3
Pinebeach Ct BH13 ...214 G8
Pinecliff Rd BH13 .....214 G8
Pinecliffe Ave BH6 ...206 A4
Pinecliffe Rd BH25 ...209 C7
Pinefield Rd SO18 ....79 F2
Pinegrove Rd SO19 ...103 F4
Pineholt Cl BH24 ......140 A5
Pinehurst
  10 Milford on S SO41 ..211 C4
  6 Southampton SO17 ..79 A1
Pinehurst Ave BH23 ...207 F5
Pinehurst Cl PO7 .....112 C2
Pinehurst Pk BH22 ....165 F8
Pinehurst Rd
  West Moors BH22 .....138 F7
Pinelands Ct SO16 ....78 C4
Pinelands Rd SO16 ...78 F8
Pines The Godshill SP6 .70 F2
  Poole BH13 ....204 A2
  Porchester PO16 ......132 A1
  Southampton SO18 ....78 B3
Pineside BH9 ....205 A8
Pinesprings Dr BH18 ..186 E2
Pinetops Cl SO21 .....197 B3
Pinetree Wlk BH17 ...201 F8
Pineview Cl SO31 .....105 A1
Pinewood Gosport PO13 155 E1
  Southampton SO16 ....78 F6
Pinewood Ave
  Bournemouth BH10 ....189 D5
  Havant PO9 ....135 B3
Pinewood Cl
  Bournemouth BH10 ....189 D5
  Romsey SO51 ....28 C1
  Southampton SO14 ...104 D4
  Upton BH16 ....201 A7
  Walkford BH23 ....194 A2
Pinewood Cres SO45 ..126 B2
Pinewood Ct BH22 ....138 D2
Pinewood Dr SO45 ....126 B1
Pinewood Gdns BH22 .165 D7
Pinewood Lodge 5
  PO16 ....131 B2
Pinewood Pk SO19 ...104 F5
Pinewood Rd
  Christchurch BH23 ....193 F1
  Ferndown BH22 ....165 C2
  Hordle SO41 ....195 F3
  Poole BH13 ....204 B1
  St Leonards BH24 ....139 E8
Pink Rd PO2 ....182 E8
Pinkney La SO43 ......121 E3
Pinks Hill PO16 ....131 D2
Pinnacle The 7 BH1 ...205 A3
Pinsley Dr PO14 ....133 B5
Pinto Cl PO15 ....129 C7

Pipers Ash BH24 ......141 C8
Pipers Cl SO40 ....100 D6
Pipers Dr BH23 ....208 A7
Pipers Mead PO4 .....88 A5
Pipers Wood Ind Est
  PO7 ....134 C8
Piping Cl SO21 ....56 F8
Piping Gn SO21 ....56 F8
Piping Rd SO21 ....56 F8
Pipistrelle Wlk 4 PO17 130 E8
Pipit Cl Gosport PO12 ..181 B8
  Waterlooville PO8 .....112 A6
Pippin Cl
  Christchurch BH23 ....191 E2
  8 Lymington SO41 ....197 E2
Pirelli St SO15 ....102 F4
Pirrie Cl SO15 ....78 D1
Pitcairn Mews 8 PO4 .183 B2
Pitchponds Rd SO31 ..152 C10
Pitcot La SO21 ....33 B3
Pitcroft La GU31 ......65 F5
Pitcroft Rd PO2 ......157 D1
Pitmore Cl SO50 ......56 B8
Pitmore La
  Sway,Bowling Green SO41 196 F7
  Sway,Durns Town SO41 ..172 D1
Pitmore Rd SO50 .....56 B8
Pitreavie Rd PO6 .....157 F6
Pitt Hill La PO7 ....86 F1
Pitt Rd SO15 ....102 C6
Pitt Rdbt SO22 ....10 B5
Pitter Cl SO22 ....1 B5
Pitthouse La BH23 ....191 D8
Pittmore Rd BH23 ....192 C2
Pitts Deep La SO41 ...199 C4
Pitts La SP5 ....22 C8
Pitts Rd BH15 ....195 D2
Pitwines Cl BH15 .....202 D2
Pitymoor La PO17 ....133 B4
Place Cres PO7 ....134 F5
Place House Cl PO15 ..130 C1
Place La SO21 ....31 E8
Plaitford Gr PO9 ......135 C5
Plaitford Wlk SO16 ...77 F1
Plant Cl SO51 ....51 B2
Plantagenet Cres BH11 188 D5
Plantation SO41 ......211 E8
Plantation Ct
  Lymington SO41 ......197 D4
  Poole BH17 ....187 C1
Plantation Dr
  Marchwood SO40 ......101 E1
  Walkford BH23 ....194 A2
Plantation Rd
  Hill Brow GU33 ....21 B2
  West Wellow SO51 ....74 D8
Plantation The SO32 ..82 E2
Plassey Cres BH10 ...189 C5
Platform Rd SO14 ....103 A2
Platoff Rd SO41 ......212 E8
Player Ct SP6 ....69 F3
Players Cres SO40 ...100 E5
Playfair Rd PO5 ......216 C2
Playfields Dr BH12 ...203 E6
Plaza Mews 3 SO51 ..52 F7
Plaza Par 4 SO51 ....52 F7
Pleasance Way BH25 ..194 F3
Pleasant La PO10 .....162 F7
Pleasant Rd PO4 .....183 B4
Plecy Cl BH22 ....165 D2
Plemont Cl BH12 .....188 E1
Pless Rd SO41 ....211 B5
Plough La SO32 ......85 C2
Plough Way SO22 ....215 B2
Plover Cl
  Southampton SO16 ...78 B5
  Stubbington PO14 ....179 B7
Plover Dr SO41 ....211 F4
Plover Rd SO40 ......100 C7
Plover Reach PO4 ....183 B5
Plovers Down SO22 ..10 B3
Plovers Rd PO8 ......112 A6
PLPH Rd SO45 ....151 B5
Plumer Rd BH17 .....187 A1
Plumley Wlk PO9 ....135 D7
Plumpton Gdns PO3 ..158 B3
Plumpton Gr 4 PO7 ..112 B1
Pluto Rd SO50 ....45 F5
Plymouth Dr PO14 ...179 B8
Plymouth St PO5 .....216 B2
Pococks La GU33 .....19 F7
Poets Way SO22 .....215 B6
Poinsettia Cl PO15 ...129 E3
Point The BH5 ....205 E3
Pointout Cl SO16 .....78 E3
Pointout Rd SO16 ....78 E3
Pokesdown Com Prim Sch
  BH5 ....206 B5
Pokesdown Sta PO4 ..206 A5
Poles La Hursley SO21 ..30 D6
  Lymington SO41 ......197 E1
  Otterbourne SO21 ....31 B5
Polesden Cl SO53 ....55 B8
Police Station La SO32 .61 B1
Police Training Ctr
  SO31 ....127 D5
Pollards Moor Rd SO40 75 B1
Polygon Ct SO15 .....102 E6
Polygon Sch The SO15 102 E6
Polygon The SO15 ...102 E5
Pomona Cl PO7 ......165 D6
Pompey Ctr PO4 .....183 F5
Pompey Ctr Trad Pk The
  PO4 ....182 F5
Pompey's Cnr BH21 ..165 A4

Pompey's La BH22 ....165 B2
Pond Cl Marchwood SO40 101 F2
  New Milton BH25 .....195 A3
Pond Cotts GU32 .....39 C1
Pond La PO8 ....88 B6
Pond Piece PO7 ......110 F3
Pond Rd SO31 ....128 F6
Pondhead Cl SO45 ...150 C3
Pondside Flats SO42 ..148 F1
Pondside La SO32 ....83 C8
Ponsonby Ho PO5 ....216 B2
Ponsonby Rd BH14 ..203 D4
Pony Dr BH16 ....201 D7
Pook La Fareham PO17 .131 C4
  8 Havant PO9 ....160 A8
Pooksgreen SO40 .....101 D1
Pool Lane Rdbt BH11 .188 E4
Poole Aquarium &
  Serpentarium* BH15 ..202 C1
Poole Commerce Ctr
  BH12 ....203 F5
Poole Gram Sch BH17 ..187 D2
Poole High Sch BH15 ..202 C4
Poole Hill BH2 ....204 D3
Poole Hospl BH15 ....202 C3
Poole La BH11 ....189 B5
Poole Rd
  Bournemouth BH4 ....204 C3
  Poole BH13 ....204 A4
  Southampton SO19 ..103 E4
  Wimborne Minst BH21 163 C4
Poole Sta BH15 ......202 C3
Popes La Totton SO40 ..100 F7
  Upham SO32 ....58 C4
Popes Rd BH15 ......202 C3
Popham Ct PO9 ......135 C6
Poplar Cl
  Bransgore BH23 ......193 C8
  Christchurch BH23 ...209 B8
  8 Poole BH15 ....202 B1
  Wimborne Minst BH21 163 D5
Poplar Cres BH24 ....141 B7
Poplar Dr Fareham PO14 154 E8
  Hythe SO45 ....126 B3
Poplar Gr PO11 ......185 A4
Poplar La BH23 ......193 C8
Poplar Rd
  New Milton BH25 .....195 A3
  Southampton SO19 ..103 F6
Poplar Way
  Hedge End SO30 ......79 E5
  North Baddesley SO52 .53 F5
  Ringwood BH24 ......141 B7
Poplar Wlk GU31 ....40 E1
Poplars The SO32 ....83 E3
Poppy Cl
  Christchurch BH23 ...208 D3
  Locks Heath SO31 ...128 F2
Poppy Rd SO16 ......79 C5
Poppyfields SO53 ....55 A6
Porchester Rd SO19 ..103 E3
Porlock Rd SO16 .....77 D2
Port La Hursley SO22 ..30 C8
  Winchester SO22 .....10 A2
Port Royal St 9 PO5 ..216 C2
Port Way PO6 ....157 B7
Portadene 1 BH4 ....204 D2
Portal Rd
  Bishopstoke SO50 ....56 D3
  Gosport PO13 ....155 C3
  Southampton SO19 ..104 B8
  Totton SO40 ....100 E7
  Winchester SO23 ....215 F4
Portarlington Cl BH4 ..204 D2
Portarlington Ct 44
  BH4 ....204 D2
Portarlington Rd BH4 ..204 C2
Portchester Bsns Ctr
  PO16 ....156 D8
Portchester Castle*
  PO16 ....156 F6
Portchester Com Sch
  PO16 ....156 D8
Portchester Ct 3 BH8 .205 B5
Portchester Ho 5 PO17 130 E8
Portchester Hts PO16 ..132 A1
Portchester La PO17 ..132 D4
Portchester Pl BH8 ...205 B5
Portchester Rd
  Bournemouth BH8 ....205 A5
  Portchester PO16 ....156 A8
  Portsmouth PO2 .....182 E8
Portchester Rise SO50 .56 D4
Portchester Sch 5 PO4 .183 B2
Portcreek Cotts PO6 ..158 B5
Portelet Cl BH12 .....188 D2
Portelet Ho SO16 ....77 D3
Portelet Pl SO30 .....105 D5
Porteous Cres SO19 ..55 F6
Porter's La SO14 .....103 A2
Porters Rd SO14 .....102 F3
Porters La BH21 .....164 C6
Portersbridge Mews 1
  SO51 ....52 E7
Portersbridge St SO51 .52 E7
Portesham Gdns BH8 ..190 B4
Portesham Way BH17 ..187 E3
Portfield Cl BH23 .....207 A2
Portfield Rd
  Christchurch BH23 ...207 B3
  Portsmouth PO3 .....158 B3
Portfield Sch
  Christchurch BH23 ...207 A4
  East Barley BH23 ....190 B8
Portiere Ho BH11 ....189 A4
Portland Bldgs 5 PO12 181 C5

Portland Dr PO12 ....180 D3
Portland Ho 7 PO12 ..181 D5
Portland Pl 4 PO4 ....204 F4
Portland Rd
  Bournemouth BH9 ....205 A8
  Portsmouth PO5 .....182 C2
  Waterlooville PO7 ....134 E7
Portland Sq 6 GU33 ..20 F4
Portland St
  Portsmouth PO1 .....182 B5
  Southampton SO14 ..102 F4
Portland Terr
  2 Portsmouth PO5 ...182 C2
  Southampton SO14 ..102 F4
Portman Cres BH5 ...206 B4
Portman Rd BH7 .....205 F5
Portman Terr BH5 ....206 B4
Portmore Cl BH18 ....187 C6
Portobello Gr PO16 ..132 D1
Portsdown Ave PO6 ..158 C8
Portsdown Hill Rd
  Cosham PO6 ....134 C1
  Havant PO9 ....135 A1
  Portchester PO17 ....132 D2
  Portsmouth PO6 .....133 C1
Portsdown Prim Sch
  PO6 ....157 F8
Portsdown Rd PO16 ..156 E8
Portside Cl SO40 .....102 A3
Portsmouth & Southsea Sta
  PO1 ....216 B3
Portsmouth Cath (CE)
  PO1 ....182 B4
Portsmouth City Mus & Art
  Gallery* PO1 ....182 B3
Portsmouth Coll PO3 ..183 C7
Portsmouth Ent Ctr
  PO3 ....158 B2
Portsmouth Gram Sch The
  PO1 ....182 B3
Portsmouth Harbour Sta
  PO1 ....181 F6
Portsmouth High Sch for
  Girls PO5 ....216 A1
Portsmouth High Sch for
  Girls (Juns) PO5 .....182 C2
Portsmouth Hospl (Bupa)
  PO9 ....136 D5
Portsmouth RC Cath*
  PO1 ....216 A4
Portsmouth Rd
  Bursledon SO31 .....105 A1
  Colden Common SO50 .57 C6
  Cosham PO6 ....157 C4
  Horndean PO8 ....112 C6
  Lee-on-t-S PO13 .....180 A4
  Southampton SO19 ..104 C2
Portsview Ave PO16 ..156 D8
Portsview Gdns PO16 .132 D1
Portswood Ave SO17 ..103 B8
Portswood Ctr SO17 ..79 B1
Portswood Pk 2 BH10 190 A4
Portswood Prim Sch
  SO17 ....79 C2
Portswood Rd
  Havant PO9 ....135 D6
  Portsmouth PO2 .....157 E5
  Southampton SO17 ..103 B8
Portuguese Fireplace*
  SO43 ....120 F1
Portview Rd SO18 ....79 F1
Portway Cl SO18 .....104 B7
Posbrooke La PO14 ..153 E6
Posbrooke Rd PO4 ..183 B4
Post Office Bldgs BH9 .204 F4
Post Office La BH24 ..140 A5
Post Office Rd
  18 Bournemouth BH1 ..204 F3
  Waterlooville PO7 ....134 C5
Postern Cl PO16 .....156 D8
Postern Ct 9 SO14 ...102 F3
Potash Terr PO9 .....135 E1
Potteries The PO16 ..131 B3
Potterne Way BH21 ..115 A4
Potterne Wood Cl BH21 131 A4
Potters Field GU33 ...21 A7
Potters Heron Cl SO51 .29 E3
Potters Heron La SO51 .29 E3
Potters Way BH14 ...203 C2
Pottery Junc BH14 ...203 B2
Pottery Rd BH14 .....203 B2
Poulner Cl SO19 .....104 C4
Poulner Ct PO9 ......135 C6
Poulner Cl PO9 ......135 C6
Poulner Hill BH24 ...141 E8
Poulner Inf & Jun Schs
  BH24 ....117 C2
Poulner Pk BH24 ....117 C1
Pound Cl Gosport PO13 180 E4
  Poole BH15 ....202 F5
  Ringwood BH24 .....141 B6
Pound Cotts SO32 ...61 D5
Pound Ct SO18 ......104 A7
Pound Gate Dr PO14 ..129 C1
Pound Hill SO51 .....50 D2
Pound La Ampfield SO51 29 B2
  Ashurst SO40 ....100 E3
  Burley BH24 ....142 F2
  Cadnam SO40 ....75 C1
  11 Christchurch BH23 .207 B6
  Damerham SP6 ......98 B5
  Meonstoke SO32 ....61 D5
  Platsford SO51 ......50 C5
  Poole BH15 ....202 E5
  Sherfield English SO51 .25 F2
Pound Lea PO11 .....185 A5

Pound Rd
Bursledon SO31 ....104 E1
Kings Worthy SO23 ....2 C8
Lymington SO41 ....197 B2
Portsmouth PO6 ....133 B2
Pound St SO18 ....104 A7
Pound Tree Rd SO14 ...103 A4
Poundbury Cl SO31 ...129 A6
Pounds Terr PO1 .....182 A6
Powell Cres SO40 ....100 F5
Powell Rd BH14 ......203 B3
Powell Sq 8 PO1 ....182 A5
Power Rd PO1 ....182 E6
Powerscourt Rd
Barton on S BH25 ....209 E7
Portsmouth PO2 ....182 E8
Powis Cl BH25 ....195 B3
Powlett Rd SO41 .....197 E3
Poyner Cl PO16 ......131 B2
Poynings Pl PO1 .....182 A3
Precinct The
Holbury SO45 ....150 C4
Waterlooville PO7 ....134 E7
Precosa Rd SO30 .....105 E6
Prelate Way PO4 .....129 D2
Premier Ctr The SO51 ..53 D5
Premier Par SO18 ......79 F3
Premier Way SO51 ....53 D5
Preshaw Cl SO16 ......78 B4
Preshaw St SO32 ......35 B3
Presidents Ct 12 PO12 .181 C9
Presseys Cnr SP6 ......93 A7
Preston Cl BH16 ......201 C7
Preston La BH23 .....192 D3
Preston Rd Poole BH15 .202 C6
Portsmouth PO2 ....182 F8
Preston Way BH23 ....208 D8
Prestwood Cl BH25 ...194 F1
Prestwood Rd SO30 ...105 C6
Pretoria Rd
Hedge End SO30 ....105 B5
Portsmouth PO4 ....182 F3
Prettyjohn Ho 14 PO4 .183 E2
Pricketts Hill PO17,SO32 .108 A6
Prideaux-Brune Ave
PO13 ....155 C4
Priest Croft SO45 ....150 E2
Priest Croft Dr SO45 .150 E2
Priest La BH23 ....192 B7
Priest's House Mus & Gdns*
BH21 ....163 B4
Priestfields PO14 ....129 C2
Priestlands SO51 ......52 E8
Priestlands Cl SO40 ..100 A6
Priestlands La SO41 ..197 C3
Priestlands Pl SO41 ..197 D3
Priestlands Rd SO41 ..197 D3
Priestlands Sch SO41 .197 D2
Priestley Cl SO40 ....100 D7
Priestley Rd BH10 ....189 B1
Priestwood Cl SO18 ..104 D7
Primate Rd PO14 .....129 D2
Primrose Cl
Chandler's Ford SO53 ....54 F4
Gosport PO13 ....155 C5
Hedge End SO30 ......105 C5
Primrose Ct PO7 .....135 A6
Primrose Gdns BH17 ..186 F1
Primrose La Rake GU33 .21 D4
Redlynch SP5 ....47 C6
Primrose Rd SO16 .....79 A4
Primrose Terr SO32 ..159 D2
Primrose Way
Christchurch BH23 ....208 C8
Corfe Mullen BH21 ....186 E7
Locks Heath SO31 ....128 F2
Romsey SO51 ....28 C1
Prince Albert Rd PO4 .183 A3
Prince Alfred St PO12 .181 A4
Prince George St
Havant PO9 ....135 F1
Portsmouth PO1 ......182 A5
Prince Of Wales Ave
SO15 ....102 A3
Prince Of Wales Cl 4
PO7 ....135 A7
Prince Of Wales Rd
Bournemouth BH4 .....204 C4
8 Gosport PO12 .....181 C2
Prince Rd Fareham PO14 .154 F6
Rownhams SO16 ....77 E6
Prince Regent Ct PO5 .216 E4
Prince William Ct SO50 ..56 F2
Prince's Bldgs 21 SO23 .215 E1
Prince's Ct
Ferndown BH22 ....165 D5
7 Portsmouth PO1 ....182 D7
Prince's Mead Sch SO21 ..2 E6
Prince's Pl
New Milton BH25 .....195 C3
1 Portsmouth PO1 ....182 D7
Prince's Rd SO51 ......52 E8
Prince's St
Portsmouth PO1 ......182 D7
Southampton SO14 ...103 C6
Princes Cl
Bishop's Waltham SO32 ..83 B8
Redlynch SP5 ....47 E7
Princes Cotts GU32 ...63 D8
Princes Cres SO43 ...122 B5
Princes Ct
Lyndhurst SO43 ....122 B5
8 Poole BH13 ....204 A4
2 Southampton SO14 ..103 C6
Princes Dr PO7 ....112 A1
Princes Hill SP5 ......47 E7
Princes Ho
Portsmouth PO5 ......216 A1

Princes Ho continued
3 Southampton SO14 ..103 C6
Princes Pl SO22 .....215 C3
Princes Rd
Ferndown BH22 ....165 D5
Petersfield GU32 ......40 D4
Southampton SO15 ...102 D6
Princess Anne Hospl
SO16 ....78 B3
Princess Ave BH23 ...207 B6
Princess Cl SO30 ......80 E2
Princess Ct 11 SO23 .215 E6
Princess Gdns PO8 ...112 C7
Princess Rd
Ashurst SO40 ....100 B2
Bournemouth BH4 ....204 B4
Poole BH13 ....204 A4
Pringles Cl BH22 .....165 E5
Pringles Dr BH22 .....165 E5
Prinstead Cl 6 SO23 .215 F4
Prinsted Cres PO6 ....158 D7
Prinsted La PO10 .....161 D7
Prinsted Wlk PO14 ...154 D8
Printers Row 8 SO23 .215 D6
Priors Barton SO23 ...215 D3
Priors Cl Breach PO10 .137 E1
Christchurch BH23 ....208 C7
Priors Dean Rd SO22 ...1 D4
Priors Hill La SO31 ...127 E8
Priors Leaze La PO18 .137 F1
Priors Rd BH17 ......202 A8
Priors Way SO22 ......10 B3
Priors Wlk 3 BH21 ...163 B5
Priorsdean Ave PO3 ..183 A6
Priorsdean Cres PO9 .135 D3
Priory Ave SO17 ......79 F8
Priory CE Prim Sch The
BH23 ....207 B6
Priory Cl
Bishop's Waltham SO32 ..83 B8
Southampton SO17 .....79 D1
Priory Cres PO4 ......183 A4
Priory Ct
Bishop's Waltham SO32 ..83 B8
Portchester PO16 .....156 E8
Portsmouth PO5 ......216 D2
Priory Gdns
Portchester PO16 .....156 C7
Waterlooville PO7 ....111 E1
West Moors BH22 .....166 A8
13 Winchester SO23 ..215 E6
Priory Ho
Christchurch BH23 ....207 C5
6 Southampton SO14 .103 A5
Priory Ind Pk BH23 ..208 B7
Priory Quay BH23 ....207 C5
Priory Rd
Bournemouth BH2 ....204 E2
Eastleigh SO50 ....55 F1
Fareham PO15 ....130 D2
Gosport PO12 ....181 B9
Gosport PO12 ....181 C9
Netley SO31 ....127 B6
5 Portsmouth PO4 ...183 A2
Southampton,Portswood
SO17 ....79 D1
Southampton,St Denys
SO17 ....103 C8
Southwick PO17 ......133 A6
West Moors BH22 .....166 A8
Priory Sch SO32 ......83 B8
Priory Sch (Sports Coll)
PO4 ....216 D2
Priory The SO32 ....83 B7
Priory View Cl 2 BH22 .165 E7
Priory View Pl 3 BH9 .190 A3
Priory View Rd
Bournemouth BH9 ....190 A3
Burton BH23 ....192 A2
Private Rd SO41 ......197 E5
Privet Rd BH9 ....204 F8
Privett Ho PO1 ....182 A6
Privett Pl PO12 .....180 E4
Privett Rd Fareham PO15 .130 C2
Gosport PO12,PO13 ...180 D3
High Cross GU32 ......18 E2
Waterlooville PO7 ....134 D8
Proctor Cl SO19 .....104 D5
Proctor Dr SO52 ......53 F3
Proctor La PO1 ......182 F5
Promenade BH23 .....208 B5
Promenade Ct PO1 ...182 F5
Promenade The
Emsworth PO10 ......160 F7
Hythe SO45 ....126 A5
5 Portsmouth PO2 ...157 D1
Prospect La
Durrants PO9 ....136 B7
Havant PO9 ....136 B5
Prospect Pl
Chandler's Ford SO53 ..55 C6
Hythe SO45 ....126 A5
Prospect Rd PO1 .....182 C7
Prosperous St 1 BH15 .202 C1
Protea Gdns PO14 ...130 A1
Provene Cl SO32 ......83 E4
Provene Gdns SO32 ...83 E4
Providence Ct 2 PO1 .182 C7
Providence Hill SO31 .105 A2
Providence Pk SO16 ...78 F5
Provost St SP6 ....69 F1
Pruetts La GU31 ......20 F1
Prunus Cl
Ferndown BH22 ......165 B7
Southampton SO16 ....78 C5
Prunus Dr BH22 .....165 B7
Pudbrook Ho SO30 ...106 A6

Pudbrooke Gdns SO30 .105 B8
Pudding La SO23 ....2 B5
Puddleslosh La SP6 ...69 D3
Puddletown Cres BH17 .187 F2
Puffin Cl SO16 ....78 B5
Puffin Cres PO14 .....154 B4
Puffin Gdns PO13 ....155 B3
Puffin Wlk PO8 ......111 D4
Pug's Hole SP5 ....4 B7
Pulens Cres GU31 .....41 C4
Pulens La GU31 ....41 B4
Pullman Bsns Pk BH24 .141 B6
Pullman Ct BH22 .....138 D2
Pullman Way BH24 ...141 B6
Pump La Gosport PO13 .155 C1
Waterlooville PO7 ....112 A5
Pundle Green Est SO40 .99 B6
Punsholt La SO24 .....16 F5
Purbeck Ave BH15 ...201 E1
Purbeck Cl BH16 .....201 B7
Purbeck Ct
Fareham PO14 ....154 D8
Verwood BH31 ....114 F5
Purbeck Gdns BH14 ..202 F5
Purbeck Hts BH14 ...203 B5
Purbeck Rd
Barton on S BH25 ....209 D7
Bournemouth BH4 ....204 E2
Purbeck Wlk PO14 ...154 D7
Purbrook Chase Prec
PO7 ....134 E3
Purbrook Cl SO16 .....78 C4
Purbrook Gdns PO7 ..134 C5
Purbrook Heath Rd
PO7 ....134 B5
Purbrook Ho PO7 ....134 C5
Purbrook Inf Sch PO7 .134 D5
Purbrook Jun Sch PO7 .134 D5
Purbrook Park Sch PO7 .134 D3
Purbrook Rd PO1 ....182 E5
Purbrook Way
Havant PO9 ....135 C4
Waterlooville PO7 ....134 F4
Purcell Cl PO7 ......134 E4
Purcell Rd SO19 .....104 D4
Purchase Rd BH12 ...204 C7
Purdy Ho BH11 ......189 A4
Purewell BH23 ....207 D6
Purewell Cl BH23 ....207 E6
Purewell Cross BH23 .207 E6
Purewell Cross Rd
BH23 ....207 D7
Purewell Ct 2 BH23 ..207 E7
Purewell Rdbt BH23 ..207 E6
Purkess Cl SO53 ......55 D7
Purkiss Cl SO40 ......99 C5
Purley Way SO51 ......50 B3
Purlieu La SP6 ....70 F3
Purrocks The GU32 ....40 F5
Purslane Gdns PO15 ..129 E3
Purvis Gdns SO19 ...104 B2
Pussex La BH23 ......191 A4
Putmans La GU31 .....66 F7
Pycroft Cl
North Hayling PO11 ...160 C3
Southampton SO19 ...104 A3
Pye Cl BH21 ....186 E7
Pye Cnr BH21 ....163 A8
Pye La Alderholt BH21 ..91 E6
Wimborne Minst BH21 .163 B4
Pye St PO1 ....216 B4
Pyland's La SO31 .....105 B3
Pyle Cl PO8 ....112 A4
Pylehill SO50 ....55 A4
Pylewell Park Gdns*
SO41 ....198 E4
Pylewell Rd SO45 ....126 A4
Pyramid Ctr PO3 .....158 B3
Pyramids L Ctr The
PO5 ....182 D1
Pyrford Cl Gosport PO12 .180 E3
Waterlooville PO7 ....111 E2
Pyrford Gdns 3 SO41 .197 E2
Pyrford Mews SO41 ..197 E2
Pytchley PO14 ....179 A7

Q

Quadra Point PO3 ....158 B3
Quadrangle The
Eastleigh SO50 ....56 A4
Romsey SO51 ....53 D6
Quadrant SP6 ....93 E8
Quadrant Ctr The BH1 .204 F3
Quail Way PO8 ......112 A6
Quaker Ct BH24 .....140 F6
Quantock Cl 7 BH23 .207 F8
Quantock Rd SO16 ...101 E8
Quantocks The SO45 .125 D2
Quarels Rd PO9 .....135 C6
Quarr Ho SO41 ......172 A3
Quarry Chase 4 BH4 .204 C3
Quarry Cl BH21 ......164 B7
Quarry Dr BH21 .....164 B7
Quarry Rd
Wimborne Minst BH21 .164 B7
Winchester SO23 ......11 C7
Quarterdeck Ave PO2 .157 B1
Quarterdeck The PO1 .181 E6
Quarterjack Mews 1
BH21 ....163 C4
Quartremaine Rd PO3 .158 B3
Quavey Rd SP5 ....47 E6
Quay 2000 SO14 ....103 C8
Quay Haven SO31 ....128 D8
Quay Hill SO41 ......197 F4
Quay Ho SO31 ....128 B1
Quay La PO12 ....156 B1
Quay Point
8 Poole BH15 ....202 C1
Quay Rd
Christchurch BH23 ....207 B6
Lymington SO41 .....197 F4
Quay St Fareham PO16 .131 C1
Fareham PO16 ....155 B8
Lymington SO41 .....197 F4
Quay The
Hamble-le-R SO31 ....128 A2
Poole BH15 ....202 C1
Quayle Dr BH11 .....188 F6
Quayside SO30 ......106 A6
Quayside Commerce Ctr
PO16 ....155 B8
Quayside Rd
Fawley SO45 ....151 F1
Southampton SO18 ..103 D7
Quayside Wlk SO40 ..101 F3
Quebec Gdns SO31 ...104 F1
Queen Alexandra Hospl
PO6 ....157 F8
Queen Anne Dr
Oakley BH21 ....187 E8
Wimborne Minst BH21 .164 A1
Queen Elizabeth Ave
SO41 ....197 D4
**Queen Elizabeth Country
Park Visitor Ctr *** PO8 ..64 F4
Queen Elizabeth Ct
Southampton SO17 ....79 C3
Wimborne Minst BH21 .163 B4
Queen Elizabeth Ctry Pk*
GU31 ....65 B3
Queen Elizabeth's Sch
BH21 ....162 F6
Queen Katherine Rd
SO41 ....197 E5
Queen Mary Ave BH9 .189 F2
Queen Mary Rd PO16 .156 D7
Queen Rd PO14 .....154 F6
Queen St Emsworth PO10 .161 A8
Lymington SO41 .....197 D3
Portsmouth PO1 ......182 A5
Twyford SO21 ....31 F5
Woodgreen SP6 ......47 B2
Queen's Ave BH23 ...207 B5
Queen's Cl SO51 ......53 A7
Queen's Cres PO5 ...216 B1
Queen's Ct SO15 .....102 E5
Queen's Gr PO5 .....216 B1
Queen's Inclosure Prim Sch
PO7 ....112 A1
Queen's Par
Lyndhurst SO43 ......121 F5
1 Waterlooville PO7 ..134 E7
Queen's Park Ave BH8 .205 D8
Queen's Park Gdns BH8 .205 D8
Queen's Park Inf Sch
BH8 ....190 C1
Queen's Park Jun Sch
BH8 ....190 B1
Queen's Park Rd BH8 .205 D7
Queen's Park South Dr
BH8 ....205 D7
Queen's Park West Dr
BH8 ....205 D7
Queen's Pl BH21 .....216 B1
Queen's Rd
Bournemouth BH3 ....204 D4
Chandler's Ford SO53 ..30 D1
Christchurch BH23 ....207 E6
Corfe Mullen BH21 ...196 D6
Fareham PO16 ....131 B1
Poole BH14 ....203 D4
Portsmouth PO1 ......181 F7
Portsmouth,Buckland PO2 .182 E8
Southampton SO15 ...78 C2
Warsash SO31 ....152 C10
Waterlooville PO7 ...134 D5
Winchester SO22 ....215 B5
Queen's Terr PO5 ....216 B1
Queen's Terr SO14 ...103 A3
Queen's Way PO5 ....216 B1
Queen's Hythe SO45 ..126 B3
Lee-on-t-S PO13 .....179 E3
West Moors BH22 ....138 D1
Queens Cres
Horndean PO8 ....112 C7
Stubbington PO14 ...179 D8
Queens Ct
16 Bournemouth BH4 ..204 D4
Bournemouth,Charminster
BH8 ....205 B8
New Milton BH25 ....195 D3
12 Winchester SO23 .215 D5
Queens Gate PO1 ....182 B2
Queens Gdns
Bournemouth BH4 ....204 D4
Fordingbridge SP6 .....69 F2
Queens Gr
New Milton BH25 ....195 C4
Waterlooville PO7 ...134 D5
Queens Ho 2 SO14 ..103 A3
Queens Keep
22 Bournemouth PO5 .182 C2
4 Southampton SO15 .102 F5
Queens Mead SO22 ..215 A4
Queens Rd
Ferndown BH22 ......165 D7
Lee-on-t-S PO13 .....179 F1

Queens Rd continued
Lyndhurst SO43 ....122 B5
Petersfield GU32 ......40 D4
Queens Ride SO22 .....53 E4
Queens View SO31 ...127 B6
Queens Way BH24 ....141 B7
Queensbury Mans 9
BH1 ....205 A3
Queensland Rd BH5 ..206 A5
Queensmead
Burton BH23 ....192 A1
4 Wimborne Minst BH21 .163 C5
Queenstown Rd SO15 .102 D6
Queensway
New Milton BH25 .....194 E3
North Hayling PO11 ..160 A3
Southampton SO14 ..103 A3
Queensway The PO16 .156 B8
Queenswood Dr BH8 ..190 E1
Queenswood Dr BH21 .165 D7
Querida Cl SO31 .....128 D8
Quilter Cl SO19 .....104 D4
Quince La BH21 ....163 E6
Quintin Cl BH23 .....208 F8
Quinton Cl PO5 .....216 C2
Quintrell Ave PO16 ..156 A8
Quob Farm Cl SO30 ...80 E3
Quob La SO30 ....80 E3
Quomp The BH24 ....141 A7
Quoyne Cl SO51 ....52 E7

R

R L Stevenson Ave BH4 .204 B3
Racecourse La PO6 ...157 B8
Racecourse View SO43 .121 F6
Rachel Cl Fair Oak SO50 ..57 B2
Poole BH12 ....203 C3
Rachel Madocks Sch
PO8 ....111 D4
Racton Ave PO6 .....158 B7
Racton Rd PO10 .....136 F3
Radcliffe Ct SO14 ...103 B5
Radcliffe Rd SO14 ...103 B6
Radcliffe Rd PO16 ...131 C2
Radipole Rd BH17 ...188 A2
Radleigh Gdns SO40 .100 B8
Radley Cl SO30 ....81 C1
Radnor St PO5 ......216 B2
Radstock Rd SO19 ...103 E3
Radway Cres SO15 ...102 D8
Radway Rd SO15 ......78 E1
Raebarn Cl SO24 .....14 D5
Raeburn Dr SO30 ....105 C7
Raglan Cl SO53 ....55 A4
Raglan Ct Eastleigh SO50 ..56 A6
Gosport PO12 ....181 A5
Locks Heath SO31 ...129 A5
Raglan Gdns BH11 ...189 A2
Raglan Se PO5 ......216 C3
Raglan Terr PO10 ...137 A1
Ragmore La GU32 ...118 E5
Rails La PO11 ....185 C2
Railway Cotts
Southampton SO15 ..101 C8
West Dean SP5 ....3 D3
West Moor SO32 ......37 C4
West Tisted GU34 .....17 C6
Railway Flats PO1 ...182 E5
Railway Terr SO42 ...172 F8
Railway Triangle Ind Est
PO6 ....158 B6
Railway View PO1 ...216 C3
Railway View Rd SO17 .103 C8
Rainbow Pl SO15 .....102 E8
Rake Bsns Pk GU33 ....21 E4
Rake CE Est Sch GU33 .21 F5
Rake Rd GU33 ....21 B4
Raleigh Cl
Christchurch BH23 ...207 F5
New Milton BH25 .....194 F3
Ringwood BH24 ......141 C8
Raleigh Ho 7 PO11 ..182 A5
Raleigh Rd BH12 ....188 E1
Raleigh Wlk PO13 ...180 D6
Raley Rd SO31 ......129 A2
Ralph Jessop Ct BH12 .203 D7
Ralph La SO51 ....28 A1
Ralph Rd BH21 ......186 E7
Ramalley La SO53 .....55 B8
Rambler Dr PO13 ...180 C6
Ramblers Way PO7 ..112 C1
Ramillies Ho
3 Fareham PO14 .....154 E7
16 Gosport PO12 ....181 C5
Ramley Rd SO41 .....197 B3
Rampart Gdns PO3 ..157 F5
Rampart Rd SO18 ...103 D7
Rampart Row PO12 ..181 E4
Rampart The SO41 ...197 D5
Rams Wlk GU32 ....40 F3
Ramsay Pl PO13 .....155 C2
Ramsay Rd SO23 ....2 C8
Ramsdale Ave PO9 ...135 C5
Ramsdean Rd GU32 ...39 E2
Ramsey Ct BH25 .....194 F3
Ramsey Rd BH11 ....185 A3
Ramshill GU31 ....41 A4
Rances Way SO22 ...215 C3
Randall Cl SO40 ......76 C2
Randall Rd SO53 ......30 D2
Randall's La BH24 ...142 E5
Randolph Rd
2 Bournemouth BH1 .205 E4

Randolph Rd continued
Poole BH14 ....**203** C5
Portsmouth PO2 ....**157** E2
Randolph St SO15 ......**102** C7
Ranelagh Ct 9 SO17 ...**103** A8
Ranelagh Gdns SO15 ...**102** E7
Ranelagh Rd
Christchurch BH23 .....**208** F7
Havant PO9 ....**135** D1
Portsmouth PO2 ....**157** C1
Winchester SO23 ....**215** D4
Ranfurly Gdns SO45 ....**125** E1
Range Gdns SO19 ......**104** B3
Range Gn PO2 ....**157** C3
Ranger Ct SO14 ....**103** B2
Ranmore Cl SO45 ....**125** C4
Rannoch Cl PO15 ....**130** E3
Ransome Cl PO14 ....**153** F7
Ranwilles Jun & Inf Schs
PO14 ....**154** C8
Ranvilles La PO14 ....**154** B7
Rapley Ct PO11 ....**184** E3
Rapson Cl PO14 ....**133** C1
Raptor & Reptile Ctr*
BH24 ....**141** C5
Rareridge La SO32 ....**83** E8
Rashley Mews SO41 .....**197** E3
Ratcliffe Rd
Dibden Purlieu SO45 ....**125** F1
Hedge End SO30 ....**105** C7
Rathdora Mews SO14 ....**127** F8
Ratlake La SO21 ....**29** F4
Rattigan Gdns PO15 .....**129** C8
Ravana Ct 4 BH8 ....**205** A5
Raven Cl PO13 ....**150** C6
Raven Croft PO5 ....**216** B1
Raven Rd SO14 ....**103** B6
Raven Sq SO50 ....**55** D2
Ravens Cl PO14 ....**179** D7
Ravens Way SO41 ....**211** D4
Ravenscourt Rd
Bournemouth BH6 ......**206** C5
Lymington SO41 ....**197** D2
Ravenscroft Cl SO31 ....**104** F1
Ravenscroft Way SO32 ...**81** F1
Ravensdale Cl BH12 .....**203** C6
Ravenswood PO14 ......**204** D2
Ravenswood Gdns 12
PO5 ....**182** D2
Ravenswood House Hospl
PO17 ....**130** E8
Ravine Cl BH13 ....**214** F7
Ravine Gdns 5 BH13 ....**214** F7
Ravine Rd
Bournemouth BH5 ......**206** B4
Poole BH13 ....**214** F8
Rawlinson Terr PO1 .....**182** A6
Raymond Cl
Holbury SO45 ....**150** D3
Verwood BH31 ....**115** B6
West End SO30 ....**80** F3
Raymond Rd
Portchester PO6 ....**132** E1
Southampton SO15 .....**102** D7
Rayners Dr BH12 ....**203** D6
Rayners Gdns SO16 ......**79** D4
Raynes Rd PO13 ....**180** A4
Rayscliff 21 BH4 ....**204** C2
Reading Room La SO32 ..**106** D8
Readon Cl GU31 ....**41** A4
Readon Ho GU31 ....**41** A4
Rebbeck Rd BH7 ....**206** A6
Recess The SO50 ....**56** B5
Record Rd PO10 ....**136** E1
Recreation Cotts SO51 ....**50** E3
Recreation Rd BH12 .....**203** E6
Rectory Ave
Corfe Mullen BH21 ......**162** D1
Farlington PO6 ....**158** F8
Rectory Cl Gosport PO12 .**181** A3
Stubbington PO14 ......**179** C8
Rectory Ct SO30 ....**105** F7
Rectory Hill SP5 ....**3** D3
Rectory La Breamore SP6 .**46** B1
Meonstoke SO32 ....**61** C5
Rectory Rd
Langstone PO9 ....**159** F8
Poole BH15 ....**202** C6
Red Barn Ave PO16 .....**132** C1
Red Barn Com Prim Sch
PO16 ....**156** C8
Red Barn La PO16 ....**130** E4
Red Deer Ct 2 SO42 ...**215** C6
Red Hill Cres SO16 ....**78** E4
Red Hill Way SO16 ....**78** E4
Red Horn Cl BH16 ....**201** C4
Red House Mews SO14 ...**199** E3
Red House Mus & Gdns*
BH23 ....**207** B6
Red La Corfe Mullen BH21 .**186** A8
Upham SO32 ....**58** B6
West Tytherley SP5 ....**4** A7
Red Leaves SO32 ....**83** E2
Red Lodge SO53 ....**55** B3
Red Lodge Sch SO16 .....**78** E5
Red Oaks Cl BH22 ....**165** B7
Red Oaks Dr SO31 ......**129** B5
Redan Cl BH23 ....**208** F7
Redan The PO12 ....**181** C2
Redbreast Rd BH9 ......**190** A3
Redbreast Rd N BH9 ....**190** A3
Redbridge Com Sch
SO16 ....**101** D8

Redbridge Cswy SO15,
SO16,SO40 ....**101** B8
Redbridge Flyover
SO16 ....**101** C8
Redbridge Gr PO9 ....**135** D3
Redbridge Hill SO16 ....**77** F1
Redbridge La
Nursling SO16 ....**77** D4
Southampton SO16 ......**77** C2
Redbridge Prim Sch
SO15 ....**101** D8
Redbridge Rd SO15 .....**101** D8
Redbridge Sta SO15 ....**101** C8
Redbridge Twrs SO16 ...**101** C8
Redbrook Cotts SP6 .....**94** A7
Redcar Ave PO3 ....**158** A1
Redcliffe Cl BH23 ....**192** C3
Redcote Cl SO18 ....**104** B7
Redcotts La BH21 ....**163** B5
Redcotts Rd BH21 ......**163** B5
Redcourt 2 SO16 ....**78** F4
Redcroft La SO31 ....**126** E8
Redfords The SO40 ......**76** E1
Redhill SO16 ....**78** E4
Redhill Ave BH9 ....**189** F3
Redhill Cl
Bournemouth BH10 .....**189** E3
Southampton SO16 ......**78** E4
Redhill Cres BH9 ....**189** F3
Redhill Ct 1 BH10 ......**190** A4
Redhill Dr BH10 ....**189** E3
Redhill Ho PO1 ....**216** C4
Redhill Park Homes 1
BH10 ....**189** F4
Redhill Rd PO9 ....**113** B1
Redhill Rdbt BH10 ......**189** F4
Redhoave Rd BH17 ......**187** E2
Redhouse Park Gdns
PO12 ....**180** F7
Redlands
Christchurch BH23 .....**208** A7
Poole BH12 ....**203** F5
Redlands Dr SO19 ......**103** F6
Redlands Gr PO4 ....**183** C4
Redlands La
Emsworth PO10 ....**136** F4
Fareham PO14,PO16 ....**155** A8
Redlands Prim Sch
PO16 ....**155** B7
Redlynch CE Prim Sch
SP5 ....**48** A5
Redlynch Cl PO9 ....**136** B4
Redmans View BH31 ....**114** E6
Redmoor Cl SO19 ....**103** F6
Rednal Ho PO5 ....**216** C3
Redoubt Ct PO14 ....**154** F6
Redrise Cl SO45 ....**150** B3
Redsails BH13 ....**214** B3
Redshank Cl BH17 ......**186** F1
Redshank Rd PO8 ....**112** A7
Redvers Cl SO41 ....**197** D2
Redvers Rd BH23 ....**207** E7
Redward Rd SO16 ......**77** C7
Redwing Cl PO4 ....**183** C5
Redwing Gdns SO40 ....**100** C8
Redwing Rd PO8 ....**88** C4
Redwood Cl Hythe SO45 .**125** C3
Lymington SO41 ....**197** D5
Ringwood BH24 ....**141** B7
West End SO30 ....**80** C2
Redwood Ct Bassett SO16 .**79** A6
8 Waterlooville PO7 ....**134** E8
Redwood Dr
Ferndown BH22 ....**165** C8
Portchester PO16 ......**156** B8
Redwood Gdns SO40 ....**100** C7
Redwood Gr PO9 ....**136** A4
Redwood Lodge 4
PO16 ....**131** B2
Redwood Park Sch PO6 ..**158** A6
Redwood Rd BH16 ......**201** A8
Redwood Way SO16 .....**79** A6
Reed Dr SO40 ....**101** F2
Reed's Pl PO12 ....**181** B7
Reeder Cl SP6 ....**69** E1
Reedling Dr PO4 ....**183** C5
Reedmace Cl PO7 ....**135** A6
Reeds La GU33 ....**21** D6
Reeds Mdw GU32 ....**39** D4
Reeds Rd PO12 ....**181** B8
Reeves Cl SO51 ....**50** E3
Reeves Way SO31 ......**104** F1
Regal Cl PO6 ....**157** F8
Regency Cres BH23 ....**206** F8
Regency Ct 1 PO1 .....**182** A4
Regency Gdns PO7 .....**134** D6
Regency Pl
Fareham PO15 ....**130** E1
Ringwood BH24 ....**141** A8
Regency St SO21 ....**31** C4
Regent Ct
Portsmouth PO1 ....**182** D7
17 Southampton SO17 ..**79** A1
13 Winchester SO23 ....**215** E8
Regent Dr BH7 ....**205** F8
Regent Ho SO30 ....**81** C3
Regent Mews GU32 .....**40** D4
Regent Pl PO5 ....**216** A1
Regent Rd SO53 ....**55** D6
Regent St
Portsmouth PO1 ....**182** C7
Southampton SO14 .....**102** F4
Regent Way BH23 ......**207** B6
Regent's Gr 1 SO19 ...**102** B8
Regent's Park Gdns
SO15 ....**102** B7
Regent's Park Rd SO15 .**102** A7

Regents Ct
11 Knowle Village PO17 ..**130** E7
Langstone PO9 ....**159** F8
8 Southampton SO16 ...**102** B8
Regents Gate SO31 .....**128** E5
Regents Park Com Coll
SO16 ....**102** A8
Regents Pl PO12 ....**181** D7
Reginald Rd PO4 ....**183** A3
Reid St BH23 ....**207** A8
Reigate Ho PO11 ....**88** C4
Relay Rd PO7 ....**134** D8
Reldas The 9 PO1 .....**182** A3
Reliant Cl SO53 ....**55** B4
Rempstone Rd BH21 ...**187** D8
Renault Dr BH18 ....**187** A1
Renda Rd SO45 ....**150** C4
Renny Rd PO1 ....**182** F5
Renouf Cl SO41 ....**197** C3
Renown Cl SO53 ....**55** B5
Renown Gdns PO8 ......**111** F5
Renown Ho 12 PO12 ...**181** E5
Repton Cl PO12 ....**180** E4
Repton Gdns SO30 .....**81** D2
Reservoir La
Hedge End SO30 ....**105** A6
Petersfield GU32 ....**40** F6
Resolution Ho 14 PO12 .**181** C5
Rest-A-Wyle Ave PO11 ..**185** A5
Restharrow BH1 ....**205** A4
Restynge Ho BH31 .....**114** F7
Retreat Rd BH21 ....**163** D4
Retreat The
Eastleigh SO50 ....**56** B4
Portsmouth PO5 ....**216** B1
Totton SO40 ....**101** A8
Revenge Cl PO4 ....**183** C6
Revenge Ho 15 PO12 ...**181** C5
Rewlands Dr SO22 ......**1** C4
Rex Est SO53 ....**55** D5
Reynard Ct BH15 ....**202** F3
Reynolds Ct SO51 ....**53** A6
Reynolds Dale SO40 ....**100** D5
Reynolds Rd
Fair Oak SO50 ....**57** D1
Gosport PO12 ....**181** C3
Southampton SO15 .....**102** C8
Rhinefield Cl
Bishopstoke SO50 ......**56** F2
Brockenhurst SO42 .....**145** E1
Havant PO9 ....**135** C4
Rhinefield Dr
Brockenhurst SO42 .....**145** C2
New Milton BH25 ....**170** E2
Rhiners Cl SO41 ....**172** B2
Rhyme Hall Mews SO45 .**151** B3
Rhys Ct PO4 ....**183** A4
Ribble Cl
Broadstone BH18 ....**187** A2
Chandler's Ford SO53 ...**55** D5
Ribble Ct SO16 ....**77** E1
Ribbonwood Hts BH14 ..**203** B4
Ricardo Cres SO31 .....**208** A6
Ricardo Way SO41 ......**197** D7
Rice Gdns BH16 ....**201** D4
Rice Terr BH16 ....**201** D4
Richard Cl BH16 ....**201** B8
Richard Gr PO12 ....**156** A1
Richard Moss Ho 9
SO23 ....**215** E6
Richard Taunton Pl SO17 .**79** A2
Richards Cl
Blackfield SO45 ....**150** F2
Locks Heath SO31 ......**129** B3
Richards Ct 6 SO15 ....**78** B1
Riches Mews 8 PO16 ...**131** A1
Richlans Rd SO30 ......**105** D6
Richmond Cl
Chandler's Ford SO53 ...**30** C1
South Hayling PO11 .....**184** E4
Totton SO40 ....**76** B1
Richmond Ct
12 Milford on S SO41 ....**211** C4
4 New Milton BH25 .....**195** A3
Richmond Dr PO11 .....**184** E4
Richmond Gdns
Bournemouth BH1 ......**204** F3
Southampton SO17 ......**79** B1
Waterlooville PO7 ......**134** C5
Richmond Hall 6 SO17 ..**79** C2
Richmond Hill BH2 .....**204** F3
Richmond Hill Dr BH2 ..**204** F3
Richmond Ho
1 Southampton SO15 ...**102** C6
5 Winchester SO22 ....**215** D6
Richmond La SO51 .....**28** A1
Richmond Park Ave
BH8 ....**205** A5
Richmond Park Cres
BH8 ....**205** A5
Richmond Park Rd BH8 ..**205** C7
Richmond Pk SO21 .....**31** D4
Richmond Pl
Portsmouth,Portsea PO1 ..**182** B5
Portsmouth,Southsea PO5 .**182** C2
Richmond Rd
Gosport PO12 ....**181** A5
Lee-on-t-S PO13 ....**179** D3
Poole BH14 ....**203** C4
Portsmouth PO5 ....**182** D2
Southampton SO15 .....**102** C6
Wimborne Minst SO32 ..**163** D4

Richmond Rise
Bournemouth BH8 ......**205** D6
Portchester PO16 ......**132** C1
Richmond St SO14 ......**103** B3
Richmond Terr 12 PO5 ..**182** C2
Richmond Wood Rd
SO9 ....**205** C7
Richville Rd SO16 ......**102** A8
Ridding Cl SO15 ....**78** C1
Riders Inf Sch PO9 .....**135** E5
Riders Jun Sch PO9 ....**135** E5
Riders La PO9 ....**135** E4
Ridge Cl PO8 ....**88** C4
Ridge Common La GU32 ..**40** C6
Ridge La Curbridge SO30 .**106** D3
Romsey SO51 ....**76** C8
Ridge The SP5 ....**47** D5
Ridge Top La
Froxfield Green SO32 ....**39** E6
Froxfield Green GU32 ...**40** B8
Ridgefield Gdns BH23 ..**208** D8
Ridgemede Jun Sch
SO32 ....**83** D8
Ridgemount Ave BH8 ...**78** F5
Ridgemount Gdns BH15 .**201** E3
Ridgemount La SO16 ....**78** F5
Ridgeway
Broadstone BH18 ....**187** B4
Corfe Mullen BH21 .....**186** D8
Ferndown BH22 ....**189** E8
Winchester SO22 ....**215** A3
Ridgeway Cl
Chandler's Ford SO53 ...**55** E5
Fair Oak SO50 ....**57** C3
Portchester PO6 ....**132** F1
Ridgeway House Sch
SO19 ....**103** F5
Ridgeway La SO41 ......**197** D2
Ridgeway The PO16 ....**131** E1
Ridgeway Wlk SO53 ....**55** E5
Ridgewood Cl SO45 ....**125** C4
Ridgway PO9 ....**135** D3
Ridings The Fair Oak SO50 .**57** A2
Liss GU33 ....**21** B4
Portsmouth PO2 ....**157** F3
Waltham Chase SO32 ....**83** E4
Ridley Cl SO45 ....**150** C4
Ridley Rd BH9 ....**204** F8
Ridout Cl BH10 ....**189** B1
Rigby Rd SO17 ....**103** B8
Riggs Gdns BH11 ......**188** F2
Rigler Rd BH15 ....**202** A2
Rimbury Way BH23 ....**207** A8
Rimington Gdns 1 SO51 .**28** B1
Rimington Rd PO8 .....**111** E3
Ring The SO16 ....**78** E7
Ringbury SO41 ....**197** D6
Ringlet Way 6 SO23 ...**11** C8
Ringwood CE Inf Sch
BH24 ....**141** A7
Ringwood Dr SO52 .....**53** E4
Ringwood Ho PO9 ......**135** F5
Ringwood Jun Sch
BH24 ....**141** A6
Ringwood Rd
Alderholt SP6 ....**93** A4
Bournemouth BH11 .....**188** E4
Bransgore BH23 ....**193** D5
Burley Street BH24 .....**142** E5
Ferndown BH22 ....**165** C4
Fordingbridge SP6 ......**94** A4
Fordingbridge SP6 ......**94** C4
Poole BH12 ....**203** B2
Portsmouth PO4 ....**183** B3
Ringwood BH24 ....**140** C6
Sopley BH23 ....**192** A7
St Leonards BH24 ......**124** C2
Three Legged Cross BH21 .**139** B7
Totton SO40 ....**100** C7
Verwood BH31 ....**115** F5
Walkford BH23 ....**194** B1
West Moors BH22 ......**166** A8
Ringwood Rd Nature Reserve
BH11 ....**188** E5
Ringwood Road Ret Pk
BH11 ....**188** E3
Ringwood Sch BH24 ....**141** A7
Ringwood Terr SO14 ...**103** B3
Ringwood Trad Est
BH24 ....**141** A6
Ringwood Waldorf Sch
BH24 ....**140** D6
Ripley Cl BH23 ....**165** F7
Ripley Gr PO3 ....**183** A8
Ripon Gdns BH12 ......**212** D1
Ripon Gdns 8 PO7 .....**112** B1
Ripon Rd BH9 ....**190** A1
Ripplewood SO40 ......**102** A1
Ripstone Gdns SO17 ....**79** B3
Rise The
Brockenhurst SO42 .....**145** F1
Waterlooville PO7 ......**134** D2
Ritchie Cl PO11 ....**185** A3
Ritchie Ct SO18 ....**104** B4
Ritchie Pl BH22 ....**138** D4
Ritchie Rd BH11 ....**189** B4
Rival Moor Rd GU31 ....**41** C2
River Cl SO41 ....**163** C6
River Ct SO41 ....**197** F4
River Gdns SO41 ....**211** E4
River La SO41 ....**128** A2
River La PO15 ....**130** B6
River Mews SO50 ....**56** D3
River Pk BH6 ....**206** G6
River Rd SP6 ....**70** D2
River St PO10 ....**137** B4
River View Ho SO19 ....**103** D3
River View Rd SO18 ....**79** D2

River Way
Christchurch BH23 .....**191** D2
Havant PO9 ....**136** A3
River Wlk SO18 ....**79** E3
River's St PO5 ....**216** C2
Riverbourne Ct SO18 ...**103** D8
Riverdale Ave PO7 .....**135** E3
Riverdale Cl SP6 ....**69** F2
Riverdale Cotts PO16 ...**131** D3
Riverdale La BH23 ......**207** A6
Riverdene Pl SO18 .....**103** D8
Riverhead Cl PO4 ......**183** B5
Riverland Ct 4 BH23 ...**207** A6
Riverlea Rd BH23 ......**207** A6
Rivermead Cl SO51 .....**52** D7
Rivermead Ct PO10 ....**137** A3
Rivermead Gdns BH23 ..**207** A6
Riverpark Ct SO18 .....**79** D1
Rivers Reach SO41 .....**197** F3
Riversdale 8 BH21 .....**163** C4
Riversdale Cl SO19 .....**126** E8
Riversdale Gdns PO9 ...**135** F2
Riversdale Rd BH6 ......**207** A4
Riverside
Bishopstoke SO50 ......**56** D3
6 Bournemouth BH10 ..**189** F4
Ringwood BH24 ....**140** F6
Riverside Ave
Bournemouth BH7 ......**191** C1
Fareham PO16 ....**131** D3
Riverside Bsns Pk SO41 .**197** F4
Riverside Cl Bartley SO40 ..**99** C6
Liss GU33 ....**20** F4
Riverside Cotts SO21 ...**31** F5
Riverside Ct
7 Bournemouth BH4 ...**204** D4
Southampton,Bitterne
SO18 ....**103** D8
Southampton,Bitterne Manor
SO18 ....**103** C7
West Moors BH22 ......**138** D3
Riverside Gdns SO51 ....**52** E6
Riverside Ho 4 SO23 ...**215** F6
Riverside La BH6 ....**206** F5
Riverside Mews PO17 ...**108** A3
Riverside Pk BH23 ......**207** A5
Riverside Pk Cvn & Campsite
SO31 ....**128** A5
Riverside Pl SP6 ....**69** F1
Riverside Rd
Bournemouth BH6 ......**206** F5
West Moors BH22 ......**139** C2
Riverside Terr 9 PO10 ..**137** A3
Riverslea Mews BH23 ...**207** D6
Riversmeet Ct BH23 ....**207** A5
Riverview SO40 ....**100** F5
Riverview Terr SO31 ...**128** D8
Riviera 11 BH1 ....**205** B3
Riviera Ct
Bournemouth **204** D3
6 Poole BH13 ....**214** F7
RN Submarine Mus & HMS
Alliance* PO12 ....**181** E4
RNLI Mus* BH15 ....**202** C2
Road View PO2 ....**182** C8
Roads Hill PO4 ....**88** A1
Robann Cvn Pk SO31 ...**129** D3
Robere Ho SO19 ....**103** D3
Robert Cecil Ave SO18 ..**79** F4
Robert Mack Ct 10 PO1 .**182** A5
Robert Whitworth Dr
SO51 ....**27** F1
Roberts Cl Everton SO41 .**196** E1
Wickham PO17 ....**108** A4
Roberts La BH17 ....**201** F7
Roberts Rd
Bournemouth BH7 ......**206** A6
Gosport PO12 ....**180** F6
Hythe SO45 ....**125** F4
Poole BH17 ....**187** B1
Southampton SO15 .....**102** C5
Totton SO40 ....**100** F4
Robertshaw Ho SO43 ...**121** F6
Robin Cres BH25 ......**194** D5
Robin Ct SO51 ....**102** F8
Robin Gdns
Christchurch BH23 .....**207** A8
Totton SO40 ....**100** C8
Waterlooville PO8 ......**111** F4
Robin Sq SO50 ....**55** C2
Robina Cl PO7 ....**135** A7
Robina Gn SO16 ....**78** F5
Robins Cl PO14 ....**179** C8
Robins Ct 1 BH21 ......**163** C4
Robins Mdw PO14 .....**129** C1
Robins Way BH23 ......**208** B5
Robinson Ct
Lee-on-t-S PO13 ....**179** E2
Portchester PO16 ......**132** C1
Robinson Rd PO14 .....**179** B6
Robinson Way PO3 .....**158** C3
Robinswood Dr BH22 ...**165** D7
Robsall Cl BH12 ....**203** E7
Robville Ct 3 BH7 .....**206** B6
Rochester Cl PO12 .....**181** C4
Rochester Ct 11 PO13 ..**180** D5
Rochester Rd
Bournemouth BH11 .....**189** B4
Portsmouth PO4 ....**182** F3
Rochester St SO14 .....**103** C5
Rochford Rd PO6 ......**157** D8
Rockall Cl SO16 ....**77** E5
Rockbourne Cl PO9 ....**135** C4
Rockbourne Gdns BH25 .**209** D8
Rockbourne La SP6 ....**68** D2

Rockbourne Rd SO22 ... 1 D4
Rockbourne Roman Villa* SP6 ... 68 F7
Rockery Cl SO45 ... 125 C4
Rockford Cl BH6 ... 206 F3
Rockford Ho SO50 ... 57 B1
Rockingham Way PO16 ... 156 B8
Rockleigh Dr SO40 ... 100 D5
Rockleigh Rd SO16 ... 78 D3
Rockley Mews BH15 ... 201 E2
Rockley Pk Cvn Est BH15,BH16 ... 201 B3
Rockley Rd BH15 ... 201 E1
Rockpit Cotts GU33 ... 21 B4
Rockram Cl SO40 ... 99 B7
Rockram Gdns SO45 ... 125 C4
Rockrose Way PO6 ... 133 A2
Rockstone Ct 2 SO14 ... 103 A6
Rockstone La SO14 ... 103 A6
Rockstone Pl SO15 ... 102 F6
Rockville Dr PO7 ... 134 E7
Rodbard Ho SO31 ... 104 F1
Rodbourne Cl SO41 ... 211 D8
Rodfield La SO21,SO24 ... 13 C5
Rodlease La SO41 ... 173 E2
Rodney Cl Gosport PO13 ... 180 D6
Poole BH12 ... 204 A8
Rodney Ct
Christchurch BH23 ... 208 A6
7 Poole BH15 ... 202 C1
Southampton SO19 ... 104 C4
Rodney Dr BH23 ... 207 F6
Rodney Ho 10 PO12 ... 181 D5
Rodney Rd PO4 ... 183 A5
Rodney Way PO8 ... 112 B6
Rodway BH21 ... 163 C4
Rodwell Cl BH10 ... 189 C6
Roebuck Ave PO15 ... 130 D5
Roebuck Cl Cosham PO6 ... 157 F7
New Milton BH25 ... 195 B3
Roebuck Dr PO12 ... 181 C8
Roeshot Cres BH23 ... 193 E1
Roeshot Hill BH23 ... 193 C2
Roewood Cl SO45 ... 150 C3
Roewood Rd SO45 ... 150 C3
Rogate Gdns PO16 ... 132 C1
Rogate Ho 1 PO1 ... 216 C4
Roger Penny Way
Brook SO43 ... 73 C2
Fordingbridge,Bramshaw, SP5 ... 72 D6
Fordingbridge,Godshill SP6 ... 71 B5
Rogers Cl
Bishopstoke SO50 ... 56 E4
Gosport PO12 ... 181 B7
Rogers Ho PO13 ... 179 F2
Rogers Mead PO11 ... 160 A3
Rogers Rd SO50 ... 56 E4
Roi-mar Home Pk BH8 ... 190 D4
Roker Way SO50 ... 57 B1
Roland Cl PO8 ... 112 B6
Rollesbrook Gdns SO15 ... 102 E6
Rollestone Rd SO45 ... 150 C2
Rolls Dr BH6 ... 207 B3
Roman Cl SO53 ... 55 E7
Roman Ct PO10 ... 137 D1
Roman Dr SO16 ... 78 E7
Roman Gdns SO45 ... 125 D1
Roman Gn PO7 ... 110 E4
Roman Gr PO16 ... 156 D6
Roman Ho SO18 ... 103 C7
Roman Hts BH21 ... 186 E8
Roman Mdw SP5 ... 46 F7
Roman Quay SP6 ... 69 F1
Roman Rd Chilworth SO16 ... 78 E8
Corfe Mullen BH18 ... 186 E5
Dibden Purlieu SO45 ... 149 E8
Dibden Purlieu,Applemore SO45 ... 125 C2
Hardley SO45 ... 150 B6
Havant PO10 ... 136 C1
Twyford SO21 ... 32 A5
Roman Row SO32 ... 83 D8
Roman Way
Dibden Purlieu SO45 ... 125 D1
Havant PO9 ... 135 C2
Pamphill BH21 ... 162 C5
Romans' Rd SO23 ... 215 D4
Romford Rd SO31 ... 152 D10
Romill Cl SO18 ... 80 B3
Romney Cl BH10 ... 189 E3
Romney Ct 51 BH4 ... 204 C3
Romney Rd BH10 ... 189 E4
Romsey Abbey* SO51 ... 52 E7
Romsey Abbey CE Prim Sch SO51 ... 52 E7
Romsey Ave
Portchester PO16 ... 156 A8
Portsmouth PO3 ... 183 B6
Romsey Cl SO50 ... 56 A3
Romsey Ct SO15 ... 102 D6
Romsey Hospl SO51 ... 53 A7
Romsey Ind Est SO51 ... 52 F8
Romsey Inf Sch SO51 ... 52 F7
Romsey Jun Sch SO51 ... 53 A8
Romsey Lodge 8 SO16 ... 78 A1
Romsey Rd Awbridge SO51 ... 26 E4
Cadnam SO40,SO51 ... 75 C3
Compton SO20 ... 6 D8
Eastleigh SO50 ... 56 A3
Horndean PO8 ... 88 C2
Lyndhurst SO43 ... 121 F5
Ower SO51 ... 75 F6
Southampton SO16 ... 78 A1
West Wellow SO51 ... 51 A3
Whiteparish SP5 ... 24 F3
Winchester SO22 ... 215 A4
Romsey Sch The SO51 ... 52 E8
Romsey Sta SO51 ... 52 F8
Romyns Ct PO14 ... 130 F1
Ronald Bowker Ct 1 SO22 ... 215 C6
Ronald Pugh Ct SO18 ... 79 E4
Rook Hill Rd BH23 ... 208 B6
Rookcliff 13 SO41 ... 211 C4
Rookcliff Way SO41 ... 211 C4
Rooke Ho 17 PO1 ... 182 A5
Rookery Ave PO15,SO31 ... 129 B7
Rookery Grange SO31 ... 129 B7
Rookery La SP6 ... 45 F1
Rookery The
Lumley PO10 ... 137 A1
West Dean SP5 ... 3 D3
Rookes Cl PO8 ... 112 B6
Rookes La SO41 ... 197 E2
Rookes Mews GU31 ... 41 A4
Rookesbury Park Sch PO17 ... 108 D4
Rookesbury Pk Cvn Club Site PO17 ... 108 D5
Rookley SO31 ... 127 C7
Rooks Down Rd SO22 ... 215 B3
Rooksbridge SO45 ... 125 C4
Rooksbury Croft PO9 ... 136 A5
Rooksway Gr PO16 ... 155 F8
Rookwood 3 SO41 ... 211 C4
Rookwood Cl SO50 ... 56 B6
Rookwood Gdns SP6 ... 69 D1
Rookwood View PO7 ... 110 F5
Roosevelt Cres BH11 ... 189 B6
Rope Hill SO41 ... 173 D1
Rope Wlk SO31 ... 128 A2
Rope Wlk The PO16 ... 155 B8
Ropers La BH16 ... 201 D7
Ropewalk Ho 7 SO23 ... 215 E6
Ropley Cl SO19 ... 127 A8
Ropley Rd
Bournemouth BH7 ... 206 C7
25 Havant PO9 ... 136 B5
Rosamund Ave BH21 ... 163 E1
Roscrea Cl BH6 ... 207 B4
Roscrea Dr BH6 ... 207 B4
Rose Bowl The* SO30 ... 80 F1
Rose Cl Hedge End SO30 ... 105 C8
Hythe SO45 ... 126 A2
Rose Cott PO8 ... 112 D7
Rose Cres BH15 ... 202 F6
Rose Ct BH15 ... 202 E3
Rose Farm Cl BH22 ... 165 B3
Rose Gdn The BH23 ... 191 D1
Rose Gdns BH9 ... 190 A3
Rose Hill PO8 ... 112 A5
Rose Rd
Southampton SO14 ... 103 A8
Totton SO40 ... 101 A6
Rosebank Cl SO16 ... 77 E5
Rosebank Lodge SO16 ... 77 E5
Rosebay Cl SO50 ... 81 C6
Rosebay Ct 2 PO7 ... 134 F5
Rosebery Ave
Cosham PO6 ... 158 A7
Hythe SO45 ... 126 A2
Rosebery Cl BH31 ... 115 C5
Rosebery Cres SO50 ... 56 B6
Rosebery Rd BH5 ... 206 A5
Rosebrook Ct 4 SO18 ... 103 E7
Rosebud Ave 1 BH9 ... 190 A2
Rosecrae Cl BH25 ... 194 F4
Rosedale Ave SO51 ... 53 A7
Rosedale Cl
3 Christchurch BH23 ... 207 E6
Titchfield PO14 ... 153 F8
Rosehill Cl BH23 ... 169 B1
Rosehill Dr BH23 ... 169 B1
Roseship Cl SO50 ... 57 A1
Roselands
Waterlooville PO8 ... 112 A5
West End SO30 ... 104 D8
Roselands Cl SO50 ... 57 B3
Roselands Gdns SO17 ... 79 A2
Roseleigh Dr SO40 ... 100 E6
Rosemary Ct 8 BH23 ... 209 B7
Rosemary Gdns
Hedge End SO30 ... 105 C5
Poole BH12 ... 203 B7
Whiteley PO15 ... 129 D8
Rosemary La 29 PO1 ... 182 A5
Rosemary Rd BH12 ... 203 C7
Rosemary Way PO8 ... 112 B5
Rosemary Wlk 3 PO13 ... 179 F3
Rosemoor Gr SO53 ... 30 B1
Rosemount Rd BH4 ... 204 B2
Rosendale Rd SO53 ... 55 D4
Rosery The PO12 ... 181 B2
Rosetta Rd PO4 ... 183 B4
Rosewall Rd SO16 ... 77 F3
Rosewarne Ct 9 SO23 ... 215 E7
Rosewood PO13 ... 155 E1
Rosewood Gdns
Clanfield PO8 ... 88 C5
Marchwood SO40 ... 102 A1
New Milton BH25 ... 194 F4
Rosida Gdns SO15 ... 102 E6
Rosina Cl PO7 ... 135 B8
Roslin Gdns BH3 ... 204 D7
Roslin Rd BH3 ... 204 E7
Roslin Rd S BH3 ... 204 E7
Roslyn Ho PO5 ... 216 B1
Rosoman Ct SO19 ... 103 F4
Rosoman Ho SO19 ... 103 F4
Rosoman Rd SO19 ... 103 F4
Ross Gdns
Bournemouth BH11 ... 188 C5
Southampton SO16 ... 78 A2
Ross Glades BH3 ... 204 E6
Ross Mews SO31 ... 127 A6
Ross Rd BH24 ... 117 C1
Ross Way PO13 ... 179 F4
Rossan Ave SO31 ... 152 D9
Rossington Ave SO18 ... 103 F8
Rossington Way SO18 ... 103 F7
Rossiters La SO40 ... 99 E5
Rossiters Quay BH23 ... 207 C6
Rossley Cl BH23 ... 193 E2
Rosslyn Cl SO52 ... 54 A4
Rossmore Com Coll BH12 ... 203 D8
Rossmore Par BH12 ... 203 B8
Rossmore Rd BH12 ... 203 D7
Rostrevor La 9 PO4 ... 182 E1
Rostrevor Mans 8 PO4 ... 182 E1
Rostron Cl SO18 ... 80 A3
Rosyth Rd SO18 ... 103 F7
Rotary Cl BH21 ... 163 F7
Rotary Ct SO31 ... 127 B6
Rotary Ho SO15 ... 102 D8
Rothbury Cl
Southampton SO19 ... 104 A4
Totton SO40 ... 76 D1
Rothbury Pk BH25 ... 195 B2
Rother Cl Petersfield GU31 ... 41 C4
West End SO18 ... 80 B1
Rother Dale SO19 ... 104 E3
Rother Ho GU33 ... 20 F3
Rotherbank Farm La GU33 ... 21 A6
Rothercombe La GU32 ... 40 A4
Rotherfield Rd
Bournemouth BH5 ... 206 B3
Walkford BH23 ... 194 A1
Rotherley GU32 ... 40 E4
Rotherwick Cl PO9 ... 136 B5
Rothesay Dr BH23 ... 208 E7
Rothesay Rd
Bournemouth BH4 ... 204 C5
Gosport PO12 ... 181 A8
Rothsbury Dr SO53 ... 55 B6
Rothschild Cl SO19 ... 103 E1
Rothville Pl SO53 ... 30 B2
Rothwell Cl 9 PO6 ... 133 A1
Rotterdam Dr BH23 ... 207 D7
Rotterdam Twrs SO19 ... 126 F8
Roughdown La SO45 ... 150 C1
Roumelia La BH1,BH5 ... 205 E4
Round Hill SP6 ... 69 F1
Roundabouts The GU33 ... 21 A5
Roundcopse SO45 ... 125 C3
Roundhaye Gdns BH11 ... 188 F6
Roundhaye Rd BH11 ... 188 F6
Roundhill Cl SO18 ... 80 A1
Roundhill Cross SP6 ... 45 E1
Roundhouse Ct
Lymington SO41 ... 197 D3
South Hayling PO11 ... 185 B2
Roundhouse Dr SO40 ... 100 C6
Roundhouse Mdw PO10 ... 161 A7
Roundhuts Rise 3 SO23 ... 11 C8
Roundway PO7 ... 134 F8
Roundways BH11 ... 188 F3
Routs Way SO16 ... 77 F7
Row The SP5 ... 47 D7
Row Wood La PO13 ... 155 B1
Rowallan Ave PO13 ... 180 C8
Rowan Ave PO8 ... 112 B2
Rowan Cl Bursledon SO31 ... 127 F8
Christchurch BH23 ... 208 D8
Lee-on-t-S PO13 ... 179 F2
Romsey SO51 ... 53 C6
Southampton SO16 ... 78 A3
St Leonards BH24 ... 139 D4
Swanmore SO32 ... 84 B4
Sway SO41 ... 172 B1
Totton SO40 ... 100 D6
Rowan Ct
Portsmouth PO4 ... 182 F4
Southampton SO19 ... 103 F3
Rowan Dr
Broadstone BH17 ... 186 E1
Christchurch BH23 ... 208 D8
Verwood BH31 ... 115 B4
Rowan Gdns SO30 ... 105 D6
Rowan Rd PO9 ... 136 C3
Rowan Tree Cl GU33 ... 21 A4
Rowan Way PO14 ... 154 C7
Rowans Pk SO41 ... 197 D3
Rowans The SO40 ... 101 E1
Rowbarrow Cl BH17 ... 187 E2
Rowborough Rd SO18 ... 103 F8
Rowbury Rd PO9 ... 135 D6
Rowden Cl SO51 ... 50 E2
Rowe Asheway SO31 ... 128 F3
Rowe Gdns 6 BH12 ... 203 F7
Rowena Ct PO5 ... 216 C2
Rowena Rd BH6 ... 206 F5
Rowes La SO41 ... 199 B7
Rowhay La SO32 ... 58 C5
Rowhill Dr SO45 ... 125 C3
Rowin Cl PO11 ... 185 D2
Rowland Ave BH15 ... 202 E6
Rowland Rd
Fareham PO15 ... 130 F2
Portchester PO6 ... 132 E1
Rowlands Ave PO7 ... 111 E1
Rowlands Castle Rd
Blendworth PO8 ... 112 E6
Blendworth PO8 ... 112 F7
Rowlands Castle St John's CE Prim Sch PO9 ... 136 B8
Rowlands Castle Sta PO9 ... 113 C2
Rowlands Cl SO53 ... 55 A4
Rowlands Hill BH21 ... 163 D6
Rowlands Wlk 2 SO18 ... 80 A2
Rowley Cl SO30 ... 105 F8
Rowley Dr SO30 ... 105 F8
Rowlings Rd SO22 ... 1 D3
Rowner Cl PO13 ... 155 C1
Rowner Inf Schs PO13 ... 155 D1
Rowner Jun Sch PO13 ... 155 D1
Rowner La PO13 ... 155 C1
Rowner Rd PO13 ... 180 D8
Rownhams Cl SO16 ... 77 E6
Rownhams Ct SO16 ... 77 F3
Rownhams La
North Baddesley SO52 ... 53 F5
Rownhams SO16 ... 77 F7
Rownhams,Toot Hill SO16, SO52 ... 53 F1
Rownhams Pk SO16 ... 77 E8
Rownhams Rd
Bournemouth BH8 ... 190 D3
Havant PO9 ... 135 D5
North Baddesley SO52 ... 54 A4
Southampton SO16 ... 77 F3
Rownhams Rd N SO16 ... 77 F5
Rownhams St John's CE Prim Sch SO16 ... 77 E6
Rownhams Way SO16 ... 77 E6
Rowse Cl SO51 ... 27 F1
Roxan Ct 5 SO15 ... 102 F7
Roxborough 47 BH4 ... 204 C3
Roxburgh Ho SO31 ... 129 A3
Roy's La SO32 ... 109 D8
Royal Arc 5 BH1 ... 205 E4
Royal Armouries Mus of Artillery* PO17 ... 132 B3
Royal Bournemouth Gen Hospl The BH7 ... 191 B1
Royal Crescent Rd 10 SO14 ... 103 B3
Royal Ct
Chandler's Ford SO53 ... 55 C6
Southampton SO17 ... 79 C2
Royal Gate PO4 ... 183 B2
Royal Gdns
Rowlands Castle PO9 ... 113 A1
Southampton SO15 ... 101 F7
Royal Greenjackets Mus* SO23 ... 215 D5
Royal Hampshire Cty Hospl SO22 ... 215 C5
Royal Hampshire Regiment Mus* SO23 ... 215 D5
Royal Hospl Haslar PO12 ... 181 D3
Royal London Pk SO30 ... 105 B8
Royal Marines Mus* PO4 ... 183 B2
Royal Mews 15 PO5 ... 182 D2
Royal Naval Cotts PO17 ... 132 F6
Royal Naval Mus* PO1 ... 181 F7
Royal Oak Rd BH10 ... 189 C5
Royal South Hants Hospl SO14 ... 103 A6
Royal Sovereign Ave PO14 ... 155 A5
Royal The PO11 ... 184 E2
Royal Victoria Ctry Pk* SO31 ... 127 C4
Royal Victoria Mews BH4 ... 204 D3
Royal Way PO7 ... 135 A7
Royal Winchester Mews SO22 ... 215 A5
Royden La SO41 ... 173 D3
Roydon Cl SO22 ... 215 C3
Royster Cl BH17 ... 187 C1
Royston Ave SO50 ... 56 A5
Royston Cl SO17 ... 79 B2
Royston Ct SO40 ... 76 E1
Royston Dr BH21 ... 163 D5
Royston Pl BH25 ... 210 B8
Rozel Ct SO16 ... 77 E3
Rozel Manor BH13 ... 204 B2
Rozelle Cl SO22 ... 1 A5
Rozelle Rd BH14 ... 203 C4
Ruben Dr BH15 ... 201 D2
Rubens Cl BH25 ... 195 B3
Ruby Cl SO40 ... 76 B1
Ruby Ct 1 PO7 ... 134 E8
Ruby Rd SO19 ... 104 A6
Rudd La SO51 ... 27 E7
Rudgwick Cl PO16 ... 156 B8
Rudmore Ct 3 PO2 ... 157 C1
Rudmore Rd PO2 ... 182 C8
Rudmore Sq PO2 ... 182 C8
Rudolph Ct PO7 ... 134 C5
Ruffield Cl SO22 ... 215 A8
Rufford Cl SO50 ... 56 A6
Rufford Gdns BH6 ... 206 E5
Rufus Cl
Chandler's Ford SO53 ... 55 E8
Rownhams SO16 ... 77 D6
Rufus Ct SO43 ... 122 A5
Rufus Gdns SO40 ... 100 C7
Rufus Stone* SO43 ... 98 A6
Rugby Rd Poole BH17 ... 187 A1
Portsmouth PO5 ... 216 D2
Rumbridge Ct SO40 ... 101 A6
Rumbridge Gdns SO40 ... 101 A7
Rumbridge St SO40 ... 101 A6
Runnymede
Fareham PO15 ... 130 D4
West End SO30 ... 80 D1
Runnymede Ave BH11 ... 188 E6
Runton Rd BH12 ... 203 F5
Runway The BH23 ... 208 B7
Rushall La BH21 ... 186 A5
Rushcombe Fst Sch BH21 ... 186 D5
Rushcombe Way BH21 ... 186 E6
Rushes Ct GU32 ... 40 E4
Rushes Farm GU32 ... 40 E4
Rushes Rd GU32 ... 40 E4
Rushes The SO40 ... 101 F2
Rushfield Rd GU33 ... 20 F3
Rushford Warren BH23 ... 207 F5
Rushin Ho PO16 ... 156 D8
Rushington Ave SO40 ... 100 F6
Rushington Bsns Pk SO40 ... 100 E5
Rushington La SO40 ... 100 E6
Rushmere Gate PO7 ... 86 C2
Rushmere La PO7 ... 110 E8
Rushmere Rd BH6 ... 206 D7
Rushmere Wlk PO9 ... 135 D6
Rushpole Ct SO45 ... 125 C3
Rushton Cres BH3 ... 204 F6
Ruskin Ave BH9 ... 190 B3
Ruskin Rd Eastleigh SO50 ... 56 B5
Portsmouth PO4 ... 183 A4
Ruskin Way PO8 ... 111 F4
Rusland Cl SO53 ... 55 B7
Russel Rd BH10 ... 189 C6
Russell Bldgs PO16 ... 156 C7
Russell Churcher Ct PO12 ... 180 F7
Russell Cl PO13 ... 179 F3
Russell Cotes Art Gall & Mus* BH1 ... 205 A2
Russell Cotes Rd BH1 ... 205 A2
Russell Ct 2 BH25 ... 195 A3
Russell Dr
Christchurch BH23 ... 207 D6
Dunbridge SO51 ... 5 D1
Russell Gdns
Hamworthy BH16 ... 201 C4
St Leonards BH24 ... 140 B5
Russell Pl Fareham PO16 ... 131 A1
Southampton SO17 ... 79 B1
Russell Rd Havant PO9 ... 135 F2
Lee-on-t-S PO13 ... 179 F3
Winchester SO23 ... 215 E8
Russell St Gosport PO12 ... 181 A7
11 Southampton SO14 ... 103 A3
Russell Way GU31 ... 41 A2
Russet Cl
Ferndown BH22 ... 165 D6
3 Lymington SO41 ... 197 F2
Russet Gdns PO10 ... 161 B8
Russet Ho SO30 ... 105 A6
Russett Cl SO32 ... 84 B4
Rustan Cl Fair Oak SO50 ... 57 D2
Hedge End SO30 ... 105 B6
Rustington Ho 3 PO1 ... 216 B3
Rustlings Mews PO8 ... 112 B7
Rutland Ct SO18 ... 104 A7
Rutland Gdns SO31 ... 105 A1
Rutland Manor 10 BH13 ... 204 A4
Rutland Rd
Bournemouth BH9 ... 205 B8
Christchurch BH23 ... 191 F1
Rutland Way SO18 ... 80 A1
Ruxley Cl SO45 ... 150 C4
Ryall Rd BH17 ... 187 D1
Ryan Cl BH22 ... 165 C7
Ryan Gdns
Bournemouth BH11 ... 189 B6
Ferndown BH22 ... 165 C7
Rydal Cl
Christchurch BH23 ... 191 D4
9 Portsmouth PO6 ... 133 B1
Rydal Ho
2 Bournemouth BH4 ... 204 C2
11 Portsmouth PO6 ... 133 B1
Rydal Mews BH21 ... 163 D5
Rydal Rd PO12 ... 181 A9
Ryde Pl PO13 ... 180 A4
Ryde Terr SO14 ... 103 B3
Rye Cl SO53 ... 54 F6
Rye Dale SO40 ... 100 C3
Rye Paddock La SO45 ... 151 B4
Ryecroft Havant PO9 ... 136 B1
Titchfield PO14 ... 129 C2
Ryecroft Ave BH11 ... 188 E5
Ryedown La SO51 ... 51 E4
Ryefield Cl GU31 ... 41 C3
Rylandes Ct SO16 ... 77 F3

S

Sabre Rd PO10 ... 161 A3
Sackville St PO5 ... 216 B2
Saddle Cl BH21 ... 164 C6
Saddlers Cl
Eastleigh SO50 ... 56 A6
2 Fordingbridge SP6 ... 69 F1
Sadlers La SO45 ... 126 A1
Sadlers Wlk 9 PO10 ... 161 A8
Saffron Ct
Bournemouth BH11 ... 188 D3
Locks Heath SO31 ... 128 E2
Saffron Dr BH23 ... 208 B8
Saffron Way
Bournemouth BH11 ... 188 D3
Whiteley PO15 ... 129 D8
Sage Cl PO7 ... 135 A6
Sages La GU34 ... 17 D5
Sailor's La SO32 ... 35 E1
Sailors La SO32 ... 60 C8
Sainsbury Lodge PO1 ... 216 D3
Saints Cl BH21 ... 138 E8
St Adlem's CE Comb Sch BH12 ... 204 A6
St Agatha's Rd SO31 ... 128 A4
St Agathas Way PO1 ... 216 B4

St Alban's Ave BH8 .....205 C7
St Alban's CE Prim Sch
 PO9 ....136 A3
St Alban's Cres BH8 ...205 B8
St Alban's Rd
 Bournemouth BH8 .....205 B7
 Havant PO9 ....136 A4
 Southampton SO14 ....103 B5
St Albans Rd PO4 ......182 F3
St Aldhelm's BH14 .....203 F4
St Aldhelm's Cl BH13 ..203 F3
St Aldhelm's Pl BH13 ..203 F4
St Aldhelm's Rd BH13 ..203 F4
St Andrew Cl PO8 ......88 C2
St Andrew's Bldgs SO31 .128 A2
St Andrew's Rd
 Farlington PO6 ....158 F8
 Gosport PO12 ....181 B5
 Portsmouth PO5 ......216 C2
 South Hayling PO11 ...185 B2
St Andrews BH23 ......207 A6
St Andrews Cl
 Michelmersh SO51 .....27 D6
 North Baddesley SO32 ..53 E5
St Andrews Gn SO32 ...61 C5
St Andrews Ho SO17 ..103 B8
St Andrews Pk SO50 ...81 D6
St Andrews Rd
 Broadstone BH18 .....187 A5
 Southampton SO14 ....103 A5
St Ann's Cres PO12 ....181 A7
St Ann's Ct BH11 .....205 E5
St Ann's Hospl BH13 ..214 E6
St Ann's Rd
 Horndean PO8 ....112 C7
 Portsmouth PO4 ......182 F3
St Anne's Ave BH6 ....206 E5
St Anne's Gdns SO19 ..103 E2
St Anne's Gr PO14 ....154 F7
St Anne's RC Sch SO51 .102 F6
St Anne's Rd
 Southampton SO19 ....103 E2
 Upton BH16 ....201 B7
St Anne's Sch PO13 ...179 E3
St Annes Cl SO22 .....215 A2
St Annes Gdns SO41 ..197 D3
St Annes Ho SO51 .....52 E6
St Annes La SO32 .....107 E7
St Annes Mews SO14 ..103 A8
St Anns Ct SO17 ......79 F2
St Anthony's RC Prim Sch
 PO14 ....129 D1
St Anthony's Rd BH4 ..204 F5
St Antony's BH4 ......204 D2
St Aubin's Ave PO13 ..104 B5
St Aubin's Pk PO11 ...184 D3
St Aubyns Ct BH15 ....202 B2
St Aubyns La BH24 ...117 E1
St Augustin's Rd BH2 ..204 F5
St Augustine Gdns SO17 .79 D1
St Augustine Rd PO4 ..182 F3
St Austell Cl SO50 .....56 E3
St Barbara Way PO2 ..157 F4
St Barbe Cl SO41 .....197 E4
St Barbe Mus* SO41 ..197 E4
St Bartholomew's Gdns
 PO5 ....216 C1
St Bede CE Prim Sch
 SO23 ....215 E6
St Bede's Ct SO23 ....215 E6
St Bernard Ho SO14 ..103 A3
St Birinus Rd SP5 .....47 D6
St Blaize Rd SO51 ....53 C8
St Boniface Ct SO32 ..54 B3
St Bonnet Dr SO32 ...83 C8
St Brelade Pl SO16 ...77 D3
St Brelades Ave BH12 ..188 D1
St Catherine St PO5 ..182 D1
St Catherine's Par BH23 .191 F1
St Catherine's RC Prim Sch
 BH21 ....164 B6
St Catherine's Rd
 Bournemouth BH6 .....206 F3
 Eastleigh SO50 ....56 B5
 South Hayling PO11 ...184 C4
 Southampton SO18 ....79 E1
 Winchester SO23 .....215 F4
St Catherine's Way
 BH23 ....191 D3
St Catherines BH21 ...163 C4
St Catherines Ct PO11 .184 C3
St Catherines Rd SO50 ..56 A5
St Catherines View
 SO30 ....105 A6
St Catherines Way
 PO16 ....131 E1
St Chad's Ave PO2 ....157 E2
St Christopher Ave
 PO16 ....131 C3
St Christopher Ct
 PO5 ....182 E1
St Christopher's Rd
 PO9 ....135 C4
St Christophers Cl SO52 .54 A4
St Christophers Gdns
 PO13 ....155 C2
St Christophers Hospl
 PO16 ....131 B3
St Christophers Mobile Home
 Pk PO8 ....88 D3
St Christophers Sch
 SO18 ....103 E8
St Clair Rd BH13 .....214 F7
St Clares Ave PO9 ....135 D7

St Cleeve Way BH22 ...165 C3
St Clement St SO23 ..215 D5
St Clement's & St John's CE
 Inf Sch BH1 ....205 D5
St Clement's Gdns BH1 .205 D5
St Clement's Rd BH1 ..205 D5
St Clements Cl SO51 ..52 E8
St Clements Rd BH15 ..203 A7
St Colman's Ave PO6 ..158 A8
St Contest Way SO40 ..124 F8
St Cross Ct SO23 .....215 D3
St Cross Hospl* SO23 ..215 D2
St Cross Mede SO23 ..215 C2
St Cross Rd SO23 ....215 D3
St Cuthberts Cl SO31 ..129 A4
St Cuthberts La SO31 ..129 A4
St Cyres Meml Cotts
 SO41 ....197 F5
St David's Cl SO40 ....76 C1
St David's Ct
 Bournemouth BH1 ....205 E5
 Gosport PO13 ....180 C6
 North Baddesley SO52 ..54 A3
St David's Rd
 Clanfield PO8 ....88 C5
 Portsmouth PO5 ......216 C2
 Upton BH16 ....201 B7
St Davids Rd SO31 ...128 F3
St Denys BH25 ......195 B1
St Denys Prim Sch SO17 .79 C1
St Denys Rd SO17 ....79 C1
St Denys Wlk PO9 ....135 D6
St Denys' Sta SO17 ...103 C8
St Edmondsbury CE
 PO13 ....180 D5
St Edmund Cl SO14 ..129 B1
St Edmund's Rd SO16 ..102 B8
St Edmunds RC Sch
 PO1 ....216 C3
St Edward's RC/CE Sch
 BH15 ....202 F7
St Edward's Rd
 Gosport PO12 ....181 B5
 Portsmouth PO5 ......216 B1
 Southampton SO15 ...25 A1
St Edward's Terr
 PO12 ....181 A7
St Edwards Rd SO31 ..127 B7
St Elizabeth's Ave SO18 .104 B7
St Evox Cl SO16 ......77 F5
St Faith's CE Prim Sch
 SO22 ....215 D5
St Faith's Cl PO12 ....181 A6
St Faith's Rd
 Winchester SO23 .....215 D3
St Francis Ave SO18 ..104 B8
St Francis CE Prim Sch
 SO53 ....55 A5
St Francis Cl SO45 ...177 E7
St Francis Ct
 Locks Heath PO14 ....129 C3
 Portsmouth PO2 .....157 E4
St Francis Pl PO9 ....135 E3
St Francis Rd
 Blackfield SO45 ......177 E2
 Gosport PO12 ....181 C2
St Francis Specl Sch
 SO14 ....154 C8
St Gabriel's Rd SO18 ..104 B7
St George Cl SO31 ...104 F1
St George RC Sch (Boys)
 PO1 ....79 C6
St George's Almshos
 BH15 ....202 B1
St George's Ave
 Bournemouth BH8 ....205 C8
 Havant PO9 ....136 B1
 Poole BH12 ....203 B8
St George's Beneficial CE
 Prim Sch PO1 ....182 A5
St George's Bsns Ctr
 PO1 ....182 A5
St George's Cl
 Bournemouth BH8 ....205 C8
 Christchurch BH23 ...208 D8
St George's Cotts SP5 ..47 D3
St George's Cres SP6 ..69 F3
St George's Ct
 Bournemouth BH1 ....205 E5
 North Baddesley SO52 ..54 A3
St George's Ct BH12 ..203 B8
St George's CE PO16 .216 A1
St George's Dr BH22 ..165 C4
St George's Ho SO23 ..215 E5
St George's Rd
 Cosham PO6 ....157 F8
 Portsmouth,Eastney PO4 .183 A2
 Portsmouth,Old Portsmouth
 PO1 ....182 A4
 South Hayling PO11 ...184 D3
St George's Sq SO32 ..83 C7
St George's St SO23 ..215 E6
St George's Way PO1 ..182 A5
St George's Wlk PO7 ..134 E7
St Georges Cotts
 Martin SP6 ....43 C3
 Woodgreen SP6 ......70 D8
St Georges Ct
 Fareham PO16 ....155 B8
 Ferndown BH22 ......165 E5
St Georges Dr
 Bournemouth BH11 ...188 D3
 Bransgore BH23 .....193 B8
St Georges Ho SO17 ..103 B8
St Georges Ind Est PO4 .183 A5
St Georges Mans
 BH5 ....205 F4

St Georges Rd
 Fordingbridge SP6 ....69 F2
 Locks Heath SO31 ...128 F3
St Georges Sq PO1 ...182 A5
St Georges St SO14 ..103 A4
St Georges Wlk PO12 ..181 D6
St Giles Cl SO23 .....215 F5
St Giles Hill SO23 ....215 F5
St Giles Way PO8 ....88 C2
St Helen's Mans
 PO4 ....182 E1
St Helen's Par PO4 ...182 E1
St Helen's Rd
 Gosport PO12 ....180 E3
 South Hayling PO11 ..184 D3
St Helena Gdns SO18 ..79 F3
St Helena Way PO16 ..156 C8
St Helens Cl PO4 ....182 F2
St Helens Mews SO50 ..57 D2
St Helier Pl SO16 ....77 E3
St Helier Rd
 Gosport PO12 ....181 C9
 Poole BH12 ....188 D7
St Hellen's Rd PO6 ...158 D8
St Hermans Cvn Est
 PO11 ....185 C2
St Hermans Mans PO11 .185 C2
St Hermans Rd PO11 ..185 C2
St Hilda Ave PO8 ....88 C2
St Hubert Rd PO8 ....88 C2
St Ives End La BH24 ..140 A4
St Ives Fst Sch BH24 ..140 B5
St Ives Gdns BH2 ....204 F5
St Ives Pk BH24 .....140 A5
St Ives Wood BH24 ...140 C5
St James CE Fst Sch SP6 .93 A6
St James Cl Clanfield PO8 .88 C4
 Poole BH15 ....202 B1
 Southampton SO15 ...78 C1
St James Cvn Pk SO52 ..30 A1
St James Ho SO14 ...103 A3
St James Hospl PO4 ..183 C5
St James Pk BH24 ...140 B6
St James Pk (Cvn Pk)
 SO52 ....55 A8
St James Rd
 Ferndown BH22 ......165 A6
 Sway SO41 ....172 C2
 Upper Shirley SO15 ..78 C1
 West End SO30 ......80 D2
St James' CE Prim Sch
 Bournemouth BH2 ....206 B6
 West End SO30 ......80 D2
St James' La SO22,SO23 .215 D5
St James' Rd PO10 ...136 F1
St James'Terr SO22,
 SO23 ....215 D5
St James's Villas SO23 .215 D5
St James's BH1 ......205 E3
St James's St
 Portsmouth PO1 .....182 A5
 Southampton SO15 ...102 D8
St James's Sq BH5 ...206 A5
St James's St PO1 ...182 B5
St John the Baptist CE Prim
 Sch
 Titchfield PO14 ......129 C2
 Waltham Chase SO32 ..83 E2
St John's Ave PO7 ...134 E3
St John's CE Prim Sch
 PO12 ....181 B8
St John's Cl
 Gosport PO12 ....181 B6
 Wimborne Minst BH21 ..163 D4
St John's Coll PO5 ...216 C1
St John's Ct
 Bournemouth BH1 ....205 E5
 North Baddesley SO52 ..54 B3
 Portsmouth PO2 .....157 E7
St John's Ctr SO30 ...105 B6
St John's Gdns BH9 ..189 F1
St John's Hill BH21 ...163 D5
St John's Hospital
 (Almshouses)(N)
 SO23 ....215 F5
St John's Hospital
 (Almshouses)(S)
 SO23 ....215 F5
St John's Rd
 Bournemouth BH5 ....205 E4
 Breach PO10 ....137 D1
 Christchurch BH23 ...207 A6
 Cosham PO6 ....158 A8
 Eastleigh SO50 ......56 B4
 Havant PO9 ....135 B5
 Hedge End SO19,SO30 ..105 B5
 Locks Heath SO31 ...129 B2
 Poole BH15 ....202 D4
 Winchester SO23 ....215 F5
St John's St Hythe SO45 .126 A4
 Winchester SO23 ....215 F5
St Johns CE Fst Sch
 BH21 ....163 D4
St Johns Cl
 Rownhams SO16 .....77 E2
 South Hayling PO11 ..184 D3
St Johns Dr SO41 ...101 F1
St Johns Dr SO40 ...101 E1
St Johns Gdns SO51 ..52 F8
St Johns Glebe SO16 ..77 F6
St Johns Inf Sch SO14 .102 F3
St Johns La SO32 ....107 E7
St Johns Mews
 Locks Heath SO31 ...129 C1
 Portsmouth PO5 .....216 C1

St Johns RC Prim Sch
 PO1 ....216 C3
St Johns Rd BH25 ...195 A7
St Johns Sq PO12 ...181 B6
St Joseph Cl SO31 ...129 B3
St Joseph's RC Comb Sch
 BH12 ....203 E7
St Joseph's RC Prim Sch
 BH23 ....208 A8
St Josephs Mews PO5 ..216 C1
St Jude's CE Prim Sch
 PO1 ....182 B3
St Judes Cl PO5 .....130 E1
St Judes Ct PO5 .....216 B1
St Julien's Hospl
 (Almhouses) SO14 ...103 A2
St Just Cl BH21 .....165 C3
St Katharine's CE Prim Sch
 BH6 ....207 B4
St Kitts Ho PO6 .....132 F2
St Lawrence Cl SO30 ..81 D2
St Lawrence Rd
 Eastleigh SO50 ......56 A4
 Southampton SO14 ...103 B3
St Ledger's Pl BH8 ...205 D6
St Ledger's Rd BH8 ..205 D6
St Leonard's Ave PO11 .185 A3
St Leonard's Rd
 Bournemouth BH8 ....205 B6
 Winchester SO23 ....11 C6
St Leonards Cl PO15 ..129 E3
St Leonards Farm Pk
 BH22 ....166 A8
St Leonards Hospl
 BH24 ....139 C1
St Leonards Rd SO41 ..199 B8
St Leonards Way BH24 .139 D4
St Lucia Ho PO6 .....132 F2
St Luke's CE Prim Sch
 PO5 ....216 B3
St Luke's CE Sec Sch
 PO5 ....216 B3
St Luke's Rd
 Bournemouth BH3 ....204 F7
 Gosport PO12 ....181 A7
St Lukes Cl SO30 ....81 C1
St Maradox La BH9 ..189 F2
St Margaret's Almshouses
 BH21 ....163 A5
St Margaret's Ave PO13 .207 B5
St Margaret's Cl SO18 .104 B7
St Margaret's Cotts SO32 .59 D2
St Margaret's Hill PO1 .163 A5
St Margaret's Rd
 Bishopstoke SO50 ....56 D4
 Bournemouth BH10 ...189 C2
 Poole BH15 ....204 F5
St Margarets BH2 ....204 F5
St Margarets Cl BH21 ..163 A5
St Margarets Hill BH21 .163 A5
St Margarets La SO18 ..104 B7
St Margarets Rd PO11 .185 A3
St Mark's CE Jun Sch
 BH10 ....189 C1
St Mark's Cl PO12 ...181 B2
St Mark's Pl PO12 ...181 B3
St Mark's Rd
 Bournemouth BH11 ...189 B3
 Gosport PO12 ....181 A3
 Portsmouth PO2 .....157 C1
St Marks Cl SO30 ....30 F1
St Marks Ct PO12 ...181 A6
St Marks Rd
 Lymington SO41 .....197 B3
 Southampton SO14 ..103 B5
St Martin's Cl
 Southampton SO16 ..77 C3
 Winchester SO23 ....215 B3
St Martin's Ho PO5 ..182 D1
St Martins Cl SO30 ..56 D4
St Martins Rd BH16 ..201 A7
St Martins Trad Pk
 SO23 ....215 B3
St Mary Gr SO14 ....196 B2
St Mary Magdalen
 Almshouses SO23 ...215 F5
St Mary St
 Southampton SO14 ..103 B4
 Winchester SO23 ....215 B3
St Mary's SO51 .....52 E6
St Mary's Ave PO12 ..181 A1
St Mary's CE Prim Sch
 SO14 ....103 B4
St Mary's Church Cl
 SO18 ....79 D4
St Mary's Cl
 Droxford SO32 ......61 B1
 Kings Worthy SO21 ..2 C5
 Redlynch SP5 ....47 F4
St Mary's Coll SO18 ..103 E8
St Mary's La PO8 ...88 E7
St Mary's Ho PO1 ...182 F6
St Mary's Hospl East Wing
 PO3 ....183 A6
St Mary's Hospl West Wing
 PO1 ....182 F6
St Mary's Maternity Hospl
 BH15 ....202 B2
St Mary's Mews BH22 ..165 D4
St Mary's Pl SO14 ...103 A4
St Mary's RC Comb Sch
 BH15 ....202 E5
 PO12 ....181 A6

St Mary's Rd
 Bishopstoke SO50 ...56 D4
 Bournemouth BH1 ...205 D6
 Bournemouth BH22 ..165 D5
 Liss GU33 ....20 F4
 Netley SO31 ....127 C2
 Poole BH15 ....202 E4
 Portsmouth PO1 ....182 F6
 South Hayling PO11 ..184 F3
 Southampton SO14 ..103 A6
 Stubbington PO14 ...154 C4
St Mary's Terr SO21 ..32 A1
St Marys Cl BH23 ...193 C8
St Matthews Rd SO22 ..215 B8
St Matthew's Rd PO6 ..153 F7
St Matthews Cl SO14 ..103 A5
St Matthews Ct PO12 ..181 D6
St Merrin's Cl BH10 ..189 C4
St Michael & All Angels CE
 Inf Sch SO43 ....121 F5
St Michael's BH2 ....204 D3
St Michael's CE Mid Sch
 BH21 ....163 E7
St Michael's CE Prim Sch
 BH2 ....204 D3
St Michael's Ct PO6 ..133 B1
St Michael's Gdns
 SO23 ....215 D5
St Michael's Gr PO14 ..154 F7
St Michael's Ho PO14 ..154 F8
St Michael's Mews
 BH2 ....204 D3
St Michael's Pas SO23 .215 E4
St Michael's Pl BH2 ..204 D3
St Michael's Rd
 Bournemouth BH2 ...204 E2
 Havant PO9 ....135 C3
 Portsmouth PO4 .....182 E2
 Winchester SO23 ....215 D4
St Michael's Rdbt BH4 .204 D3
St Michael's Sq SO14 ..102 F3
St Michael's St SO14 ..102 F3
St Michaels
 Blackfields SO45 ....150 F1
 Hamworthy BH15 ....201 E3
 Verwood BH31 ......114 F5
St Michaels Cl BH1 ..206 C4
St Michaels Rd
 Locks Heath SO31 ...129 A2
 Totton SO40 ....100 F8
 Verwood BH31 ......114 F4
St Michaels Way PO8 ..88 C2
St Monica Inf Sch SO19 .104 A3
St Monica Jun Sch
 SO19 ....104 A3
St Nicholas Ave SO19 ..103 A3
St Nicholas Ct SO30 ..180 C7
St Nicholas Flats
 PO2 ....157 D1
St Nicholas Rise SO23 .157 D1
St Nicholas Rd PO7 ..108 A3
St Nicholas St PO1 ...182 A2
St Nicholas' Rd PO9 ..135 C3
St Osmund's Rd BH14 ..203 D2
St Patrick's Ct SO52 ..54 A3
St Patrick's La GU33 ..21 D7
St Patrick's RC Prim Sch
 SO19 ....103 E3
St Paul's Hill SO22 ...215 B6
St Paul's La BH8 ....205 B4
St Paul's Pl BH8 ....205 B4
St Paul's Rd
 Bournemouth BH8 ...205 B4
 Portsmouth PO5 .....216 C2
 Sarisbury SO31 .....128 C6
St Paul's Sq PO5 ....216 A2
St Pauls Ct SO22 ....215 B6
St Pauls Rd SO23 ...215 D6
St Pauls RC Prim Sch
 PO6 ....157 B8
St Peter St SO23 ....215 E6
St Peter's Ave PO11 ..160 C2
St Peter's Ct
 Petersfield GU32 ....40 F3
 Poole BH14 ....203 A4
St Peter's Gr PO5 ...216 C1
St Peter's RC Comp Sch
 BH6 ....206 F4
St Peter's RC Prim Sch
 SO22 ....10 B5
St Peter's RC Sch BH7 .206 B8
St Peter's Rd
 Bournemouth BH1 ...205 A3
 Petersfield GU32 ....40 F3
 Poole BH14 ....203 A4
St Peter's Rdbt BH1 ..205 A3
St Peter's Sq PO10 ..160 F8
St Peter's St SO32 ...83 C8
St Peter's Wlk BH1 ..204 F3
St Peters Cl SO32 ...106 D8
St Peters Ct
 Petersfield GU32 ....40 F3
 Emsworth PO10 .....161 A8
St Peters RC Prim Sch
 PO7 ....134 F5
St Peters Rd PO11 ...160 C3
St Philip's Way SO18 ..104 B7
St Pirans Ave PO3 ...183 A7
St Quentin Ho PO14 ..154 E7
St Richards Gdns PO7 .134 C5
St Ronan's Ave PO4 ..182 E2
St Ronan's Rd PO4 ..182 E2
St Saviours Cl PO7 ..134 C5
St Sebastian Cres PO16 .131 B3
St Simon Cl SO31 ...129 B3
St Simons Rd PO5 ..182 D2
St Stephen's Ct BH2 ..204 E4

St Stephen's Rd
Bournemouth BH2 .... 204 E3
Winchester SO22 .... 215 B8
St Stephen's Way 4
BH2 .... 204 F3
St Stephens La BH1 .... 115 A7
St Stephens Rd PO2 .... 182 E8
St Swithun Cl SO22 .... 83 B8
St Swithun St SO23 .... 215 E5
St Swithun Wells RC Prim
Sch SO53 .... 55 E5
St Swithun's Cl SO51 .... 28 D1
St Swithun's RC Prim Sch
PO5 .... 182 D2
St Swithun's Rd BH1 ...... 205 B4
St Swithun's Rd S BH1 .... 205 B4
St Swithun's Rdbt BH1 .... 205 B3
St Swithun's Sch SO21 .... 11 D8
St Swithuns St 6 SO14 ... 103 A6
St Swithuns Rd PO2 .... 157 F2
St Theresas Cl PO9 .... 135 C3
St Thomas Ave PO11 ...... 184 D3
St Thomas Cl
Bournemouth BH10 ...... 189 D2
Fareham PO16 .... 131 C3
St Thomas Ct SO50 .... 57 D2
St Thomas Garnet's RC Sch
BH5 .... 206 A5
St Thomas Mews 3
SO23 .... 215 D5
St Thomas More's RC Prim
Sch PO9 .... 135 D3
St Thomas Pk SO41 .... 197 D3
St Thomas St SO23 .... 215 D5
St Thomas's Ct 6 PO1 .... 182 A4
St Thomas's Rd PO12 ..... 181 B9
St Thomas's St
Lymington SO41 .... 197 E3
Portsmouth PO1 .... 182 A3
St Tristan Cl SO31 .... 129 B2
St Ursula Gr PO3 .... 216 C1
St Valerie Rd
Bournemouth BH2 .... 204 F5
Gosport PO12 .... 181 B4
St Vigor Way SO21 .... 56 F8
St Vincent Coll PO12 ..... 181 B6
St Vincent Cres PO8 ...... 112 B6
St Vincent Rd
Gosport PO12 .... 181 B7
Portsmouth PO5 .... 182 D2
St Vincent St PO5 .... 216 A2
St Walburga's RC Prim Sch
BH9 .... 190 B1
St Winifred's Rd
Bournemouth BH2 .... 204 F5
Southampton SO16 .... 78 C2
St Winifred's Sch SO17 .... 79 A1
Salcombe Ave PO3 .... 158 A1
Salcombe Cl SO53 .... 55 B4
Salcombe Cres SO40 ...... 100 E6
Salcombe Rd
Southampton SO15 .... 102 C7
Totton SO40 .... 100 E6
Salcot Rd SO23 .... 215 E8
Salem St SO15 .... 78 C1
Salerno Dr PO12 .... 180 F4
Salerno Ho
Fareham PO14 .... 154 F7
Romsey SO51 .... 53 B7
Salerno Pl BH15 .... 201 D2
Salerno Rd
Portsmouth PO2 .... 157 D4
Southampton SO16 .... 78 C5
Salet Way PO7 .... 112 B1
Salisbury Cl SO50 .... 56 B4
Salisbury Cl 1 SO40 ...... 56 B4
Salisbury Rd
Awbridge SO51 .... 52 B6
Bournemouth BH1 .... 205 E4
Breamore SP6 .... 46 C2
Burton BH23 .... 192 D2
Cosham PO6 .... 158 A7
Ellingham BH24 .... 116 F5
Fordingbridge SP6 .... 70 A5
Ibsley BH24 .... 94 A1
Ower SO51 .... 75 D8
Ower,Stonyford SO51 .... 75 F4
Poole BH14 .... 203 C5
Portsmouth PO4 .... 182 F2
Ringwood BH24 .... 140 F8
Sopley,Winkton BH23 .... 192 B5
Southampton SO17 .... 79 A3
Totton SO40 .... 76 C3
West Wellow SO51 .... 51 B1
Salisbury Road Arc 4
SO40 .... 100 F7
Salisbury St
Fordingbridge SP6 .... 69 F1
6 Southampton SO15 ... 102 F6
Salisbury Terr PO13 ...... 179 F2
Salmon Dr SO50 .... 56 F2
Salt La SO24,SO32 .... 34 E3
Salt Meat La PO12 .... 181 D7
Salter Rd BH13 .... 214 C3
Salterne Ho 2 SO41 ..... 197 E2
Salterns Ave PO4 .... 183 B6
Salterns Cl PO11 .... 185 C3
Salterns Est BH14 .... 214 B8
Salterns Est PO16 .... 155 B7
Salterns La
Burelam SO31 .... 128 A7
Fareham PO16 .... 155 B7
South Hayling PO11 ...... 185 C3
Salterns Point BH14 ..... 214 B8
Salterns Quay BH14 ..... 214 B8
Salterns Rd Poole BH14 .. 203 A3
Stubbington PO13,PO14 .. 179 B5
Salterns Sch SO40 .... 101 A7

Salterns Way BH14 .... 214 B8
Salters Acres SO22 .... 1 C3
Salters La SO22 .... 1 B2
Saltgrass La SO41 .... 212 A3
Saltings Rd BH16 .... 201 B6
Saltings The
Farlington PO6 .... 158 E7
Langstone PO9 .... 159 F6
Saltmarsh La PO11 ...... 184 E5
Saltmarsh Rd SO14 ...... 103 B3
Saltmead SO17 .... 79 C1
Salvia Cl PO7 .... 135 A6
Salwey Rd SO30 .... 105 D5
Samantha Cl BH10 .... 189 E3
Samber Cl SO41 .... 197 C4
Sammy Miller Motorcycle
Mus* BH25 .... 194 E5
Sampan Cl SO31 .... 128 E1
Samphire Cl SO41 .... 197 E5
Samples Way BH17 ...... 202 F8
Sampson Rd
Fareham PO14 .... 154 F6
Portsmouth PO1 .... 181 F7
Samson Cl PO13 .... 180 D7
Samson Rd BH15 .... 201 D2
Samuel Rd PO1 .... 182 F6
San Diego Rd PO12 ..... 181 B7
San Remo Twrs 4 BH5 .. 205 E3
Sancreed Rd BH12 ...... 203 E7
Sancroft Ho BH21 .... 164 A1
Sand Cl SO51 .... 50 E3
Sandbanks Bsns Ctre
BH13 .... 214 B3
Sandbanks Rd BH14,
BH15 .... 203 A2
Sandbourne Rd
Bournemouth BH4 ...... 204 C1
Poole BH15 .... 202 D4
Sandcroft Cl PO12 ...... 180 E3
Sandecotes Rd BH14 .... 203 C3
Sandell Ct SO16 .... 79 B5
Sanderling Rd PO4 ...... 183 D5
Sanderlings BH24 .... 141 C6
Sanderlings The PO11 ... 185 A2
Sandford Ave PO12 ..... 180 D4
Sandford Cl BH9 .... 190 C3
Sandford Way BH18 ..... 186 F2
Sandhill La PO13 .... 180 A6
Sandhills Cl BH17 ...... 187 D2
Sandhurst Ct PO5 .... 216 C1
Sandhurst Dr BH21 ...... 139 A7
Sandhurst Rd SO15 ..... 102 E6
Sandilands Way 7
SO45 .... 126 A1
Sandisplatt PO14 .... 154 C8
Sandle Copse SP6 .... 69 B2
Sandleford Rd PO9 ...... 135 D7
Sandleheath Ind Est SP6 . 69 B2
Sandleheath Rd SP6 ..... 92 F8
Sandlewood Cl
Clanfield PO8 .... 88 C5
Totton SO40 .... 100 C8
Sandmartin Cl BH25 .... 209 F7
Sandown Cl PO12 .... 180 D3
Sandown Rd
Christchurch BH23 ...... 207 E6
Cosham PO6 .... 157 E7
Southampton SO15 ...... 78 B1
Sandpiper Cl
Broadstone BH17 .... 186 F1
Horndean PO8 .... 112 A7
Marchwood SO40 .... 101 E1
Sandpiper Rd SO16 ..... 78 B6
Sandpipers PO6 .... 158 E7
Sandpit La SO41 .... 199 D5
Sandport Gr PO16 ...... 156 B7
Sandringham Cl
Bournemouth BH9 ...... 190 B4
Chandler's Ford SO53 ... 54 F4
Sandringham Ct
Bournemouth BH6 ...... 205 C6
13 Gosport PO12 ...... 181 C9
5 Southampton,Millbrook
SO15 .... 102 A6
14 Westwood Park SO17 . 79 A1
Sandringham Gdns BH9 . 190 B4
Sandringham La PO1 .... 216 D3
Sandringham Rd
Fareham PO14 .... 154 C8
Petersfield GU32 .... 40 F4
Poole BH14 .... 203 C3
Portsmouth PO1 .... 216 D3
Southampton SO18 ..... 79 E1
Sandsbury La GU32 ..... 40 C5
Sandy Balls Holiday Ctr
SP6 .... 70 D2
Sandy Beach Est PO11 .. 185 F1
Sandy Brow PO7 .... 134 D3
Sandy Cl Petersfield GU31 . 41 C3
Wimborne Minst BH21 .. 164 A8
Sandy Down SO41 ...... 173 C4
Sandy La
Abbotswood SO51 .... 28 B3
Bournemouth BH6 ...... 206 B5
Bransgore BH23 .... 191 E2
Fair Oak SO50 .... 57 B2
Lyndhurst SO43 .... 121 F4
North Baddesley SO52 ... 54 B5
Pamphill BH21 .... 162 B5
Rake GU33 .... 21 E4
Rowlands Castle SP6 .... 47 E7
St Leonards BH24 .... 140 A5
Steep Marsh GU32 ...... 41 B8
Three Legged Cross BH21 . 114 E2
Titchfield PO14 .... 153 F8
Upton BH16 .... 201 B6
Verwood BH31 .... 115 A6
Waltham Chase SO32 .... 83 C2

Sandy La continued
Wimborne Minst BH21 .. 164 A8
Sandy Mead Rd BH8 .... 190 F1
Sandy Plot BH23 .... 207 C8
Sandy Point Rd PO11 ... 185 E1
Sandy Way BH10 .... 189 E4
Sandyfield Cres PO8 .... 111 E3
Sandyhurst Cl BH17 .... 187 C1
Sanross Cl PO14 .... 179 A6
Santoy BH13 .... 214 D5
Saplings The SO45 ...... 150 B5
Sapphire Cl 1 PO12 .... 181 C8
Sapphire Ridge PO7 .... 135 A7
Saracen Cl SO41 .... 197 C1
Saracens Rd SO53 ...... 55 F7
Sarah Cl BH7 .... 206 B8
Sarah Robinson Ho 22
PO1 .... 182 A5
Sarah Sands Cl BH23 ... 207 D8
Sarisbury CE Jun Sch
SO31 .... 128 E5
Sarisbury Gate 4 SO31 . 129 B5
Sarisbury Inf Sch SO31 .. 128 E4
Sark Rd BH12 .... 203 D8
Sarnia Cl SO16 .... 77 E3
Sarum Ave BH22 .... 138 E4
Sarum Cl SO22 .... 215 A5
Sarum Ct Poole BH14 ... 203 C4
Winchester SO22 ...... 215 B5
Sarum Rd
Chandler's Ford SO53 ... 55 E6
Winchester SO22 .... 10 B7
Sarum Road Hospl
SO22 .... 215 A5
Sarum St 12 BH15 ..... 202 B1
Sarum View SO22 .... 10 B7
Sarum Wlk SO41 .... 197 D6
Satchell La SO31 .... 128 A4
Saturn Cl SO16 .... 77 F4
Saulfland Dr BH23 ...... 208 D8
Saulfland Ho BH23 ...... 208 D8
Saulfland Pl BH23 ...... 208 D8
Saunders Ct PO13 ..... 180 A7
Saunders Ho PO6 ...... 132 E1
Saunders La SO51 ...... 26 E6
Saunders Mews 5 PO4 . 183 B2
Savernake Cl
Gosport PO13 .... 155 D2
1 Romsey SO51 .... 28 B1
Saville Cl
Bishopstoke SO50 ...... 56 D5
Gosport PO12 .... 180 F3
Saville Ct SO31 .... 163 D3
Saville Gdns PO16 ..... 131 A3
Savoy Bldgs 6 PO5 .... 131 B1
Savoy Ho SO40 .... 101 A7
Sawmills The SO32 ..... 82 B5
Sawyer Cl SO22 .... 1 B6
Saxe Ct 12 PO17 ...... 130 E7
Saxholm Cl SO16 ...... 78 A6
Saxholm Dale SO16 .... 78 F6
Saxholm Way SO16 .... 78 F6
Saxley Ct PO9 .... 135 C6
Saxon Cl Horndean PO8 . 88 C5
Locks Heath SO31 ..... 128 E1
Portchester PO16 ...... 132 B1
Saxon Ct 17 SO23 ..... 215 E6
Saxon Gdns SO30 ...... 105 A5
Saxon Ho 17 SO14 .... 103 C6
Saxon Hts PO6 .... 206 E5
Saxon King Gdns BH6 .. 207 B4
Saxon Mdw SP5 .... 46 F7
Saxon Rd SO41 .... 197 D6
Saxon Rd Blackfield SO45 . 150 F1
Southampton SO15 ..... 102 D5
Winchester SO23 ...... 215 E7
Saxon Shore Inf Sch
PO6 .... 156 E8
Saxon Sq Sh Ctr BH23 .. 207 B6
Saxon Way Alderholt SP6 . 93 A5
Romsey SO51 .... 53 C7
Saxon Wlk SO53 .... 55 E5
Saxonbury Rd BH6 ..... 206 E5
Saxonford Rd BH23 .... 208 C7
Saxonhurst Cl BH10 ... 189 E5
Saxonhurst Gdns BH10 . 189 E4
Saxonhurst Rd BH10 ... 189 E4
Sayers Rd SO50 .... 56 E3
Scafell Ave PO14 ...... 154 D8
Scallows La SO41 .... 50 E6
Scantabout Ave SO53 .. 55 F7
Scantabout Prim Sch
SO53 .... 55 F7
Scarf Rd BH17 .... 202 F7
Scarp Cl PO15 .... 185 B2
Scholars' Wlk PO6 ..... 158 C7
School Cl
Chandler's Ford SO53 ... 55 B5
Verwood BH31 .... 115 A7
School Hill SO32 .... 85 C6
School La
Bournemouth BH11 .... 189 B6
Bransgore BH23 .... 169 E4
Chandler's Ford SO53 ... 55 B5
Compton PO7 .... 90 F2
Denmead PO7 .... 110 D5
Emsworth PO10 .... 160 F8
Hamble-le-R SO31 ..... 128 A2
Kings Worthy SO23 .... 2 B4
3 Liss GU33 .... 20 F4
Lymington SO41 .... 197 D4
Lymington,Warborne SO41 . 197 F8
Milford on S SO41 ...... 211 E6
Petersfield GU32 .... 41 B6
Poole BH15 .... 202 C5
Ringwood BH24 .... 141 A7
Southbourne PO10 ...... 161 F7

School La continued
St Leonards BH24 ...... 140 A4
Three Legged Cross BH21 . 138 F7
Westbourne PO10 ...... 137 B5
Wimborne Minst BH21 .. 163 B5
School Pl SO19 .... 103 E4
School Rd
Bransgore BH23 .... 169 E4
Burseldon SO31 .... 128 A8
Fawley SO45 .... 151 B3
Gosport PO12 .... 155 F1
Havant PO9 .... 135 E1
Hythe SO45 .... 126 A4
Nomansland SP5 .... 73 C8
Redlynch SP5 .... 48 A5
Romsey SO51 .... 28 C1
West Wellow SO51 ..... 50 F2
Wickham PO17 .... 108 A3
Schooner Way
Locks Heath SO31 ..... 128 E1
Portsmouth PO4 .... 183 C6
Schooners Ct PO13 .... 179 F4
Scimitars The PO14 ... 179 B8
Scivier's La SO32 ...... 58 C2
Scotland Cl SO50 ...... 57 E2
Scotney Ct 18 PO9 .... 136 B6
Scott Cl Poole BH12 ... 188 F1
Stubbington PO14 ..... 154 C4
Scott Ho 2 PO2 .... 157 C2
Scott Rd Eastleigh SO50 . 55 F2
Poole BH12 .... 188 F1
Poole BH12 .... 203 F8
Portsmouth,Hilsea PO3 . 157 F5
Portsmouth,Portsea Island
PO1 .... 181 F7
Southampton SO19 .... 103 F1
Scott's Gn BH23 ...... 207 F8
Scott-Paine Dr SO45 .. 126 B4
Scotter Rd
Bishopstoke SO50 ...... 56 D3
Bournemouth BH7 ...... 206 B6
Scotter Sq SO50 .... 56 D3
Scotts Cl
Colden Common SO21 ... 57 A8
Downton SP5 .... 46 E8
Scotts Hill La BH23 .... 207 D7
Scratchface La
Havant PO9 .... 135 B2
Waterlooville PO7 ..... 134 F4
Scullards La 1 SO14 .. 102 F4
Scylla Ind Est SO23 .... 11 C8
Sea Breeze Gdns PO4 .. 183 C3
Sea Crest Rd PO13 .... 179 F2
Sea Front PO11 .... 184 E3
Sea Front Est PO11 ... 185 B2
Sea Grove Ave PO11 ... 185 A2
Sea Kings PO14 .... 179 B7
Sea La PO13 .... 179 A5
Sea Mill Gdns 33 PO1 . 182 A5
Sea Pines 9 SO41 ..... 211 C4
Sea Point 8 BH13 ..... 214 F7
Sea Rd Barton on S BH25 . 209 E8
Bournemouth BH5 ..... 205 E4
Bournemouth,Southbourne
BH6 .... 206 F3
Milford on S SO41 ..... 211 E4
Southampton SO19 .... 103 D4
Sea View Cotts PO10 .. 160 F8
Sea View Est SO31 .... 127 B5
Sea View Rd
Cosham PO6 .... 134 D1
Poole BH15 .... 203 A6
Upton BH16 .... 201 A7
Sea Vixen Ind Est BH23 . 208 A8
Seabank Cl BH16 ...... 201 A7
Seabird Way PO10 ..... 155 B7
Seabourne Pl 8 BH5 ... 206 B5
Seabourne Rd BH5 .... 206 B5
Seabreeze Way SO41 .. 211 B6
Seacliff Ct BH6 .... 206 D3
Seacombe Gn SO16 .... 77 D1
Seacombe Rd BH13 .... 214 B3
Seacroft Ave BH25 .... 209 E8
Seafarers Wlk PO11 ... 185 F1
Seafield Cl BH25 ...... 209 F7
Seafield Dr BH6 .... 206 E5
Seafield Park Rd PO14 . 179 B6
Seafield Rd
Barton on S BH25 ..... 209 E8
Bournemouth BH6 ..... 206 D4
Christchurch BH23 ..... 208 C2
Portchester PO16 ..... 156 B7
Portsmouth PO3 .... 158 A1
Southampton SO19 .... 79 F3
Seafield Terr PO12 .... 181 C4
Seafields PO10 .... 160 E8
Seaford Cl SO31 ...... 104 F1
Seagarth Cl SO16 ..... 78 D3
Seagarth La SO16 ..... 78 D3
Seager's Ct PO1 ...... 181 F4
Seagram Rd BH9 ...... 190 C3
Seagrove Rd PO2 ...... 157 D1
Seagull Cl PO4 .... 183 C6
Seagull Ct PO10 ...... 136 F1
Seagull La PO10 .... 136 F1
Seagull Rd BH8 .... 190 F2
Seagulls The PO13 .... 180 A4
Seahorse Wlk PO12 ... 181 D6
Sealark Rd PO12 ...... 180 E3
Seaman's La SO43 .... 98 C4
Seamead PO14 .... 179 A6
Seamoor La BH4 ...... 204 B3
Seamoor Rd BH4 ...... 204 B3
Searles Hill SO21 ...... 32 A6
Seathrift Cl PO13 ..... 179 E3

Seathwaite Ho 15 PO6 .. 133 B1
Seaton Ave PO3 .... 183 A8
Seaton Cl
Christchurch BH23 ..... 209 B8
Lymington SO41 .... 197 E5
Stubbington PO14 ..... 179 C7
West End SO18 .... 80 C1
Seaton Rd BH23 .... 209 B8
Seatown Cl BH17 ...... 188 A1
Seaview Ave PO16 .... 132 E1
Seaview Ct
9 Bournemouth PO12 .. 180 D3
Lee-on-t-S PO13 ...... 179 F2
Seaward Ave
Barton on S BH25 ..... 209 D7
South Hayling PO11 ... 185 D3
Walkford BH23 .... 194 C1
Seaward Ct
Barton on S BH25 ..... 209 F7
Bournemouth BH6 ..... 206 B4
Seaward Gdns SO19 ... 103 E4
Seaward Rd SO19 ..... 103 E4
Seaward Twr 11 PO12 . 181 E5
Seaway BH25 .... 210 B8
Seaway Ave BH23 ..... 208 C7
Seaway Cres PO4 ..... 183 D4
Seaway Gr PO16 ...... 156 C6
Seaweed Cl SO19 ..... 126 E8
Seawinds SO41 .... 211 A5
Sebastian Gr PO7 ..... 135 A8
Second Ave Cosham PO6 . 158 C8
Farlington PO6 .... 158 E8
Havant PO9 .... 136 B2
Southampton SO15 .... 101 D7
Southbourne PO10 .... 161 D8
Second Marine Ave
BH25 .... 210 A6
Second St SO45 .... 150 E8
Sedberg Ho SO16 ..... 77 D1
Sedbergh Rd SO16 .... 77 D1
Seddon Cl BH25 ...... 210 B8
Seddul-Bahr SO30 .... 80 E5
Sedgefield Cl
Portchester PO6 ...... 156 F8
Totton SO40 .... 100 C8
Sedgeley Gr PO12 .... 181 A8
Sedgemead SO31 ..... 127 B5
Sedgemead Ct SO31 .. 127 B5
Sedgewick Cl PO13 ... 180 D8
Sedgewick Rd SO19 .. 104 C5
Sedgley Cl PO5 .... 216 C2
Sedgley Rd BH9 ...... 204 E8
Sedgwick Cl SO50 .... 56 D3
Sedgwick Rd SO50 .... 56 D3
Seed Warehouse The 3
BH15 .... 202 C1
Segars La SO21 .... 31 F1
Segensworth E Ind Est
PO15 .... 129 D5
Segensworth N Ind Est
PO15 .... 129 E5
Segensworth W Ind Est
PO15 .... 129 C5
Selangor Ave PO10 ... 136 D1
Selborne Ave
Havant PO9 .... 135 D5
Southampton SO18 ... 104 C3
Selborne Cl GU32 .... 40 F5
Selborne Ct 8 SO51 .. 28 B1
Selborne Gdns PO12 . 181 A5
Selborne Pl SO22 .... 215 B3
Selborne Wlk SO18 .. 104 C8
Selbourne Rd SO50 ... 56 A4
Selbourne Rd
Havant PO9 .... 135 D5
Totton SO40 .... 100 B8
Selbourne Terr PO1 .. 216 D3
Selby Cl PO18 .... 187 A3
Seldon Cl SO22 .... 10 B4
Seldown BH15 .... 202 D3
Seldown Bridge BH15 . 202 D3
Seldown La BH15 ..... 202 D3
Seldown Rd BH15 .... 202 D3
Self Rd SO45 .... 202 A2
Selfridge Ave BH6 ... 207 B3
Selfridge Cl BH6 ..... 207 B3
Selhurst Ho PO1 ..... 216 C4
Selhurst Way SO50 .. 57 C1
Seliot Cl BH15 .... 202 D5
Selkirk Cl BH21 ...... 163 E1
Sellwood Rd SO31 ... 127 C6
Sellwood Way BH25 .. 209 D8
Sells Cl BH15 .... 182 D2
Selman Cl SO45 ...... 126 B4
Selsdon Ave SO51 .... 53 B8
Selsey Ave Gosport PO12 . 181 A9
Portsmouth PO4 ..... 183 A2
Selsey Cl
South Hayling PO11 ... 185 F2
Southampton SO16 ... 77 E2
Selsmore Ave PO11 ... 185 B3
Selsmore Rd PO11 .... 185 B3
Selwood Pk BH10 ..... 189 C7
Selworth La SO32 .... 85 B3
Selworthy Cl BH14 ... 203 A2
Selwyn Ct 8 PO6 ..... 157 F7
Selwyn Gdns SO50 ... 56 A5
Sengana Cl SO30 ..... 105 D6
Senlac Rd SO51 ...... 53 B7
Sennen Pl PO6 .... 157 A7
Sentinel Cl BH15 .... 202 E3
Sentinel Cl PO7 ...... 112 A3
Seps 4 Rd SO45 ...... 151 C4
September Cl SO30 ... 80 D1

Serle Cl SO40 ....100 B7
Serle Gdns SO40 ....100 C6
Sermon Rd SO22 ....215 A7
Serotine Cl PO17 ......130 C7
Serpentine Rd
 Fareham PO16 ....131 B2
 Poole BH15 ....202 C3
 [7] Portsmouth PO5 ...182 C2
 Waterlooville PO7 ...134 C3
Service Rd PO16 ....157 D8
Set Oaks Cvn Site BH25 .171 E5
Set Thorns Rd SO41 ....172 C2
Setley Gdns BH8 ....190 E3
Setters Cl SO21 ....56 F8
Settle Cl [4] SO16 ......102 B8
Settlers Cl PO1 ....216 C4
Sevenoaks Dr BH7 ......206 A8
Sevenoaks Rd PO6 ......157 E8
Severn Cl
 Portchester PO16 ....156 A8
 Poole BH16 ....133 B1
Severn Rd
 Ferndown BH22 ......166 A5
 Southampton SO16 ...101 E8
Severn Way SO30 ....80 C1
Seward Rd SO45 ....126 B3
Seward Rise SO51 ......53 C8
Seymour Cl
 Chandler's Ford SO53 ..55 E5
 Portsmouth PO2 .....182 C7
 Southampton SO16 ....78 C3
 Totton SO40 ....76 C1
Seymour Ho SO16 ....78 D3
Seymour La SO52 ......53 F4
Seymour Rd
 Lee-on-t-S PO13 .....180 A4
 Ringwood BH24 ......117 B1
 Southampton SO16 ....78 D3
Shackleton Ho [2] PO2 ..157 E2
Shackleton Rd PO13 ...180 D8
Shackleton Sq BH23 ...159 B6
Shadwell Ct [9] PO2 ....157 C2
Shadwell Rd PO2 ......157 C2
Shaftesbury Ave
 Chandler's Ford SO53 ..55 C4
 Southampton SO17 ....79 B2
 Waterlooville PO7 ....134 E5
Shaftesbury Cl BH22 ...138 F2
Shaftesbury Ct BH3 ...204 F6
Shaftesbury Rd
 Bournemouth BH8 ....205 C6
 Gosport PO12 ....181 C4
 Poole BH15 ....202 D3
 Portsmouth,Southsea PO5 .182 C2
 West Moors BH22 ....138 F2
Shaftesbury St SP6 .....69 F1
Shaftsbury Rd
 Gosport PO12 ....181 C4
 Gosport PO12 ....181 C5
Shags Mdw SO43 ....122 A5
Shakespeare Ave SO17 .103 B8
Shakespeare Bsns Ctr
 SO50 ....56 B4
Shakespeare Dr SO40 ...76 D2
Shakespeare Gdns PO8 .111 E3
Shakespeare Inf Sch
 SO50 ....56 A5
Shakespeare Jun Sch
 SO50 ....56 A5
Shakespeare Mews
 PO14 ....154 A8
Shakespeare Rd
 Bournemouth BH6 ....206 D7
 Eastleigh SO50 ....56 A4
 Portsmouth PO1 .....182 E7
 Waterlooville BH21 ..163 C6
Shakespeare Terr [12]
 PO1 ....182 A3
Shalbourne Rd PO12 ...181 A8
Shalcombe SO31 ....127 C7
Shaldon Cl SO16 ....78 C4
Shaldon Rd [8] PO9 ....136 B6
Shales Rd SO18 ....104 B7
Shallow La BH11 ......188 E5
Shallows The SP6 ......70 C7
Shamblehurst La N SO32 .81 D3
Shamblehurst La S SO32 .81 C1
Shamblehurst Prim Sch
 SO30 ....105 C8
Shamrock Cl PO12 .....181 D5
Shamrock Ct [2] BH21 ...163 C4
Shamrock Quay SO14 ..103 D5
Shamrock Rd SO19 .....103 D3
Shamrock Villas [3] SO17 .79 C1
Shamrock Way SO45 ...126 A5
Shanklin Cres SO15 .....78 D1
Shanklin Rd
 Portsmouth PO4 .....182 E4
 Southampton SO15 ....78 D2
Shannon Cl PO15 ......130 D2
Shannon Ct [7] PO12 ...181 C9
Shannon Ho [9] SO14 ..103 C5
Shannon Rd
 Gosport PO14 ....155 A5
 Stubbington PO14 ...179 B8
Shannon Way SO53 .....55 B6
Shappel Ave BH41 .....188 C5
Shappen Hill La BH24 .142 F1
Shapton Cl SO45 ......150 B4
Shapwick Rd BH15 ....202 A1
Shard Cl BH31 ....115 A6
Sharland Pl [6] PO14 ...154 E7
Sharlands Cl BH18 ....187 B3
Sharlands Rd PO14 ....155 A6

Sharon Ct [4] PO12 .....181 C6
Sharon Rd SO30 ....80 C2
Sharp Rd BH12 ....204 A7
Sharp's Copse Prim Sch
 PO9 ....136 B5
Sharp's Rd PO9 ....136 B5
Sharpley Cl SP6 ....69 E3
Sharpness Cl PO14 ....154 C8
Sharps Cl PO3 ....158 B3
Sharps Rd PO9 ....136 C8
Sharvells Rd SO41 ....211 C5
Shavard La SO32 ......61 D6
Shaves La BH25 ......195 A5
Shaw Cl Totton SO40 ..100 D7
 West End SO18 ......80 A2
Shaw Rd BH24 ....117 C2
Shawcross Ind Pk PO3 .158 A5
Shawford Cl
 Southampton SO16 ...78 E4
 Totton SO40 ....100 B7
Shawford Gdns BH8 ...190 D2
Shawford Gr PO9 ......135 C5
Shawford Rd
 Bournemouth BH8 ....190 D3
 Twyford SO21 ....31 F6
Shawford Sta SO21 ....31 E6
Shayer Rd SO15 ......78 C1
Shear Hill GU31 ......41 B5
Sheardley La SO32 .....62 A1
Shearer Rd PO1 ......182 E7
Shears Brook Cl BH23 .169 B1
Shears Rd SO50 ....56 C3
Shearwater Ave PO16 .155 E8
Shearwater Cl PO11 ..155 B2
Shearwater Dr PO6 ...158 F7
Sheep Pond La SO32 ...61 B3
Sheep St SO12 ....40 F3
Sheepwash La SO47 ...133 F8
Sheet Prim Sch GU32 ..41 B6
Sheffield Cl SO50 ......56 D5
Sheffield Ct [11] PO13 ..180 C6
Sheffield Rd PO1 .....216 D3
Sheiling Sch The BH24 .140 C6
Shelbourne Cl BH8 ....205 D6
Shelbourne Rd BH8 ...205 B6
Sheldrake Gdns
 Hordle SO41 ....196 B3
 Southampton SO16 ...78 B5
Sheldrake Rd BH23 ...208 A5
Shelford Rd PO4 ......183 B5
Shell By Sailing Ctr*
 BH19 ....214 A1
Shell Ct SO40 ....101 F2
Shellcroft SO31 ......152 D10
Shelley Ave PO6 ......132 E1
Shelley Cl
 Bournemouth BH1 ...205 E5
 Christchurch BH23 ..208 C7
 St Leonards BH24 ...139 E5
 Winchester SO22 ....215 B6
Shelley Ct
 [10] Bournemouth BH1 .204 C3
 Ferndown BH22 .....165 D5
 Southampton SO15 ..102 E5
Shelley Gdns
 Bournemouth BH1 ...205 E5
 Waterlooville PO8 ..111 E3
Shelley Hamlets BH23 .208 D7
Shelley Hill BH23 ....208 D7
Shelley Ho [9] BH25 ...195 A2
Shelley La SO51 ....75 E8
Shelley Rd
 Bournemouth BH1 ...205 E5
 Eastleigh SO50 ......55 F1
 Poole BH12 ....203 D5
 Southampton SO19 ..104 E6
 Totton SO40 ....76 D2
Shelley Rd E PO4 .....205 F5
Shelley Way SO41 ....211 D5
Shelton Rd BH6 ......206 C6
Shenley Cl PO15 .....130 C2
Shenstone Ct [2] BH25 .195 A1
Shepards Cl PO14 ....154 C8
Shephard's Way PO12 .181 C3
Shepherd Cl BH23 ....193 F1
Shepherds Cl
 Bartley SO40 ....99 B6
 Winchester SO22 ....10 B4
Shepherds Down Specl Sch
 SO21 ....31 C6
Shepherds Hey Rd SO40 .76 B1
Shepherds Hill BH24 ..116 C6
Shepherds La
 Compton SO21 ......31 C6
 Ellingham BH24 .....116 B6
Shepherds Purse Cl
 SO31 ....128 F2
Shepherds Rd
 Bartley SO40 ....99 C6
 Winchester SO23 ...11 C8
Shepherds Way
 Bournemouth BH7 ..206 A7
 Everton SO41 ......196 D1
 Nursling SO16 ......77 C5
Sheppard Cl PO8 .....112 A6
Sheppards Field [4]
 BH21 ....163 B6
Shepperd Terr [14] PO13 .180 C6
Sherborn Cres BH17 ..188 A2
Sherborne Cl SO50 ....56 A6
Sherborne Dr BH22 ..165 D4
Sherborne House Sch
 SO53 ....55 D8
Sherborne Rd SO17 ...79 B3
Sherborne Way SO30 .105 C6
Sherbrooke Cl
 Kings Worthy SO23 ....2 C8

Sherbrooke Cl continued
 Lee-on-t-S PO13 ......180 A6
Sherecroft Gdns SO30 .106 B7
Sherfield Ave PO9 .....136 A5
Sherfield Cl BH8 ......190 D2
Sherfield English La
 SO51 ....50 C6
Sherfield English Rd SP5 .50 B4
Sherfield Ho [10] SO15 .102 E7
Sheridan Cl
 Southampton SO19 ..104 D5
 Winchester SO22 ....215 A3
Sheridan Gdns
 Swanwick PO15 .....129 C8
 Totton SO40 ....100 D7
Sheringham Rd
 Poole BH12 ....203 F5
 Portsmouth PO6 ....133 D1
Sherley Gn SO31 .....105 A1
Sherrin Cl BH15 ......202 D5
Sherringham Cl SO45 .151 B3
Sherwin Wlk PO12 ...181 A4
Sherwood Ave
 Ferndown BH22 .....165 C3
 Hedge End SO30 ....105 C4
 Poole BH14 ....203 A3
Sherwood Cl
 Christchurch BH23 ..206 F7
 Liss GU33 ....21 A7
 Southampton SO18 ..78 E3
Sherwood Dr BH31 ...115 B6
Sherwood Gdns SO31 .128 E4
Sherwood Rd
 Chandler's Ford SO53 ..30 E1
 Gosport PO12 ....181 A5
Sherwood Way SO45 ..177 E2
Shetland Cl
 Portsmouth PO6 .....133 F1
 Totton SO40 ....100 B8
Shetland Rise SO31 ..129 B7
Shetland View BH31 ..115 A6
Shillinglee PO7 ....134 E4
Shillingstone Dr BH9 ..190 B3
Shillingstone Gdns [3]
 BH12 ....203 F7
Shillito Rd BH12 .....203 E5
Shinewell Gdns [4] SO16 .101 E8
Shingle Bank Dr SO41 .211 D4
Shinwell Ct [8] SO15 ..78 B1
Ship Leopard St [12] PO1 .182 A5
Shipbuilding Rd [13] PO1 .181 F8
Shipcote La SO32 .....59 D2
Shipley Rd SO21 ......32 A7
Shipstal Cl BH16 .....201 C4
Shipton Gn PO9 .....135 D6
Shipwrights Wlk SO31 .212 B3
Shire Cl Swanwick PO15 .129 B7
 Waterlooville PO7 ..112 C1
Shires Cl BH24 ......141 A4
Shires Copse BH6 ....206 F3
Shires Mead BH31 ...115 A6
Shires The SO30 .....105 A6
Shires Wlk SO40 .....100 B7
Shirley Ave
 Portsmouth PO4 ....183 C4
 Southampton SO15 ..102 C8
Shirley Cl
 Bransgore BH23 ....169 B1
 West Moors BH22 ...138 E2
Shirley High St SO15 ..102 B8
Shirley Holms SO41 ..173 B1
Shirley Inf Sch SO15 ..78 C1
Shirley Park Rd SO16 .102 B8
Shirley Pk SO16 ......78 C2
Shirley Rd
 Bournemouth BH9 ...190 A1
 Poole BH16 ....203 B6
 Portsmouth PO5 ....182 E2
 Southampton SO15 ..102 C7
 Upton BH16 ....201 C7
Shirley Twrs SO15 ...102 C8
Shirley Warren Prim Sch
 SO16 ....78 A2
Shirrel Ct [7] SO17 ...180 D3
Shoblands Way BH23 .126 A1
Shoe La Meonstoke SO32 .61 C6
 Upham SO32 ....58 F6
Sholing Ct PO9 ......135 D6
Sholing Inf Sch SO19 .104 A5
Sholing Jun Sch SO19 .104 A5
Sholing Rd SO19 .....103 E4
Sholing Sta SO19 ....103 F2
Sholing Tech Coll The
 SO19 ....104 A4
Shoot Hill PO7,PO17 .109 D3
Shoot La PO13 ....180 A8
Shooters Hill Cl SO19 .104 A5
Shop La SO19,SO31 ...104 E2
Shore Ave
 Portsmouth PO4 ....183 B6
 Upton BH16 ....201 C6
Shore Cl
 Milford on S SO41 ..211 D4
 Upton BH16 ....201 C6
Shore Cres SO32 .....83 D7
Shore Gdns BH16 ....201 B6
Shore Ho SO31 ......128 C1
Shore La
 Bishop's Waltham SO32 .83 D7
 Upton BH16 ....201 C6
Shore Rd Hythe SO45 .126 B3
 Poole BH13 ....214 D6
 Warsash SO31 ......128 C1
Shoreacres BH13 .....214 C3
Shorefield Country Pk
 SO41 ....211 A6
Shorefield Cres SO41 .211 C5

Shorefield Rd
 Marchwood SO40 ...101 F2
 Milford on S SO41 ..211 A6
Shorefield Way SO41 .211 C5
Shorehaven PO6 .....156 F8
Shorewood Cl SO31 ..128 F1
Short Cl BH12 ......204 A8
Short Hill Nomansland SP5 .73 B8
 Romsey SO51 ....28 C1
Short Rd PO14 ......179 A7
Short Row PO1 .....182 A6
Short's Farm SO51 ...50 D7
Shorts Cl BH23 .....192 C1
Shorts Rd SO50 .....57 C2
Shorwell SO31 ......127 C7
Shotterfield Terr GU33 .20 F4
Shotters Hill Cl SO31 ..80 D1
Shotts La SO41 .....196 D4
Shottsford Rd BH15 ..202 C5
Shraveshill Cl SO40 ..76 D1
Shrubb's Ave SO41 ..197 E4
Shrubbery Cl PO16 ..156 C7
Shrubbery The PO12 .180 F7
Shrubbs Hill Gdns SO43 .121 F4
Shrubbs Hill Rd SO43 .121 F4
Shrubland Cl SO18 ..104 B8
Sibland Cl PO14 ....154 D8
Siblings The SO19 ..104 E6
Sicily Ho [7] PO4 ....154 E7
Siddal Cl SO19 .....104 C4
Sidings The Downton SP5 .47 A8
 Netley SO31 ....127 D5
Sidlesham Cl PO11 ..185 F2
Sidmouth Ave [1] PO3 .183 A8
Sidney Gdns [2] BH9 ..190 B4
Sidney Smith Ct BH17 .187 E2
Sidney St SO41 .....196 A2
Silchester Cl BH2 ...204 F5
Silchester Pl [13] SO22 .215 E7
Silchester Rd PO3 ...183 B7
Silhouette Ct PO11 ..185 D1
Silkin Gdns SO40 ...100 D6
Silkstead Ave PO9 ..135 F6
Silkstead La SO21 ...30 F7
Sillen La SP6 ......43 A3
Silver Birch Ave PO14 .154 E8
Silver Birch Cl Liss GU33 .21 A4
 Poole BH13 ....204 A4
 Southampton SO19 ..104 C4
Silver Birch Way [1]
 PO15 ....129 D8
Silver Birches SO31 .127 F8
Silver Birches Pk BH23 .207 F7
Silver Hill SO23 ....215 E5
Silver St
 [5] Christchurch BH23 .207 B6
 Hordle SO41 ....196 C5
 Lyndhurst SO43 ....121 D5
 [1] Portsmouth PO5 ..216 A1
Silver Way BH23 ....208 E2
Silverdale BH25 ....210 B7
Silverdale Cl BH18 ..186 A4
Silverdale Cres PO9 ..93 A6
Silverdale Ct [5] SO15 .102 E7
Silverdale Dr PO7 ...111 C3
Silverdale Rd SO15 ..102 E7
Silverlock Pl PO10 ..137 B5
Silvers End [2] SO45 ..126 A1
Silvers Wood SO40 ...76 C1
Silversands Ct PO11 .185 F2
Silversands Gdns PO11 .185 B2
Silverthorne Way PO7 .134 D8
Silvertrees
 Emsworth PO10 ....136 F2
 Sarisbury SO31 ....128 E6
Silverweed Cl SO53 ...54 F7
Silverweed Ct SO31 .128 E2
Silverwood Cl
 Merley BH21 ....163 D2
 Winchester SO22 ...215 B3
Silvester Rd PO8 ....111 F2
Silwood Cl SO22 ...215 C7
Simmonds Cl BH15 ..202 D5
Simmons Cl SO30 ...105 C8
Simmons Gn PO11 ..185 C3
Simnel St [8] SO14 ..102 F3
Simon Cl SO30 .....104 E7
Simon Way SO18 ....104 E6
Simonds Ct [6] SO23 .215 E8
Simpkins Ct [15] SO53 ..30 E1
Simpson Cl PO16 ....156 E6
Simpson Rd PO2 ....157 C1
Sinah La PO11 ......184 C4
Sinclair Ct [4] BH14 ..203 A4
Sinclair Prim Sch SO16 .78 A5
Sinclair Rd SO16 ....78 A5
Singleton Dr BH10 ..189 C2
Singleton Gdns PO8 ..88 D4
Singleton Way SO40 .100 B8
Sir Christopher Ct SO45 .126 B4
Sir Galahad Rd SO53 .54 F6
Sir George's Rd SO15 .102 D6
Sir Harold Hillier Gardens &
 Arboretum* SO51 ...28 C4
Sir John's Mews SO32 .35 B3
Sir Lancelot Cl SO53 ..54 F6
Sirdar Ho SO17 .....79 C3
Sirdar Rd SO17 ....79 C3
Sirius Ct PO5 ......216 B2
Sirius Ho [10] PO5 ...182 D2
Siskin Cl
 Bishop's Waltham SO32 .83 A8
 Ferndown BH22 ....165 B7
 Southampton SO16 ..78 B5
Siskin Gr PO7 .....135 A6
Siskin Inf Sch PO13 .180 D6
Siskin Jun Sch PO13 .180 D6
Siskin Rd PO4 ......183 C5

Sissinghurst Cl SO19 ..104 A1
Sissinghurst Rd PO16 .156 A7
Siward Ho GU32 ......40 E3
Six Dials SO14 ......103 A5
Six Oaks Rd SO52 ....54 A4
Sixpenny Cl
 Locks Heath PO14 ..129 A1
 Poole BH12 ....203 F7
Sixth Ave PO6 ......157 E8
Sizer Way SO45 ....125 B3
Skew Rd PO17 .....132 D2
Skinner St BH15 ....202 C1
Skintle Gn SO21 .....56 F8
Skipper Cl SO40 ....102 A3
Skipper Way PO13 ..180 A5
Skipton Cl BH18 ....187 A2
Skipton Rd SO53 ....55 C4
Sky End La SO41 ....196 A2
Skye Cl PO6 ....133 F1
Skylark Ct PO4 .....183 C5
Skylark Mdws
 Fareham PO15 .....130 A6
 Whiteley PO15 .....129 F5
Skys Wood Rd SO53 ..54 F6
Slab La Redlynch SP5 ..47 C6
 West Wellow SO51 ...50 E3
Slade Cl SO41 ......196 A3
Slade The GU32 .....18 F2
Slade's La BH10 ....204 C8
Slader Bsns Pk BH17 .187 E1
Slades Farm Rd BH10 .189 D2
Slades Hill SO45 ....150 F2
Slater App PO2 .....157 A1
Slater Cl SO40 .....100 B8
Sleepbrook Cl BH31 .114 E6
Sleeper's Hill SO22 ..215 B4
Sleeper's Hill Ho SO22 .215 B4
Sleepers Delle Gdns
 SO22 ....215 C4
Sleepers Hill Gdns
 SO22 ....215 B4
Sleight La BH21 ....186 C8
Slepe Cres BH12 ....203 F8
Slindon Cl PO8 .....88 D5
Slindon Gdns [4] PO9 .135 F1
Slindon St PO1 .....216 A3
Slingsby Cl PO1 ....216 A1
Slinn Rd BH23 .....207 E7
Slip Way BH15 .....202 B2
Slipper Cvn Pk PO10 .161 A8
Slipper Rd PO10 ...161 A8
Slipway The PO6 ...157 A7
Sloane Ave SO45 ...150 D4
Sloane Ct SO32 ....107 D7
Sloane Stanley Ct PO12 .181 B7
Slocum Ho [10] PO12 .181 C5
Sloe Tree Cl SO31 ..129 C2
Slough La BH16 ....201 A6
Small Cl GU31 .....41 A5
Smallcutts Ave PO10 .137 D1
Smeaton Cl PO15 ...129 E4
Smeaton St [12] PO2 ..157 C2
Smeeton Rd PO13 ...179 F3
Smith Cl SO45 .....150 F2
Smith Gr SO30 .....105 C5
Smith La PO10 .....161 D1
Smith St PO12 .....181 A6
Smith's Field SO51 ...28 A1
Smithe Cl SO50 .....56 A3
Smithfield Pl BH9 ..189 F1
Smiths La SO32 ....107 F8
Smithson Cl BH12 ..204 C8
Smithy La BH25 ....194 F6
Smithy The PO7 ....110 C4
Smugglers La BH21 .163 E2
Smugglers La N BH23 .193 C1
Smugglers La S BH23 .208 B8
Smugglers Reach BH23 .208 A5
Smugglers Wood Rd
 BH23 ....193 C1
Smythe Rd SO19 ...104 D3
Snailing La GU33 ...20 C8
Snails La BH24 .....117 B3
Snakemoor La SO32 ..81 E5
Snapdragon Cl SO31 .128 F2
Snape Cl PO13 .....180 C6
Snell's Cnr PO8 .....88 D3
Snellgrove Cl SO40 ..76 C2
Snellgrove Pl SO40 ..76 C2
Snooks La SO41 ....198 B6
Snowberry Cres PO9 .136 C3
Snowdon Dr PO14 ..154 E8
Snowdon Rd BH4 ...204 C4
Snowdrop Cl SO31 ..128 F2
Snowdrop Gdns BH23 .193 B1
Soake Rd PO7 .....111 E3
Soalwood La GU32 ...18 F1
Soberton Ho
 Portsmouth PO1 ...216 C4
 [22] Southampton SO17 .79 A1
Soberton Rd
 Bournemouth BH8 ..205 D6
 Havant PO9 ....135 E4
Soberton Twrs SO32 ..85 B6
Solar Ct BH13 .....204 C4
Soldridge Cl [5] PO9 .136 B6
Solent Ave
 Lymington SO41 ....198 A3
 Southampton SO19 ..104 A4
Solent Breezes Cvn Site
 SO31 ....152 F6
Solent Bsns Ctr SO15 .152 D5
Solent Bsns Pk PO15 .129 C7
Solent Cl
 Chandler's Ford SO53 .55 C4
 Lymington SO41 ...197 F3
Solent Ct
 [6] Milford on S SO41 .211 C4

Solent Ct continued
[26] Portsmouth PO5 ....182 C2
Southampton SO19 ....103 E1
Stubbington PO14 ....179 C7
Solent Ctr PO15 ....129 E7
Solent Dr
Barton on S BH25 ....210 A7
Hythe SO45 ....125 F4
South Hayling PO11 ....184 F2
Warsash SO31 ....152 D8
Solent Gate
Gosport PO14 ....155 B5
[12] Portsmouth PO5 ....182 E1
Solent Ho Fareham PO16 ....155 A7
Havant PO9 ....136 A3
Solent Homes SO19 ....104 E6
Solent Hts
Lee-on-t-S PO13 ....179 E2
Portsmouth PO4 ....183 B2
Solent Ind Ctr SO15 ....102 C6
Solent Ind Est SO30 ....81 B1
Solent Inf Sch PO6 ....158 D8
Solent Jun Sch PO6 ....158 D8
Solent Lo [8] BH25 ....195 A1
Solent Mdws SO31 ....128 A2
Solent Mead SO41 ....197 E3
Solent Pines [2] SO41 ....211 B4
Solent Rd
Barton on S BH25 ....209 D7
Bournemouth BH6 ....207 A3
Cosham PO6 ....158 C8
Havant PO9 ....136 A3
Hythe SO45 ....149 E8
Southampton SO15 ....102 E4
Stubbington PO14 ....179 A6
Walkford BH23 ....194 B2
Solent View
Bournemouth BH6 ....207 A3
Calshot SO45 ....178 F8
Lee-on-t-S PO13 ....179 D4
Portchester PO16 ....132 B1
Walhampton SO41 ....198 B3
Solent Village PO15 ....129 E6
Solent Way
Beaulieu SO42 ....148 F8
Gosport PO12 ....180 F3
Milford on S SO41 ....211 F4
Solihull Ho PO5 ....216 A2
Solly Cl BH12 ....203 E7
Solomon Way BH15 ....201 D2
Solomons La SO32 ....83 F2
Solona Cl SO53 ....55 F7
Solway Ho [10] SO14 ....103 C6
Somborne Ct [17] SO17 ....79 A1
Somborne Dr PO9 ....135 F5
Somborne Ho SO19 ....103 F1
Somerby Rd BH15 ....202 B6
Somerford Ave BH23 ....208 B8
Somerford Bsns Pk
BH23 ....208 A7
Somerford Cl SO19 ....104 A6
Somerford Ct BH23 ....208 E7
Somerford Prim Com Sch
BH23 ....207 E7
Somerford Rd BH23 ....207 F7
Somerford Rdbt BH23 ....208 A8
Somerford Way BH23 ....207 E6
Somerley Rd BH9 ....205 A8
Somerley View [1] BH24 ....141 A8
Somers Cl SO22 ....215 B3
Somers Park Prim Sch
PO5 ....216 C3
Somers Rd
Portsmouth PO5 ....216 C2
Portsmouth PO5 ....216 C3
Somers Rd N PO1 ....216 D3
Somerset Ave SO18 ....104 C7
Somerset Cres SO53 ....55 D3
Somerset Ct [6] SO15 ....102 C6
Somerset Ho PO7 ....111 C1
Somerset Rd
Bournemouth BH7 ....206 A5
Christchurch BH23 ....206 E8
Portsmouth PO5 ....182 D1
Southampton SO17 ....79 C2
Somerset Terr SO15 ....102 C6
Somerstown Flats PO9 ....136 A1
Somerton Ave SO18 ....104 B7
Somerton Cl BH05 ....195 D3
Somervell Cl PO12 ....181 A3
Somervell Dr PO16 ....131 A3
Somerville Cl BH25 ....194 F3
Somerville Pl [1] PO2 ....157 C2
Somerville Rd
Bournemouth BH2 ....204 D3
Ringwood BH24 ....2 C8
Ringwood BH24 ....141 C8
Sommers Ct SO19 ....103 C3
Sonata Ho PO6 ....157 A7
Sonnet Way PO7 ....135 B8
Sonning Way BH8 ....190 B2
Sopers La
Christchurch BH23 ....207 A6
Poole BH17 ....187 B1
Sopley Cl BH25 ....209 D8
Sopley Common Nature
Reserve* BH23 ....191 C8
Sopley Ct [16] PO9 ....136 B6
Sopley Farm Bldgs
BH23 ....192 B6
Sopley Prim Sch BH23 ....168 C1
Sopwith Cl BH23 ....208 B6
Sopwith Cres [1] BH24 ....163 E2
Sopwith Rd SO50 ....55 F3
Sopwith Way BH23 ....128 F8
Sorrel Cl Romsey SO51 ....28 C1
Waterlooville PO7 ....135 A6
Sorrel Dr PO15 ....129 D7

Sorrel Gdns BH18 ....186 F2
Sorrel Cl SO31 ....128 F2
Sorrell Ct BH23 ....208 B8
Sorrell Way BH23 ....208 B8
South Ave Fawley SO45 ....150 E3
Holbury SO45 ....150 C5
New Milton BH25 ....195 B2
Portsmouth PO2 ....157 E4
South Baddesley Rd
SO41 ....198 B4
South Baddesley CE Prim Sch
SO41 ....198 E6
South Bay PO10 ....161 A3
South Cl Gosport PO12 ....180 F2
Havant PO9 ....160 A8
Romsey SO51 ....28 C1
South Cliff Rd BH2 ....204 F2
South Cross St PO1 ....181 D5
South Ct
Hamble-le-R SO31 ....127 E2
Milford on S SO41 ....211 E4
South Downs Coll PO7 ....135 A3
South Dr Arundage SO51 ....27 B3
Littleton SO22 ....1 B4
West Moors BH24 ....168 E7
South East Cres SO19 ....104 A4
South East Rd SO19 ....104 A4
South End Cl SO21 ....30 B7
South Front
[9] Romsey SO51 ....52 F7
Southampton SO14 ....103 A4
South Gr SO41 ....197 F3
South Hampshire Ind Pk
SO40 ....76 D2
South Haven Cl SO31 ....201 B3
South Hill Alderholt SP6 ....93 A6
Droxford SO32 ....85 A8
Southampton SO16 ....79 A4
South Kinson Dr BH11 ....189 B4
South La Breach PO10 ....137 E2
Buriton GU31 ....65 D4
Clanfield PO8 ....88 B6
Downton SP5 ....46 E7
Horndean PO8 ....89 B3
Nomansland SP5 ....73 C7
Woodmancote PO10 ....137 D3
South Lodge
Fareham PO15 ....130 B1
Poole BH13 ....214 G7
South Mill Rd SO15 ....102 A7
South Millers Dale SO53 ....55 B7
South Normandy [4]
PO1 ....182 A4
South Par
Portsmouth PO5 ....182 D1
[8] Totton SO40 ....100 F7
South Parade Pier*
PO5 ....182 E1
South Park Rd BH1 ....204 A8
South Pl PO13 ....180 A4
South Rd
Bournemouth BH7 ....205 E5
Corfe Mullen BH21 ....186 E6
Cosham PO6 ....158 C7
Horndean PO8 ....88 C1
Poole BH15 ....202 C2
Portsmouth,Paulsgrove
PO6 ....133 A2
Portsmouth,Portsea Island
PO1 ....182 E7
South Hayling SO17 ....184 F3
Southampton SO17 ....103 C8
Southwick PO17 ....105 A8
South Road Comb Sch
BH15 ....202 C2
South Spur PO6 ....133 B2
South Sq [9] PO7 ....130 E7
South St Eastleigh SO50 ....80 A8
Emsworth PO10 ....160 F8
Cosham PO6 ....158 D7
Havant PO9 ....135 F1
Hythe SO45 ....126 A4
Lymington SO41 ....197 C2
Portsmouth PO5 ....216 A1
Titchfield PO14 ....129 D3
South Stoneham Ho
SO18 ....79 D3
South Sway La SO41 ....196 D7
South Terr PO1 ....182 A5
South Trestle Rd SO45 ....151 B5
South View
Bournemouth BH2 ....204 F5
Waterlooville PO8 ....112 A3
Winchester SO22 ....215 C6
South View Park Homes
SO22 ....215 A1
South View Pl [1] BH2 ....204 E3
South View Rd
Christchurch BH23 ....207 A6
Southampton SO15 ....102 D8
Winchester SO22 ....10 B4
South Weirs SO42 ....172 D8
South Western Cres
BH14 ....203 B2
South Wood Gdns SO31 ....128 F2
Southampton Airport
(Parkway) Sta SO18 ....79 F4
Southampton Central Sta
SO15 ....102 E5
Southampton City Coll
SO14 ....103 B4
Southampton Gen Hospl
SO16 ....78 B2
Southampton Hill SO40 ....129 F1
Southampton Ho [6]
PO9 ....136 B3
Southampton International
Airport SO18 ....79 F4

Southampton Maritime
Mus* SO14 ....102 F3
Southampton Oceanography
Ctr SO14 ....103 B2
Southampton Rd
Bartley SO40 ....99 B7
Brockenhurst SO42,SO41 ....173 A4
Cadnam SO40 ....76 B8
Eastleigh SO50 ....56 B1
Fareham PO16 ....131 B2
Fordingbridge SP6 ....70 B1
Hythe SO45 ....125 F4
Locks Heath PO15 ....129 C5
Locks Heath SO31 ....129 C4
Lymington SO41 ....197 D5
Lyndhurst SO43 ....122 B6
Portsmouth PO6 ....157 D8
Ringwood BH24 ....141 B8
Romsey SO51 ....53 A6
Titchfield PO14 ....129 D3
Southampton Solent Univ
SO14 ....103 A5
Southampton Solent Univ
Marine Operations Ctr
SO40 ....102 A2
Southampton St [3]
SO15 ....102 F6
Southbourne Ave
Cosham PO6 ....158 B7
Emsworth PO10 ....161 B8
Holbury SO45 ....150 C4
Southbourne Coast Rd
BH6 ....206 F3
Southbourne Cross Roads [5]
BH6 ....206 E3
Southbourne Gr BH6 ....206 C4
Southbourne Jun & Inf Schs
PO10 ....161 E8
Southbourne Lane Central [6]
BH6 ....206 C4
Southbourne Lane E [5]
BH6 ....206 C4
Southbourne Lane W
BH6 ....206 B4
Southbourne Overcliff Dr
BH6 ....206 D3
Southbourne Rd
Bournemouth BH6 ....206 C4
Lymington SO41 ....197 C3
Southbourne Sands
BH6 ....206 D3
Southbourne Sta PO10 ....161 E8
Southbrook Cl
Langstone PO9 ....159 F8
Poole BH17 ....188 A2
Southbrook Mews [5]
SO32 ....83 C8
Southbrook Rd
Langstone PO9 ....159 F8
[5] Southampton SO15 ....102 E5
Southcliff PO13 ....179 E4
Southcliff Rd SO14 ....103 A4
Southcliffe Ho [1] SO14 ....103 A4
Southcote Rd
Barton on S BH25 ....209 D7
Christchurch BH23 ....208 C6
Southcote Rd BH1 ....205 C4
Southcroft Rd PO12 ....180 F5
Southdale Ct SO53 ....55 C6
Southdene Rd SO53 ....55 C5
Southdown Ct [1] BH23 ....207 F8
Southdown Rd
Compton SO21 ....31 D5
Cosham PO6 ....158 A8
Horndean PO8 ....88 B2
Horndean PO8 ....88 C3
Southdown View PO7 ....111 C2
Southdown Way BH22 ....138 F1
Southend La SO32 ....109 D8
Southern Ave BH22 ....139 A1
Southern Gdns SO40 ....100 E7
Southern La
Barton on S BH25 ....209 F8
Old Milton BH25 ....194 F1
Southern Oaks BH25 ....194 F1
Southern Rd
Bournemouth BH6 ....206 C4
Fawley SO45 ....151 F1
Lymington SO41 ....197 D3
Southampton SO15 ....102 E4
West End SO30 ....80 E1
Southernhay PO7 ....110 F4
Southernhay Rd BH31 ....115 B6
Southey Rd BH23 ....207 F7
Southfield BH24 ....141 A6
Southfield La BH24 ....143 D2
Southfield Mews [6]
BH24 ....141 A6
Southfield Wlk PO9 ....135 C7
Southfields Cl SO32 ....83 C8
Southgate St SO23 ....215 D5
Southgate Villas SO23 ....215 D5
Southill Ave SO31 ....203 C6
Southill Gdns BH9 ....190 A1
Southill Rd
Bournemouth BH9 ....190 A1
Poole BH12 ....203 D7
Southlands Cosham PO6 ....158 A8
Lymington SO41 ....197 C2
Southlands Ave
Bournemouth BH6 ....206 D4
Corfe Mullen BH21 ....186 D6
Southlands Cl BH21 ....186 D6
Southlands Ct BH18 ....187 A3
Southlands Sch & The Wing
Ctr SO41 ....197 F1
Southlaws Wlk BH25 ....194 F1
Southlea Ave BH6 ....206 F4

Southleigh Gr PO11 ....184 F4
Southleigh Rd
Emsworth PO10 ....136 F3
Havant PO9 ....136 C3
Southmead Rd PO15 ....130 E1
Southmoor La PO9 ....159 D7
Southsea Castle* PO5 ....182 C1
Southsea Cvn Pk PO4 ....183 D2
Southsea Inf Sch PO5 ....182 E2
Southsea Terr PO5 ....216 A1
Southview Droxford SO32 ....61 B1
[4] Portsmouth PO4 ....182 F2
Southville Rd BH5 ....206 B5
Southwater SO13 ....179 E3
Southway Gosport PO13 ....155 D3
Titchfield PO15 ....129 E3
Southways PO14 ....129 F7
Southwick Ave PO16 ....132 E1
Southwick Cl SO22 ....1 D4
Southwick Ct PO14 ....155 A6
Southwick Hill Rd PO6 ....133 C1
Southwick Ho [5] PO1 ....216 C4
Southwick Pl BH6 ....206 C7
Southwick Rd
Bournemouth BH6 ....206 C6
Portsmouth PO7 ....110 E4
Portsmouth PO6 ....133 C2
Wickham PO17 ....107 C3
Southwood Ave
Bournemouth BH6 ....206 C4
Walkford BH23 ....194 B1
Southwood Cl
Ferndown BH22 ....165 C6
Walkford BH23 ....194 A1
Southwood Rd
Portsmouth PO2 ....157 E4
South Hayling PO11 ....185 D1
Sovereign Ave PO12 ....181 C8
Sovereign Bsns Ctr
BH15 ....202 B6
Sovereign Cl
Bournemouth BH7 ....205 F8
Portsmouth PO4 ....183 C5
Totton SO40 ....100 C8
Sovereign Cres PO14 ....129 A1
Sovereign Ct
[4] Eastleigh SO50 ....56 A2
Southampton SO17 ....79 A1
Sovereign Ct [5] BH1 ....205 E4
Sovereign Dr
Hedge End SO30 ....105 E6
Portsmouth PO4 ....183 C5
Sovereign La PO7 ....134 E3
Sovereign Pl BH24 ....140 F7
Sovereign Way SO50 ....75 E6
Sowden Cl SO30 ....105 B7
Sowley La SO41 ....199 D5
Spain Bldgs GU32 ....40 E3
Spain The GU32 ....40 E3
Spalding Rd SO19 ....104 E5
Spaniard's La SO51 ....53 A3
Sparkford Cl
Bournemouth BH7 ....206 B8
Winchester SO22 ....215 C4
Sparkford Rd SO22 ....215 C5
Sparrow Cl PO8 ....111 F4
Sparrow Ct PO13 ....179 F4
Sparrow Sq SO50 ....55 D2
Sparrowgrove SO21 ....31 D4
Sparrowhawk Cl PO3 ....158 A4
Sparsholt CE Prim Sch
SO21 ....2 C6
Sparsholt Rd
Southampton SO19 ....126 F8
Winchester SO21,SO22 ....9 C3
Spartan Cl
Stubbington PO14 ....154 C5
Thorney Island PO10 ....161 A3
Spartina Dr SO41 ....197 E5
Spear Rd SO14 ....103 A8
Spearywell Wood Woodland
Wlk* SO51 ....5 C4
Specks La PO4 ....183 A5
Speedfield Pk PO14 ....155 A5
Speedwell Cl
Chandler's Ford SO53 ....55 B5
Locks Heath SO31 ....128 F2
Speedwell Dr BH23 ....208 B8
Speggs Wlk [2] SO30 ....105 C6
Spelthan Hill PO7 ....88 D2
Spencer Cl PO4 ....183 D5
Spencer Ct
[1] New Milton BH25 ....195 B2
[2] Portsmouth PO5 ....182 D2
Stubbington PO14 ....179 E7
Spencer Dr PO13 ....179 F2
Spencer Gdns PO8 ....111 C3
Spencer Rd
Bournemouth BH1 ....205 C4
Eastleigh SO50 ....55 E2
Emsworth PO10 ....136 E4
New Milton BH25 ....195 B2
Poole BH13 ....214 F8
Portsmouth PO4 ....183 C5
Southampton SO19 ....104 D6
Spenlow Cl PO2 ....182 D8
Spenser Cl SO31 ....152 D10
Spetisbury Cl BH9 ....190 B3
Spice Quay [1] PO1 ....182 A3
Spicer La PO1 ....188 E5
Spicer St PO1 ....216 B4
Spicer's Hill SO40 ....100 F5
Spicer's Way SO40 ....100 E6
Spicers Ct [2] SO22 ....215 D6
Spicewood PO15 ....130 E2
Spinacre BH25 ....210 B8
Spindle Cl
Broadstone BH18 ....186 F2

Spindle Cl continued
Havant PO9 ....136 C3
Spindle Warren PO9 ....136 C3
Spindlewood Cl
[10] Old Milton BH25 ....195 A1
Southampton SO16 ....79 A6
Spindlewood Way SO40 ....124 F8
Spinnaker Cl
Gosport PO13 ....180 D7
South Hayling PO11 ....184 E4
Spinnaker Ct
Netley SO31 ....127 B6
[7] Portsmouth PO1 ....182 A5
Spinnaker Dr PO12 ....157 D4
Spinnaker Grange PO11 ....160 C4
Spinnaker Ho PO6 ....157 E4
Spinnaker Pl [6] PO10 ....161 A8
Spinnaker Quay PO11 ....181 F4
Spinnaker Twr* PO1 ....181 F5
Spinnaker View PO9 ....153 A1
Spinnakers The PO13 ....179 E2
Spinners Cl BH22 ....138 E1
Spinners Gdn* SO41 ....173 E1
Spinney Cl
St Leonards BH24 ....139 D4
Waterlooville PO8 ....111 E3
Spinney Dale SO45 ....126 B2
Spinney Gdns SO45 ....126 B2
Spinney The
Bramdean SO24 ....15 C5
Compton SO21 ....31 C7
Denmead PO7 ....110 E3
[8] Eastleigh SO50 ....56 A2
Fair Oak SO50 ....57 A2
Gosport PO13 ....155 D1
Portchester PO16 ....131 F1
Southampton SO16 ....79 A6
St Leonards BH24 ....139 F6
Totton SO40 ....76 C1
Waterlooville PO8 ....112 A6
Spinney Way BH25 ....195 B6
Spinney Wlk SO18 ....79 F3
Spinneys La SO41 ....197 E5
Spinningfield Ho [1]
GU32 ....40 F4
Spitfire Cl SO31 ....103 D3
Spitfire End [2] SO23 ....11 D8
Spitfire Quay SO19 ....103 C4
Spitfire Way SO31 ....127 F3
Spithead Ave PO12 ....181 C2
Spithead Ho PO16 ....155 A7
Spithead Hts PO4 ....183 D5
Spittlefields BH24 ....141 B7
Sportsman Pl SO30 ....80 E1
Spouts La SO51 ....50 D6
Spring Cl Fair Oak SO50 ....57 C2
Verwood BH31 ....114 F5
Spring Cres SO17 ....103 B8
Spring Ct Poole BH12 ....203 D5
Spring Firs SO19 ....103 E3
Spring Garden La PO12 ....181 C6
Spring Gdns
[2] Emsworth PO10 ....161 A8
North Baddesley SO52 ....54 A4
Poole BH12 ....203 D5
Portsmouth PO1 ....216 A3
Spring Gr SO31 ....105 A1
Spring Hills SO19 ....104 D4
Spring House Cl SO21 ....32 A1
Spring La
Bishopstoke SO50 ....56 D3
Colden Common SO21 ....31 F1
New Milton BH25 ....195 D2
Swanmore SO32 ....84 B5
Spring Pl [2] SO51 ....52 E7
Spring Rd
Bournemouth BH1 ....205 D4
Hythe SO45 ....125 E3
Lymington SO41 ....198 A2
Sarisbury SO31 ....128 F6
Southampton SO19 ....104 A5
Southampton,Merry Oak
SO19 ....103 F6
Spring St PO1 ....216 B3
Spring The PO1 ....110 F3
Spring Vale
Swanmore SO32 ....84 A4
Waterlooville PO8 ....112 B4
Spring Wlk PO1 ....216 B4
Springbank Rd BH7 ....205 D8
Springbourne Ct BH1 ....205 D5
Springbourne Mews
BH1 ....205 C5
Springcroft PO13 ....155 B5
Springdale Ave BH18 ....186 F5
Springdale Ct [3] SO40 ....100 F7
Springdale Fst Sch
BH18 ....186 E4
Springdale Gr BH18 ....186 E4
Springdale Rd BH18,
BH21 ....186 E4
Springfield [2] GU33 ....20 F4
Springfield Ave
Bournemouth BH6 ....207 A4
Christchurch BH23 ....191 D2
Holbury SO45 ....150 D3
Springfield Cl
Havant PO9 ....135 B2
Lymington SO41 ....198 A3
Verwood BH31 ....114 F5
Wickham PO17 ....108 A1

Springfield Cres
Poole BH14 ....**203** B4
Redlynch SP5 ....**47** D5
Springfield Ct S019 .....**103** F2
Springfield Dr S040 ....**100** E6
Springfield Gdns BH25 ..**195** D2
Springfield Gr S045 ....**150** D4
Springfield Rd
Poole BH14 ....**203** A4
Verwood BH31 ....**114** F5
Springfields Sch PO6 ....**158** C7
Springfield Way PO14 ...**179** C6
Springfields Cl 3 S021 ...**31** F1
Springford Cl S016 ....**78** B4
Springford Cres S016 .....**78** B3
Springford Gdns S016 ....**78** B4
Springford Rd S016 ....**78** B4
Springhill RC Prim Sch
S015 ....**102** E6
Springhill Rd S053 ....**55** D6
Springles La PO15 ......**130** A5
Springvale Ave
Bournemouth BH7 ....**205** F8
Kings Worthy S023 ....**2** B6
Springvale Rd S023 ....**2** B7
Springwater Cl BH11 ....**189** A3
Springwater Ct BH23 ....**207** D6
Springwater Dr BH23 ....**207** D6
Springwater Rd BH11 ...**189** A3
Springwell 3 PO9 ....**135** F1
Springwood Ave PO7 ....**134** F6
Spruce Ave PO7 ....**135** A6
Spruce Cl
Broadstone BH17 ....**186** E1
Warsash SO31 ....**152** D10
Spruce Dr
Southampton S019 ......**104** E5
Totton S040 ....**100** B8
Spruce Wlk 8 PO13 .....**179** F3
Spur Cl BH21 ....**164** C6
Spur Hill Ave BH14 .....**203** D3
Spur Rd Cosham PO6 .....**157** F8
Poole BH14 ....**203** D3
Waterlooville PO7 ....**134** E7
Spur The Gosport PO12 ...**180** F2
Wickham PO17 ....**108** A4
Spurgeon Rd BH7 ....**206** B6
Spurlings Ind Est PO17 ..**131** D3
Spurlings Rd PO17 ......**131** D4
Square Cl BH21 ....**164** F3
Square The
Bournemouth BH2 ....**204** F3
Compton PO18 ....**90** F2
Fawley S045 ....**151** B3
Gosport PO12 ....**181** C9
Hamble-le-R S031 ....**128** A2
Lymington S041 ....**197** C3
Petersfield GU32 ....**40** F3
Sherfield English S051 ....**26** B4
Southbourne PO10 ....**161** D7
Titchfield PO14 ....**153** F8
West Moors BH24 ....**166** B8
Westbourne PO10 ....**137** B3
Wickham PO17 ....**108** A3
Winchester S023 ....**215** E5
Squarey Cl SP5 ....**46** F6
Squires Wlk S019 ....**103** E1
Squirrel Cl
Bishopstoke S050 ....**56** F2
1 Christchurch BH23 .....**129** B5
Squirrel Dr S019 ....**104** A3
Squirrel Wlk BH31 ......**114** F5
Squirrel's Cl BH23 ......**191** D2
Squirrels Wlk S040 ......**125** F2
Stable Cl PO14 ....**129** D2
Stable Colts S043 ....**74** A3
Stable La 6 GU31 ....**40** F3
Stables The
Christchurch BH23 ....**206** F7
Locks Heath S031 ....**129** A2
Stacey Cl BH12 ....**203** C7
Stacey Ct Havant PO9 ....**135** D7
Portsmouth PO5 ....**182** C1
Stacey Gdns BH8 ....**190** F2
Stadium Way BH15 ......**202** C3
Staff Rd S051 ....**6** B1
Stafford Rd
Bournemouth BH1 ....**205** A4
Petersfield GU32 ....**40** F5
Portsmouth PO5 ....**216** C1
Waterlooville PO7 ....**102** D6
Staffriwise Bsns Ctr PO6 .**157** F7
Stag Bsns Pk BH24 ......**141** A5
Stag Cl Bishopstoke S050 ..**56** F2
New Milton BH25 ....**194** E4
Stag Dr S030 ....**105** D8
Stag Gates S045 ....**150** E1
Stag Way PO15 ....**130** B5
Stagbrake Cl S045 ....**150** B3
Stags La S021 ....**33** A5
Stagshorn Rd PO8 ....**112** C7
Stagswood BH31 ....**114** D6
Stainer Cl S019 ....**104** D3
Staith Cl S019 ....**104** C5
Stake's La S032 ....**59** E8
Stakes Hill Inf Sch PO7 ..**134** F6
Stakes Hill Rd PO7 ......**134** F6
Stakes La S032 ....**58** F4
Stakes Rd PO7 ....**134** D4
Stalbridge Dr BH22 .....**165** D4
Stalbridge Rd PO17 .....**202** A7
Stalham Rd BH12 ....**203** F6
Stallard Cl PO10 ....**136** E1
Stallards La BH24 ....**140** F7

Stalybridge Cl S031 .....**129** A6
Stamford Ave PO11 ......**184** E3
Stamford Cl S031 ....**184** E3
Stamford Lodge PO11 ....**184** E3
Stamford Rd BH6 ....**206** D5
Stamford St PO1 ....**216** D4
Stamford Way S050 ......**57** C1
Stampsey Ct 8 PO2 .....**157** D2
Stanshaw Cl 7 PO2 .....**157** D1
Stanshaw Inf Sch PO2 ...**157** D1
Stanshaw Rd PO2 ....**157** D1
Stanbridge Earls Sch
S051 ....**27** B3
Stanbridge La S051 ....**27** B3
Stanbridge Rd PO9 ......**136** B3
Standard Way PO16 .....**131** D3
Standen Rd S016 ....**77** C5
Standford St S014 ....**103** B4
Standing Hill SP5 ....**3** F8
Stanfield Cl BH12 ....**203** D7
Stanfield Rd
Bournemouth BH9 ....**204** E8
Ferndown BH22 ....**165** C6
Poole BH12 ....**203** D7
Stanford Cl PO6 ....**157** D8
Stanford Ct
28 Havant PO9 ....**136** B5
Southampton S019 ......**104** D3
Stanford Gdns S041 ....**197** D2
Stanford Hill S041 ......**197** D3
Stanford Rd S041 ....**197** D3
Stanford Rise S041 ......**172** B2
Stanhope Gate 1 PO5 ...**182** C2
Stanhope Rd PO1 ....**216** B3
Stanier Way S030 ....**81** C2
Staniforth Ct BH23 .....**207** D6
Stanley Ave PO3 ....**183** B8
Stanley Cl
Bishopstoke SP5 ....**22** B8
Fareham PO15 ....**130** E2
Gosport PO12 ....**156** A1
Verwood BH31 ....**115** A5
Stanley Ct
Bournemouth BH1 ....**205** C5
Poole BH15 ....**202** C6
Stanley Green Cres
BH15 ....**202** C5
Stanley Green Fst Sch
BH15 ....**202** C6
Stanley Green Ind Est
BH15 ....**202** C6
Stanley Green Rd
Poole BH15 ....**202** C5
Poole BH15 ....**202** C6
Stanley La PO5 ....**182** C2
Stanley Pearce Ho
BH17 ....**187** C1
**Stanley Pk (Crn & Chalet
Site)** BH25 ....**195** C6
Stanley Rd
Bournemouth BH1 ....**205** C5
Christchurch BH23 ......**209** A8
Emsworth PO10 ....**161** A8
Holbury S045 ....**150** D4
Lymington S041 ....**198** A2
Poole BH15 ....**202** C1
Portsmouth PO2 ....**157** C1
Southampton S017 ....**79** C1
Totton S040 ....**76** D1
Stanley Sq PO5 ....**182** C2
Stanmore La S022 ......**215** B3
Stanmore Prim Sch
S022 ....**215** C3
Stannington Cl BH25 ....**195** B2
Stannington Cres S040 ..**100** F8
Stannington Way S040 ..**100** F8
Stanpit BH23 ....**207** E5
Stanstead Rd S050 ....**55** F4
Stansted Cl PO10 ....**113** C1
Stansted Cres PO9 ......**136** B6
Stansted Ct PO9 ....**113** C2
Stansted Rd PO5 ....**216** D2
Stanswood Rd
Blackfield S045 ....**178** C6
Havant PO9 ....**135** D6
Stanton Bldgs S015 .....**102** A7
Stanton Lacy 12 BH13 ..**214** F7
Stanton Rd
Bournemouth BH10 .....**189** C2
Petersfield GU32 ....**40** E4
Southampton S015 ......**102** A7
Stanton Rd Ind Est
S015 ....**102** A7
Stapehill Cres BH21 ....**164** C5
Stapehill Mus & Gdns*
BH21 ....**164** E5
Stapehill Rd BH21 ......**164** F4
Staple Ash La GU32 ......**39** C7
Staple Cl PO7 ....**111** D1
Staple Close La BH15 ...**202** C6
Staple Cross
Burton BH23 ....**207** E8
Southwick PO17 ....**132** C8
Staplecross La BH23 ....**207** D8
Stapleford Ave BH22 ....**165** F6
Stapleford Cl S051 ....**28** B2
Stapleford La S032 ....**81** F5
Staplehurst Cl S019 ....**104** B1
Staplers Reach PO13 ....**155** B2
Stapleton Rd 6 PO3 ....**183** A8
Staplewood La
Ashurst S040 ....**124** C7
Marchwood S040 ....**101** C1
Star Cotts PO17 ....**108** A3
Star La BH24 ....**140** F7
Stares Cl PO13 ....**180** C7
Starina Gdns PO7 ....**135** B8
Starlight Farm Cl BH31 ..**115** A7

Starling Sq S050 ....**55** D2
Station App
Broadstone BH18 ....**187** A4
Brockenhurst S042 ......**146** A1
23 Portsmouth PO1 .....**182** A5
Station Cl PO17 ....**108** A4
Station Cotts S042 .....**123** D1
Station Hill Botley S030 ..**106** C7
Burnsledon S031 ....**128** B8
Eastleigh S050 ....**56** B3
Winchester S023 ....**215** D6
Station La S053 ....**55** C5
Station Rd Alderholt SP6 ..**92** F6
Bishop's Waltham S032 ...**83** C7
Burley BH24 ....**170** D7
Bursledon S031 ....**128** B8
Christchurch BH23 ......**207** A7
Christchurch,Highcliffe
BH23 ....**193** E2
Cosham PO6 ....**158** C7
Fordingbridge SP6 ....**69** D1
Gosport PO12 ....**180** F7
Liss GU33 ....**83** B4
Locks Heath S031 ....**129** A5
Netley S031 ....**127** B5
New Milton BH25 ....**195** A2
Nursling S016 ....**77** A5
Petersfield GU32 ....**40** E4
Poole,Lower Hamworthy
BH15 ....**202** A1
Poole,Lower Parkstone
BH14 ....**203** B4
Portchester PO16 ....**156** D8
Portsmouth PO3 ....**183** A8
Romsey S051 ....**52** E7
Soberton S032 ....**85** C7
South Hayling PO11 .....**184** E4
Southampton,Redbridge
S015 ....**101** C8
Southampton,Sholing
S019 ....**103** F3
Sway S041 ....**172** B1
Verwood BH31 ....**114** D7
West Moors GU32 ....**37** C4
West Moors BH22 ....**138** D2
Wickham PO17 ....**108** A4
32 Winchester S023 ....**215** D6
Station Rd N S040 ......**101** A7
Station Rd S S040 ......**101** A7
Station St
Lymington S041 ....**197** F4
Portsmouth PO1 ....**216** B3
Station Terr Twyford S021 ..**31** E6
Station Yd SP6 ....**92** E6
Staunton BH2 ....**204** F2
Staunton Ave PO11 .....**184** D3
Staunton Ctry Pk* PO9 ..**136** A7
**Staunton Ctry Pk Vistors
Ctr*** PO9 ....**136** A6
Staunton Park Com Sch
PO9 ....**136** B7
Staunton Rd PO9 ....**135** E2
Staunton St PO1 ....**216** B4
Stead Cl PO11 ....**185** B3
Stedman Rd BH5 ....**206** B5
Steel St PO5 ....**216** A1
Steele Cl S053 ....**55** C4
Steels Dro SP6 ....**70** E7
Steep Cl S016 ....**77** F6
Sheep Cl E Prim Sch GU32 .**40** F7
Steep Cl
Portchester PO16 ....**132** C1
Southampton S018 .....**104** C8
Steepdene BH14 ....**203** B3
Steeple Cl BH17 ....**187** D3
Steeple Way S031 ......**127** C7
Steepleton Rd BH18 ....**187** A2
Steerforth Cl PO2 ......**182** D8
Stein Rd PO10 ....**137** D2
Steinbeck Cl PO15 ......**129** C8
Stella Ct
18 Christchurch BH23 ...**209** B7
Southampton S016 ....**78** C4
Stem La BH25 ....**194** E4
Stenbury Way S031 .....**127** C7
Stenhurst Rd BH15 .....**202** E6
Step Terr S022 ....**215** C6
Stephen Cl PO8 ....**112** B2
Stephen Langton Dr
BH11 ....**188** D5
Stephen Lodge PO5 .....**216** B1
Stephen Martin Gdns
SP6 ....**69** E2
Stephen Rd PO15 ....**130** F1
Stephens Ct S051 ....**52** E6
Stephens Wlk BH24 ....**140** F7
Stephenson Cl PO12 ....**181** A3
Stephenson Rd S040 .....**76** D2
Stephenson Way S030 ...**81** C3
Steplake La S051 ....**25** C1
Steplake Rd S051 ....**50** D7
Stepnell Reach BH16 ...**201** D5
Sterte Ave BH15 ....**202** B4
Sterte Avenue W BH15 .**202** B4
Sterte Cl BH15 ....**202** C4
Sterte Esp BH15 ....**202** C4
Sterte Ind Est BH15 ....**202** B4
Sterte Rd BH15 ....**202** C4
Steuart Rd S018 ....**103** D7
Stevenson Cres BH14 ...**203** E3
Stevenson Rd BH6 ......**207** A3
Stevensons Cl 3 BH23 ..**163** C4
Steventon Rd S018 .....**104** C7
Stewart Cl 5 BH8 ......**205** C5
Stewart Ho S053 ....**30** C1

Stewart Pl PO1 ....**182** E7
Stewart Rd BH8 ....**205** B6
Stewarts Gn PO7 ....**86** C3
Stewarts Way BH22 .....**165** E7
Stibbs Way BH23 ....**169** C1
Stillmore Rd BH11 ......**188** D3
Stillwater Pk BH24 .....**117** C2
Stinchar Dr S053 ....**55** A5
Stinsford Cl BH9 ....**190** B4
Stinsford Rd BH11 .....**187** D1
Stirling Ave PO7 ....**134** F7
Stirling Bsns Pk BH21 ..**164** F7
Stirling Cl
New Milton BH25 ....**195** B3
Totton S040 ....**77** A1
Stirling Cres
Hedge End S030 ....**81** C1
Totton S040 ....**101** A8
Stirling Ct
3 Bournemouth BH4 ...**204** C2
Fareham PO15 ....**130** E3
11 New Milton BH25 ....**195** B3
Stirling Rd BH3 ....**204** E7
Stirling St PO2 ....**182** D8
Stirling Way BH23 .....**208** B6
Stirling Wlk S051 ....**52** E7
Stirrup Cl Upton BH16 ...**201** D7
Wimborne Minst BH21 ..**164** C6
Stock La SP5 ....**49** D6
Stock's Cross S043 ......**73** F4
Stock's La S032 ....**61** E5
Stockbridge Cl
Havant PO9 ....**136** B5
Poole BH17 ....**188** B2
Stockbridge Rd
Michelmersh S051 ....**27** C7
Winchester S022 ....**215** B7
Stocker Pl PO13 ....**155** D1
Stockers Ave S022 .....**215** B7
Stockheath La PO9 .....**135** E3
Stockheath Rd PO9 .....**135** F4
Stockheath Way PO9 ...**135** F4
Stockholm Dr S030 .....**105** C5
Stockley Cl S045 ....**150** C3
Stocks La GU34 ....**37** A2
Stockton Cl S030 ....**105** C7
Stockton Ave S019 .....**103** F6
Stodham La
Hill Brow GU33 ....**21** A2
Liss GU33 ....**20** F1
Stoke Common Rd S050 .**56** E5
Stoke Gdns PO12 ......**181** C5
Stoke Hts S050 ....**57** B3
Stoke Park Dr S050 ......**56** D4
Stoke Park Inf Sch S050 .**56** F2
Stoke Park Jun Sch
S050 ....**56** E2
Stoke Rd Gosport PO12 ..**181** C5
Southampton S016 ....**78** A1
Winchester S022 ....**2** A3
Stoke Wood Cl S050 .....**57** B2
Stoke Wood Rd BH24 ...**117** C2
Stokes Ave BH15 ....**202** D4
Stokes Bay Mobile Home Pk
PO12 ....**180** D2
Stokes Bay Rd PO12 ....**180** D2
Stokes Ct 2 S015 ......**102** E6
Stokesay Cl S045 ......**150** A8
Stokewood Rd BH3 .....**205** A8
Stone Copse Cl S031 ...**128** F2
Stone Gdns BH8 ....**191** A2
Stone La Gosport PO12 ..**181** B4
5 Gosport PO12 ......**181** B5
Wimborne Minst BH21 ..**163** A6
Stone Lane Ind Est
BH21 ....**163** B6
Stone Sq PO9 ....**216** A1
Stone Terr S021 ....**31** A1
Stonechat Cl
Ferndown BH22 ....**165** B8
Petersfield GU31 ....**41** C7
Stonechat Dr S040 .....**100** B8
Stonechat Rd PO8 ......**112** A7
Stonecrop Cl BH18 .....**186** E2
Stoneham Cemetery Rd
S018 ....**79** F4
Stoneham Cl
Petersfield GU32 ....**40** D4
Southampton S016 ....**79** D5
Stoneham Ct S016 ....**79** B5
Stoneham Gdns S031 ...**104** F1
Stoneham La S016 ....**79** E5
Stoneham Pk GU32 ......**40** D4
Stoneham Way S016, ...**79** E5
S018 ....**79** E5
Stonehills S045 ....**151** C3
Stoneleigh 3 BH13 .....**214** F8
Stoneleigh Ave S041 ...**195** F4
Stoneleigh Cl PO16 .....**156** B8
Stoner Hill Rd GU32 .....**19** B1
Stoners Cl PO13 ....**155** B3
Stoney Croft Rise S053 ..**55** C2
Stoney Ct S022 ....**215** C8
Stoney La S022 ....**215** C8
Stony La Burton BH23 ...**192** C2
Christchurch BH23 ......**207** C7
Damerham SP6 ....**68** B4
Portsmouth PO1 ....**182** A6
Stony Lane S BH23 .....**207** D6
Stonymoor Cl S045 .....**150** C3
Stopples La S041 ....**195** F3
Storrington Rd PO8 ......**88** D5
Story La BH18 ....**187** A1
Stour Cl Ferndown BH21 ..**164** D4

Stour Cl continued
Petersfield GU31 ....**40** E2
West End S018 ....**80** A3
West Wellow S051 ....**50** D3
Stour Ct 6 BH13 ....**204** A4
Stour Pk BH10 ....**189** E6
Stour Rd
Bournemouth BH8 ......**205** D6
Christchurch BH23 .....**207** A6
Stour Rdbt BH23 ....**206** F5
Stour View Gdns BH21 ..**162** E1
Stour Way BH23 ....**191** D1
Stour Wlk
Bournemouth BH8 ......**190** D4
Wimborne Minst BH21 ..**163** D3
Stourbank Rd BH23 ....**207** A6
Stourcliffe Ave BH6 ....**206** C4
Stourcroft Dr BH23 .....**191** E1
Stourfield Inf & Jun Schs
BH6 ....**206** D6
Stourfield Rd BH5 ......**206** B4
Stourpaine Rd BH17 ....**187** D2
Stourton Cl 21 BH4 ....**204** C3
Stourton Rd BH21 ......**206** D8
Stourvale Gdns BH5 .....**55** D5
Stourvale Pl 3 BH5 .....**206** B5
Stourvale Rd BH6 ......**206** C6
Stourwood Ave BH6 ...**206** C6
Stourwood Mans 4
BH6 ....**206** C4
Stourwood Rd BH6 .....**206** D4
Stouts La BH23 ....**169** B1
Stove Cres PO15 ....**130** D2
Stowe Cl S030 ....**81** D1
Stowe Rd PO4 ....**183** B4
Stradbrook PO13 ....**155** B1
Stragwyne Cl S052 .....**53** F5
Straight Mile The S051 ...**28** E2
Strand S014 ....**103** A4
Strand St BH15 ....**202** C1
Strand The PO13 ....**185** C1
Stranding St S050 ......**56** F2
Stratfield Dr 9 S053 ....**30** B1
Stratfield Gdns PO9 ....**135** D7
Stratfield Pk PO7 ......**134** C8
Stratfield Pl BH25 .....**194** E3
Stratford Ct 10 S023 ...**215** E8
Stratford Ho PO5 ......**216** B2
Stratford Pl
Eastleigh S050 ....**56** B4
Lymington S041 ....**197** D5
Stratford Rd PO7 ......**135** A8
Strathmore Dr BH31 ...**115** B6
Strathmore Rd
Bournemouth BH9 ......**190** A4
Gosport PO12 ....**181** C5
Stratton Cl PO6 ....**157** C8
Stratton Rd
Bournemouth BH9 ......**190** A4
Southampton S015 ....**78** C1
Winchester S022 ....**11** C7
Strawberry Fields
East Boldre S042 ....**175** D6
Hedge End S030 ....**105** A6
Strawberry Hill S031 ...**128** D3
Strawberry Mead S050 ..**57** B1
Streamleaze PO14 ......**129** C2
Street End S052 ....**54** B5
Street The SP5 ....**24** A4
Streets La BH24 ....**141** C4
Strete Mount 1 BH23 ...**207** E7
Stretton Ct BH14 ......**203** B4
Stride Ave PO3 ....**183** B6
Strides La BH24 ....**140** F7
Strides Way S040 ......**100** B7
Strode Gdns BH24 .....**140** B5
Strode Rd PO2 ....**157** C2
Strongs Cl S051 ....**53** B8
Stroud Cl
Portsmouth PO6 ....**133** A1
Wimborne Minst BH21 ..**164** A6
Stroud End GU32 ....**40** B4
Stroud Gdns BH23 .....**207** E6
Stroud Green La PO14 ..**154** D5
Stroud La BH23 ....**207** E6
Stroud Park Ave BH23 ..**207** E6
Stroud Sch S051 ....**53** E8
Stroude Ave BH5 ......**205** C8
Strouden Court Prec
PO9 ....**135** D7
Strouden Ct PO9 ....**135** D7
Strouden Rd BH9 ......**190** A1
Stroudley Ave PO6 .....**158** C6
Stroudley Way S030 .....**81** D2
Stroudwood Rd
Fair Oak S032 ....**58** A4
Havant PO9 ....**136** A3
Struan Cl BH24 ....**139** F6
Struan Ct BH24 ....**140** A6
Struan Dr BH24 ....**140** A6
Struan Gdns BH24 .....**139** F6
Stuart Bridgewater Ho
S018 ....**104** A7
Stuart Cl
Stubbington PO14 ......**179** C7
Upton BH16 ....**201** B7
Stuart Cres S022 ....**215** C3
Stuart Ct 4 PO6 ....**157** F8
Stuart Rd BH23 ....**209** B8
Stubbermere PO10 .....**136** E7
Stubbington Ave PO2 ...**157** E1
Stubbington La PO14 ...**179** B6
Stubbington La PO14 ...**179** A7
Stubbington Way S050 ..**57** D1
Stubbs Dro S030 ....**105** D7
Stubbs Rd S019 ....**104** C3
Stuckton Rd SP6 ....**94** B8
Student Village BH12 ...**204** D8

Studland Cl SO16 77 D1
Studland Ct 20 BH4 204 C3
Studland Dr SO41 211 C5
Studland Rd
Bournemouth BH4 204 C1
Lee-on-t-S PO13 179 E3
Southampton SO16 77 D1
Studley Ave SO45 150 C3
Studley Cl BH23 209 C8
Studley Ct BH25 209 D8
Sturgess Ct 14 PO16 131 B1
Sturminster Ho 4 SO16 78 A1
Sturminster Rd 1 BH9 190 B4
Styles The SP5 22 C8
Sudbury Rd PO6 157 D8
Suetts La SO32 83 F7
Suffolk Ave
Christchurch BH23 191 F2
Southampton SO15 102 D7
Suffolk Cl
Chandler's Ford SO53 55 C2
Wimborne Minst BH21 164 C6
Suffolk Dr
Chandler's Ford SO53 55 C2
Swanwick PO15 129 B7
Suffolk Gn SO53 55 C2
Suffolk Rd
Bournemouth BH2 204 E3
Portsmouth PO4 183 B3
Suffolk Rd S BH2 204 D3
Sullivan Cl PO6 156 E8
Sullivan Rd SO19 104 D3
Sullivan Way PO7 134 E5
Sultan Rd
Emsworth PO10 136 F1
Portsmouth PO1,PO2 182 D7
Sumar Cl PO14 154 D5
Summer Field Cl BH21 164 A4
Summer Flds BH31 114 F4
Summer La SO42 176 F8
Summercroft Way BH22 138 E3
Summerfield Cl BH23 192 C2
Summerfield Ct PO3 158 B4
Summerfield Gdns SO16 79 D5
Summerfields
Bournemouth BH7 205 F7
Locks Heath SO31 129 B1
Summerhill Rd PO8 112 A3
Summerlands BH22 165 D6
Summerlands Rd SO50 57 C2
Summerlands Wlk 17
PO9 136 B5
Summerleigh Wlk PO14 154 D5
Summers Ave BH11 189 B6
Summers La BH23 192 D1
Summers St SO14 103 C6
Summersfield GU33 20 F3
Summertrees Ct BH25 195 D4
Summit Way SO18 79 F1
Sumner Rd GU31 65 D5
Sun Ct PO5 216 C2
Sun St PO1 182 A5
Sun Valley Bsns Pk SO23 2 C1
Sunbeam Way PO12 181 B4
Sunbury Cl BH11 189 A6
Sunbury Ct
24 Bournemouth BH4 204 C3
Fareham PO15 130 E4
Suncourt Villas PO12 180 F8
Sunderland Dr BH23 208 B7
Sunderton La PO8 88 C5
Sundew Cl
Christchurch BH23 193 C1
New Milton BH25 195 D4
Sundew Rd BH18 186 E2
Sundowner SO14 103 B2
Sundridge Cl PO6 157 F8
Sunlight Cotts SO21 29 E8
Sunningdale
41 Bournemouth BH4 204 C3
Christchurch BH23 206 F6
Colden Common SO21 31 F1
Hythe SO45 125 F3
6 Poole BH15 202 E3
Sunningdale Cl
Bishopstoke SO50 56 F2
Gosport PO13 155 C1
Sunningdale Cres BH10 189 C4
Sunningdale Gdns
Broadstone BH18 187 A5
Southampton SO18 104 B7
Sunningdale Rd
Portchester PO16 156 D7
Portsmouth PO3 183 A7
Sunny Hill Ct BH12 203 D5
Sunny Hill Rd BH12 203 D5
Sunny Way SO40 100 F7
Sunny Wlk PO1 182 A6
Sunnybank Dr BH21 164 B6
Sunnybank Rd BH21 164 B6
Sunnybank Way BH21 164 B6
Sunnydown Rd SO22 10 A3
Sunnyfield Rd BH25 210 A8
Sunnyfield Rise SO31 105 A1
Sunnyfields PO6 158 C7
Sunnyheath PO9 135 E4
Sunnyhill Rd BH6 206 C5
Sunnylands Ave BH6 206 F4
Sunnymead Dr PO7 111 D2
Sunnymoor Rd BH11 189 A1
Sunnyside Pk BH24 140 C5
Sunnyside Rd BH12 203 D6
Sunnyside Wlk PO9 135 D7
Sunridge Cl BH12 204 A6
Sunrise Ct BH22 165 D5
Sunset Ave SO40 100 E8
Sunset Lo BH13 204 A2
Sunset Rd SO40 100 E8
Sunshine Ave PO11 185 B2
Suntrap Gdns PO11 185 B2
Sunvale Cl SO19 104 B3
Sunwood Rd PO9 135 D5
Surbiton Rd SO50 56 B5
Surrey Cl
Christchurch BH23 191 F2
Totton SO40 100 D5
Surrey Ct
Chandler's Ford SO53 55 D3
Southampton SO15 102 C6
Surrey Gdns BH4 204 C4
Surrey Lo 8 BH4 204 D4
Surrey Point 7 SO16 78 E3
Surrey Rd
Bournemouth BH4,BH12 204 B4
Chandler's Ford SO53 55 D4
Southampton SO19 103 D2
Surrey Rd S BH4 204 C4
Surrey St PO1 216 B3
Sussex Cl BH9 190 B4
Sussex Ct
6 Gosport PO12 181 C9
Portsmouth PO5 216 B1
Sussex Gdns GU31 40 F2
Sussex Pl
Portsmouth PO5 216 B1
Portsmouth,Landport PO1 216 B4
Sussex Rd
Chandler's Ford SO53 55 D3
Petersfield GU31 41 B1
Portsmouth PO5 216 B1
Southampton SO14 103 A4
Sussex St SO23 215 D6
Sussex Terr PO5 216 B1
Sutherland Ave BH18 186 E5
Sutherland Cl 6 SO51 28 B1
Sutherland Rd
Portsmouth PO4 182 E4
Southampton SO16 77 F5
Sutherlands Ct SO53 55 C6
Sutherlands Way SO53 55 B6
Sutton Cl Poole BH17 188 B2
Portsmouth PO3 158 B4
Waterlooville PO8 111 D3
Sutton Ct PO14 130 F1
Sutton Gdns SO23 215 E6
Sutton Hill Camping Site
BH21 114 B8
Sutton Pl SO42 146 A1
Sutton Rd
Bournemouth BH9 190 B1
Totton SO40 76 E1
Waterlooville PO8 111 D3
Swale Dr SO53 55 A7
Swallow Cl
Broadstone BH17 201 F8
Havant PO9 136 B2
Totton SO40 100 C6
Swallow Ct Clanfield PO8 88 B6
Lee-on-t-S PO13 179 F4
Swallow Dr SO41 211 E4
Swallow Sq SO50 55 D2
Swallow Way BH21 164 A7
Swallow Wood PO16 131 B3
Swan Cl Emsworth PO10 161 A8
Lower Swanwick SO31 128 D7
Swan Ct Bursledon SO31 128 C8
Gosport PO13 155 B4
Swan Ctr The SO50 56 B2
Swan Gn 3 BH23 207 A5
Swan La SO23 215 E6
Swan Mead BH24 141 C6
Swan Quay
Portchester PO16 155 D8
Southampton SO18 103 D8
Swan St GU32 40 E3
Swanage Cl SO19 103 E3
Swanage Rd PO13 179 E3
Swancote PO16 155 F8
Swanley Cl SO50 56 A5
Swanmore Ave SO19 104 C3
Swanmore Bsns Pk SO32 83 F5
Swanmore CE Prim Sch
SO32 84 B5
Swanmore Cl
Bournemouth BH7 206 B7
Winchester SO22 1 D4
Swanmore Coll of Tech
SO32 84 A4
Swanmore Park Ho SO32 84 C8
Swanmore Rd
Bournemouth BH7 206 B7
Droxford SO32 84 E7
Havant PO9 135 D7
Swanmore SO32 84 A6
Swans Wlk PO11 185 B3
Swansbury Dr BH8 191 B2
Swanton Cl PO14 179 D8
Swanton Gdns SO53 55 B7
Swanwick Bsns Ctr
SO31 128 D7
Swanwick La
Lower Swanwick SO31 128 E8
Swanwick SO31 129 A8
Swanwick Nature Reserve*
SO31 128 F8
Swanwick Shore Rd
SO31 128 D7
Swanwick Sta SO31 129 B6
Swarraton Rd PO9 136 A3
Sway Ct 20 Havant PO9 136 B5
Sway SO41 196 C8
Sway Gdns BH8 190 D2
Sway Park Ind Est SO41 172 B1
Sway Rd
Brockenhurst SO42 172 F7
Lymington SO41 197 B6
Sway Rd *continued*
New Milton BH25,SO41 195 C6
Sway Sta SO41 172 B1
Swaythling Prim Sch
SO17 79 B3
Swaythling Rd
Havant PO9 135 D6
West End SO30 80 B2
Swaythling Sta SO18 79 D4
Swedish Hos SO41 198 E8
Sweep The BH24 140 F7
Sweetbriar Gdns PO7 134 F5
Sweethills Cres PO15 129 C8
Sweyns Lease SO42 175 C6
Swift Cl Broadstone BH17 201 F8
Eastleigh SO50 55 D2
Horndean PO8 112 A7
Lee-on-t-S PO13 179 F4
Winchester SO22 215 B3
Swift Gdns SO19 103 D1
Swift Hollow SO19 103 D1
Swift Rd
Southampton SO19 103 D1
Thorney Island PO10 161 A3
Swinburn Gdns PO8 111 F4
Swincombe Rise SO18 80 B1
Swiss Rd PO7 134 E7
Switch House Rd SO45 151 E2
Swivelton La PO17 132 A3
Sword Cl Clanfield PO8 88 B5
Gosport PO12 180 E2
Sword Sands Rd PO2 183 C7
Swordfish Dr BH23 208 B7
Sycamore Ave SO53 30 C1
Sycamore Cl
Broadstone BH17 186 F1
Bursledon SO31 127 F8
Christchurch BH23 206 D8
Clanfield PO8 88 D5
Gosport PO13 155 E1
Milford on S SO41 211 C5
North Baddesley SO52 53 F5
Romsey SO51 53 C6
Titchfield PO14 129 C1
Waterlooville PO8 111 E3
Sycamore Ct
4 Fordingbridge SP6 69 F1
Ringwood BH24 117 C2
Sycamore Dr
Holbury SO45 150 B5
Kings Worthy SO23 2 B8
South Hayling PO11 184 F4
Sycamore Pl BH21 164 D5
Sycamore Rd
Bishop's Waltham SO32 83 E7
Hordle SO41 195 F4
Hythe SO45 125 F3
Southampton SO16 78 A2
Sycamore Wlk
Botley SO30 105 F7
Petersfield GU31 40 E1
Sycamores The SO45 126 A4
Sydenham Ct PO1 216 D3
Sydenham Terr
Portsmouth PO1 216 D3
Westbourne PO10 137 B5
Sydling Cl BH17 188 B2
Sydmanton Cl SO51 53 A6
Sydmonton Ct 2 PO9 136 B6
Sydney Ave SO31 127 E3
Sydney Ho PO1 216 B4
Sydney Rd
Bishopstoke SO50 56 D4
Broadstone BH18 187 A3
Christchurch BH23 191 E1
Gosport PO12 181 B5
Southampton SO15 78 B1
Syers Cl GU33 20 F4
Syers Rd GU33 20 F4
Sylmor Gdns BH9 190 A2
Sylvan Ave SO19 104 C6
Sylvan Cl Hordle SO41 196 B2
St Leonards BH24 139 D4
Sylvan Dr SO52 53 F3
Sylvan Fst Sch BH12 203 B6
Sylvan La SO31 128 A2
Sylvan Rd BH12 203 B6
Sylvan View PO7 134 F6
Sylvans The SO45 125 D3
Sylvia Cres SO40 76 E1
Symes Rd
Hamworthy BH15 201 E4
Romsey SO51 53 B7
Symonds Cl SO53 55 D4
Symonds St SO23 215 E5
Synor Ho 12 SO15 103 A6
Sywell Cres PO3 158 C4

T

Tadburn Cl
Chandler's Ford SO53 55 D5
Romsey SO51 53 B7
Tadburn Gn SO51 52 E6
Tadburn Rd SO51 53 A6
Tadden Cotts BH21 162 D7
Tadden Wlk BH18 186 F2
Tadfield Cres SO51 53 A7
Tadfield Rd SO51 53 A7
Tadhurst Ho 4 PO1 216 C3
Tait Cl BH17 202 E7
Tait Pl PO13 155 D1
Talbot Ave BH3 204 E7
Talbot Cl Havant PO9 135 D3
Southampton SO16 78 F4
Talbot Comb Sch BH12 204 B8
Talbot Ct
Bournemouth BH9 189 F1
21 Southampton SO14 103 A3
Talbot Dr
Christchurch BH23 193 F2
Poole BH12 204 B8
Talbot Heath Sch BH4 204 C5
Talbot Hill Rd BH9 204 D8
Talbot House Prep Sch
BH9 204 E7
Talbot Manor BH3 204 D8
Talbot Mdws BH12 204 B8
Talbot Mews BH10 189 B1
Talbot Rd
Bournemouth BH9 204 E7
Dibden Purlieu SO45 125 E1
Havant PO9 135 D3
Portsmouth PO4 182 E4
Titchfield PO15 129 E2
Talbot Rdbt BH3 204 D7
Talbot Rise BH10 189 C2
Talisman Bsns Ctr SO31 129 B6
Talland Rd PO14 129 B1
Tamar Cl Ferndown BH22 166 A5
Portchester PO16 132 A1
Tamar Down PO7 135 A7
Tamar Gdns SO18 80 B2
Tamar Gr SO45 125 E3
Tamarisk Cl
Portsmouth PO4 183 C3
Stubbington PO14 179 C6
Waterlooville PO7 135 A5
Tamarisk Gdns SO18 103 E8
Tamarisk Rd SO30 105 B8
Tamella Rd SO30 105 E6
Tammys Turn PO14 154 B8
Tamorisk Dr SO40 100 C6
Tamworth Ct 3 PO12 181 B4
Tamworth Rd
Bournemouth BH7 205 F5
Portsmouth PO3 183 A6
Tan Howse Cl BH7 206 B8
Tanfield La PO17 108 A3
Tanfield Pk PO17 108 A3
Tangier La SO32 83 A8
Tangier Rd PO3 183 B7
Tanglewood
Fareham PO16 131 A3
Marchwood SO40 102 A1
Tanglewood Cl PO7 134 C4
Tanglewood Ct 1 BH25 195 B3
Tanglewood Lo BH17 201 F8
Tangley Wlk PO9 136 B5
Tangmere Cl BH23 208 B6
Tangmere Dr SO16 78 A4
Tangmere Pl BH17 202 E7
Tangmere Rise SO53 55 D4
Tangyes Cl PO14 179 D8
Tanhouse Cl SO30 105 D5
Tanhouse La SO30 105 D5
Tankerdale La GU33 41 C8
Tankerton Cl 2 PO6 157 E8
Tankerville Rd SO19 103 D3
Tanner St 7 SO23 215 E5
Tanner's Brook Inf Sch
SO15 101 F7
Tanner's Brook Jun Sch
SO15 101 F7
Tanner's Brook Way
SO15 101 F6
Tanner's La PO7 111 A5
Tanner's Ridge PO7 134 E3
Tanneries Ind Est The
PO9 135 E1
Tanneries The PO14 154 A8
Tanners La
Fareham PO14 154 F5
Sandleheath SP6 68 F3
South Baddesley SO41 199 A4
West Wellow SO51 51 D7
Tanners Rd SO52 54 A3
Tanners The PO14 129 C1
Tansy Cl PO7 135 A6
Tansy Mdw SO53 54 F4
Tanyard Cotts GU32 41 B6
Tanyards The SO53 30 B1
Taplin Dr SO30 105 C8
Taplings Cl SO22 1 D3
Taplings Rd SO22 1 D3
Tapper Ct BH21 163 E4
Taranto Rd SO16 78 C4
Tarbery Cres PO8 112 C7
Tardif Ho SO16 78 B2
Target Rd PO2 157 C2
Tarius Cl PO13 155 D3
Tarleton Rd PO6 133 B1
Tarn Dr BH17 201 F8
Tarn Rise PO8 88 C2
Tarrant Cl BH17 187 E2
Tarrant Gdns PO9 135 D3
Tarrant Rd BH9 190 B3
Tarrants The 12 BH2 204 D4
Tasman Cl
Christchurch BH23 206 F8
Southampton SO14 103 B2
Tasman Ct SO14 103 B2
Taswell Rd PO5 182 D2
Tatchbury La SO40 99 F8
Tatchbury Mount Hospl
SO40 76 A2
Tate Ct SO15 101 C7
Tate Mews SO15 101 C8
Tate Rd SO15 101 C8
Tates Rd SO45 126 B3
Tatnam Cres BH15 202 C3
Tatnam Rd BH15 202 C4
Tattenham Rd SO42 172 F8
Tattershall Cres PO16 156 B7
Tatwin Cl SO19 104 D5
Tatwin Cres SO19 104 D5
Taunton Dr SO18 104 B7
Taunton Row SO53 55 D3
Taunton's Coll SO15 78 E1
Tavell's La SO40 101 E1
Tavells Cl SO40 101 E1
Taverner Cl BH15 202 D2
Taverners Cl SO19 104 D3
Tavistock Cl 4 SO51 28 B1
Tavistock Gdns 3 PO9 136 B1
Tavy Cl SO53 55 B6
Taw Dr SO53 55 B6
Tawny Owl Cl PO14 154 B4
Taylor Cl SO19 103 D1
Taylor Dr BH8 190 D4
Taylor Rd PO12 181 C3
Taylor Way BH31 115 A6
Taylor's Bldgs 6 BH15 202 C1
Taylors Cnr SO23 2 B5
Teachers Terr 7 GU33 20 F4
Teachers Way SO45 150 B4
Teak Cl BH13 214 H8
Teal Cl Horndean PO8 112 A7
Portchester PO16 155 F8
South Hayling PO11 185 B3
Totton SO40 100 C7
Teal Wlk PO13 155 B3
Teapot Row 2 PO4 183 B2
Teasel Way BH22 138 E1
Teazle Cl GU31 41 C2
Tebourba Cotts SO41 172 B1
Tebourba Dr PO12 181 A4
Tebourba Ho 6 PO14 154 E8
Tebourba Way
Curdridge SO30 106 D7
Southampton SO16 101 F7
Technology Rd BH17 202 A8
Ted Bates Ct 7 SO15 102 E6
Ted Bates Rd 9 SO14 103 B3
Ted Kelly Ct 43 PO1 182 A5
Tedder Cl BH11 189 B3
Tedder Gdns BH11 189 B3
Tedder Rd
Bournemouth BH11 189 B3
Gosport PO13 155 D3
Southampton SO18 104 A8
Tedder Way SO40 100 D7
Teddington Rd PO4 183 A3
Tee Ct 10 SO51 52 E7
Tees Cl SO53 55 A7
Tees Farm Rd SO21 56 F8
Tees Gn SO21 56 F8
Teg Down GU31 41 B4
Teg Down Meads SO22 215 A7
Teglease Gn PO9 135 D7
Teignmouth Rd
Gosport PO12 180 F7
Portsmouth PO3 183 A8
Telegraph Rd SO30 80 E1
Telegraph Way SO21 12 B7
Telephone Rd PO4 182 E4
Telford Gdns SO30 81 E2
Telford Pl SO41 211 E4
Telford Rd
Ferndown BH21 165 A8
Portsmouth PO2 157 E3
Telford Way SO31 129 C5
Teme Cres SO16 101 E8
Teme Rd SO16 101 E8
Temeraire 11 SO15 102 F8
Tempest Ave PO7 135 A8
Templar Ct 2 SO14 103 A7
Templars Mede SO53 55 B3
Templars Way SO53 55 B3
Temple Gdns SO19 103 F2
Temple La GU32 63 E8
Temple Mews BH1 205 D6
Temple Rd Liss GU33 21 A6
Southampton SO19 103 F2
Temple St PO1 216 B4
Temple Trees 45 BH4 204 C3
Templecombe Rd SO50 56 F1
Templemere PO14 154 B7
Templer Cl BH11 188 F1
Templeton Cl PO2 157 E3
Tenby Cl SO18 104 A8
Tenby Dr SO53 55 A4
Tench Way SO51 52 F8
Tennyson Cl
Bishop's Waltham SO32 83 E8
Holbury SO45 150 B5
Tennyson Cres PO7 111 D1
Tennyson Ct
2 Portswood SO17 79 B1
22 Southampton SO17 79 A1
Tennyson Gdns PO16 131 A2
Tennyson Rd
Bournemouth BH9 189 F2
Eastleigh SO50 55 F2
1 Poole BH14 203 A3
Portsmouth PO2 182 F8
Southampton SO17 79 B1
Totton SO40 76 D2
Wimborne Minst BH21 163 C6
Tenon Ct BH23 207 B7
Tensing Cl PO16 131 A3
Tensing Rd BH23 207 E8
Tenterton Ave SO19 104 B1
Terence Ave BH17 187 C1
Terence Gdns PO4 182 E2
Terence Rd BH21 186 C5
Terminus Terr SO14 103 B3
Tern Cl SO45 126 B2
Tern Ct BH6 206 D6

Tern Wlk Gosport PO13 ...155 B3
6 Portsmouth PO4 ......183 B5
Terrace Rd BH2 ....204 E3
Terrace The
Damerham SP6 ....68 D5
Rockbourne SP6 ....68 F8
Terrier Cl SO30 ....81 C3
Terrington Ave BH23 ....193 E1
Terriote Cl SO53 ....55 C7
Test Cl GU31 ....40 E2
Test Ho SO23 ....215 F4
Test La SO16 ....77 B2
Test Rd SO14 ....126 B8
Test Valley Bsns Ctr
SO16 ....77 C2
Test Valley Bsns Pk
SO52 ....54 A5
Testbourne Ave SO40 ...100 D7
Testbourne Cl SO40 .....100 D7
Testbourne Rd SO40 ....100 D6
Testcombe Rd PO12 .....181 B4
Testlands Ave SO16 ......77 D6
Testwood Ave SO40 ......76 E1
Testwood Cres SO40 .....76 D2
Testwood La SO40 ....76 F1
Testwood Pl SO40 ....101 A8
Testwood Rd
Havant PO9 ....135 D5
Southampton SO15 ......102 B6
Testwood Sch SO40 ......76 F1
Tethering Dro SP6 ....47 D3
Tetney Cl SO16 ....77 E3
Tetsome Cotts PO17 ....130 E7
Teviot Ho 9 SO14 ......103 C6
Teviot Rd SO53 ....55 A5
Tewkesbury Ave
Fareham PO15 ....130 C3
Gosport PO12 ....181 B8
Tewkesbury Cl PO6 .....157 D8
Texas Dr SO22 ....10 B3
Thackeray Mall 10 PO16 .131 B1
Thackeray Rd SO17 .....103 B8
Thackeray Sq 11 PO14 ...131 C1
Thacking Gn SO21 ....56 F8
Thames Cl
Ferndown BH22 ....166 A6
West End SO18 ....80 B3
Thames Ct 1 PO8 ....111 F4
Thames Dr PO15 ....130 C4
Thames Mews 11 SO2,2 .202 B1
Thames St BH15 ....202 B1
Thameshead Cl PO12 ...180 F7
Thatched Cottage Cvn Pk
SO43 ....122 B6
Thatchers La
Norleywood SO41 ......198 F8
Sopley BH23 ....168 F3
Theatre Mews 17 PO5 ..182 D2
Theobald Rd BH23 ......191 A8
Theseus Rd PO13 ....179 D4
Thessaly Ct 4 BH4 .....205 F4
Thetchers Cl BH25 .....195 B5
Thetford Gdns SO53 ....55 A7
Thetford Rd
Gosport PO12 ....180 F7
Poole BH12 ....203 F5
Thicket The
Gosport PO13 ....155 E1
Portchester PO16 ......131 F1
Portsmouth PO5 ....216 C1
Romsey SO51 ....53 C6
Waterlooville PO7 ......134 D3
Third Ave Cosham PO6 .157 E8
Havant PO9 ....136 A2
Southampton SO15 .....101 F6
Thirlmere SO50 ....55 F2
Thirlmere Cl PO14 .....154 D4
Thirlmere Ho 12 PO6 ..133 B1
Thirlmere Rd PO6 ......157 F8
Thirstane Firs SO53 ....55 B4
Thistle Cl BH23 ....208 C8
Thistle Rd
Chandler's Ford SO53 ...54 F5
Hedge End SO30 ....105 B6
Thistlebarrow Rd BH7 ..205 E6
Thistledown PO8 ....112 B5
Thistledowne Gdns
PO10 ....161 B8
Thomas Cl SO40 ....100 D6
Thomas Grant Ave
PO12 ....181 D7
Thomas Lewis Way SO17 .79 C2
Thomas Lockyer Cl
BH31 ....115 A5
Thomas Rd
North Baddesley SO52 ..54 A4
Petersfield GU31 ....41 A5
Thompson's La
Colden Common SO50,SO21 .57 E7
Colden Common,Hensting
SO50 ....57 C7
Thompsons La PO7 .....110 C6
Thoresby Ct BH25 .....194 E3
Thorn Cl Eastleigh SO50 ...70 F2
Petersfield GU31 ....41 C2
Thorn Rd BH17 ....187 D3
Thornbrake Rd PO12 ...181 C4
Thornbury 18 BH4 .....204 C3
Thornbury Ave
Blackfield SO45 ....177 F8
Southampton SO15 .....102 E2
Thornbury Ct PO14 ....154 C8
Thornbury Ho 10 PO6 ..132 F2
Thornbury Hts SO53 ...30 F1
Thornbury Rd BH6 .....207 A4

Thornbury Wood SO53 ...30 F1
Thornby Ct PO3 ....158 B4
Thorncliffe Cl PO2 .....157 F4
Thorncombe Cl
Bournemouth BH9 ......190 B4
Poole BH17 ....187 E2
Thorncroft Rd PO1 .....182 E5
Thornden Sch SO53 .....55 F8
Thorndike Cl SO16 ......78 A2
Thorndike Rd SO16 .....77 F2
Thorne Cl BH31 ....114 E6
Thorne Way BH21 ......139 B6
Thorner's Homes,Centre Ct
15 SO15 ....102 B8
Thorner's Homes,North Ct 14
SO15 ....102 B8
Thorner's Homes,South Ct 16
SO15 ....102 B8
Thorner's Homes,West Ct 13
SO15 ....102 B8
Thorness Cl 8 SO15 ...102 F6
Thorness Cl SO16 ....77 C1
Thorney Cl PO14 ....154 D8
Thorney Island Com Prim Sch
PO10 ....161 A3
Thorney Old Pk PO10 ..161 D1
Thorney Rd PO10 ......161 B6
Thorney View PO11 ....160 C2
Thornfield Cl PO8 ......88 C2
Thornfield Dr BH23 ....193 F1
Thorngate SP5 ....4 B8
Thorngate Ct 5 PO12 ..181 A7
Thorngate Way 5
PO12 ....181 D5
Thornham La SO30 .....161 C6
Thornham Rd BH25 ....195 D3
Thornhill Ave SO19 ....104 D6
Thornhill Cl SO45 ......150 F2
Thornhill Park Rd SO18 .104 D7
Thornhill Prim Sch
SO19 ....104 C5
Thornhill Rd
Blackfield SO45 ....150 F2
Southampton SO16 .....78 D4
Thorni Ave PO15 ....130 C3
Thornleigh Rd SO19 ...103 E2
Thornley Rd BH10 .....189 D4
Thornton Ave SO31 ....128 C1
Thornton Cl
Corfe Mullen BH21 ....186 C5
Cosham PO7 ....134 B2
Thornton Rd PO12 .....181 B9
Thornworthy 4 SO45 ..125 E1
Thornycroft Ave SO19 ..103 D2
Thorogood Ct 4 BH15 .202 E4
Thorold Ct SO18 ....79 E1
Thorold Rd
Chandler's Ford SO53 ...30 E1
Southampton SO18 .....79 E1
Three Acre Dr BH25 ...209 F8
Three Acres PO7 ....111 A3
Three Cross Rd BH21 ...138 E6
Three Horse Shoes La
SO24 ....16 E2
Three Legged Cross Fst Sch
SO24 ....114 E1
Three Lions Cl 9 BH21 .163 B5
Three Oaks SO19 ......104 E5
Three Tun Cl 13 PO1 ..182 A5
Threefield La SO14 ....103 A3
Thresher Cl PO7 ....112 C1
Throop Cl BH8 ....191 A2
Throop Rd
Bournemouth,Holdenhurst
BH8 ....191 A2
Bournemouth,Throop BH8 .190 D4
Throopside Ave BH9 ...190 D4
Thrush Rd BH12 ....188 C1
Thrush Wlk PO8 ....111 E4
Thruxton Cl SO19 ......103 E5
Thruxton Rd PO9 ......135 D5
Thurbern Rd PO2 ......157 E2
Thurmell Cl SO30 ......105 C4
Thurmell Wlk SO30 ....105 C4
Thurmond Cres SO22 ..215 A4
Thurmond Rd SO22 ....215 A4
Thursby Rd BH23 ......193 F1
Thurston Cl SO53 ......55 D7
Thwaite Rd PO3 ....204 B5
Thyme Ave PO15 ....129 D8
Thyme Ct 2 PO15 .....129 D8
Tichborne Gr PO9 .....135 D5
Tichborne Rd
Eastleigh SO50 ....80 A8
Southampton SO18 ....104 D8
Tichborne Way PO13 ..155 D1
Tichborne Ho SO30 ....105 C7
Tickleford Dr SO19 ....104 A1
Tickner Cl SO30 ....105 E5
Ticonderoga Gdns
SO19 ....103 E1
Tidcombe Gn PO9 .....135 D5
Tidemill Cl BH23 ....207 A8
Tides Reach SO18 .....103 D8
Tides Way SO40 ....101 F2
Tideway Gdns PO4 ....135 F4
Tidworth Rd PO9 ......135 F4
Tiffany Cl SO41 ....195 F4
Tiffield Cl PO3 ....158 C4
Tiger Rd PO1 ....181 F8
Tilbrook Rd SO15 ......101 E6
Tilburg Rd BH23 ....207 D7
Tilbury Ct SO41 ....31 D5
Tile Barn Camp Site
SO42 ....173 A8
Tilebarn La SO42 ......173 A6
Tilford Rd PO8 ....111 F6

Tiller Gdns BH11 ....189 A5
Tillingbourn PO14 .....129 C3
Tillington Gdns PO8 ...88 D4
Tilmore Gdns GU32 ...40 F5
Tilmore Rd GU32 ......40 A5
Timberlane PO7 ....134 D4
Timberley Ho 2 PO1 ..216 C3
Timberley La SP5 ......48 A6
Timberly Cl SO45 .....150 C4
Timbermill St SP6 .....93 F8
Timbers The PO15 ....130 C1
Timor Cl PO15 ....129 C8
Timothy Cl BH10 .....189 D5
Timpson Rd PO1 ......216 A4
Timsbury Cres PO9 ...135 E2
Timsbury Ct SO19 ....103 F4
Timsbury Dr SO16 ....77 F1
Tincknell Ct SO16 ....100 C6
Tincleton Gdns BH9 ..190 B4
Tindale Rd SO16 ......77 E2
Tinker Alley SO30 .....80 A7
Tinkers Cross SP6 ....69 E4
Tinneys Cl SP5 ....47 D4
Tintagel Cl SO16 ......78 C6
Tintagel Way PO6 ....157 B7
Tintern Cl PO6 ....133 A1
Tintern Gr SO15 ......102 E5
Tintern Rd PO12 ......181 A5
Tipner Cl PO2 ....157 C3
Tipner La PO2 ....157 B3
Tipner Rd PO2 ....157 C2
Tiptoe Gn 17 PO9 .....136 B6
Tiptoe Prim Sch SO41 .195 D8
Tipton Cl BH11 ....171 B1
Tipton Ho PO5 ....216 B2
Tiptree Cl SO50 ......56 A5
Tisted Ct 9 PO9 ......136 B5
Titchfield Abbey*
PO15 ....153 F1
Titchfield Haven Visitor Ctr*
PO14 ....153 F1
Titchfield Hill PO14 ...154 A8
Titchfield La PO17 ....107 D3
Titchfield Park Rd
PO15 ....129 D3
Titchfield Prim Sch
PO14 ....129 F1
Titchfield Rd PO14 ....154 B6
Tithe Barn SO41 ......197 E5
Tithe Mead SO51 .....27 F1
Tithe The PO7 ....111 D8
Tithelands La SO24 ...15 F4
Titus Gdns PO7 ....135 A8
Tiverton Ct
34 Bournemouth BH4 .204 C3
1 Fareham PO16 .....131 C2
Tivoli Cl PO13 ....55 F7
Tivoli Ct PO2 ....182 F8
Toby St PO1 ....216 B4
Todber Cl BH11 ......188 D3
Tolstoi Rd BH14 .....203 D2
Tokar St PO4 ....143 F6
Tokio Rd PO3 ....158 A1
Tolefrey Gdns SO53 ..54 F6
Tollard Cl BH12 ......203 D8
Tollbar Way SO30 ....105 A8
Tollgate BH13 ....187 D2
Tollgate Cl SO22 .....55 C2
Tollgate Ests SO51 ..27 B3
Tollgate Rd SO31 ....128 C8
Tollgate The
Fareham PO16 ....131 B2
3 Winchester SO23 .215 E2
Tolpuddle Gdns BH9 .190 B4
Tolworth Rd PO6 .....157 A8
Tomkyns Cl SO23 ....54 F6
Tommy Green Wlk SO50 .55 F3
Toms La BH24 ....118 B8
Tonbridge St PO5 ....182 C2
Tonge Rd BH11 ....188 B8
Tonnant Cl PO14 .....179 D2
Toogoods Way SO16 ..77 D5
Toomer Cl SO45 .....150 C4
Toothill Rd SO51 .....53 D1
Top La BH24 ....141 A7
Topaz Gr PO7 ....134 A1
Topiary Gdns SO19 ..129 B4
Topiary The BH14 ...202 F5
Tor Cl Porchester PO7 ..134 E3
Waterlooville PO7 ....134 F3
Tor Way GU31 ....41 A3
Torbay Rd BH14 .....203 C3
Torberry Dr GU31 ....41 B2
Torch Cl SO30 ....105 E5
Torcross Cl SO19 ....103 C2
Torfrida Ct PO14 .....154 D8
Tormead SO45 ......125 F3
Tornay Gr SO52 .....52 E4
Toronto Pl PO12 .....181 B6
Toronto Rd PO2 .....157 E3
Torquay Ave
Gosport PO12 ....181 A4
Southampton SO15 ...102 A5
Torque Cl SO19 ......104 E4
Torre Cl SO50 ....56 A5
Torridge Gdns PO8 ..111 C3
Torrington Cl SO19 ...104 A4
Tortoise La PO14 ....129 B1
Torvain Pk BH14 ....203 A2
Torwood Gdns SO50 ..56 F2
Tosson Cl 3 SO16 ...100 E6
Totland Cl SO16 .....101 E8
Totland Ct 4 BH4 ...204 C3
Totland Rd Cosham PO6 ..157 E7
Gosport PO13 ....155 C2
Totmel Rd BH17 .....188 A2
Totnes Cl SO50 ......55 F5

Tottehale Cl SO52 .....53 F3
Tottenham Rd PO1 ....216 D4
Totton & Eling Heritage Ctr*
SO40 ....101 A6
Totton By Pass SO40 ..101 A7
Totton Coll SO40 .....100 D8
Totton Sta SO40 ......101 A7
Totton Western By-Pass
SO40 ....100 C5
Totton Wlk PO9 ......135 D6
Tournerbury La PO11 ..185 B4
Tourney Rd BH11 .....188 E6
Tovey Pl SO23 ....2 C7
Towans The BH13 ....214 C3
Tower Cl PO12 ....180 D3
Tower Ct
Bournemouth BH2 ....204 E2
Warsash SO31 ....128 C1
Tower Gdns 4 SO16 ...78 F4
Tower Ho SO19 ....103 E1
Tower Ind Est The SO50 .56 C2
Tower La Eastleigh SO50 .56 C2
Wimborne Minst BH21 .163 D6
Tower Park Rdbt BH15 .202 F7
Tower Pl SO30 ....80 D1
Tower Rd
Bournemouth BH1 ....205 E5
Poole BH13 ....204 B2
Portsmouth PO4 .....182 F3
Winchester SO23 ....215 D6
Tower Rd W BH13 ....204 A1
Tower St Emsworth PO10 .161 A8
Portsmouth PO1 .....184 F4
Winchester SO23 ....215 D6
Tower Rd The PO12 ..181 A5
Towers Farm PO17 ...107 D5
Towers Gdn PO9 ......159 F6
Towers The SO31 ....122 E8
Towers Way PO9 .....186 D7
Town Hall Rd PO9 ....135 F1
Town Quay
Portsmouth PO1 .....181 F4
Southampton SO15 ..102 F2
Towngate Bridge PO15 .202 C3
Towngate Sh Ctr 1
BH15 ....202 C3
Townhill Inf Sch SO18 .80 A2
Townhill Jun Sch SO18 .80 A2
Townhill Way SO18 ...80 B2
Townsend Cl BH11 ...189 B6
Townsend La Martin SP6 .43 A4
Pentridge SP6 ....42 E4
Townsend Prim Sch
BH8 ....191 A2
Townsville Rd BH9 ....190 F4
Towpath Mead PO4 ..183 C4
Toynbee Cl SO50 .....56 A3
Toynbee Rd SO50 ....56 A3
Toynbee Sch The SO53 .55 F5
Tozer Cl BH11 ....188 D3
Tracey Ct 8 BH23 ....209 A7
Trafalgar
Chandler's Ford SO53 ..55 B5
Hermitage PO10 .....161 D8
Trafalgar Ct
Christchurch BH23 ...207 F5
6 Portsmouth PO5 ..182 D2
Trafalgar Ho SO45 ...126 B3
Trafalgar Pl
Lymington SO41 .....197 F4
Portsmouth PO1 .....216 A4
Trafalgar Rd
Bournemouth BH9 ....190 F4
Southampton SO14 ..103 A2
Southampton,Freemantle
SO15 ....102 C6
Trafalgar Sq PO12 ...181 A6
Trafalgar St SO23 ....215 D6
Trafalgar Way 3 SO45 .126 B1
Trampers La PO17 ...57 B1
Tranby Rd SO19 ......103 F2
Tranmere Cl SO41 ...197 F2
Tranmere Rd PO4 ....158 A6
Treadwheel Rd PO8 ..113 B6
Treagore Rd SO40 ....76 C1
Trearnan Cl SO16 ....101 D8
Treble Cl SO22 ....10 B4
Treeside Rd SO15 ....102 A7
Treeside Ave SO40 ...101 A8
Trefoil Cl Denmead PO7 .132 A7
Trefoil Way 8 PO7 ...208 C8
Tregantle Mews PO12 .181 A5
Tregaron Ave BH10 ..189 B5
Tregonwell 18 BH2 ...204 E2
Tregonwell Rd BH2 ..204 E2
Treharne Cl 6 BH31 ..114 E6
Treloen Ct 9 BH4 ....204 C3
Treloyhan Cl SO53 ...55 D4
Tremona Ct SO16 ....78 E3
Tremona Rd SO16 ....78 D2
Trenley Cl SO40 .....150 B3

Trent Way continued
West End SO30 ....80 D2
Trent Wlk PO16 ......156 A8
Trentham Ave BH7 ...206 B8
Trentham Cl BH7 ....206 B8
Tresillian Cl BH23 ...194 B2
Tresillian Gdns BH23 .80 B2
Tresillian Way BH23 ..194 B2
Trevis Rd PO4 ....183 C4
Trevone Cl SO53 ....195 B3
Trevone Ct SO40 ....100 C5
Trevor Rd PO4 ......182 E3
Trevose Cl
Chandler's Ford SO53 ..55 D4
Gosport PO13 ....155 C1
Trevose Cres SO53 ...55 D5
Trevose Way PO14 ...129 B1
Triangle Gdns PO16 ..77 D3
Triangle La PO14 ....153 E4
Triangle The
Bournemouth BH2 ...204 E3
Upton BH16 ....201 B7
Whiteparish SP5 .....24 B4
Tribe Rd PO12 ....181 A6
Tricketts La PO7 .....165 F6
Trigon Rd BH15 .....202 D7
Trimaran Cl SO31 ....128 E1
Trimaran Rd SO31 ...128 E1
Trimm's Dro SP6 .....70 E8
Trimmer's Ct PO1 ...181 F5
Trinidad Cl 1 PO6 ...132 F2
Trinidad Cres 1 ....203 C8
Trinidad Ho PO1 .....203 C8
Trinity 2 BH1 ....205 E3
Trinity Cl Fst Sch BH31 .114 F8
Trinity Cl PO13 ......181 E5
Trinity Ct
Chandler's Ford SO53 ..55 D6
8 Southampton SO15 .102 C6
9 Totton SO40 ......76 E2
Trinity Gdns
Fareham PO16 ......131 A1
2 Winchester SO23 .215 E6
Trinity Ind Est
Southampton SO15 ..101 F7
Wimborne Minst BH21 .163 E3
Trinity Rd
Bournemouth BH1 ...205 A4
Southampton SO14 ..103 A5
7 Southampton SO16 .131 B1
Tripps Mobile Home Pk
SO30 ....105 D7
Tristan Cl SO16 ......178 E2
Tristram Cl SO53 ....54 F4
Triton Ctr The SO51 ..53 D5
Triumph Rd PO14 ...154 F5
Troak Cl BH23 ....207 D8
Trojan Way PO7 ....134 F3
Troon Cl BH18 ....134 C1
Troon Rd BH14 .....203 D3
Trooper Bottom GU32 .19 B3
Trosnant Jun Sch PO9 .135 E3
Trosnant Rd PO9 ....135 E3
Trotters La SO40 ....101 C3
Trotts La SP5 ....12 F4
Troublefield Nature
Reserve* BH23 .....191 A8
Trowbridge Cl 7 PO1 .182 D7
Trowbridge Cl SO16 ..77 E5
Truman Rd BH11 ....189 B6
Truro Ct PO13 ....180 B8
Truro Rd PO12 ......132 F1
Truro Rise SO50 .....56 E3
Truscott Ave BH9 ...205 C4
Trussell Cl SO22 .....1 D3
Trussell Way SO22 ..1 D2
Trystworthy 3 BH2 ..204 E3
Tuckers La PO11 .....1 D3
Tucks Cl BH23 ....193 A8
Tuckton Cl BH6 .....206 D6
Tuckton Rd
Bournemouth,Southbourne
BH6 ....206 F5
Bournemouth,West Southbourne
BH6 ....206 E4
Tuckton Rdbt BH6 ..206 E4
Tudor Cl Lee-on-t-S PO13 .178 F3
Tudor Ct Alderholt SP6 ..93 A5
Gosport PO13 ....180 D8
South Hayling PO11 ..184 F2
Tudor Cres PO6 .....157 F6
Tudor Ct
Bournemouth PO6 ...157 F8
Fareham PO14 ......154 F7
Poole BH15 ....202 E6
Tudor Gdns PO13 ...105 A5
Tudor House Mus & Gdn*
SO14 ....103 A2
Tudor Rd SO18 ......104 D8
Tudor Wood Cl SO16 .78 F4
Tuffin Cl SO16 ......78 F4
Tukes Ave PO13 .....155 B4
Tulip Gdns Havant PO9 .135 C1
Salisbury SP1 ....129 E2
Tumulus Cl SO19 ....104 A4
Tunstall Rd
Portsmouth PO6 ....133 D1
Southampton SO19 ..104 E4

Tunworth Ct PO9 ....136 B5
Tupman Ho ⁴ PO1 ....182 D7
Tuppenny La PO10 ....161 C8
Turbary Cl BH21 ....203 D8
Turbary Ct
  Bournemouth BH12 ....189 A1
  Ferndown BH22 ....165 F6
  Upton BH16 ....201 C8
Turbary Hts BH11 ....188 F1
Turbary Park Ave BH11 ...189 A2
Turbary Rd
  Ferndown BH22 ....165 F6
  Poole BH12 ....203 D8
Turbary Ret Pk BH11 ......188 F3
Turf Croft Ct BH23 ....194 B2
Turk's La BH14 ....203 A1
Turlin Moor Com Fst Sch
  BH16 ....201 C4
Turlin Moor Com Mid Sch
  BH16 ....201 C4
Turlin Rd BH16 ....201 C4
Turnberry Cl BH23 ....206 F6
Turner Ave PO13 ....180 E8
Turner Rd PO1 ....182 D7
Turners Farm Cres
  SO41 ....196 A2
Turners Oak Cl SO15 ......78 C1
Turnpike Down SO21 ......11 C8
Turnpike Way SO30 ....105 B7
Turnstone Gdns SO16 .....78 B5
Turnworth Cl BH18 ....187 C3
Turtle Cl PO14 ....154 B4
Turvy King Ct PO7 ....110 F4
Tuscan Wlk SO53 ....55 E6
Tuscany Way PO7 ....135 B8
Tussocks The SO40 ....101 F2
Tutland Rd SO52 ....53 F4
Tutor Cl SO31 ....127 F3
Tutt's La SO51 ....50 E4
Tweed Cl SO53 ....55 A7
Tweed La SO41 ....197 D8
Tweedale Rd BH9 ....190 C3
Twemlow Ave PO12 ......202 F3
Twiggs End Cl SO31 ......128 F4
Twiggs La
  Marchwood SO40 .....124 E7
  Marchwood SO40 .....124 E8
Twiggs Lane End SO40 ...124 C5
Twin Oak Pk BH23 ....192 D6
Twin Oaks SO19 ....103 F3
Twin Oaks Cl BH18 ....187 A3
Twitterns Way PO9 ....115 A1
Twyford Ave
  Portsmouth PO2 ......157 D1
  Southampton SO15 ...78 C4
Twyford Cl BH8 ....190 D2
Twyford Ct ⁵ SO23 ....215 E8
Twyford Ct PO13 ....179 F3
Twyford Ho
  Southampton SO15 ...102 F7
  Trickett's Cross BH22 .165 F6
Twyford Rd SO50 ....156 B8
Twyford Sch SO21 ....32 A6
Twyford St Mary's CE Prim
  Sch SO21 ....31 F5
Twyford Way BH17 ....188 A2
Twynham Ave BH23 ......207 A7
Twynham Cl SP5 ....46 F6
Twynham Rd BH6 ....206 F4
Twynham Sch BH23 ......207 A6
Twynhams Hill SO32 .....108 A8
Tyler Ct PO9 ....135 E5
Tylers Cl SO41 ....197 D5
Tyleshades The SO51 .....53 A6
Tyne Cl SO53 ....55 A5
Tyne Way SO30 ....80 E2
Tynedale Cl
  Bournemouth BH9 ....190 B4
  Gosport PO12 ....180 E4
Tyneham Ave BH12 ......203 C8
Tynham Ct BH23 ....207 C6
Tyrrels La BH24 ....142 E4
Tyrrel Lawn PO9 ....135 D7
Tyrrel Rd SO53 ....55 C7
Tyrrell Gdns BH8 ....191 A2
Tyrrells Ct BH23 ....169 B1
Tyseley Rd PO5 ....216 B2
Tytherley Gn
  Bournemouth BH8 ....190 D2
  ⁵ Havant PO9 ....136 B5
Tytherley Rd SO18 ......104 C8

U

Ubsdell Cl BH25 ....195 A3
Uddens Dr BH21 ....164 D7
Uddens Trad Est BH21 ...164 E6
Ullswater SO50 ....56 A1
Ullswater Ave SO18 ......80 B1
Ullswater Ho ⁴ PO6 ......133 B1
Ullswater Rd
  Southampton SO16 ...77 E1
  Wimborne Minst BH21 .163 C2
Undercliff Dr BH1 ....205 C2
Undercliff Gdns SO16 ....77 E1
Undercliff Rd BH5 ....205 E3
Underdown Ave PO7 .....134 D2
Undershore SO41 ....197 E6
Undershore Rd SO41 ....198 A4
Underwood Cl
  Poole BH17 ....187 B1
  Southampton SO16 ...78 E4
Underwood Rd
  Bishopstoke SO50 ....56 E3
  Southampton SO16 ...78 E4
Unicorn Rd
  Lee-on-t-S PO13 ......179 D4

Unicorn Rd continued
  Portsmouth PO1 ....216 B4
Unicorn Training Ctr The
  PO1 ....216 A4
Union La SO32 ....61 A1
Union Pl PO1 ....216 C4
Union Rd Havant PO9 ....135 E1
  Southampton SO14 ...103 C6
Union St Fareham PO16 ..131 C1
  ⁵ Portsmouth PO1 ....182 A5
  Winchester SO23 .....215 F6
Univ Coll Winchester
  SO22 ....215 C5
Univ of Portsmouth
  PO1 ....216 A3
Univ of Portsmouth (Eldon
  Bldg) PO1 ....216 B2
Univ of Portsmouth
  (Langstone Campus)
  PO4 ....183 D5
Universal Marina SO31 ..128 C6
University Cres SO17 .....79 B3
University Parkway SO16 .54 D1
University Rd SO17 ......79 B3
University Rdbt BH10 ....204 C8
Unwin Cl SO19 ....103 D1
Upham CE Prim Sch
  SO32 ....58 E5
Upham St SO32 ....58 D5
Uphill Rd SO22 ....1 C5
Upland La GU33 ....20 B7
Uplands Ave BH25 ....210 A8
Uplands Cl BH22 ....166 A8
Uplands Cres PO16 ......131 B2
Uplands Gdns BH8 ......190 C2
Uplands Prim Sch PO16 .131 A3
Uplands Rd
  Bournemouth BH8 ....190 C2
  Cosham PO6 ....158 C8
  Denmead PO7 ....110 C6
  Rowlands Castle PO9 ..113 C2
  West Moors BH22 ....139 A1
  Winchester SO22 .....1 E3
Uplands Sch BH14 ....203 C3
Uplyme Cl BH17 ....188 A2
Upmill Cl SO18 ....80 B3
Uppark (NT)* GU31 ......90 F8
Upper Arundel St PO1 ...216 B3
Upper Banister St ¹
  SO15 ....102 F6
Upper Barn Copse SO50 .57 B3
Upper Bere Wood PO7 ...134 E7
Upper Brook Dr SO31 ....128 F2
Upper Brook St SO23 ....215 B5
Upper Brownhill Rd
  SO16 ....77 F3
Upper Bugle St SO14 ....102 F3
Upper Church Rd SO32 ..107 E7
Upper Common Rd
  SO41 ....196 F4
Upper Cornaway La
  PO16 ....132 B1
Upper Crabbick La PO7 ..110 C6
Upper Crescent Rd ⁵ 53 F5
Upper Deacon Rd SO19 ..104 C6
Upper Gn GU33 ....19 E7
Upper Golf Links Rd
  BH18 ....187 B5
Upper Gordon Rd ⁵ 194 A1
Upper Heyshott GU31 ...41 A3
Upper High St SO23 .....215 D6
Upper Hinton Rd BH1 ....204 F3
Upper House Ct PO17 ....108 A3
Upper House Farm SO24 .16 D2
Upper Market St SO50 ...56 B3
Upper Mead Cl SO50 ....57 D2
Upper Moors Rd
  Brambridge SO50 ....31 F1
  Colden Common SO21,SO50 .56 F8
Upper Mount GU33 ......20 E3
Upper Mullins La SO45 ..125 E3
Upper New Rd SO30 .....80 D1
Upper Northam Cl
  SO30 ....105 A6
Upper Northam Dr
  SO30 ....105 A5
Upper Northam Rd
  SO30 ....105 B6
Upper Norwich Rd ⁶
  BH2 ....204 E3
Upper Old St PO14 ......154 B4
Upper Piece PO7 ....111 A3
Upper Rd BH12 ....203 C6
Upper Shaftesbury Ave
  SO17 ....79 B2
Upper Shirley Ave SO15 .78 C1
Upper Spinney SO31 .....152 C10
Upper St Helens Rd
  SO30 ....105 B5
Upper St Michael's Gr
  PO14 ....154 F8
Upper Terrace Rd BH2 ...204 E3
Upper Toothill Rd SO16,
  SO51 ....53 E1
Upper Wardown GU31 ...41 B4
Upper Weston La SO19 ..104 A2
Upper Wharf PO14 ......155 C8
Uppleby Rd BH12 ....203 C6
Upton Cl Havant PO9 ....135 D7
  Upton BH16 ....201 B7
Upton Cres SO16 ....78 F4
Upton Cross Mobile Home Pk
  BH16 ....201 C7
Upton Ct BH16 ....201 D7
Upton Ctry Pk* BH17 ....201 F6
Upton Grey Cl SO22 .....1 D3
Upton Heath Est BH16 ..201 D7

Upton Ho ³ SO16 ....78 A1
Upton Ind Est BH16 .....201 D6
Upton Inf Sch BH16 .....201 A7
Upton Jun Sch BH16 ....201 A7
Upton La SO16 ....77 C6
Upton Rd BH17 ....201 F7
Upton Way BH16 ....186 F3
Upwey Ave BH15 ....201 E3
Usborne Cl PO13 ....179 F4
Utrecht Cl BH23 ....207 D7
Uxbridge Cl SO31 ......128 F6

V

Vadne Gdns PO12 ....181 B7
Vaggs La SO41 ....195 E6
Vale Cl BH14 ....203 E4
Vale Dr SO18 ....79 F1
Vale Gr PO12 ....181 A8
Vale Lodge BH1 ....205 D5
Vale Mans ⁴ BH1 ....205 D4
Vale Rd
  Bournemouth BH1 ....205 D4
  Poole BH14 ....203 E4
  Redlynch SP5 ....47 C6
  Winchester SO23 .....11 C6
Vale The Horndean PO8 ..88 C1
  Hythe SO45 ....125 F3
  Locks Heath SO31 ....129 B2
  Portsmouth PO5 .....182 C2
Vale View Pk SO41 ......195 F7
Valencia Cl BH23 ....191 D4
Valentine Ave SO19 .....104 C3
Valentine Cl PO15 ......130 C2
Valentine Ct
  Southampton SO19 ...104 C3
  Waterlooville PO7 ....135 A8
Valentines Inf Sch
  SO19 ....104 C2
Valerian Ave PO15 ......129 F3
Valerian Cl SO50 ....81 C6
Valerian Rd SO30 ....105 D8
Valetta Pk PO10 ....160 E8
Valetta Rd PO10 ....161 D1
Valette Rd BH9 ....190 A3
Valiant Gdns PO2 ....157 D4
Valiant Way BH23 ......208 B7
Valley Cl Blackfield SO45 .150 F1
  Christchurch BH23 ...191 E3
  Colden Common SO21 ..56 F8
  Redlynch SP5 ....47 D6
  Waterlooville PO7 ....134 C3
Valley Ct The SO22 .....215 B4
Valley Park Dr PO8 .....88 D4
Valley Rd
  Bournemouth BH8 ....190 F3
  Chandler's Ford SO53 ..55 C7
  Littleton SO22 ....1 B5
  Totton SO40 ....100 F5
Valley Rise SO31 ....128 E4
Valley View Poole BH18 .204 B7
  Southampton,Sholing
  SO19 ....104 A4
  Southampton,Sholing Common
  SO19 ....104 A5
Valleydene SO45 ....125 F2
Vallis Cl BH15 ....202 D1
Vanburgh Way ⁶ SO30 ..30 B1
Vancouver Wharf SO19 ..103 C4
Vanguard Ct PO4 ....183 D3
Vanguard Rd
  Bournemouth BH8 ....190 E1
  ⁶ Poole BH15 ....202 C2
  Southampton SO18 ...104 A8
Vanstone Rd PO13 ......180 D7
Vantage Way BH12 .....188 B2
Vardy Cl SO19 ....104 D3
Varna Rd SO15 ....102 C6
Varos Cl PO12 ....181 A7
Varsity Rd PO10 ....161 D1
Vaudrey Cl SO19 ....104 E5
Vaughan Cl SO19 ....104 E5
Vaughan Rd SO45 ......125 C4
Vauxhall Way GU32 .....60 E3
Veal's La SO40 ....125 A7
Year's La SO21 ....57 A8
Vecta Cl BH23 ....208 C6
Vectis Ct ¹ SO41 ....78 F4
Vectis Rd
  Barton on S BH25 ....209 D7
  Gosport PO12 ....180 E3
Vectis Way PO6 ....157 F7
Velder Ave PO4 ....183 B5
Vellan Ct SO16 ....77 C1
Velmore Rd SO53 ......55 B4
Velsheda Ct SO45 ......126 A5
Velvet Lawn Rd BH25 ...195 A3
Venator Pl BH21 ....163 C6
Venerable Rd PO13 .....179 E4
Vengeance Rd PO13 ....179 F4
Venice Cl PO7 ....135 A8
Venning Ave PO11 .....188 E5
Ventnor Cl SO16 ....79 C5
Ventnor Rd
  Gosport PO13 ....155 B3
  Portsmouth PO4 .....182 E4
Ventnor Way PO16 .....131 B1
Ventry Cl BH13 ....203 F4
Ventura Ctr The BH16 ..186 A7
Ventura Pl BH16 ....186 A7
Venture Ct PO3 ....158 C4
Venture Ind Pk PO3 ....158 A5

Venture Rd SO16 ....54 D1
Verbena Cres PO8 ......112 B4
Verbena Way SO30 .....105 C6
Verdon Ave SO31 ....127 F3
Verger Cl PO14 ....129 C3
Verity Cres BH17 ......188 A1
Vermont Cl SO16 ....78 F4
Vermont Rd SO16 ......78 E4
Vernalls Cl BH10 ....189 A4
Vernalls Ct BH25 ......195 C5
Vernalls Gdns BH10 ....189 D5
Verne Rd BH31 ....115 A5
Verney Cl BH11 ....189 B3
Verney Rd BH11 ....189 A3
Vernham Rd SO22 ......215 C8
Verno La BH23 ....193 C1
Vernon Ave PO4 ....183 A5
Vernon Cl
  Bishop's Waltham SO32 .59 D2
  Gosport PO12 ....181 A6
Vernon Ct ³ PO2 ....157 E2
Vernon Hill SO32 ....59 D2
Vernon Mews ² PO4 ....183 A5
Vernon Rd Gosport PO12 .181 A6
  Portsmouth PO4 .....183 A5
Vernon Wlk ⁸ SO15 ....102 F6
Verona Ave BH6 ....206 D5
Verona Rd SO53 ....55 F6
Verulam Pl ⁸ BH1 ......204 F3
Verulam Rd Poole BH14 .202 F4
  Southampton SO14 ..103 B7
Verwood CE Fst Sch
  BH31 ....114 C5
Verwood Cres BH6 .....207 B4
Verwood Ind Est BH31 ..115 A6
Verwood Rd
  Ellingham BH24 .....116 A1
  Havant PO9 ....136 B6
  Ringwood BH24 .....140 C8
  Three Legged Cross BH21 .114 F1
  Woodlands Common BH21 .114 A7
Veryan PO14 ....130 E1
Vesca Rd SO31 ....129 B6
Vespasian Cl SO18 .....103 D7
Vespasian Rd SO18 ....103 D7
Vespasian Way SO53 ...55 F7
Vesta Way SO53 ....55 F7
Vetch Cl BH23 ....208 C8
Vian Cl PO13 ....155 C4
Vian Ct BH25 ....194 F3
Vian Pl SO23 ....2 C8
Vian Rd PO7 ....134 E5
Vicarage Cotts BH8 ....190 F3
Vicarage Dr SO30 .....105 B5
Vicarage Farm Bsns Pk
  SO50 ....57 C5
Vicarage Gdns SO41 ...196 A2
Vicarage La Cadnam SO40 .75 B1
  Curdridge SO32 .....106 C8
  Hambledon PO7 .....86 D3
  Hordle SO41 ....196 A2
  Stubbington PO14 ...179 C8
  Swanmore SO32 ....84 C6
Vicarage Pk SP5 ......47 D6
Vicarage Rd
  Bournemouth BH9 ...189 F1
  Marchwood SO40 ...101 F1
  Poole BH15 ....202 C6
  Redlynch SP5 ....48 A5
  Verwood BH31 ......114 F6
Vicarage Terr PO12 ....180 F8
Vicarage Way BH23 ....192 D2
Vice La SO43 ....74 A4
Viceroy Rd SO19 ......104 A3
Vickers Cl BH8 ....191 B2
Vickery Way BH23 .....207 D8
Victena Rd SO50 ......57 C2
Victor Cl SO18 ....104 D6
Victor Rd
  Portsmouth PO1 .....182 F7
  Thorney Island PO10 .161 D1
Victor St SO15 ....78 B1
Victoria Ave
  Bournemouth BH9 ...189 E1
  Portsmouth PO1 .....182 B3
  South Hayling PO11 ..184 F3
  Waterlooville PO7 ...134 B3
Victoria Bldgs SO32 ...83 B8
Victoria Cl
  Corfe Mullen BH21 ...186 D5
  Locks Heath SO31 ...129 A1
Victoria Cottage Hospl
  PO10 ....160 F8
Victoria Cres PO12 ....203 D6
Victoria Ct Durley SO32 .82 C7
  Netley SO31 ....127 A6
  ⁶ Portsmouth PO1 ...182 D7
  South Hayling PO11 .184 E3
Victoria Gdns
  Ferndown BH22 .....165 D6
  Fordingbridge SP6 ...69 D1
  Ringwood BH24 .....141 A6
Victoria Glade SO31 ...127 C5
Victoria Gr ² PO5 ......216 C1
Victoria Ho
  ¹ Fareham PO16 .....131 B1
  ⁵ Winchester SO23 ..215 D6
  Victoria Hospl BH21 ..163 A4
Victoria Mews ⁶ PO7 ...130 E7
Victoria Park Pl ⁴ BH9 ..189 F1
Victoria Park Rd BH9 ...189 E1
Victoria Pl
  Bournemouth BH1,BH8 .205 C5
  ⁶ Gosport PO12 .....181 B5
  ⁴ Lymington SO41 ...197 E2
  Romsey SO51 ....52 E7
  Wimborne Minst BH21 .163 B5

Victoria Rd
  Bishop's Waltham SO32 .83 B8
  Bournemouth BH1 ....205 C5
  Christchurch BH23 ...207 E5
  Eastleigh SO50 ......56 B5
  Emsworth PO10 .....136 E1
  Ferndown BH22 .....165 D6
  Fordingbridge SP6 ...69 D1
  Milford on S SO41 ...211 C4
  Netley SO31 ....127 A6
  Poole BH12 ....203 C6
  Portsmouth PO1 .....182 A6
  Southampton SO19 ..103 D2
  Stoke PO11 ....159 F2
  Waterlooville PO7 ...134 E7
  Wimborne Minst BH21 .163 B5
  Winchester SO23 ....215 D5
Victoria Rd N PO5 .....216 C2
Victoria Rd S PO5 .....182 D2
Victoria Sch BH13 ....203 F4
Victoria Sq PO13 .....179 A3
Victoria St Gosport PO12 .181 C6
  Portsmouth PO1 .....182 D7
  Southampton SO14 ..103 C5
Victoria Terr
  ³ Cosham PO6 ......157 F7
  Lumley PO10 ....137 A1
  Southbourne PO10 ..161 C8
  Westbourne PO10 ...137 B3
Victoria Wlk SO30 ....80 E2
Victory Ave PO8 ......112 A6
Victory Cl
  Chandler's Ford SO53 .55 B4
  Three Legged Cross BH21 .139 B6
Victory Cotts SO31 ....128 D7
Victory Cres SO15 ....102 B6
Victory Ct PO13 ......155 C1
Victory Gn PO2 ....157 C2
Victory Ho PO6 ....157 A7
Victory Rd
  ² Portsmouth PO1 ...182 A5
  Southampton SO15 ..102 B6
  Stubbington PO14 ...179 C7
Victory Ret Pk PO2 ....182 C7
Victory Sq SO15 ......102 B6
Victory Trad Est PO3 ..158 B2
Victory Way SO16 ....77 F7
Viewside Cl BH21 .....186 C5
Viking Cl Blackfield SO45 .177 F8
  Bournemouth BH6 ...207 A4
  Southampton SO16 ..77 E4
  Stubbington PO14 ...179 B8
Viking Way
  Bournemouth BH6 ...207 A4
  Christchurch BH23 ...208 A5
  Horndean PO8 ......88 C3
Vikings The SO51 .....53 B7
Villa Gdns PO7 ....134 F8
Village Cl PO14 ....201 A4
Village Ctr SO40 ......101 F1
Village Gate PO14 ....153 F8
Village Mews SO40 ...101 F1
Village Rd PO12 ......181 A3
Village St GU32 ......41 B6
Village The SP5 ......4 A8
Villas The BH25 ......195 A2
Ville De Paris Rd PO14 .155 A5
Villeneuve St Georges Way
  SO50 ....55 E3
Villette Cl BH24 ......192 A1
Villiers Ct
  ¹⁰ Portsmouth PO5 ..182 C2
  Winchester SO23 ...215 D5
Villiers Rd Hythe SO45 .149 F8
  Portsmouth PO5 ....182 C2
  Southampton SO15 ..102 C8
Vimoutiers Ct SP6 ....69 F1
Vine Ho ⁵ PO1 ....154 E8
Vince Cl BH11 ....189 B5
Vincent Ave SO16 ....78 C2
Vincent Gr PO16 .....156 C7
Vincent Rd
  ¹ New Milton BH25 ..195 A2
  Southampton SO15 ..102 C8
Vincent St SO15 ......102 C8
Vincent's Gr SO15 ...102 B8
Vincent's Wlk SO14 ...103 A4
Vine Bank SO18 ......104 D5
Vine Cl Bournemouth BH7 .206 A7
  Warsash SO31 ......127 F2
Vine Coppice PO7 ....134 E4
Vine Ct ⁸ PO6 ....157 F7
Vine Farm Cl BH12 ...204 C8
Vine Farm Rd BH12 ...204 B8
Vine Hill BH21 ....162 A5
Vine Ho SO31 ....129 A5
Vine Rd SO18 ....104 D5
Vine Sch The SO32 ...106 D8
Vinegar Hill SO41 ....211 D3
Vineries Cl BH21 .....163 F6
Vinery Gdns SO16 ....78 C1
Vinery Rd SO16 ......78 C2
Vinery The BH25 .....195 B2
Vineside PO13 ....155 E1
Viney Ave SO51 .....53 B8
Viney Rd SO41 ......197 F1
Vineyard Cl SO19 ....103 C3
Vineyards The SO32 ..54 A4
Vinnells La GU32 ....37 D6
Vinneys Cl BH23 ....192 C2
Vinson Rd GU33 ....21 A4
Violet Ave PO14 ....179 B7
Violet Cl SO53 ......55 A6

Violet Farm CI BH21 ....186 D8
Violet La BH25 ....195 A4
Violet Rd SO16 ....79 A4
Virginia CI BH12 ....203 C7
Virginia Park Rd PO12 ..180 F6
Viscount Ct BH11 ....188 D5
Viscount Dr BH23 ....208 B7
Viscount Wlk BH11 .....188 D5
Vista Marina BH13 .....214 D6
Vita Rd PO2 ....157 E3
Vitre Gdns SO41 ....197 E2
Vivash Rd PO1 ....216 D3
Vixen CI PO14 ....179 B7
Vixen Wlk BH25 ....195 B5
Vokes CI SO19 ....104 B5
Vokes Cotts SO23 ....2 A5
Vulcan CI SO15 ....101 F7
Vulcan Rd
  Southampton SO15 ....101 F7
  Thorney Island PO10 ..161 D1
Vulcan The **10** PO1 ..182 A4
Vulcan Way BH23 ......208 B7
Vyse La **15** SO14 ...102 F3

W

Wade Court Rd PO9 ....160 A8
Wade La PO9 ....160 A8
Wadham Rd PO2 ....157 D2
Wadhurst Gdns SO19 ..127 A8
Wadhurst Rd SO30 .....105 C6
Wadmore CI SO45 .....126 B4
Wagtail Dr BH25 ....194 F2
Wagtail Rd PO8 ....112 A6
Wagtail Way PO16 .....155 F8
Wainscot Rd PO4 ......183 A2
Wainsford CI SO41 .....197 B2
Wainsford Ct SO41 .....197 C2
Wainsford Rd SO41 ....196 E2
Wainwright CI PO6 .....158 C6
Wainwright Gdns SO30 ...8 E1
Wait End Rd PO7 ......134 E6
Waite End Prim Sch
  PO7 ....134 E6
Wake Lawn PO4 ....183 C3
Wakefield Ave
  Bournemouth BH10 ...189 E5
  Fareham PO16 ....130 F3
Wakefield Ct **2** SO18 ..80 A1
Wakefield PI PO12 .....181 A3
Wakefield Rd SO18 ....80 A1
Wakeford CI SO31 .....52 F7
Wakeford PI SO31 .....129 A1
Wakefords Way PO9 ...136 B6
Wakely Gdns BH11 ....189 A5
Wakely Rd BH11 ......189 B5
Walberant Bldgs **2**
  PO3 ....157 F4
Walberton Ave PO6 ...158 A8
Walberton Ct **1** PO6 ..158 A8
Walburton Way PO8 ...88 D4
Walcheren PI BH15 ...201 C3
Walcote CI SO23 .....215 D6
Walcott Ave BH23 ....191 F1
Waldegrave CI SO19 ..103 D1
Walden Gdns PO8 ....112 B7
Walden Rd PO2 ......157 C2
Walditch Gdns BH17 ..187 E2
Waldon Gdns SO18 ...80 B2
Waldren CI BH15 ....202 E2
Wales St SO23 ......215 F6
Walford Bldgs PO3 ...183 A7
Walford CI BH21 .....163 C6
Walford Gdns BH21 ..163 B6
Walford Mill Craft Ctr*
  BH21 ....163 B6
Walford Rd PO6 .....133 C1
Walhampton Hill SO41 .197 F5
Walker Gdns SO30 ...81 C1
Walker PI Gosport PO13 .155 D1
  Hamble-le-R SO31 ...127 F2
Walker Rd PO2 ......157 C2
Walker's La S SO45 ..177 F8
Walkers CI SO30 ....57 D2
Walkers La N SO45 ..150 F1
Walkford La BH25 ...194 D3
Walkford Rd BH23 ...194 C2
Walkford Way BH23 ..194 B1
Walking Field La BH15 .202 D2
Walkwood Ave BH7 ...206 B8
Wallace CI BH18 ....187 A3
Wallace La SO42 ....175 C6
Wallace Rd
  Broadstone BH18 ....187 A3
  Portsmouth PO2 .....182 F8
  Southampton SO19 ...103 F1
Wallington Ct PO14 ...154 F6
Wallington Dr SO53 ..155 B6
Wallington Hill **8** PO16 .131 C2
Wallington Rd PO2 ...157 F1
Wallington Shore Rd
  Fareham PO16 ....131 C2
  1 Portchester PO16 .131 D1
Wallington Way PO16 .131 C2
Wallis Gdns PO7 ....111 E1
Wallis Rd
  Bournemouth BH10 ..189 B1
  Waterlooville PO7 ....111 E1
Walliscott Rd BH11 ..189 A1
Wallisdean Ave
  Fareham PO14 ....154 F8
  Portsmouth PO3 .....183 B7

Wallisdean Jun & Inf Schs
  PO14 ....154 F8
Wallisdown Rd BH10 .204 C8
Wallisdown Rdbt BH12 .189 A1
Wallrock Wlk PO10 ...136 F4
Walmer CI SO50 .....56 A7
Walmer Rd PO1 .....182 E5
Walnut Ave SO18 ....79 E5
Walnut CI
  Chandler's Ford SO53 ..30 C2
  New Milton BH25 ....194 F3
  Southampton SO16 ...77 F1
Walnut Dr PO14 .....179 B7
Walnut Gr
  Southampton SO16 ...77 F1
  Winchester SO22 ....215 B7
Walnut Tree CI PO11 .184 F3
Walnut Tree Dr PO10 .137 E3
Walnut Way La SO31 .128 E8
Walpole Rd
  Bournemouth BH1 ...205 E5
  Gosport PO12 ....181 D5
  Southampton SO22 ..215 A3
Walpole Terr **8** PO12 .181 D4
Walsall Rd PO3 .....183 A6
Walsford Rd BH4 ...204 C5
Walsingham CI PO6 ..133 D1
Walsingham Dene BH7 .205 F8
Walsingham Gdns SO18 .79 F3
Waltham Bsns Pk SO32 .84 A4
Waltham CI Droxford SO32 .61 A2
  Portchester PO16 ....132 C2
Waltham Cres SO16 ..78 B4
Waltham Rd BH7 ....206 B6
Waltham St PO5 ....216 A2
Walton CI Gosport PO12 .181 A5
  Waterlooville PO7 ....134 E5
Walton Ct Fareham PO15 .130 D4
  10 Portsmouth PO1 .182 A4
Walton PI SO22 .....215 B3
Walton Rd
  Bournemouth BH10 ..189 C2
  Cosham PO6 ....158 C5
  Gosport PO12 ....181 A5
  Poole BH15 ....203 A6
  Southampton SO19 ..104 D3
Waltons Ave SO45 ...150 D4
Wandesford PI PO12 .156 F1
Wangfield La SO32 ..82 C1
Wansbeck CI SO53 ..55 B5
Wansbeck Rd BH24 .117 B1
Walton Rd
  Bournemouth BH10 ..189 C2
War Meml Hospl
  Gosport PO12 ....181 A5
  Milford on S SO41 ...211 E4
Warbler CI
  Fareham PO16 ....112 A7
  Southampton SO16 ..78 B6
  Upton BH16 ....201 B8
Warblington Ave PO9 .136 B1
Warblington Ct **2** PO1 .182 A4
Warblington Rd PO10 .160 E8
Warblington Sch PO9 .136 B1
Warblington St **2** PO1 .182 A4
Warblington Sta PO9 .136 B1
Warborne La SO41 ..197 F8
Warbrook Ct **8** PO9 .136 B5
Warburton CI SO19 ..104 E4
Warburton Rd
  Poole BH17 ....202 E8
  Southampton SO19 ..104 E4
Ward Cres PO10 ....137 E3
Ward Ct PO11 ......184 E2
Ward Ho PO1 ......182 A6
Ward Rd PO4 ......183 A2
Wardens CI SO30 ...80 D1
Wardens CI PO11 ..184 F5
Wardens Ct **2** PO12 .181 B6
Wardle Rd SO50 ....56 D7
Wardroom Rd PO2 ..157 B1
Wareham Ct
  Bournemouth BH7 ...206 B6
  Hamble BH15 ....201 E2
Wareham Rd BH21 ..186 D5
Warfield Ave PO7 ...134 E7
Warfield Cres PO7 ..134 F7
Warland Way PO1 ..186 E7
Warlock CI SO19 ...104 D3
Warmwell CI
  Bournemouth BH9 ...190 B4
  Poole BH17 ....187 F2
Warnborough Ct **6**
  PO9 ....136 B6
Warner Ct **12** SO23 .215 E8
Warner Mews SO30 .106 A7
Warnes La BH24 ....142 F7
Warnford CI PO12 ..181 A5
Warnford Cres PO9 .135 D5
Warnford Ct SO15 ..102 F7
Warnford Rd
  Bournemouth BH7 ...206 B7
  Meonstoke SO32 .....61 D7
Warren Ave
  Chandler's Ford SO53 ..55 E5
  Christchurch BH23 ..207 F5
  Portsmouth PO4 .....183 B5
  Southampton SO16 ..78 B2
Warren CI
  Chandler's Ford SO53 ..55 E5
  South Hayling SO41 ..184 C4
  Southampton SO16 ..78 A2
Warren Cres SO16 ..78 A2
Warren Dr BH24 ....140 D5
Warren Edge CI BH6 .206 F3
Warren Edge Ct BH6 .206 F3
Warren Edge Rd BH6 .206 F3
Warren Gdns SO51 ..28 B1

Warren La
  Bucklers Hard SO42 ..200 E7
  Owslebury SO21 .....33 E8
  St Leonards BH24 ...140 D5
Warren Corner GU32 .19 B5
Warren Park Prim Sch
  PO9 ....135 D7
Warren Pk SO41 ....211 A6
Warren PI SO40 ....100 C2
Warren Rd
  Bournemouth BH4 ...204 B2
  Liss GU33 ....21 B7
  Poole BH14 ....203 D4
  Winchester SO23 ....11 C8
Warren The SO45 ..150 B5
Warren Wlk BH22 ..165 B7
Warrior Bsns Ctr The
  PO6 ....158 E7
Warrior CI SO53 ....55 B4
Warrior Pk SO53 ...55 B4
Warrys CI SO45 ....150 A8
Warsash CI PO9 ....135 E6
Warsash Ct SO31 ...128 C1
Warsash Gr PO13 ..155 B2
Warsash Maritime Ctr
  (Southampton Solent Univ)
  SO31 ....152 C9
Warsash Rd
  Locks Heath PO14 ...153 C8
  Warsash SO31 ......128 E1
Warspite CI PO2 ...157 D4
Warton CI SO42 ...175 C6
Warwick Ave BH25 .195 B3
Warwick CI
  Chandler's Ford SO53 .55 A4
  Lee-on-t-S PO13 ....180 A4
  14 Winchester SO23 .215 E8
Warwick Cres PO5 .216 B2
Warwick Ct
  8 Emsworth PO10 ..160 F8
  15 Winchester SO23 .215 E8
Warwick Ho **18** SO14 .103 C6
Warwick PI
  1 Bournemouth BH7 .206 A5
  West Wellow SO51 ...50 E3
Warwick Rd
  Bournemouth BH7 ...206 A5
  Poole BH14 ....203 C3
  Southampton SO15 ..78 D2
  Totton SO40 ....100 F8
Warwick Way PO17 .108 A4
Wasdale CI PO8 ....88 C2
Washbrook Rd PO6 .133 D1
Washington Ave PO1 .205 D6
Washington Ct **4** PO4 .183 A5
Washington Rd
  Emsworth PO10 .....136 F1
  Portsmouth PO2 ....182 D8
Wastwater Ho **14** PO6 .133 B1
Watcombe Rd BH6 ..206 D5
Water CI SO23 .....215 E5
Water La
  Bournemouth BH6 ...206 D7
  Hythe SO45 ....125 E2
  2 Southampton SO15 .102 F7
  Totton SO40 ....100 E8
Water Lane Farm BH10 .189 E6
Water's Edge SO30 ..105 B6
Waterbeech Dr SO30 .105 C8
Waterberry Dr PO7 ..111 C1
Waterditch Rd BH23 .193 A4
Waterford CI
  Lymington SO41 ....197 F3
  Poole BH14 ....203 A2
Waterford Gdns BH23 .209 A7
Waterford La SO41 ..197 F2
Waterford Lodge BH23 .208 B6
Waterford PI BH23 ..209 B7
Waterford Rd
  Christchurch BH23 ..209 B7
  New Milton BH25 ....195 C3
  Northmoor Mus* BH25 .202 B1
Watergardens BH8 ..205 A5
Watergate **12** PO12 .181 E5
Waterhouse La SO15 .102 B7
Waterhouse Way SO15 .102 B7
Waterlock Gdns PO4 .183 D4
Waterloo CI PO8 ....111 D3
Waterloo Ho BH17 ..187 B1
Waterloo Ind Est SO30 .81 B1
Waterloo Rd
  Bournemouth BH9 ...204 F7
  Corfe Mullen BH21 ..204 F7
  Gosport PO12 ....181 C2
  Havant PO9 ....135 F2
  Lymington SO41 ....197 F4
  Poole BH17 ....202 C8
  Southampton SO15 ..102 D6
Waterloo Sch The PO7 .134 E7
Waterloo St SO15 ..216 B2
Waterloo Terr SO15 .102 F7
Waterloo Way BH24 .146 A2
Waterman Terr PO5 .216 D1
Watermans La SO45 .125 E1
Watermead **5** BH2 .216 A2
Watermead Rd PO6 .158 E7
Watermill CI **2** PO9 .135 F1
Watermill Rd BH23 .207 A8
Waters Edge
  Lee-on-t-S PO13 ....179 F1
Waters Edge Gdns
  PO10 ....160 F8
Waters Gn SO42 ...146 A2
Waters Green CI SO42 .146 A2
Waters The PO17 ...130 E5
Watersedge PO17 ..108 A4

Watersedge Rd PO6 .157 A8
Watershed Ct **2** PO6 .133 A1
Watership Dr BH24 .141 D6
Waterside
  Christchurch BH23 ..207 F4
  Downton SP5 ....47 A7
  Hythe SO45 ....126 A5
Waterside CI BH24 .117 B1
Waterside Gdns PO16 .131 B1
Waterside Heritage Ctr*
  SO45 ....126 B4
Waterside La PO16 .156 E6
Waterside Prim Sch
  SO45 ....126 B2
Waterside Rd SO51 .28 A1
Waterside Sch PO2 .157 B3
Waterside Sch (Unit)
  PO4 ....183 C4
Waterside Sq SO45 .125 F5
Watersmead SO23 .215 D3
Watersmeet
  Fareham PO16 ......155 B7
  5 Winchester SO22 .215 F5
Watersmeet Ct BH23 .207 B5
Waterston CI BH17 .187 F2
Waterworks Rd
  Farlington PO6 ......158 D7
  Otterbourne SO21 ...31 D4
  Petersfield GU32 ....41 A6
Watery La
  Christchurch BH23 ..208 A8
  Upton BH16 ....201 A7
Watkin Rd
  8 Bournemouth BH5 .205 F4
  Hedge End SO30 ....81 D2
Watley CI SO16 ....77 D5
Watley La SO21 ...32 B6
Watson Wlk SO40 .100 C7
Watton CI BH8 ....191 A2
Watton La SO32 ..61 E2
Watton Rd SO45 ..150 C3
Watts CI SO15 ....77 F3
Watts Rd
  Hedge End SO30 ...105 C7
  Portsmouth PO1 ....182 D7
Wavecrest CI SO40 .140 A3
Wavell Ave BH17 ..187 A1
Wavell Rd
  Bournemouth BH11 .189 B4
  Gosport PO13 ......155 D3
  Southampton SO18 .102 A1
Wavell Way SO22 .215 A3
Wavendon Ave BH25 .209 E8
Waveney CI PO13 ..179 F3
Waveney Gn SO16 .77 F2
Waverley **14** BH4 .204 C3
Waverley Ave SO31 .127 C5
Waverley CI
  Fordingbridge SP6 ..69 F3
  Romsey SO51 ......50 A3
Waverley Gr PO4 ..182 E2
Waverley Path PO12 .180 E3
Waverley Rd
  Cosham PO6 ....158 C7
  Fordingbridge SP6 ..69 F3
  New Milton BH25 ...195 C3
  Portsmouth PO4 ...182 E2
  Southampton SO15 .102 C3
Wayfarer CI
  Hayling SO31 ......128 F1
  Portsmouth PO4 ...183 C5
Wayfarers PO13 ...180 D7
Wayground Rd BH21 .162 E1
Waylands PI SO30 .105 C8
Wayman Rd BH21 ..162 E6
Wayne Rd BH12 ...203 B6
Waynflete CI **11** SO32 .83 C8
Waynflete PI SO22 .215 A4
Wayside SO31 .....128 D8
Wayside CI SO41 ..211 D5
Wayside Rd
  Bournemouth BH6 ..206 E4
  St Leonards BH24 ..166 F8
Wayte St PO6 .....157 F7
Waytown CI BH17 .187 F2
Weald CI SO31 ...129 A4
Weardale Rd SO53 .55 D4
Weavers CI BH22 ..138 E1
Weavers Gn PO9 ..135 E6
Weavers PI SO53 ..55 B8
Weavills Rd SO50 ..57 A1
Webb CI PO11 ....185 A2
Webb's Way BH11 .188 F1
Webbers Way PO12 .181 C3
Webbs CI BH23 ...139 D6
Webbs Gn SO23 ..85 C3
Webbs Way BH24 .136 E6
Webburn Gdns SO18 .80 A2
Webster Rd
  Bournemouth BH9 ..190 A3
  Winchester SO22 ..215 A7
Wedgewood CI
  Holbury SO45 ......126 A2
  Stubbington PO14 ..179 A6
Wedgwood Way PO8 .112 A3
Wedgwood Dr BH14 .203 A2
Wedgwood Gdns BH23 .126 C1
Wedmore CI SO22 .110 A3
Weeke CI SP5 .....46 D7
Weeke Manor CI SO22 .215 B8
Weeke Prim Sch SO22 .215 B8
Weevil La PO12 ...181 D7
Weirs The **3** SO23 .215 F4

Welbeck Ave SO17 ..79 B2
Welbeck Ct SO17 ...79 B2
Welburn Ct SO18 ...80 A1
Welch Rd Gosport PO12 .181 A8
  Portsmouth PO4 ....182 E2
Welch Way SO16 ...77 F5
Welchwood Ct PO8 .111 F6
Weldon Ave BH11 ..188 E5
Welch CI BH25 ....194 F2
Well Copse CI PO8 .88 C1
Well Hill PO7 ......110 D7
Well House Rd SP6 ..45 B3
Well House La SO22 ..1 E5
Well La Godshill SP6 .70 E2
  Hamble-le-R SO31 ..128 A2
  Poole BH15 ....202 C4
Well Mdw PO9 ....135 E6
Welland Gdns SO18 .80 B2
Welland Gdns SO16 .101 E8
Welland Rd BH21 ..163 D4
Wellands Rd SO43 .122 A5
Wellbrooke Gdns SO53 .55 B7
Weller Ho PO1 ....182 D7
Wellers CI SO45 ..150 A8
Welles Rd SO53 ..55 D6
Wellesley Ave BH23 .208 C2
Wellesley CI PO7 .134 E7
Wellington Ave
  Christchurch BH23 ..208 C2
  Southampton SO18 .104 B7
Wellington Ct
  Dibden Purlieu SO45 .125 D1
  Horndean PO8 .....112 D6
Wellington Ct **7**
  Bournemouth,Dean Park
  BH8 ....205 A5
  Bournemouth,Westbourne
  BH2 ....204 D3
  3 Gosport PO12 ...181 C9
  10 Havant PO9 ....135 F1
  New Milton BH25 ...195 A3
  Southampton SO15 .102 B6
  West End SO30 ....80 C2
Wellington Dr PO13 .180 A5
Wellington Gr PO16 .156 C7
Wellington Pk SO30 .81 A1
Wellington Rd
  Bournemouth BH8 ..205 A5
  Poole BH14 ....203 C3
  Southampton SO15 .79 E2
Wellington St PO5 .216 B2
Wellington Way **2** PO4 .134 E7
Wellingtonia Gdns
  SO41 ....195 F4
Wellman Ct **2** SO53 .55 B7
Wellow CI Havant PO9 .135 D3
  Southampton SO18 .104 C7
Wellow Dr SO18 ...103 E8
Wellow Dro SO51 .50 E7
Wellow Gdns PO14 .129 C1
Wellow St SO51 ..50 F3
Wellow Wood Rd SO51 .50 D8
Wells CI Portsmouth PO3 .183 B6
  Swanwick PO15 ...129 C8
Wells PI SO50 ....56 B2
Wells Rd SO50 ...56 B2
Wellsmoor PO14 ..129 C2
Wellswood Gdns PO9 .113 C3
Wellsworth La PO9 .113 C3
Wellworthy Rd SO41 .197 D6
Wembley Dr PO6 ..158 B6
Wembley Way SO50 .57 C1
Wendover CI BH23 .194 F1
Wendover Rd PO9 .135 E2
Wendy Cres BH22 .165 F3
Wenlock Ct **9** BH23 .207 F8
Wensley Gdns PO10 .136 F3
Wentwood Gdns PO14 .179 A6
Wentworth Ave BH5 .206 B4
Wentworth CI
  Broadstone BH18 ..187 B5
  Christchurch BH23 .206 F6
  Poole BH14 ....112 B7
Wentworth Gdns
  Holbury SO45 .....150 D3
  Southampton SO19 .104 B1
Wentworth Gr SO45 .150 D3
Wentworth Grange **48**
  SO22 ....204 C3
Wescott Way BH11 .188 E4
Wesermarsch Rd PO8 .112 A4
Wesley CI
  8 Bournemouth BH8 .205 C5
  Southampton SO19 .104 D4
Wesley Gr PO3 ...216 D3
Wesley Grange **48** BH4 .204 C3
Wesley Ho
  Trickett's Cross BH22 .165 F6
  15 Winchester SO23 .215 E6
Wesley Rd
  Kings Worthy SO23 ..2 C7
  Poole BH21 ....203 C5
  Wimborne Minst BH21 .163 E5
Wessex Ave BH25 .195 A2
Wessex CI
  Blackfield SO45 ....177 F8
  Christchurch BH23 .208 C7
  Lee-on-t-S PO13 ...180 A6

Wessex Ct
Southampton,Sholing
SO19 . . . . .104 A4
8 Southampton,Westwood Pk
SO17 . . . . .103 A8
22 Winchester SO23 . . . . .215 D6
Wessex Dr SO22 . . . . . . .215 C8
Wessex Est BH24 . . . . . .141 C8
Wessex Gate
Bournemouth BH8 . . . . . .205 C6
2 Southampton SO15 . . .102 E7
Wessex Gate Ind Est
PO8 . . . . .112 C6
Wessex Gate Ret Pk
BH15 . . . . .202 B6
Wessex Gdns
Portchester PO16 . . . . . .156 B7
Romsey SO51 . . . . .53 B7
Wessex La SO18 . . . . . . .79 D4
Wessex Nuffield Hospl
SO53 . . . . .31 A1
Wessex Rd Horndean PO8 . .88 D3
Poole BH14 . . . . .203 A3
Ringwood BH24 . . . . .141 B8
Wessex Trade Ctr BH12 . .203 A7
Wessex Way
Bournemouth,Springbourne
BH8 . . . . .205 C5
Bournemouth,Westbourne
BH2,BH4 . . . . .204 D3
Canford Common SO21 . . . .57 A8
West Ave BH21 . . . . .138 E8
West Bargate 2 SO14 . . .102 F4
West Battery Rd PO2 . . . .157 B1
West Bay Rd SO15 . . . . . .102 C5
West Borough BH21 . . . . .163 B5
West Cl Lymington SO41 . .197 B2
Verwood BH31 . . . . .114 D6
West Cliff BH2 . . . . .204 F4
West Cliff Cotts BH2 . . . .204 E2
West Cliff Gdns BH2 . . . .204 E2
West Cliff 4D BH4 . . . . . .204 C3
West Cliff Gdns BH2 . . . .204 E2
West Cliff Mews BH2 . . . .204 E2
West Cliff Rd BH4 . . . . . .204 E2
West Close Ho BH6 . . . . .207 A4
West Comm SO45 . . . . . .177 E6
West Ct
Portsmouth,Buckland PO1 .182 E7
Portsmouth,Eastney PO4 .183 A3
Southampton SO17 . . . . . .103 F1
West Downs Cl PO16 . . . .131 A4
West Downs Student Village
SO22 . . . . .215 B5
West Dr Bishopstoke SO50 . .56 D4
West Moors BH22 . . . . .66 B8
West End Cl SO22 . . . . . .215 C6
West End Cotts 2
PO16 . . . . .131 A1
**West End Local History Mus
& Heritage Ctr*** SO30 . . .80 D1
West End Rd
Burslodon SO31 . . . . .104 F3
Southampton SO18 . . . . . .104 A8
West End Terr SO22 . . . . .215 A2
West Hayes Rd PO11 . . . .185 D1
West Hayes
Lymington SO41 . . . . .197 F3
Winchester SO22 . . . . . . .215 B5
West Hill Cl SO15 . . . . . .102 E5
West Hill Dr Hythe SO45 . .125 F5
Winchester SO22 . . . . . . .215 A2
West Hill Park Sch
PO14 . . . . .153 E8
West Hill Pk SO22 . . . . . .215 B6
West Hill Pl 8 BH2 . . . . .204 E3
West Hill Rd BH2 . . . . . . .204 E2
West Hoe La SO32 . . . . . . .83 F7
West Horton Cl SO50 . . . . .56 F2
West Horton La SO50 . . . . .56 F1
West Howe Cl BH11 . . . . .189 A4
West Howe Ind Est
BH11 . . . . .188 E3
West La Everton SO41 . . . .196 E1
North Baddesley SO52 . . . . .53 E5
North Hayling PO11 . . . . . .184 F6
West Links SO53 . . . . .55 C2
West Lodge PO13 . . . . . . .179 D4
West Mans 3 BH4 . . . . . .204 C3
West Marlands Rd SO14 .102 F5
West Meon CE Prim Sch
GU32 . . . . .37 B5
West Mews 4 PO17 . . . . .130 E7
West Mill St SP6 . . . . .69 E1
West Moors Mid Sch
BH22 . . . . .138 F1
West Moors
Ferndown BH22 . . . . .165 D7
Three Legged Cross BH21 .138 E7
West Moors BH22 . . . . . . .138 D3
**West Moors St Mary's CE Fst
Sch** BH22 . . . . .138 D3
West Overcliff Dr BH4 . . .204 D3
West Park Dr SP6 . . . . .68 D5
West Park La SP6 . . . . . . .68 C5
West Park La 30 SO17 . . . .79 A1
West Park Rd SO15 . . . . .102 F5
West Point PO13 . . . . . . .179 E3
West Quay SO14 . . . . . . .102 F4
West Quay Rd
Poole BH14 . . . . .202 B2
Southampton SO15 . . . . . .102 E4
West Rd
Bournemouth BH5 . . . . . .206 B4
Bransgore BH23 . . . . .193 A8
Dibden Purlieu SO45 . . . . .125 D1
Emsworth PO10 . . . . .160 E8
Fawley SO45 . . . . .150 C8
Hedge End SO30 . . . . .104 F6

West Rd *continued*
Milford on S SO41 . . . . . . .211 A5
Southampton,Woolston
SO19 . . . . .103 E2
Southwick PO17 . . . . .133 A6
West Row BH21 . . . . .163 B4
West Row Mews BH21 . . .163 B4
West St Emsworth PO10 . .160 F8
Fareham PO16 . . . . .131 B1
Fordingbridge SP6 . . . . . . .69 E1
Hambledon PO7 . . . . .86 C2
Havant PO9 . . . . .135 F1
Havant,Bedhampton PO9 . .135 E1
Portchester PO16 . . . . . . .156 C8
Portchester PO16 . . . . . . .156 D8
Portsmouth PO1 . . . . .181 F4
Ringwood BH24 . . . . .140 E7
Soberton SO32 . . . . .85 C5
Southampton SO14 . . . . . .102 F3
Southwick PO17 . . . . .133 E6
Titchfield PO14 . . . . .153 F8
Wimborne Minst BH21 . . . .163 B5
West Station Terr BH4 . . .204 D3
West Street Ct 6 BH21 . .163 A8
West Tytherley CE Prim Sch
SP5 . . . . .4 A8
West Undercliff Prom
BH2 . . . . .204 D1
West View Cotts PO10 . . .137 E2
West View Rd
Christchurch BH23 . . . . . .207 E6
Poole BH15 . . . . .202 C4
**West Walk (North) Forest
Wlk*** PO17 . . . . .108 E7
**West Walk (South) Forest
Wlk*** PO17 . . . . .108 F5
West Way
Bournemouth BH9 . . . . . .190 B2
Broadstone BH18 . . . . . . .186 F3
Lymington SO41 . . . . .197 C2
West Way Cl BH9 . . . . .190 B1
Westbeams Rd SO41 . . . .172 B1
Westborn Rd PO16 . . . . . .131 B1
Westbourne Ave
Emsworth PO10 . . . . .137 A2
Holbury SO45 . . . . .150 C4
Westbourne Cl
Bournemouth BH4 . . . . . .204 C3
Emsworth PO10 . . . . .137 A3
Westbourne Cres SO17 . . .79 A1
Westbourne Ct 5 PO9 . . .203 D8
Westbourne Gate 19
BH4 . . . . .204 C3
Westbourne Mans 1
SO17 . . . . .79 A1
Westbourne Park Rd
BH4 . . . . .204 B2
Westbourne Prim Sch
PO10 . . . . .137 B4
Westbourne Rd
Portsmouth PO2 . . . . .182 F8
Westbourne PO10 . . . . . . .137 A3
Westbrook Cl
Bournemouth BH10 . . . . .189 D2
Locks Heath SO31 . . . . . .129 A6
Westbrook Ctr The 7
PO7 . . . . .134 D3
Westbrook Gr PO7 . . . . . .134 D4
Westbrook Rd PO16 . . . . .156 D6
Westbrook Way SO18 . . . .79 D4
Westbrooke Cl PO8 . . . . .134 A2
Westbrooke Cotts GU32 . . .38 E1
Westbury Cl
Barton on S BH25 . . . . . .210 B8
Bransgore BH23 . . . . .193 A7
Christchurch BH23 . . . . . .193 D1
22 Portsmouth PO6 . . . . .133 B1
Westbury Ct
Hedge End SO30 . . . . .105 C6
1 Poole BH13 . . . . .203 B4
Westbury Mall 3 PO16 . .131 B1
Westbury Manor Mus*
PO16 . . . . .131 B1
Westbury Rd
Fareham PO16 . . . . .131 B1
Ringwood BH24 . . . . .141 B7
Southampton SO15 . . . . . .101 F7
Westbury Sq 9 PO16 . . . .131 B1
Westby Rd BH5 . . . . .205 F4
Westcliff Cl PO13 . . . . . . .179 E4
Westcliff Ho 8 BH4 . . . . .204 C3
Westcliff Mews SO19 . . . .103 D3
Westcliff Palms 10 BH4 .204 C2
Westcliff Wlk SO45 . . . . .125 F5
Westcot Rd SO45 . . . . . . .150 B3
Westcroft Par 7 BH25 . . .195 A2
Westcroft Pk BH18 . . . . . .187 C4
Westcroft Rd PO12 . . . . . .180 F5
Westdown Rd BH11 . . . . .189 A5
Westerham Rd BH13 . . . . .204 B3
Westerham Cl PO6 . . . . . .158 B7
Westerham Rd BH4 . . . . . .204 B3
Westering SO51 . . . . .53 C8
Westerleigh 12 BH4 . . . . .204 C2
Westerley Cl SO31 . . . . . .128 E1
Western Ave
Barton on S BH25 . . . . . .209 D8
Bournemouth BH10 . . . . .189 D4
Emsworth PO10 . . . . .160 D8
Poole BH13 . . . . .203 F2
Southampton SO15 . . . . . .102 A6
Western CE Prim Sch
SO22 . . . . .215 B6
Western Ct BH10 . . . . . . .189 D5

Western Com Hospl
SO16 . . . . .77 F1
Western Ct 3 PO16 . . . . .131 A1
Western District Cut
SO15 . . . . .102 D7
**Western Downland CE Prim
Sch**
Damerham SP6 . . . . .68 D4
Rockbourne SP6 . . . . .44 F1
Western Espl
Southampton SO14,SO15 . .102 F3
Southampton SO15 . . . . . .102 E5
Western Par
Emsworth PO10 . . . . .160 E7
Portsmouth PO5 . . . . .182 B2
Western Rd
Chandler's Ford SO53 . . . . .30 E1
Fareham PO16 . . . . .131 B1
Fawley SO45 . . . . .151 E1
Havant PO9 . . . . .135 C2
Liss GU33 . . . . .20 F4
Lymington SO41 . . . . .197 D4
Poole BH14 . . . . .204 A2
Poole,Canford Cliffs BH13 .214 F8
Portsmouth PO6 . . . . .157 D7
West End SO30 . . . . .80 D1
Winchester SO22 . . . . . . .215 C6
Western Terr PO2 . . . . . . .157 C2
Western Way
Fareham PO16 . . . . .131 A1
Gosport PO12 . . . . .180 E2
Portsmouth PO1 . . . . .181 F8
Westergate 15 BH23 . . . .204 B3
Westfield 16 BH21 . . . . . .163 B5
Westfield Ave
Fareham PO14 . . . . .154 F8
South Hayling PO11 . . . . .184 F3
Westfield Cl
Hamble-le-R SO31 . . . . . .127 E2
Horton Heath SO50 . . . . . .81 D7
Wimborne Minst BH21 . . . .163 B5
Westfield Comm SO31 . . . .79 E5
Westfield Comm SO31 . . .127 E2
Westfield Cres SO31 . . . . .55 C4
Westfield Dr SO32 . . . . . . .84 D2
Westfield Dro SO24 . . . . . .34 F8
Westfield Ho SO18 . . . . . . .79 E4
Westfield Ind Est
Gosport PO12 . . . . .181 A5
Horndean PO8 . . . . .112 D7
Westfield Jun Sch PO6 . . .156 E8
Westfield Oaks PO11 . . . .184 F3
Westfield Rd
Bournemouth BH6 . . . . . .206 E4
Chandler's Ford SO53 . . . . .55 C3
Gosport PO12 . . . . .181 A5
Littleton SO22 . . . . .1 B5
Lymington SO41 . . . . .198 A2
Portsmouth PO4 . . . . .183 A3
Southampton SO15 . . . . . .102 A7
Totton SO40 . . . . .100 F8
Westgate PO14 . . . . .179 C6
Westgate Mews SO31 . . . .80 E1
Westgate Mus* SO23 . . . .215 D6
Westgate Sch The SO22 . .204 B3
Westgate St 14 SO14 . . . .102 F3
Westgrove SP6 . . . . .69 E1
Westgrove Gdns PO10 . . .160 F8
Westham Cl BH17 . . . . . . .187 A3
Westheath Rd BH18 . . . . .187 B4
Westland Dr PO7 . . . . . . .134 F4
Westland Gdns PO12 . . . .181 A4
Westlands Cl BH23 . . . . . .193 A8
Westlands Dr BH13 . . . . . .214 F8
Westlands Gr PO16 . . . . . .156 C7
Westley Cl SO22 . . . . .215 B7
Westley Gr PO14 . . . . .154 F8
Westlie SO51 . . . . .28 A3
Westman Rd SO22 . . . . . . .1 D3
Westmarch Ct 1 SO17 . . .79 C2
Westmead Rd PO11 . . . . .184 E3
Westminster Ct BH25 . . . .209 F7
Westminster Gate SO22 . .1 A8
Westminster Gdns
PO14 . . . . .129 C3
Westminster Pl PO12 . . . .182 D7
Westminster Rd
Milford on S SO41 . . . . . . .211 A4
Poole BH13 . . . . .204 B1
Westminster Rd E BH13 . .204 B1
Westmoreland Ct BH7 . . .206 A5
Westmorland Way SO53 . . .55 C5
Weston Cl SO19 . . . . .103 F1
Weston Cres SO18 . . . . . .104 C7
Weston Ct SO19 . . . . .126 F8
Weston Dr BH1 . . . . .205 B3
Weston Grove Rd SO19 . .103 D2
Weston Ho GU32 . . . . .40 E3
Weston La Nursling SO16 . . .77 A4
Southampton SO19 . . . . . .103 F1
Weston Par SO19 . . . . . . .126 E8
Weston Park Boys Sch
SO19 . . . . .103 F1
Weston Park Inf Sch
SO19 . . . . .104 A1
Weston Park Jun Sch
SO19 . . . . .104 A1
Weston Rd Colehill BH21 .163 F7
Eastleigh SO50 . . . . .56 A3
Petersfield GU31 . . . . .41 A3
Weston Shore Inf Sch
SO19 . . . . .126 F8
Westover La BH24 . . . . . .140 C5
Westover Prim Sch PO3 .183 B8

Westover Rd
Bournemouth BH1 . . . . . .204 F3
Milford on S SO41 . . . . . . .211 D4
Portsmouth PO3 . . . . .183 B8
Southampton SO16 . . . . . .101 C8
Westover Retail Pk BH9 .190 A4
Westquay Ho 6 PO16 . . . .131 C1
Westray Hall BH4 . . . . . . .204 C1
Westridge Ct 4 SO17 . . . .79 B1
Westridge Rd
Portswood SO17 . . . . .79 B1
Southampton SO17 . . . . . .103 B8
Westrow Gdns SO15 . . . .102 F7
Westrow Rd SO15 . . . . . . .102 F7
Westside View PO7 . . . . . .111 C1
Westview Rd SO22 . . . . . . .1 D6
Westward Rd SO30 . . . . . .105 C8
Westway PO15 . . . . .129 E3
Westways Havant PO9 . . .158 F8
Stubbington PO14 . . . . . . .179 D7
Westwood Ave BH22 . . . .165 D6
Westwood Cl PO10 . . . . . .137 A2
Westwood Ct
12 Southampton SO17 . . .103 A8
Totton SO40 . . . . .76 E2
West End SO30 . . . . .80 D1
Westwood Gdns SO53 . . . .55 E7
Westwood Mans 28 SO17 .79 A1
Westwood Rd
Lyndhurst SO43 . . . . .121 F6
Netley SO31 . . . . .127 B7
Portsmouth PO2 . . . . .157 E4
Southampton SO17 . . . . . .103 A8
Westwood Park SO17 . . . . .79 A1
Westwood View SO24 . . . .14 E1
Westwoods & Glendene Pk
BH25 . . . . .194 D6
Wetherby Cl BH18 . . . . . .187 A2
Wetherby Ct SO40 . . . . . .100 D8
Wetherby Gdns SO40 . . . .100 C8
Wetherdown GU31 . . . . . . .41 A3
Weybridge Cl SO31 . . . . .128 F6
Weyhill Cl Havant PO9 . . .135 D5
Portchester PO16 . . . . . . .132 C1
Weyman's Ave BH10 . . . .189 C6
Weymouth Ave BH12 . . . .206 B3
Weymouth Ave PO12 . . . .180 F8
Weymouth Rd
Poole BH14 . . . . .203 C5
1 Portsmouth PO2 . . . . . .157 D1
Whaddon Chase PO14 . . .179 B7
Whaddon Ct PO10 . . . . . .135 C6
Whaddon La
Colden Common SO21 . . . . .58 A8
Owslebury SO21 . . . . .33 A3
Whale Island Way PO2 . .157 C1
Whalesmead Cl SO50 . . . . .56 F1
Whalesmead Rd SO50 . . . .56 F1
Whaley Rd PO2 . . . . .157 B1
Wharf Cl BH12 . . . . .203 E6
Wharf Hill SO23 . . . . .215 F4
Wharf Rd
Portsmouth PO2 . . . . .182 C8
Southampton SO19 . . . . . .103 D3
Wharfdale Rd
Bournemouth BH4 . . . . . .204 D4
Poole BH13 . . . . .203 E6
Wharncliffe Ct BH23 . . . .208 F7
Wharncliffe Gdns BH23 . .209 A7
Wharncliffe Ho SO19 . . . .103 D3
Wharncliffe Rd
Bournemouth BH5 . . . . . .205 D4
Christchurch BH23 . . . . . .209 A7
Southampton SO19 . . . . . .103 D3
Whartons Cl SO40 . . . . . .100 C3
Whartons La SO40 . . . . . .100 C3
Whatleigh Cl BH15 . . . . . .202 C1
Wheat Cl SO53 . . . . .54 F6
Wheatcroft Dr SO18 . . . . .80 B1
Wheatcroft Rd PO13 . . . .179 F3
Wheatear Dr GU31 . . . . . .41 C2
Wheatears Dr SO51 . . . . . .50 E3
Wheatland Cl SO22 . . . . .215 B3
Wheatlands PO14 . . . . . . .129 C4
Wheatlands Ave PO11 . . .185 E1
Wheatlands Cres PO11 . . .185 E1
Wheatley Gn PO9 . . . . . . .135 C6
Wheaton Grange 4
BH4 . . . . .204 D4
Wheaton Rd BH7 . . . . . . .206 A5
Wheatplot Park Homes 2
BH10 . . . . .189 F4
Wheatsheaf Ct SO30 . . . .105 B6
Wheatsheaf Dr PO8 . . . . .111 D3
Wheatstone Rd PO4 . . . . .182 F3
Wheeler Cl PO12 . . . . . . .181 B7
Wheelers La BH11 . . . . . .188 D6
Wheelers Mdw SO31 . . . .104 F1
Wheelers Wlk SO45 . . . . .177 E8
Wheelhouse Cvn Pk
SO52 . . . . .30 A1
Wheelwright Mews SP5 . . .86 F2
Whernside SO16 . . . . .101 F8
Wherwell Ct 14 PO9 . . . .136 B5
Whichers Gate Rd PO9 . .136 B8
Whichers Cl PO9 . . . . . . .136 B8
Whimbrel Ave PO4 . . . . . .183 C5
Whimbrel Ct BH23 . . . . . .208 A6
Whinchat Cl
Fareham PO15 . . . . .130 C4
Southampton SO16 . . . . . . .78 B6
Whincroft Cl BH22 . . . . . .165 E2
Whincroft Dr BH22 . . . . . .165 E6
Whinfield Rd SO45 . . . . . .149 E8
Whinwhistle Rd SO51 . . . .51 B2
Whippingham Cl PO6 . . . .157 D7

Whistler Cl SO19 . . . . . . .104 C3
Whistler Rd SO19 . . . . . . .104 C3
Whitaker Cres SO41 . . . . .197 C3
Whitby Ave BH18 . . . . . . .187 A2
Whitby Cl BH23 . . . . .191 D4
Whitby Cres BH18 . . . . . .187 A2
Whitby Ct 3 SO41 . . . . . .211 B4
Whitby Rd SO41 . . . . .211 B4
Whitchurch Ave BH18 . . .187 C3
Whitchurch Ct SO19 . . . . .103 C3
Whitcombe Cl SO40 . . . . .108 E7
Whitcombe Gdns PO1 . . .182 E6
White Barn Cres SO41 . . .196 A3
White Beam Rise PO8 . . . .88 C5
White Cl BH15 . . . . .203 A4
White Cloud Pk PO4 . . . .182 F3
White Cloud Pl PO4 . . . . .182 F3
White Cotts SP5 . . . . .47 D7
White Dirt La PO8 . . . . . . .88 D1
White Farm Cl BH10 . . . .204 D8
White Gates SO32 . . . . . . .82 B5
White Harmony Acres Ind Est
SO30 . . . . .80 E5
White Hart La
Cadnam SO40 . . . . .98 F8
Portchester PO16 . . . . . . .156 C7
White Hart Rd
Fair Oak SO50 . . . . .57 C1
4 Gosport PO12 . . . . . . .181 B5
Portsmouth PO1 . . . . .182 A8
White Heather Ct SO45 . .126 A6
White Ho The SO41 . . . . .211 D3
White Horse Dr BH15 . . . .202 C5
White Horse La PO7 . . . . .111 A6
White Horse BH25 . . . . . .200 F7
White House Gdns GU32 . .40 E5
White Knights BH25 . . . . .209 F7
White La SO21 . . . . .32 A8
White Ladies SO51 . . . . . .28 B7
White Ladies Cl PO9 . . . .136 A1
White Lion Ctyd BH24 . . .140 F7
White Lion Wlk PO12 . . . .181 D6
White Lodge Gdns
BH25 . . . . .130 E4
White Oak Wlk 12 PO9 . .136 E4
White Oaks Ct 9 SO16 . .102 B8
White Rd SO50 . . . . .56 D4
White Row SP5 . . . . .46 C8
White Swan Rd PO1 . . . . .216 A3
White Way The
Meonstoke SO32 . . . . .61 A7
Warnford SO32 . . . . .36 A1
White Wings Ho PO7 . . . .110 F3
White's Rd SO19 . . . . . . .104 A6
Whiteacres Cl 4 PO12 . . .181 B6
Whitebeam Cl
Colden Common SO21 . . . . .57 A8
2 Fareham PO14 . . . . . .154 E8
Waterlooville PO8 . . . . . . .112 D5
Whitebeam Rd SO30 . . . .105 D6
Whitebeam Way
North Baddesley SO52 . . . . .54 A5
Verwood BH31 . . . . .115 D3
Whitechimney Row
PO10 . . . . .137 B3
Whitecliff Cres BH14 . . . .203 A2
Whitecliff Pl BH14 . . . . . .202 F2
Whitecliffe Ave PO3 . . . . .183 A7
Whitecliffe Ct PO13 . . . . .180 D4
Whitecroft SO45 . . . . .126 A2
Whitecross Cl BH17 . . . . .187 E3
Whitecross Gdns 1
PO2 . . . . .157 F3
Whitedell La PO17 . . . . . .131 D5
Whitefield Farm SO45 . . .177 F6
Whitefield Rd
Holbury SO45 . . . . .150 C3
New Milton BH25 . . . . . . .195 A2
Poole BH14 . . . . .203 A2
Whitehall BH23 . . . . .207 B6
Whitehart Fields BH24 . . .141 C8
Whitehaugh Cl SO50 . . . . .56 E4
Whitehaven
Horndean PO8 . . . . .112 D6
Portchester PO16 . . . . . . .156 B7
Whitehaven Cvn Pk
SO45 . . . . .177 E8
Whitehaven Home Pk
SO45 . . . . .177 E8
Whitehayes Cl BH23 . . . . .192 D2
Whitehayes Rd BH23 . . . .192 D1
Whitehill Cl SO18 . . . . . . .104 C7
Whitehorn Dr SP5 . . . . . . .73 D8
Whitehouse Gdns SO15 . .102 A6
Whitehouse Rd BH21 . . . .163 D6
Whitelands
Bransgore BH23 . . . . .169 D4
Droxford SO32 . . . . .85 B8
Whitelaw Rd SO15 . . . . . .102 B7
Whiteleaf La PO7 . . . . .86 B7
Whitelegg Way BH10 . . . .189 F5
Whiteley Farm Rdbt
PO15 . . . . .106 E1
Whiteley La
Swanwick PO15 . . . . .129 F5
Whiteley PO15 . . . . .129 C5
Whiteley Prim Sch
PO15 . . . . .129 C7
Whiteley Sh Ctr PO15 . . .129 E8
Whiteley Way PO15 . . . . .129 E7
Whitemoor La SO40,SO51 . .75 C3
Whitemoor Rd SO42 . . . . .145 D2
Whitenap Cl SO51 . . . . . . .53 B6
Whitenap La SO51 . . . . . . .53 C6

Whiteparish All Saints CE Prim Sch SP5 ....24 B3
Whites Ct 4 PO2 ....157 D1
Whites Hill SO21 ....33 A3
Whiteshoot SP5,SP6 ....47 F4
Whiteshoot Hill SP5 ....47 E4
Whiteshute La SO23 ....215 C3
Whitestone Cl SO16 ....101 F8
Whitethorn Rd PO11 ....185 B3
Whitewater Rise SO45 ....125 F1
Whiteways BH21 ....163 E6
Whitfield Pk BH24 ....140 B5
Whitledwood Ave SO15 ....102 D8
Whithers La SO42 ....175 C2
Whitingham Ct 1 BH5 ....206 B5
Whitley Cl PO10 ....137 B5
Whitley Row PO4 ....183 C5
Whitley Way BH25 ....195 B5
Whitmore La BH21 ....114 A7
Whitsbury Cl BH8 ....190 D2
Whitsbury Cross SP6 ....69 C8
Whitsbury Rd Fordingbridge SP6 ....69 E3
Havant PO9 ....136 A5
Whitstable Rd PO6 ....157 E8
Whittington Cl SO45 ....125 F3
Whittle Ave PO15 ....129 C5
Whittle Rd BH21 ....164 F7
Whittles Way BH15 ....202 B2
Whitwell SO31 ....127 C7
Whitwell Rd PO4 ....182 E1
Whitworth Cl PO12 ....181 B5
Whitworth Cres SO18 ....103 D8
Whitworth Ct SO18 ....103 D7
Whitworth Rd Gosport PO12 ....181 A6
Portsmouth PO2 ....182 F8
Southampton SO18 ....103 D8
Whyke Ct 3 PO9 ....135 E2
Whyte Cl SO45 ....150 B3
Whyteways SO50 ....55 F4
Wick 1 Ind Est BH25 ....194 E2
Wick 2 Ind Est BH25 ....194 E2
Wick Cl BH25 ....194 E2
Wick Dr BH25 ....194 E2
Wick Farm BH6 ....207 B5
Wick La Bournemouth BH6 ....207 A5
Christchurch BH23 ....207 B6
Downton SP5 ....46 B8
Wick Point Mews BH23 ....207 B5
Wicket Rd BH10 ....189 C5
Wicket The SO45 ....125 F2
Wickfield Ave BH23 ....207 B6
Wickfield Cl BH23 ....207 B6
Wickford Ho BH23 ....207 A6
Wickham CE Prim Sch PO17 ....108 A4
Wickham Croft PO17 ....108 A3
Wickham Ct Fareham BH22 ....165 E6
3 Gosport PO12 ....180 D3
Wickham Dr BH21 ....186 D4
Wickham Ho 3 Portsmouth SO17 ....79 B1
10 Southampton SO17 ....79 A1
Wickham Rd Bournemouth BH7 ....206 A5
Droxford SO32 ....85 A5
Fareham PO16,PO17 ....131 B5
Wickham St PO1 ....182 A5
Wickham Vineyard* SO32 ....107 B7
Wicklea Rd BH6 ....207 B4
Wicklow Dr SO53 ....55 A5
Wickmeads Rd BH6 ....207 A5
Wickor Cl PO10 ....137 A2
Wickor Way PO10 ....137 A2
Wickor Mill La PO16 ....156 B7
Wicor Path PO16 ....156 D6
Wicor Prim Sch PO16 ....156 B8
Widbury Rd SO41 ....197 C2
Widden Cl SO41 ....172 B2
Widdicombe Ave PO7 ....203 E2
Wide La SO18 ....79 E5
Wide Lane Cl SO42 ....145 F1
Widecombe Dr SO45 ....125 E3
Widgeon Cl Gosport PO12 ....181 B8
Southampton SO16 ....78 B6
Widgeon Cl PO10 ....155 F8
Widget Cl BH11 ....189 B2
Widlers La SO32 ....58 F6
Widley Court Dr PO6 ....158 A7
Widley Ct 3 Cosham PO6 ....158 A7
Fareham PO14 ....155 A6
Widley Gdns PO7 ....134 D3
Widley Rd Cosham PO6 ....158 A8
Portsmouth PO2 ....157 D2
Widley Wlk PO6,PO7 ....133 F3
Widworthy Dr BH18 ....186 F5
Wield Cl PO9 ....135 C4
Wigan Cres BH9 ....135 B2
Wight View Lee-on-t-S PO13 ....179 D4
South Hayling PO11 ....185 C1
Wight Wlk BH22 ....121 B1
Wightway Mews SO31 ....128 C1
Wigmore Ho PO1 ....216 C4
Wilberforce Rd 2 SO22 ....215 A4
Wilberforce Rd Gosport PO12 ....181 C2

Wilberforce Rd continued Portsmouth PO5 ....216 B1
Wilby La PO3 ....158 C4
Wilcon Ct SO50 ....81 D7
Wild Arum Way SO53 ....54 F5
Wild Cherry Way SO53 ....55 A6
Wild Grounds Nature Reserve* PO13 ....180 C6
Wild Ridings PO14 ....154 C8
Wild Rose Cres SO31 ....128 E2
Wildburn Cl SO40 ....76 C2
Wilde Cl SO40 ....100 D7
Wildern Cl SO31 ....128 F3
Wildern Ct SO30 ....105 B8
Wildern La SO30 ....105 C7
Wildern Sch SO30 ....105 C7
Wilderness Hts SO18 ....80 C1
Wilderton Rd BH13 ....203 F3
Wilderton Rd W BH13 ....204 A4
Wildfell Cl BH23 ....192 A1
Wildground Inf Sch SO45 ....125 F1
Wildground Jun Sch SO45 ....125 F1
Wildground La 4 SO45 ....126 A1
Wildmoor Wlk 4 PO9 ....136 B5
Wildown Gdns BH6 ....207 A3
Wildown Rd BH6 ....207 A3
Wilfred Rd BH5 ....205 F4
Wilkins Cl PO8 ....88 B6
Wilkins Way BH15 ....202 B8
Wilkinson Dr BH8 ....191 B2
Wilkinson Ho 15 PO4 ....183 B2
Wilks Cl SO16 ....77 C5
Willersley Cl PO6 ....133 C1
Willett Rd BH21 ....163 A2
William Booth Ho 1 PO1 ....182 B5
William Cl Stubbington PO14 ....179 D6
Walkford BH23 ....194 A2
William Ct 11 Christchurch BH23 ....209 B7
5 Portsmouth PO4 ....183 B4
William George Ct PO13 ....179 E2
William Gilpin CE Prim Sch SO41 ....173 F1
William Macleod Way SO16 ....78 A1
William Panter Ct 2 SO50 ....56 A2
William Price Gdns PO16 ....131 B2
William Rd Bournemouth BH7 ....205 F7
Lymington SO41 ....197 E5
William St SO14 ....103 C5
William's Ind Pk BH25 ....194 E2
Williams Cl Gosport PO13 ....180 D7
Holbury SO45 ....150 D7
Williams Rd PO3 ....158 B3
Willis Ave SO52 ....54 B4
Willis Rd Gosport PO12 ....181 C5
Portsmouth PO1 ....216 B3
Southampton SO16 ....79 C5
Willis Way BH15 ....202 B6
Willis Waye SO23 ....2 C6
Willment Marine & Bsns Pk SO19 ....103 D5
Willow Ave SP6 ....69 F2
Willow Cl Bournemouth BH4 ....204 B5
Havant PO9 ....136 A1
Hedge End SO30 ....105 D6
St Leonards BH24 ....139 D4
Upton BH16 ....201 D5
West End SO30 ....80 E3
Willow Ct Bournemouth BH4 ....206 C6
Fareham PO14 ....130 D1
Southampton SO16 ....78 A3
Willow Dr Christchurch BH6 ....207 A5
Marchwood SO40 ....124 F8
Ringwood BH24 ....141 A5
Wimborne Minst BH21 ....164 C6
Willow Gdns North Baddesley SO52 ....53 F5
Westbourne PO10 ....137 B4
Willow Gn SO21 ....57 A8
Willow Gr SO50 ....57 D2
Willow Herb Cl SO31 ....128 E2
Willow La BH23 ....169 D3
Willow Lo 1 BH1 ....205 D4
Willow Mead Bournemouth BH8 ....190 D4
Hedge End SO30 ....105 B8
Willow Pk BH14 ....203 A3
Willow Pl Christchurch BH23 ....207 C6
Gosport PO12 ....181 B6
Willow Rd Bishop's Waltham SO32 ....83 E7
Liss GU33 ....21 A4
Willow Tree Ave PO8 ....112 B2
Willow Tree Gdns PO14 ....154 E8
Willow Tree Ho SO41 ....197 C2
Willow Tree Rise BH11 ....189 B3
Willow Tree Wlk SO19 ....104 B3
Willow View BH16 ....201 C4
Willow Way Christchurch BH23 ....207 A5
Ferndown BH22 ....165 D2
Willow Wlk BH25 ....210 B7
Willow Wood Rd PO11 ....185 A3
Willowdale Cl GU32 ....40 A4

Willowdene Cl Havant PO9 ....135 B4
New Milton BH25 ....195 C3
Willows The Barton on S BH25 ....210 B8
Chandler's Ford SO53 ....55 C3
Denmead PO7 ....110 F4
Wills Cl BH21 ....186 D4
Wills Rd BH12 ....203 F4
Wills Way SO51 ....53 A6
Willwood Cl BH17 ....187 E3
Wilmcote Gdns 5 PO5 ....216 C3
Wilmcote Ho PO5 ....216 C3
Wilmer Rd SO50 ....56 B2
Wilmington Cl SO18 ....79 F3
Wilmot Cl SO30 ....56 E5
Wilmott Cl PO12 ....180 F5
Wilmott La PO12 ....180 F5
Wilmur Cres BH11 ....202 E6
Wilson Ct 6 SP6 ....69 F1
Wilson Gr PO5 ....216 C1
Wilton Cl Christchurch BH23 ....191 D1
5 Gosport PO12 ....180 F4
Wilton Cres SO15 ....78 D1
Wilton Ct SO15 ....102 D8
Wilton Dr PO8 ....112 A5
Wilton Gdns New Milton BH25 ....194 F3
Southampton SO15 ....78 D1
Wilton Pl 10 Bournemouth BH4 ....204 C2
Portsmouth PO5 ....182 D2
Wilton Rd Bournemouth BH7 ....205 F6
Southampton SO15 ....78 D1
Wilton Terr PO5 ....182 D2
Wiltshire Gdns BH23 ....192 F8
Wiltshire Rd Bransgore BH23 ....192 F8
Chandler's Ford SO53 ....55 D3
Wiltshire St PO5 ....216 A2
Wilverley Ave Bournemouth BH8 ....190 F2
Havant PO9 ....135 D3
Wilverley Cl SO41 ....197 B2
Wilverley Inclosure Forest Walks* BH25 ....171 C7
Wilverley Pl SO45 ....150 E1
Wilverley Rd Brockenhurst SO42 ....145 F1
Christchurch BH23 ....208 A7
New Milton BH25 ....170 F3
Wimbledon Park Rd PO5 ....182 D2
Wimborne Ho BH21 ....163 B5
Wimborne Rd Bournemouth SO16 ....77 F1
Trickett's Cross BH22 ....165 F7
Wimborne Inf & Jun Schs PO4 ....183 A4
Wimborne Minster Model Town & Gdns* BH21 ....163 B4
Wimborne Rd Bournemouth,Dean Park BH9 ....204 F5
Bournemouth,Kinson BH11 ....189 C6
Bournemouth,Moordown BH9 ....204 F8
East End BH21 ....162 F1
Poole,Longfleet BH15 ....202 D4
Poole,Oakdale BH15 ....202 D6
Portsmouth PO4 ....183 A4
Wimborne Minst BH21 ....163 A5
Wimborne Rd E Ferndown BH22 ....165 B6
Trickett's Cross BH22 ....165 E7
Wimborne Rd W Ferndown BH21 ....164 E6
Wimborne Minst BH21 ....164 B4
Wimpole Ct PO1 ....216 C4
Wimpole St PO1 ....216 C4
Wimpson Gdns SO16 ....77 F1
Wimpson La SO16 ....77 E1
Wincanton Way PO7 ....112 B1
Winchcombe Rd PO6 ....133 B1
Winchelsea Specl Sch BH12 ....188 D1
Winchester By Pass SO23 ....2 C3
Winchester Cath* SO23 ....215 B5
Winchester Christian Sch SO22 ....215 B3
Winchester City Mill* SO23 ....215 F5
Winchester Cl SO31 ....127 B6
Winchester Cl SO23 ....215 F4
Winchester Ct 16 Gosport PO13 ....180 D5
5 Romsey SO51 ....53 D1
Southampton SO15 ....78 C1
Winchester Cty Mus* SO23 ....215 B5
Winchester Hill SO51 ....53 B8
Winchester Ho 8 Havant PO9 ....136 A5
Romsey SO51 ....53 A7
Winchester Mews 19 SO17 ....103 A8
Winchester Pl 5 BH15 ....202 C2

Winchester Rd Bishop's Waltham SO32 ....83 B8
Chandler's Ford SO53 ....55 E7
Durley SO32 ....81 E4
Fair Oak SO50 ....57 C4
Langrish GU32 ....39 E4
New Milton BH25 ....195 C4
Petersfield GU32 ....40 D4
Portsmouth,Stroud GU32 ....40 B4
Portsmouth PO2 ....182 E8
Romsey SO51 ....52 F7
Romsey,Woodley SO51 ....28 C1
Shedfield SO32,PO17 ....107 E6
Southampton SO16 ....78 C2
Upham SO21,SO32 ....58 C3
Waltham Chase SO32 ....83 E2
Wickham PO17 ....108 A3
Winchester Sch of Art SO23 ....215 F6
Winchester St Botley SO30 ....106 A7
4 Southampton SO15 ....102 F6
Winchester Sta SO23 ....215 D6
Winchester Trad Pk SO23 ....2 C1
Winchester Way SO40 ....100 C7
Winchfield Cl SO19 ....104 A4
Winchfield Cres PO9 ....135 C4
Winchfield Ho 4 PO12 ....181 E5
Wincombe Cl BH22 ....165 D3
Wincombe Dr BH22 ....165 D4
Windbury Rd SO16 ....77 E2
Windermere Ave Southampton SO16 ....77 E2
Stubbington PO14 ....154 D4
Windermere Gdns SO40 ....100 E8
Windermere Ho PO6 ....157 B8
Windermere Rd Bournemouth BH3 ....205 A7
Portsmouth PO2 ....157 F3
West End SO18 ....80 B1
Windfield Dr SO51 ....53 B8
Windgreen Est BH21 ....186 E7
Windham Mews BH1 ....205 D5
Windham Rd BH1 ....205 D5
Windmill Cl Clanfield PO8 ....88 C6
5 Milford on S SO41 ....211 D5
St Leonards BH24 ....140 D4
Windmill Copse SO45 ....125 F1
Windmill Field PO7 ....111 A4
Windmill Gr PO16 ....156 C6
Windmill La Burseldon SO31 ....105 A2
St Leonards BH24 ....140 D4
Windover Cl SO19 ....104 C6
Windrush Gdns PO7 ....134 D7
Windrush Rd SO16 ....101 E8
Windrush Way SO45 ....126 A3
Windsor Cl Hordle SO41 ....195 E4
St Leonards BH24 ....139 F4
Windsor Ct Bishopstoke SO50 ....56 D4
3 Christchurch BH23 ....209 A7
6 Cosham PO6 ....157 F8
Poole BH14 ....203 B3
11 Portsmouth PO5 ....182 C2
14 Southampton,Bevois Mount SO17 ....103 A8
2 Southampton,Bitterne SO18 ....103 C7
6 Southampton,Millbrook SO15 ....101 E5
6 Southampton,Westwood Pk SO17 ....103 A8
Windsor Gate SO50 ....56 A6
Windsor Ho 3 Portsmouth PO1 ....216 C3
1 Winchester SO23 ....215 F6
Windsor Mans 1 BH6 ....206 E3
Windsor Rd Bournemouth BH5 ....205 E4
Christchurch BH23 ....206 E7
Cosham PO6 ....157 F7
Gosport PO12 ....181 A5
Petersfield GU32 ....40 F4
Poole BH14 ....203 B3
Portchester PO16 ....156 D6
Waterlooville PO7 ....111 D2
Windsor Way SP6 ....93 A6
Windward Ct 12 BH2 ....205 E4
Wine Cross PO17 ....109 A1
Winecross Cotts PO17 ....109 A2
Winfield Way PO10 ....136 F4
Winfrid Ho SO40 ....100 D7
Winfrith Cres BH12 ....203 E8
Winfrith Way SO16 ....77 D5
Wingate Rd Gosport PO12 ....155 F1
Totton SO40 ....100 D8
Wingfield Ave Christchurch BH23 ....193 D1
Poole BH15 ....202 D6
Wingfield St BH1 ....205 C3
Wingfield St PO1 ....182 D7
Winghams La SO51 ....29 B3
Wingrove Rd SO40 ....100 C3
Winifred Cl SO50 ....57 C3
Winifred Rd Poole BH15 ....202 E5
Waterlooville PO7 ....134 E8
Winkfield Row PO8 ....112 B5
Winkle St SO14 ....103 A2
Winkton Cl Burton BH23 ....192 C3
Havant PO9 ....135 C4
Winkton Gdns BH23 ....192 C5
Winkton Gn BH23 ....192 C4
Winn Cl SO17 ....102 E7
Winn Ct SO17 ....102 C7
Winn Mans 18 SO17 ....79 A1
Winn Rd SO17 ....79 A1

Winnall Cl SO23 ....2 C1
Winnall Manor Rd SO23 ....11 C8
Winnall Prim Sch SO23 ....11 C8
Winnall Trad Est Winchester SO23 ....11 C8
Winchester SO23 ....2 C1
Winnall Valley Rd SO23 ....11 C8
Winnards Cl BH22 ....165 E2
Winnards Pk SO31 ....128 E2
Winnham Dr PO16 ....132 A1
Winnington PO15 ....130 D4
Winnington Cl PO15 ....130 D4
Winscombe Ave PO8 ....112 A2
Winsford Ave SO50 ....57 A1
Winsford Cl Bishopstoke SO50 ....57 A1
Christchurch BH23 ....193 D1
Winsford Gdns SO50 ....57 A1
Winslade Rd Havant PO9 ....135 D5
Winchester SO22 ....1 C3
Winsley Ave BH6 ....206 C4
Winslow Ct PO6 ....158 D8
Winsor Cl PO11 ....185 D1
Winsor La SO40 ....99 E7
Winsor Rd Bartley SO40 ....98 D8
Cadnam SO40 ....75 D1
Totton SO40 ....101 A6
Winspit Cl PO15 ....201 E3
Winstanley Rd Nursling SO16 ....77 C5
Portsmouth PO2 ....157 C1
Winston Ave PO11 ....204 A6
Winston Churchill Ave PO5 ....216 B2
Winston Cl Eastleigh SO50 ....56 A4
South Hayling PO11 ....184 E3
Southampton SO16 ....77 F2
Winston Ct 1 Christchurch BH23 ....207 A7
4 Old Milton BH25 ....195 A1
Winston Gdns BH12 ....204 A6
Winston Par 13 BH25 ....195 A1
Winston Pk BH12 ....204 A6
Winston Rd BH9 ....190 A3
Winston Way BH24 ....141 B8
Winstone Bldgs SO16 ....78 E3
Winstone Cres SO52 ....54 A3
Winter Rd PO4 ....183 A3
Winterbarrow Cotts SO32 ....36 E3
Winterborne Ct BH15 ....202 D4
Winterbourne Rd Poole BH15 ....202 D5
Portchester PO6 ....132 F1
Romsey SO51 ....28 B1
Winterhayes Cl BH17 ....187 E3
Wintersfield Rd PO6 ....157 D8
Winters Cl SO45 ....150 D3
Winters Hill SO32 ....82 E8
Winters Rd SO32 ....84 A1
Winterslow Dr PO9 ....135 E6
Winton Boys' Sch BH10 ....189 D1
Winton Cl Lymington SO41 ....197 F3
Winchester SO22 ....215 D8
Winton Ct 8 Petersfield GU32 ....40 F3
West End SO30 ....80 D1
Winton Prim Sch SO22 ....189 E2
Winton Rd Petersfield GU32 ....40 F4
Portsmouth PO2 ....157 F2
Winton St 8 SO14 ....103 A5
Winton Way Bournemouth BH10 ....189 D1
New Milton BH25 ....195 B5
Wisbech Way SO41 ....195 F3
Wisborough Rd PO5 ....182 E2
Wises Ct 1 PO12 ....181 E5
Wish Pl PO5 ....216 D1
Wishart Gdns BH9 ....190 B5
Wistaria Ho 7 BH10 ....115 C4
Wisteria Dr BH31 ....136 B4
Witchampton Cl PO9 ....136 A5
Witchampton Rd BH18 ....186 F2
Witham Cl SO53 ....55 A6
Witherbed La Titchfield PO15 ....129 D4
Titchfield PO15 ....129 D4
Withermoor Rd BH9 ....204 E8
Withewood Mans 2 SO15 ....102 C7
Withies Rd PO13 ....180 D8
Withingham Rd BH13 ....203 F3
Withington Cl 3 PO6 ....133 B1
Withy Cl SO51 ....52 F8
Witley PO14 ....130 B3
Witley Rd PO8 ....111 F6
Witney Rd BH17 ....187 D1
Witt Rd SO50 ....57 C2
Wittensford La SO43 ....98 C8
Wittering Rd South Hayling PO11 ....185 F2
Southampton SO16 ....78 A4
Witts Hill SO18 ....79 E7
Wivenhoe Ho BH17 ....165 F6
Woburn Cl SO50 ....56 A6
Woburn Rd SO16 ....78 B5
Wode Cl PO8 ....88 C3
Wodehouse Rd SO19 ....103 E4
Woking Rd BH14 ....203 C4
Wolfe Cl Christchurch BH23 ....207 D7
Winchester SO22 ....215 A3
Wollaston Rd BH6 ....206 F3
Wollaton Cres BH22 ....165 C3
Wollaton Rd BH22 ....165 C3

Wollstonecraft Rd 🅱
BH5 . . . . .205 F3
Wolseley Rd Poole BH12 . .203 D6
Southampton SO15 . . . . . .102 C7
Wolsey Way SO41 . . . . . . .211 D5
Wolverton Rd SO24 . . . . . .204 A5
Wolverley Ct
🔟 Bournemouth BH4 . . . .204 C3
Southampton SO16 . . . . . .78 D3
Wolverton Rd
Bournemouth BH7 . . . . . .205 F5
Havant PO9 . . . . .135 C5
Southampton SO14 . . . . . .103 B5
Wolvesey Castle (Old
**Bishop's Palace)*
SO23 . . . . .215 C5
Wolvesey Pl SO53 . . . . .55 A4
Wolvesey Terr 🅰 SO23 . .215 F4
Wonderholm Par BH11 . . .189 B2
Wonston Ct PO9 . . . . .136 C6
Wonston Rd SO16 . . . . .78 B4
Wood Cl SO19 . . . . .104 C3
Wood End Rd BH24 . . . . . .141 E5
Wood End Way SO53 . . . . . .55 A6
Wood Glade Cl SO40 . . . . .101 F1
Wood Ho 🅶 BH13 . . . . . . .204 B3
Wood La
Bournemouth BH11 . . . . .188 E6
Bramdean SO24 . . . . .15 E6
Milford on S SO41 . . . . . .211 C4
Southwick PO17 . . . . .133 A6
Wood Lawn Cl BH25 . . . . .209 F8
Wood Lodge SO40 . . . . . . .76 B1
Wood Rd SO40 . . . . .100 B2
Wood Row BH9 . . . . .190 E4
Wood View BH21 . . . . .164 A8
Wood's Cnr BH24 . . . . .143 C5
Woodacre Gdns BH22 . . .165 E4
Woodberry La
Emsworth PO10 . . . . .137 A6
Rowland's Castle PO9 . . . .136 F8
Rowlands Castle PO9 . . . .113 D1
Woodbind Wlk SO31 . . . .128 F2
Woodbourne Cl
Fareham PO15 . . . . .130 D1
Liss GU33 . . . . .21 A4
Woodbury
Bournemouth BH1 . . . . . .205 A2
Brockenhurst SO42 . . . . .145 D1
Woodbury Ave
Bournemouth BH8 . . . . . .190 F2
Langstone PO9 . . . . .159 F8
Petersfield GU32 . . . . .40 E5
Woodbury Cl BH23 . . . . . .191 E3
Woodbury Gr PO8 . . . . . . .111 F5
Woodcock La SO41 . . . . . .196 B4
Woodcocks Cres BH7 . . . .206 A8
Woodcot Cres PO9 . . . . . .136 B5
Woodcot Prim Sch
PO13 . . . . .155 B4
Woodcote Cotts SO44 . . . .15 D4
Woodcote Dr BH16 . . . . . .201 B6
Woodcote La PO14 . . . . . .155 A3
Woodcote Rd SO17 . . . . . .79 C3
Woodcroft Gdns PO8 . . . .111 F5
Woodcroft La PO8 . . . . . . .111 F5
Wooden House La SO41 . .174 B2
Woodend Rd BH9 . . . . .204 F8
Woodenson Cl SO40 . . . . . .57 B3
Woodfalls Cross SP5 . . . . .74 C8
Woodfern SP6 . . . . .70 D2
Woodfield Ave PO6 . . . . . .134 F1
Woodfield Cotts GU32 . . . .19 B3
Woodfield Dr SO22 . . . . . .10 B6
Woodfield Gdns BH23 . . .193 D1
Woodfield Ho 🅷 PO2 . . . .157 E3
Woodfield Park Rd
PO10 . . . . .161 B8
Woodfield Rd BH11 . . . . . .189 A5
Woodford Cl BH24 . . . . . . .141 C7
Woodford Ho PO15 . . . . . .130 D2
Woodford Rd BH1 . . . . . . .205 C4
Woodgaston La PO11 . . . .160 C1
Woodgreen Ave PO9 . . . . .135 D3
Woodgreen Dr BH11 . . . . .188 D4
Woodgreen Rd SO22 . . . . . . .1 D4
Woodgreen Wlk SO40 . . . .76 B1
Woodhay SO43 . . . . .121 E5
Woodhay Wlk 🔟 PO9 . . . .136 B6
Woodhayes Ave BH23 . . .193 E2
Woodhill Sch
Botley SO30 . . . . .105 F1
Chandler's Ford SO53 . . . . .55 D7
Woodhouse Ct SO30 . . . . .105 C8
Woodhouse La
Finchdean PO8 . . . . .113 A6
Hedge End SO30 . . . . . . .105 E8
Rowlands Castle PO8,PO9 .113 C4
Woodhouse Rd PO8 . . . . . .112 F7
Woodington Cl PO9 . . . . .136 A6
Woodington Rd SO51 . . . . .51 C6
Woodlake CI BH17 . . . . . . .187 D1
Woodland Ave BH5 . . . . . .206 A4
Woodland Cl
Southampton SO18 . . . . .104 D7
Verwood BH31 . . . . .114 E7
West Wellow SO51 . . . . . . .51 B2
Woodland Ct BH24 . . . . . .205 F5
Woodland Dro SO21 . . . . . .32 A3
Woodland Mans BH14 . . .203 B5
Woodland Mews SO30 . . . .80 D1
Woodland Pl 🅱 SO15 . . . .102 C4
Woodland St PO1 . . . . .216 D4
Woodland View
Bursledon SO31 . . . . .127 F8
Horndean PO8 . . . . .111 F6

Woodland Way
Christchurch BH23 . . . . . .208 D8
Milford on S SO41 . . . . . .211 C4
Woodland Wlk
Bournemouth BH6 . . . . . .206 A4
Ferndown BH22 . . . . .165 F7
Woodlands
Fareham PO16 . . . . .131 D2
🅱 Poole BH13 . . . . .204 A4
Woodlands Ave
Emsworth PO10 . . . . .136 F3
Warminghurst BH15 . . . . .201 F3
Woodlands Cl
Bransgore BH23 . . . . .193 A8
Chandler's Ford SO53 . . . . .30 D1
Dibden Purlieu SO45 . . . .125 F1
Gosport PO13 . . . . .180 C6
Sarisbury SO31 . . . . .128 F6
Woodlands Com Sch
SO18 . . . . .104 D8
Woodlands Cotts SO24 . . .16 D2
Woodlands Cres BH15 . . .201 F3
Woodlands Ct
Dibden Purlieu SO45 . . . .125 F1
Poole BH12 . . . . .204 B2
🅱 Winchester,Hyde SO23 .215 E7
Winchester,Weeke SO22 . .215 A8
Woodlands Cvn Pk
SO41 . . . . .196 A3
Woodlands Dr SO31 . . . . .127 D6
Woodlands Dro SO40 . . . .100 A3
Woodlands Ed Ctr PO8 . .111 E4
Woodlands Gdns 🅱
SO51 . . . . .28 B1
Woodlands Gr PO7 . . . . . .134 D5
Woodlands La
Hill Brow GU33 . . . . .21 B3
South Hayling PO11 . . . . .184 E5
Woodlands Rd
Barton on S BH25 . . . . . .209 E7
Brockenhurst SO42 . . . . .172 F7
Woodlands SO40 . . . . .99 E3
Woodlands The
Chandler's Ford SO53 . . . . .30 A1
Kings Worthy SO23 . . . . . . .2 C6
Woodlands Way
Bursledon SO31 . . . . .127 F8
Havant PO9 . . . . .135 F4
New Milton BH25 . . . . . . .195 B5
North Baddesley SO52 . . . .53 F4
Southampton SO15 . . . . .102 F8
St Leonards BH24 . . . . . .139 F4
Woodlane Cl SO04 . . . . . . .15 D5
Woodlark Gdns GU31 . . . . .41 C3
Woodlea Cl SO22 . . . . . . .215 C8
Woodlea Gdns SO30 . . . . . .80 E1
Woodlea Ho SO53 . . . . .55 C3
Woodlea Way SO51 . . . . . . .29 F2
Woodleaze Cl BH18 . . . . . .187 B6
Woodleigh Ct PO9 . . . . . . .136 C3
Woodley Cl SO51 . . . . .28 C2
Woodley Close Flats
SO51 . . . . .28 C2
Woodley Gdns SO41 . . . . .197 D5
Woodley La SO51 . . . . .28 C2
Woodley Rd
Gosport PO13 . . . . .181 C5
Southampton SO19 . . . . .103 D3
Woodley Ways SO51 . . . . . .28 C2
Wooding Cres SP6 . . . . . . .70 D2
Woodlinken Cl BH31 . . . . .115 B4
Woodlinken Dr BH31 . . . . .115 B5
Woodlinken Way BH31 . . .115 C4
Woodmancote La PO10 . . .137 E4
Woodmancote Rd PO4 . . .183 A4
Woodmill La SO18 . . . . . . .79 E2
Woodmoor Cl SO40 . . . . . .102 A1
Woodpath PO5 . . . . .216 B1
Woodpath Ho PO5 . . . . . . .216 B1
Woodpecker Cl
Havant PO9 . . . . .136 B1
Verwood BH31 . . . . .114 F5
Woodpecker Copse
SO31 . . . . .129 B3
Woodpecker Dr
Broadstone BH17 . . . . . .201 F8
Marchwood SO40 . . . . . .101 E1
Woodpecker Way
Eastleigh SO50 . . . . .55 D2
Portsmouth PO3 . . . . . . .158 A4
Woodpeckers SO23 . . . . .215 E8
Woodpeckers Dr SO22 . . .215 A8
Woodrising BH13 . . . . .214 B3
Woodrisings The 🅶
BH2 . . . . .204 D4
Woodroffe Wlk PO10 . . . .136 F4
Woodrow PO7 . . . . .110 E4
Woodruff Cl BH23 . . . . . . .208 C8
Woodrush Cres SO31 . . . .128 E2
Woods Edge BH18 . . . . . . .187 A2
Woods Ho 🅶 GU32 . . . . . . .40 F4
Woods View Rd BH9 . . . . .204 D8
Woodsedge PO7 . . . . .135 A6
Woodside
Brockenhurst SO42 . . . . .173 A8
Chilworth SO16 . . . . .54 E2
Gosport PO13 . . . . .155 B5
Portsmouth PO5 . . . . . . .216 B1
Woodside Ave
Eastleigh SO50 . . . . .55 B7
Lymington SO41 . . . . . . .197 E1
Woodside Cl
Ferndown BH22 . . . . .165 E6
🔟 Lymington SO41 . . . . .197 E2
Marchwood SO40 . . . . . . .101 E1
Woodside Cres SO16 . . . . .54 E2
Woodside Ct 🅱 SO17 . . . .103 B8
Woodside Gdns SO40 . . . .100 C3

Woodside La SO41 . . . . . .197 E1
Woodside Rd
Bournemouth BH5 . . . . . .206 B4
Eastleigh SO50 . . . . .55 E4
Ferndown BH22 . . . . .165 E6
North Baddesley SO52 . . . .53 F4
Poole BH14 . . . . .203 C3
Southampton SO17 . . . . .103 B8
West Moors BH22 . . . . . .138 D4
Woodside Way SO30 . . . . .105 A5
Woodstock Ave PO8 . . . . .112 A5
Woodstock Cl
Fareham PO14 . . . . .130 C1
Hedge End SO30 . . . . . . .105 D5
Poole BH14 . . . . .203 B2
Woodstock Dr SO17 . . . . . .79 A1
Woodstock La BH24 . . . . .141 A6
Woodstock Rd
Burton BH23 . . . . .192 D2
Gosport PO12 . . . . .181 C4
Havant PO9 . . . . .135 D2
Poole BH14 . . . . .203 A2
Woodthorpe Gdns SO31 . .128 F6
Woodvale PO15 . . . . .130 D2
Woodvale Gdns BH25 . . . .195 A2
Woodview SO16 . . . . .79 A6
Woodview Cl SO16 . . . . . . .79 A6
Woodville Dr SO30 . . . . . .106 C7
Woodville Dr PO1 . . . . . . .182 B3
Woodville Rd
Fawley SO45 . . . . .151 B3
Havant PO9 . . . . .135 B2
Woodward Cl PO12 . . . . . .180 F4
Woofferton Rd PO6 . . . . . .133 A1
Wool Rd BH12 . . . . .203 B8
Woolfield La GU32,GU34 . .18 B3
Woolford Cl 🅱 SO23 . . . .215 A4
Woolley Ho 🅷 SO14 . . . . .103 A5
Woolmer Cl 🔟 PO9 . . . . . .136 B5
Woolmer La BH24 . . . . . . .117 A2
Woolmer St PO10 . . . . . . .136 E4
Woolner Ave
Cosham PO6 . . . . .158 A8
Petersfield GU32 . . . . .40 F4
Woolridge Ind Est
BH21 . . . . .139 A6
Woolsbridge Rd BH24 . . .139 E5
Woolslope Cl BH22 . . . . . .138 C1
Woolslope Gdns BH22 . . .138 C1
Woolslope Rd BH22 . . . . .138 C1
Woolston Ct 🅴 PO12 . . . .180 D3
Woolston Rd SO19 . . . . . .103 E2
Woolston Sch
Havant PO9 . . . . .135 C6
Netley SO31 . . . . .127 C7
Woolston Sch (Language
Coll) SO19 . . . . .103 F2
Woolston Sta SO19 . . . . . .103 D3
Woolven Cl BH14 . . . . .203 A5
Wooton SO31 . . . . .127 C7
Wootton Farm Rd BH25 . .170 E2
Wootton Gdns BH1 . . . . . .205 A3
Wootton Mount BH1 . . . . .205 A3
Wootton Rd
Lee-on-t-S PO13 . . . . . . .180 A4
🅱 Portsmouth PO3 . . . . .195 D7
Wootton St PO6 . . . . .133 C1
Wootton Rough BH25 . . . .195 B8
Worbarrow Gdns BH12 . . .203 C8
Worcester Cl 🅴 PO13 . . . .180 C6
Worcester Ct 🅵 PO13 . . . .180 C6
Worcester Pl
🅱 Lymington SO41 . . . . .197 F2
Southampton SO19 . . . . .104 B2
Wordsworth Ave
Bournemouth BH8 . . . . . .190 E1
Portchester PO16 . . . . . . .132 C1
Wordsworth Cl
Bishop's Waltham SO32 . . .83 E8
Winchester SO22 . . . . . . .215 B6
Wordsworth Inf Sch
SO15 . . . . .78 B1
Wordsworth Pl PO15 . . . . .106 C1
Wordsworth Rd SO15 . . . . .78 C1
Worgret Rd BH15 . . . . . . .202 D7
Workhouse La SO41 . . . . . .38 D1
Workmans's La SO31 . . . . .152 E8
Workshop Rd PO4 . . . . . . .133 A2
Worldham Rd PO9 . . . . . . .136 B6
Worrell Dr BH12 . . . . .203 C8
Worsley Rd PO5 . . . . .216 B1
Worsley St PO4 . . . . .183 A2
Worth Apts PO5 . . . . .182 D1
Worthing Ave PO12 . . . . . .180 F8
Worthing Rd PO5 . . . . .182 D1
Worthington Cres BH14 . .203 A3
Worthy Cl PO7 . . . . .136 B5
Worthy Ho SO16 . . . . .78 B1
Worthy La SO23 . . . . .215 B7
Worthy Rd
New Milton BH25 . . . . . . .195 A3
Winchester SO23 . . . . . . .215 E8
Wortley Rd BH23 . . . . .209 A2
Wr Twr Rd BH14 . . . . .187 C4
Wraxall Cl BH17 . . . . .187 D1
Wraysbury Park Dr
PO10 . . . . .136 F4
Wren Cl
Christchurch BH23 . . . . . .208 B5
New Milton BH25 . . . . . . .194 F2
Ringwood BH24 . . . . .141 C6
Winchester SO22 . . . . . . .215 B4
Wren Cres BH12 . . . . .204 A4
Wren Ctr The PO10 . . . . . .137 A3
Wren Gdns SP6 . . . . .93 B5
Wren Rd SO50 . . . . .55 E1
Wrenway PO16 . . . . .155 F8

Wrexham Gr PO8 . . . . .88 B2
Wright Cl PO15 . . . . .129 F6
Wright Way SO45 . . . . . . .151 E1
Wright's Hill SO19 . . . . . .104 A2
Wrights Wlk SO31 . . . . . . .104 F1
Wriothesley Ct PO14 . . . .153 F8
Wroxall Rd PO12 . . . . .203 F5
Wroxham Rd PO12 . . . . . .164 D5
Wryneck Cl SO16 . . . . .78 B6
Wyatts Cl BH21 . . . . .186 D6
Wyatts Ave BH21 . . . . .186 D6
Wyatts La BH21 . . . . .186 D6
Wyborn Cl PO11 . . . . .185 A2
Wych La PO13 . . . . .155 B3
Wychwood Cl
Hedge End SO30 . . . . . . .105 D5
Poole BH14 . . . . .203 B2
Woodstock Dr SO17 . . . . . .79 A1
Wychwood Dr
Blackfield SO45 . . . . .177 E7
Bournemouth BH2 . . . . . .204 F4
Wychwood Gr SO53 . . . . . .55 E8
Wychwood Grange 🅱
BH2 . . . . .204 F4
Wycliffe Rd
Bournemouth BH9 . . . . . .204 F8
Southampton SO18 . . . . . .80 A1
Wycote Rd PO13 . . . . .155 B4
Wyeford Cl 🅴 PO9 . . . . . .136 B6
Wyelands Ave BH21 . . . . .164 D5
Wyke Mark SO22 . . . . .215 A8
Wykeham Ave PO7 . . . . . .157 F2
Wykeham Cl Netley SO31 . .127 B6
Poole BH17 . . . . .202 E8
Southampton SO16 . . . . . .78 D4
Wykeham Ct PO11 . . . . . . .108 A3
Wykeham House Sch
PO16 . . . . .131 C1
Wykeham Ind Est The
SO23 . . . . .2 C2
Wykeham Pk SO21 . . . . . . .122 A7
Wykeham Pl
Lymington SO41 . . . . . . .197 E3
Winchester SO22 . . . . . . .215 B4
Wykeham Rd
Netley SO31 . . . . .127 B6
Portsmouth PO2 . . . . . . .157 E1
Wykeham Terr 🅵 SO23 . . .215 E7
Wylde Green La GU33 . . . . .21 B5
Wylds La GU32 . . . . .65 C8
Wyllie Rd PO2 . . . . .157 E4
Wylye Cl SO18 . . . . .80 B3
Wymering La PO6 . . . . . . .133 C1
Wymering Manor (Youth
Hostel)* PO6 . . . . .157 D8
Wymering Manor Cl 🅶
PO6 . . . . .157 D8
Wymering Rd PO2 . . . . . . .182 E8
Wyn Sutcliffe Ct 🅱 PO4 .183 A3
Wyncombe Rd BH5 . . . . . .206 B5
Wyndcliffe Rd PO4 . . . . . .182 E3
Wyndham Cl
Bournemouth BH6 . . . . . .206 A8
Waterlooville PO8 . . . . . .112 B4
Wyndham Ct SO15 . . . . . .102 E5
Wyndham Mews PO1 . . . .182 A3
Wyndham Pl 🅴 SO15 . . . .102 E5
Wyndham Rd
Poole BH14 . . . . .203 B3
Poole BH12 . . . . .194 B2
Wynford End PO4 . . . . .27 F4
Wynford Rd
Bournemouth BH9 . . . . . .190 B4
Poole BH14 . . . . .203 C4
Wynne Cl BH18 . . . . .186 F4
Wynter Cl BH7 . . . . .205 F7
Wynter Rd SO18 . . . . .104 B8
Wynton Way PO15 . . . . . . .130 C3
Wynyards Gap SO52 . . . . . .53 F4
Wyre Cl SO53 . . . . .55 B6
Wyvern Cl
Chandler's Ford SO53 . . . . .55 D6
Poole BH12 . . . . .203 D7
Wyvern Tech Coll SO50 . . .57 C1

Y

Yachtsman Cl SO31 . . . . . .128 C8
Yaldhurst Ct 🅴 PO9 . . . . .136 B6
Yaldhurst La SO41 . . . . . . .197 B3
Yapton St PO1 . . . . .216 B3
Yarborough Rd PO5 . . . . . .216 B1
Yardlea Cl PO9 . . . . .113 B1
Yardley Ct PO3 . . . . .158 C4
Yardley Rd SO30 . . . . .105 C5
Yarmouth Cl BH12 . . . . . .204 A5
Yarmouth Gdns 🅵 SO15 . .78 B1
Yarmouth Rd BH12 . . . . . .203 F6
Yarrell Mead SO41 . . . . . .197 B3
Yarrells Cl BH16 . . . . .201 C6
Yarrells Dr BH16 . . . . .201 B7
Yarrells La BH16 . . . . .201 C6
Yarrells Sch BH16 . . . . . . .201 B7
Yarrow Cl
🅰 BH23 . . . . .208 B8
Yarrow Rd BH12 . . . . .203 A8
Yarrow Way SO31 . . . . . . .128 C2
Yateley Ct PO9 . . . . .135 C5
Yaverland SO31 . . . . .127 A6
Yeatmans Old Mill 🔟
BH15 . . . . .202 B1
Yeatminster Rd BH17 . . . .187 F2
Yeatton Ho SO41 . . . . .196 A1
Yelverton Ave SO45 . . . . . .150 A8
Yelverton Rd 🔟 BH1 . . . .204 F3
Yeo Ct PO4 . . . . .183 C4
Yeoman Pk SO16 . . . . .77 C1
Yeomans Ind Pk BH8 . . . .190 F2
Yeomans Lodge 🅶
BH25 . . . . .195 B2
Yeomans Rd BH8 . . . . .190 E3

Yeomans Way
Bournemouth BH8 . . . . . .190 E2
Totten SO40 . . . . .100 F8
Yeovil Chase SO18 . . . . . .104 B8
Yeovilton Cl SO41 . . . . . . .196 E1
Yerville Gdns SO41 . . . . . .195 F3
Yew La BH25 . . . . .195 C4
Yew Rd SO18 . . . . .104 A8
Yew Tree Ave PO8 . . . . . . .112 B2
Yew Tree Cl
Fair Oak SO50 . . . . .57 C3
Hedge End SO30 . . . . . . .105 B6
Wimborne Minst BH21 . . .163 D5
Yew Tree Ct
Fordingbridge SP6 . . . . . . .93 E8
🅱 New Milton BH25 . . . .195 B1
Swanwick PO15 . . . . .129 B7
Yew Tree Dr PO15 . . . . . . .129 C7
Yew Tree Gdns
Denmead PO7 . . . . .110 E4
🅱 Ringwood BH24 . . . . .141 A6
Yew Tree Pl GU33 . . . . .21 A4
Yew Tree Rd PO11 . . . . . . .185 A8
Yewberry Way SO53 . . . . . .54 E6
Yews The PO8 . . . . .112 D7
Yewside PO13 . . . . .155 D2
Yewtree Cl SO45 . . . . .150 A8
Yewtree La SO16 . . . . .77 C3
Yoells Cres PO8 . . . . .111 F6
Yoells La PO8 . . . . .111 F6
Yokesford Hill SO51 . . . . . .27 E4
Yokesford Hill Est SO51 . . .27 F5
Yonge Cl SO50 . . . . .56 B3
York Ave BH25 . . . . .195 B3
York Bldgs SO14 . . . . .103 A4
York Cl Broadstone BH18 . .187 A2
Chandler's Ford SO53 . . . . .54 F4
Christchurch BH23 . . . . . .209 E7
Horton Heath SO50 . . . . . .81 D7
Petersfield GU32 . . . . .40 D3
Southampton SO14 . . . . .103 C6
🅱 Winchester SO23 . . . . .215 E8
York Pl Bournemouth BH7 .206 A5
🅱 New Milton BH25 . . . .195 B3
Portsmouth PO1 . . . . . . .182 B6
York Rd
Bournemouth BH1 . . . . . .205 B4
Broadstone BH18 . . . . . . .187 A2
Eastleigh SO50 . . . . .80 A8
Netley SO31 . . . . .127 A6
Southampton SO15 . . . . .102 C7
York Terr PO2 . . . . .157 F5
Yorkdale SO31 . . . . .128 C3
Yorke St PO5 . . . . .216 B2
Yorke Way SO31 . . . . .127 E3
Yorkwood GU33 . . . . .20 F4
Youngbridge Ct PO16 . . . .155 A7
Youngs Rd BH11 . . . . .189 A5
Yves Mews PO5 . . . . .182 B2

Z

Zamek Cl BH11 . . . . .189 A5
Zetland Ct BH4 . . . . .204 B1
Zetland Rd
Farlington PO6 . . . . .158 D7
Gosport PO12 . . . . .181 B6
Zeus La PO7 . . . . .134 F3
Zinnia Cl BH10 . . . . .189 E2

Addresses

Name and Address	Telephone	Page	Grid reference

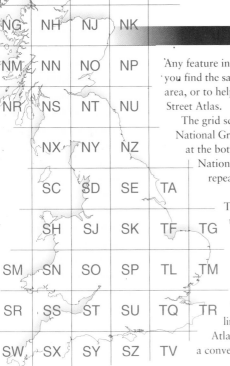

Using the Ordnance Survey National Grid

Any feature in this atlas can be given a unique reference to help you find the same feature on other Ordnance Survey maps of the area, or to help someone else locate you if they do not have a Street Atlas.

The grid squares in this atlas match the Ordnance Survey National Grid and are at 500 metre intervals. The small figures at the bottom and sides of every other grid line are the National Grid kilometre values (**00** to **99** km) and are repeated across the country every 100 km (see left).

To give a unique National Grid reference you need to locate where in the country you are. The country is divided into 100 km squares with each square given a unique two-letter reference. Use the administrative map to determine in which 100 km square a particular page of this atlas falls.

The bold letters and numbers between each grid line (**A** to **F**, **1** to **8**) are for use within a specific Street Atlas only, and when used with the page number, are a convenient way of referencing these grid squares.

Example *The railway bridge over DARLEY GREEN RD in grid square B1*

Step 1: Identify the two-letter reference, in this example the page is in **SP**

Step 2: Identify the 1 km square in which the railway bridge falls. Use the figures in the southwest corner of this square: Eastings **17**, Northings **74**. This gives a unique reference: **SP 17 74**, accurate to 1 km.

Step 3: To give a more precise reference accurate to 100 m you need to estimate how many tenths along and how many tenths up this 1 km square the feature is (to help with this the 1 km square is divided into four 500 m squares). This makes the bridge about **8** tenths along and about **1** tenth up from the southwest corner.

This gives a unique reference: **SP 178 741**, accurate to 100 m.

Eastings (read from left to right along the bottom) come before Northings (read from bottom to top). If you have trouble remembering say to yourself "Along the hall, THEN up the stairs"!

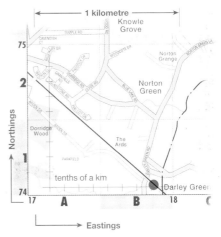

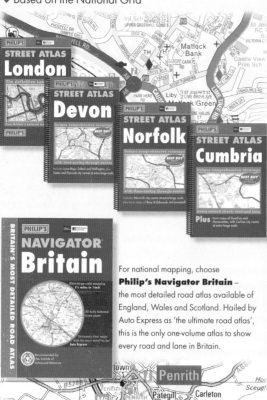